MW01678512

Publisher:

BLAISE PASCAL MAGAZINE

ALL ABOUT DELPHI AND DELPHI PRISM(.Net), LAZARUS & PASCAL AND RELATED LANGUAGES

Pascal

J. Braun,
M. van Canneyt,
M. Gärtner,
S. Heinig,
F. Monteiro de Cavalho,
I. Ouedraogo,
M. Weustink

LAZARUS
THE COMPLETE GUIDE

Developmental Editor: Detlef Overbeek
Production Editor: Detlef Overbeek
Technical Editor: Peter Bijlsma
Proofreaders: Peter Bijlsma, Howard Page-Clark, James Duff, Rik Smit, Anton Vogelaar
Translators: Kenneth Cox, Evelien Snel
Correctors: Howard Page-Clark, James Duff

Cover Designer: Detlef Overbeek
This book is an English translation of the German original:
Lazarus : Arbeiten mit IDE und Klassenbibliothek Published by C&L

1. Auflage 2010,
2. Auflage 2011

Email: **Office@blaisepascal.eu** **http://www.blaisepascalmagazine.eu**

This edition is registered by the Nederlandse Koninklijke Bibliotheek

ISBN: 978-94-90968-02-1

Content

Chapter 3: The IDE 93

By Swen Heinig

Chapter 4: Projects 233

By Felipe Monteiro de Carvalho

Chapter 5: Target Platforms 279

By Felipe Monteiro de Carvalho

Chapter 6: The Class Libraries 328

By Michael Van Canneyt

Chapter 7: Porting Delphi components 494

By Michael Van Canneyt

Chapter 8: Files and Devices 514

By Felipe Monteiro de Carvalho and Jörg Braun

Chapter 9: Graphics Programming 560

By Felipe Monteiro de Carvalho

Chapter 10: Processes and threads 595
By Felipe Monteiro de Carvalho

Chapter 11: Network Programming 614
By Inoussa Ouedraogo

Chapter 12: Database Access 651
By Michael Van Canneyt

INDEX 719

Foreword

Software development is still a youthful science.
Some would term it an art. Whatever your perspective, no one can deny that from the outset it has been a rapidly changing field, and an area of human enterprise more prone than many to domination by fashions, and the 'rule of cool'.
However in 2011 the best in the software development world are mature enough to embrace not only commercial applications produced at the dictates of the market, but research and academic contributions, and the gamut of open source expertise.

Lazarus is a development tool whose history bears the imprint of all these worlds: commercial, academic and open source.
Its survival in the absence of any commercial sponsorship, and growing strength, is a tribute both to the genius of Niklaus Wirth who bequeathed us the Pascal language (among others), and a tribute to the strength of collaboration among a stable and expanding team of international expert software designers drawn from all walks of life (including professional programmers, academics and amateurs).

Lazarus took the RAD concept of Delphi and its well-designed (but Windows-centric) visual library, opening it up for cross-platform development by building on the strengths of the Free Pascal compiler and its mature and well-tested cross-platform runtime library.

Object Pascal traces a valuable middle path between the ease of use of Visual Basic (without that language's lack of true object-orientation) and the greater complexity and slower compilation of C++.
The elegance and simplicity (and slight verbosity) of Object Pascal and its compiler-checked typing gives well-written Lazarus sources a readability that enhances a new programmer's ability to maintain and reuse code he (or she) may inherit.

This book is the first available to English-speaking developers that will enable you to maximise your use of the Lazarus IDE, learn vital details of its underlying libraries and design, and benefit from thousands of lines of code examples written specifically to help that learning process.
Code written, like Lazarus itself, by the team who have developed this impressive tool to the capabilities it offers today's programmers. You will find online a friendly community of Lazarus users and developers (including the authors of this book) who are willing to offer their help (if you can be courteous in asking).
All this is free. Lazarus lets you have your software cake, and eat it too.
Just bear in mind that screenshots here are based mostly on Lazarus releases available towards the end of 2010, and some details of interface and functionality may differ if you are using a more recent version, since Lazarus developers are an active and industrious group, and the development of this tool is forging ahead fast towards a stable 1.0 release.

This book's authors are all member of the Lazarus or Free Pascal development teams. Michael van Canneyt (a core member of the Free Pascal team) has written extensively about the LCL and database integration. He has put enormous effort into this edition, solving many technical questions for us. Michael and I spent a lot of time working together to make this English edition possible. He has endless patience, and was prepared to work at solving any problem I threw at him. It has been a joy to work with him.

Howard Page-Clark is our corrector and even though the book has several authors whose text has been transmitted through several translators, he was able to create a unifying style for the book and often clarified the English by rewriting or rephrasing.

Peter Bijlsma helped in many ways, as a proof-reader, corrector, and technical editor. Likewise Rik Smit's comments, corrections, and editing helped to discover and remove many sneaky errors.

The translation from the original German was undertaken by Kenneth Cox, Evelien Snel, Peter Bijlsma, Michael van Canneyt, James Duff and myself. We needed so many people to get this large book (which treats Lazarus so comprehensively) to press within a reasonable timescale. Our translators did an excellent job and I am very grateful to them.

Detlef D. Overbeek – Editor in Chief

Chapter 1
The Architecture of Lazarus

By Mattias Gärtner

Lazarus is an integrated development environment (IDE) for the Object Pascal language. The Free Pascal Compiler provides the backend for Lazarus. This combination of backend engine and integrated development environment is comparable to Visual Studio for C++ or Borland Delphi. It yields efficient, highly optimized native source code. Whereas Java and C# development environments produce bytecode that must be interpreted in a runtime environment or converted into poorly optimized code by a JIT compiler.

Among the strong points of the Lazarus IDE are its RAD capabilities, which greatly simplify and accelerate the development of graphic programs. They are largely similar to Delphi's capabilities. However Delphi is based on the Delphi compiler, while Lazarus is based on the Free Pascal Compiler (FPC), which is broadly compatible with Delphi 2007. In addition, Lazarus runs not only under Windows, but also in native mode on Linux, MacOS X, BSD and other platforms. The Free Pascal Compiler is itself written in Pascal, just as Lazarus is written entirely in Lazarus. FPC also includes language extensions from other Pascal dialects, which makes it easy to port existing source code. In line with its strong focus on platform independence, FPC detects code that may not be portable and generates a warning.
Lazarus's graphic component library is called the Lazarus Component Library (LCL). Many of its units, classes and identifiers have the same names and work the same way as in Delphi, so Delphi code can be ported directly to Lazarus. However, Lazarus is not a Delphi clone, but instead an extension of the Delphi concept that supports platform independence using native applications, with no need for emulators. The price that must be paid for this is that full compatibility with Delphi's component library (the VCL) is not possible. The LCL has native components. On all platforms LCL-based applications look the same as other native applications, and they are used the same way. The LCL achieves this by using native widget-sets, such as WinAPI for Windows, Gtk 2 for Linux/BSD, and Carbon/Cocoa for MacOS X.

The main differences from Delphi are that Lazarus is fully open source, that it currently runs on more than fifteen platforms, that it is free even for commercial users, and that it is based on a flexible licensing scheme. Thanks to the efforts of the open source community, many Delphi libraries have been ported to Lazarus and extended to other platforms. Also new libraries that are only available under Lazarus have been written. Numerous forums, mailing lists and websites offer fast, straightforward help.

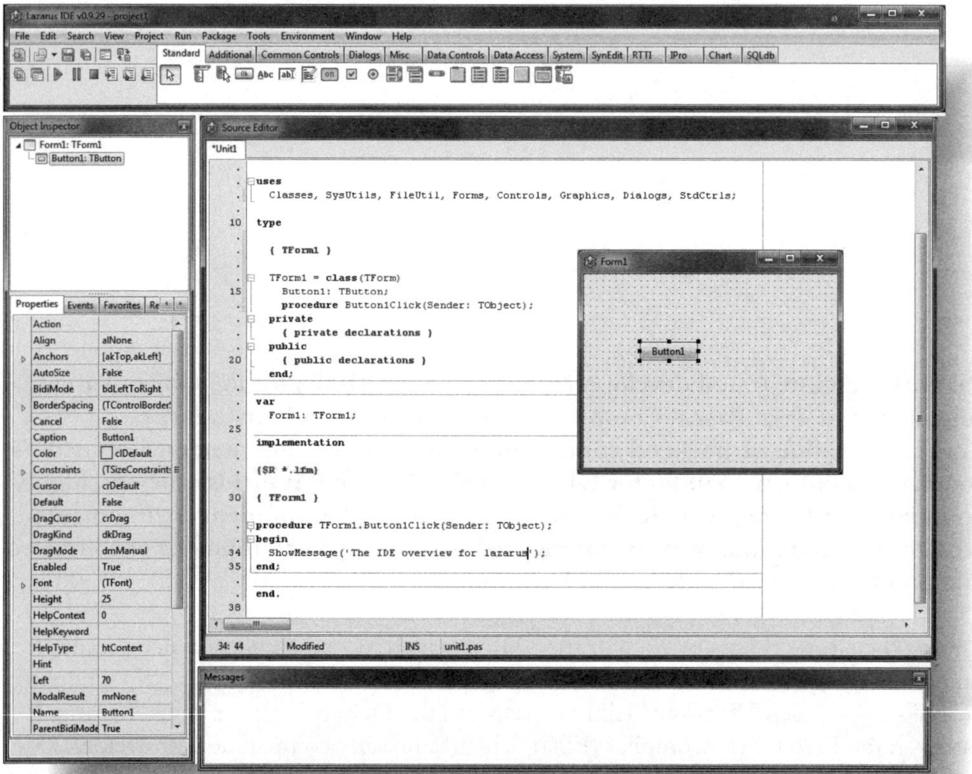

Figure 1.1: A familiar environment for Delphi users: Form Editor, Object Inspector and Code Explorer

The Free Pascal Compiler and its accompanying libraries form a sound foundation for Lazarus. Although they are closely related, FPC and Lazarus are different projects. The first version of Free Pascal appeared in 1993, while work on Lazarus began in 1999. Free Pascal is a 32- and 64-bit compiler for Windows 32, Windows 64, WinCE, Linux, FreeBSD, MacOS X/Darwin, DOS, OS/2, Netware (libc and classic) and MorphOS, running on the Intel x86, AMD64/x86_64, PowerPC, PowerPC64, Sparc and ARM architectures. Like Delphi, the compiler is very fast, but not quite as fast as Delphi because FPC is optimized for more than one platform in the interest of extensibility. In terms of size and speed, under Windows the resulting compiled code is comparable to that produced by Delphi (sometimes FPC is better, and sometimes Delphi), and under Linux or MacOS X the code is comparable to that produced by the GNU C/C++ compiler.

Lazarus currently lacks .NET support, and there are no packages comparable to those in the Delphi .bpl libraries. However normal libraries can be compiled and bound on all platforms.
Native graphic applications, Windows services, Linux daemons, command-line tools, libraries, plugins, database applications, Web applications and much more can be programmed with Lazarus. The functional scope of the IDE can be expanded with design-time packages.

Lazarus enables cross-compilation, such as generating Windows programs on a Linux system or WinCE applications on a Windows system. Code navigation and code completion operate intelligently in these situations. The configuration can be changed in the IDE without restarting. The Free Pascal compiler supports conditional compilation, which allows code to be generated selectively according to the operating system, CPU type or other criteria.
The IDE allows macros in all search paths, which means for example that units and *include* files can be selected according to the operating system. Particularly when more than two platforms are involved, this yields a clean, comprehensible structure.
The LCL itself is based on this concept. It appears to the programmer as a platform-independent set of components, while macros in the search paths enable modules tailored to specific operating systems to access native widget-sets.

The Lazarus package concept allows units to be combined into larger entities with their own compiler configurations. This ensures that code can easily be ported to other computers with different paths and different operating systems. All that is necessary for this is to copy the files and open the package. There is no need to modify paths or configure switches, which considerably simplifies package updating.
The *LCL*'s visual components are event-driven. This means that it is not necessary to write complete applications sequentially. Instead, programmers can develop methods that respond to events. The status of the *LCL* components is determined entirely by properties. They can be modified in virtually any desired sequence, and forms can conveniently be put together graphically in the IDE. If a desired function is missing, any component class can be used as the basis for a user-defined class and used graphically in the IDE. Users may also generate their own component libraries.

Windows can be edited graphically in the IDE. Each unit may have at most one window. Windows can be based on other windows (inherited) or nested as subwindows (frames). Their properties are stored in `.lfm` files. Of course, windows can also be generated using code. The key to all of this is that the Form Editor is linked closely to the Source Code Editor.

When a new component is placed on a form, a new variable is generated in the source code, and if the *OnClick* event of a button is set, a new method is generated in the source code. The program can be compiled immediately and run; nothing else is necessary.
A programming language should have both a simple syntax, and a mechanism for combining files for compilation. This is implemented very conveniently in FPC.

In other languages such as C or C++, compiling multiple files is often specified by *make* files. Generating and maintaining *make* files is not easy, so there are innumerable tools available to help C users generate *make* files.

The good news for FPC users is that *make* files are often unnecessary. Even better, they can still be used if desired. And to make things perfect, there are tools that generate *make* files automatically.
The task of a makefile is to simplify and standardize the compilation process.
It ensures that modified files are automatically compiled in the right sequence, and it specifies the appropriate compiler parameters. The Free Pascal Compiler automatically compiles all modified units, does this considerably faster than a makefile, and works with checksums. These checksums are especially important when the files are located in network directories, with a good possibility of different time of day references in client and server systems. Many C programmers are familiar with the warning that something is wrong with a file's time-stamp. FPC has fewer problems with this, so programmers can simply give FPC the main file and allow the compiler to find all the auxiliary files itself.

For example,

```
fpc program1.pas
```

automatically calls correctly all the files needed by program1. A second compiler will be necessary for cross-compilation to a different processor architecture.
This second compiler will of course also be an FPC, but one that compiles code for the target architecture.
The compiler begins by reading the source file, and when it encounters a *uses* clause, it automatically looks for the corresponding units. If it finds precompiled .ppu files, it uses them.
If it finds only source files (or the source files are newer than the `.ppu` files) it compiles the source files. If these files need other units, these other units are compiled recursively.

This all goes very fast – the compilation rate is normally between ten thousand and one hundred thousand lines per second. The compiler finds the specified files and automatically compiles all modified files in the correct sequence.
In contrast to C compilers, most of the compiler parameters are easy to understand. This is partly because many of the settings are located in the source code, and partly because the compiler and the system libraries originate from the same sources on all platforms .

As a result, the compiler command-line parameters are mostly limited to specifying search paths, and the notorious `./configure` for collecting the system parameters is unnecessary. This is all in line with Lazarus' motto "Write Once, Compile Anywhere'. For example, a call to *configure* under C checks the size of an *int* variable, among other things. With Free Pascal, the type sizes are known directly from the code.

Tests to determine which *libc* version to use are unnecessary with Free Pascal because the runtime library uses only core functions, which experience shows are modified very rarely. For this reason, a Pascal program runs on multiple distributions in the same way as a comparable C program. As Pascal does not directly need the C header files, specific tests for which libraries to use are not necessary.
Lazarus extends the unit concept to include *packages* and *projects*.

A **package** is a set of files with information on how they should be compiled and which packages are necessary for this. A package may be a library, or it may simply be a logical entity in an extensive project. A Lazarus **project** is also a set of files, but it includes additional information necessary for building a program. In addition, for each project the IDE saves the names of files open in the Editor, together with debugging information and other data. You could say that a Lazarus package or project is an enhanced makefile. This allows even large, mutually independent libraries to be compiled without makefiles. The command-line program *lazbuild* is responsible for this.

For example, a project always has a `projectname.lpi` file that holds all the metadata. The `.lpi` file is an XML file, and all data in the file can be configured easily using the IDE. Manual editing is therefore unnecessary (unless you want to rename several hundred files at once). In addition, there is usually a main file with a name and suffix assigned by the user. By default, the IDE assigns the name `project1.lpr` to the main file.

Here we have briefly described how Lazarus combines files to form larger entities called packages and projects. Thanks to the principle of independence, packages from very diverse programmers and external suppliers can be handled as a group. The next section explains how the Lazarus Source Code Editor helps users take advantage of this knowledge during programming.

1.1 The Source Code Editor

The Source Editor epitomizes the concept of integration in the IDE. It is based on the *SynEdit* components, and uses its own tools called *codetools* for cross-project navigation and editing. The Form Editor, the debugger and the FPDoc editor are also closely linked to the Source Code Editor. This is one of the strong points of Lazarus, and in many respects it goes beyond the Delphi editor's capabilities.

All functions may be assigned keyboard shortcuts, which are configured under *Environment → Options → Editor → Key Mappings*. Keyboard shortcuts may consist of one or two keys with any desired combination of modifier keys. The modifier keys under Windows are [Ctrl], [Shift] and [Alt].

1.1.1 Code tools

The IDE uses *codetools* to read the source code rather than using the compiler for this. Codetools have the following advantages compared to the compiler:

- They are error-tolerant, especially with regard to missing units. They can read Delphi, Kylix and FPC code.
- They can be used in every directory with their own compiler parameters.
- When editing cross-platform, the codetools allow users working on a particular platform to edit code for another platform as though they were working on the other platform. For instance, it is not necessary to install a cross-compiler in order to edit Windows code on a Linux platform.
- Speed: when you edit the base unit of a large project, a compiler would have to recompile all dependent units. The codetools are optimized to update only what is actually necessary.
- The codetools also work with comments and code disabled by *IFDEFs*, although syntax checking is less reliable in comments.

1.1.2 Fast navigation through code

The key combinations [Ctrl]+[Shift]+↑ and [Ctrl]+[Shift]+↓ can be used to jump back and forth between the declaration and implementation of a procedure. These functions, which are called *Find procedure definition* and *Find procedure method*, can be used to jump between methods, procedures in the interface section, and forward procedures. They can be used almost everywhere:

```
procedure DoSomething(i: Integer); // from here

implementation

procedure DoSomething(i: Integer);
begin
  // to here, or vice versa
end;
```

If a matching procedure is not found, the function looks for the closest-match procedure, and positions the cursor at the first difference.
For example, if the parameter *i* above is renamed to *Parameter1*, [Ctrl]+[Shift]+↑ jumps to the implementation. The IDE positions the cursor at the first difference, which in this case is the parameter *i*. There the variable can be renamed.

```
procedure DoSomething(Parameter1: Integer); // from here

implementation

procedure DoSomething(i: Integer);
begin                    // ? to here
```

1.1.2 Fast navigation through code

The function *Find declaration* (key combination [Alt]+↑) searches for the declaration of an identifier, and always jumps to the nearest declaration. For example:

```
type    TMyInteger = 1..2; // does not find any other
        TMyInteger = 1..3; // jumps to the first TMyInteger
var i: TMyInteger;  // jumps to the second TMyInteger
```

If the cursor is located at a forward declaration, the function jumps to the actual declaration. In case of identifiers that use a forward declaration, the function normally jumps to the forward declaration because it is closest. If you want to have the IDE jump directly to the actual declaration, this can be configured in the codetools.

```
type TDog = class; // jumps downward to the actual declaration
     TPaw = class

     public
       Dog: TDog;    // jumps upward
                     // or directly downward, depending on the setting
     end;

     TDog = class
     public
       Paws: array[1..4] of TPaw;
     end;
```

Code context (Ctrl]+[Shift]+[Space])
If the cursor is located in a parameter list, the *Code context* function shows the declaration. If the cursor is located inside the parentheses of the constructor parameter list in the source code:

```
fs := TFilestream.Create( );
```

Code context shows all constructors of class *TFileStream*, including the parameter lists, and the parameter currently under the cursor is highlighted. The context information disappears when the user presses [Escape] or the cursor leaves the parameter list.

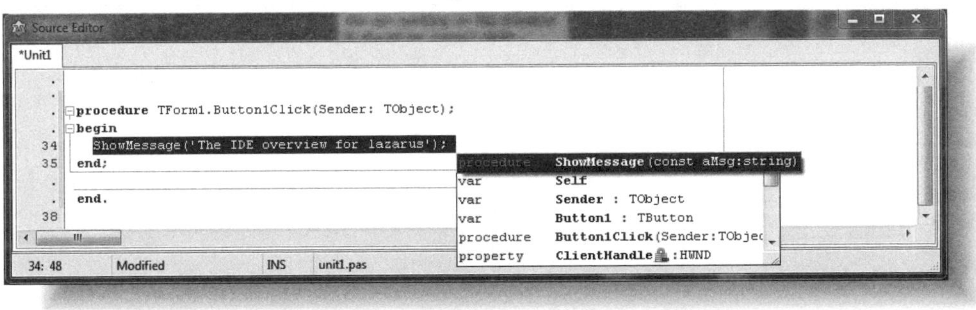

Figure 1.2: Parameter tips can be displayed by pressing [Ctrl]+[Shift]+[Space]

The Code Explorer

The Code Explorer is a separate window (*View → Code Explorer*) that displays all the Pascal identifiers of the current unit (as in Delphi). They are sorted either alphabetically or by category. A directive browser is also displayed in a second pane. It provides a list of all directives in the source code. This simplifies the task of searching for conditional code or finding include directives.

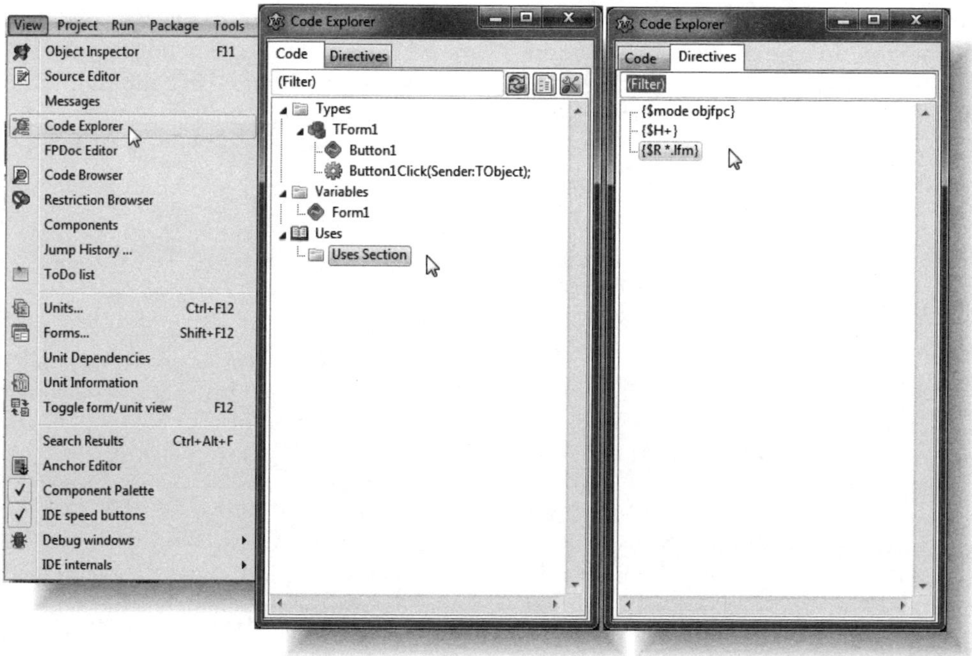

Figure 1.3: The two panes of the Code Explorer window

Starting with Lazarus 0.9.28, the View menu has a new option called *Code Observer,* which shows a window listing code segments that may be coded poorly.

1.1.3 Autocompletion

Identifier completion ([Ctrl]+[Space])
Identifier completion displays a list of a class's methods or properties. This list is filtered while the letters of the method name are being typed. The user can use the mouse or the keyboard arrow keys to scroll through the list and select the desired method.
This function is enabled by pressing the [Ctrl]+[Space] key combination.
If the cursor is positioned on the '.' after the identifier L in the following source code:

```
  var  L : TStrings;
       I : integer;
begin
  for I := 0 to L.
```

pressing [Ctrl]+[Space] causes a list of the properties and methods of the class *TStrings* to be displayed (because variable L is of type *Tstrings*).

Edit →Complete code ([Ctrl]+[Shift]+[C])
The effect of the code completion function depends on the cursor position.
If the cursor is located in the declaration section of a class, class completion is enabled. In this case, the IDE attempts to complete the class declaration and generate empty implementations for all of the procedures in the declaration. In this process, it recognizes property getters and setters and uses intelligent heuristics to guess what should be converted in the fields or methods.
For example, if code completion is triggered by pressing [Ctrl]+[Shift]+[C] in the following declaration:

```
type
  TMyComponent = class(TComponent)
  public
  property Active: Boolean Read FActive Write SetActive;
end;
```

the IDE modifies the source code to the following:

```
TMyComponent = class(TComponent)
private
  FActive: Boolean;
  procedure SetActive(const AValue: Boolean);
public
  property Active: Boolean Read FActive Write SetActive;
end;

{ TMyComponent }
procedure TMyComponent.SetActive(const AValue: Boolean);
begin
  if FActive = AValue then Exit;
  FActive := AValue;
end;
```

Here it recognizes *SetActive* as a method and *FActive* as a field, which by default it generates in the private section of the class declaration. It also creates the body of the method *SetActive* and fills it with initial code. Of course, it does this only for property setters, which means methods located after the keyword *Write*. This example contains only a few property definitions, but the IDE does the same thing for every incomplete method or property it encounters.
The reverse operation is also possible. For example, if the following procedure is added to the implementation of the class:

```
procedure TMyComponent.CheckActive;
begin
  if not Active then RaiseException;
end;
```

then the following procedure declaration is added if code completion is triggered while the cursor is located anywhere between the keywords *procedure* and *end:*

```
TMyComponent = class(Tcomponent)
private
  FActive: Boolean;
  procedure CheckActive;
  procedure SetActive(const AValue: Boolean);
public
  property Active: Boolean Read FActive Write SetActive;
end;
```

Another type of code completion is *variable completion.* In the source code

```
procedure TForm1.Button1Click(Sender: TObject);
begin
  for i := 0 to L.Count - 1 do

end;
```

the variable *i* is defined as an integer if code completion is triggered while the cursor is positioned on the variable *i* in the *for* statement:

```
procedure TForm1.Button1Click(Sender: TObject);
  var i: Integer;
begin
  for i := 0 to L.Count - 1 do
```

Here the code completion function deduces the type of the variable. This also works with parameters:

```
procedure TForm1.FormCreate(Sender: TObject);
begin
  SetBounds(Left, Top, Width, Height);
end;
```

If code completion is triggered when the cursor is positioned on the new variable *Left*, the parameter signature of the declaration of the *SetBounds* method is used to declare *Left* as an integer thus:

```
procedure TMainForm.FormCreate(Sender: TObject);
  var Left: Integer;
begin
  SetBounds(Left, Top, Width, Height);
end;
```

Code completion can even be used to generate complete event handlers in the code. This capability is present in Delphi's Object Inspector, which generates a complete declaration and implementation when an event handler is assigned to a component. This can additionally be done in the code.
In the source code:

```
procedure TForm1.Button1Click(Sender: TObject);
  var l: TStringList;
begin
  L.OnChange := @DoListChange;
end;
```

if code completion is triggered when the cursor is positioned on the identifier *DoListChange*, the IDE recognizes that this involves assigning an event handler and generates a handler with the appropriate signature in the class:

```
procedure TForm1.DoListChange(Sender: TObject);
begin

end;
```

In addition to code completion, the IDE supports *code templates*. These are short, predefined code segments that can be inserted in the source code with a single key combination ([Ctrl]+[J]). Each of these code segments has a name and a short description. To insert a code template, type its name and then press the code template completion key combination [Ctrl]+[J]. In response, the IDE will insert the code at the cursor position. Incidentally, it is not necessary to type the full name; a unique initial string is sufficient. If there is more than one template with the same initial string, a selection window is displayed in the same way as for identifier completion.
Lazarus has many predefined code templates available.

For example, if the cursor is located at the end of the word *trye* in the source code

```
begin
  trye
end;
```

pressing the key combination [Ctrl]+[J] causes the IDE to expand *trye* to

```
begin
  try

  except
  end;
end;
```

The cursor is positioned between the key words *try* and *except*, where it is ready for the rest of the source code to be entered. If [Ctrl]+[J] is pressed when the cursor is positioned where no name is present (on a blank line), the IDE displays a list of templates so the user can select one of them. The available templates can be edited in the *Code Templates* dialog, which is accessed via *Environment →Code Templates.*

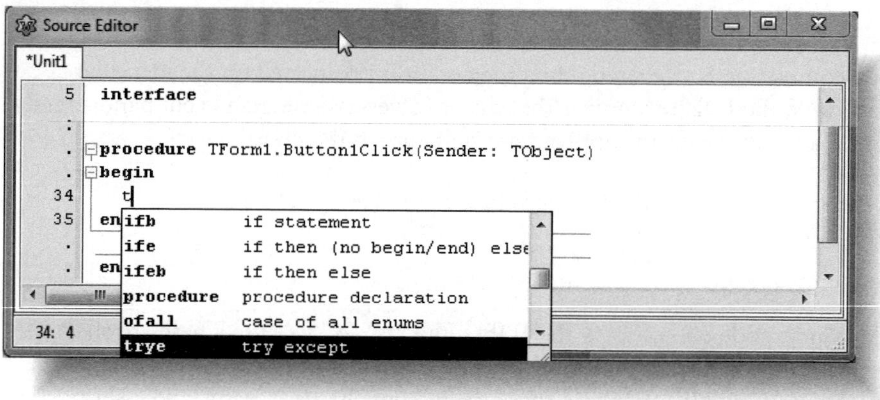

Figure 1.4: pressing [ctrl]+[j] lets the codesample template appear

Three conditions must be fulfilled for each code template:

- Its name must be known (the entered string is compared with the initial letters of its name).
- The short description must be present.
- The source text to be entered in place of the name must be present.

The source code is entered as though it were entered manually. The cursor is positioned at the start of the source code segment or on the pipe symbol '|' if this symbol is present in the template code. The code template for *trye* is:

```
try
  |
except

end;
```

In addition to the pipe symbol, various macros are allowed. They can be enabled with the *Insert Macro* button.
Templates can also be triggered automatically with the [Enter] or [Space] key.
Starting with version 0.9.28, Lazarus completes code blocks automatically. If the cursor is positioned after *repeat* in the source code

```
begin
  repeat

end;
```

and the [Enter] key is pressed, the IDE automatically inserts the missing *until*:

```
begin
  repeat

  until;
end;
```

If you object to this degree of automatic code generation, you can disable it under *Environment →Options →Editor →Completion and Hints →Add close statement for Pascal blocks.*
Many editors are able to provide syntax highlighting for more than one language. Lazarus also does this. Several syntax highlighters preconfigured for Free Pascal and Lazarus are available from the SynEdit project. Unlike the Delphi IDE, all Lazarus tools can process *include* files, which are especially handy for splitting platform-specific code into individual files in order to avoid unreadable *IFDEF* structures. This is particularly helpful when it is necessary to support more than two platforms.

The appropriate *include* file for each platform can be easily and automatically selected by macros in the search paths.
Include files are more common in Free Pascal and Lazarus code than in Delphi.

Large files
Even large files with several hundred thousand lines of code can be edited reasonably. The codetools also offer programmers a variety of refactoring tools, as described below.

Identifier renaming
All instances of an identifier can be renamed. This involves a context-sensitive Find-and-Replace operation.

Method extraction
Users can mark a set of statements and relocate them to a separate method. The IDE displays various options for this (see Figure 1.5).

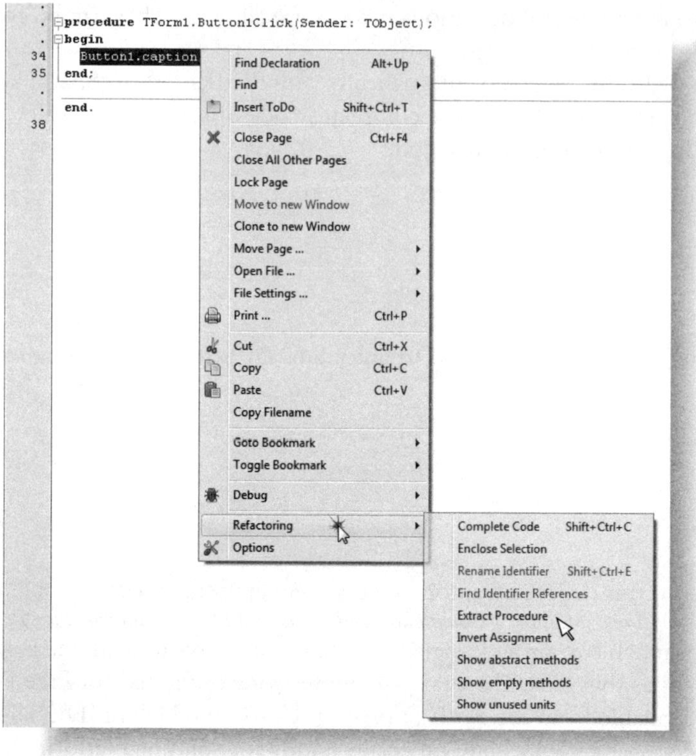

Figure 1.5: Method extraction with the code tools

This allows the size of procedures to be reduced, enhancing the clarity of the source code and making it easier to understand.

Automatic completion of classes often results in empty methods. They can be found and removed automatically with *Environment →Options →Editor →Completion and Hints →Auto remove empty methods.*

Show unused units analyses the uses clauses of the current unit and shows unused units in two categories. You access this dialog from the Source Editor by right-clicking a Pascal unit to show a popup menu, then choosing from a submenu under *Refactoring.*

Here 'unused' means that no identifier is used directly, but identifiers may be used indirectly if the unit uses the initialization section to register global objects. For example, the image formats of the LCL operate in this manner. Binding the *laztga* unit is sufficient to ensure that all *TOpenPictureDialogs* understand the .tga image format. Lazarus forms also use the *initialization* section to load form data. If a form is not used, the data is also unnecessary. The compiler sees the *initialization* section, so it does not report that the unit is not used. As a result, the unused data is also not removed by smart linking. This dialog finds such 'unused' units and allows these dependencies to be removed easily.

The codetools can also be used to find abstract procedures. If the cursor is positioned in a class declaration, the *Show abstract methods* function (accessed from the same popup menu mentioned above) shows a list of parent classes that still need to be overridden.

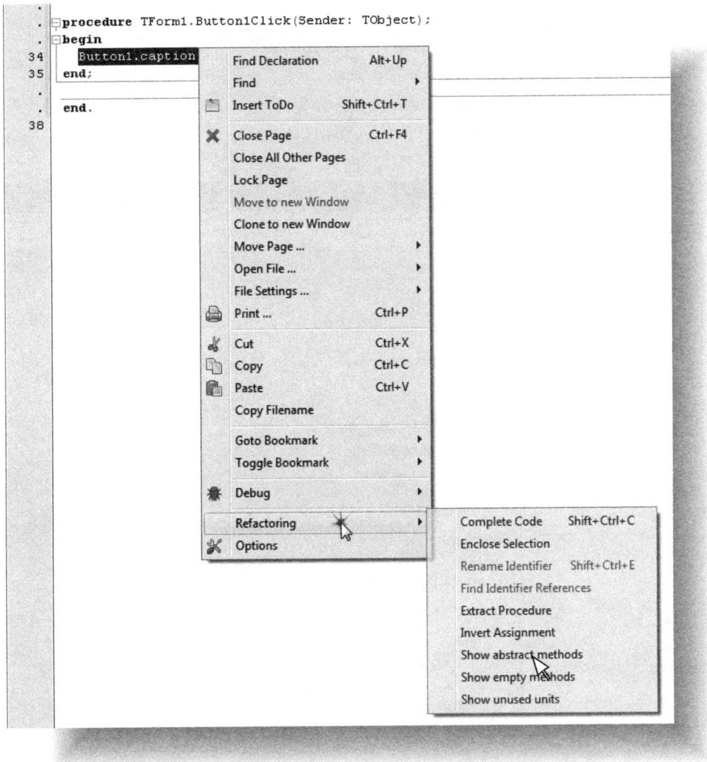

Figure 1.6: The Show Abstract Methods refactoring tool simplifies the implementation of abstract classes

The desired methods can then be selected, after which the IDE generates the appropriate declarations and body implementations.
Like all editors, Lazarus also has a set of find-and-replace functions, including *Find whole words only* and *Find regular expressions.*

Searching may optionally be set to case-sensitive and may be restricted to specific terms if necessary. Multi-line expressions can also be entered as search terms. The search range can be set to the current selection or the current file, and the search direction can be set to up or down.
It is also possible to search more than one file, including all open files, all project files, or all files in a directory (with an optional file mask and optionally subdirectories).
Figure 1.7 shows the options for searching in multiple files.

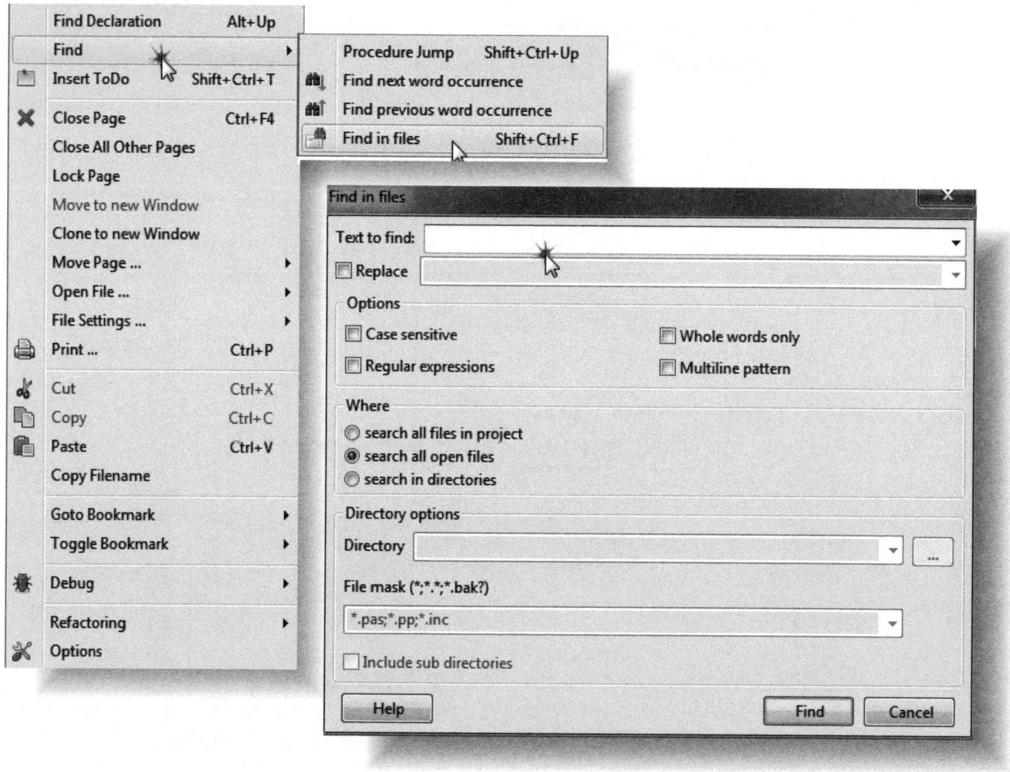

Figure 1.7: The Find in Files dialog supports searching in multiple files

Naturally, the search string may be replaced by the entered replacement string.

1.2 Language Basics

The Free Pascal Compiler is a complete object-oriented compiler for Object Pascal, which is itself written in Pascal. Lazarus makes extensive use of the capabilities of FPC. Object Pascal is very suitable for writing fast, efficient code comparable to C or C++, but it is easier to learn and the source code is easier to read. This is especially beneficial for novice programmers, indeed Pascal was originally designed as a teaching language for programming.

Of course, the language has been extended since, but the basic principles are still valid. The original Pascal has been extended to allow embedding of inline assembly language (i.e. assembly language source code can be placed directly in the Pascal code), and new objects and classes have been added.
Programs compiled with Free Pascal are less dependent on C libraries, with the result that they usually run on many more Linux or BSD distributions than comparable C programs. For example, a program that has been compiled for a Linux system can run on many versions of SUSE, Red Hat, Ubuntu and other distributions without recompilation. The extent of this depends on the libraries that are used.

It arises from the independence of the run-time library (RTL), which provides basic functions such as file operations. The run-time libraries are programmed to utilize if possible only kernel functions and the kernel functions are subject to the fewest modifications.
As with C and C++, recompilation is necessary when changing to a later release of the Free Pascal Compiler.

The standard version of the Free Pascal Compiler comes with an internal assembler, but a different assembler may be used if desired. Various assemblers can be integrated, of which the most important is the GNU *as* assembler.

The compiler translates all assembly-language instructions it finds in the source code into the desired output format: GNU *as*, NASM, or Watcom assembler. It is also possible to write and edit assembly-language code in a separate file before sending it to an assembler. Starting with version 2.2.0, FPC under Windows has its own linker, which works much faster and handles Pascal code better with smart linking.
The default for Linux and BSD is *ld*, the same as for the GNU C and C++ compilers. It is not yet known if and when the FPC internal linker will also be used for Linux and BSD.
Apple's own linker is used under MacOS X. The new linker provided by Apple with MacOS X 10.6 and later does a better job of handling the *dwarf* debugging format. Accordingly, in MacOS X 10.5 FPC should be called with the -gw option to instruct it to use this format.
The compiler generates debugging data for the GNU *gdb* debugger. This is a command-line tool that the Lazarus IDE uses in the background. As *gcc* also supplies this data, it is quite possible to debug mixed-language programs. However, the Lazarus debugger cannot process C source code files.
The GNU *gprof* profiler can be used on all platforms, although it does not work with multithreaded programs and is difficult to install under Windows. The *valgrind* profiler can also be used under Linux, BSD and MacOS X.

The Free Pascal Compiler continues the tradition of user-friendly Pascal compilers: no `make` files or associated tools are necessary, since the compiler has sufficient intrinsic intelligence to link different code segments without the aid of the developer. This is all made possible by the concept of units, which are pieces of reusable source code.
The developer only needs to tell the compiler where to find the various compiled units, and the compiler takes care of everything else itself.

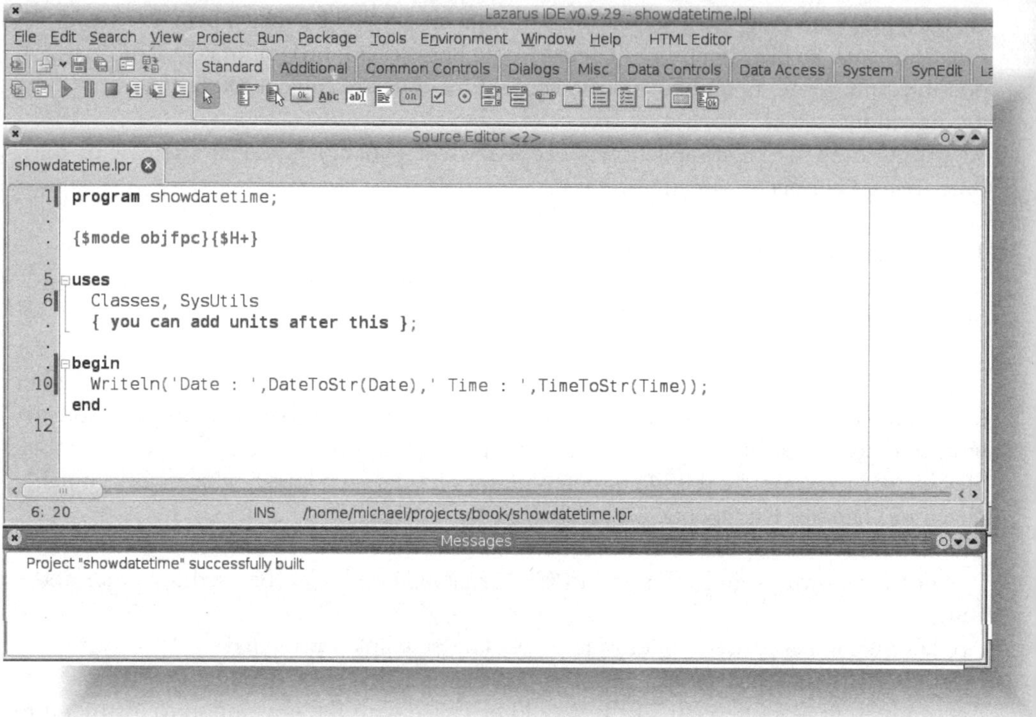

Figure 1.8: The IDE with a small program that outputs the date and time of day

The unit concept also supports name spaces, which means that the same identifier (the name of a function, variable or type) can be reused in different units. In case of ambiguity, the compiler itself knows which identifier is valid unless the identifier and the unit have the same name (which of course should be strictly avoided in normal practice). The compiler and the RTL are written in Object Pascal, which makes them largely independent of the C library. You are able to easily write code that avoids linking to external libraries, since the generated code calls the system core functions directly. This allows programs generated with FPC to run under many different versions of operating systems or on different distributions of a particular operating system. Despite this independence, existing C libraries can be bound easily to Object Pascal programs. This only requires writing a unit that provides an Object Pascal translation of the library interface, so that the compiler has access to all the data it needs to use the library. Free Pascal is supplied with the *h2pas* command line tool, which performs this translation automatically.

In addition to C libraries, many existing C tools can be used. For example, the generated code can be debugged using readily available tools, including GNU tools. The executable files can be generated with the GNU assembler and linker, and *gdb* can be used for debugging (as with Lazarus). Profiling can be performed with *gprof* or *valgrind.*

The compiler runs on more than twenty platforms. Particular attention is given to platform independence, so the notorious *./configure* call is not necessary for FPC programs. The run-time library is based solely on kernel functions, so FPC programs run on different distributions without recompilation.

1.2.1 Basic types

Like C, Object Pascal has a set of basic types. Table 1.1 lists the basic Pascal integer types and their counterparts in C.

Object Pascal type	Corresponding C data type
Integer	int
Cardinal	unsigned int
ShortInt	char
Byt	eunsigned char
Word	16-bit unsigned int
LongWord	unsigned int
Int64	long int
Qword	unsigned long int

Table 1.1:Object Pascal and C integer types

Floating-point type	Length (bytes)
Single	4
Double	8
Extended	10 (if supported, otherwise the same as Double)
Comp	8
Currency	8

Table 1.2:Floating-point types in Object Pascal

Object Pascal also has various string types.

String type	Features
Char	Single 1-byte character.
Widechar	Single 2-byte character.
Shortstring	String of 1-byte characters. The maximum string length is 255 characters. The length of the string is stored in the 0th character. Memory is reserved on the stack.
AnsiString	String of 1-byte characters. In contrast to Shortstring, there is no length restriction. Memory is requested from the heap. An indexed type.
WideString	String of 2-byte characters (DBCS). No length restriction. Memory is requested from the heap.
Resourcestring	A resource string similar to AnsiString, which is defined in the source code, but loaded from a resource file, which means that it can be translated into other languages.

Table 1.3: String types in Object Pascal

There are also other data types in Object Pascal.

Type	Description
Pchar	A pointer to a character
Pointer	An untyped pointer
Boolean	Has two possible values: True or False
Longbool	A boolean value with an internal size of 4 bytes
Shortbool	A boolean value with an internal size of 1 word

Table 1.4: Other data types

The unit *Ctypes*, which is supplied with Free Pascal and Lazarus, contains a set of type definitions for the most commonly used C types.

```
program CDemo1;
uses  CTypes;
  var  i: cint;          // corresponds to "int i;" in C
       j: cint16;        // corresponds to "int16 j;" in C
       k: cunsigned;     // C: "unsigned k;" or "unsigned int k;"
       l: cushort;       // C: "unsigned short l;"
       m: cfloat;        // C: "float m;"
begin
  i := 3;
end.
```

In addition to these basic types, Object Pascal has *enumerated* types, *range* types, *sets*, *records* and *classes*. They must be defined as types in a type declaration block. This block begins with the keyword *type*, followed by the definitions of one or more types separated by semicolons.
For example:

```
type
  TWeekDay = (Monday, Tuesday, Wednesday, Thursday, Friday, Saturday,
                                                            Sunday);
```

defines an enumerated type. A range is defined as follows:

```
TDice = 1..6;
```

A record definition takes the following form:

```
TPoint = record
  X : Integer;
  Y : Integer;
end;
```

A record with variables is called a variant record in Pascal. There are two types of variant record:

```
MyVariant = record
  A: Integer;
  case Integer of
    1 : (B    : ShortString);
    2 : (C, D: ShortString;);
end;
```

The variant portion of the record begins with the *case* identifier, followed by a type. After this comes a value for each variant part, which is usually a sequential number, and a definition located inside parentheses. It is also possible to reserve memory for each number by stating a field name for this:

```
MyVariant = record
  A: Integer;
  case E: Integer of
    1 : (B    : String);
    2 : (C, D: String;);
end;
```

Here it should be noted that the numbers are provided solely for the sake of readability; they are ignored by the compiler.
Here is an example of a set definition:

```
TDays = set of TWeekDay; // see the declaration of TWeekDay above
```

or

```
Throws = set of TDice;    // see the declaration of TDice above
```

A typed pointer points to a variable of a particular type, as in the following example:

```
PInteger = ^Integer;
```

This corresponds to the following C definition:

```
PInteger = int *;
```

Letter case is not important in Object Pascal because the Pascal language is not case-sensitive. This means that all of the following definitions are equivalent:

```
PInteger = ^Integer;
Pinteger = ^Integer;
pInteger = ^Integer;
pinteger = ^Integer;
```

It also means that an attempt to define an identifier twice with different letter case will lead to an error. The following instructions will result in a 'Duplicate identifier' error:

```
type
  MyInteger = ^Integer;
  MYINTEGER = ^Integer;
end;
```

In Pascal, all identifiers must be declared before they are accessed. This yields clearly structured code and has the advantage that Pascal compilers can compile source code in just one pass, which is one of the reasons for the extremely high speed of all Pascal compilers. C compilers are much slower because C and C++ have significantly laxer declaration conventions.
The following is an example of a record definition containing an element of a linked list. A straightforward definition would take the form:

```
TData = record
  TheData: Integer;
  Next   : ^TData;
end;
```

The *Next* field is a pointer to the next *TData* record. However, *TData* is not completely defined at the point where the *Next* field is declared.

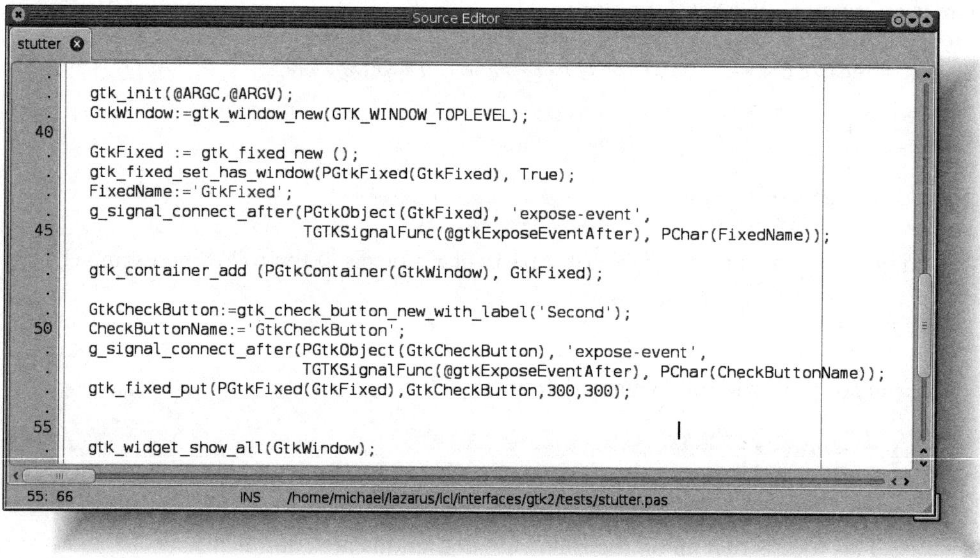

Figure 1.9: C code can often be converted directly to Pascal

This example illustrates the point of a *forward declaration*, which is a partial declaration that is completed further on in the source code. Forward declarations can be used for pointer types, class types and functions. The forward declaration of a pointer type takes the form:

```
PData = ^TData;
TData = record
  TheData: Integer;
  Next   : PData;
end;
```

Here the field *Next* of the record *TData* is of type *PData*. It is defined as a pointer to a type named *TData*. This type of definition is a forward definition because *TData* itself is not yet defined at this point. A forward definition of this sort must always be completed in the *type* block containing the reference.

There is a similar situation with classes:

```
TFirstClass   = class;         // forward declaration
TSecondClass = class
  First: TFirstClass;
end;

TFirstClass = class            // actual declaration
  Second: TSecondClass
end;
```

As *TFirstClass* has a field of type *TSecondClass*, the latter field must be declared before *TFirstClass*. However, *TFirstClass* must be defined before *TSecondClass* because *TSecondClass* itself has a field of type *TFirstClass*. To solve this predicament, a forward declaration for *TFirstClass* can be used as illustrated in the above example. There *TFirstClass* is initially defined simply as a class; the full definition comes later. This technique can also be applied to functions. A function may be declared forward, which means that it can be used in the subsequent source code even though its actual implementation comes later.
This is a forward declaration:

```
function Second: Boolean; forward;

function First : Integer;
begin
  Result := Ord(Second);
end;
```

The function *Second* can be used in the implementation of the function *First* even though the definition of *Second* is not yet complete. Of course, the implementation of *Second* must occur in the source code somewhere after the implementation of *First*, otherwise the compiler will report an error because it will not be able to resolve all forward declarations.
Types, variables and constants are defined in declaration blocks. Unlike C and C++, these blocks cannot be located arbitrarily in the source code, but instead must be located in the header of the unit or program, or in a function or a procedure header.
A type declaration block starts with the keyword *type*, followed by the declaration of one or more types.
A variable declaration block starts with the keyword *var* or *ThreadVar*, followed by the declaration of one or more variables.
The following are valid variable declaration blocks:

```
var  I: integer;

var  I: Integer;
     S: String;
```

A constant declaration block starts with the keyword **const**, followed by one or more constant definitions. The keyword *Resourcestring* marks the definition(s) of one or more string constants. Only string constant definitions may follow this keyword, as illustrated in the following example:

```
const  MyInteger = 10;
       MyString  = 'A String';

Resourcestring    SOK     = 'OK';
                  SCancel = 'Cancel';
```

1.2.2 Structure and operation of units

Unlike the system of header and body files used in C and C++, Object Pascal utilizes the concept of *units*. A unit is an individual, self-contained source code file. It is divided into two sections:

- *Interface* section: This corresponds to the header file in C and contains only definitions of types, constants, variables and functions. Everything defined in this section is externally accessible, which means it can be accessed by other units.
- *Implementation* section: This corresponds to the body code file in C and contains the implementations of the functions and procedures defined in the interface section. It may also contain private definitions and declarations, which are not available to other units that access this unit.

An example of a minimum unit structure is:

```
unit unita;

interface

  procedure Hello;

implementation

  procedure Hello;
  begin
    Writeln('Hello, World');
  end;
end.
```

As already mentioned, the unit concept supports name spaces, since the same identifier may be defined in more than one unit. A source code segment that accesses different units with the same identifiers can distinguish between the two by prefixing the identifier with the unit name.

1.2.2 Structure and operation of units

There are several standard units available that provide basic routines used in nearly all programs, as listed in Table 1.5

Unit name	Contents
System	Standard I/O routines and basic conversion functions
SysUtils	Extended I/O, many conversion routines, and handlers for date and time, the file system and exceptions
Math	Mathematical routines
StrUtils	Routines for processing character strings
DateUtils	Routines for processing date and time
Classes	Basic classes and streaming system

Table 1.5: The standard units offered by Free Pascal

The *LibC* library in C also comprises these basic components.
To enable access to a unit, its name must appear in the *uses* clause of a program or a unit, as illustrated in the following example:

```
uses  SysUtils, Classes;
```

This statement binds the *SysUtils* and *Classes* units. This corresponds to the following preprocessor directives in C:

```
#include <sysutils.h>
#include "Classes.h"
```

Note that Pascal does not distinguish between < > and " " in the #include statement as is the case in C. All units in the search path are searched and bound to the resulting program only once. This is a fundamental principle of Free Pascal.
The following is a complete example:

```
unit unit1;
interface
  uses Math; // This unit can use the functions in the Math unit,
             // but they are not inherited automatically by MiniProgram.
  var  FirstNumber: Integer;      // public definition
implementation
  var  SecondNumber: integer;     // Private definition (visible only inside unit1)
end.
```

The program file of the unit is:

```
program MiniProgram;
uses Classes, SysUtils, unit1;
begin
  FirstNumber := 0;          // Allowed: unit1 is listed in the uses clause
  unit1.FirstNumber := 1;    // The same, but with explicit naming
                             // of the unit where the identifier comes from
  SecondNumber := 3 ;        // Prohibited: SecondNumber is private in unit1
  Math.Min (1, 3);           // Prohibited: Math unit is not listed in the uses clause
end.
```

As previously mentioned, identifier names are not case-sensitive in Object Pascal. However, there are a few exceptions to this rule. They apply in particular to file systems in which case is significant in file names, which is generally true in Unix-like systems and some MacOS systems.
In such systems, the compiler first looks for the unit name as it is written in the *uses* clause, then the name with all lower-case letters, and finally the name with all upper-case letters. Consequently, it has become common practice to write all file names in lower case. The file names of all FPC and Lazarus units are also written in lower case, and they can be written in any desired manner in the uses clause. For this reason, when a new unit is saved the IDE asks whether the name should be set to lower case, which should be answered with "Yes". This query can be suppressed in *Environment →Options → Environment →Naming*, where automatic renaming to lower case can also be specified.
Aside from this, there are only a few rules. The following conventions should be adhered to when assigning names:

- types always begin with "T";
- private fields of classes begin with "F";
- property setter methods begin with "Set";
- property getter methods begin with "Get".

For example:

```
TAClass = class
private
  FName: String;
  FValue: Integer;
  function GetName: String;
  procedure SetValue(const AValue: Integer);
public
  property Value: integer read FValue write SetValue;
  property Name: String read GetName write FName;
end;
```

These conventions are not mandatory, but they are advisable. It is also advisable to use CamelCase/Incaps notation, in which the first letter of the identifier and the first letter of each part of the identifier corresponding to a word is capitalized, as in the following example:

```
MyOwnVariable: Integer;
TSearchRec = record ... end;
```

1.2.3 Object orientation in Lazarus

As suggested by the name, object oriented code can be generated with Object Pascal. Object orientation is an integral part of the language, but it is optional. There are two types of objects: the older type (from the Turbo Pascal era) and the new type, which consists of classes. Lazarus and the LCL are written in accordance with the class concept, for which reason only the class concept is described below.
A class is a type, so it must always be defined in a type declaration block. In contrast to C++, only the methods are declared in the class declaration; the actual code is implemented in a separate block. A class declaration consists of several sections:

- *private* section: all identifiers in this section are available only inside the current unit
- *protected* section: all identifiers in this section are available in the current unit and in classes derived from it
- *public* section: identifiers in this section are globally available
- *published* section: similar to a public section, but the compiler generates run-time type information (RTTI) for declarations in this section. Each section may hold variables (fields), methods, class methods and properties. The following class declaration is valid:

```
TMyClass = class(TComponent)
private
  FMyInteger : Integer;
public
  property MyInteger: Integer Read FMyInteger Write FMyInteger;
end;
```

Note that the keyword *Read* followed by a fieldname in the property declaration of *MyInteger* indicates that the field *FMyInteger* is accessed directly.
A property can also be set or retrieved using a method, as in this example:

```
unit unit1;

interface
uses Classes;
type
  TMyClass = class(TComponent)
  private
    FMyInteger: Integer;
    Function GetMyInteger: Integer;
    Procedure SetMyInteger(const AValue: Integer);
  public
    Property MyInteger: Integer Read GetMyInteger Write SetMyInteger;
  end;

implementation
function TMyClass.GetMyInteger: Integer;
begin
  Result := FMyInteger;
end;

procedure TMyClass.SetMyInteger(const AValue: Integer);
begin
  FMyInteger := AValue;
end;
```

A mix of direct field access with getter and setter methods is also possible. Methods may be simple static methods (as above), or they may be defined as *virtual*, *abstract* or *class* methods.
A method is defined as virtual by placing the keyword *virtual* after its declaration:

```
function GetMyInteger: Integer; virtual;
```

If this method is implemented by a derived class, the definition must be repeated and the keyword *virtual* must be replaced by *override*:

```
function GetMyInteger: Integer; override;
```

If the keyword *override* is missing, the method will not be overridden.

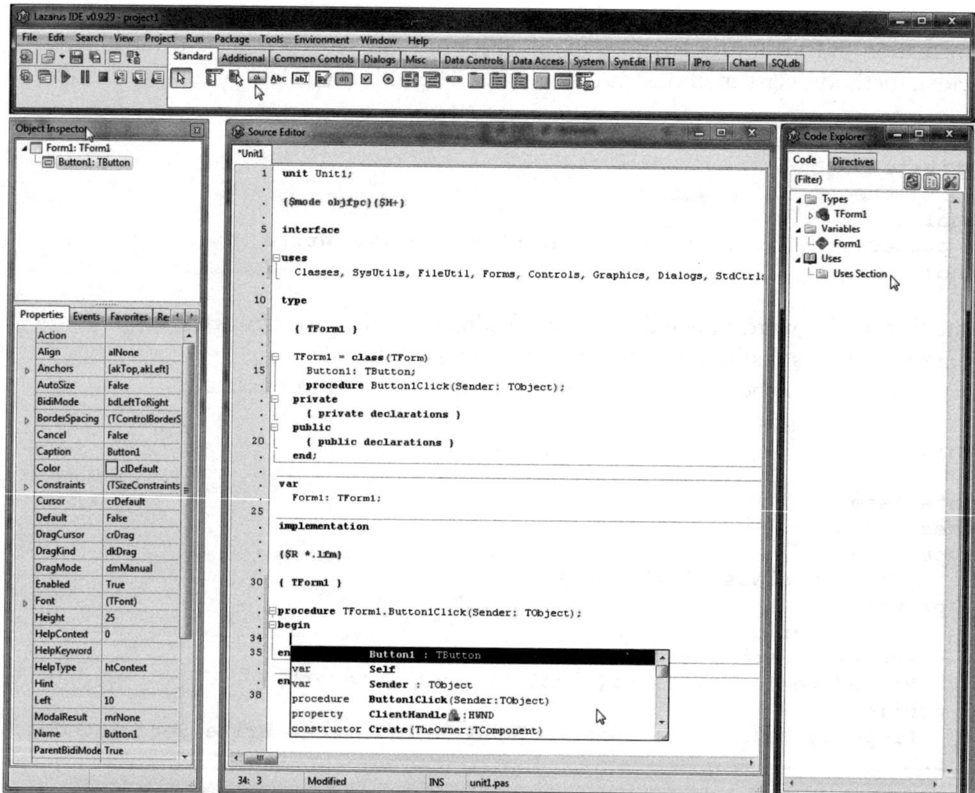

Figure 1.10: Classes can be browsed in the following dialogs: Source Editor, Object Inspector, Identifier Completion and Code Explorer

A virtual method may also be declared as *abstract.* In this case, there is no implementation of the method in the class; derived classes *must* override and implement the method. The compiler issues a warning if a class is constructed using abstract methods. Calling an unimplemented abstract method yields a runtime error. This is an example of an abstract declaration:

```
function GetMyInteger: Integer; virtual; abstract;
```

A *class* method is a method that is specific to a class but not to the instances of the class. The implementation of a class cannot access the fields or the properties of the class, and it cannot call any regular methods of the class. A class method is declared by placing the keyword *class* at the start of the declaration:

```
class function InstanceSize: Cardinal;
```

If a class is derived from an ancestor class, the class declaration only needs to contain the name of the parent class:

```
TMyChildClass = class(TMyParentClass)
  function GetMyInteger: Integer; override;
end;
```

In this example, *TMyChildClass* is declared as a child of *TMyParentClass* and the method *GetMyInteger* is overridden. Unlike C++, Object Pascal does not support multiple inheritance. It is not possible to specify more than one parent class when a derived class is created. However, Object Pascal has a limited sort of multiple inheritance in the form of *interfaces.* Every class may implement one or more interfaces. An interface defines a set of methods. No source code is associated with these methods, and no variable or field definitions can be present in an interface. The following is an example of a valid interface definition:

```
IStreamPersist = interface ['{B8CD12A3-267A-11D4-83DA-00004F60B2DD)']
  procedure LoadFromStream(Stream: TStream);
  procedure SaveTostream(Stream: TStream);
end;
```

If a class wishes to implement this interface, it must state the name of the interface in its declaration section and provide an implementation for each of the methods in the interface definition. In the following example, a class derived from *TPersistent* is defined and the interface *IStreamPersist* is implemented:

```
TStreamPersistent = class(TPersistent, IStreamPersist)
protected
  procedure LoadFromStream(Stream: TStream);
  procedure SaveToStream(Stream: TStream);
end;
```

Note that both methods of *IStreamPersist* are present in the implementation of the class.

1.2.4 Arrays in Free Pascal, compared to C

Arrays are generated in C by using pointers, which can be done in Pascal as in the following example:

```
type
  PExample = ^Example;
var
  ExampleArray: ^Example;
```

Here the type *Example* may be any desired type, such as Byte or Longint.
The first line defined a typed pointer named *PExample*, which corresponds to the following definition in C:

```
typedef Example* PExample;
```

The second line defines the array, although it still needs memory space, which must be reserved. This is done by the following call:

```
GetMem(ExampleArray, Sizeof(Example) * Number);
```

GetMem allocates memory and works the same way as *malloc* in C. As in C, the function *sizeof* returns the size of the type in bytes. *GetMem* allocates a memory area of the stated size on the heap and saves the pointer in *ExampleArray*. If *ExampleArray* already points to a memory area, it is not released. If the call fails, it throws an *Out of memory* exception and the new area is not initialized. The area is usually aligned to the best processing size for the processor.
The array must be initialized with the function *FillByte*:

```
FillByte(ExampleArray^, SizeOf(Example) * Number, 0);
```

FillByte fills a variable with a byte pattern. As the memory area referenced by the pointer *ExampleArray* must be cleared, rather than the pointer itself, it is necessary to pass *ExampleArray^* (with a carat). If the dereferencing operator is omitted, the variable will be overwritten, probably along with adjacent variables, because *FillByte* is fast but it does not provide any memory protection.
Memory that has been requested with *GetMem* is subsequently released with FreeMem:

```
FreeMem(ExampleArray);
```

A more convenient option is the procedure *ReAllocMem*, which can request, release, enlarge and shrink memory areas. Its operation is similar to that of *realloc* in C:

```
ExampleArray := NIL;     // NIL is the constant for undefined pointers or objects;  similar to NULL in C

ReAllocMem(ExampleArray, SizeOf(Example) * number);
```

If 0 is passed for *number*, no memory is reserved and *ExampleArray* remains nil. Otherwise this function corresponds to *GetMem*.

```
ReAllocMem(ExampleArray, SizeOf(Example), number_size);
```

If the memory area needs to be enlarged, the function tests whether the subsequent memory area is free and it is only necessary to adjust the heap. This goes very fast.
If insufficient additional memory is available, a new area is allocated and the previous contents are copied, after which the old area is released and *ExampleArray* is adjusted. The additional memory is not initialized. If the new area is smaller, only the smaller area is copied.

If zero bytes are requested and ExampleArray points to an area, this area is released and *ExampleArray* is set to NIL.

```
ReAllocMem(ExampleArray, 0);
```

The elements of the array can be accessed using the same pointer arithmetic operations as in C:

```
Value := ExampleArrary[3];      // read the value of the fourth element
Value := ExampleArray^;         // ^ is the dereferencing operator;
                                // it has the same effect as := ExampleArray[0];
```

To fetch the pointer to an element:

```
var
  Runner: PExample;
...
  Runner := @ExampleArray[2];             // @ returns the pointer to the third element
  Value  := Runner^;                      // Read the value of the third element
  Runner := Runner + SizeOf(Example);     // Next element
  Inc(Runner);                            // Next element
                                          // Inc works the same way for all types
  Inc(Runner, 2);                         // The next plus one element
  Dec(Runner);                            // The previous element; the opposite of Inc
```

Memory areas can be copied with the *Move* function of the *System* unit:

```
Move(ExampleArray[0], ExampleArray[10], SizeOf(Example) * 3);
```

This copies the values of the first three elements to the values of the eleventh to thirteenth elements.
Fixed-size arrays can also be defined. In contrast to C, numbering may start at any desired value:

```
var FixedArray: array[1..3] of Integer;
```

The array *FixedArray* has a fixed size of three elements, with the first element in position 1. Enumerated types can also be used to specify array limits:

```
   type TColor = (Red, Green, Blue);
   var  ColorArray: array[TColor] of integer;
begin
   ColorArray[Red] := 3;
end;
```

To move through each element of an array:

```
  var Color: TColor;
      i    : Integer;
begin
   for Color := Low(TColor) to High(TColor) do
     WriteLn(ColorArray[Color]);
   for i := Low(FixedArray) to High(FixedArray) do
     WriteLn(FixedArray[i]);
end;
```

Dynamic arrays are an extension of pointer arrays. Dynamic arrays store their own length, which can be found using *Length*. Their size can be changed with *SetLength*. They have indices, for which reason they are released automatically and can be copied quickly. The indices reference only the array as an entity, not the individual elements. *SetLength* initializes automatically if this is necessary.

```
   var DynArray: array of Integer;
begin
   SetLength(DynArray, 3);
   for i := 0 to Length(DynArray) - 1 do WriteLn(DynArray[i]);
  // The compiler handles the release
end;
```

To allow a dynamic array to be passed to a function, it must be defined as a type:

```
   type ArrayOfInteger = array of Integer;
Procedure Sum(a: ArrayOfInteger);
```

C has a construct that allows an undefined number of function arguments to be specified with an ellipsis. This can also be implemented in Object Pascal by using the keyword *varargs*.
The *printf* function in the standard C library uses the ellipsis:

```
int printf(char * fmt, ...);
```

This is bound in Object Pascal with

```
function printf(Fmt: PChar); CDecl; varargs;
```

This construct is only possible with the *cdecl* calling convention. It is also useful for external function declarations, for Object Pascal functions that accept a variable number of elements, for open arrays, and for arrays of constants. Open arrays are possible if all arguments are of one and the same type. In this case a function can be declared as follows:

```
function DoSomething(const Fmt:String; Args:array of String):Integer;
```

Caution: do not confuse this with a dynamic array!
The elements of this array are accessed in the same way as those of a normal array, with the limits *Low(Args)* and *High(Args)* being specified in advance as in the following example:

```
function DoSomething(const Fmt: String; Args: array of String):
                                                              Integer;
  var i: Integer;
begin
  for i := Low(Args) to High(Args) do Write(Args[i]);
end;
```

If it is necessary to pass a variable number of arguments of different types, an array of constants (*const* array) is a good choice. The *Format* function is a good example:

```
function Format(const Fmt: String; Args: array of const): String;
```

The *Args* array is implemented internally as an array of *TVarRec* in this function, as though it were declared as follows:

```
function Format(const Fmt: String; Args: array of TVarRec): String;
```

The compiler automatically builds the necessary *TVarRec* records when the function is called. Accordingly, the following calls of the *Format* function are valid:

```
Format('There are %d entries', [12]);
Format('There are %d entries and %d errors', [12, 4]);
Format('There were %d errors, with message : %s', [3,
                                                  'Error occurred']);
```

The argument types can be examined using the *vType* field of the *TVarRec* record:

```
function ArrayofConst(Args : array of const): Integer;
  var  A: TVarRec;
       I: Integer;
begin
  for I := Low(Args) to High(Args) do
  begin
    A := Args[i];
    case A.vType of
      vtInteger: WriteLn('Argument ', I,
                           ' is an integer with value: ',A.vInteger);
      vBoolean: WriteLn('Argument ', I,
                           ' is a boolean with value: ', A.VBoolean);
    end; { case }
  end; { for }
end; { function }
```

The above example does not examine all possible values. This can be remedied by using the Lazarus IDE codetools, which can list all possible values in the *TVarRec* structure.

1.2.5 Compiler directives

Some of the compiler directives and pragmas used in C have counterparts in FPC. The term 'pragma' is not used in FPC; what is called a pragma in C is known as a compiler directive in FPC. The most important directives for Object Pascal are described briefly here. Detailed descriptions of all directives are available in the *Free Pascal V2 User's Guide* by Michaël Van Canneyt from the same publisher as this book (ISBN 978-3-936546-43-8).

Include files

Include directives allow several files to be bound into a single file. They have the following syntax:

```
{$include file_name}
```

or in short form:

```
{$i file_name}
```

This works the same way as *#include* in C. Encountering a {$i ...} directive in a file the compiler proceeds to read the included file, then returns to the original file, and carries on reading it. The Free Pascal Compiler has its own search path for *include* files, which can be extended with the *-Fi* parameter. The file suffix of an include file can be freely chosen by the programmer, although *.inc* is commonly used to distinguish it from a Pascal unit.
As include files have their own search path and search paths may contain macros, a different include file can be bound for each platform.

For example, if an implementation differs for Windows, Linux and OS X, three different include files can be generated and all assigned the same name (e.g. *example.inc*), but stored in separate, appropriately named subdirectories. They can then be called automatically according to the operating system type.

Conditional compilation

The directives *$IF*, *$IFDEF*, *$IFNDEF*, *$ELSE*, *$ENDIF*, *$DEFINE* and *$UNDEF* address exceptions specific to individual compiler versions, processors and operating systems. Their operation is largely the same as their C counterparts. For example:

```
{$IFDEF MSWindows}
// code for Windows
{$ELSE}
// code for non-Windows
{$ENDIF}
```

Along with *MSWindows* and its synonym *Windows*, there are many other flags for operating systems (Linux, Darwin, FreeBSD); families (MS Windows, Unix, BSD); processors (CPUi386, CPU32, CPU64); endianess (ENDIAN_LITTLE, ENDIAN_BIG); compiler versions (FPC, VER2, VER2_3, VER2_3_1); and for modes, tests and features.
The actual flags are defined in Lazarus under
Environment →Code Tools Defines Editor →Free Pascal Compiler.
The specific meaning is described in the Free Pascal documentation.

Macros

Macros are virtually indispensable in C, but they are rarely necessary in Free Pascal. Although the Free Pascal Compiler supports macros for compatibility reasons and to simplify the implementation of C libraries, they are disabled by default and are not recognized by Lazarus. The only exception is *extdecl*. Many platform-independent libraries use different calling conventions on different systems. This involves how and in which order function parameters are placed on the stack. The calling convention must be stated in the form of a keyword for each individual function; the macro *extdecl* can relieve the programmer of this task. An example from the *Gl* unit:

```
{$MACRO ON}
{$IFDEF Windows}
    {$DEFINE extdecl := stdcall)
{$ELSE}
    {$DEFINE extdecl := cdecl}
{$ENDIF)

procedure glAccum ( op : GLenum ; value : GLfloat ) ; extdecl ;
// other functions
```

Macros are valid only inside the unit and are not passed to other units. Starting with version 2.3.1 of FPC, there is a new directive that can be used to switch calling conventions: *{$callingconvention stdcall}*.

{$IFDEF Windows}	*{$callingconvention stdcall}*
{$ELSE}	*{$callingconvention cdecl}*
{$ENDIF}	

The directive applies to all subsequent procedures until the next *{$callingconvention}*.

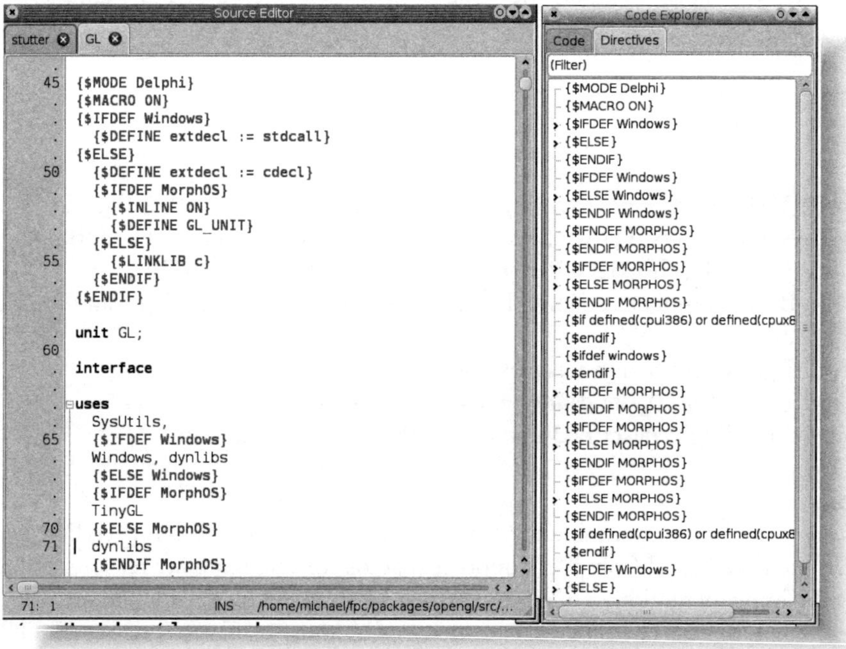

Figure 1.11: Code Explorer is helpful for getting your bearings in long units with many directives

1.3 Projects

Delphi and Lazarus projects have a lot in common. They usually generate programs. In particular, packages in Delphi generate Windows libraries (`.bpl` files), while in Lazarus packages are primarily used to modularize relatively large projects. Both projects and packages have been developed in Lazarus differently from Delphi with particular attention to the needs and constraints of platform independence.

Project files

In Delphi, a project is defined by its `.dpr` file. This file contains information about which forms, units and packages belong to the project, and which parameters must be passed to the compiler. Depending on the Delphi version, additional information (such as search paths) is contained in other files. In Lazarus, a project is defined by its `.lpi` file. A project usually has an `.lpr` file, which is the main file and has a structure similar to that of a Delphi `.dpr` file. However, a project may have more units than those listed in the `.lpr` file, and it can use more packages.

All of the complier settings are stored in the `.lpi` file. Like all Lazarus configuration files, this file is generated in XML format. All data in the file can be edited in the IDE dialogs.
To recap all of this for the sake of clarity: the `.lpr` file is largely managed by the IDE, as in Delphi, but the `.lpi` file is more important.
For example, a Delphi `.dpr` file has the following entry in the *uses* clause:

```
unit1 in 'Directory\Unit1.pas' {Form1};
```

Delphi recognizes from the **in** keyword which unit belongs to the project and where it is located. By contrast, Lazarus uses search paths and does not generate *in* paths, because they can cause problems on non-Windows platforms. For example, letter case must be taken into account under Linux, BSD and MacOS X. It is also essential to write 'Directory' with an initial capital and the rest lower case.
Furthermore, Lazarus saves the session data for each project, which allows the IDE to restore the full status the next time the project is opened. If the IDE has been closed or another project was opened in the meantime, it restores everything to the way it was when the IDE or project was last closed, including open files, cursor positions, breakpoints, jump history and much more. The session data is normally saved in the `.lpi` file, but it can be saved in a separate file if this option is configured in *Project →Project Options →Session.*
A tool that simplifies converting Delphi projects to Lazarus projects is available under *Tools →Convert Delphi project to Lazarus project....*
Delphi can bundle several projects into a project group. This is not yet implemented in Lazarus, where large projects are structured using packages.
All file names and search paths are saved in relative form in Lazarus projects, which makes it easy to copy a project to another computer, even if it runs a different operating system. No conversions are necessary. This allows projects to be managed using a version control system such as SVN, and it allows several programmers to work on a project at the same time using different operating systems. The development of Lazarus itself is a good example of this.

The relatively few absolute search paths are implemented using macros. For instance, the macro *$(LazarusDir)* stands for the current Lazarus directory. Thanks to packages, absolute paths are almost unnecessary. How this works is explained elsewhere in this book.
In contrast to Delphi, there is no global directory holding all of the precompiled units in the form of `.ppu` files (which correspond to Delphi's `.dcu` files). Each project and each package has its own directories for this. This strict segregation allows well-defined, conflict-free compiler configurations to be defined for each package, and it facilitates fast, clean changes between different versions and targets.

For example, a program to be run under Windows can be compiled either for Windows 32 or Windows CE. Special package installation is also unnecessary. This is described in more detail elsewhere in this book.
A Delphi package is a set of units compiled into a library (DLL or `.bpl`).

The main file has the suffix `.dpk`. A Lazarus package is a set of files along with their own compiler configurations and data related to i18n, FPDoc and inheritance (i18n stands for 'internationalization', which means translation of strings into different languages, and FPDoc is a Free Pascal tool for documenting Pascal code). Although a package may generate a library, Lazarus packages are normally used to structure relatively large projects or to distribute and reuse units. The main file has the suffix `.lpk`, and like all Lazarus configuration files it is an XML file. Each package has its own settings and search paths. Furthermore, each package can itself use other packages and be used by other packages. What is inherited for this purpose can be defined.
The following compiler settings can be inherited:

- search paths (units, object files, linker and source code)
- compiler parameters
- linker parameters

All in all, there are quite a few differences, so Lazarus users coming from a Delphi background are advised to read the entire 'Packages' section (see below at Section 1.5). Each package can have its own compilations, which utilize resources. During compilation, FPC generates a `.rst` file for each unit that has resource strings.
If the *i18n* option is enabled and a subdirectory is specified, Lazarus automatically creates `.po` files. These are simple text files that are recognized by many open-source internationalization programs, and editors for `.po` files are available on all platforms.
Each package can provide documentation and help for the source code.
Lazarus has built-in support for FPDoc and a subset of the *pasdoc* notation. To activate this, FPDoc support must be enabled under *Options →Project Options →i18n* for the package or the project, and the directory where the FPDoc documents are to be saved must be specified. At present, FPC can only generate normal dynamic libraries; the Delphi package concept cannot be ported to other platforms. This means that the initialization and finalization sections are not called automatically, and the RTL packages and other FPC packages are not yet available as ready-made DLL or `.so` files.
The main difference for experienced Delphi users is that Delphi works predominantly with global search paths, which hampers the segregation of packages, versions and projects and makes it difficult to copy projects and packages to other computers. Lazarus relies almost exclusively on context-sensitive search paths, which means that each search path is assigned to a project or a package. For this reason, Lazarus projects and packages can easily be copied to other computers and operating systems without modifying any paths. As a result, the number of paths that must be modified is less than under Delphi, and in most cases it is only necessary to delete paths when converting Delphi projects into packages. Actually, search path editing is only necessary under Lazarus if the path contains macros and dynamic distinction between operating systems is desired. If too many search paths are entered under Delphi, this usually does not have any adverse consequences, but under Lazarus it may cause the compiler to find source files belonging to other packages and compile them more than once. This is discussed in more detail in Section 1.5. There is a tool that simplifies the task of converting Delphi packages into Lazarus packages. It is located under *Tools →Convert Delphi package to Lazarus package....*

1.4 Components

Despite its name, Delphi's VCL (Visual Component Library) also contains non-visual components, while Lazarus's LCL contains only visual components. The non-visual components, such as database components, are found in FPC or are available from external sources. In FPC, this group of components is called the Free Pascal Component Library (FCL). Some VCL components are not present in the LCL or the FCL, while on the other hand there are components present in the LCL or the FCL that are not available in Delphi. Furthermore, the components are not emulations – some of the properties are not present, and some of them have different characteristics.
For every property, the *Restricted Properties* tab of Lazarus's Object Inspector shows the extent to which it can be used on different platforms.
Communication between the LCL and the graphical user interface of the operating system is event-driven. Events are messages that are exchanged and processed using message pipes. For example, if the user clicks the mouse, a message containing the mouse coordinates is sent to the window beneath the cursor.
The VCL components utilize the Windows messaging API and forward the messages through the levels. The LCL is based on the same system, but in its case the messages do not come directly from Windows. Instead, they come from the relevant interface to the LCL, such as GTK, Qt or Windows.
These messages are forwarded largely unchanged under Windows, but on all other platforms the messages are generated artificially in the interest of compatibility with the VCL. This means that by no means all Windows API messages are generated, and some parameters operate differently. To enable programs written and tested to run under Windows to also run on other platforms, the Windows 32/64 interface of the LCL forwards only certain messages and changes some of the parameters if necessary.
Only messages and parameters that are portable are possible in the LCL, and of course they exist only if a Lazarus developer has taken the trouble to implement them. In practice, this means that messages can only be sent to LCL components; they cannot be sent to the LCL interface. Caution is especially necessary when porting Delphi components that utilize Windows API messages. Events in different widget-sets occur in different sequences or with different frequencies.
For example, one widget-set may first forward a *MouseDown* event and only afterwards respond to it, while another widget-set may reverse this order. Consequently, particular attention must be given to examining and testing messages when porting Delphi components, and the best approach is to replace them by LCL methods.
It is only natural that functionality that is not provided by Delphi's VCL or RTL that is needed in Delphi programs will be implemented with the aid of direct Windows API functions, since all Delphi programs are developed to run under Windows. Since the LCL is compatible with Delphi's VCL but not with Windows, and is by no means a Windows emulator, Delphi components relying directly on the Windows API must be replaced for other platforms.
The open-source community has already ported a large number of libraries to FPC and Lazarus, and they have generated platform-independent libraries for nearly everything you might need.

Naturally, the Windows units can be used under Windows with LCL as well, but in this case the components should be marked with *{$IFDEF MSWindows}*. Please do not copy Borland's mistaken practice of using *{$IFDEF Linux}* to mark non-Windows code, since most code for Linux also runs on BSD and MacOS X platforms. The proper name of the higher-level family is *unix* in FPC.

1.5 Packages

Packages group several units into a larger logical entity. Packages have their own directories, their own compiler configurations, and their own translation files.
This makes them independent entities that can easily be copied to other computers and other operating systems. Like projects, they can use other packages, but unlike projects, they can also inherit attributes. Lazarus 0.9.28 allows only one *project* to be open at a time, but it allows any number of *packages* to be open.
Consequently, packages are primarily useful for modularizing projects.
Moreover, platform independence is a high priority with Lazarus, so packages can easily be reused and can be compiled on other platforms without any changes to paths or settings. In addition, they can be installed in the IDE in order to add new components, menu items and much more.
Up to and including version 0.9.28, the distinction between design time, run time and design-and-run-time, as under Delphi, is just an indication; it is not obligatory. It may become more important if and when the FP compiler supports dynamic packages.

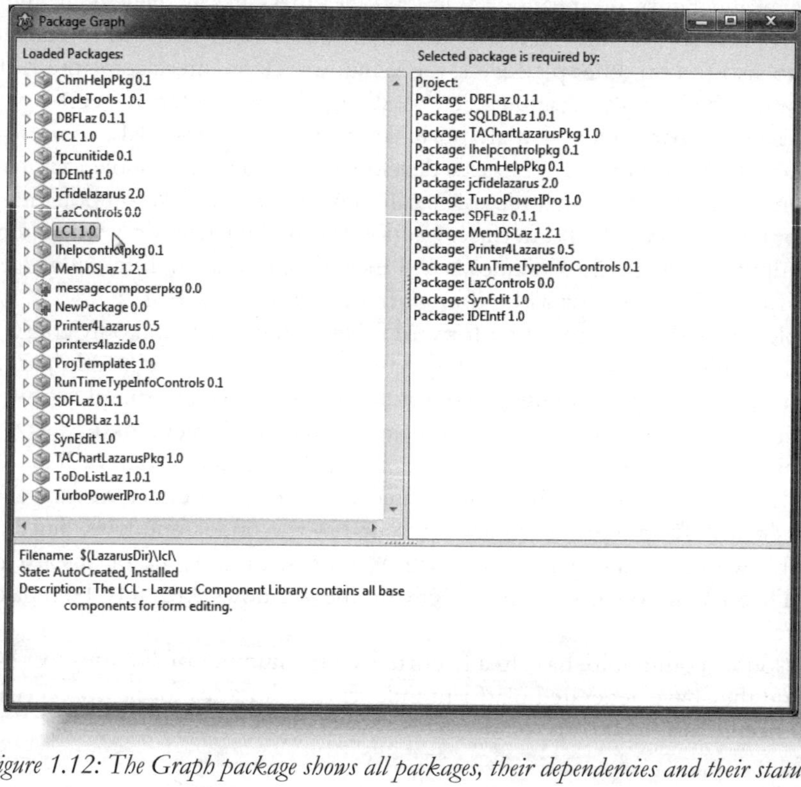

Figure 1.12: The Graph package shows all packages, their dependencies and their status

It is not necessary for all of the files of a package to be units; other types of files, such as include files, form files (`.lfm`) and binary files (such as images and databases) can also be added to a package. Generally speaking, all files necessary for compiling the package should be included in the package, since the IDE automatically recompiles the package if any of these files is modified. More specifically, this occurs when the change date of the file is later than the date of the automatically generated `package_name.compiled` file. The IDE saves the `.compiled` file in the output directory of the package after every successful compilation (see Section 3.1.8).
The files may be located in different directories, and they need not necessarily be located in subdirectories, although this is usually more convenient for package users.
All file and directory names are saved relative to the `.lpk` file. As a result, a package with all of its files can easily be copied to another system and compiled with no need to modify the path names. All that is necessary is to open the `.lpk` file on the other system and click *Compile* or *Install*. As Windows systems use '\' as a director separator while Linux and other system use '/', this information is stored in the `.lpk` file and the paths are converted when the file is opened. Drive letters such as 'C:' and 'D:' are used only in Windows systems (and in OS/2, for which Lazarus support is lacking due to the failure some time ago of over-ambitious projects initiated in the community).

1.5.1 C libraries in Free Pascal

C libraries can be used in Pascal programs. This can be done in two different ways:

- Static:
  With static binding, the entry points of the library are declared as though they were part of a program or a unit, after which they can be used as such. The library must always be present in the system in which the program is compiled and run.
  This is because the library is loaded when the program is launched, and it searches for the entry points in the library.
  If an error occurs in this process, the program cannot be run.
- Dynamic:
  With dynamic binding, procedure variables (pointers) are defined for all of the functions in the C library. The library is loaded into memory and the addresses of the entry points, obtained by querying the library, are stored in the corresponding variables. This means that the binary file is always loaded, and problems arising from situations where the library is not loaded, for example because it is not installed on the system, can be resolved with suitable code.

Static binding requires the declaration of the necessary entry points.

There are three things worth noting in the following example:

```
procedure Free(P: Pointer); StdCall; external 'msvcrt' name 'free';
```

Firstly there is the *StdCall* modifier, which indicates the calling convention.
Under Windows it is *StdCall*, while on most other systems it is *Cdecl*.
Secondly, the name of the library comes after the keyword *external*.

A file extension is not necessary here; the system looks after this.
Thirdly, the name of the entry point is indicated by the keyword *name*. This part may be skipped if the name of the entry point is the same as the declared name of the function. However, caution is necessary here because the name of the entry point, unlike the names of identifiers in Object Pascal, is usually case-sensitive.
Consequently, the above declaration takes the following form under Linux:

```
procedure Free(P: Pointer); CDecl; external 'c' name 'free';
```

The following source code performs dynamic binding:

```
uses dynlibs;
  type  TfreeProc = Procedure(P: Pointer); CDecl;
  var   Free: TfreeProc;
        H   : TlibHandle;
begin
  H := LoadLibrary('msvrt');
  if H <> NilHandle then
    Pointer(Free) := GetProcedureAddress(H, 'free');
end.
```

The unit *Dynlibs* contains the definitions of *TLibHandle* and *NilHandle* as well as the procedures *LoadLibrary* and *GetProcedureAddress*. These definitions are platform-independent and work on all systems. However, the library name may vary, as may the calling convention.

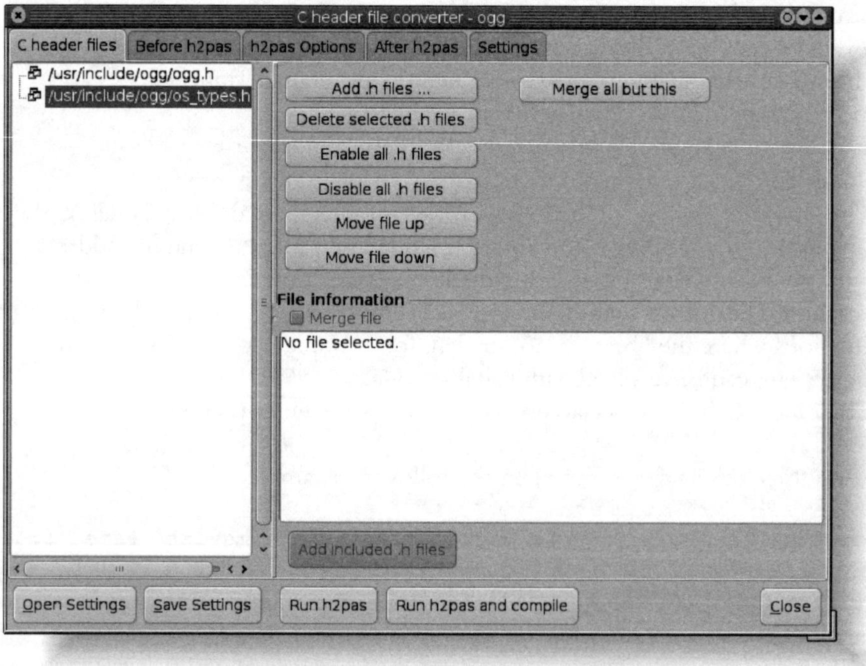

Figure 1.13: The GUI wizard h2paswizard

Regardless of which method is used to load a library, it is always necessary to have a unit that defines the types and entry points of the library. It may be created manually, but there is also a tool that can convert C header files `(.h)` to Pascal. Although the command-line tool *h2pas* is not perfect, it is certainly useful when C constructs must be converted to Pascal. It is included with Free Pascal. Lazarus has a GUI wizard called *h2paswizard* that helps with the configuration of the options of *h2pas*. This wizard is a Lazarus package, and it is installed via *Package →Configure installed packages....* As input it takes one or more C header files that describe a library, and as output it generates a Pascal unit that can be used to statically bind the library to a Free Pascal program.
The most commonly used options are enabled by default; the other options are primarily related to the generated code and are self-explanatory. They may be configured as desired. More information on *h2paswizard* is available at
`http://wiki.lazarus.freepascal.org/Creating_bindings_ for_C_libraries.`
If the Pascal bindings are distributed over several files, they should be grouped in a Lazarus package.

1.5.2 Free Pascal libraries in C

Lazarus can be used to generate dynamically loadable libraries that can be called from any C program, or more precisely, from any program written in a language that can bind libraries. All that is necessary for this is to generate a library instead of a program.
A library is similar to a program; the difference is that it begins with the keyword *library* instead of the keyword *program*. In addition, the keyword *exports* indicates which functions and procedures in the library can be exported.
The following code exports a function named *free*:

```
library newfree:

procedure Free(P: Pointer); Stdcall;
begin
  FreeMem(P);
end;

exports
  free;         // case-sensitive!
end.
```

When the source code is compiled, a library named `newfree.dll (libnewfree.so` on Unix systems) is generated; this library exports the function *free* (everything in lowercase). Note the calling convention *Stdcall* – no current C compiler understands the default Free Pascal calling convention *register*. Also note that some Pascal constructs are not allowed in a library. In particular, character *strings* and *classes* cannot be exported from libraries or imported from libraries. This is because the Pascal *string* type is unknown in C and because Pascal classes are not binary-compatible with C++ classes.
The names of the Free Pascal procedures are modified in the process; the name appearing in the declaration is not the same as the name in the assembler. For this reason, it is better to write the name in the *exports* clause in the same way as it is exported.
In the above example, the function with the name in lowercase letters is exported.

1.5.3 Installing new components in the IDE

The example described in this section demonstrates how to generate your own package and a new component, and how to install it in the IDE.
The first task is to create a new package by selecting *Package →New package....*
The Package dialog then opens with a new package named *NewPackage.*
The toolbar at the top of the window has icons for the most common actions, such as save and compile, and the files and details are shown below. All other actions, such as renaming and deinstalling, can be accessed from the pop-up menu.

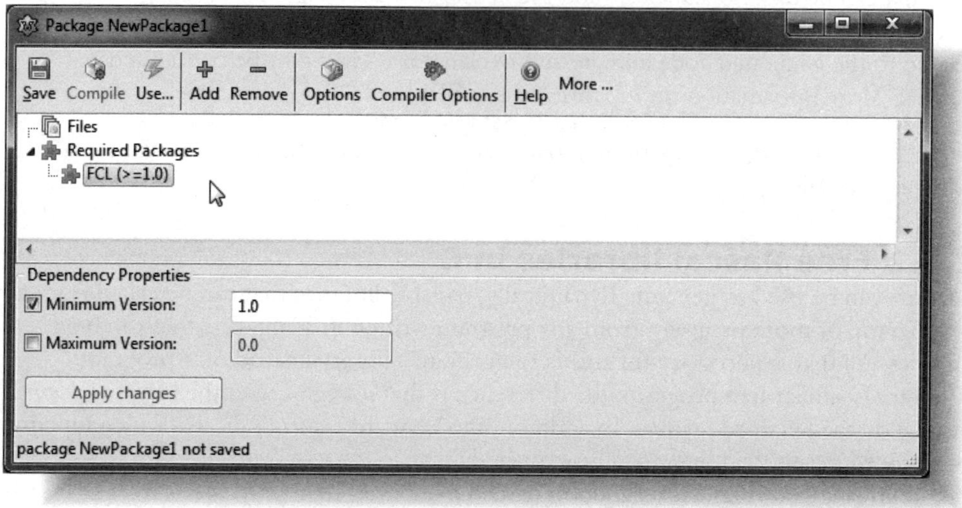

Figure 1.14: All configuration settings of a package can be edited in the Package dialog

Clicking the *Save* icon opens the Save dialog. It is advisable to create a new directory in order to avoid overlap or conflicts with existing packages and projects. Avoid using special characters or spaces in the directory name, since some tools do not like them. The file name must be a valid Pascal identifier and must have the suffix `.lpk`. If this suffix is missing, it is automatically appended to the file name. Many platforms distinguish between upper case and lower case, so the file name should be all lower case. The IDE treats the project name and the file name separately, so there is no danger in using upper-case letters as desired in the project name.
If you enter a file name such as *MyPackage1* in the dialog, the IDE will ask whether the file name should be written in lower case. If so, the package name will be *MyPackage1* and the file name will be `mypackage1.lpk`. Note that a unit with the same name is created automatically. This unit is generated by the IDE and overwritten each time a change is made, so its contents cannot be edited. The name can be changed later via the Package dialog pop-up menu.
Like all Lazarus configuration files, the new `.lpk` file is a human-readable XML file. This means that it can be searched or edited manually if necessary. The IDE notes the file name, and from this point on the package can only be found using this name.
It also appears in the dialog opened by *Open recent package...* in the *Package* menu.

1.5.3 Installing new components in the IDE

A new component can easily be added by clicking *Add* in the Package dialog. This opens a dialog for generating and adding files and dependencies. The key parameters of the new component can be entered on the *New Component* tab. For example, suppose you wish to create a new *TButton* that displays a short message when it is clicked.
For this purpose, select *TButton* as the base class (parent type). In response, the IDE enters default values in all other fields. Here we assume that the class name should be *TMessageButton*, and it should appear on the *Misc* tab in the Component Palette. If you wish, you can also enter a new palette tab name, such as *My Components*. The usual Pascal rules apply to the new file and unit names, and the unit cannot have the same name as the package. After you click *OK*, the new unit appears in the Source Editor:

```
unit MessageButton;
{$mode objfpc}{$H+}
interface

uses  Classes, SysUtils, LResources, Forms,
      Controls, Graphics, Dialogs, StdCtrls;
type
 TMessageButton = class(TButton)
 private
 { Private declarations }
 protected
 { Protected declarations }
 public
 { Public declarations }
 published
 { Published declarations }
 end;

procedure Register;
implementation
  procedure Register;
  begin
    RegisterComponents('Misc', [TMessageButton]);
  end;
end. { Unit }
```

The unit is automatically added to the package and saved in the main directory of the package. It contains the new class *TMessageButton* and the procedure *Register*.
The IDE calls these entities during initialization. The procedure *RegisterComponents* registers the new class in the Misc palette page. Other IDE extensions may also be registered here. The IDE also adds the unit *Buttons*, which contains the base class *TButton*, to the *uses* clause. As the unit *Buttons* belongs to the package LCL, a dependency is added for it. It is shown on the *Files* tab of the Package dialog. As a result of this dependency, the search paths of the package are automatically extended so that all units of the LCL can be used. Next, click *Install* in the Package dialog. This saves and compiles the new package, checks the dependencies, and compiles the new IDE. In this process, the IDE shows a dialog that describes what will happen and requests confirmation of recompilation of the IDE. Compilation may take several minutes the first time.
After this, the operating system has the data available in working memory and compiling the IDE should take only a few seconds.

In the default configuration, Lazarus will now restart automatically. If it does not, this must be initiated manually.
After the restart, the new component appears in the component palette on the *Misc* tab. As no icon was specified for the new class, the standard icon is used. This component can now be placed on a form, the same as any other component.

1.5.4 Units in multiple projects

Over the course of time, most programmers develop several handy functions and units that they use in nearly all of their projects. Under Delphi, the directory holding these units is simply added to the Unit search path. Although this is in principle also possible under Lazarus, this method has some drawbacks. If these units are transferred to a different computer, all of the search paths must be updated. Furthermore, the compiler generates `.ppu` files from the units, and these files are generated using the current compiler configuration. If another project has a different configuration, the `.ppu` files will not be regenerated automatically, which can lead to strange errors. Lazarus packages bundle units into well-defined entities and can be generated with just a few mouse clicks. Suppose the units are located in the directory `C:\Sundry`. The new package is generated by clicking *Packages →New Package*, which opens the Package dialog. Clicking *Save at* the top left of this dialog opens a file selection dialog, where the file named `C:\Sundry\Sundry.lpk` should be selected. Depending on the configuration, the IDE asks whether the file should be renamed to lowercase, which should be answered with "Yes". As a result, the new package is called *Sundry* and has the file name `C:\Sundry\sundry.lpk`.
The next step is to add the units by clicking *Add* in the Package dialog. This opens a dialog with several tabs. On the *Add Files* tab, select *Browse*. This opens a file selection dialog where the units can be selected. You may also include `.lfm` files and other types of files. After the file selection window is closed, the selected files are listed in the dialog. This list can be edited if desired. Then click *Add files to package*. When the dialog is closed, the files are added to the package and listed in the Package dialog. A final click on *Save* records the package on disk.
If the *Sundry* units only access the standard units of the FCL, the package is complete at this point. If the package needs to contain form files or needs units belonging to the LCL, the LCL package must be added to the list of required packages. To do this, click *Add* in the Package dialog, select the *New Requirement* tab, and select the LCL package in the *Package Name* field. After you click OK to close the dialog, LCL will appear under *Required Packages*. The effect can be seen on the *Inherited* tab of the Package dialog *Compiler Options* tab.
To check whether all dependencies have been resolved, click *Compile* in the Package dialog. If the compiler cannot find a unit, Sundry needs another package.
Once the package *Sundry* has been compiled, it is an autonomous package that can easily be copied to any desired destination, including other computers. The IDE also gives the package its own output directory to hold the generated `.ppu` files.
To use the package in the project, click *More...→Add to project* in the Package dialog. Select *Package →Open recent package...* to re-open the Package dialog for *Sundry*. The dependencies of the project are listed under *Project →Project Inspector*. There you can delete dependencies or add new dependencies.

The package *Sundry* can also be used in other packages.
If you follow all these steps, you will see that each path has been specified only once. All search paths are derived from the packages or projects. This is what makes Lazarus packages platform-independent and allows them to be relocated easily. Furthermore, other developers who wish to use the packages do not need to worry about how the package is structured, and they do not need to adapt any search paths at all.

1.5.5 Virtual units

Every component class of the Component Palette needs a unit and a package. If a unit defines a component class but does not register it, it can be included virtually in a package. An example of this is the unit `ibconnection.pp`, which is a standard Free Pascal unit. The package *SQLDBLaz* defines a virtual unit *ibconnection*, which registers the component class *TIBConnection* for the unit `ibconnection.pp`. The result is that a package and a package file are registered with the class.

1.5.6 Units for different platforms

Many packages run on highly diverse platforms. Usually a uniform external API is provided, with different code internally for each platform. Conditional compilation is sufficient for minor differences:

```
{$IFDEF MSWindows}
    // Code for Windows 98, ME, NT, 2K, XP, WinCE, etc.
{$ELSE}
    // Code for Linux, BSD, OS X, Solaris, etc.
{$ENDIF}
```

This quickly becomes unwieldy with large differences or many different platforms, so it is better to create a separate *include* file for each platform or unit:

```
uses
{$IFDEF MSWindows}
 WindowsUnit
{$ENDIF}
{$IFDEF Unix}
 UnixUnit
{$ENDIF}
;
```

Here the two units *WindowsUnit* and *UnixUnit* should be added to the package, but they do not always need to be compiled with the package. To prevent automatic compilation of a unit, select it in the Package dialog to display the file properties at the bottom of the dialog, and disable the Use *unit* option. After this, the IDE will continue to check the change date of the unit (e.g. *Windows*Unit), but it will not automatically compile the unit with the package. The compiler does this recursively, due to the previously mentioned *IFDEF* directive

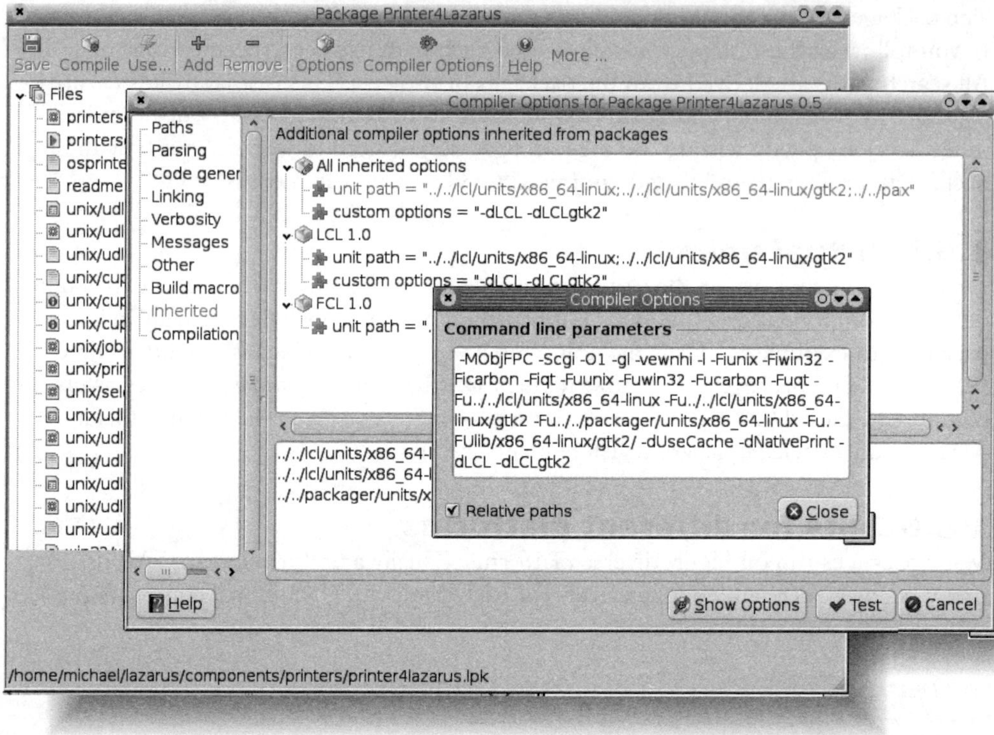

Figure 1.15: The package Printer4Lazarus provides access to three different print libraries, depending on the operating system. The compiler parameters are displayed under Compiler Options Show Options. The Inherited table shows the sources of other parameters

If there are several such units, this method also quickly becomes unwieldy. For this reason, Lazarus allows macros to be used in search paths. For example, suppose the unit *Handy* is available in two versions: one for Windows 32 and the other for Linux. These two units are stored in subdirectories, which in accordance with the Free Pascal names of the operating system are named:

```
MyPackage/
   mypackage.lpk
   mypackage.pas
   mainunit.pas
   win32/handy.pas
   linux/handy.pas
```

Include files are often used instead of units.
The entry under *Compiler Options →Paths →Other Unit Files* in the Package dialog should now be:

```
$(TargetOS)
```

with no additional path.
A suffixed directory separator is OK, such as the following entry under Windows:

```
$(TargetOS)\
```

or under Linux:

```
$(TargetOS)/
```

Starting with Lazarus 9.26, the macro *TargetOS* takes one of the following values, depending on the operating system: *darwin*, *freebsd*, *linux*, *netbsd*, *openbsd*, *solaris*, *win32*, *win64*, *wince*. Other useful macros in this connection are:

Macro	Target
TargetCPU	i386, powerpc, m68k, x86_64, sparc, arm
TargetOS	windows, unix

A frequent combination for conditional compilation is:

```
$(TargetOS)-$(TargetCPU)
```

These macros modify the search path according to the operating system, with the result that the compiler and the code tools automatically find the right *handy.pas* unit during compilation. Note that with this method the code is completely free of *IFDEF*s. Another option is provided by the macro *$Env()*, which returns the values of environment variables. For example, an environment variable named *LIBPATH* containing the path to special libraries can be defined. *$Env(LIBPATH)* allows this value to be used in every Lazarus path.

1.5.7 Finding packages

A package is identified by its name and its version. The name must be a valid Pascal identifier, which means that the first character must be a letter (A…Z, a…z) or an underscore, while all subsequent characters may be letters or digits. Letter case is only significant for file names. In theory, the name may be up to 256 characters long, but some linkers impose a length restriction of 255 characters for the entire path name. This leads to problems where you have nested procedures with long names. Fortunately, linking tools of this sort are becoming less common.

The version number consists of up to four numbers, which are called *Major*, *Minor*, *Release* and *Build* in Lazarus. Version numbers lacking the trailing positions are automatically padded with zeros.

A package file name always begins with the package name, with deviations in letter case allowed, and ends with the suffix `.lpk` (which stands for 'Lazarus package'). File names should preferably be written in lower case to ensure that the files can be found easily under all operating systems. Like all IDE configuration files, `.lpk` files are XML files, and they can be read and written using the *TXMLConfig* component. They can also be edited manually using a text editor. The format is backward compatible, so that new versions of the IDE can read older versions.

Although an older version of the IDE can also read new versions of the files, it will ignore newer parameters and discard them when the files are saved.
When a project is opened, the IDE automatically loads all required packages in the background. The project normally has a list only of the used packages, with their names and the minimum and maximum version numbers. For each name and version range, the IDE searches for the matching `.lpk` file, opens it, loads its package list and so on, until all dependencies have been resolved.
First it searches the list of recently opened packages, which is stored in `Configdirectory/packagefiles.xml`. This list is related to the list displayed by *Package →Open recent package...*, but it is larger because it is not limited to a specific number of files and also saves version numbers. An entry is placed on this list every time the programmer opens a new package file. The entry is updated when a package is moved to a new location. For this reason, when a new package is created the `.lpk` file only has to be identified once for the IDE; after this every project and package can find the `.lpk` file automatically.
If no package with a suitable name and version is found in the `packagefiles.xml` list, the IDE searches the source code directory under *packager/globallinks/* for `.lpl` (Lazarus package link) files. An `.lpl` file has a name and version in its file name. For instance, the file `packager/globalinks/cgilaz-0.lpl` looks after all packages named *cgilaz* with version number 0.0.0.0 or higher.
If there is also another `.lpl` file named `cgilaz-1.0.lpl`, it takes precedence for all dependencies with version numbers greater than 1.0.0.0. The `.lpl` file contains only a single line with the path name of the `.lpk` file. This path name may include macros.
The `.lpl` files can be used by external suppliers or administrators, for example when a package needs to be installed for all users of a system. The `.lpl` file allows the source files of the packages to be stored in the system somewhere in a central location.
Next, the IDE looks for the `.lpk` files in the same directory as the project or package to which the dependencies belong.
Finally, every package and every project can define its own locations for `.lpk` files.
To do this, right-click on a dependency in the Package dialog or the Project Inspector and select *Store dependency filename*. This saves the relative path to the package that is currently being used. This is a good idea with the example projects supplied with the package or with large libraries containing several interdependent `.lpk` files. This allows them to reference each other and allows the user to start anywhere. For example, the user can open an example project and the IDE will find and automatically load the appropriate `.lpk` file from a nearby directory. To find out which packages the IDE is currently aware of, open *View →IDE internals →Package links....*
With Lazarus 0.9.26, it is only possible to view packages here.
Two packages with the same name cannot be open at the same time. If one of these packages is opened, the other is automatically replaced. This happens even if a package with version 1.0 is installed and a project that needs that package with version 2.0 or higher is opened. In this situation, the IDE automatically loads a package with version 2.0 or higher and replaces the previous package in memory. However, only the administrative data is replaced; the installed components and the registered IDE extensions are retained.

The new components of the version 2.0 package are installed only when the IDE is recompiled and restarted. This allows users to work with different versions of a package conveniently. Manual editing of search paths or files, as required with Delphi, is not necessary.

1.5.8 Directories and search paths

Each package has its own output directory and its own search paths. The paths are configured in the Package dialog under *Compiler Options*. All search paths are saved relative to the `.lpk` file, and they may contain macros. Macros may be used to bind different units and include files for different platforms, as described in Section 1.5.6. The compiler configurations are largely the same as those of the project. The linker configuration is not important for normal packages and is ignored by the compiler. The compiler configuration is needed when the package itself is compiled; it is not passed on to other packages. However, it is affected by the packages that are used. The inherited paths and options are listed on the *Inherited* tab.
Along with the compiler configuration, packages may pass on their search paths and settings to other packages. This is configured in the Package dialog for the package under *Options →Usage*. All fields on this tab are normally empty with the exception of the *Units* search path, which contains the entry *$(PkgOutDir)/*. The macro *PkgOutDir* stands for the output directory of the package as configured in the compiler options. All compiled units (`.ppu` files) of the package are placed in the output directory. If a project needs this package, the output directory of the package is appended to the search path of the project. This can be checked under *Project →Compiler Options →Inherited*. In this way, the compiler can find the `.ppu` files of the package, but not its source files. This separation between source files and `.ppu` files is very important, since it prevents the compiler from inadvertently using the compiler configuration of the project to compile the source files of the package.
For users with a Delphi background, we repeat here the advice to refrain from arbitrarily adding search paths in response to a 'Unit not found' error. Instead, you should first check whether the package is listed as a dependency in the Project Inspector or the Package dialog, and after this run the test in the *Compiler Options* dialog, which checks for a variety of common configuration errors. The search path should be extended only if a unit that belongs to the package is not found during compilation.
Each package has its own compiler configuration, which means it has its own search paths for units, include files, source files, object files and libraries, and its own compiler parameters, so the project settings do not have any affect on the packages. The only exception to this occurs when a package uses global macros, such as *$(TargetOS)* or *$(LCLWidgetType)*. These macros are defined by the project. The settings apply to every directory in which package units are located, and to every directory in the units' search path. If you want to view the settings of a directory, open the pop-up menu of a unit in the Source Editor and select *File Settings...→Unit Info*. The resulting dialog shows the search paths for the unit, include files and source files. If no paths are shown here, it usually means that the IDE is not able to associate any files in the directory with a package or a project.

The package to which a source file belongs can be seen by selecting *Open File...* in the pop-up menu of the Source Editor. If the file belongs to a package, the package is shown here. To prevent mixing of the compiler options of the package and the project, the source directories must be separated. Normally only the output directory of the package, which contains the `.ppu` files, is visible to the project.

1.5.9 Dependencies and inheritance

Every package may use a group of packages. This means that the inherited search paths and compiler parameters are appended to the package's own paths and parameters.
The dependencies are configured in the Package dialog. Dependencies can be added under *Add →New Requirement* in the Package dialog. The minimum and maximum version numbers can also be specified there. To remove a dependency, select the dependency (required package) and then select *Remove dependency* in the pop-up menu.
The search paths and parameters are inherited under *Options →Usage* in the Package dialog. The compiler configuration is not inherited, but it contains the inherited paths of the packages that are used. If a package depends on a second package that in turn depends on a third package, the first package inherits all of these settings of the other two packages.
The IDE manages the packages internally in a graph, which means it can also handle circular dependencies. However, the IDE issues a warning if such dependencies arise and refuses to compile the packages until the circular dependencies have been eliminated.
All dependencies and packages can be viewed under *Package →Package Graph....* The IDE always arranges the packages topologically in the internal graph.

1.5.10 Compiling Packages

The IDE compiles all packages topologically, which means that it compiles packages without dependencies first. By default, packages are recompiled if a file belonging to the package or the environment has changed. The environment includes the compiler and the compilation parameters. After compilation, this data is saved in the file *packagename.compiled.* An example of such a file is:

```
<?xml version="1.0"?>
<CONFIG>
  <Compiler Value="/usr/bin/ppc386" Date="1204315279"/>
  <Params Value=" -S2cgi -OG1 -gl -vewnhi -l -
                                         Fu../../ideintf/units/i386-linux/
  -Fu../../lcl/units/i386-linux/ -Fu../../lel/units/i386-linux/gtk2/
  -Fu../../packager/units/i386-linux/ -Fu. -FUlib/i386-linux/ -dLCL
  -dLCLgtk2 runtimetypeinfocontrol s.pas"/>
</CONFIG>
```

As can be seen, this file holds the path of the compiler, the change date of the compiler, and the parameters. From this, the IDE can see whether a different compiler has been installed or the widget set has been replaced by a different one. As this information is saved with the package instead of in the configuration directory of the IDE, it is possible for several IDEs to use the same package at the same time.

Furthermore, a package can be compiled without Lazarus, based on its contents. The command-line program *lazbuild*, which can be used to compile packages and projects directly, has been available since Lazarus 0.9.24. Starting with version 0.9.26, *lazbuild* can also compile the IDE with packages. If a package should not be compiled every time something changes, this can be suppressed automatically under *Options →IDE Integration → Update* in the Package dialog. The options for non-automatic compilation are 'Manual compilation', which means that the package is compiled only via the *Compile* button of the Package dialog, or 'Auto-rebuild when rebuilding all', which means that the package is compiled only if the programmer selects *Run →Build all or More...→Recompile all required* in the Package dialog.

1.5.11 Translating packages

All messages and strings in a package that need to be translated into different languages can be defined as resource strings:

```
Resourcestring
  rsTitle = 'Title';
  rsOk    = 'Ok';

procedure TMainForm.FormCreate(Sender: TObject);
begin
  Caption          := rsTitle;
  OkButton.Caption := rsOk;
end;
```

The compiler extracts the resource strings of each unit into a `.rst` file. There are no translation editors for these files, so Lazarus can automatically convert the `.rst` files into `.po` files. This widely used format can be translated using the tools of the GNU translation project. For this purpose, enable the *i18n* option under *Options →Enable i18n* and select a subdirectory, such as *languages* or *po*. Like all file names, the subdirectory of the package is referenced to the `.lpk` file. The directory must already be present, since it is not created automatically by Lazarus. When the package is compiled, the compiler generates the *.rst* file in the output directory and Lazarus creates the `.po` file in the `i18n` directory. It has a simple format:

```
msgid ""
msgstr "Content-Type: text/plain; charset=UTF-8"

#: unit1.rsok
msgid "Ok"
msgstr ""

#: unit1.rstitle
msgid "Title"
msgstr ""
```

For every resource string, there is an original text and a translation. This is the base file, which is generated automatically and should not be edited.

A copy of this file must be created for each national language, with the country code included in the file name. For example, a German translation file named `messagebutton.de.po` can be created from an original `.po` file named `messagebutton.po`. This file can then be translated manually or edited more conveniently using a program such as POEdit (see below) or kbabel.
If new resource strings are added, the IDE automatically adds all of the `.po` files after each compilation. As the LCL uses UTF-8 everywhere from version 0.9.26 onward, the `.po` files should also be written in UTF-8. The IDE loads the `.po` files automatically for the installed packages, while the programmer is responsible for this in the programmer's own application. This can be done by including the following code in the main program (`.lpr` file):

```
program ...
uses  ..., Translations, gettext;

procedure Translate;
  var  PODirectory, Lang, FallbackLang: String;
begin
  // all .po files are located in the pofiles/ subdirectory
  PODirectory  :=  'pofiles' + PathDelim;
  Lang         := '';
  FallbackLang := '';
  GetLanguageIDs(Lang, FallbackLang);   // in unit gettext
  Translations.TranslateUnitResourceStrings('LCLStrConsts',
      PODirectory + 'lclstrconsts.%s.po',
      Lang,
      FallbackLang);
  Translations.TranslateUnitResourcestrings('MessageButton',
      PODirectory + 'messagebutton.%s.po',
      Lang,
      FallbackLang);
end;

begin
  Translate;
  Application.Initialize;
  Application.CreateForm(TMainForm, MainForm);
  Application.Run;
end.
```

This routine presumes that all `.po` files are located in the `pofiles/` subdirectory when the program is run. It is the responsibility of the programmer to group the `.po` files of all of the packages in the same place. The LCL's `.po` files are saved in `lazarus/lcl/languages/`.
This operation should also be performed automatically in a future version of Lazarus.
The actual translation is performed by calling *Translation.TranslateUnitResourceStrings*.
The first parameter is the name of the unit of the `.po`, and the second parameter is a string containing the file name and a placeholder for the language code (ISO 3166-1 country code). It is important to call the procedure *Translate* as early as possible, since it translates only the resource strings and ignores any strings that have already been copied.

Tedious manual editing of `.po` files is not necessary. POEdit, an editor designed specifically for this task, makes the job significantly easier and even checks the character strings for errors. POEdit also generates binary POT files from the `.po` files, but these files are not needed with Lazarus.
POEdit is available with all Linux distributions and with FreeBSD. The Windows and OS X versions can be downloaded from the website `www.poedit.net`. Manual compilation is not advisable because a considerable number of dependencies must be resolved, including Berkeley DB and wxWidgets.

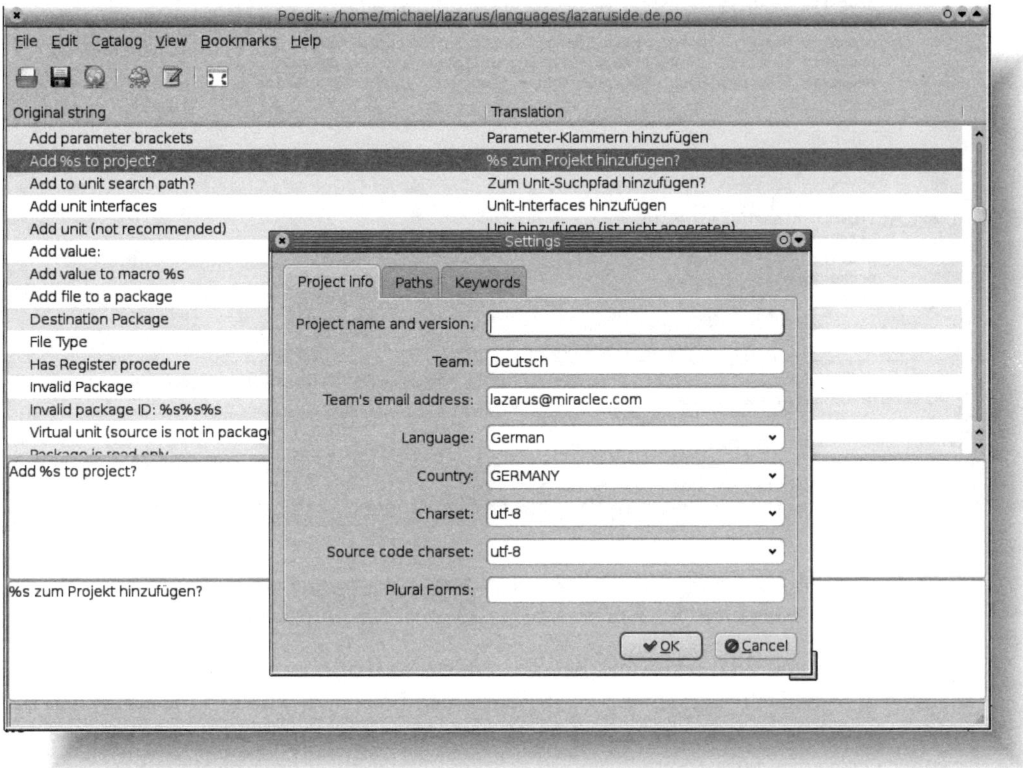

Figure 1.16: The German language file of the Lazarus IDE in POEdit

1.6 Source code documentation

Although Pascal code is inherently easy to read, the code should be documented. One option is to write comments and mark them with special characters so that tools such as *pasdoc* can generate documentation from the comments. However, it is not possible to include executable examples and complete descriptions in the source code when using pasdoc. For this reason, Free Pascal offers the *FPDoc* tool. For each unit, this tool generates an XML file that can hold a short description, an explanation, examples, links and other information for each identifier. FPDoc supports a subset of HTML formatting tags.
FPDoc is designed to be very flexible and extensible, and it contains various output modules. Modules are presently available for Latex, HTML, PDF and chm.

A Documentation Editor was introduced with Lazarus version 0.9.24. It is a complete FPDoc editor that can be used to edit multiple FPDoc XML files, with the XML elements shown in a convenient tree structure. There was also a simple integrated editor for the IDE, which showed the corresponding entry in the FPDoc XML file for the currently selected identifier in the source code and allowed simple changes.

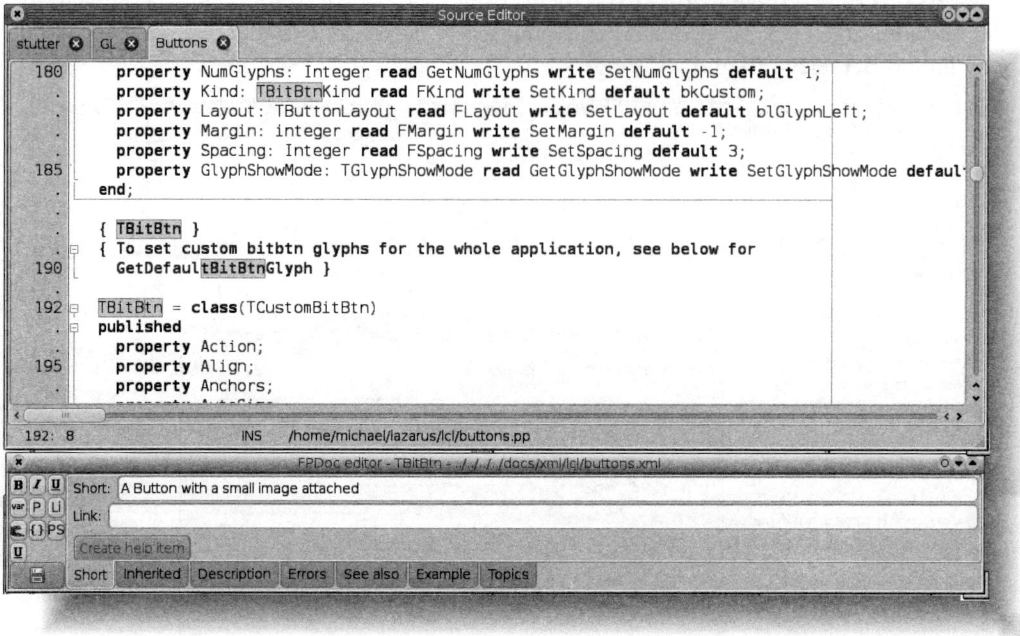

Figure 1.17: The integrated FPDoc editor tracks the cursor in the Source Editor and enables the documentation of the currently selected identifier

Since then this integrated editor has been extended, so that now FPDoc XML files can be generated automatically and almost all attributes can be edited. The FPDoc editor can be displayed by selecting *View →FPDoc Editor*. If the cursor is positioned on an identifier in the source code, the editor initially shows that no entries for it are present yet. Clicking the *Create help item* button opens a directory dialog.

A separate subdirectory (folder) in the package or project directory should be created for the FPDoc files, for example with the name *doc*. This sets the path under *Options →IDE Integration →FPDoc files path* in the Package dialog and creates the first FPDoc file with the name of the unit. The same procedure can be used for a unit of the current project. This allows programmers to generate documentation directly, and the documentation is immediately visible in the IDE. For example, when the mouse pointer hovers over an identifier the IDE shows all comments, pasdoc comments and FPDoc short descriptions for this identifier.
In addition, the IDE automatically searches for all ancestors and overloaded procedures and shows their help information as well. This means that it is sufficient to document the base class; all derived classes are automatically documented as a result. The procedure for generating complete help files in HTML, PDF, Latex or CHM format from the XML files is described in detail in the FPDoc description on the Free Pascal website (`http://www.freepascal.org/docs.var`), see 'fpdoc documentation tool reference manual'.

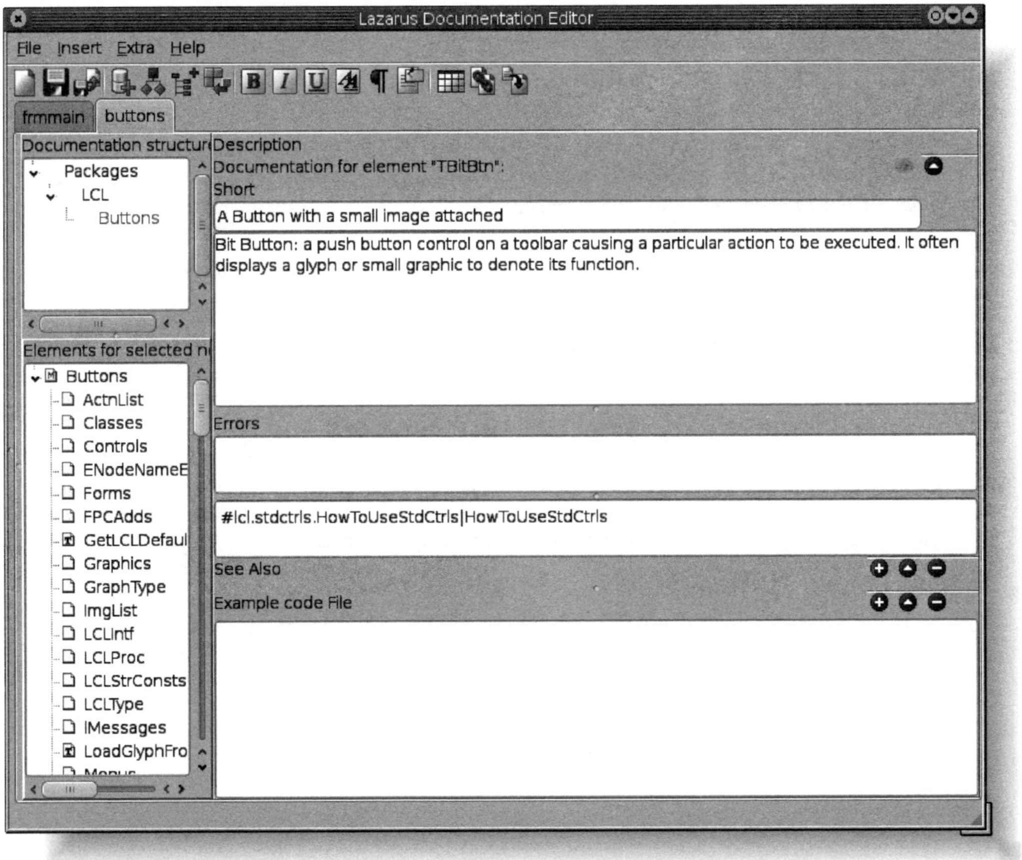

Figure 1.18: The Lazarus Documentation Editor (LazDE) is a stand-alone application that simplifies the task of documenting complete units

1.7 Unicode

For a long time the VCL supported only *AnsiString*. This did not change until Delphi 2009. Furthermore, all displayed captions had to be composed from characters found in the current code page. From version 0.9.26 onward, the LCL is based on UTF-8 on all platforms. This means that all characters, including non-English characters, can be used. UTF-8 is an eight-bit Unicode encoding that is ASCII-compatible in the range of 0 to 127 and specifically designed to simplify the porting of existing code to Unicode.
The World Wide Web is in part based on UTF-8, as are the graphic user interfaces of Linux and MacOS X. BSD supports UTF-8 only very rudimentarily and reluctantly.
For Delphi programs ported to Lazarus and for older Lazarus programs, this means that:

- Strings remain 8-bit strings.
- English constants and strings can be copied unchanged.
- Constants and strings containing non-English characters or non-ASCII characters must be checked. In many cases it is sufficient to change the encoding of the source file. For example, in Lazarus a source file can be converted to UTF-8 by selecting *File Settings…→Encoding* in the pop-up menu of the Source Editor. Entire projects or packages can be converted by selecting *Tools →Convert encoding of projects/packages….*
- File operations: The RTL still uses the system encoding, so strings used there must be converted. The RTL functions *AnsiToUTF8* and *UTF8ToAnsi* are provided for this purpose. In addition, the LCL provides a set of UTF… functions in the units *LCLProc* and *FileUtil*. The most important ones are:

```
function UTF8ToSys(const s: String): String;      // Like UFT8ToAnsi, but
                                                   // optimised for the LCL
function SysToUTF8(const s: String): String;      // Like UFT8ToAnsi, but
                                                   // optimised for the LCL
function UTF8ToConsole(const s: String): String;  // encode UTF8 string for
                                                   // WriteLn
```

The following functions and procedures are the UTF-8 counterparts of the corresponding calls to the Free Pascal runtime library:

```
function  FileExistsUTF8(const Filename: String): Boolean;
function  FileAgeUTF8(const FileName: String): Longint;
function  DirectoryExistsUTF8(const Directory: String): Boolean;
function  ExpandFileNameUTF8(const FileName: String): String;
function  ExpandUNCFileNameUTF8(const FileName: String): String;
function  ExtractShortPathNameUTF8(const FileName : String): String;
function  FindFirstUTF8(const Path: String; Attr: Longint;
        out Rslt: TSearchRec): Longint;
function  FindNextUTF8(var Rslt: TSearchRec): LongInt;
procedure FindCloseUTF8(var F: TSearchrec);
function  FileSetDateUTF8(const FileName: String; Age: Longint):
LongInt;
function  FileGetAttrUTF8(const FileName: String): LongInt;
function  FileSetAttrUTF8(const Filename: String; Attr: Longint):
LongInt;
function  DeleteFileUTF8(const FileName: String): Boolean;
function  RenameFileUTF8(const OldName, NewName: String): Boolean;
function  FileSearchUTF8(const Name, DirList : String): String;
function  FileIsReadOnlyUTF8(const FileName: String): Boolean;
function  GetCurrentDirUTF8: String;
function  SetCurrentDirUTF8(const NewDir: String): Boolean;
function  CreateDirUTF8(const NewDir: String): Boolean;
function  RemoveDirUTF8(const Dir: String): Boolean;
function  ForceDirectoriesUTF8(const Dir: String): Boolean;

function  ParamStrUTF8(Param: Integer): String;
function  GetEnvironmentStringUTF8(Index: Integer): String;
function  GetEnvironmentVariableUTF8(const EnvVar: String): String;
function  GetAppConfigDirUTF8(Global: Boolean): String;

function SysErrorMessageUTF8(ErrorCode: Integer): String;
```

Many text files do not contain any information about their character encoding; they usually use the encoding of the operating system. Under Windows this is usually the current Windows code page (for example, in the German versions of Windows it is code page 1250, in Russian it is code page 1251). UTF-8 is standard for the graphic user interfaces of Linux and MacOS X and is used to very limited extent in BSD, although the 8-bit ISO encodings are generally preferred in BSD, with ISO 8859-15 being used for Western Europe.
The *LCL* unit *Lconvencoding* enables platform-independent reading and writing of text files. It provides functions that determine the system encoding and convert the encodings of text files. When a text file is opened, the encoding must first be determined.
The function *GuessEncoding* attempts to guess the encoding of a string. First it looks for typical markings such as the UTF byte order mark (BOM). If it does not find any marking, it checks the text against UTF-8. UTF-8 uses multibyte codes with special bit patterns for non-ASCII characters These bit patterns are specifically designed such that texts encoded with Windows code pages are very likely to violate the patterns.
This makes it easy to recognize UTF-8. If the text is not encoded with UTF-8, *GuessEncoding* returns the system encoding.

The function *ConvertEncoding* can be used to convert strings. Internally *ConvertEncoding* calls various conversion functions such as *CP1250ToUTF8*, which converts a string encoded with the Windows 1250 code page into a string encoded with *UTF-8*. The following function reads in a text file, converts the text to UTF-8, and returns the text and the original encoding:

```
function LoadTextFile(const FileName: String; out EncodingFile:
                                                    String): String;
  var fs: TFileStream;
begin
  EncodingFile := EncodingUTF8;
  fs           := TFileStream.Create(FileName, fmOpenRead);
  try
    SetLength(Result, fs.Size);
    if Result <> '' then fs.Read(Result[1], Length(Result));
    EncodingFile := GuessEncoding(Result);
    Result  := ConvertEncoding(Result, EncodingFile, EncodingUTF8);
  finally
    fs.Free;
  end;
end;
```

The text can be displayed elsewhere, such as in a *TMemo* component:

```
Memo1.Lines.Text := LoadTextFile('test.txt', CodingFile);
```

The following procedure saves the result:

```
procedure SaveTextFile(const FileName, Contents, EncodingFile: String);
  var  fs: TFileStream; s : String;
begin
  fs := TFileStream.Create(FileName, fmCreate);
  try
    s := ConvertEncoding(Contents, EncodingUTF8, EncodingFile);
    if s <> '' then fs.Write(s[1], Length(s));
  finally
    fs.Free;
  end;
end;
```

The following statement saves the contents of the *TMemo* component with the original encoding:

```
SaveTextFile('test.txt', Memo1.Lines.Text, CodingFile);
```

Bear in mind that UTF-8 encompasses the entire Unicode character set, including all Windows code pages, but the opposite is not true. For example, CP1250 contains only the ASCII characters and the characters of many European languages, such as German umlaut characters.
This means that when UTF-8 is converted to CP1250, characters not present in CP1250 (such as Japanese characters) are silently eliminated.

Chapter 2
Installing Lazarus

By Jörg Braun, Swen Heinig and Felipe Monteiro de Carvalho

Naturally, you have to install Lazarus before you can use it, just as you do for other programs of any complexity. Although the operating system that Lazarus runs on does not significantly affect how you work with Lazarus, there are some differences in the installation procedure on different platforms. Consequently, in this chapter we describe separate Lazarus installation procedures for the most commonly used operating systems. If you work on another operating system, you should first check the Lazarus and Free Pascal websites to find out whether it is possible to install Lazarus on your system. If it is, the instructions given here will help to guide you. If you have any problems, you may be able to obtain further help from the Lazarus forum or the mailing list.

Without doubt, Lazarus is most often installed under Windows, perhaps because an erstwhile Delphi user wants to develop 64-bit Windows programs or program for the Windows CE platform, or because he's reluctant to pay for expensive annual updates with perhaps few benefits. Furthermore, anyone who is considering switching and first wants to get a feel for Lazarus is better off to install it first under the operating system they are used to, rather than embarking on the adventure of trying out both a new operating system and a new development environment at the same time.
Compared with other platforms, Lazarus under Windows also has a major advantage if you are a user with a Delphi background: you can continue to use many Delphi components with few (if any) changes. Certainly, there is much more to consider when you start developing truly cross-platform software with the LCL than when you simply move from Delphi to Lazarus on Windows.

So this chapter begins by describing how to install Lazarus under Microsoft Windows. It does not matter whether you are using Windows 2000, XP, Vista, 7, or one of the server versions. Lazarus runs stably on all these platforms.
In principle you can install different Lazarus versions in parallel, each in its own directory. However, the installed versions may interfere with each other. Eliminating the interference takes a certain amount of effort, so installing a different version on a virtual machine is usually a simpler solution.
There are basically three versions of Lazarus that you can install, including under Windows:

- the official stable version
- a current daily snapshot
- an SVN repository with the current source files

The Lazarus project administers the changes to the source code in an SVN repository. Lazarus is provided under an Open Source licence, and makes the complete source code available. The easiest way to obtain it is from the SVN repository.
The snapshots are taken every night from the current SVN data. This involves generating an executable installation file for Windows 32 (e.g. `lazarus-0.9.29-23728-fpc-2.5.1-20100218 -win32.exe`), RPM files for Linux, and a disk image package (`.dmg` *file*) for MacOS X.
The installation archive contains all necessary files, including the Free Pascal Compiler. In contrast to the stable version, the new installation files are not tested for proper operation, so you use them at your own risk. However, past experience has shown that problems arise only very rarely.
A stable version is built when, in the opinion of the developers, enough changes have occurred to justify a new version number. In this case, the last number of the version number is always an even number (e.g. 0.9.28.2). As with the snapshots, an executable installation file is generated for Windows. In contrast to the snapshots which are not tested at all, extensive testing is performed on the stable releases to verify that the new installation files function correctly. A disadvantage of the stable versions is that they do not include the very latest developments, owing to the usually relatively large time interval between successive stable versions. If you encounter an error in a stable version, you should first check whether the error has already been corrected in a current version. Another remark on the stable versions: they are always released together with a particular version of the Free Pascal Compiler. For example, this is FPC 2.2.4 for Lazarus 0.9.28.2, and it will probably be version 2.4.0 for Lazarus 0.9.30. If a new version of the compiler is released in between, there is no guarantee that the stable version of Lazarus will also work flawlessly with the new version of the compiler, and the same holds true for the development versions of the compiler. If you need the very latest compiler versions, you are advised to use the SVN or the snapshot versions.

2.1 Downloading from a Version Management system

By Jörg Braun

As with most open source projects, there are several ways to obtain the source code for Lazarus (and for Free Pascal). The simplest option is to download either the release sources or the current daily version as an archive from the Internet. The stable releases may be obtained from SourceForge at
`http://sourceforge.net/projects/lazarus/files/`.
The current daily sources may be obtained from
`http://www.hu.freepascal.org/lazarus/`, or better from a mirror site such as `http://snapshots.lazarus.shikami.org/` in France or
`http.//michael-ep3.physik.uni-halle.de/lazarus/` in Germany.
There are links to the primary download sources at
`http://www.lazarus.freepascal.org`. You can also find Lazarus and Free Pascal on the FTP server of the Free Pascal project at
`ftp://ftp.freepascal.org/pub/lazarus/`. The source code of the releases is available on this site under `releases/Lazarus%20Zip%20_ %20GZip`, while the snapshots of the current daily files are located in the subdirectory `snapshots/`.

If you just need a snapshot, for example if you want to compile Lazarus directly from the source, you only need to download the source archive. Another reason for downloading the source is that you already have Free Pascal fully installed and you do not want to install it twice, or that you work with FreeBSD, for which no binary version is available.
A disadvantage of downloading the source is that whenever you need new source files (perhaps only a few days later), you must download everything again.
If this is the case, or if you want to participate in the project, or simply wish to keep track of the changes, you should obtain the files from the version management system. This way only the files that have changed since the previous version are downloaded. The source repository of Free Pascal and Lazarus is based on Subversion. Read access to the files is very easy, and it is even more convenient under Windows than under Unix.

2.1.1 Installing TortoiseSVN

The preferred SVN client under Windows is TortoiseSVN from `http://www.tortoisesvn.org.`
As part of ongoing product development, new releases of the client are constantly being published.

However, you must be very careful with TortoiseSVN with respect to the installed Windows version. The current version (1.6x) requires at least Windows 2000.
The installer works flawlessly on Windows XP and higher, but on Windows 2000, the gdiplus library (available from Microsoft) must be installed prior to attempting to install TortoiseSVN.

Support for Windows 9x and Windows ME was discontinued at version 1.2.
TortoiseSVN is a Windows shell extension and is multilingual.

The basic installation supports English, with support for other languages provided by installing supplementary language packs. As with every shell extension, the operating system must be restarted after installation.
Installations with separate core and language files are available for both Windows 32 and Windows 64.
Both versions may be installed in parallel under Windows 64, and this is actually recommended because the extension is then valid for 32-bit programs as well.
In this case, a total of four files (two basic installations and two language installations) must be downloaded and configured. The system only needs to be restarted once, following the final installation.
Installation is very easy: launch the downloaded .msi file to start the installation program, select Custom Setup, and then deselect everything except the basic package (see Figure 2.1). You should accept the default installation path. Next, select the language file. No options need to be configured here. After this, restart your system.

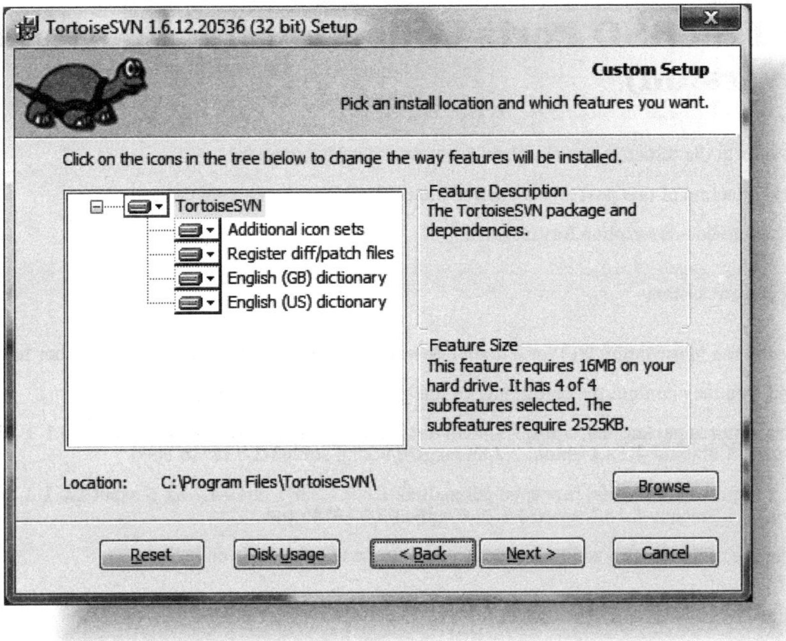

Figure 2.1: Only the basic package is necessary for anonymous download from the SVN directories; the dictionaries and supplementary packages are not required

2.1.2 The Subversion package

The command-line program *svn* is available for Linux, BSD, MacOS X and Windows.
In Unix derivatives, it is installed as part of the *subversion* program package using the system's package management utility. This package contains a very large number of programs, most of which are not needed for anonymous downloading of extracts from a repository.
In fact, only the *svn* program is needed for this purpose.
The source archive can also be obtained from `subversion.apache.org` (formerly `http://subversion.tigris.org`), but there is no real need to compile the programs from the source. It is also necessary to resolve dependencies, as described in the info file of the FreeBSD port shown in Figure 2.2.

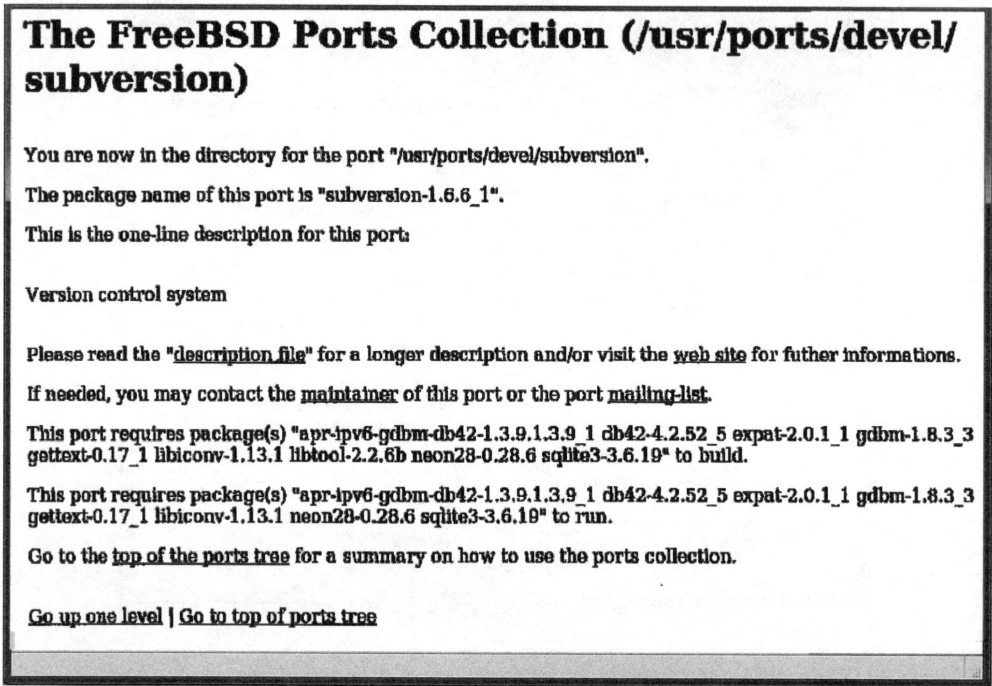

Figure 2.2: The FreeBSD port indicates which programs and libraries are necessary

If you do not wish to wish to or cannot work with TortoiseSVN under Windows, another option is to install the command-line package in the Cygwin environment (see `http://cygwin.com/`), but there are also a fair number of Windows compilations available. Links to them can be found at
`http://subversion.apache.org/packages.html#windows.`
They all have the same user interface as the Unix version. The download addresses for other operating systems are also available on the same page.
If you choose the Cygwin option, note that this environment works with Free Pascal (and therefore with Lazarus) only if the path to the Free Pascal Compiler is not included in the Windows search path, because the `cygwin1.dll` file included with the package and needed by the GNU binutils is not compatible with the other Cygwin programs. However, under Windows the compiler does not need to be in the Windows search path to enable Lazarus to compile programs. The `make.exe` file included with Free Pascal, which is located in the same directory as the compiler, launches the compiler and the other programs in the suite even if the directory is not included in the system variable PATH. If a *Makefile* file is present in the current directory, it is sufficient to state the complete path when calling make. For example, with compiler version 2.2.4 the call statement is:

```
C:\lazarus\fpc\2.2.4\bin\i386-win32\make
```

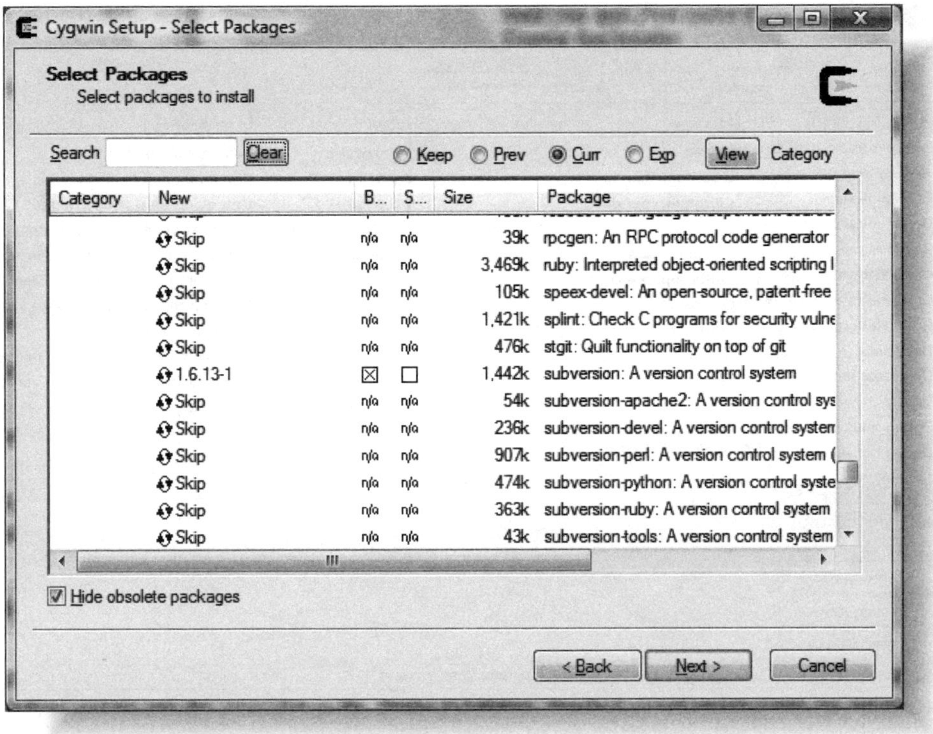

Figure 2.3: Subversion is also available in Cygwin

The easiest way to install the package under Debian or Ubuntu is to use *synaptic*.
A search for 'subversion' yields around 75 packages, of which only the basic package is needed (see Figure 2.4) and should be selected for installation.
A few other specific library modules are additionally installed as dependencies.

After the SVN client has been installed, you can use it to check out any desired SVN directories. All you need to know for this purpose is the name of the associated basic path.

SVN directories are always located on HTTP servers, for which reason they can also be viewed with a web browser.
However, with a browser you can only view and download individual files, but never the entire history, which is located in hidden directories named `.SVN`.

2.1.2 The Subversion package

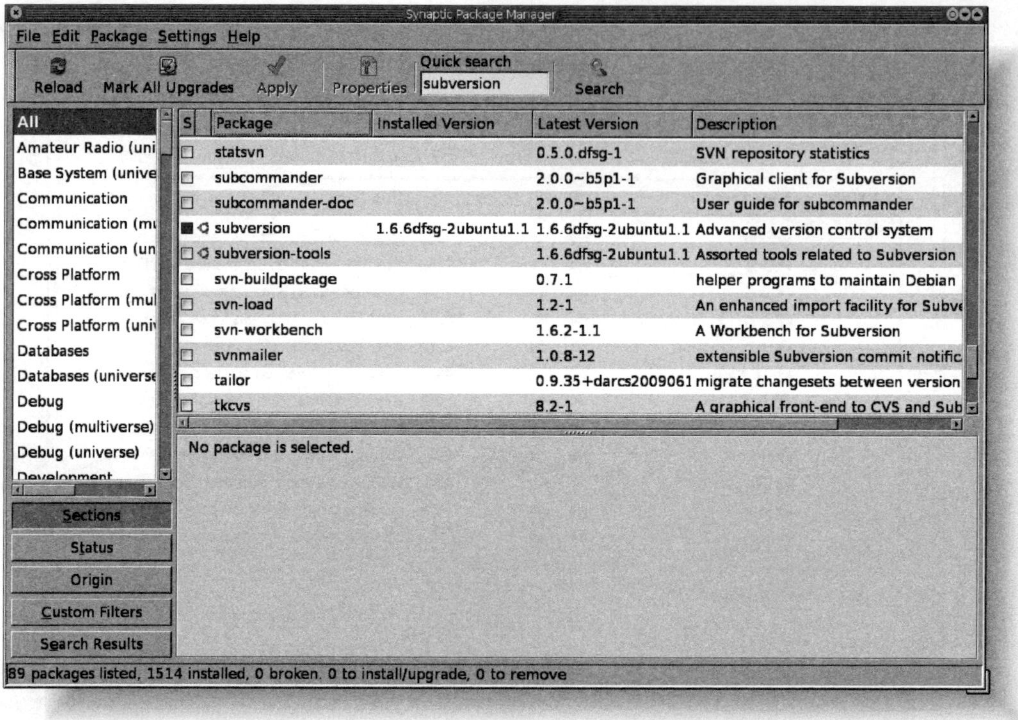

Figure 2.4: Installation with synaptic under Debian GNU/Linux

2.1.3 SVN directories for Lazarus and FPC

Before you can work with SVN repositories, you need to understand how they are organized and the basic aspects of how files are handled in version management systems such as CVS and SVN.

Every version management system is organized as a tree structure. It has a trunk, to which releases are attached using tags. For each release, a separate branch with its own subversions splits off from one of these tags. Each version of a file is backed up in a subdirectory named `.SVN`. The advantage of this is that if an error has been introduced somewhere, the version in which the error appeared can be searched and the error can be corrected, or a rollback can be performed to eliminate the bad branch. As can be seen from this brief description, version management systems are similar to database systems. In principle, a version management system is simply a database of all files of a software project and all changes that have been made to the files and to the project.
Free Pascal and Lazarus provide several SVN base directories, from which the components of the project can be downloaded using an SVN client. Downloading is generally allowed; no user account or password is necessary for this purpose. Specific permissions are only necessary for checking files into the system. This type of downloading is called 'anonymous SVN', analogous to anonymous FTP.

Address	Entry	Entry
`http://svn.freepascal.org/svn/fpc/`		
	... branches/	
	... patches/	
	... tags/	
	... trunk/	
`http://svn.freepascal.org/svn/fpcbuild`		
	... binaries/	
	... branches/	
	... scripts/	
	... tags/	
	... trunk/	
`http://svn.freepascal.org/svn/lazarus/`		
	... binaries/	
	... branches/	
		... fixes_0_9_24/
		... fixes_0_9_26/
		... fixes_0_9_28/
		... (etc.)
	... tags/	
		... binairies_0_9_26/
		... binairies_0_9_26/
		... binairies_0_9_26/
		... Lazarus_0_9_4/
		... ...
		... Lazarus_0_9_4/
	...trunk/	

Table 2.1: The Free Pascal SVN directories

Basic access to the Free Pascal SVN is possible via `http://svn.freepascal.org/svn/fpc/` or `http://svn.freepascal.org/svn/fpcbuild/`; the Lazarus SVN can be accessed via `http://svn.freepascal.org/svn/lazarus/` (see Table 2.1).
The two base directories of Free Pascal are directly equivalent to the two archives `fpc-<version_number>.source.tar.gz` (or `.zip`) and `fpcbuild-<version_number>.tar.gz` (or `.zip`).
The first directory or first source archive contains only the actual compiler data, with everything that is necessary for compiling the compiler suite in *fpcbuild*. However, this is not sufficient for building your own Free Pascal distribution. This is possible only after you *check out* the files from the SVN.

As already mentioned, a version management system has a trunk, tags and branches. Table 2.1 also lists several other directories: *binaries*, *patches* and *scripts*. These are supplementary directories, and they are normally ignored when the source files are checked out. Information on what is located in the directories and whether it is worthwhile to download the contents of the other directories can be found by searching with your web browser. If you wish to download a portion of the files from the SVN, you can enter any desired path in the repository as the source. For example, if you wish to download all the files for Lazarus (which would take a very long time, since all of the previous versions would be included), enter `http://svn.freepascal.org/svn/ lazarus/` in the Source field; if you wish to download only the current developer version, enter `http://svn.freepascai.org/svn/lazarus/trunk/` in the Source field.
Subversion 0.9.28.2, which is a leaf of the version 0.9.28 branch, can be found with the path `http://svn.freepascal.org/svn/lazarus/tags/lazarus_0_9_28_2/`.
How you check out files depends on which SVN client you use.

2.1.4 Basic command-line operations

Command-line instructions are used to download data from the repository using the program *svn*. Three parameters are passed to this program: first the command that tells it what to do, then the source path, and finally the target directory. Only two of the many commands available with *svn* are necessary for the anonymous checkout procedure described here. First a local mirror of the SVN repository is created, and then the data is exported from it. The following instruction copies the developer version of Lazarus to the local SVN directory `/pub/svn`:

```
# svn co http://svn.freepascal.org/svn/lazarus/trunk/ /pub/svn/lazarus
```

Here *co* is the abbreviation of 'checkout'. If a relative path is passed to *svn* instead of an absolute path, the data is copied to the corresponding subdirectory. After being checked out, the data should be exported from the local repository:

```
# cd /usr/local
# svn export /pub/svn/lazarus lazarus
```

This copies the complete structure from the local repository to the current Lazarus subdirectory. However, only the current version is exported; the version history and the `.svn` directories are discarded.
This export is not absolutely necessary, since all of the data is available in processable form in the SVN copy, but working with the original data has two drawbacks:

- If you create an archive of the data, it will be considerably larger than what is obtained from the exported tree because the SVN archive contains the entire version tree, which is removed in the export process.
- If you make changes to files in the SVN mirror or delete files, these files must be replaced or modified on the occasion of the next checkout to keep the mirror properly synchronized.

No other *svn* commands are necessary if you only want to check out data from the SVN repository. To find out what else is possible, enter:

```
# svn help
```

However, you should use *more* or *less* to display the output pagewise.
If you want to stay current, you also need the update command (which can be abbreviated to *up*). SVN is smart enough that all you need to do is to change to the local SVN directory and enter

```
# svn up
```

The program determines the source path from the version data available in this directory. Updating a directory that is presently already current takes the following form (in a system without language-specific local definitions for the build sources of Free Pascal):

```
# svn up

Fetching external item into 'fpcsrc'
External at revision 14918.

Fetching external item into 'fpcdocs'
U    fpcdocs/prog.tex
U    fpcdocs/db.xml

Updated external to revision 636.
Fetching external item into 'logs'
U    logs/fpcdocs-trunk.log
U    logs/lazarus-all.log
U    logs/fpcprojects-all.log
U    logs/fpc-trunk.log
U    logs/fpcbuild-trunk.log
U    logs/fpc-all.log
U    logs/fpcbuild-all.log
Updated external to revision 22353.

Updated to revision 753.
```

2.1.5 Checkout with TortoiseSVN

There are two different ways to initiate a checkout with TortoiseSVN under Windows. This simplest way is to change the protocol after scrolling through the SVN tree. With TortoiseSVN installed, you can initiate a checkout by specifying *tsvn:* instead of *http:* as the protocol in the URL field (e.g. `tsvn:http://svn.freepascal.org/svn/fpc/trunk`). This opens a window in which you are asked to specify the program to be used for this protocol (see Figure 2.5). Naturally, in this case you should select the SVN client.

Figure 2.5: TortoiseSVN handles the TSVN protocol

When you select TortoiseSVN, its configuration dialog is displayed automatically.
Here you should check that the source address is correct, and then select a suitable target folder that you will be able to find later on. A folder under `My Documents` or a directory in the drive root (e.g. `C:\SVN`) is a better choice.
If you tick the *HEAD Revision* button under *Revision*, the current version (head) will be downloaded. Alternatively, you can download an older version by entering its version number.

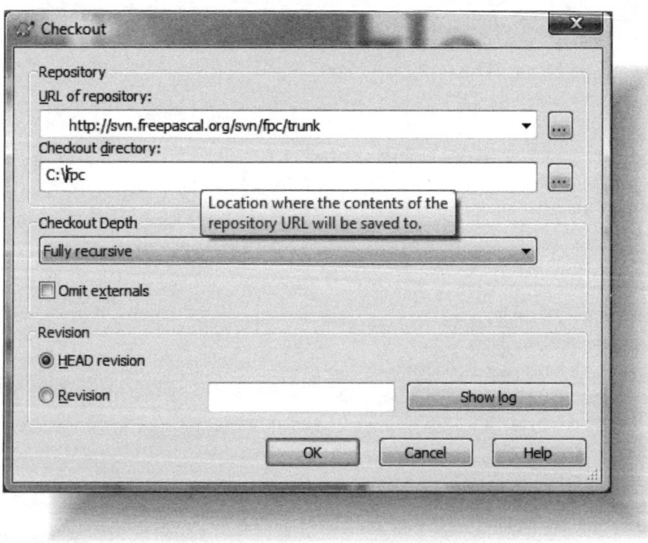

Figure 2.6: You should choose a suitable target directory

After entering the data, click OK to confirm the entry and start the checkout.
The other way to initiate a checkout starts in a local directory instead of on the server. This is possible because TortoiseSVN, as a shell extension, can be accessed equally well from the pop-up menu of Windows Explorer. First create an empty directory, such as `C:\SVN`, and then open the Windows Explorer pop-up menu in this directory and select `SVN Checkout…`.
This opens the same dialog as the one opened when you call TortoiseSVN from the browser, but in this case the source path is empty and the current directory is entered in the target directory field. To check out the source files for the developer version of Lazarus, you only need to enter `http://svn.freepascal.org/svn/lazarus/trunk/` in the empty URL field and hit OK or the [Enter] key to start the checkout.
The project is fairly sizeable, so it will take quite a while before the local tree is complete. However, in the progress window you can see how the new subdirectories are created in the specified directory. The folders have special markings: the green ones with tick marks are OK, while the red ones with crosses are damaged. They can be repaired with another checkout.

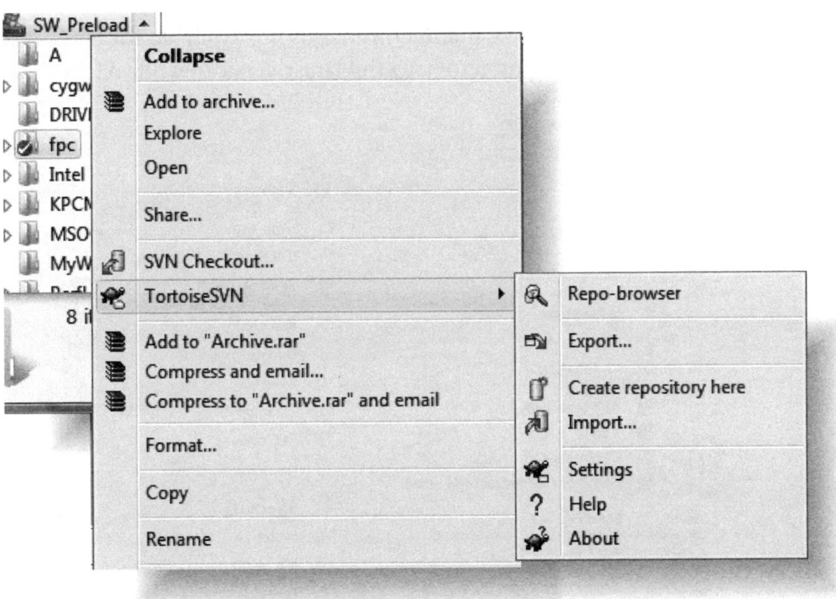

Figure 2.7: Windows Explorer pop-up menu with supplementary TortoiseSVN commands

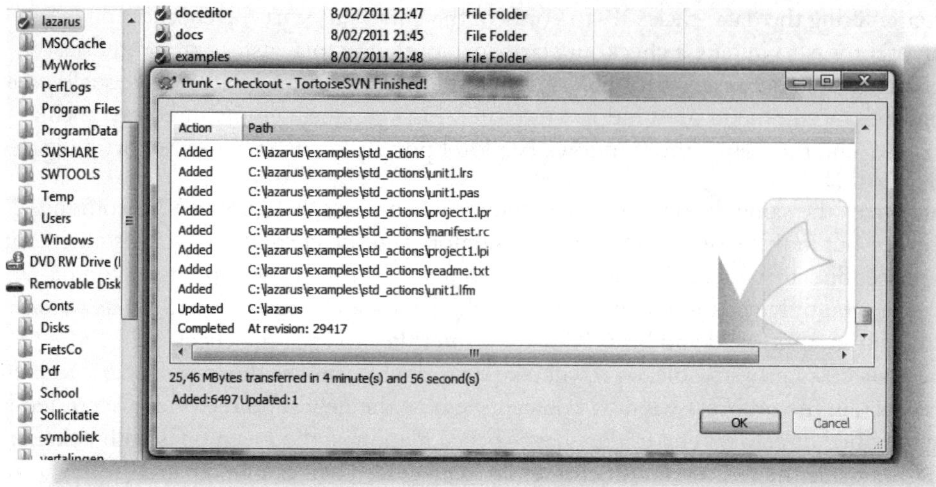

Figure 2.8: A successful checkout with TortoiseSVN

After a successful checkout, two new menu commands are available for SVN directories: *SVN Update* updates the working directory to the latest version, while *SVN Commit…* copies it back to the server.

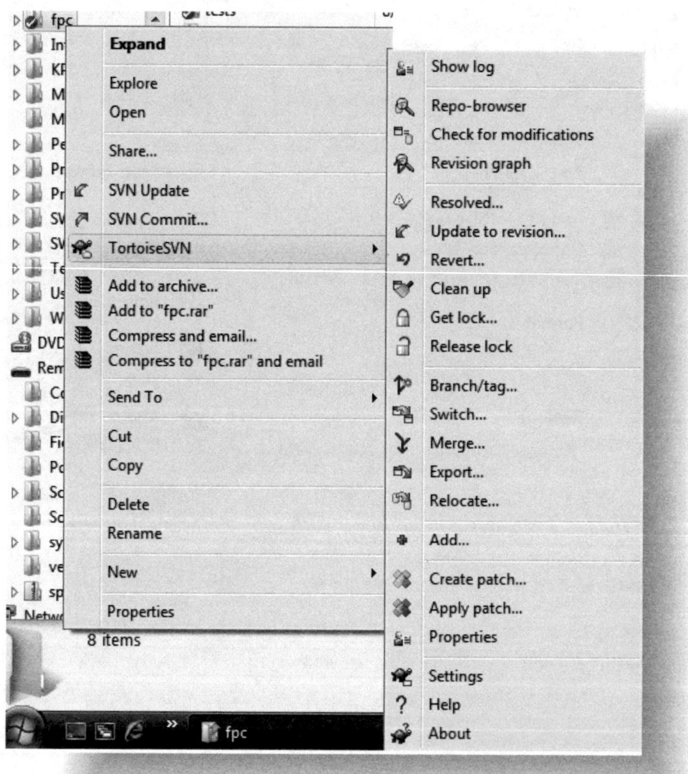

Figure 2.9: Extended SVN menu with new menu commands for the SVN mirror

The latter operation is not possible unless you have a user account (user name and password) with write permission for the repository.
Figure 2.9 shows a considerably larger number of submenu items for TortoiseSVN than in Figure 2.7. The only command of real significance for outside observers of a project is *Export*. This copies the mirror data to a different directory and deletes the version data. However, directories and files can also be copied to any desired empty directory on the hard disk with an ordinary drag & drop operation.

2.2 Installation on Windows

By Swen Heinig

Lazarus runs under all Windows versions from Windows 98 onward, but Windows 98 and Windows ME should not be used as development platforms. If you wish to implement current technologies in your applications, you should also use the latest version of Windows. For obvious reasons, the Lazarus IDE cannot be used under Windows CE (mobile), but it can be used to write applications for Windows CE. This is described in Section 5.1.2.

A computer with 512 MB of working memory should be adequate for running the IDE under Windows XP, although there's naturally no harm in having more memory than this. The processor has relatively little effect on the operation of the IDE itself, but a slow processor will make compiling programs irritatingly slow. A Pentium IV or comparable processor should be adequate in most cases. At least 500 MB of free space should be available on the hard disk for installing the IDE. As you will also need space for your own projects later on, the recommended amount of free space on the disk drive is at least 1 GB. A monitor with a resolution of at least 1024 x 768 pixels is desirable for displaying the Lazarus IDE. Although it is possible to run Lazarus with lower resolution, it will not be possible to work truly efficiently under these conditions. A fast Internet connection is advantageous not only for downloading the installation files, but also for accessing online help. However, an Internet connection is not indispensable for installing or working with Lazarus. The easiest way to obtain the latest Lazarus installation file is to download it from the Web. Two links are available in the box on the left at `www.lazarus.freepascal.org`: There *Downloads* takes you to the stable versions, while *Daily Snapshots* takes you to the snapshots.
The stable and snapshot versions are both supplied with an executable installation file. After you download this file, double-click it to start the installation.
You need Administrator permissions for installation under Windows XP and later versions. Note that under Vista, even administrators do not have full system access. In addition to installing and configuring Lazarus, the installation program installs the Free Pascal Compiler and a few selected packages. Incidentally, the version number of the installed compiler can usually be seen from the name of the installation file.
The setup language depends on your Windows' language configuration, so the language configured as Windows' default input language is proposed as Lazarus' setup language. However, you can select a different language if desired. It is advisable to close any programs you do not need before starting the installation.

However, no specific incompatibilities are known at present. Next you must specify the directory where you want Lazarus to be installed. The default is `C:\lazarus`, but you can enter any desired directory name here. Note that `\lazarus` is appended automatically, so if you enter `C:\Program Files\lazarus` the program files will be installed in the directory `C:\Program Files\lazarus\lazarus`.

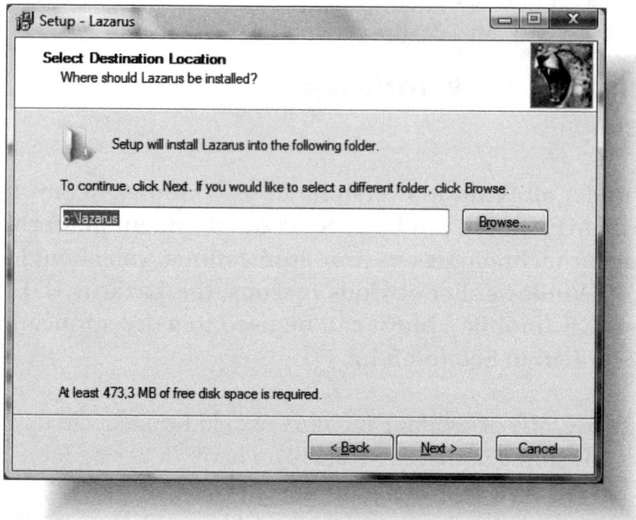

Figure 2.10: Selecting the target directory. Note that spaces are not allowed

Some auxiliary tools used by Lazarus have problems with space characters in path names, so spaces should be avoided as much as possible. Note also that the displayed path name is not always the same as the actual path name. For example, under Windows Vista the directory name `C:\Program Files` (which contains a space character) is shown as `C:\Programme` if the language is set to German.
The next step consists of associating typical Lazarus file extensions with Lazarus, so that these files can be opened with Lazarus directly from Windows Explorer.
If another program uses the same extension and so associating it with Lazarus is not desirable, that extension may be de-selected. With the 32-bit version of the Windows installation program, it is also possible to set up a DLL file, which is needed (under Windows) if you intend to build the Lazarus IDE using the Qt widget-set. However, this does not eliminate the need to install the actual Qt libraries.
You can accept the default name for the shortcut in the Start folder without causing any problems. You may wish to add the version number to the shortcut name.
The installation program can also create a shortcut to Lazarus on the desktop.
This is handy for at least two reasons: you can then easily start Lazarus with additional parameters or with extended permissions. You can also create a shortcut manually at any desired time after the program has been installed.

The selected options are displayed once again before the actual installation starts. If you see that you made a mistake (such as selecting the wrong installation directory) you can use the *Back* button to revise the settings.

When the 'Completing the Lazarus Setup Wizard' screen appears, installation of Lazarus has been completed successfully. Now you can launch Lazarus from the entry in the *Start* menu or the desktop shortcut, if it is available.

2.2.1 64-bit Windows

Windows has been available in a 64-bit version since Windows XP. A 64-bit operating system is necessary to effectively use 4 GB or more of working memory. As a Lazarus user, you basically have two options: you can use the 32-bit version of Lazarus to generate 32-bit applications, which also run without problems under Windows 64, or you can use the 64-bit version, which as available in both snapshot and stable versions. The installation procedure is the same as for the 32-bit version. As Lazarus allows you to write both 32-bit and 64-bit applications, the decision should be based on the available test software. For example, if you want to develop a database application and you have a locally installed database server and associated client libraries available for testing, the client library should be the decisive factor, since a 64-bit application cannot access a 32-bit library or vice versa. If you have a 32-bit library available, you should use the 32-bit version of Lazarus.

2.2.2 Removing Lazarus

The installation program also creates a shortcut in the Start menu for removing Lazarus. It may happen that a few files in the Lazarus installation directory are not deleted when Lazarus is removed. For this reason, you should always check the directory after removing the program and manually delete any remaining files.

Some settings, such as the list of installed packages or the path settings, are stored in the user directory of the current user, which is
`C:\Documents and Settings\user_name\Local Settings\Application Data\lazarus` under Windows 2000/XP or
`C:\Users\user_name\AppData\Local\lazarus` under Vista or later.
The advantage of this is that if Lazarus is reinstalled, a single recompilation is all that is required to restore your IDE to match your previous configuration settings.
However, problems may occur if the new Lazarus version differs from the previously installed version, for example with respect to the compiler. In this case the old configuration settings will lead to error messages. If you intend to install a newer version of Lazarus, you should first check the entries in the user directory and delete them if necessary.

2.3 Installation on Linux

By Swen Heinig

A single installation file, such as that available for Windows, is not available for Linux. You should bear in mind that there is actually no such thing as 'the Linux operating system', but rather a variety of distributions, such as Debian or Red Hat, which form systems assembled around a Linux core. An installation file would therefore need to work properly with all of these different distributions, which is presently not feasible. Nevertheless, Lazarus can be installed from the source under Linux and under FreeBSD.

Snapshots (presently only in `*.rpm` format) and stable versions are also available for Linux. Both of these can be installed using the system's package manager. Essentially the same download options as for the Windows versions are available on the Lazarus website, with different downloads for 32- and 64-bit versions.
The versions with `...i386...` in their file names are 32-bit versions. Many distributions now offer their own Lazarus packages as well. They contain the stable versions of Lazarus and FPC,
which can be installed relatively easily using the package manager. However, things are relatively fluid in this area, so changes may occur between the release dates of different distribution versions. In addition, past experience shows that it is entirely possible for one or more dependencies to be overlooked or for an entire package to be missing.
In such cases, however, it is always possible to remedy the situation with a download from the Lazarus website. A missing package usually leads to error messages the fist time Lazarus is launched. It is advisable to work with the latest distribution as much as possible.
If an earlier version of Lazarus has already been installed, problems may sometimes occur when it is updated using the package manager. In this case, it usually helps to completely remove the previous version and then install the new version.

The hardware requirements under Linux are the same as under Windows. Approximately 500 MB of free space on the hard disk is needed for the Lazarus and FPC packages. The monitor resolution should be at least 1024 x 768 pixels.
The procedure for installing Lazarus is described below using openSUSE 11.2 (Milestone 8) as an example, assuming that Lazarus is not available as a package in the repository.
Three packages must be downloaded from the download site for the stable versions:

- `fpc-2.2.4-0.i386.rpm` (contains the Free Pascal Compiler)
- `fpc-src-2.2.4-0.i386.rpm` (contains the source for Free Pascal)
- `lazarus-0.9.28-0.i386.rpm` (contains the Lazarus files)

With the 64-bit version of openSUSE, the corresponding `.rpm` files should be taken from the Lazarus *Linux x86_64 RPM* section. Although the file names will change with new releases of Lazarus or Free Pascal, the basic principle remains the same.

First the two packages containing the compiler and the Free Pascal source must be installed. The Lazarus package has several dependencies in addition to the compiler, which are primarily related to graphic display using GTK.

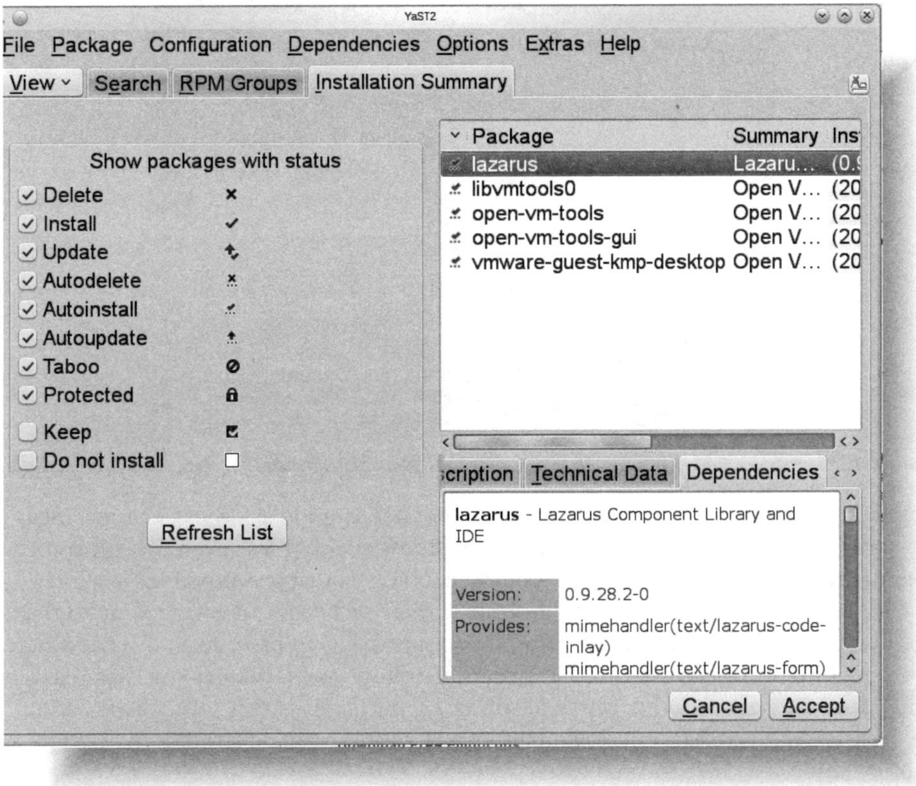

Figure 2.11: An extract of the dependencies of the Lazarus package under openSUSE 11.2

The installation of the Lazarus package will fail if the dependencies are not installed. They include the development packages, such as *gdk-pixbuf-devel* for *gdk-pixbuf*. However, some of the dependencies may have already been installed with other programs. To find out which ones still need to be installed, you can try installing the Lazarus packages. If this fails, you can see from the error message which dependencies are still missing.

Once these packages have been installed, Lazarus is ready to run. After successful installation, an entry for launching Lazarus is located in the KDE menu. If the language is set to English, the category is called **Development**.

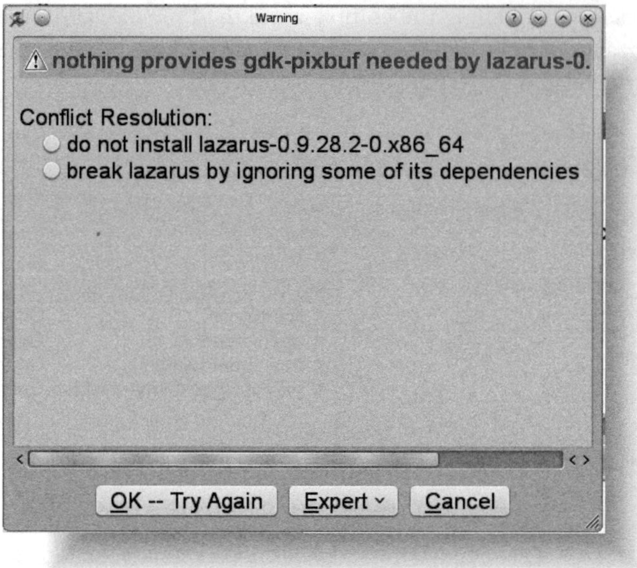

Figure 2.12: Error message from YaST indicating that some dependencies are missing in the installation

The package managers of some distributions are not as good as others. For instance, with some distributions it is apparently possible to install Lazarus even though some dependencies are missing. Another common problem is that it is possible to launch Lazarus, but it fails in the compilation phase with a *'can't find...'* message. Due to the large number of potential combinations, it is not possible to provide an overview here of what does or does not work with the various distributions. If you get stuck the Lazarus mailing list may help. Another possible source of problems is that some distributions have non-standard paths for installing libraries. Consulting the distribution documentation may help in such cases.

There are other alternatives to the installation options already mentioned. However, it is not possible to predict how these alternatives will evolve, or whether they will continue to be available in the future (and in the same place). For openSUSE there is the openSUSE build service, which is available via `http://software.opensuse.org/search`. In the Search field, enter a relevant term such as 'Lazarus'. Then click the *1-Click Install* button to install the desired package. Here you should check that the selected package matches your distribution, since the build service also provides packages for other distributions, including Mandriva and Ubuntu. For Debian-based systems such as Ubuntu, there are supplementary repositories that often hold versions of Lazarus that are newer than the versions in the official repositories. This arises in part from the release cycle of the major distributions, which is usually six months, as well as the 'feature freeze' phenomenon, which sometimes causes a delay of up to nine months before a new version of Lazarus appears in the repositories. If you bind one of these supplementary repositories into your own system (if the repository is digitally signed, the key must be bound first), you can simply use the package manager to perform the Lazarus installation. An example of such a repository is *deb* `http://ppa.launchpad.net/ximion/ppa/ubuntu karmic main`.

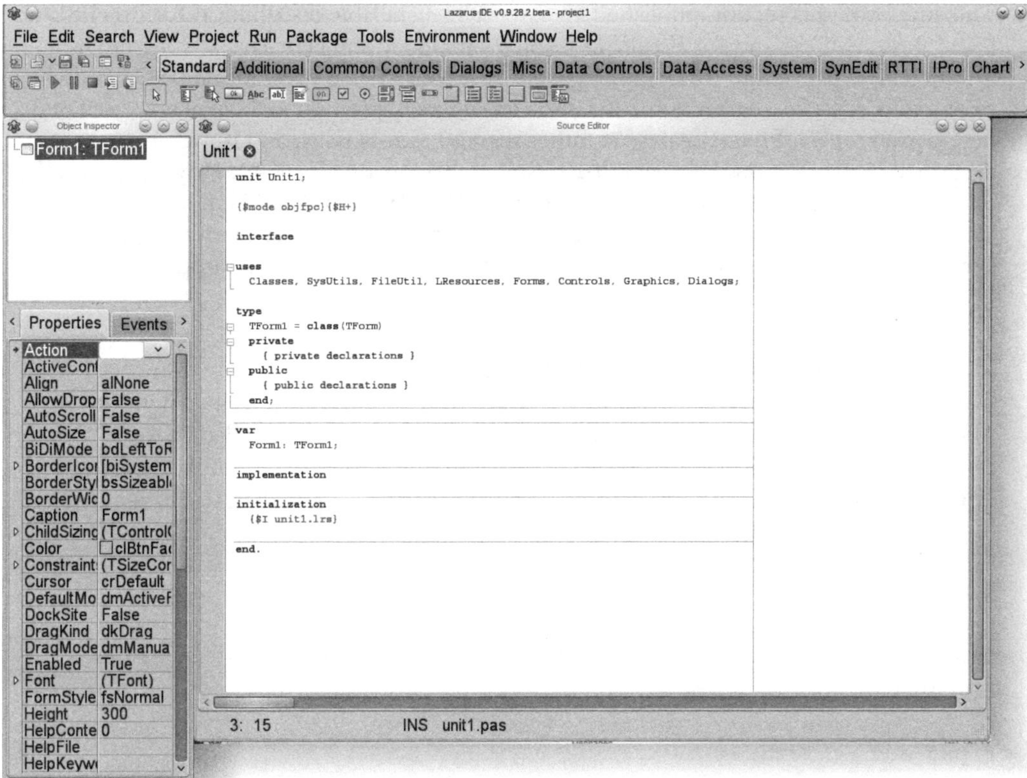

Figure 2.13: The Lazarus IDE under openSUSE 11.2 with the Gtk 2 settings

The package manager also has to be called for uninstallating. If you also want to remove the FPC packages, it usually helps to search for the term 'Pascal'. After uninstalling, it may be worthwhile to delete the configuration files under `/home/user_name/.lazarus`. If you wish to delete the directory in a file manager dialog, it may be necessary to first change the view settings, since directory names beginning with a dot are normally hidden under Linux.

2.4 Installation on FreeBSD

By Jörg Braun

Lazarus can be installed on all Unix-like platforms which will run a recent Free Pascal compiler. Besides Linux/I386 and Linux/AMD64 this means principally FreeBSD (thanks to the work of Marco Van De Voort). As of Free Pascal version 2.4.2, a stable compiler is available for FreeBSD, not only in an I386 version but also for the 64-bit platform AMD64 or X86_64.

The author of this section published an externally installable distribution for FreeBSD 7, 8 and 9 on AMD64 and for FreeBSD 8 and 9 on i386 in the February 2010 issue of Toolbox. The procedure for compiling Free Pascal and Lazarus on a FreeBSD/amd64 platform is described in Section 2.4.3. Generating a distribution archive is not discussed here because it is a Free Pascal issue rather than a Lazarus issue, and it was anyhow described in detail in the February 2010 issue of *Toolbox* (in German). However, it can be assumed that sooner or later an official port for FreeBSD/amd will be made available. The earliest opportunity for this would be the distribution upgrade from compiler version 2.2.4 to 2.4.0, since previous versions of the compiler do not support FreeBSD/amd64.

2.4.1 Installing from the ports

The Lazarus project creates packages which are ready to install for Linux, Windows and MacOS. However, for FreeBSD the primary and recommended installation route uses the Ports system. Theoretically the simplest way to do this is to make sure that the latest Ports directory is installed (for example with *portsnap fetch extract*), then to change to the directory */usr/ports/editors/lazarus and execute this command:*

```
# make install
```

With some luck, a prepared port exists on the internet, which can be installed directly with the command:

```
# pkg add -r lazarus
```

Compiling Lazarus assumes that Free Pascal can be compiled, which is split in FreeBSD across a large number of packages (over 20). Additionally, using the default settings, a large number of possible database clients are compiled, even if you don't want to do database development.

Unfortunately, the Ports system (as of February 2011) does not install all the dependencies you really need. After a test installation of Lazarus 0.9.28.3 using *pkg_add -r ,* the installed IDE was not ready to run, because the Free Pascal compiler and GNU make were missing. The Port definition is incomplete, and so the packages *gmake* and *fpc* must be installed manually.

Unfortunately, even this is not enough. To recompile Lazarus (needed because packages are linked in statically) the Port packages *fpc-fcl-res* (containing the Free Pascal Resource compiler) and the library *gdk-pixbuf-2* are also needed. An advantage of the Ports system is that it asks which GUI toolkit should be used as the basis for the Lazarus installation. The dialog offers the choice between GTK2 or QT4 (see Figure 2.1). You must choose one (and only one) option. Although both options can be checked, if you do so then the port will not work, and you will have to reconfigure it using *make config.*

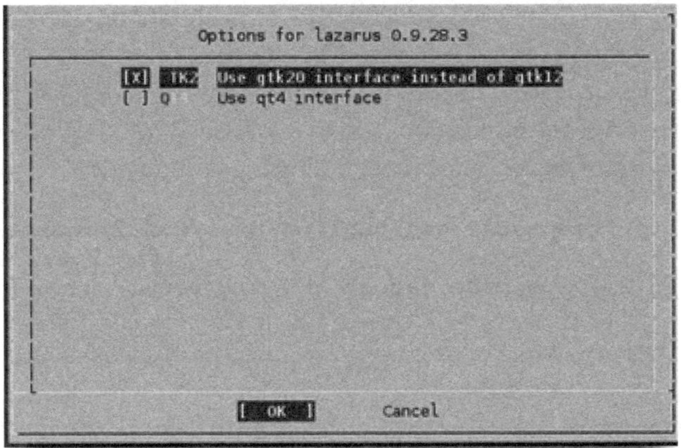

Figure 2.14: : The configuration dialog for Lazarus in FreeBSD ports. Choose only one of the options. Which one depends on the system. People using KDE 4 should choose Qt4, people preferring Gnome of XFCE 4 should pick GTK 2.

This has been nicely solved by the maintainer of the Free Pascal and Lazarus-Ports.
Less well solved are the paths which are used to copy Lazarus to `/usr/local/share/lazarus/`, but without the examples and documentation, which are copied to `/usr/local/share/doc/lazarus/` and are then symlinked to.
A further stumbling block when building Lazarus from Ports is that it needs the sources of Lazarus and Free Pascal. The Free Pascal sources are not installed with the port, and this prevents the proper functioning of the IDE (even after all this preparatory work).
Since both source archives are available after building from Ports, this is only a minor annoyance. You need to change to the IDE directory, and extract the Free Pascal source archive.
Care must be taken with Free Pascal, since there are two different source archives. The smaller one is sufficient for Lazarus, and is named fpc-<VersionNumber>source.tar.gz, so for version 2.4.2 this is fpc-2.4.2.source.tar.gz. Also available are the compiler sources, used to compile the compiler itself. The archive file is named fpcbuild-<VersionNumber>.tar.gz. For compiler version 2.4.2 this archive is called fpcbuild-2.4.2.tar.gz. When the compiler version 2.4.2 is installed from Ports, the smaller file can be extracted (if not yet deleted), or the large one can be extracted:

```
# cd /usr/local/share/lazarus
# tar -xvzf /usr/ports/distfiles/freepascal/fpcbuild-2.4.2.tar.gz
```

Extracting is done in a subdirectory of Lazarus, resulting in a subdirectory called fpc-<Version> or fpcbuild-<Version>. When *fpcbuild* is used, you can reclaim some disk space with:

```
# cd fpcbuild-2.4.2 && rm -r demo fpcdocs install
```

Only the directory fpcsrc is used, and this directory should be selected when Lazarus is first started in the dialog that asks for the FPC sources.
If Free Pascal and Lazarus were installed in binary form using *pkg_add* then the FPC sources were not needed for installation, and you will need to download them separately from the FTP server, for example using the following commands:

```
# wget ftp://ftp.freepascal.org/pub/fpc/dist/2.4.2/source/
                                                   fpc-2.4.2.source.tar.gz
# tar -xvzf fpc-2.4.2.source.tar.gz -C /usr/local/share/lazarus
```

In the small archive fpc-<VersionNumber>.source.tar.gz the sources are located in the directory fpc-<VersionNumber>.
Some small changes are needed now to add the Lazarus IDE to the menu of KDE (or Gnome or XFCE 4). These changes are also necessary when installing manually. It makes sense to copy the lazarus.desktop file (more about this later). If the included file is not patched in the FreeBSD manner, then a corrected version must be made in the *files* directory of Ports and it must be copied in *post-install*:

```
post-install:
 @${MKDIR} ${LOCALBASE}/share/applications
 @${CP} ${PORTSDIR}/${PORTNAME}/files/lazarus.desktop \
                                              ${LOCALBASE}/share/application
 @${CAT} ${PKGMESSAGE}
```

Lastly, the file lazarus-mime.xml is missing, and it must also be copied from the subdirectory install to /usr/local/share/mime/application. The Lazarus Ports is not perfect on several fronts!
If the Port is changed, then its *PORTREVISION* must be set or increased:

```
PORTNAME     =   lazarus
PORTVERSION  =   0.9.28.3
PORTREVISION =   1
CATEGORIES   =   editors devel
```

2.4.2 Manual Installation

To compile and install Free Pascal and Lazarus manually, some conditions must be met which are normally taken care of by the Ports system (although not completely, in the case of Lazarus). These details – with minor changes – are also valid for Linux and Windows. GNU make is not installed by default on FreeBSD as it is on Linux. Additionally, GTK2 must be installed, because Lazarus uses it as the default widget set as of version 0.98.2. You also need the Gdk-Pixbuf-2 library, which can be installed conveniently using the graphics/gdk-pixbuf2 port. Doing so will also correctly resolve further dependencies such as Gtk2. The most important requirement for the compilation of Free Pascal is the installation of GNU make, from the port /usr/ports/devel/gmake. Change to this directory, and with the command:

```
# make install clean
```

GNU make is installed. Alternatively, the binary version of GNU make can be installed from FreeBSD's FTP-Repository using *pkg_add -rgmake*.
The next step is to download the following packages from the Internet:

- The current binary distribution of Free Pascal for FreeBSD.
  Make sure it is the correct one for your platform, so either i386 or x86_64.
- The Free Pascal source archive (the small version is sufficient for FreeBSD 7 and 8).
  For older versions of FreeBSD or for 9-CURRENT, you will need to compile FPC manually, and the large source archive will be required for you to build it.
- The Lazarus source distribution, preferably the development version, not the 0.98.3 version which is found in ports (as of February 2011) – it is not very stable under FreeBSD.

The first two files can be downloaded directly from:
ftp://ftp.freepascal.org/pub/fpc/dist
It is important to download the correct files for the latest stable version.
For version 2.4.2 of the compiler, they are located *respectively* at:
ftp://ftp.freepascal.org/pub/fpc/ dist/2.4.2/i386-freebsd
and
ftp://ftp.freepascal.org/pub/fpc/ dist/2.4.2/x86_64-freebsd
The Free Pascal source archive at:
ftp://ftp.freepascal.org/pub/fpc/source
For the binary file it is important – if applicable – to download the version for the correct kernel version. As of Free Pascal 2.4.2 two files are available: *freebsd7.tar and *freebsd8.tar*.
When the correct compiler for the current operating system is found, there is no need to recompile it except to verify that it functions correctly. If you want to download it, then from the source directory of the FTP server, the file fpcbuild-<Version>.tar.gz must be downloaded. For compiler version 2.4.2 the filename is
ftp://ftp.freepascal.org/pub/fpc/dist/2.4.2/source/fpcbuild-2.4.2.tar.gz
This file can be downloaded with *wget*. This is definitely necessary when the correct operating system is not available, for instance when Lazarus must be installed on FreeBSD 9-CURRENT. Both archives are also available as zip files, but these files are less suitable due to missing file attributes. They are also larger than the .tar.gz files.
The archive files should be downloaded to an appropriate directory, for example /usr/ports/distfiles/freepascal, where other downloaded source files are located, or to /usr/tmp.
In the next step, the binary package of Free Pascal must be extracted. It makes sense to create a directory /usr/local/src for this and to extract the archive there.
This can be done as follows:

```
# mkdir /usr/local/src
# cd /usr/local/src
# tar -xvf /usr/ports/distfiles/freepascal/fpc-2.4.2.i386-freebsd8.tar
```

The tar file contains files named `install.sh`, `binary.i386-freebsd.tar`, `demo.tar.gz` and `doc-pdf.tar.gz`. They are extracted to the current directory, and can be deleted after the installation of the binary package. The installation script can be started with the command

```
# sh install.sh
```

It cannot be started directly, since the executable flag is not set. During installation, everything should be installed in the default locations, and the typical FreeBSD settings such as the prefix `/usr/local should be accepted`.After the installation is finished, use the command *fpc* to test whether the compiler is functioning. As a last step, it is necessary to correct the ownership of `/usr/local/lib` using the command:

```
# chown root:wheel /usr/local/*
```

Failure to do so is likely to stop FreeBSD from booting at the next restart. The changing of the ownership of the library directory under FreeBSD is a long-standing error in the installation of Free Pascal, which has fatal consequences! At system start the FreeBSD system linker `/libexec/ld-elf.so.1` uses only directories which are owned by *root* for security reasons. If important libraries in `/usr/local/lib` are needed (for example, when bash is used as shell) nothing functions any more without the change of ownership outlined above.

Vitally important: After installing Free Pascal using the installer, check the ownership directories in `/usr/local` using `ls -la /usr/local` and correct the ones changed by the installation routine using

```
# chown root:wheel /usr/local/*
```

In the next step, the compiler can or must (depending on your situation, see above) be recompiled. For instance if no compiler is available, or if you are using version 9-CURRENT and the compiler for FreeBSD 7 or 8 was installed, then everything must be extracted to the directory `/usr/local/src`:

```
# tar -xvzf /usr/ports/distfiles/fpcbuild-2.4.2.tar.gz
# cd fpcbuild-2.4.2
```

Recompiling the compiler in this directory now will not produce anything. First, you need to change to the directory `fpcsrc/rtl/freebsd/i386` and with the command:

```
# sh identpatch.sh
```

the version number of the operating system must be patched. This is only possible with the 32-bit version! In the directory for FreeBSD/AMD64 (x86_64) this script is not available, so the number must be changed manually.

The entry in the file rtl/freebsd/i386/cprt0.as looks as follows
(it is the same for versions 2.2.4, 2.4.0 and 2.4.2):

```
# ... Comments in the file
#
# freebsd 5.4 504000
# freebsd 6.3 (prerelease) : 603100
# freebsd 7.0 700055
#

        .file   "cprt0.as"
        .ident  "FreePascal 2.2.x series dynlinked to libc"
.section        .note.ABI-tag,"a",@progbits
        .p2align 2
        .type   abitag, @object
        .size   abitag, 24
abitag:
        .long   8
        .long   4
        .long   1
        .string "FreeBSD"
        .long   504000
```

The last line in this listing is important. It shows that by default, operating system version FreeBSD 5.4 is selected. This entry must be changed. Here are some version numbers for comparison:

```
FreeBSD 6.4 STABLE      = 604100
FreeBSD 7.4 RELEASE     = 704100
FreeBSD 8.0 RELEASE     = 800107
FreeBSD 8.0 STABLE      = 800500
FreeBSD 8.2 PRERELEASE  = 802500
FreeBSD 9.0 CURRENT     = 900009 (Early 2010), 900032 (Early 2011)
```

The last 3 digits – as is clear from the examples – are not important and change during a release. The Free Pascal Port enters the current version number with the following patch in the Makefile:

```
post-patch:
# patch fpc rtl
        @${REINPLACE_CMD} -i "" -e 's|504000|${OSVERSION}|g' \
         ${WRKDIR}/${FPCSRCDIR}/rtl/freebsd/${ARCH}/cprt0.as
```

The correct number is not something you will know, but it can be determined by running the program *file* on a dynamically linked program from the `/bin` directory,
here for FreeBSD 8.2-RC:

```
# file /bin/sh
/bin/sh ELF 32-bit LSB executable, Intel 80386, version 1 (FreeBSD),
dynamically linked (uses shared libs), for FreeBSD 8.2 (802500),
stripped.
```

When the file has been corrected, the command:

```
# gmake all
```

should build the compiler. GNU make is needed for this, the FreeBSD make command (*make*) only produces an error message. However, we are not there yet!
An error message is produced:

```
Makefile:2264: *** No libgda.a found, supply NOGDB=1 to disable
debugger support. End.
```

The message shows us what to do, namely all *gmake* commands must be followed by the `NOGDB = 1` option:

```
# gmake NOGDB=1 all
```

This will take a while. If the work has been successfully completed, FPC can be installed with the command

```
# gmake NOGDB=1 install
```

This will overwrite the previously installed version.
If you don't want to recompile the compiler, you need only unpack the small archive:

```
# tar -xvzf fpc-2.4.2.source.tar.gz
```

This is something which must always be done, even when Lazarus was installed from Ports, because Lazarus needs the sources for the IDE CodeTools to work correctly.
If disk space is an issue, the large archive can be deleted and the smaller one can be extracted – it contains all needed files. Then you only need two downloads.
The next step is to compile Lazarus. It is important to decide which version to use. Either the sources of the stable version – available on SourceForge – or the sources of the development version can be downloaded. The latter can be downloaded from the snapshot server or a mirror thereof, or from the Subversion server. Ideally, the .tar.bz2 file of the fixes or developer version are downloaded. Extract the files into the *lazarus* directory. This avoids the problem that a file called `lazarus-0.9.31-29426-20110209-src.zip` *of* date 9.2.2011 is extracted to a subdirectory with the same lengthy name. The file is extracted to `/usr/local/src`, for example with the following commands:

```
# cd /usr
# tar -xvzf /usr/ports/distfiles/lazarus-0.9.31-29426-20110209-src.tar.bz2
# cd lazarus
# gmake all
# strip lazarus startlazarus lazbuild
```

The work is not yet complete, but is now at the same point as the – much shorter – installation using Ports, and the additional steps mentioned earlier in this section can now be performed.

Lazarus Post-installation steps

After installation of Lazarus, the window environment (whether it is Gnome 2, KDE or XFCE 4) must be informed about this. Better still – although not necessary – is to complete the MIME database.
For this, 2 files must be copied: from the Lazarus *install* directory, the file `lazarus-mime.xml` must be copied to `/usr/local/share/mime/application/`, and the file `lazarus.desktop` must be copied to `/usr/local/share/applications/`.
In the latter file, the entry for the executable program must be corrected. Depending on the installation directory (for installation using FreeBSD Ports, this is `/usr/local/share/lazarus`) the path in the file must be corrected. It will probably look like this:

```
Exec=/usr/local/share/lazarus/startlazarus %f
```

This will make Lazarus appear in the window environment, but without an icon.
To restore the missing icon, a second entry must be corrected in the file.
The location of the icon must be changed from `Icon=lazarus.png to`

```
Icon=/usr/local/share/lazarus/images/icons/lazarus.ico
```

Of course this has no influence on the functionality of Lazarus itself.
The next step is to start Lazarus from X-Windows for the first time.
This will produce a message box, stating that the path to the Free Pascal sources is not correct.
The path to the Free Pascal sources and to *gmake* should be set in the settings dialog under *Environment* → *Options* on the *Environment* page. (Note that some recent versions of Lazarus have the *Environment* menu merged into the *Tools* menu).
In principle, you should shrink the Lazarus executable, not only on FreeBSD, but on all installations. This should be done when installing with gmake, but also when Lazarus recompiles itself. The command:

```
# strip lazarus startlazarus lazbuild
```

not only saves disk space, but also drastically improves start-up time. From its original size of 90MB, the Lazarus executable size is reduced to 10MB. Debug symbols should only be left in an executable when you actually want to debug it.

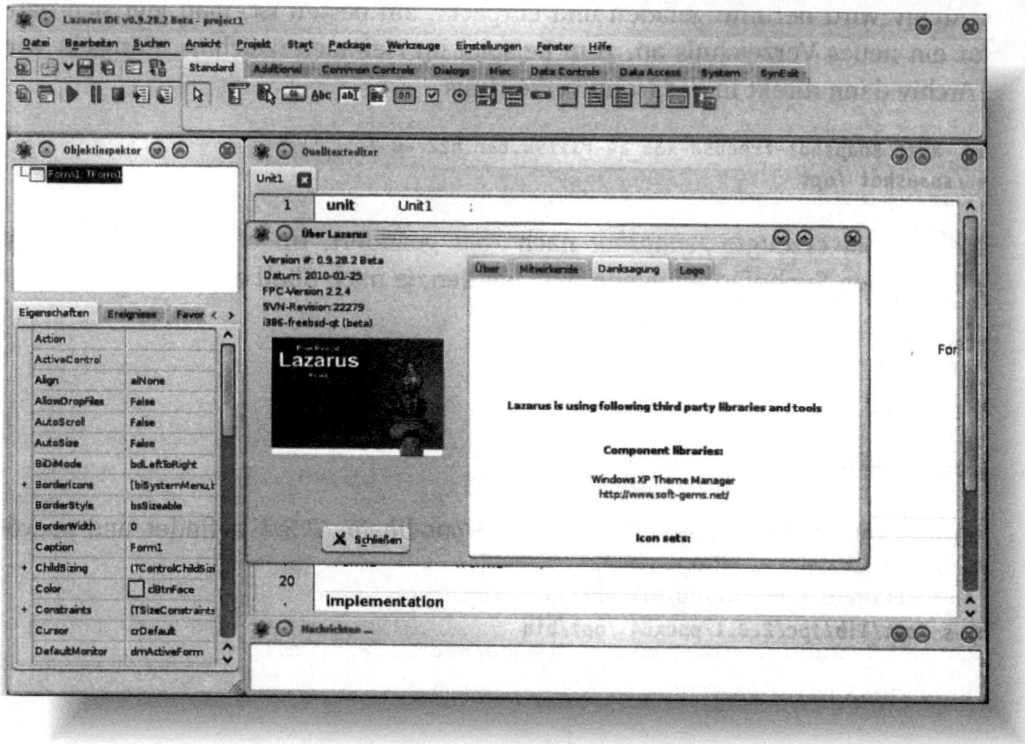

Figure 2.15: Lazarus with the Qt 4 widgets under FreeBSD and KDE 4

2.5 Installation on MacOS X

By Felipe Monteiro de Carvalho

Installing Lazarus on a Macintosh platform is very simple, although installation of Free Pascal is a prerequisite (the same as for Linux, unlike Windows). The first step is to download three archives from SourceForge or from the Free Pascal FTP server.
For Lazarus 0.9.28.2 and Free Pascal 2.2.4, you need the following disk image files:

- `fpc-2.2.4.intel-macosx.dmg` (contains the compiler)
- `fpcsrc-2.2.4-intel-macosx.dmg` (contains the compiler source files)
- `lazarus-0.9.28.2-i386-macosx.dmg` (contains the IDE)

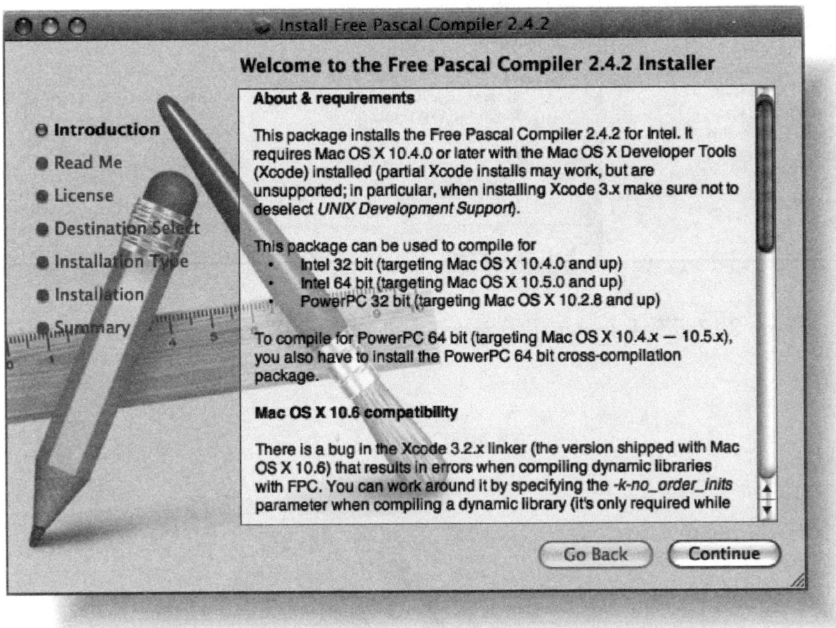

Figure 2.16: Initial dialog for installing Free Pascal

You must also verify that Xcode has been installed from the Apple DVD.
Next, double-click the disk image file `fpc-2.4.0.intel-macosx.dmg` and launch the file `fpc-2.4.0.intel-macosx` in the disk image. It installs two compilers: one for Intel x86 and the other for Intel x86_64. Another package is available for PowerPC cross-compilation, if this is desired.
Then use exactly the same procedure to install the source code files and the IDE.

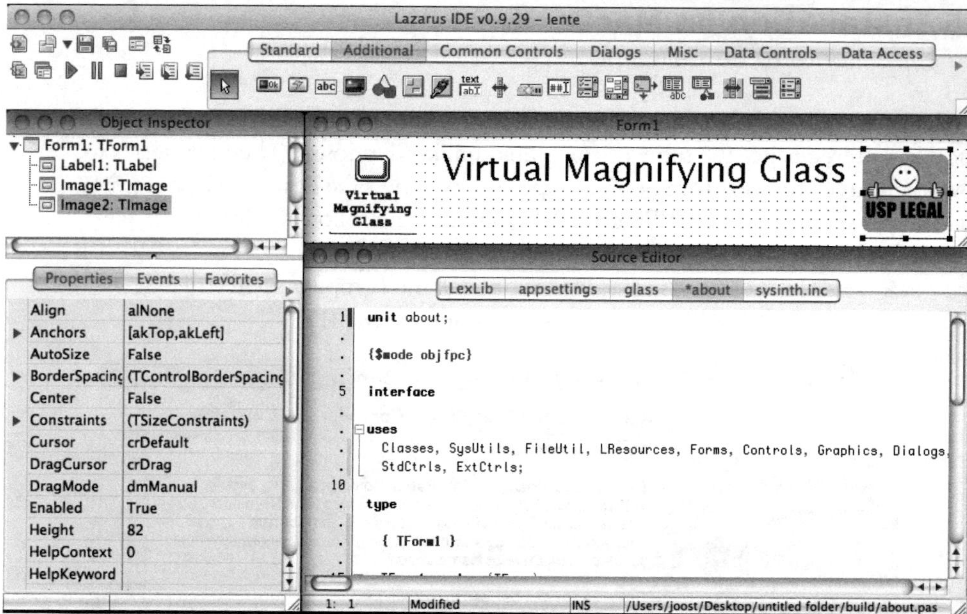

Figure 2.17: The Lazarus IDE installed under MacOS X, along with an application

Chapter 3
The IDE

by Sven Heinig

Once the installation has been successful, you can start the Lazarus IDE. The IDE is made up of several independent windows which you can arrange as you wish. You may be familiar with this type of multi-windowed development environment from other programs such as GIMP. One advantage of this arrangement is the flexibility you have to adjust individual parts of the IDE to your own needs, such as displaying text in the Editor in an extra large font.

The *main window* is located at the upper edge of the Lazarus IDE. It contains the main menu, the Component Palette and some speed buttons for frequently used functions. When you close the main window, all the other Lazarus IDE windows close too.

The Object Inspector is the window to the left side of the screen. Here at design time you can check and set component properties and events. The source code Editor is located towards the centre of the screen. Below the Editor is the *Messages* window. During program compilation this window displays any compiler messages. If an error has slipped into the program code, the appropriate error message comes up in the Messages window.

The Form Designer (or Form Editor) is sometimes located behind the text Editor. You can switch the focus between code Editor and Form Designer by pressing the [F12] function key. When you have more than one form unit open in the Editor, pressing [F12] brings the form corresponding to the current unit's source to the foreground.

The window positions described here are the default settings, but you can alter the windows' size and position to your liking. In additional to the windows mentioned, there are further informational windows available through the *View* option on the main menu. If you ever lose track of a window you have opened, use the *Window* menu to get you back on track.

3.1 The Lazarus Main Menu

The Lazarus menu at the top of the main window offers access to the functions you need in everyday programming. Beyond these built-in functions, the IDE can be customised to your own wishes in various ways such as setting your own keyboard shortcuts for menu options you use frequently (*Environment* → *Options* → *Editor, Key Mappings*).

3.1.1 The File Menu

The File menu gives you access to the basic functionality you need to work with files.

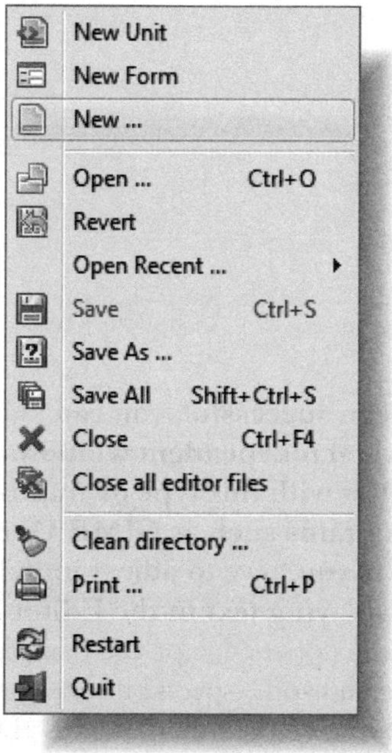

Figure 3.1: The File menu

Few programs have only one file, and at some point you will need further files. You generate a new (empty) form with *File → New form*. Because every form is based on a unit, a new unit is automatically generated with the new form.
When you want to keep a group of functions or procedures separate, use the *File → New Unit* option. This gives you an empty unit (without a form) where you can put those procedures.

For new projects and other situations where these two options are not sufficient, there is another option *File → New…*. More information about the various types of project can be found in Chapter 4.

File → Open… and *File → Close* are self-explanatory options.
File → Open Recent presents you with a list of the last few files that you opened (by default the last ten files). The number of recent files to be shown can be changed via *Environment → Options…→ Environment → Files → Max recent files.*

When a *complete project* has to be saved with another name (to distribute it to another programmer for instance) using *Project → Publish Project…* is easier than dealing with individual files one at a time.

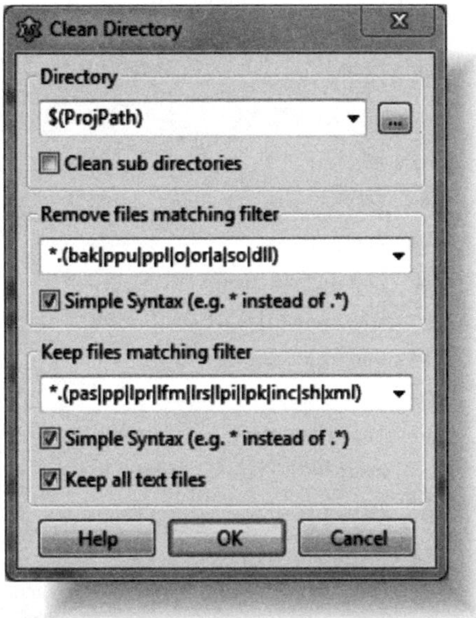

Figure 3.2: The Clean Directory dialog

As you work on a project you will collect a lot of inessential files (such as backup copies). When you convert a Delphi project to Lazarus, the old Delphi files still remain in the directory although they are no longer needed. Such files can be removed by the use of the *File* → *Clean directory…* option. In the resulting dialog you enter in the *Directory* field the directory you want to be cleaned up. If you have opened a project, its directory is shown by default. When you also want the sub-directories to be cleaned, click the appropriate checkbox.
To select the files that will be removed (cleaned) set a filter using the *Remove files matching filter* combobox. You can use one of the provided filters or type in your own custom filter.
Files that are *not* to be deleted are entered into the *Keep files matching filter* field. These files are kept even when they are included in the filter *Remove files matching filter*. You may get confused if these two filters have overlapping entries! Files are identified as 'text' files when the first 1000 bytes contain no special characters.

The *File* → *Print* option is only shown when the Lazarus package *printers4lazide* has been installed. If this is not the case, you can install it using *Package* → *Install/Uninstall packages….*
If you use the *Print* option when any text is selected in the Editor, a dialog will ask whether you want the entire text or only the selection to be printed.
If you change any Lazarus settings (such as the language to use), the changed settings are applied the next time you start Lazarus. A faster way is to use the *File* → *Restart* option.

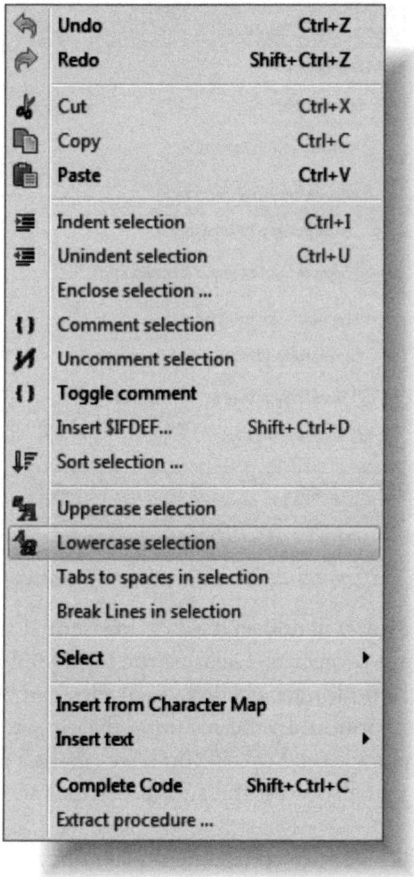

Figure 3.3: The Edit menu

3.1.2 The Edit Menu

The *Edit* menu contains the commands you might expect for using the clipboard and manipulating source code. When you press the wrong button or key while editing, or if an option did not have the desired effect, you can reverse the action with the *Undo* option ([Ctrl] [Z]).

The editor then restores the situation to the point before your mistake. Should you mistakenly undo too much, *Redo* will reverse the effect of *Undo*.

The *Edit* menu contains many commands for formatting source code. However, there are no universally accepted rules about formatting source code.

As long as you follow Pascal's syntax rules (for instance by putting a semicolon at the end of each statement), the compiler will not complain about your source code's format.

However, you can enhance the readability of your code by following certain conventions such as indenting procedures by two characters.

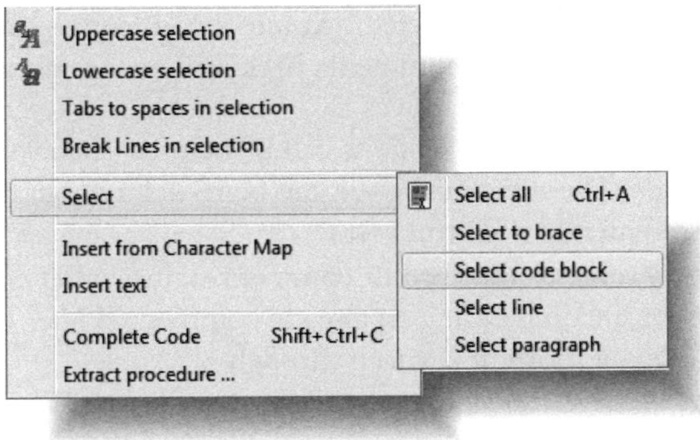

Figure 3.4: The text selection options available on the Edit menu

The formatting commands assume that some (or all) of the text has been selected. You can select text manually or by using the *Edit* → *Select* menu.
The *Indent selection* option moves the selected text to the right, and *Unindent selection* moves the selected text to the left by a certain number of characters.

The number of characters to indent by can be changed using *Environment* → *Options…*→ *Editor* → *General* → *Indent and Tabs* → *Block indent.*
The default value is two spaces.
The *Edit* → *Enclose selection…* menu presents you with a dialog where you can choose which enclosing structure you want be added around the selected text. This can be a loop (for instance *while .. do*) or a sequence (such as *begin .. end*).

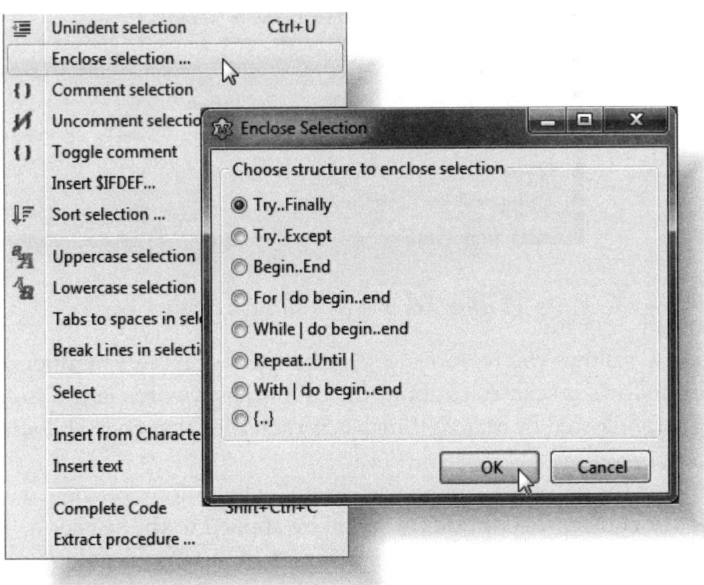

Figure 3.5: The dialog for enclosing selected text,
accessed via Edit → Enclose selection…

Edit → *Comment selection* turns the selected text into a comment by adding two // at the beginning of the line(s). Changing comments back into code is done via *Edit* → *Uncomment selection*, which removes all // comment markers.
Temporarily commenting out code sections can be helpful when you have a problem with part of your code. The remaining code can be tested without this part, saving you from deleting and re-entering doubtful code.
Edit → *Toggle comment* reverses the current comment status, either commenting an uncommented line, or uncommenting an already commented line. To make this function readily accessible assign a shortcut key to it through *Environment* → *Options…* → *Editor, Key mappings.*

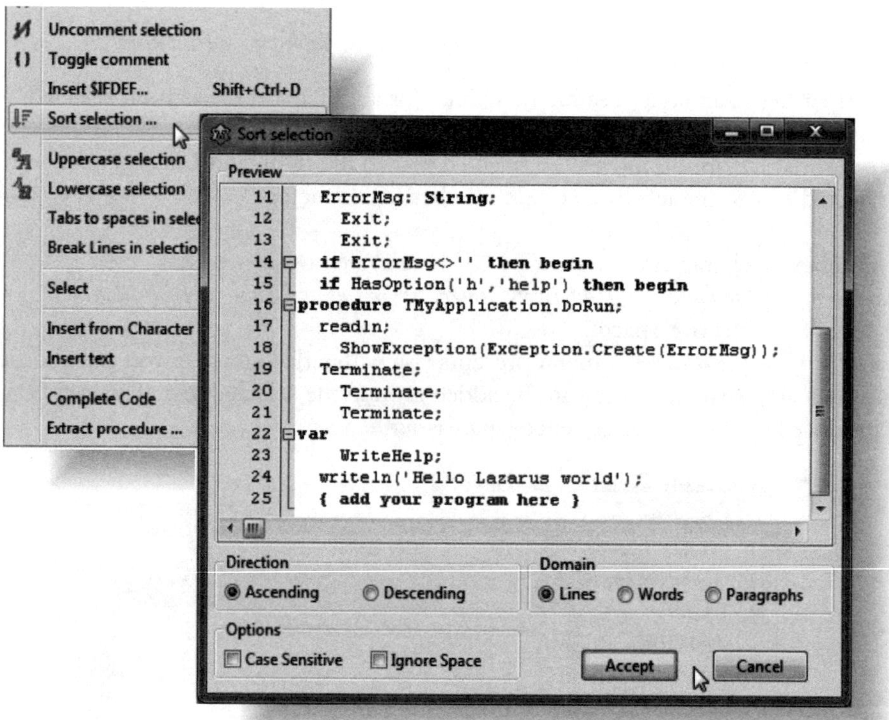

Figure 3.6: The Sort selection dialog

Edit → *Sort selection* allows you to sort the selected Editor text in a number of ways. Because Pascal follows certain rules about the order of keywords in the source code (*begin* comes first, followed by an *end*) it makes no sense to sort code alphabetically within a procedure.
However sorting a list of values can be very useful. The dialog's preview window shows the result of your chosen sort options as it will be applied to the selection. The D*irection* option lets you sort either *Ascending* or *Descending*. *Ascending* means going up, for instance *a, b, c*. *Descending* means going down as in *c, b, a*.

Use the *Domain* option to set the level at which sorting is done:
Lines sorts on the first characters of each line, for example :

```
1.  procedure Button1Click(Sender: TObject);
2.  procedure FormCreate(Sender: TObject);
3.  procedure FormMouseMove(Sender: TObject; Shift: TShiftState; X, Y: Integer);
4.  procedure FormPaint(Sender: TObject);
5.  procedure FormMouseUp(Sender: TObject; Button: TMouseButton;
                                Shift: TShiftState; X, Y: Integer);
6.  procedure FormMouseDown(Sender: TObject; Button: TMouseButton;
                                Shift: TShiftState; X, Y: Integer);
7.  procedure FormDestroy(Sender: TObject);
```

becomes:

```
1. procedure Button1Click(Sender: TObject);
2.  procedure FormCreate(Sender: TObject);
7.  procedure FormDestroy(Sender: TObject);
6.  procedure FormMouseDown(Sender: TObject; Button: TMouseButton;
                                Shift: TShiftState; X, Y: integer);
3.  procedure FormMouseMove(Sender: TObject; Shift: TShiftState; X, Y: integer);
4.  procedure FormMouseUp(Sender: TObject; Button: TMouseButton;
                                Shift: TShiftState; X, Y: integer);
5.  procedure FormPaint(Sender: TObject);
```

Words sorts like a dictionary, for example the following uses clause

```
Classes, SysUtils, FileUtil, LResources, Forms, Controls, Graphics, Dialogs;
```

becomes

```
Classes, Controls, Dialogs; FileUtil, Forms, Graphics, LResources, SysUtils,
```

With Paragraph the selected text is divided into paragraphs and then sorted. A paragraph starts with less indented text. The previous example:

```
1.  procedure Button1Click(Sender: TObject);
2.  procedure FormCreate(Sender: TObject);
3.  procedure FormMouseMove(Sender: TObject; Shift: TShiftState; X, Y: Integer);
4.  procedure FormPaint(Sender: TObject);
5.  procedure FormMouseUp(Sender: TObject; Button: TMouseButton;
                                Shift: TShiftState; X, Y: Integer);
6.  procedure FormMouseDown(Sender: TObject; Button: TMouseButton;
                                Shift: TShiftState; X, Y: Integer);
7.  procedure FormDestroy(Sender: TObject);
```

becomes

```
1.  procedure Button1Click(Sender: TObject);
2.  procedure FormCreate(Sender: TObject);
7.  procedure FormDestroy(Sender: TObject);
6.  procedure FormMouseDown(Sender: TObject; Button: TMouseButton;
                                Shift: TShiftState; X, Y: Integer);
3.  procedure FormMouseMove(Sender: TObject; Shift: TShiftState; X, Y: Integer);
4.  procedure FormMouseUp(Sender: TObject; Button: TMouseButton;
                                Shift: TShiftState; X, Y: Integer);
5.  procedure FormPaint(Sender: TObject);
```

When the *Case Sensitive* option is set, the sorting takes account of difference between a lowercase and an uppercase letter. Setting the *Ignore Space* option causes the sort to treat multiple spaces as if they were a single space.

The next menu option *Edit → Uppercase selection* converts all characters in the selected text to uppercase, just as they are all converted to lowercase with *Edit → Lowercase selection.*
Consistent casing of identifier names and keywords increases the clarity of your code and the ease of searching for identifiers. When you don't format your source code as you write, you can still do this afterwards.
Using *Edit → Tabs to spaces in selection* converts tabs to spaces using the setting from *Environment → Options…→ Editor → General → Indent and Tabs → Tab widths.*
The number of spaces is not fixed, but is needed to fill out the tabulator's remaining space. When a line in the selection exceeds 80 characters, it can be word-wrapped by using the option *Edit → Break lines in selection*, continuing at the next line. The maximum Line length before wrapping occurs is the setting found at *Environment → Options… → Editor → Display → Right margin.* The default value of 80 can be altered as desired.
As well as the insertion of the clipboard's contents the IDE provides for the insertion of other elements. *Edit → Insert from Character Map* enables you to insert special characters which cannot normally be typed with standard keystrokes. The character map is divided into two pages, one for ANSI characters and one for Unicode, enabling faster access to the character you need. A single click on a character inserts it in front of the cursor in your code.
Predefined words or phrases (boiler-plate text) can be inserted using *Edit → Insert text* which offers the submenus: *CVS keyword, General, Insert ToDo. CVS keyword* is used to insert a specific control word for a version control system. For the meaning of the individual control words listed in the submenu refer to the documentation of the version control system.
The *General* submenu offers various documentation elements you might want included in the unit, and the ability to generate and insert a text GUID. *Insert ToDo* shows a dialog where you enter details of your *ToDo* note which are then formatted into a *ToDo* comment inserted at the current cursor position in the Editor. You can review all your *ToDo* notes via *View → ToDo list.*

When your source code becomes too lengthy or too complex, you should organise sections of code into separate procedures. *Edit → Extract procedure…* is available for this. When in the example

```
procedure DoSomething;
begin
  CallSomething;
end;
```

the line CallSomething; (including the ;) is selected and the option Extract procedure is chosen, the dialog shown in Figure 3.8 is displayed.

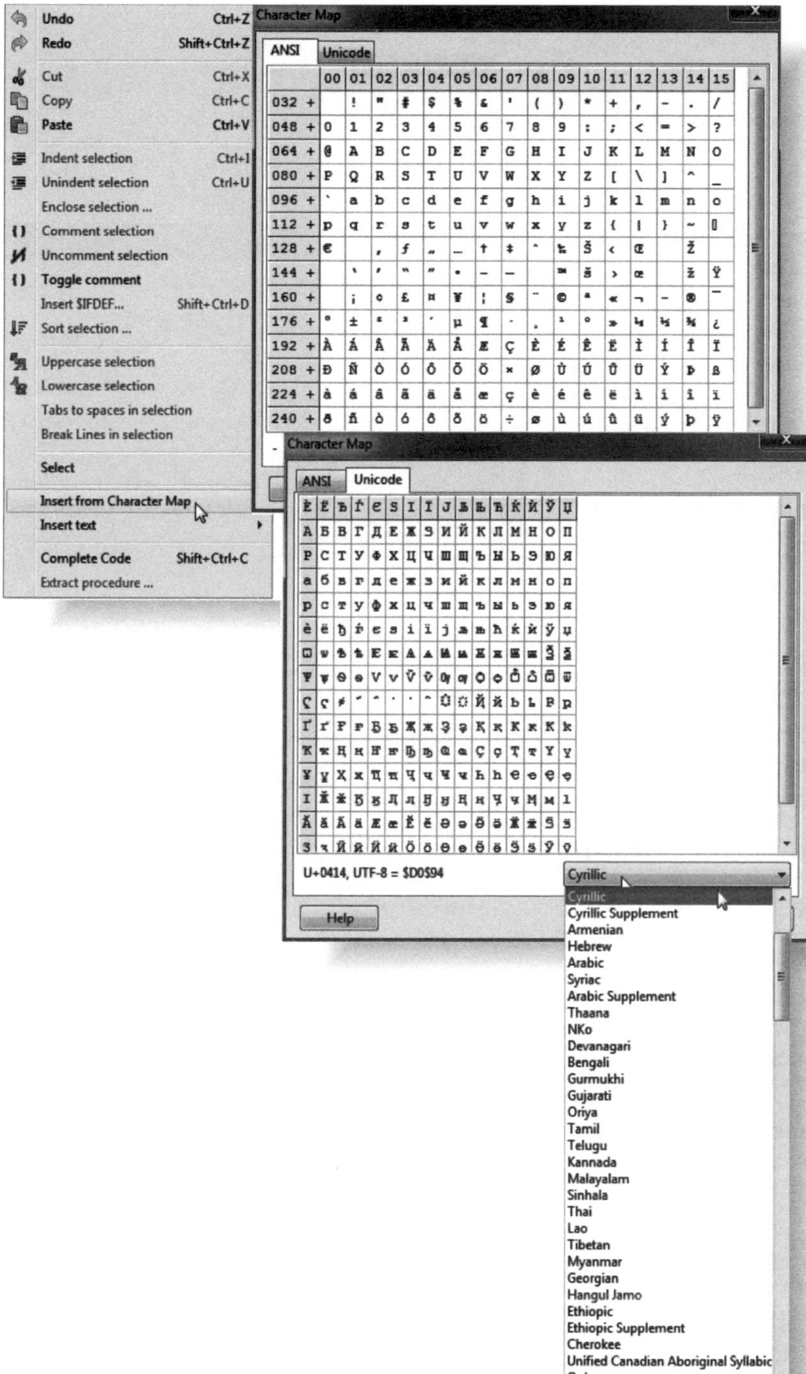

Figure 3.7: The characters available in the Character Map, accessed via Edit → Insert from Character Map

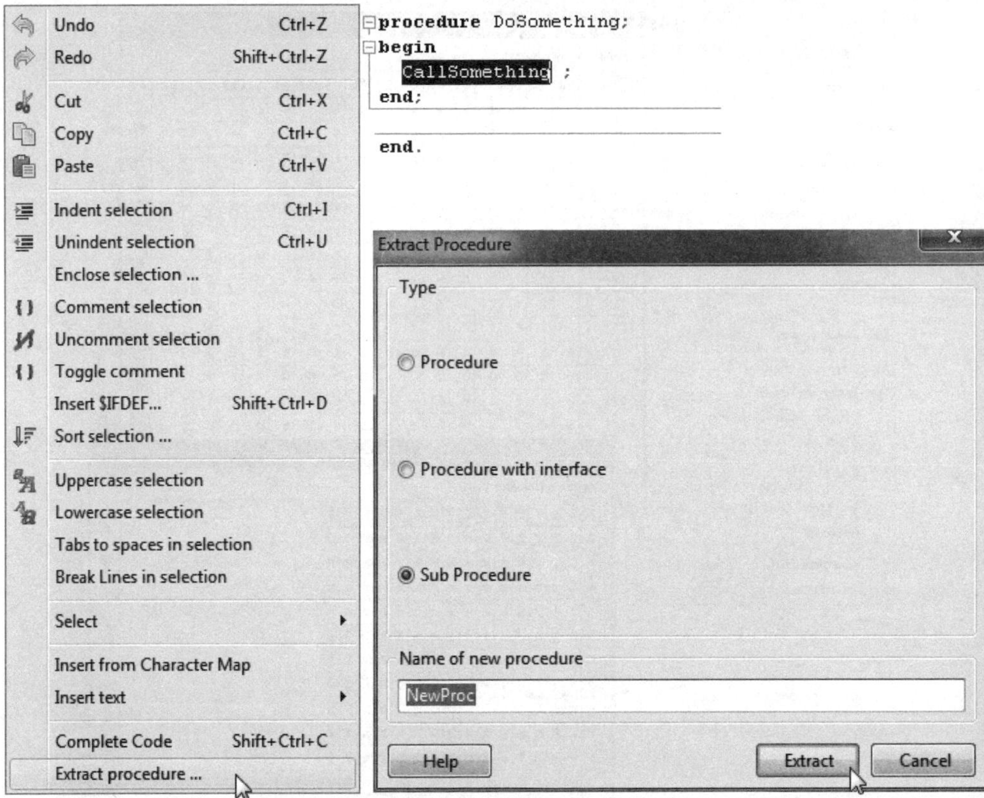

Figure 3.8: The Edit → Extract procedure… dialog

Choosing the Procedure radio button and leaving NewProc as the Name of new procedure alters your code to the following:

```
procedure NewProc;
begin
  CallSomething;
end;

procedure DoSomething;
begin
  NewProc;
end;
```

A new procedure is generated from the selected code, and that original code is replaced by a call to the new procedure. *Extract procedure…* scans for any variables used, and automatically generates a parameter list and the local variables. For instance, consider this method of Form1:

```
procedure TForm1.DoSomething(var Ernie, Bert);
  var
  i: Integer; // comment
begin
  Ernie := Ernie + Bert;
  for i:= Ernie to 5 do begin
  end;
end;
```

Select the *for* loop and generate a new procedure *NewProc.* Because the variable *i* is found only in the selected code, it is moved to the new procedure. *Ernie* is used outside the selected code and therefore it becomes a parameter.

```
procedure NewProc(const Ernie: Integer);
  var
  i: Integer; // comment
begin
  for i:= Ernie to 5 do begin
  end;
end;

procedure TForm1.DoSomething(var Ernie, Bert: Integer);
begin
  Ernie := Ernie + Bert;
  NewProc(Ernie);
end;
```

As well as the variable *i,* the comment is also moved to the new procedure.
Since Pascal is a very extensive language you may find that *Extract procedure* does not support every possible Pascal construct.

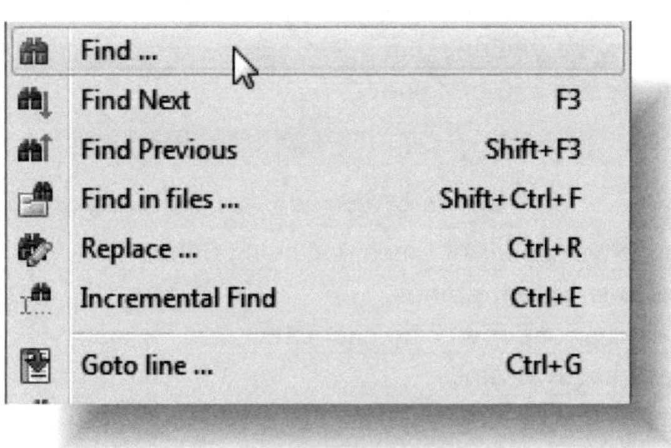

Figure 3.9: The Search menu

3.1.3 Searching

Object oriented programming has the disadvantage that as your overall design is modularised over more and more objects, its complexity increases. This makes the availability of powerful search features very important, so you can quickly locate key bits of your source code. One of the benefits of the open source nature of Lazarus is being able to search its source code as well your own code. You will often be looking for a half-remembered identifier whose exact spelling is unknown. Lazarus helps the developer by offering a set of *regular expressions* which you can use in the search field, to save you thinking of endless different variant spellings to try, hoping one will produce a hit.

Meta character	Meaning
\	Tells the search to treat the metacharacter following as a literal character instead.
^	Stands for the beginning of the line.
.	Stand for any character (except the start of a line). *Example:* a.c represents abc, aBc, a3c etc.$Stands for the end of a line.
|	Change.
()	Grouping, for example : (abc)+ represents abc, abcabc, abcabcabc etc.
[]	Defines a character set, for example [abc], [a-z], [a-zA-Z0-9]
[^]	Inverse set of characters, for example [^a-z].

Table 3.1: The meaning of the special characters (metacharacters) used in regular expression searches.

You can use the backslash \ to revert the meaning of a special character like a point to its normal text meaning. Some backslashed symbols have special meanings in the context of a search.

Symbol	Meaning
\.	Represents a .
\d	Represents a number from 0 to 9.
\D	Represents a non-numeric character.
\s	Represents an empty or control character (><,#9,#10,#12,#13).
\S	Represents a non-empty or non-control character.
\w	Represents an alphanumeric character (a to z, A to Z, 0 to 9).
\W	Represents a non-alphanumeric character.
\b	Represents a word delimiter.
\B	Represents a non-word delimiter.
\A	Represents the beginning of a line.
\Z	Represents the end of a line.

Table 3.2: Symbols available in regular expressions

Symbol	The number of repeats of the regular expression to allow
*	Matches any number of times, including none.
+	Matches one or more times.
?	Either zero or one matching character.
{n}	Matches exactly n times.
{n,}	Matches at least n times.
{n,m}	Matches at least n times but no more than m times.

Table 3.3: Regular expression weightings.

3.1.3 Searching

In some dialogs a *Simple Syntax* can be activated by a checkbox, enabling the use of the *wildcards* used by other programs. The simpler syntax is converted internally to the following regular expressions :

. becomes \.
* becomes .*
? becomes .
, becomes |
; becomes |

The dialogs presented by *Search* → *Find* and *Search* → *Replace* are basically identical. When called through [Ctrl] [F], the replace options and toggles are disabled. When called by [Ctrl] [R] these are enabled. The *Text to Find* and *Replace With* comboboxes contain the most-recently-searched texts and filters. With the down-arrow key ↓ one can go back in the history and select a previously searched text. Tip: you can set whether you want the dialog be prefilled with the word at the cursor, or just with an empty field, using *Environment* → *Options…* → *Editor* → *General* → *Misc* → *Find text at cursor.*

There are several settings for the interpretation of the searched text :

- *Case sensitive.* Distinguishes between uppercase and lowercase characters (a is not A).
- *Whole words only.* The text found must start at the beginning of the word and end at the end of the word.
- *Regular expressions.* The search text may contain regular expressions.
- *Multiline pattern* The search does not stop at line endings, so the text found can contain more than one line. Multiple lines can be copied and pasted from the source editor into the *Text to Find* field. If using regular expressions the backslash-n combination *n* symbolises a line end to search for.
- *Prompt on replace*: You will be asked to confirm replace actions (only enabled in the *Replace* dialog).

In the *Origin* section you can set where the search is to begin:

- *From cursor.* The search starts from the cursor position. If the direction is forwards, searching is done towards the end of the file.
- *Entire scope.* If the search direction is forwards the search starts at the beginning of the file towards the end of it.

The *Scope* section determines the extent of the search:

- *Selected text.* Only the selected text is searched.
- *Global.* The entire file is searched.
  Tip: To search several files use the *Search* → *Find in files…* menu.

The *Direction* section lets you set the search direction:

- *Backwards search.* The file is searched from end to the beginning. Every line is searched from left to right. (Lazarus allows languages that are written from right to left to be used in the IDE, but Pascal sources are always written from left to right whatever the setting).
- *Forward search.* The file is searched from beginning to the end. Every line is searched from left to right

Search → Find Next (usually invoked with the [F3] key) starts a new search for the search text you last entered, and no dialog is shown unless the search is unsuccessful. After a replace action also the next hit will be replaced (if you consent to the confirmation message). Similarly *Search → Find Previous* ([Shift] [F3]) locates the previous occurrence of the search text. After a replace action also the previous hit will be replaced if you confirm this.

The *Search → Find in files* menu lets you set search and replace filters for searching multiple files. It's logical that only text files are searched. This includes source text files (`.pas, .pp, .inc, .rc, .po, .txt` etc.) but not the compiled files and libraries. When you have set all options appropriately you start the search with a click on the *Find* button. Any hits are displayed in the *Search Results* window. This window can be opened later at any time using *View → Search Results* since the results of your last search are remembered.
Naturally it is almost useless to search for a general term like *unit* or *end* because the resulting hit list may be very long. Hence a *Cancel* button is provided to abandon such a fruitless search.
There are several settings which affect the way *Search* interprets text in the *Text to find* field.

- *Case sensitive:* Distinguishes between uppercase and lowercase characters (a is not A).
- *Whole words only:* The text found must start at the word beginning and end at the word end.
- *Regular expressions:* The search text may contain regular expressions.
- *Multiline pattern:* The search does not stop at line endings, so the text found can contain more than one line. Multiple lines can be copied and pasted from the source editor into the *Text to Find* field. If using regular expressions the backslash-n combination *\n* symbolises a line end to search for.

You set where the search has to take place in the *Where* section:

- *Search in all files in project:* All files included in the project are searched.
- *Search all open files:* All files opened in the editor are searched.
- *Search in directories:* You can specify any search directory, and specify additional settings using the *File mask* field. Using the default filter provided, the search will be limited to standard file types. The combo box contains the last filters you used.
- The checkbox *Include sub directories* is important when big or unknown directories need to be searched. When checked, all sub directories are searched recursively. This can take a long time.

3.1.3 Searching

The *Search* menu contains several *jump* options besides the search options. So you can jump to a specific line number, to an error that occurred, or to a bookmark (and naturally there are also options to set bookmarks). Jumps can be forwards or backwards, or to the beginning or end of the current file.
The option *Find Declaration at cursor* locates the place where the identifier or method under the cursor is declared, opening another file if the identifier is declared outside the current file. This option is especially useful when you need identifier information which can only be found where it is declared and there is no tooltip to help you.
When a unit refers to another unit (linked though the *uses* clause), this other unit can be opened using *Open filename at cursor* if the cursor is at the unit name.

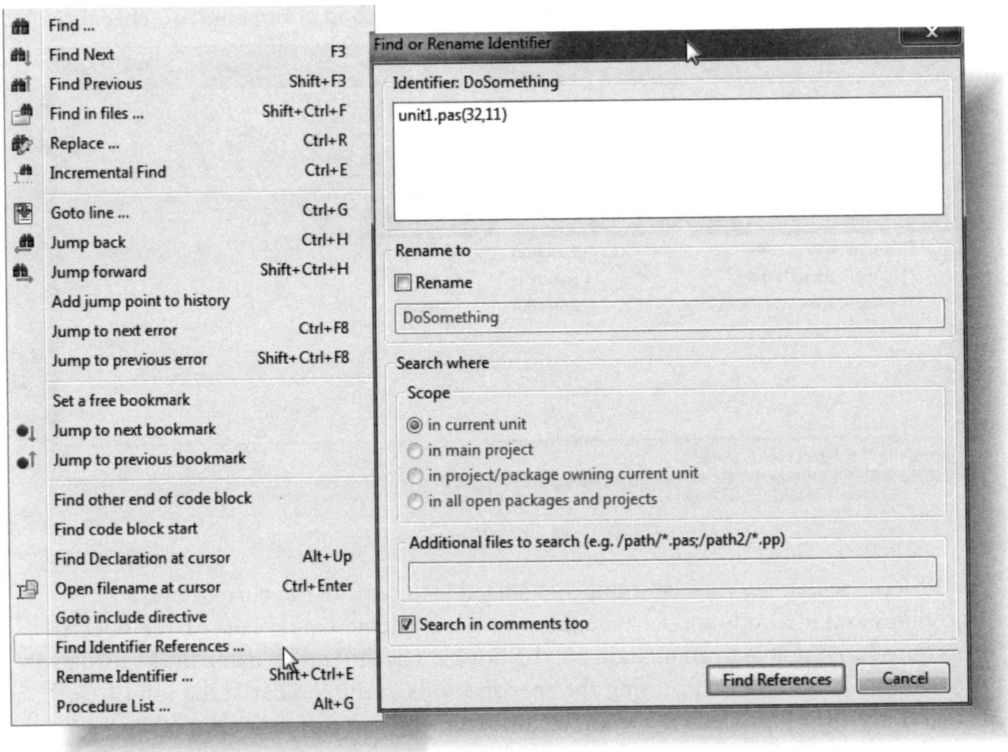

Figure 3.10: Search → Find Identifier References... shows this dialog for locating (and optionally renaming) identifiers

Lazarus lets you search for (and perhaps rename) identifiers using the *Search menu options Find Identifier References... and Rename Identifier...* .
You have to place the cursor on an identifier in your source code to make this option work. The Rename to area is only enabled when called from the Rename Identifier menu. The name of the identifier searched for is shown in the title of the Identifier group box. Below are shown any locations where the identifier is found in that unit or its include files.

Rename lets you enter the identifier's new name when it needs to be renamed.
The search can be limited to specific files or directories :

- in current unit: Search and rename only in the current unit.
- in main project: Search and rename only in the current project files.
- in project/package owning current unit: Once you select the project (or package), search and rename is executed on all files in the project (or package).
- in all open packages and projects: As above but more extensive, since search and rename changes all dependent packages or projects.

When the search needs to include more files, these can be entered in the Additional files to search field.
Searching the comments can be included using the Search in comments too checkbox.

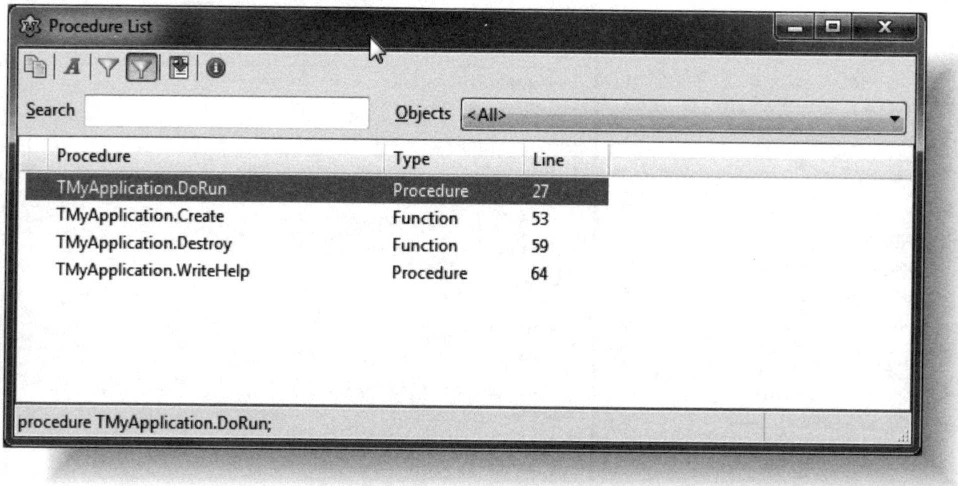

Figure 3.11: The Procedure List

The Procedure List makes a lightning fast sorted listing of all the current unit's procedures and methods and lets you jump to the implementation part of the selected procedure (even if it is in an include file) by double-clicking on its name in the listing. You can call several functions using the speedbuttons in the toolbar at the top of the dialog. If the list of procedures becomes too long, you can search for a specific procedure or method with help of the Search field which filters the list dynamically as you type a partial method name.

3.1.4 The View Menu

The View menu allows you to call a number of specific windows (or bring a particular window into the foreground if you can't see it).
Detailed information about the Object Inspector and the Source Editor, the first two items in the View menu, is found in Chapter 3.2 .

3.1.4 The View Menu

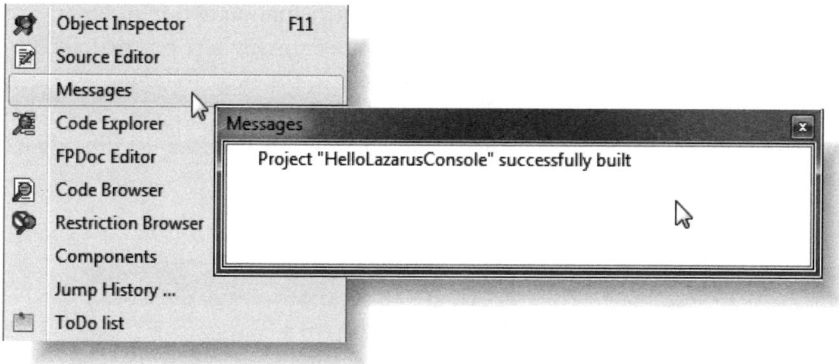

Figure 3.12: The Messages window.

The *Messages* window is located by default below the source Editor, but can be relocated elsewhere if you wish. The *Messages* window displays messages from Lazarus's Codetools, from the Free Pascal compiler and from the linker. These messages are filtered so that only the messages the Lazarus developers consider most important are shown.
Using the context menu (right-click anywhere inside the *Messages* window) messages can be copied to the clipboard where you can view them at your leisure.
When you compile Lazarus itself you may wish to disable the checkbox *Restart after building IDE (Tools → Configure "Build Lazarus"…)* because the messages window will be emptied at a restart.
You can jump to the place in your source code referred to by a message simply by clicking on it. Whether this jump needs a single or a double-click can be set at *Environment → Options…→ Environment → Desktop → Jump from message to source line on double click (otherwise: single click).*
The context menu for the *Messages* window offers several useful actions. *Clear* removes all messages from the list. *Copy selected messages to clipboard* copies your selection to the clipboard. The exact message will be important if you are reporting a bug.
Copy all shown messages to the clipboard copies all displayed messages (you might have to scroll to see them all), but excludes the messages hidden by Lazarus. When you wish to see every possible message *Copy all shown and hidden messages to clipboard* is what you want.
Behind the message shown in Figure 3.12 the following compiler output is hidden:

```
Hint: Start of reading config file C:\lazarus\fpc\2.4.3\bin\i386-win32\fpc.cfg
Hint: End of reading config file C:\lazarus\fpc\2.4.3\bin\i386-win32\fpc.cfg
Free Pascal Compiler version 2.4.3 [2011/02/05] for i386
Copyright (c) 1993-2010 by Florian Klaempfl
Target OS: Win32 for i386
Compiling HelloLazarusConsole.lpr
Compiling resource C:\LazProjects\LazarusBook\lib\i386-
win32\HelloLazarusConsole.or
Linking HelloLazarusConsole.exe
47 lines compiled, 2.5 sec , 1205744 bytes code, 295256 bytes data
2 hint(s) issued
Project "HelloLazarusConsole" successfully built
```

There is also a Help option which may give more information about an error, provided you select the message first, and provided a volunteer somewhere has provided information on that particular error and recorded it in the help system.
Sometimes copying messages to the clipboard is ruled out, but you can always Save all messages to file. This stores the messages (including hidden messages) directly to a text file that you specify.

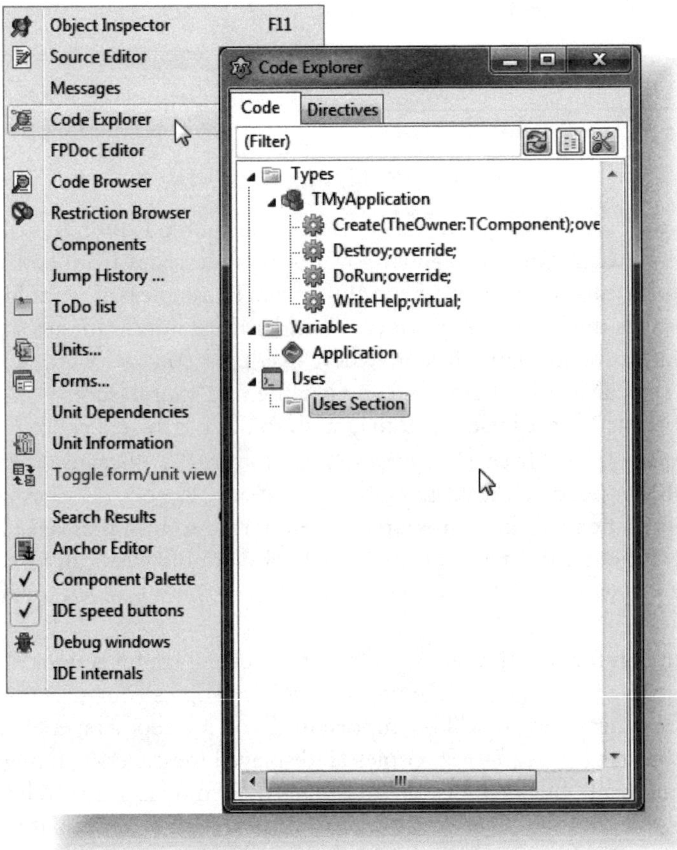

Figure 3.13: Navigating source code using the Code Explorer

The *Code Explorer* is a tool to help you see the both the organisation and the detail of a unit and to speed navigation through source code. The *Code* tab shows the Pascal structure of the unit (types, variables, constants, classes and so on). Clicking an element jumps to the corresponding place in the source code.
The filter limits the entries so that only entries matching the filter are shown.
The *Refresh* button renews the list, if you change the source code. You can edit various settings that configure the Code Explorer using the tools speedbutton (it has a spanner and screwdriver icon). The Code Explorer settings can also be configured via *Environment* → *Options...* → *Code Explorer.*
The *Directives* tab shows the occurrence of any compiler directives. Again, a click on a specific directive jumps to its position in your source.

The *FPDoc Editor* is designed to help you document your code, and view existing documentation. You are able to add comments and explanations for every identifier declared in the interface part of a unit. The XML help file generated (`<unitname>.xml`) is usually stored in a 'docs' subdirectory. When help information is available in such a file it is automatically shown in a tooltip window when the cursor hovers over a documented identifier.

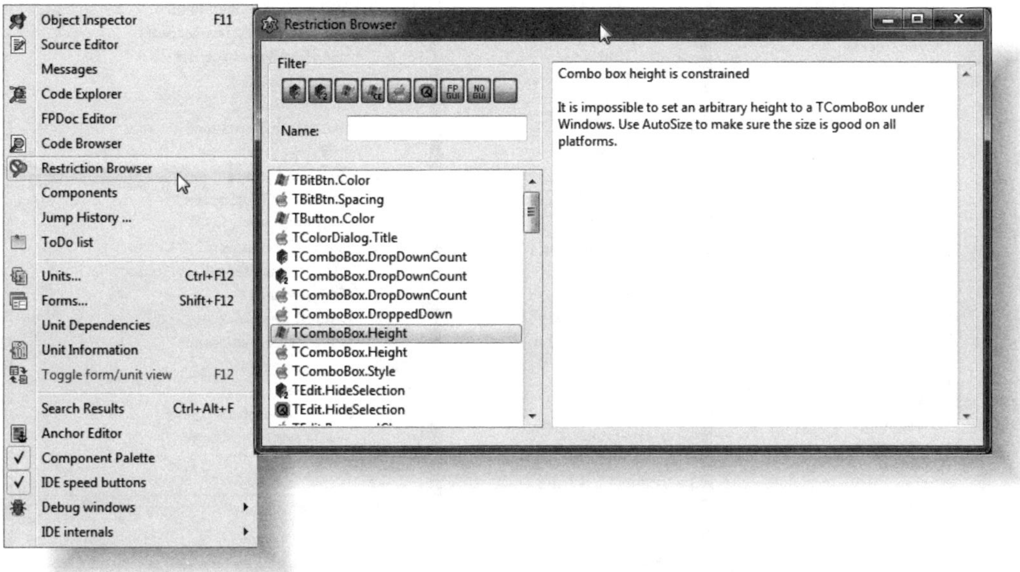

Figure 3.14: The View menu's Restriction Browser

The *Restriction browser* centralizes detailed information about visual components' behaviour in the various widget-sets Lazarus supports. Cross-platform GUI programming requires you to understand what restrictions some properties have in certain widget-sets, or perhaps certain properties are completely absent on some platforms. Maybe in the future a solution will be found for some presently restricted properties which will allow them full platform independence. For other properties this will never be the case.

The *Filter* section (a row of speedbuttons) lets you set the widget-set(s) of interest (default: all sets). The properties in question are shown in the list on the left. The memo on the right shows the relevant information. At the moment this information is only available in English.

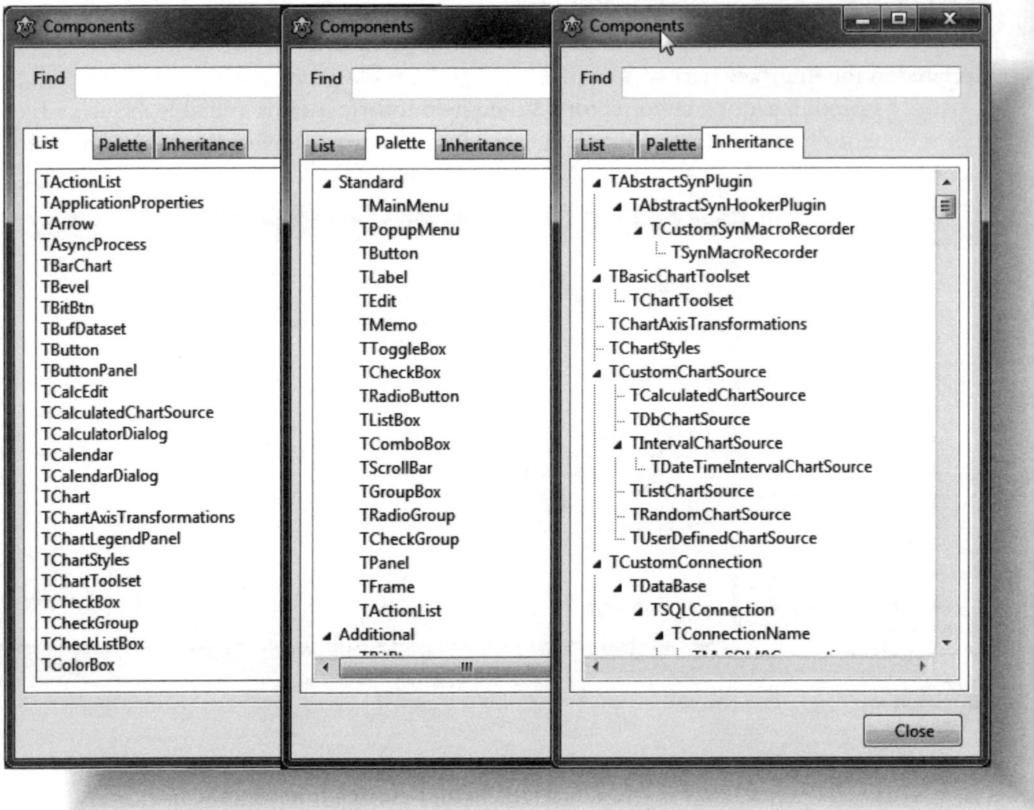

Figure 3.15: The three alternative pages listing installed Components via View → Components

View → Components shows a dialog which lets you search for a specific (installed) component and insert it in the current form. The lower part is divided into three pages offering alternative ways of organising the component list. *List* sorts all components alphabetically, while *Palette* shows them according to their location on the various Component Palette tabs. *Inheritance* shows the component inheritance hierarchy (and thus includes many components not available on the Component Palette).
The upper search field dynamically limits the list to only those components whose names contain the letters typed so far. A double-click on the selected component inserts a new instance of the component at the cursor location in your source code, and visual components are additionally added to the associated form.

The *Jump History…* window records all the jumps you have made in the current session. A click on an item takes you back again to that place in the source code.

The menu options *Units* and *Forms* list respectively all the units and forms used in the project. A double-click on an entry opens the selected file in the Source Editor (for units) or the Form Designer (for forms).

The *ToDo list* shows all the ToDo entries from all files in the project (that is, all files listed in the current .lpr file, including package units). *Refresh* searches the project files again for ToDo items.
Double-clicking a ToDo entry in the list (or selecting an entry and clicking *Go*) jumps to that ToDo entry in the source.

The *Unit Dependencies* menu option opens a dialog showing these dependencies in their hierarchical order.

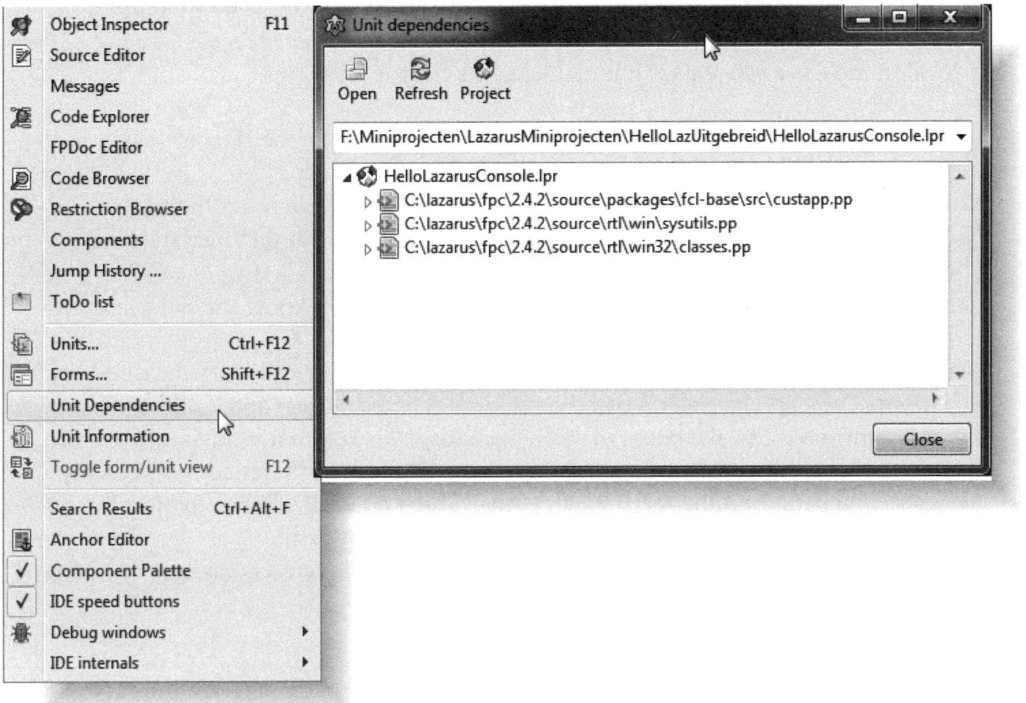

Figure 3.16: The Unit Dependencies dialog

If you open *Unit Dependencies* when a project is open, the project's main source code file (.lpr) is opened by default. Other files can be selected and opened using the *Open* button. When changes have been made, *Refresh* will rebuild the list. The *Project* button selects the main project file.
The sub-entries are the units listed in the *uses* clause. When present, the interface and implementation are separated by a red line. Circular references are shown by an icon with a double arrow. A double-click on a unit opens it in the Editor.

The *Unit information* menu option opens a dialog that shows information about the current unit open in the Source Editor. The dialog box has four pages: *General, Unit paths, Include paths* and *Source paths.*

The *General* page contains overall information about the unit. *Name* is the name of the unit as it is referred to in the source code; otherwise it is the filename without extension and path. *Type* is the type of highlighter (which can be changed via the Editor's context menu). *In Project* states whether that unit is part of the project. You can change this using the *Project* menu via *Project → Add editor file to Project* or *Project → Remove from Project…* *Size* is the unit's size in bytes. *Lines* is the number of code lines. *Path* is the complete filename. *Included by:* This file is the last one included by the unit (for instance with a *{$I filename.inc}* directive). This is set automatically when the unit containing the *Include* directive is analyzed by the IDE. When you need to jump to the *Include* directive of the previous file, use *Search → Goto include directive.*
A click on the *Clear include cache* button clears the field *Included by:*

The *Unit paths* page lists all the unit paths which are needed by the IDE to search for `.ppu, .pas, .pp` and `.p` files.
Normally these paths are passed to the compiler but this is not always the case.
The unit paths defined in the configuration file (fpc.cfg) are not the ones shown here. These paths are generated following the rules established via *Environment → CodeTools defines editor….* All files in a directory know the same search paths (unit paths, include paths, …).
When it concerns a project directory, all project unit paths are added. If the directory is part of a package, the package's paths are added. When a project and a package are saved into the same directory, the paths of both are added. Therefore it is advisable to store projects and packages each in their own directory. There are differences between the *compiler* search paths and the *IDE* search paths (which normally do not matter).
The compiler is called in a directory with a series of search paths.
Consider this example of a project using four packages, where each package compiles its files into its source directory :

- `/home/user/package1/package1.lpk`
- `/home/user/package2/package2.lpk`
- `/home/user/package3/package3.lpk (uses package1 and package2)`
- `/home/user/package4/package4.lpk (uses package1 and package2)`

Package3 will be compiled in `/home/user/package3` using the unit paths `/home/user/package1; /home/user/package2/`
When the compiler finds a unit in the directory `/home/user/package2/` and compiles it, it uses all unit paths including the path to `/home/user/package3/`. Normally this is not the recommended way and this is why a standard package defines an *output directory.* In this example it is assumed that the package compiles its files into the source directory. When the compiler is called for *package4* it is started in a different directory with different search paths, in the example `/home/user/package4/` with the unit path `/home/user/package1; /home/user/package2/`.
When the compiler finds a unit in the directory `/home/user/package2/` and compiles it, it uses all unit paths including the path to `/home/user/package4/`.
This is unsatisfactory because the result depends on the order of the paths, namely if *package3* is compiled before *package4* or other way round. This occurs more often than you may realise, and when packages contain units with the same names, the order of the file paths in the search paths becomes important.

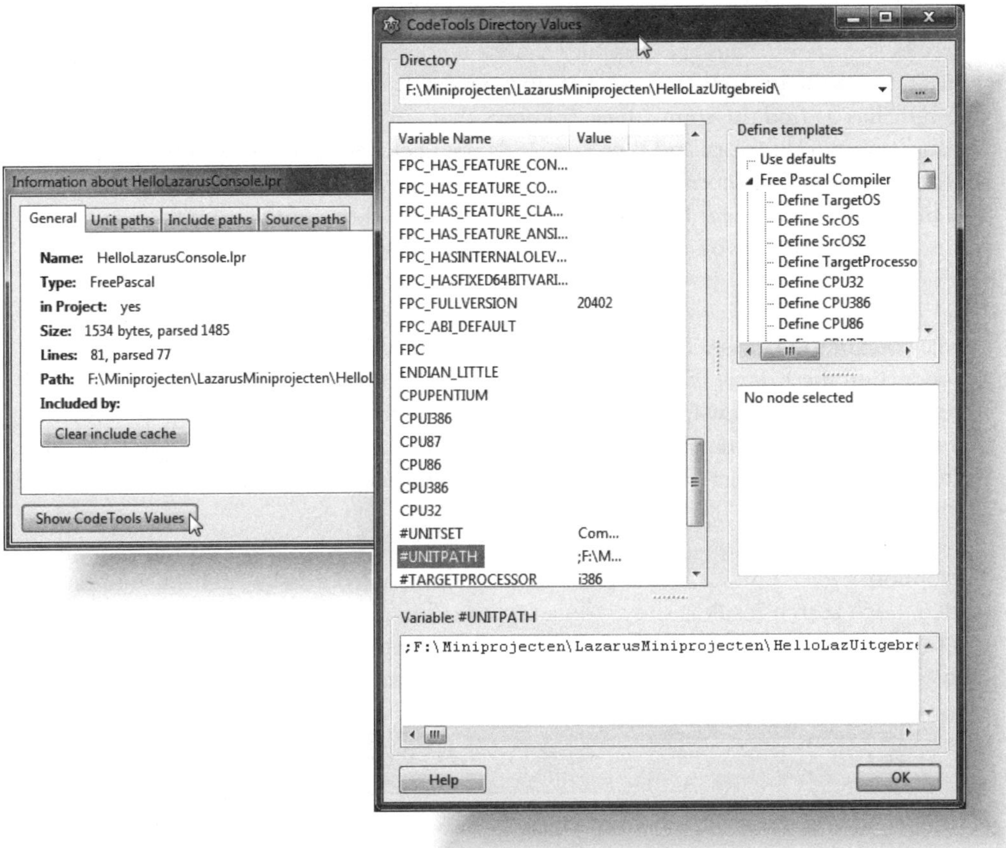

Figure 3.17: The CodeTools Directory Values dialog is invoked by the Show CodeTools Values button at the bottom of the Unit information dialog invoked via the View → Unit Information menu option.

The IDE solves this by collecting the search paths from each directory. This means for instance that the search paths for the Lazarus sources have their own unit paths and not the unit paths of their project. A directory that is not part of the project does not get the unit paths of the project. This way Delphi-VCL and Lazarus-LCL sources can be searched without ambiguities arising even though they both include identically-named units. What is true for *Unit paths* (the second tab) is also true for *Include paths* (the third tab) which are search paths for files specified using the include directive (*{$I filename.inc}* or *{$INCLUDE filename.inc}*).

The paths listed in the *Source paths* tab are the result of the *Unit paths* together with the path to the compiled sources. Here is an example:

There is a project at `/home/user/project` and a package at `/home/user/package/lib`. The project binds the package. The package sources are at `/home/user/package` and the result files (`.ppu`) of the package are located at `/home/user/package/lib`.

The project's unit path includes the path to the package's output directory.

When it compiles the project the compiler finds the package's `.ppu` files but not its source files (`.pas`). Thus the compiler cannot recompile the package, which is a good thing, because the project's compiler settings probably differ from the package's settings. The IDE has to find the source files. It knows that `/home/user/package/lib` is the package's output directory and therefore adds the package's unit paths to the project's source code path. This combination is called the *Compiled Source Path.*
The button *Show CodeTools Values* opens a dialog which shows these values.
In the *Directory* section you can choose a directory whose CodeTools values you want to see.
View → Toggle form/unit view switches focus between the form in the Designer and its source code in the Editor. The [F12] shortcut key has the same function. As more units are opened in the Editor, the switch works on the active unit. If you pull down the *Window* main menu you will see all forms and units listed, so you can switch to a form in that menu list. Or you may find it faster to use the keyboard, pressing [F12] to focus the Editor, change to another unit with [Ctrl]+[Tab] and switch to that unit's form with [F12] again.

The option *View → Search results* shows all the results of your last search since Lazarus started. Each search result is shown on a separate line. Double-clicking on the line takes you to the same line in the source. If you have completed several searches the results of each search are shown on separate pages, whose tabs are titled with the search texts used.

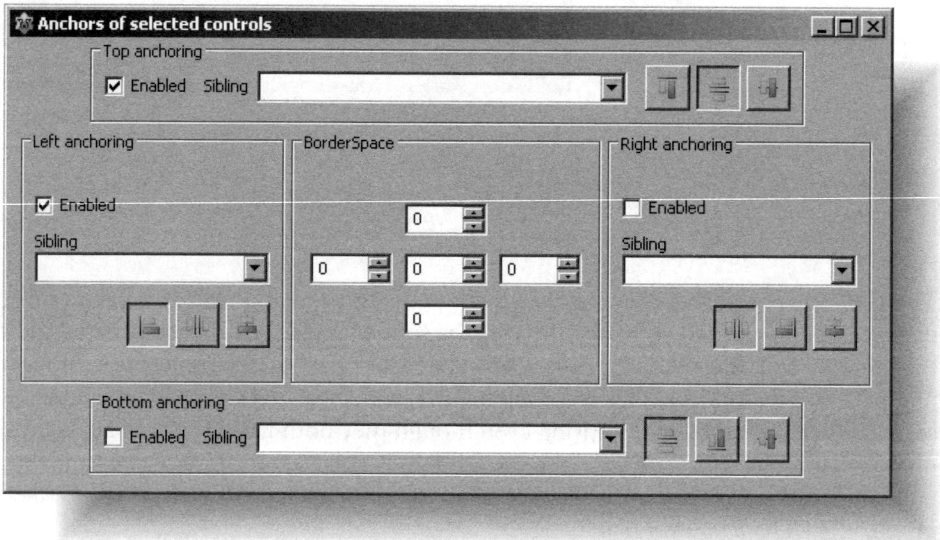

Figure 3.18: The Anchor Editor

The *Anchor Editor* menu opens a dialog where you can set parameters for anchoring visual controls to specific sides of a form (or to each other). Each of the four sides of a control (Left, Top, Right, Bottom) can be anchored to the side of another control. For example, you could anchor the left side of a *TEdit* to the right side of a *TLabel.*

Every time the anchored label is moved or resized the anchored edit's left side will follow, which normally results in the edit following in parallel with the label.
The *Enabled* checkboxes correspond to the *Anchors* property of the control(s).
The Top side uses the *akTop* enum, the Left side the *akLeft* enum and so forth.
The *Sibling* is the *AnchorSide*[xxx].*Control* property. You can leave it empty (nil), set it to the *Parent* of the control(s) or one of the siblings (controls with the same *Parent*).
The three speed buttons correspond to the *AnchorSides*[xxx].*Side* property.
The border spacing has five properties: *Around, Left, Top, Right* and *Bottom.*
The *Around* property is the centre edit field. The *Top* is the top edit field and so on.
When the desktop gets too small, the Component Palette and IDE speed buttons can be turned off (and turned on when needed) using
View → Component Palette and *View → IDE speed buttons.*

The *Debug windows* menu is described in detail at the section Tools / Debugger at the end of this chapter.

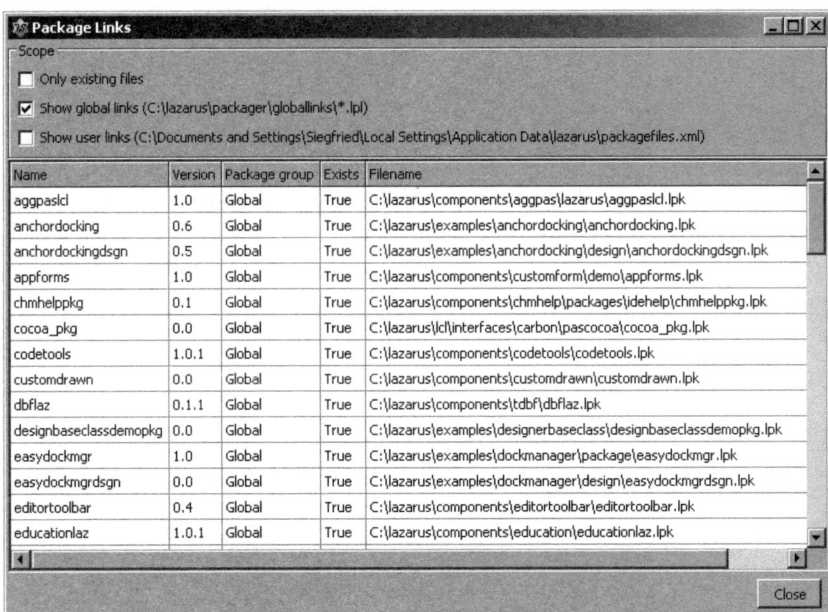

Figure 3.19: The Package Links dialog

View → IDE internals has a submenu *Package links* which opens a view showing the package links used by Lazarus. You can filter the packages shown by a combination of three options. Since version 0.9.29 two further submenus are available: *About FPC* and *About IDE.*
About IDE shows a window listing the Lazarus version and various global IDE settings and environment variables. *About FPC* shows both this and further information about many FPC settings.

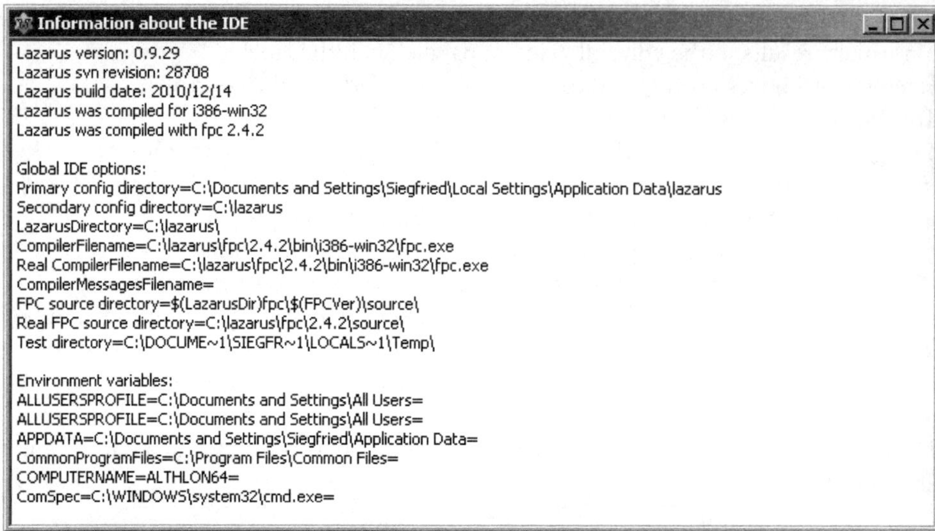

Figure 3.20: View → IDE internals → About IDE shows the information above

3.1.5 The Project Menu

What is a project? To quickly write a Pascal program any text editor will do. Naturally you can do that with the Lazarus IDE also. This will hardly stretch its capabilities. But when an application becomes more extensive, with source code divided into several files and with resource files added – then the simple text editor is not sufficient. Moreover, bigger projects usually have several programmers working cooperatively together, as for example the Lazarus project itself.

A *project* is defined as the totality of files an application needs. Clearly this includes all source code files and any project settings files. For example the following files would be part of a simple project:

- `unit1.pas` : a Pascal source file
- `unit1.ppu` : a compiled unit
- `unit1.lfm` : a file with the form's layout information generated by unit1.pas (as set in the Object Inspector)
- `unit1.lrs` : a generated resource file (not to be confused with the Windows resource file)

- project1.lpr : the main program file, which could look like this, for example:

```
program project1;
{$mode objfpc}{$H+}

uses
  {$IFDEF UNIX}{$IFDEF UseCThreads}
  cthreads,
  {$ENDIF}{ENDIF}
  Interfaces, // this includes the LCL widgetset
  Forms
  { you can add units after this }, Unit1;

begin
  Application.Initialize;
  Application.CreateForm(TForm1, Form1);
  Application.Run;
end.
```

- `project1.lpi` : the main project file (which corresponds to Delphi's `.dpr` file)

- `project1.exe` : the generated executable file

The *Project* menu lets you change project-specific settings. If a project offers functionality to be used by other projects (such as the Lazarus IDE for example) then it is called a package (see the *Package* menu).

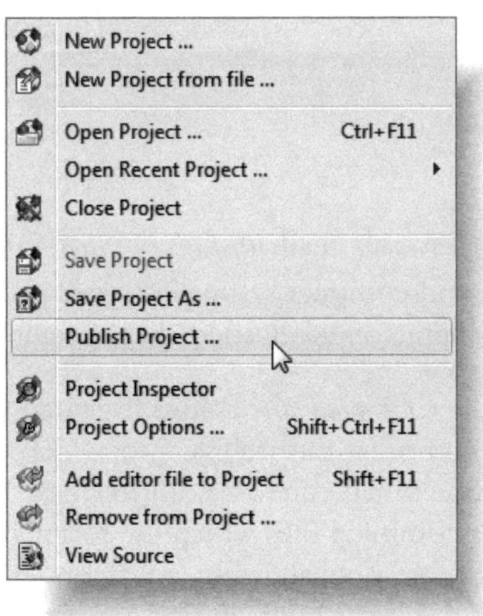

Figure 3.21: The Project menu

The first options in the *Project* menu are for opening, storing and generating new projects. The simplest way to open a project is to use *Open Project* rather than opening each file using *File → Open.*

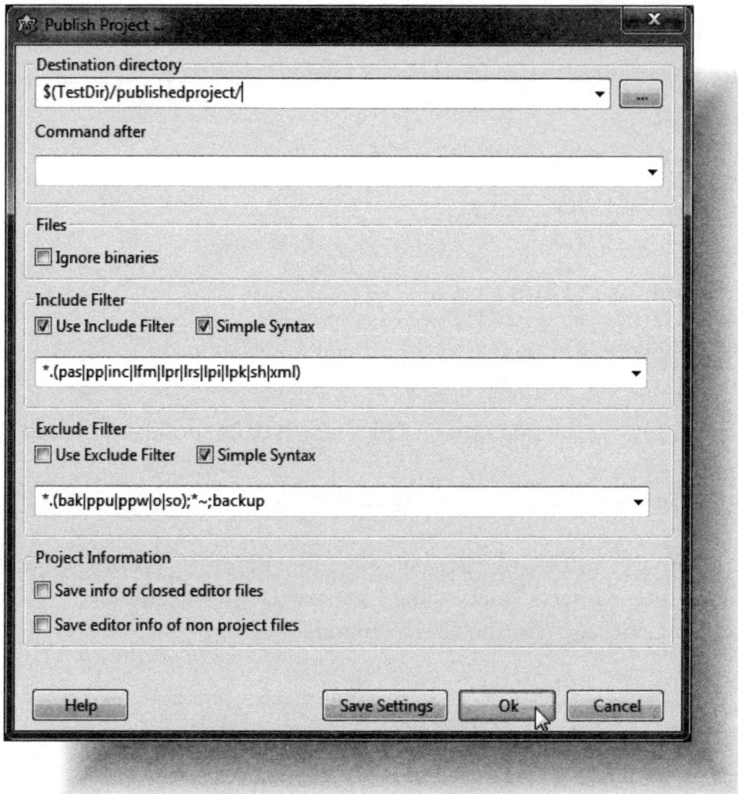

Figure 3.22: The Project → Publish Project dialog

You can generate a copy of a project with *Project → Publish Project.* This is the easiest way you can pass on the source and compiler settings of your project to other programmers. The *Destination directory* is generated and cleaned. The default value is `$(TestDir)/publishedproject/`.

The command entered in the *Command after* field is executed after Lazarus has copied the files. You could use this to compress the archive into a `.zip` file.

Check the *Ignore binaries* option when you just want to share the sources, but not the (large) executable and other compiled files which the recipient can generate for himself.

You specify exactly which files to publish using two filters. *Include Filter* specifies the files to be copied. When no *Include Filter* is used, all files are copied. For the effect of the *Simple Syntax* option see paragraph 3.1.3. The *Exclude Filter* specifies which files should not be copied (for example backup files or compressed files). When no *Exclude* filter is used all files are copied.

With *Save info of closed editor files* information about all files that you have opened in the editor is stored into the published `.lpi` file.

If *Save editor info of non project files* is checked, then information about edited files that do not belong to the project is stored in the published `.lpi` file

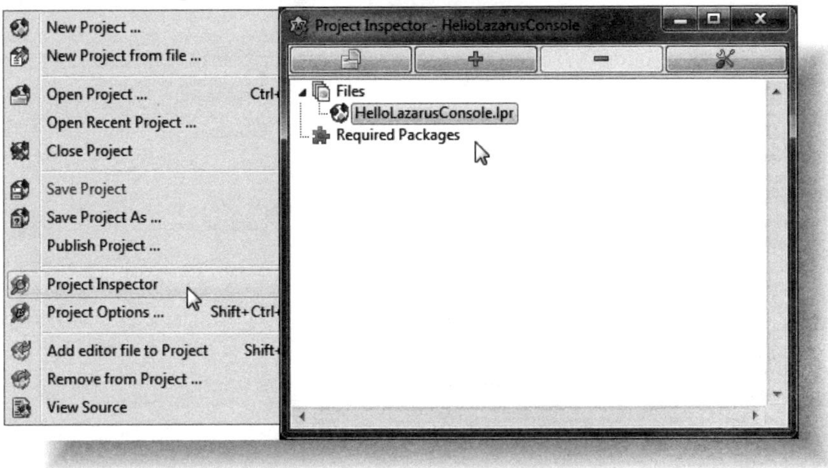

Figure 3.23: The Project Inspector

The Project Inspector is a tool that shows all of a project's files and dependencies. The first button opens the selected file or package. To add a new file or dependency click the second [+] button.

To remove a file or dependency from the project click the third [-] button. Right-clicking on a dependency shows a context menu with a range of options.

The project's settings can be reached with the rightmost button which shows the Project Options dialog (also accessible via *Project* → *Project Options...*) .
The changes you make via Project Options (in contrast to the *Environment* → *Options*... settings) concern only the current project.

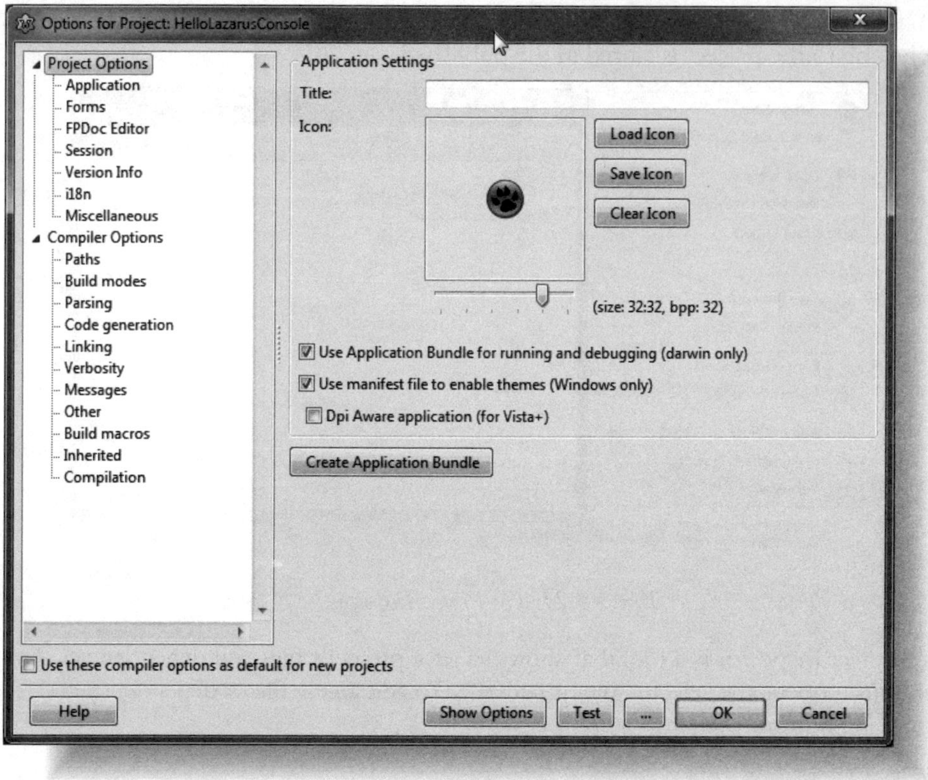

Figure 3.24: The Project Options → Application page.

The *Application* page of the *Project Options* dialog allows you to set several application parameters. The name that is entered in the *Title* field can also be set in code with `Application.Title := 'A string value';`.

Showing of the title varies with the operating system.

The project's icon can be specified – loaded (several icon formats are allowed), saved, or (if you change your mind) deleted from the project. You can also change the icon size to adapt it for several platforms.

Mac developers should check the option *Use Application Bundle for running and debugging (Darwin only)* so that the IDE starts or debugs the application bundle instead of the linked executable. (Darwin is the basis of OS X). This setting is irrelevant to users of all other operating systems. If no application bundle exists, you can create one with the *Create Application Bundle* button.

To be able to use Windows themes (XP and later) a manifest file is needed. This is generated by enabling the *Use manifest file to enable themes (Windows only)* option.

The *Target file name* field sets the name of the generated executable file. When it includes a relative path, it is extended with the project directory path (i.e. the location of the `.lpi` file). There are three buttons at the bottom of the dialog that can be accessed from all tabs. *OK* saves the changes you have made, and *Cancel* discards them. *Help* opens a Lazarus wiki page about project settings.

The *Forms* page of the *Project Options* dialog lets you change form settings. Forms can be auto-created at your application's start-up.
To enable this for a form you move it from the *Available forms* list to the *Auto-create forms* list. Reversing the procedure prevents a form from being auto-created.
You create forms in code with `Application.CreateForm(FormX, TFormX)`.

The checkbox *When creating new forms, add them to auto-created forms* saves you writing this code.
Note: automatically generated forms are not automatically shown. Form display happens only when the *Visible* property is set to *True*. This happens for instance with a call to *FormX.Show* or *FormX.ShowModal.*

The *Miscellaneous* page of the *Project Options* dialog lets you set several project options. Normally the `.lpr` file is the main unit of the project.
If this task has to be taken over by a Pascal source (`.pas`) file, you must enable the setting *Main Unit is Pascal Source.*

The *Main Unit has Uses Section containing all Units of project* setting forces the IDE to update the main unit's uses section whenever a unit is added or removed from the project.

Enabling the *Main Unit has Application.CreateForm statements* setting causes the IDE to add `Application.CreateForm(FormX, TFormX)` whenever a new form is added to the project and remove the statement when a form is removed.

The IDE neither adds, deletes or changes any *CreateForm* statements if the setting is disabled.

Enabling the *Main Unit has Application.Title statements* setting causes the IDE to add `Application.Title: = SomeTitle;` (provided *Project Options* → *Application* → *Title* has a value) when a new form is added to the project, and remove the statement if the form is removed. When *Title* is empty, the statement is removed.

When *Title* changes the line changes accordingly.
With the setting disabled the instructions are ignored (*Application.Title* statements are not deleted, added or changed).

The setting *Project is runnable* determines if the project can be called by the debugger (assuming that a debugger is available for the desired platform).

If the option *Always build (even if nothing is changed)* is disabled, the IDE checks before starting if the project has changed.
If not, compiling is skipped.

For this Lazarus checks the compiler settings, the date and filename of the executable as listed in the *projectname.compiled* file and the file contents of the files listed in the Project Inspector.
Lazarus does not check the `fpc.cfg` or the files in the project directories either (only those listed in the Project Inspector) or any included units.

That's why changes to the included units that are not listed in the Project Inspector are ignored, even when they are included by the project and opened in the source editor.

The *Save .lrs files in the output directory* setting saves the generated resource files in the output directory. From the *FPDoc Editor* page you can set the path to FPDoc help files you create for documenting your project.

Every project has a current *session*, which holds meta-information about files opened in the source editor, any bookmarks set, the jumps you made moving through files, and file execution information. Information about the latest editing session can be saved, if you wish.

The settings for this facility are found on the *Session* page of the *Project Options* dialog. The IDE saves editor information (cursor position, headers, page index, bookmarks, jump list) even for closed files and restores them when the files are opened again if you enable the *Save editor info for closed files* checkbox.

With *Save editor info only for project files* the IDE saves information for each project file (editor information, file execution information and resource name).
Normally the IDE stores this information together with the project session information either in the .lpi project file (or separately in a `.lps` file).
Disable this setting to stop saving this information.
You can arrange where the active project's session information is saved:

- *Save in .lpi file*: a disadvantage of saving in the `.lpi` is that it changes frequently which complicates version control.
- *Save in .lps file in project directory*: session information is saved in a separate `.lps` file, not in the `.lpi` file.
  This is helpful when the `.lpi` file is under version control, for example with SVN.
- *Save in the IDE config directory*: for instance if the project directory is write protected.
- *Do not save any session info*: this option will suit paranoid developers.

The *Version Info* page controls how version information is added to the executable file. This functionality may not be reliable on every non-Windows platforms.

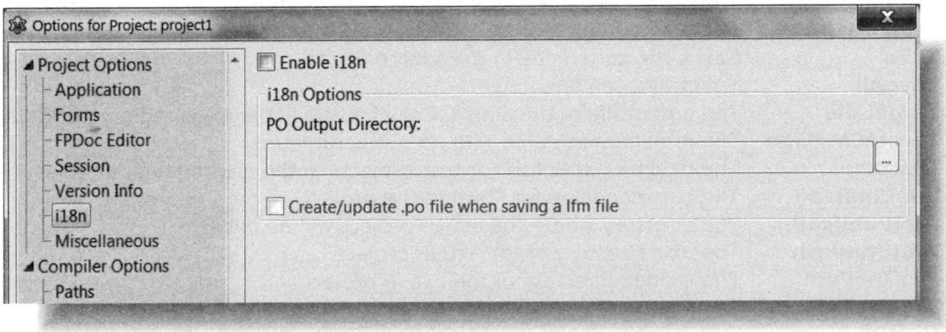

Figure 3.25: The Project Options → i18n page

To enable internationalisation for your project you have to tick the *Enable i18n* checkbox and enter a directory path in the *PO Output Directory* of the *i18n* page of the *Project Options* dialog. Any resource strings you define in your project are then converted to a `.po` file in the PO output directory.
The first .po file is generated automatically when compiling your project. You then have to translate the .po file into the other languages you need.

3.1.6 Compiler Options

The *Project Options* dialog offers eleven pages of *Compiler Options* which are details about how the project should be built, which can be set individually for each project.
The values you set in the various fields of the *Compiler Options* pages become parameters which Lazarus passes to the compiler to constrain the compilation according to your instructions. If you call the compiler from the command line, you would have to enter these parameters manually. Much more information about the compiler options available is documented in the Free Pascal programming manual, also published by this book's publisher.

Macro name	Meaning
Col	The active column in the source Editor.
Row	The active row in the source Editor.
CompPath	The compiler path set in the Environment settings.
CurToken	The character at the cursor in the source Editor.
EdFile	The name of the current file in the source Editor.
ExeExt	The executable file extension.
FPCSrcDir	The FPC source code directory set in the Environment settings.
LazarusDir	The Lazarus source directory set in the Environment settings.
LCLWidgetType	The widget-set used by the project.
TargetCPU	The CPU type the project is developed for.
Target OS	The operating system the project is developed for.
Src OS	Unix for Linux, Darwin, BSD. Win for win32, win64, winCE.
FPCVer	The FPC version (available since Lazarus 0.9.25).
LanguageID	The IDE language, for example en for English and de for German.
LanguageName	The native, translated name of the language used in the IDE, for example *Deutsch* for German.
Params	The active project's run parameters.
Prompt	Asks the user for a value (this is an interactive macro).
ProjFile	The complete file name of the main program file (.lpr) for the active project.
ProjPath	The project directory (the directory of the .lpi file).
Save	Saves the ac tive file in the source Editor.
SaveAll	Saves all open files.
TargetFile	The output file of the active project (usually the executable orpackage).
TargetCmdLine	The project executable with its run parameters.
TestDir	The directory specified for test projects in the Environment settings.
RunCmdLine	The command line for starting the project.
ProjPublishDir	The directory where the active project will be published.
ProjUnitPath	The unit directory of the active project.
ProjIncPath	The include directory of the active project.
ProjSrcPath	The source directory of the active project.
ConfDir	The directory where the IDE stores its configuration files.
MakeExec	The path to the make program (or gmake under BSD).
Project()	Macro function for several values shown below:
Project(UnitPath)	The unit path of the project instance.
Project(SrcPath)	The source path of the project instance.
Project(IncPath)	The include path of the project instance.
Project(InfoFile)	The info path of the project instance.
Ext()	Macro for ExtractFileExt.
Path()	Macro for ExtractFilePath.Name()Macro for ExtractFileName.
NameOnly()	Macro for ExtractFileNameOnly.
MakeDir()	Macro for AppendPathDelim.
MakeFile()	Macro for ChompPathDelim.
Env(name)	Macro for the environment parameters passed to the IDE (not to the project or to the debugger).
PkgDir()	Macro for the directory of a package-ID (the location of the .lpk file) passed as a parameter.
PkgSrcPath()	Macro for the source path of a package-ID passed as a parameter.
PkgUnitPath()	Macro for the unit path of a package-ID passed as a parameter.
PkgIncPath()	Macro for the include path of a package-ID passed as a parameter.
PkgOutDir()	Macro for the output directory of a package (for instance where the .ppu files are generated).

Table 3.4: Macros available for use in dialogs requiring path and file names.

The *Paths* page contains the path settings needed for the IDE to collaborate with the compiler. Relative paths are extended with the paths of the project (or package). These paths are added to the search paths.
When a package includes a project or package, those search paths are included too. The inherited search paths can be seen on the *Inherited* page. The Free Pascal Compiler has its own configuration file `fpc.cfg` defining further search paths. Multiple search paths are separated by a semicolon, and leading spaces are ignored. *Macros* are permitted in these paths. The macros available currently are listed in Table 3.4 (though future Lazarus versions may add new macros or remove existing macros).

Other Unit Files is the search path for Pascal units (`.ppu, .pp, .pas, .p`) of the project or package. This path is handed to the compiler which adds this to its Unit path. When units or packages are added to the project the Unit path is automatically updated. *Warning*: when a package has a separate output directory for its `.ppu` files, its source code directories must *not* be added to this path otherwise the compiler will generate new `.ppu` files and place them in the project directory. This leads to multiple instances of these `.ppu` files, and this can generate sometimes misleading error messages (for instance – 'Cannot find unit…') whose cause can be very difficult to track down.

Include Files is the search path for the Include files (for instance `.inc` or `.lrs` files). This path is handed to the Free Pascal Compiler which adds this to its Include path, which is used by the include directive *{$I filename.inc}* or *{$INCLUDE filename.inc}*.

Other sources is the search path for Pascal source files. It is only valid for the IDE and not for the compiler. For a project with separate directories for `.pas` and `.ppu` files, the `.ppu` directory is listed at *Other Unit Files* and the .pas directory at *Other sources*. This way the compiler can find the .ppu files and does not have to generate them each time. And the IDE can find the sources for its searching and declaration functions.

Libraries contains the search path for libraries (`.DLL, .so, .dylib`, or `.a` files).

The *Unit output directory* is the directory where the compiler stores all output files (for instance `.ppu, .o, or .rst` files).

The directories listed in *Debugger path addition (none):* are added to the search path of the IDE debugger when it searches for source code files (for instance Units or Include files).

The *Build modes* page lets you define the meaning of macros for the Default build mode, and create new build modes for targeting other platforms. When cross compiling you will need to change the default widget-set, so you can choose a different widget-set for the LCLWidgetType macro here. The widget-sets available are: gtk, gtk2, win32 (win64), wince (or Windows CE), carbon (for OS X), qt, fpGUI, noGUI, cocoa (for OS X) and android. The default widget-set of a package is the widget-set of the active project. This again depends on the operating system.

The *Parsing* page contains settings governing the compiler's analysis and interpretation of the code you send it. Using the *Syntax mode* settings it is possible to write source code so that it will be accepted by other compilers. However, compiled units cannot be mixed between compilers that have no binary compatibility. The mode chosen in these settings is used when no directive is given in the unit. Unit directives (such as *{$mode objfpc}*) override settings made in this dialog.
Despite the chosen *Syntax mode* the compiler may not be able to process an individual instruction. You should then test if this instruction can be replaced. Fuller details of the various language modes can be found in the Free Pascal manual.

FreePascal:	The original compiler language which lacks classes, interfaces and exceptions (in contrast to the Object Pascal mode).
Delphi:	Compatible up to Delphi version 7 (except for Delphi.Net).
Turbo Pascal:	Compatible to the extent of Turbo Pascal (which was limited to 16-bit code).
Object Pascal:	The default value which is close to Delphi mode but stricter. Ansi strings are not the default; the need to use the @ address operator when referencing procedure variables and event handlers; name assignment restrictions (a class cannot have a parameter or local variable with the same name as a property of that class).
Mac Pascal:	Compatible with several Macintosh-Pascal dialects.

Syntax options

In the *Syntax options* section several exceptions to the Object Pascal language rules are allowed:

C Style operators	allows some common C operators (such as **+=**) in Pascal code.
Include Assertion Code	allows Assert statements in the code.
Allow LABEL and GOTO	causes the compiler to support jump instructions with GOTO and LABEL declarations. This setting is necessary when labels are used in assembler blocks.
C++ styled INLINE	allows inline procedures.
C Style Macros	allows macros. This and the previous option support methods to replace sections of text.
Constructor name	must be 'init' (destructor must be 'done') is self-explanatory.
Static Keyword in Objects	allows declaration of static methods (which do not need the Self variable).
Strings	are shortstrings by default (compatible with Turbo Pascal) which you can change by enabling Use Ansi Strings.

Assembler style

For historical reasons the Free Pascal assembler writes AT&T assembler syntax (the *Default*). The *Assembler style* section lets you alter the way the compiler handles assembler instructions. This can be important when using existing assembler code in a Lazarus application. Choosing the *Intel* syntax forces Intel instructions to be translated internally to AT&T format before processing.

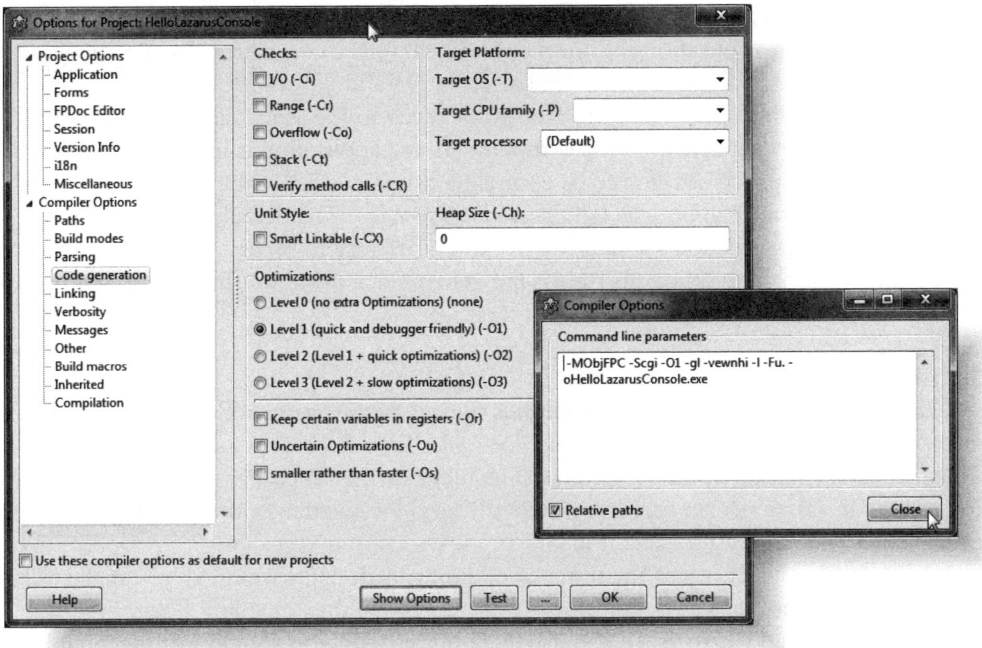

Figure 3.26: The Code generation page of the Compiler Options in the Project Options dialog.

The *Code generation* page under *Compiler Options* lets you set options for compiler checks, for the target platform and for optimizations. Enabling one of the *Checks* checkbox options causes the compiler to add appropriate instructions for that check to be performed.

Stack checks for stack overflow.
If found, the program terminates with runtime error 202.
I/O checks every input and output call. Any errors then generate a runtime error.

Overflow causes the runtime library to give the message (Overflow at xxx) when integer overflow occurs, which terminates the program with runtime error 215.

Range checks the *Self* pointer. Should it be NIL, runtime error 210 is triggered.
Verify method calls checks that the virtual method table (VMT) is valid when calling a method.

Unit Style

You have to enable *Smart Linkable* for Smart Linking to function. While this slows the compiler, it can significantly reduce the size of the linked executable.
Heap size isn't an issue for modern operating systems, but Lazarus lets you set the *Heap Size* anyway, allowing integral values greater than 1024. 0 indicates a suitable default.

Target Platform

When generating an application for another platform (cross compiling), the target operating system and CPU can be entered at *Target OS* and *Target CPU family*.
When cross compiling special attention has to be given to the availability of libraries and other tools on the computer used for compiling. If the application is to be executed on an x86-compatible processor (for cross compiling this is essential), the supported processor instructions can be selected from *Target processor*. The default (and minimum) setting is the i386 instruction set. But MMX- and more recent instructions can also be used. Using additional instructions means the generated application runs faster, but is less portable (and may not run on older computers).

Optimizations

Optimizations Level 0 means no optimization is done. *Optimizations Level 1* (the default) means peephole-optimization of the machine code. *Level 2* removes additional known sub-expressions (reload optimizing). *Level 3* includes further uncertain optimizations. *Keep certain variables in registers* replaces frequently used local variables or parameters by register calls, enabling faster execution.
Uncertain Optimizations enforces the removal of known sub-expressions. If you make calls to variables using pointers (whether directly or indirectly), then enabling *Uncertain Optimizations* will lead to errors. If you use this optimization you should test thoroughly to be sure it does not produce errors.

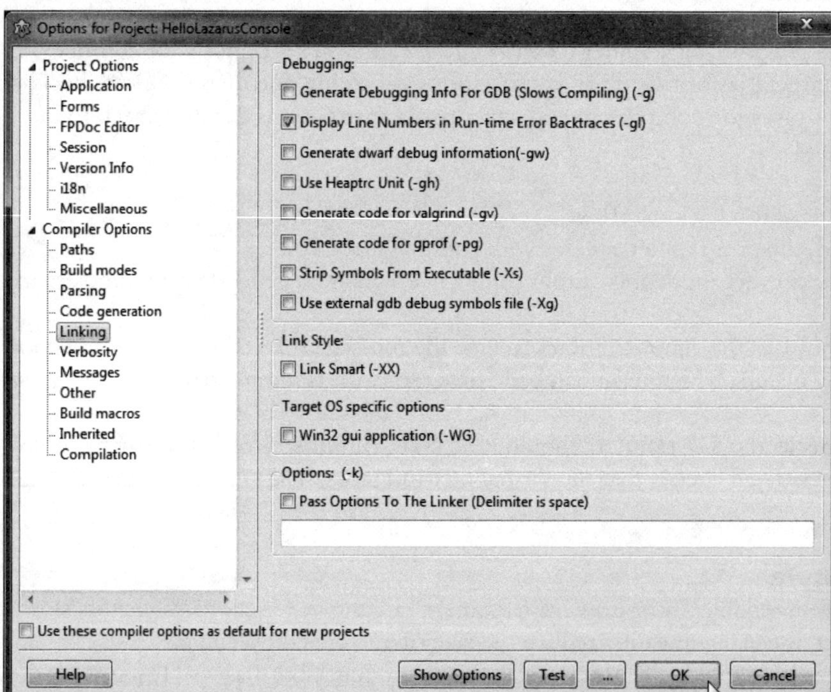

Figure 3.27: The Linking page of Compiler Options

The Linking page

The *Linking* page collects together all the settings for linking the project.
The *Debugging* section defines what kind of additional information (if any) needs to be generated for a debugger to work with Lazarus. Including debug information will result in a larger executable file.

Option	Effect
-g	Add information for the GNU debugger.
-gl	Include line number information.
-gw	Generates debug information in DWARF format (`http://dwarfstd.org`).
-gh	The *heaptrc* unit is a tool to check for memory leaks. Enabling this option includes the *heaptrc* unit which generates a report when the compiled program ends.
-gv	*valgrind* is a (Linux/Darwin) tool for error trapping and performance analysis. (`www.valgrind.org`) The code needed for this program is generated with the switch -gv.
-pg	After starting the compiled program an output file is generated, which can be examined with the GNU-profiler.
-Xs	All debug information is removed.
-Xg	The debug information is exported to a separate file.

Table 3.5: Options for generating debug information

Link Style

The *Link Style* section offers a single option *Link Smart (-XX)*. Enabling this causes linking only of those parts of the source code that are actually used.
The executable file can be significantly smaller, however compiling takes longer, and the program is usually harder to debug.

Target OS specific options

There is presently only one setting available as *Target OS Specific Options* and it relates only to Windows. Enabling this makes the application GUI only. Disabling this provides an additional empty console window (DOS box). This can be an optical annoyance, or a useful window to view debug and error console output during development.

Options

It is not possible to list all the compiler switches with their own checkbox. *Options* offers access to important compiler switches which have no specific settings page.
To pass, say, a -k parameter for the compiler to bind a particular library, you can list it at the option *Pass Options To The Linker*. Multiple switches should be separated by spaces.

The Verbosity page

Verbosity controls which messages are seen in the *Messages* window during compilation. Too many messages add to the complexity of interpreting output, and too few may hinder a search for errors. Prudent enabling/disabling of the options on this page allows you to find a happy medium. The switch -va (Show everything) is implemented for emergencies, when an inexplicable error shows up, whereas normally this would overwhelm you with countless messages.

Stop after number of errors (-Se) means the number of errors before compiling stops. The default is a single error which is usually the best option, since in the end that error has to be solved before the application can be successfully compiled.

The *Messages* page lets you set the display (or hiding) of every possible compiler message you might encounter. All possible message types are listed and by default all are active. Messages that are not necessary can be switched off (such as *(H) Parameter "$1" not used*). The character in parentheses shows the type of message:
(H) for Hint; (N) for Note; (W) for Warning.

The *Other* page allows you to pass more parameters to compiler, that you cannot set in any of the other pages. You can also specify a compiler configuration file. Most Lazarus users rely on the default compiler configuration file, *fpc.cfg*. If you want to work with a different configuration file for testing purposes, *Use additional Compiler Config File* lets you specify a secondary configuration file.

The *Custom options* field lets you set any compiler options. It is provided for switches that cannot be set on another page. Note that the IDE does not take account of any custom option that changes Search paths. The Free Pascal manual lists all the many possible compiler switches.

The *Inherited* page shows all compiler settings that are inherited from packages. (Packages provide all the components). You can investigate here when a project is not functioning as expected. Where are certain search paths or settings coming from? Does a package inherit particular settings? Why is unit X from package Y not being found? In the worst case you can at least rule out the package as a cause. Clicking on an entry shows the corresponding details in the field below.

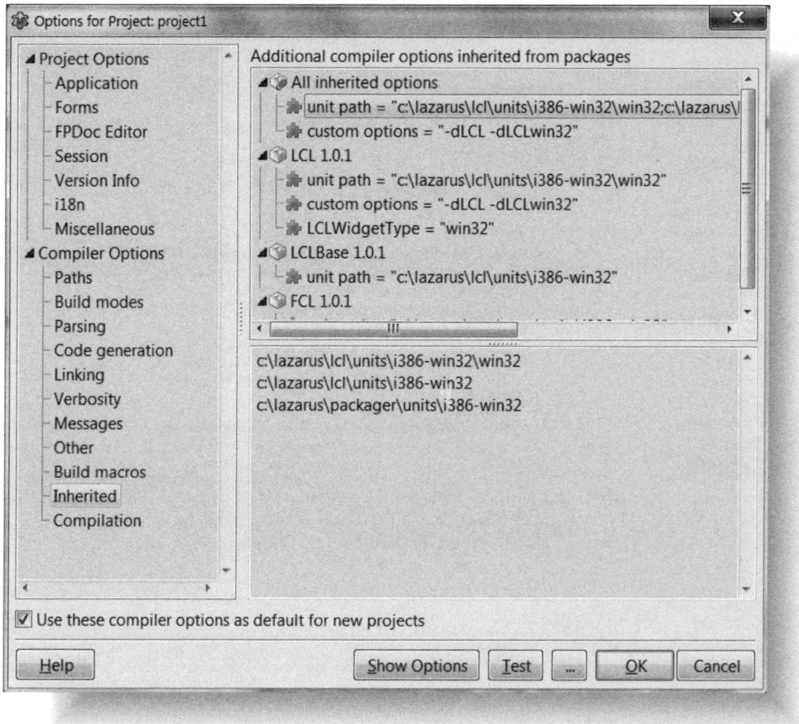

Figure 3.28: The Inherited page of Compiler Options

The *Compilation* page lets you specify if and when additional commands are executed while compiling the project. If you have a Make file for your project, the project can be compiled from the command-line later. Enabling the *Create Makefile* option causes the IDE to create a Make file and a `Makefile.fpc`.
The section *Execute before* stores commands are that are executed before the call to the compiler.

The *Call on:* section has the following options:

- **Compile** Execute with a normal compilation [F9].
- **Build** Execute only when everything is generated anew.
- **Run** Execute with a fast compilation.

When a project is started, the IDE checks whether a new compilation is necessary.
If this is not the case, the IDE skips the compiling step. With this setting enabled, the command is always executed, even when compiling is skipped.

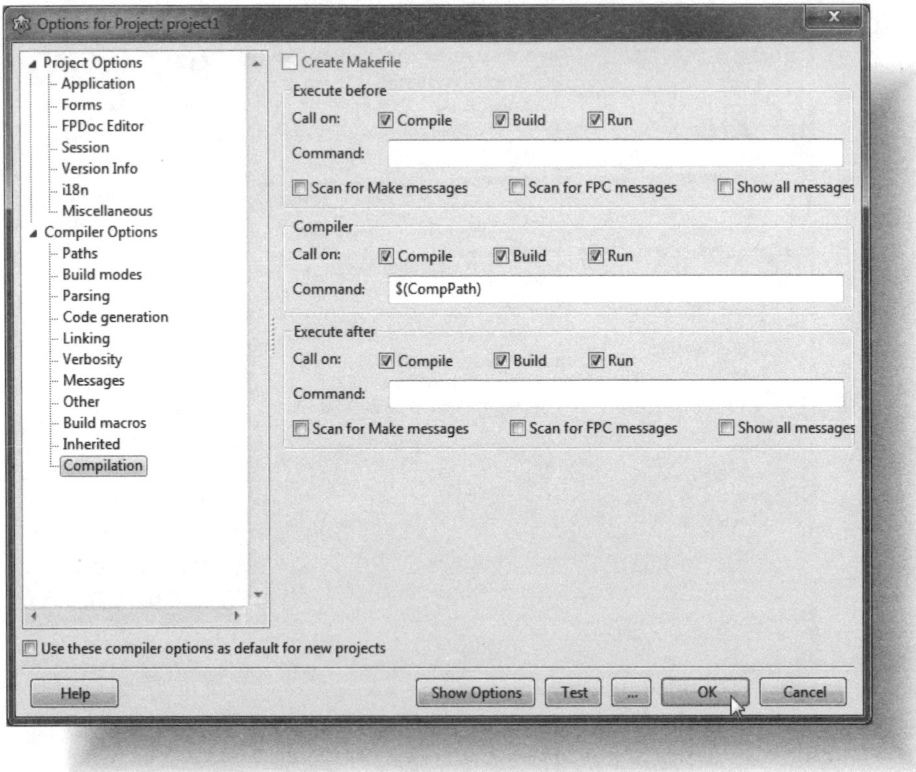

Figure 3.29: The Compilation page of the Compiler Options.

The IDE can analyze and filter the output of the command and stop if an error occurs. You can set which messages to watch for.
The path to the compiler can be set in the *Compiler* section. The default is the macro `$(CompPath)`, which is replaced by the compiler file name found in the *Environment* settings.
The *Execute after* section mirrors the settings in the *Execute before* section.

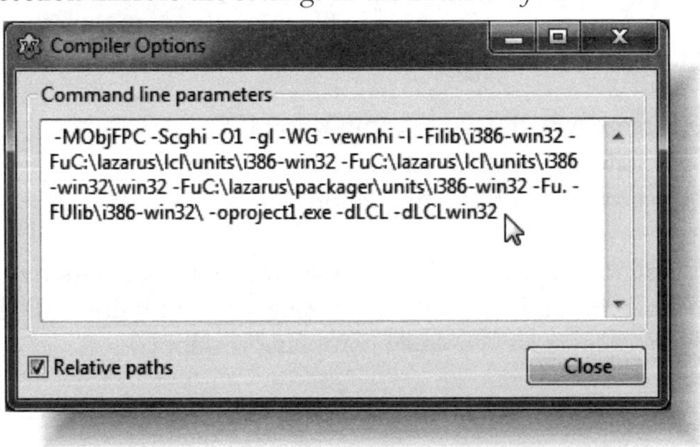

Figure 3.30: An overview of the current compiler settings.

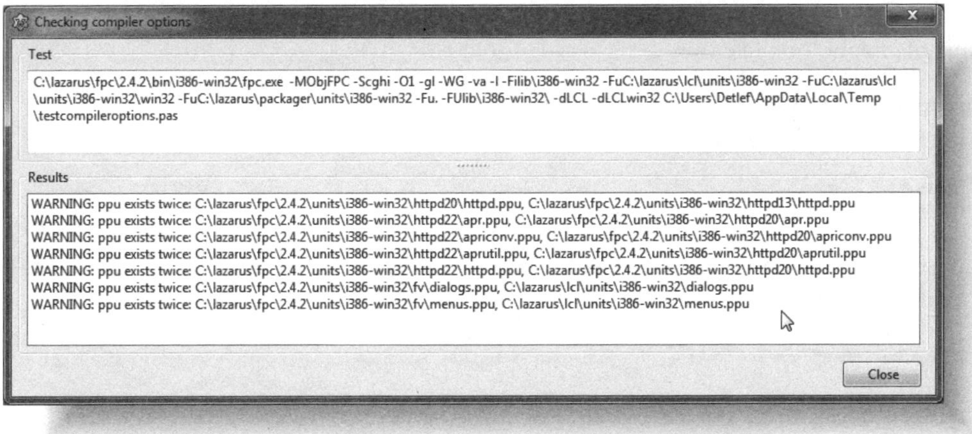

Figure 3.31: A window showing the test results of the compiler settings

At the lower edge of the *Project Options* dialog are several buttons which can be accessed from all pages of the *Compiler Options* dialog.
The *Help* button brings up a page from the Lazarus wiki with information about compiler settings.

Show options opens a dialog with the current command line parameters, and *Test* executes several tests to find common configuration errors. If you get a *Unit not found* error, there is a good chance you may find the cause here.

The (called ellipsis)[…] button opens a dialog which saves (or restores) the current compiler settings to or from an XML file. The [OK] button applies all changes and closes the dialog. [Cancel] reverses all changes and closes the dialog.

Project → Add editor file to Project adds the current editor file to the current project, if it is not already a project file. When a file needs to be removed from the project, use the option *Project → Remove from Project.* A list with all project files is shown, from which you can select the file to remove.

View Source opens the main program file (`*.lpr`) of the project in the Editor.
This file might look like this:

```
program Project1;
{$mode objfpc}{$H+}

  uses
  {$IFDEF UNIX}{$IFDEF UseCThreads}
  cthreads,
  {$ENDIF}{$ENDIF}
  Interfaces, // this includes the LCL widgetset
  Forms, Unit1
  { you can add units after this };

  {$R *.res}

begin
  RequireDerivedFormResource := True;
  Application.Initialize;
  Application.CreateForm(TForm1, Form1);
  Application.Run;
end.
```

Usually you don't need to change any code in the `.lpr` file.

3.1.7 The Run menu

The important options affecting generating and debugging a program are all located on the *Run* menu.

Build initiates a fresh compilation of every file in the current project that has changed since the last build. *Build all* does the same as *Build*, but in addition recompiles any unchanged files. *Quick compile* compiles only the current unit, without generating any assembler results or making any call to the linker. If you start a build by mistake (or something seems to have gone wrong with the build) you can choose *Abort Build* to stop the compiler process running further.

Clicking the *Run* menu option (or pressing [F9]) is the usual way to compile an application and have Lazarus run the resulting executable. Naturally, an unsuccessful build does not produce a runnable program.
The linker is called automatically following the compilation and after that the linked application is called. If your application does not work with one of the IDE components without problems (sometime this happens with the debugger) then it is best to first close Lazarus and run the application independently.

Pause interrupts the execution of the running application, perhaps to let you check the generated output. To resume the execution press [F9] again. *Stop* halts the execution, returning you to the Lazarus IDE.

Run parameters

You arrange for any starting command-line parameters to be passed to the application using the *Run parameters* menu. The dialog has two pages: *Local* and *Environment.*

The *Local* page
When the project executable and the executable to be debugged are not the same, you specify the other executable in the *Host application* field.
You enter any starting command-line parameters, in the *Command line parameters (without application name)* field.

If the project is to be started with the help of a script in a terminal, or with a special debugger or profiler you must enable the checkbox *Use launching application.* Enter the path to the launching program in the field below.

The multiple Linux desktops available under X (Gnome, KDE, xfce) are accessible through *Use Display.* For instance setting the display command-line variable to : 1 (rather than the default: 0) shows the application on the second desktop.

The value for showing on another computer can be 192.168.1.17:0 or hydra: 0,1.
This setting is ignored under Windows.
The working directory of a tested (debugged) project is normally the project directory. This means that all relative file names are extended with the path of the working directory. You can change this directory by setting *Working directory* to another location.

The *Environment* page
Normally the tested program starts with the same environment variables as the IDE itself. The *System variables* field shows you what the current settings are.
User Overrides lets you set specific environment variables to different values just for the tested program's running environment.

These are not to be mistaken for command-line parameters of configuration variables. Your program can call those variables with functions such as *GetEnvironmentVariable*, *GetEnvironmentVariableCount* or *Application.GetEnvironmentList.*

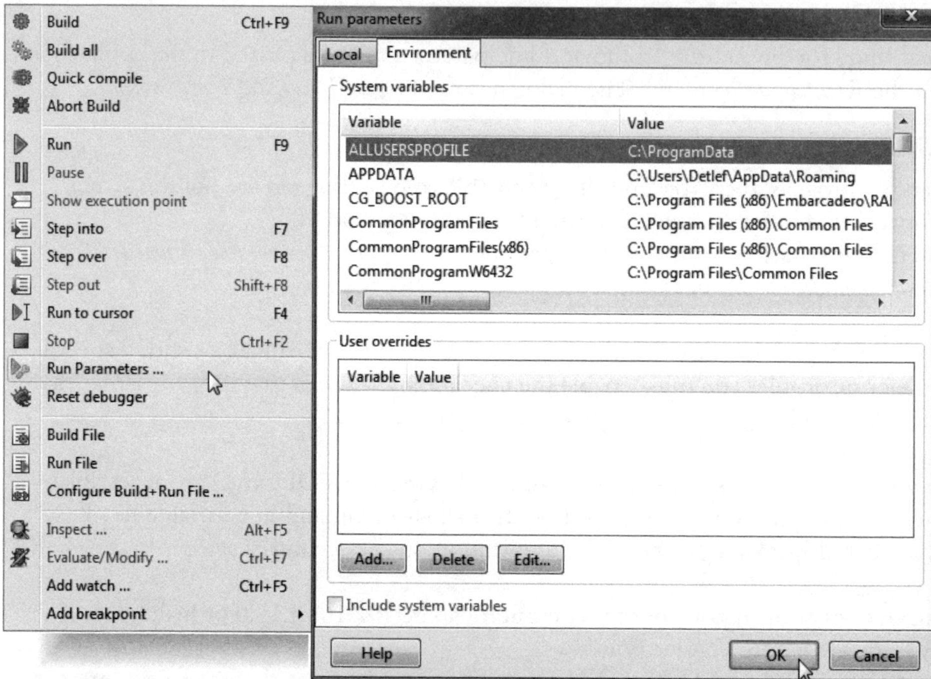

Figure 3.32: The Environment page of the Run → Run parameters dialog

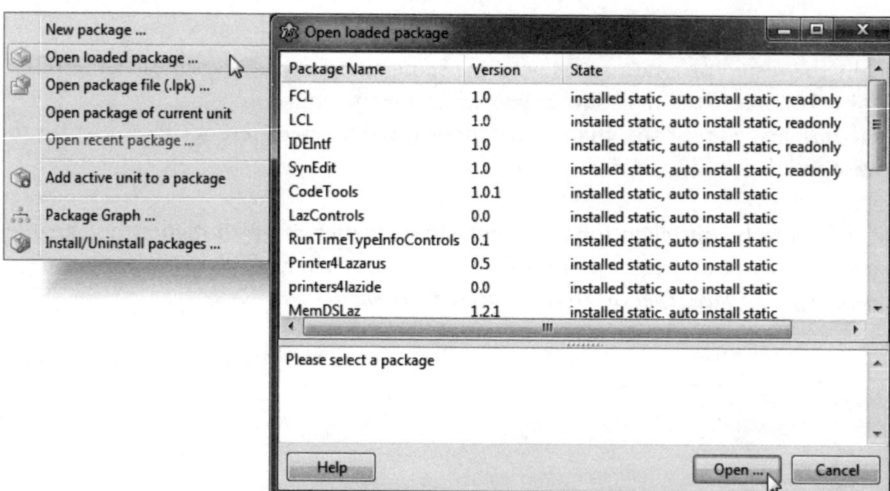

Figure 3.33: The dialog behind the menu Package → Open loaded package

3.1.8 Packages

New components are installed in the IDE using a *package*.
The most important commands for using packages are all on the *Package* menu.
Open loaded package lists all loaded (installed) packages in a dialog from which you can select one. Double-clicking the selection (or clicking on *Open*) opens the selected package in the Package Editor entitled *Package <packagename>*. Package files are stored in XML format (which makes it possible to easily work with the file outside the Lazarus IDE). They contain all the information about the package and how the Lazarus configuration files are kept.

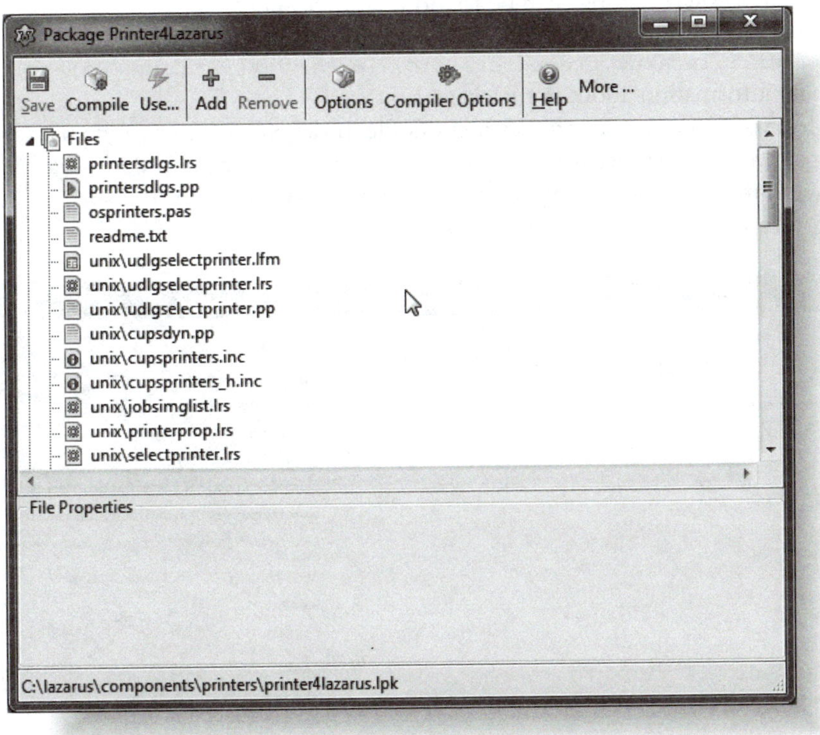

Figure 3.34: The printer4lazarus package opened in the Package Editor which is accessed via Package→ Open loaded package…

The Package Editor

The Package Editor has extensive functionality, and toolbuttons that change to offer appropriate functions. The Package Editor is the tool to use to make any changes to a package. Changes are saved using the *Save* button. If a new package has to be installed, click on *Install* and Lazarus arranges the necessary steps (including compilation).
To install a package into the IDE, it is compiled together with its dependencies, and it is added to the list of packages waiting to be installed (there may be entries selected earlier). A dialog shows you what packages will be added and removed from the IDE, and if you confirm the changes the IDE is recompiled (this may take a long time).

If the new package is not a package to be installed in the IDE, click on *Compile*, which makes the package and it dependencies available to the application at run time. Some packages depend on external libraries. Database packages, for instance, need the database client libraries. You can, however, compile database applications without the libraries, but may then find that Lazarus won't restart because of the missing libraries. It is worth paying attention to what dependencies there are therefore, before you start compilation.
To add a new element (a unit, a file, a dependency, a component), click on *Add*. The *Add to package* dialog which appears offers comprehensive options.
The general packages settings can be found with *Options* button.
The *Help* button brings up a Lazarus wiki page:
`(http://wiki.lazarus.freepascal.org/IDE_Window:_Package_Editor)`
containing information about the Package Editor.
Remove lets you remove a selected element (a file or dependency) from the package after confirmation. There is access to the package's compiler settings via the *Compiler Options* button, and many further functions are accessible via the *More* button (such as showing missing files, or bringing up the ToDo list).

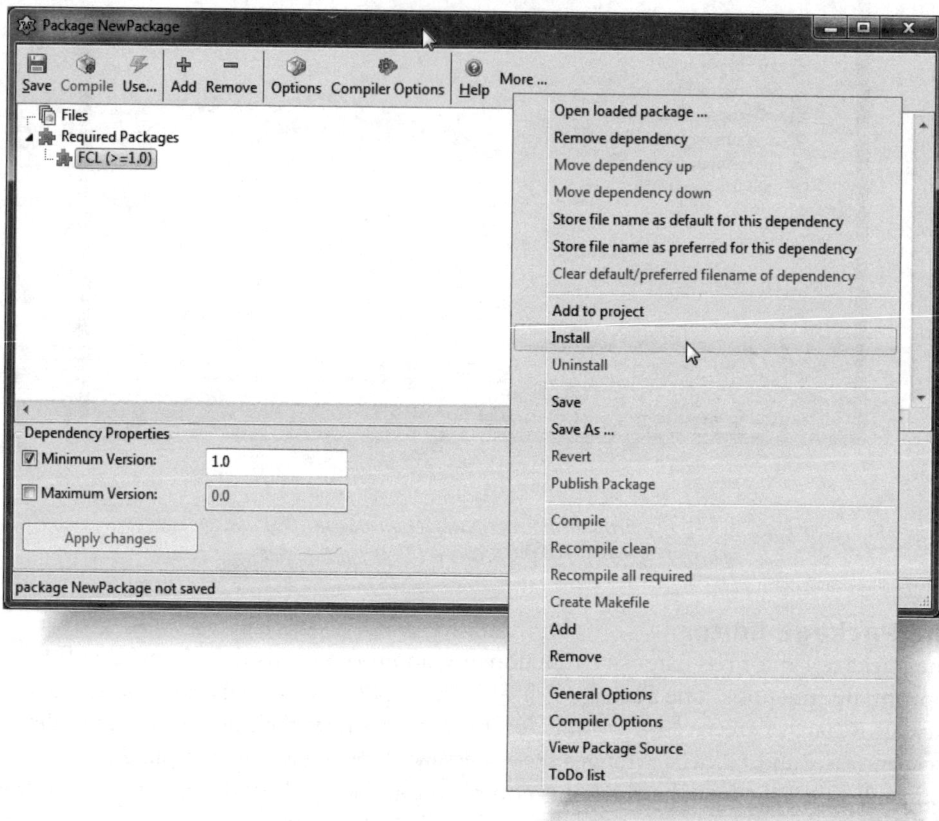

Figure 3.35: The Package Editor's context menu

The Package Editor's context menu offers an alternative way to access most of the functionality available from the various toolbuttons. You can sort, relocate, rename and change the file type of a package's component files. You can *Install* a package and then confirm that you want to recompile to see it incorporated into the IDE.

Uninstall removes the package and all dependencies from the list of the packages to be installed in the IDE. After a confirmation dialog the IDE is rebuilt.
To uninstall a static package, the IDE needs to be rebuilt and restarted.
At the moment all IDE packages are static.

Save stores the changes into the .lpk file. *Save as* opens a dialog to choose a new filename for the `.lpk` file. Although the package has been renamed, the files in it are not relocated or renamed. If you save the `.lpk` file in a new directory you need to check the paths in the compiler settings.

Revert drops all proposed changes and reloads the `.lpk` file from disk.

Publish Package opens the *Publish Package* dialog to copy the package and its files to a different directory. This is useful to generate a package without compiled and version files and to pack them into a ZIP file.

Compile compiles the package and any needed dependencies.
Normally the compiler checks every unit and avoids recompiling if it is not necessary.
The *Recompile clean* menu, however, forces every unit of the package to be compiled.
If a needed package has to be compiled also, this is done first. 'Clean' in this context means that all compiled files (mainly the `.ppu` files) are deleted first.
This option can be helpful with rebuilding Lazarus, when there are problems with one of the files in the package, because *Clean all* in the *Tools → Configure "Build Lazarus"* dialog does not always affect the installed packages.
If this happens, you are advised to rebuild the package using *Recompile clean* first.

Rebuild all required does the same as *Recompile clean* but also for each required package. However some of the basic packages like the FCL and LCL are set not to be compiled automatically and therefore are not rebuilt by this call.

Create makefile generates a make file for this package `Makefile.fpc` which you can use to compile the package outside the IDE. The make file script is deliberately quite simple assuming that all packages (including Lazarus packages) can be found on the specified paths. Therefore if you copy the make file to another computer, it will probably have to be adapted before it will work.

Add opens the *Add to package* dialog (see below) to add a new element (unit, file or dependency…) to the package. *Remove* removes the selected element from the package after a confirmation. *General options* opens the *Package Options* dialog to edit operational settings, version information and other general package settings.

Compiler options opens the *Compiler options* dialog for the selected package.
View Package Source opens the main source file of the package.
The IDE regenerates this file automatically with each recompilation and so it should not be edited manually otherwise all changes may be lost.
View ToDo list shows the ToDo list (see *Project → ToDo list*).

The Add to package *dialog*
The Package Editor's *Add* button opens a new four-page dialog for adding new elements to the package (the dialog's appearance is still being changed by the Lazarus team).

The *New File* page:
Here you can choose a file type and with a click on the *Create new file* button a new file of that type is generated and added to the package.

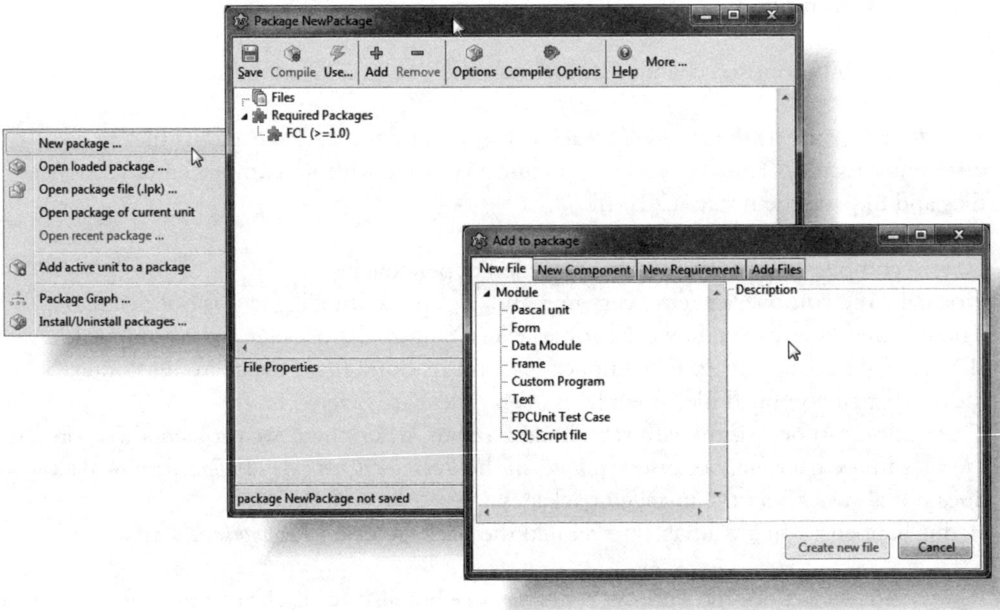

Figure 3.36: The New File page of the Add to Package dialog

The New Component page:
This page creates a new unit for a component with fields where you enter appropriate details for the new component. *Ancestor Type* specifies which class the new component descends from. For instance you would derive a new button component from *TButton.* Naturally the new class name has to differ from the ancestor class. The new button could be named *TImprovedButton,* for example.
The *Palette Page* combobox lets you choose where the new component is to be located on the Component Palette when the package is installed into the IDE. You can choose an existing tab (for example *Additional*) or a type a new name to create a new tab. The unit also needs a file name, which is entered in the *Unit File Name* field (for example `mycomponentunit.pas`).

The *Unit Name* (for example *MyComponentUnit*) is the name other packages and units will use to call this unit later on.
The icon linked to the component (if any) will be shown on the Component Palette to identify this component in place of the default Lazarus component icon.

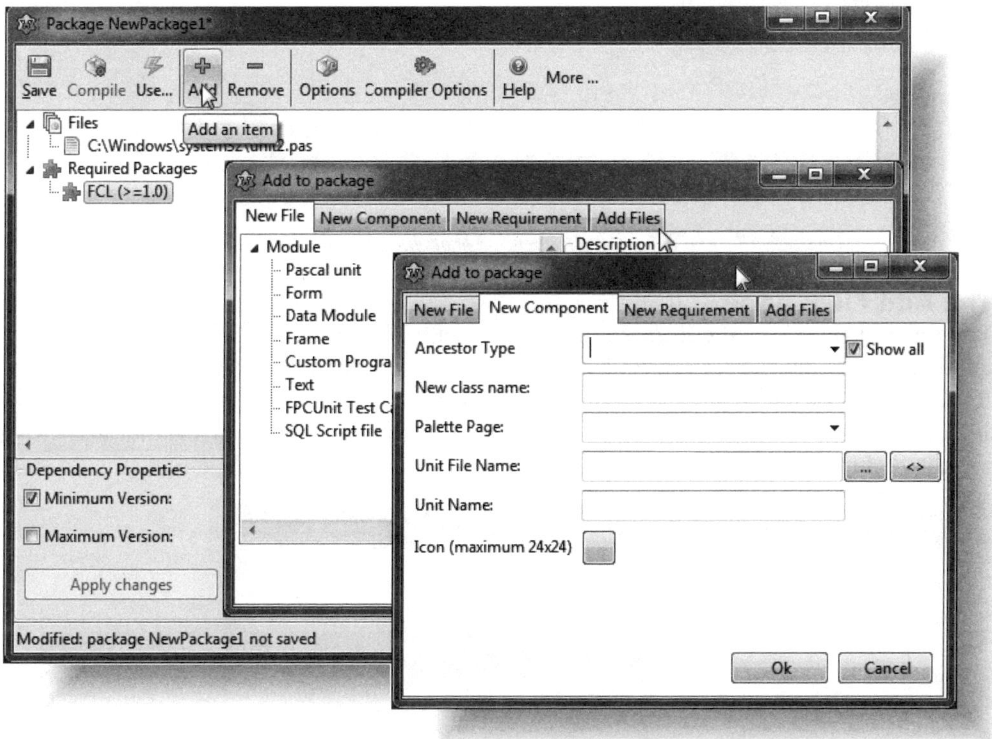

Figure 3.37: The New component page of the Add to package dialog

The New Requirement page

You can add a new dependency to a package with the *New Requirement* page. *Package name* can be any package known to the IDE.
If the package you want is not in the combobox list, just open the package once to inform the IDE of its existence, and then return to this dialog.
All packages are versioned. With *Minimum Version* and *Maximum Version* you can provide an optional range for the required package's version number.
For instance, if your package depends on functionality recently introduced into the FCL, you would set the minimum version to the first FCL version that introduced that functionality.

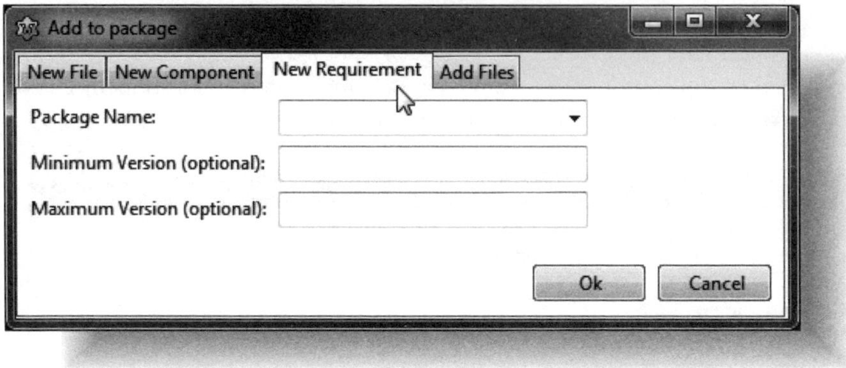

Figure3.38: The New Requirement page of the Add to Package dialog

The Add Files page

You can add any file in the file system to the package from the *Add files* page. Any number of existing files can be added to the package and their file types are guessed. The *Browse* button opens a dialog to locate a single file whereas *Add directory* is designed for adding the contents of a directory to the package. If the directory contains multiple files to be added to the package, this is faster than selecting and adding single files.

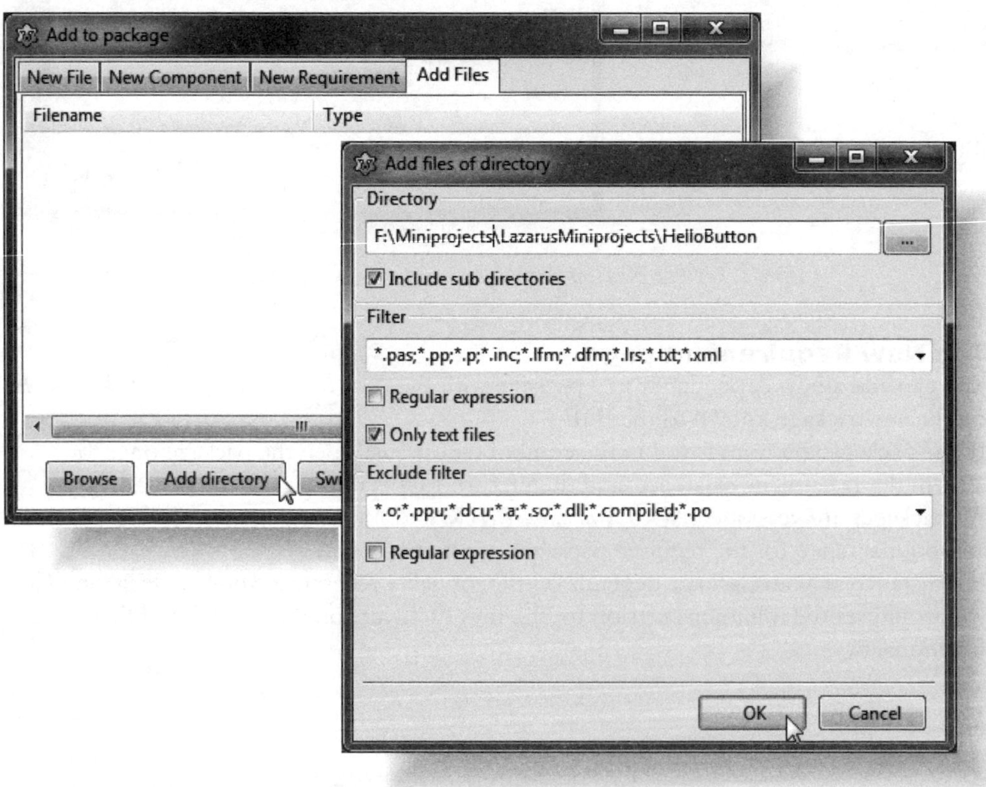

Figure 3.39: The Add files of directory dialog

Clicking the *Add directory* button opens the *Add files of directory* dialog where you can browse for a directory with the [...] elipsis button (or enter the complete path by hand), if you are looking for files which are not in the project directory (where the dialog first opens). If you want to add files in subdirectories to the package, then enable the *Include sub directories* checkbox.
If only selected files of the directory should be added, then enable a relevant *filter*. If the filter field is left empty, all files (including hidden files) are included.

Normally the filter uses a simple syntax, but you can enable full *Regular expressions* with the checkbox so labelled. If you enable addition of *Only text files* then binary files like pictures will be left out.
You can also implement filtering by excluding categories of files. The *Exclude filter* determines which files will not be added to the package. If the field stays empty, no files are excluded. You can force use of a *Regular expression* here too.

If after clicking OK you see files listed that should not be there, you can select them and use the *Delete* button to remove them from the list.
The *Switch Paths* button toggles between showing absolute or relative file paths. Once your file list is complete, you add the listed files to the package with the *Add files to package* button.

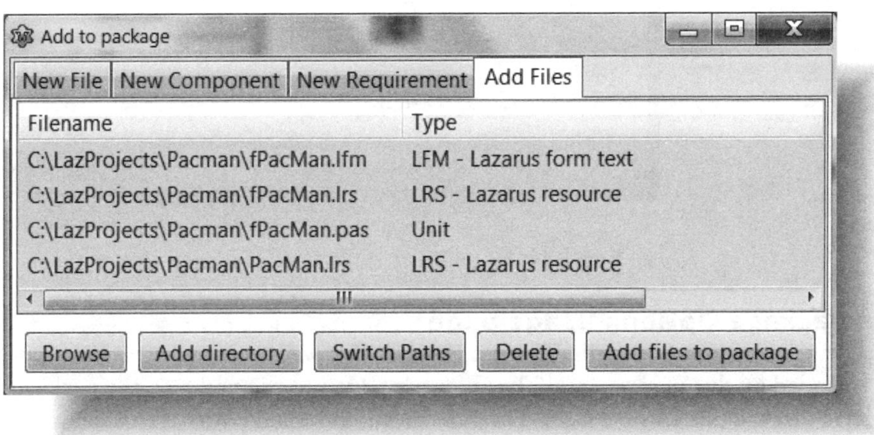

Figure 3.40: The Add Files page of the Add to Package dialog after a directory has been opened

The Package Options dialog

The Package Editor's *Options* toolbutton opens a five-page *Package Options* dialog.

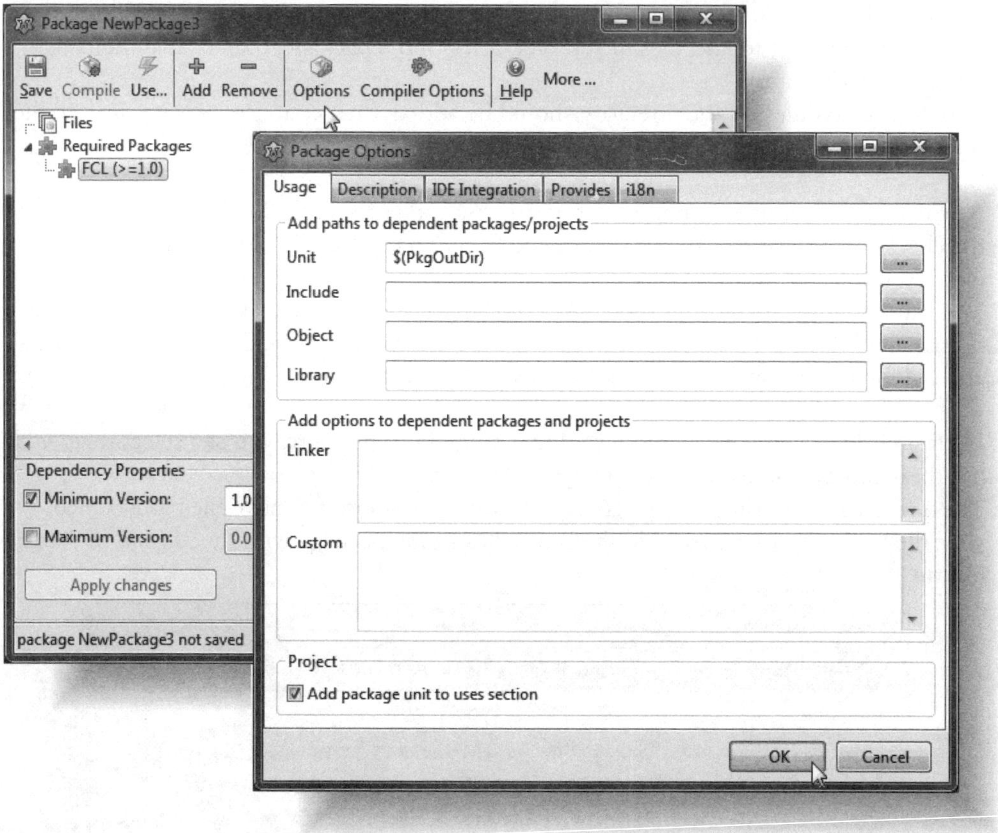

Figure 3.41: The Usage page of the Package Options dialog

The Package Options Usage page

Usage lets you set various paths. The paths set in *Add paths to dependent packages/projects* are not included by this package itself, but they are added to the paths of the packages and projects that include this package. They are called 'inherited paths'. For example suppose Package A needs Package B which uses Package C. All usage settings of C are added to the settings of B and A. The unit paths can contain macros, are separated by a semicolon and are added to the unit paths of all packages and projects that include this package. What is true for Unit paths is also true for Include paths with the only difference that they must be valid paths for any include files. Likewise for Object paths which must be valid for the object files. And likewise for Library paths with the only difference that they must be valid for libraries. New settings for dependent packages and projects can be referenced for the linker (in the *Linker* field) as well as made user-defined (in the *Custom* field). Both *Linker* and *Custom* options can contain macros, are separated by spaces (not semicolons) and are added to the linker settings of all packages and projects that include this package. Carriage returns are converted to spaces, and multiple spaces are treated as one except when placed between quotes.

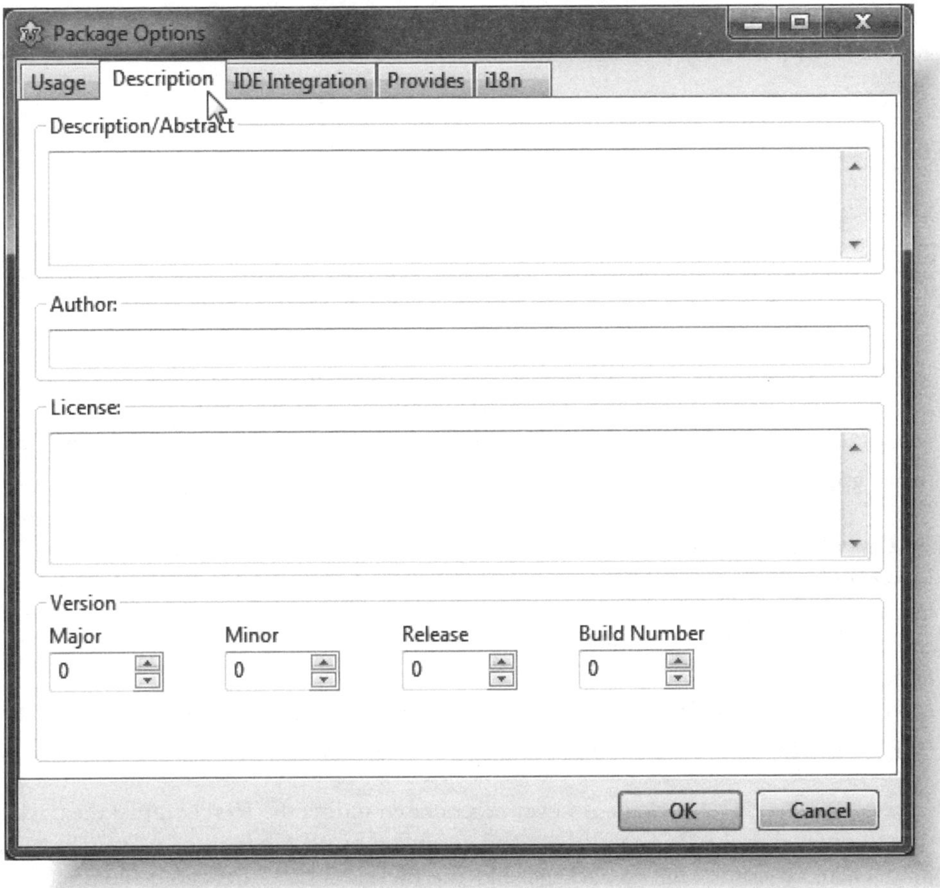

Figure 3.42: The Description page of the Package Options dialog

The Package Options Description page

The package can be documented in detail on the *Description* page.

The *Description/Abstract* field is intended to hold a brief summary of what the package does, if possible in a language understood by many users.

The developer's name (usually this would be your own name) is entered in the *Author* field.

If the package is designed be published, distributed or sold, the licence terms can be listed in the *License* field.

The various *Version* parts can mean whatever you like, but the following pattern is typical:

Major : Is incremented when the package has major changes such as extension to a previously unsupported platform.

Minor : Is incremented when the package has minor changes such as new features or changes to a method's parameter list.

Release : Is incremented when the package is released.

Build-number : Incremented every time the package is recompiled.

The Package Options IDE Integration page

The *IDE Integration* page contains information about the kind of package and how it is updated.

The P*ackageType* shows how the package is used in the IDE:

Designtime only: The package is a plug-in for the IDE and never included by normal applications. It is only relevant at design time. A design time package needs the package *IDEinf*, which contains the IDE interface functions. The IDE gives a warning when a design time package is included in a project.

Runtime only: The package has no IDE functionality and therefore should not be installed in the IDE. For example such a package might offer special file management.
Designtime and Runtime: The package offers functionality both for the IDE as well as for normal applications.

The *Update/Rebuild* section governs the frequency of package updates:
Automatically rebuild as needed: Every time a project or package that includes this package is regenerated (directly or indirectly), the IDE will check if any package file has altered. If so, the package will be recompiled.

Auto rebuild when rebuilding all: This covers the same situation as the previous option, except in this case the trigger is the user choosing to recompile.

Manual compilation: The package is never regenerated indirectly. To recompile the package it has to opened in the Package Editor and compiled by clicking on the *Compile* button.
Note: There are some built-in packages like the FCL and LCL that can be compiled only in a special way (for instance with *Make* or *Lazbuild*). Recent versions of Lazarus may be able to treat the LCL like any other package.
You can set the paths for any FPDoc help files (documenting the package) using the *FPDoc files path* field.

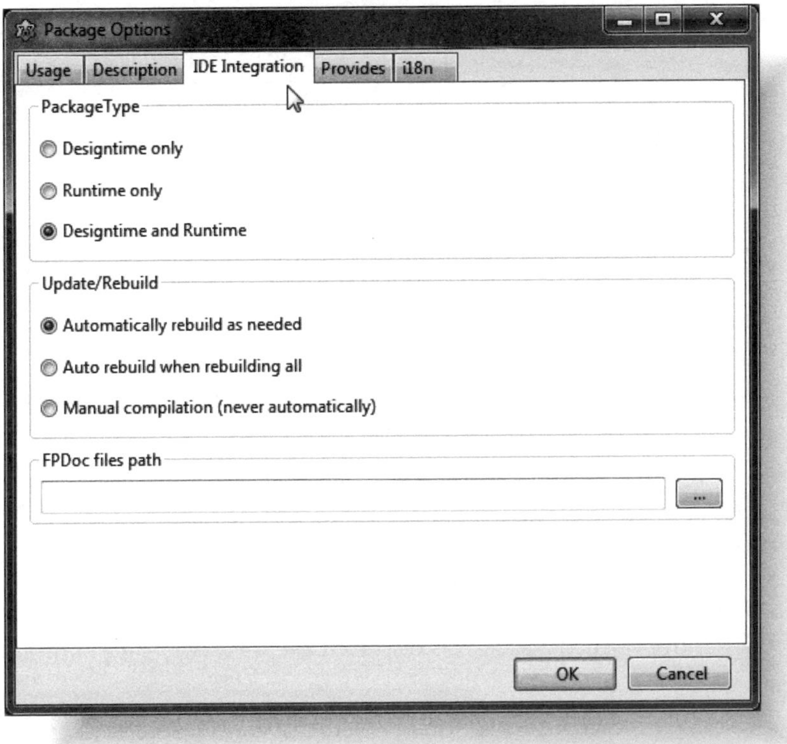

Figure 3.43: The IDE integration page of the Package Options dialog

The Package Options Provides page

The *Provides* page lets you test whether a package provides the same functionality as another package known to the IDE (for instance the various dialog components). This is useful if you have to work with an alternative to the LCL and need an overview of what the package and the LCL have in common.

The Package Options i18n page

The *i18n* page lets you activate several languages for the package (*i18n* is an abbreviation for 'internationalization'). Here Lazarus makes use of the GNU *gettext* library.
All strings displayed in the package GUI are declared as resource strings, and when compiled generate a .po file (a special-format text file).
This is translated into other languages using a tool such as *poedit.*
You can find help for generating the resource strings via *Tools → Make Resource String…*
You then have to enable the *Enable i18n* checkbox and set the path where Lazarus will save the .po file. (You have to create this directory yourself, Lazarus does not create it for you). A proven technique is to store the `.po` file in a subdirectory of the package directory named 'languages', but any directory can be used.
Compiling the package will then generate the first .po file. The developer has to make translations of the original `.po` file into as many languages as he wants to support. Each language requires a separate `.po` file.

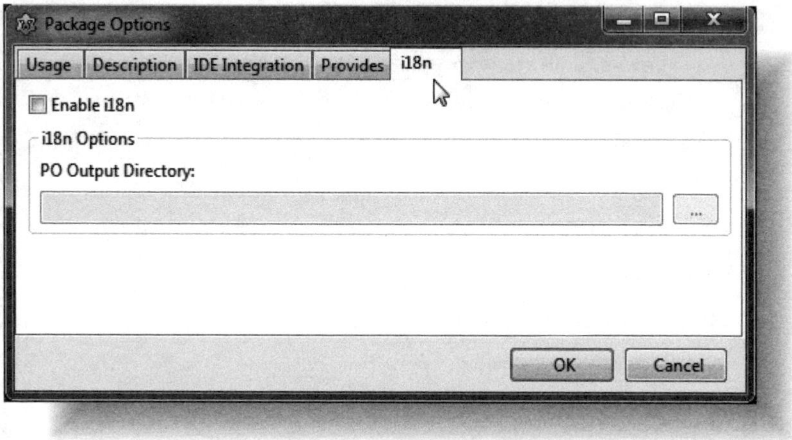

Figure 3.44: The i18n page in the Package Options dialog

Package → Open package of current unit
If the current directory belongs to a package, it can be opened in the package editor with the menu *Open package of the current unit.*
A list of the last five opened packages is displayed using *Package → Open recent packages.*

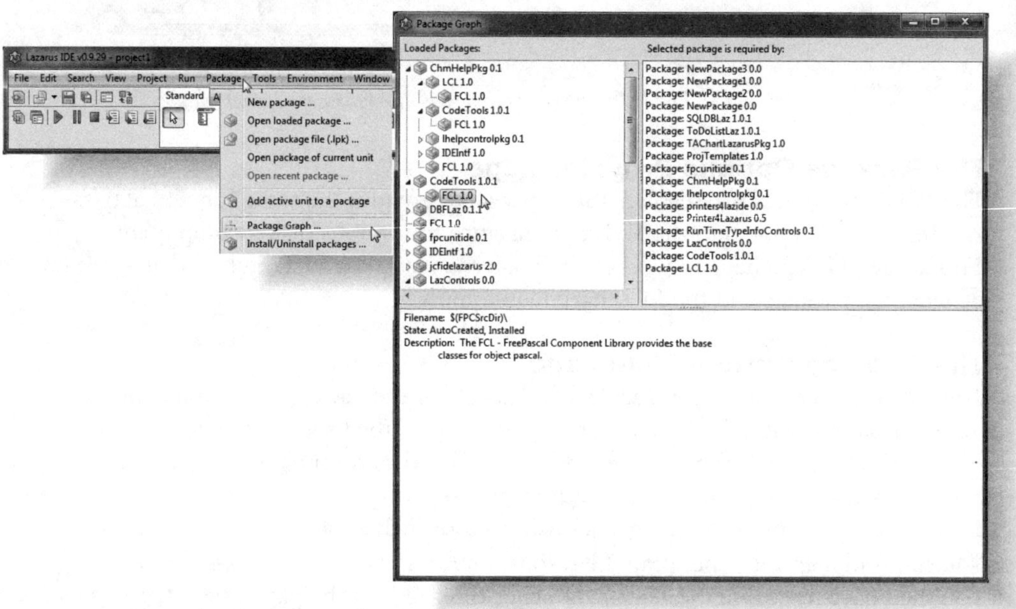

Figure 3.45: The Package Graph dialog accessed via Package → Package Graph.

3.1.8 Packages

Package → Package Graph
The package graph shows the packages currently loaded in the IDE, and their inter-dependencies. The upper left window lists all packages and the nodes are the packages they require. The upper right window show which packages need the selected package. Package details are shown in the memo below. Double-clicking any package opens it in the Package Editor.
A package can be in one of the following states :
Installed : The package is installed and compiled in the IDE making the package's classes and components available on the Component Palette.
Autocreated : The package is part of the IDE and therefore it cannot be uninstalled.
Install on next start : The package is installed and compiled into the IDE when the IDE is restarted.

Package → Install/Uninstall packages…
You install packages in the IDE using the `Install/Uninstall packages` dialog. The *Install* list includes all Lazarus packages, and other packages that have been installed before. When a package is not known to the IDE, you have to open it first using *Package → Open package file.*

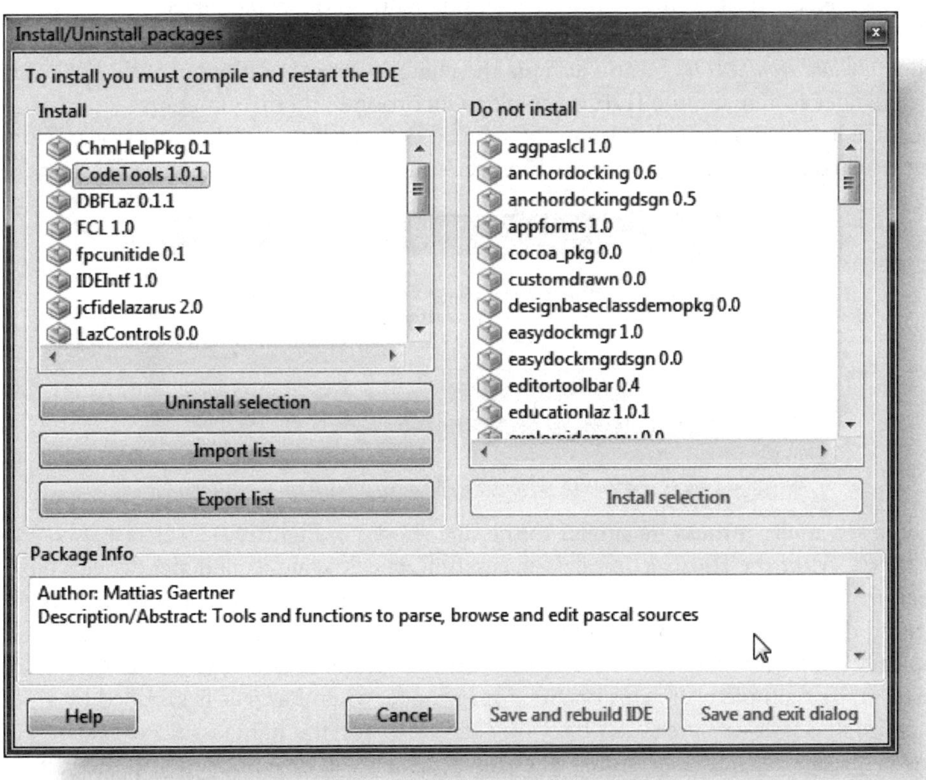

Figure 3.46: Overview of the installed and available packages in the dialog accessed via Package → Install/Uninstall packages…

Install lists those packages that are installed already or provided for installation by the developer. You can select here any package that has to be uninstalled. *Do not install* lists packages that are available for installation, but not selected to be installed. Selecting a package shows information about it in the *Package Info* field (for instance the author).

This information must have been recorded in the package using the *Description* page of the Package Options dialog. If this has not been completed this field will be empty, which is not a Lazarus error but a sign of the author's negligence. However, open source developers are often more focused on the delivery of a functional package and the task of documenting their work is ignored at first.

The *Install selection* button will mark the selected package for installation, and the *Uninstall selection* button marks it for removal. In this way several packages can be marked before the IDE is rebuilt.
Because Lazarus presently works only with static packages, the IDE has to be rebuilt after each package change before the change is effective.

If problems arise during installation or uninstall, select one package at a time and rebuild the IDE. Keep in mind that some packages depend on other packages!
The *Cancel* button rejects all changes and closes the dialog.
The *Save and rebuild IDE* button accepts the changes, and if you confirm that you want the changes to remain, the IDE is rebuilt to incorporate them. Sometimes an error message intervenes, usually because of a failed dependency. Another possibility is that the selected package needs a higher FPC version than the developer has available.

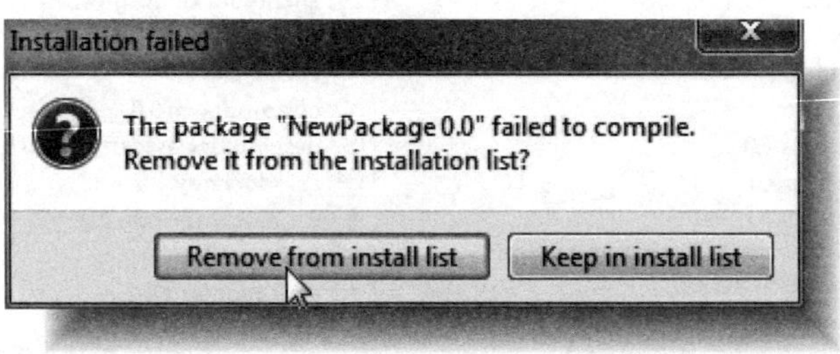

Figure 3.47: An error message during package installation

If you see an error message similar to the one shown in Figure 3.46, select *Remove from install list.* After the IDE recompiles successfully, check again if all dependencies have been met. Another possible error message arises if the programmer does not have file-writing rights for the Lazarus directory. In this case writing the executable fails. This typically happens when Lazarus was installed with administrator rights and the package is installed by a simple user. This occurs, for instance, when Lazarus is installed by a package manager (`.rpm` or `.deb` files) on Linux. Sorting the rights issue cures the problem. *Save and exit dialog* stores all changes, which will be compiled into the IDE when it is next rebuilt, but not immediately as with the *Save and rebuild IDE* button.
You can also store the changes you made in an XML file with the *Export list* button (or read such a previously saved file using the *Import list* button).

3.1.9 The Tools Menu

The *Tools* menu includes integrated tools, Delphi conversion tools, commands to rebuild the IDE, and a facility to add external tools to the IDE.

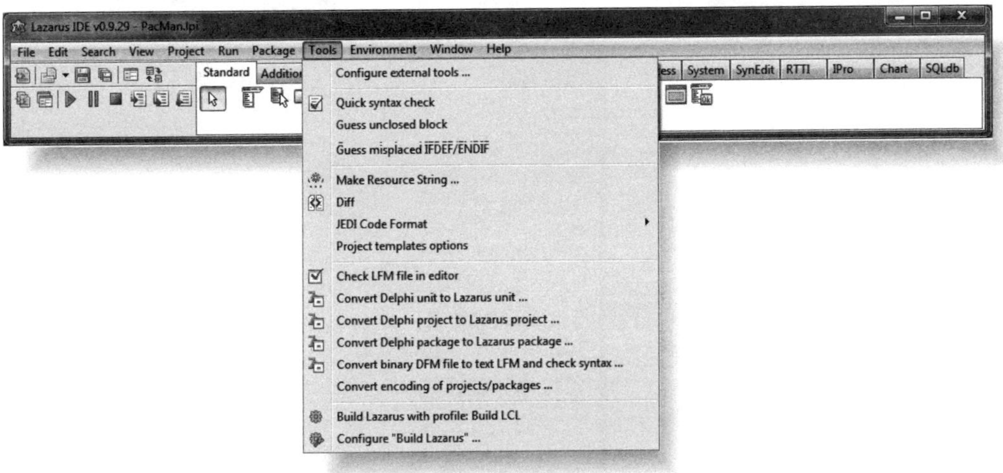

Figure 3.48: The Tools menu

Although the Lazarus IDE offers a wide range of functions, you can include external programs in the IDE to make their additional functionality easily available from inside the Lazarus environment. You set up the parameters for external tools using *Tools → Configure external tools.* These settings are global, available to all projects. In the *External tools* dialog the *Add* button opens the *Edit Tool* dialog, for adding new tools. *Edit* opens the same dialog where the currently selected tool settings can be edited. *Remove* deletes the currently selected tool, after you confirm the action. With *Up* and *Down* the current tool can be moved to a new position in the list of tools. Clicking on *OK* saves the changes and closes the dialog.

The *Edit Tool* dialog makes including a new tool in the IDE quite straightforward. The name of the tool added to the Tools menu is the name you enter in the *Title* field. The *Program Filename* must contain the complete path to the tool. The *Parameter* field is where you pass any command-line parameters to the tool, for instance: *-l test.pas*. The *Working Directory* is the directory where the tool starts. All relative paths are relative to this directory. If the tool generates output messages, the IDE can search these for compiler and/or make messages. You will have to enable the appropriate checkboxes for that. Macros can be used in the *Program Filename*, *Parameters* and *Working Directory* fields. While the cursor is in one of these fields, select a macro from the scrollable list and click *Add* to insert the macro at the cursor position.

You can also assign a keyboard shortcut to an external tool, though this is optional, since the tool can be called from the *Tools* menu too.

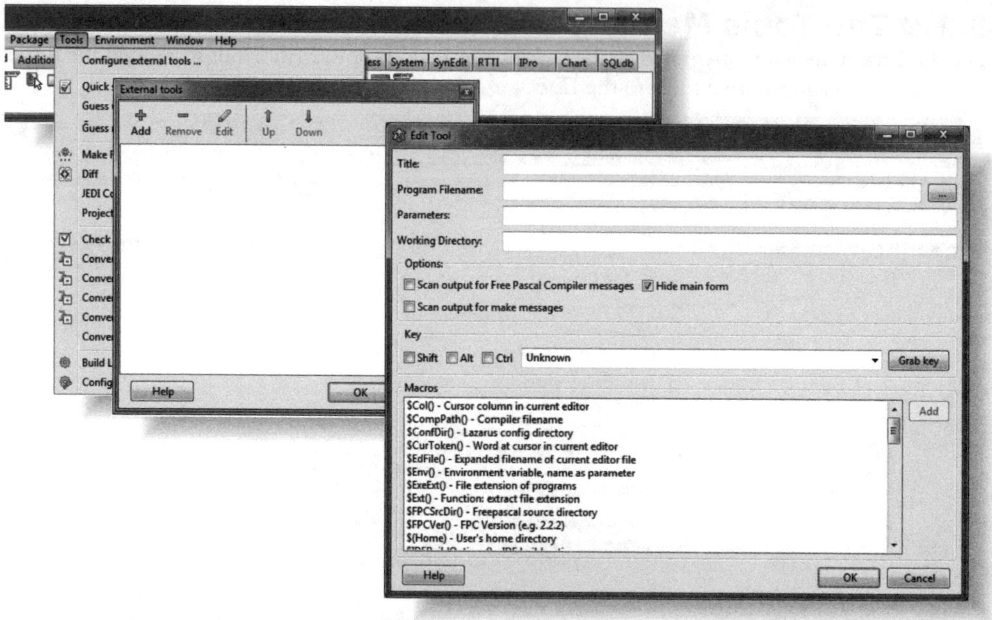

Figure 3.49: The Add button of the External tools dialog opens the Edit Tool dialog

Generating resource strings via *Tools → Make Resource String…*
You can offer your application's interface in several languages by using *resource strings* which have the advantage that new languages can be added without needing to recompile the application. To internationalize your application in this way means declaring all strings shown anywhere in the interface as named resource strings.
The *Make Resource String* dialog helps with the conversion of string constants and string literals into resource strings in preparation for internationalization.
First, a resource string section has to be available. You create this simply by entering the keyword *resourcestring* before any string declarations in the interface of the unit in question. (Before the next compile at least one resource string has to be added otherwise an error will be generated). Make sure that the cursor is placed on a string constant and select *Tools → Make Resource String*. This opens the *Make Resource String* dialog and a new identifier is automatically generated by combining a prefix (by default *rs*) with a suggested name. You can change the prefix in the *Identifier prefix* field. This not only alters the prefix in the currently generated name, but subsequent calls to *Make Resource String* will also use your custom prefix. The suggested name for a string constant is its own name, and for a string literal the suggested name is based on the string.

For example (assuming you already have a *resourcestring* section), if you type the following:

```
Button1.Caption := 'Click here';
```

and you place the cursor anywhere in the string 'Click here' and invoke *Make Resource String*, accepting the defaults and clicking the *OK* button will generate the following:

```
resourcestring
  rsClickHere = 'Click here';
...
Button1.Click := rsClickHere;
```

The new identifier replaces the former string literal or string constant name, and its string value is declared in the *resourcestring* section.

The IDE registers the prefixes for each unit, to be able to suggest the right prefix for the current unit. The *Identifier length* is the maximum length of the automatically generated identifier.

If you prefer to name the resource string yourself instead of using an automatically generated identifier, just type the name you want in the *Custom identifier* field.
The *Resourcestring section* combobox contains all the *resourcestring* sections declared in the current unit and in the interface parts of the units in the current unit's *uses* clause.

If strings with identical content are found, the *Strings with same value* combobox contains all *resourcestring* identifiers with the same content as the new resourcestring.
You can choose if you want to use one of them.

Three options govern the placing of the new resource string in the *resourcestring* section:

- *Append to section* The new identifier is added to the end of the section.
- *Insert alphabetically* The identifier is inserted alphabetically.
- *Insert context sensitive* The source code above and below the current cursor position is searched for resourcestring identifiers. If one is found, the new identifier is added there, otherwise it is appended at the end of the section.

The *Source preview* shows how the string constant will be replaced, and below a dashed line you can see how the resourcestring declaration will look. The *String constant in source* list shows all the present string constants so you can decide whether to convert more string constants into resource strings.

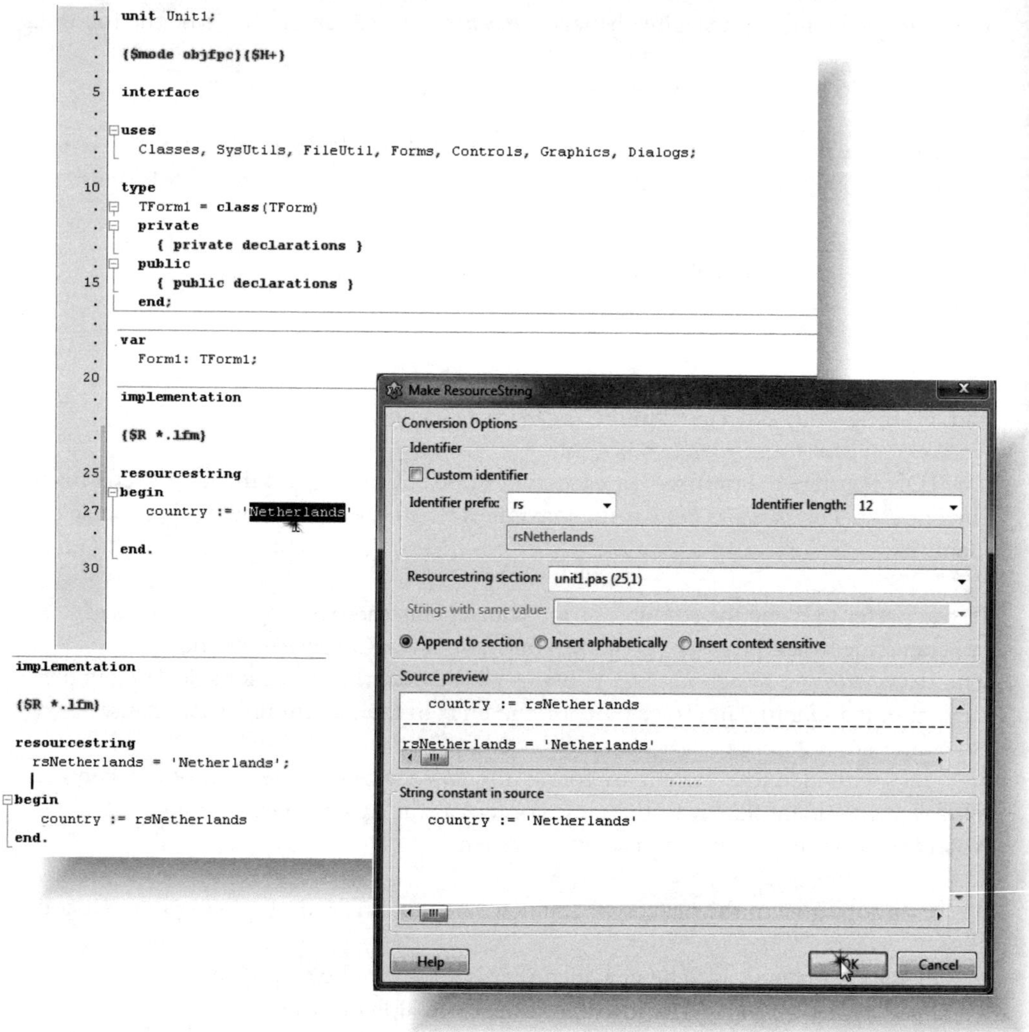

Figure 3.50: The Tools → Make Resource String… dialog

Comparing text files

The *Tools* → *Diff* menu enables you to compare two text files and generate a *diff* listing their differences. In the *Diff* dialog *Text1* and *Text2* are the two files to be compared.
If text has been selected, only this selection is compared. The comparison is line-by-line (not word or section based) and therefore works only with text files (such as Pascal sources), not with binary files.
A *diff* is a difference set of two files. With the diff and the result file it is possible to reconstruct the changed file.
The notion of diffs stems from a time when bandwidth for file transmission was limited, and a diff is often far smaller than the complete (changed) file.

When two parties have the result file, it is sufficient to exchange only the diff to enable the other party to have the changed file. In an ADSL communications era the importance of diffs is receding, but it still has value. For instance, many mailing lists (the Lazarus list is one of them) limit attachment size. If a file to be sent exceeds this size, you can always fall back on the diff.
Several settings control the comparison.
Enabling *Case Insensitive* ignores any differences in case.
Enabling *Ignore spaces at start of line,* disregards indented spaces (including tabs) when comparing two lines.
Ignore difference in line ends treats a Unix line end #10 as if it were a Windows line end #13#10 and *vice versa.* This setting can be useful when the files to be compared originate from different computers.
Ignore spaces ignores all spaces. *A B* becomes the same as *AB.*
Ignore if empty lines were added or removed ignores empty lines.
Ignore spaces at end of line ignores terminating spaces when comparing two lines.
Ignore amount of space chars treats any number of spaces as if they were one space.
When all desired comparisons are complete, you close the *Diff* dialog with *Close. Open Diff in editor* closes the dialog and shows the diff in a new Editor page. To store the diff file click the *Save* button. It is advisable to store the diff with its own file extension to be able to recognize it later on as such. There is no default for such a file extension.

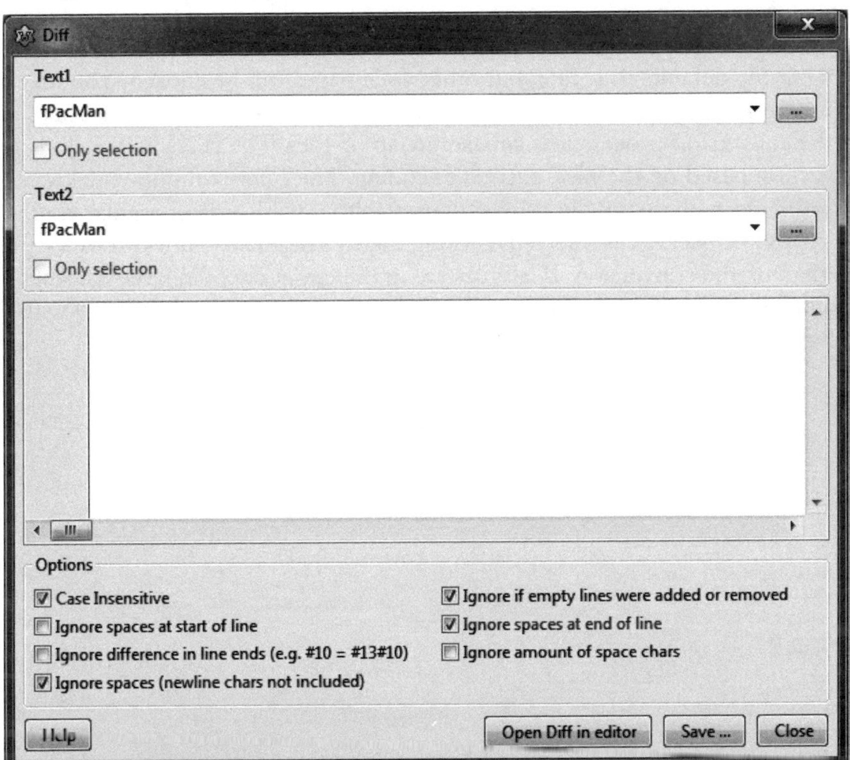

Figure 3.51: The dialog for generating a diff accessed via Tools→ Diff

Tools → JEDI Code Format
The menu option *JEDI Code Format* is only present when the *jcfidelazarus* package is installed, which recent versions of Lazarus install by default. Integrating the functions of the *JEDI Code Format* project into the Lazarus IDE is continuing steadily. The *JEDI Code Format* menu contains information about the JEDI format project if you select *About*. The actual formatting settings are found in the Editor *Options* menu (right-click in the Editor and choose the last context menu item *Options*), and may be available in the *Tools* menu by the time you read this. Everyone has an opinion about the best style for formatting source code. You may agree with the author of the JEDI formatter. This book uses a more compact, readily legible format.

Tools → Convert encoding of projects/packages
Convert encoding of projects/packages converts the string encoding of the text in a project or package. From version 0.9.26 onwards Lazarus has used Unicode (UTF8) strings on all platforms. You can use this menu option to easily convert the encoding of older projects, and avoid seeing strings of nonsense or ???? characters. German users usually notice faulty encoding when the 'umlaut' is not displayed correctly, for instance *über* displays as ?ber (or something even worse).
Clicking on the menu option opens the *Convert encoding* dialog in which you can choose from the *Convert project or package* combobox the project or package to convert. This combobox lists all projects and packages currently loaded in the IDE (excluding the LCL and FCL), so you need to open a project in the IDE before you can convert its encoding. The *New encoding* defaults to UTF8, but other code pages can be chosen. You may not need every project file to be converted, so the *File filter* section is provided where you can restrict the conversion process to a smaller group of files. The checkbox options restrict the conversion based on the files' current encoding. The *Filter* combobox restricts files to be converted on the basis of file extension using either wildcards or regular expressions. Once a project or package is selected, clicking the *Update preview* button shows a preview of the effect of the conversion. If all files are in the target encoding, the list stays empty. In not, all files needing conversion are shown. The actual conversion is done with the *Convert* button. When finished, the *Close* button closes the dialog.

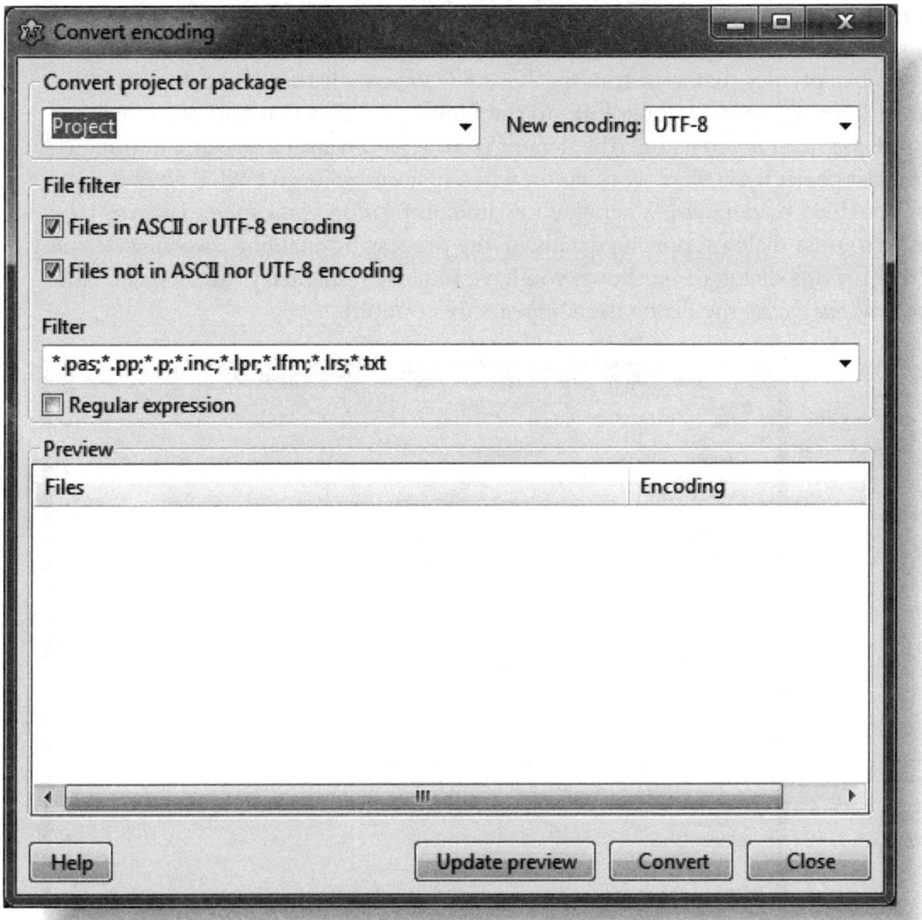

Figure 3.52: The dialog for converting encoding, accessed via Tools → Convert encoding of projects/packages

The options *Build Lazarus* and *Configure build Lazarus* are covered in detail in separate section at the end of this chapter.

3.1.10 The Environment menu

While the *Project* menu gives you comprehensive control of specific project settings, the *Environment* menu controls the appearance and behaviour Lazarus itself, and settings made here affect all projects.

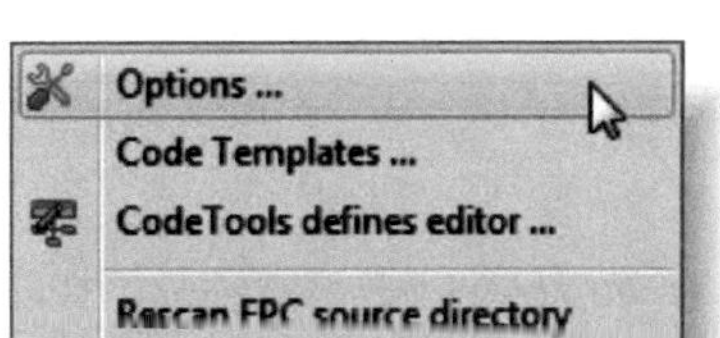

Figure 3.53 The options offered on the Environment menu

The Files page

The *Files* page contains important file and path settings. *Max recent files* sets an upper limit to the number of files that appear in the *File* → *Open recent* listing (the default is 10). *Max recent project files* sets an upper limit to the number of files that appear in the *Project* → *Open recent project* listing (the default is 5). If you want Lazarus to automatically open the last project you were working on when it starts, you can enable *Open last project at start* (it is enabled by default). When you initiate compilation you can get Lazarus to display a progress dialog reporting details of the process by enabling *Show compile dialog*. If you ask for this dialog to be shown you have to close it manually unless you enable *Auto close compile dialog* (the dialog itself repeats this option).

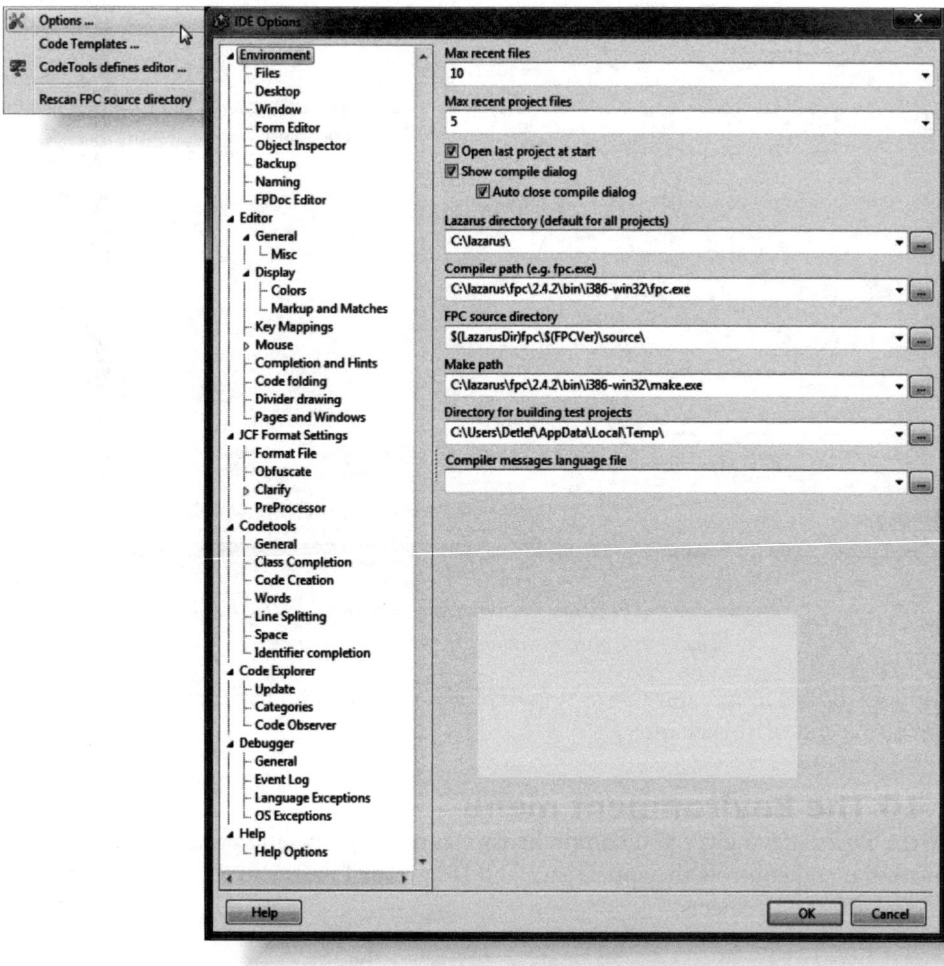

Figure 3.54: The Files page of the IDE Options dialog accessed via Environment → Options…

The *Lazarus directory* specifies the root directory for all Lazarus source code. It contains many subdirectories such as *ide, converter, components* and *lcl* where you will find the LCL sources.

The *Compiler path* contains the full path to the compiler. Typical paths are `/usr/bin/ppc386` on Linux, `/usr/bin/ppcppc` on OS X and `c:\Lazarus\fpc\2.4.3\bin\i386-win32\fpc.exe` on Windows.
Clearly the actual file path will depend on your particular compiler installation.
The *FPC source directory* contains the Free Pascal sources.
It has subdirectories such as *compiler, packages, rtl* and *fcl*. On Linux, BSD or OS X the value is typically `/usr/share/fpsrc`.
Note: do not confuse the FPC *source* directory with the FPC *unit* directory which might be `../units/i386-win32/`. This contains only the compiled `.ppu` files and is structured differently from the source directory.

Make path contains the path to the *make* tool. If the path is empty, the operating system presets are used, and these have to checked to be sure they are correct. The *make* tool is installed by default on almost all Linux and OS X systems because many Linux and Mac projects use it to compile extensive sources. For BSD *gmake* is available. Further information on make can be found at `http://www.gnu.org/software/make`.

The current project is saved and compiled in the *Directory for building test projects*, if so far you have not set a separate directory for it.

The Desktop page

You change settings for the IDE's interface on the *Desktop* page. *Language* changes the language of all the IDE menu phrases as well as the text of all the different dialogs and components (such as the *Caption* property of *TBitBtn*).
The *Language* setting has no effect on the Pascal programming language which is always a subset of English. The *Automatic (or English)* setting for *Language* means that your operating system's language setting is used. If this is a language Lazarus does not support then English is used. To make a changed *Language* setting effective, you have to restart the IDE. The *Auto save* function was not implemented at the time of writing.

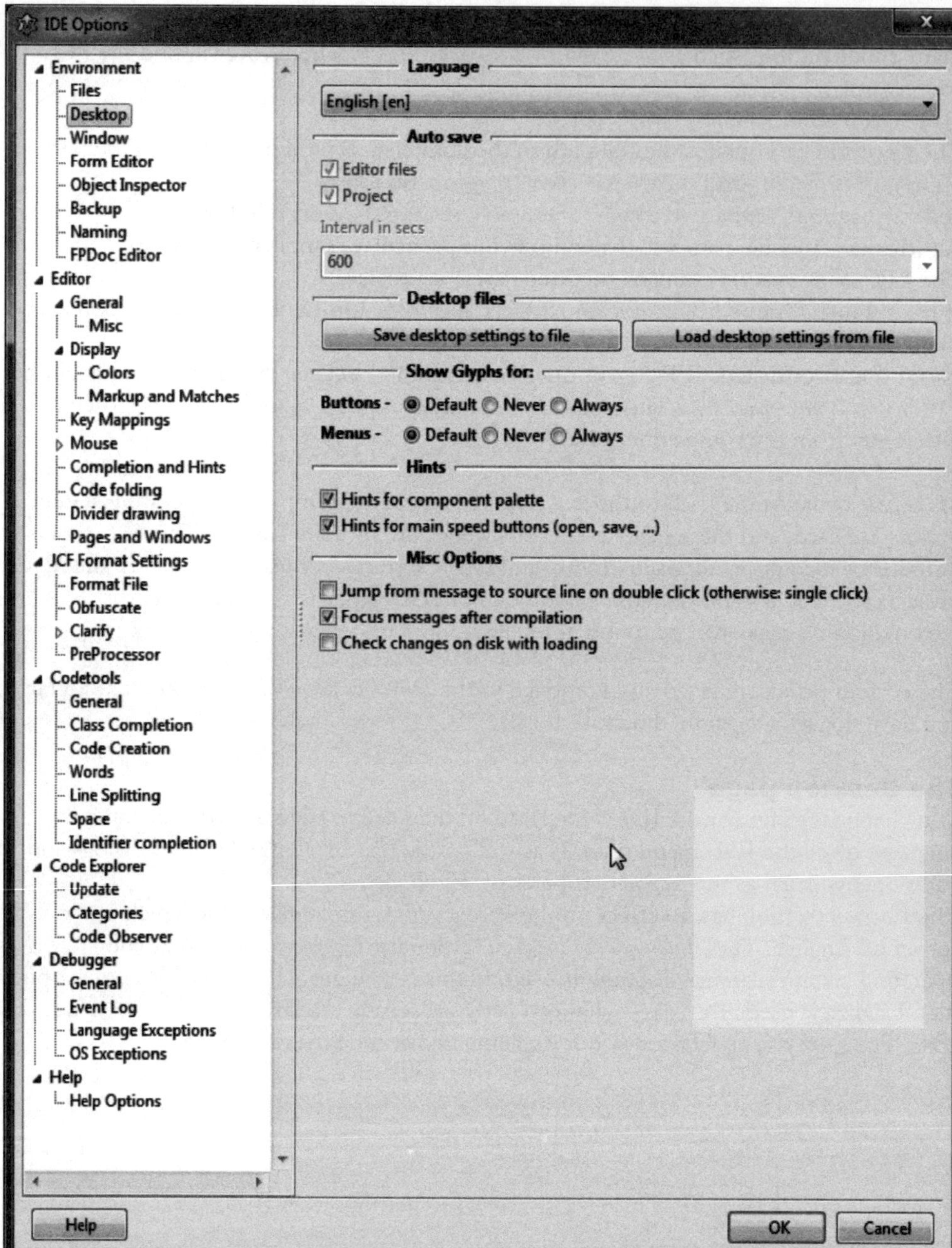

Figure 3.55: The Desktop page in the IDE Options dialog accessed via Environment → Options…

The desktop settings can be stored to a file or read from a file. The file extension `.lds` (**L**azarus **D**esktop **S**ettings) is proposed. Some components like *TBitBtn* have a *Glyph* property, which allows a small icon to be shown on the component. You set when these glyphs should be shown with the *Show Glyphs for* radiobuttons. These allow separate settings for buttons and menus. The display options are: *Default, Never* and *Always. Default* results in the glyphs never being shown on Windows but always being shown on all other operating systems. *Always* is the best setting for compatibility, especially if the application was first developed on an older version of Lazarus, since this avoids surprises with glyphs not appearing. Keep in mind that this setting is immediately noticeable when your application runs, whereas during development the glyphs are always shown.
You can override the Desktop setting by using the *Application.ShowButtonGlyphs* property which can take one of the values *sbgAlways, sbgNever or sbgSystem.*
When you move the mouse over the main menu you can see hints according to the settings *Hints for component palette* (which usually displays the name of the component) and *Hints for main speed buttons* (which may offer the name of the speedbutton function, or a fuller explanation of it).

Normally a single click on a message in the *Messages* window will take you to the appropriate location in the source. If you prefer a double-click to activate this you should enable the *Jump from message to source line on double click* option.
If you have many windows open, the *Messages* window may be hidden. When an error occurs during compilation it can be difficult to search for the *Messages* window to track down the exact error. Enabling the *Focus messages after compilation* setting means the *Messages* window will be placed in front of all other Lazarus windows when compilation finishes. When the IDE checks for changes to an editor file on disk, it normally just reads the file's timestamp. To have Lazarus reload the file and compare its contents, you can enable the *Check changes on disk with loading* option.

The Window page

The *Window* page provides several options for changing IDE window settings.
By default all Lazarus windows are listed separately in the operating system's window list (the *Taskbar* in Windows). Enabling *Show single button in TaskBar* reduces the listing to a single Lazarus item (or icon).
When a project is compiled and run from within the IDE (*Run* → *Run*) the open IDE windows can be annoying. Enabling *Hide IDE windows on run* hides the entire IDE, which is then restored when the running application ends.

In recent Lazarus versions the *Messages* window identifies different types of messages with icons. You can remove these icons by enabling *Hide message icons.*
Normally the IDE uses *Lazarus IDE vX.Y.Z - project1* as its caption in the operating system taskbar. Recent Lazarus versions let you show the project name first in the title, because most taskbars are too short for you to see more than just *Lazarus ....* Enabling the *IDE title starts with project name* checkbox is useful when starting multiple instances of the IDE to work on several different projects at the same time, since it is then easier to identify which taskbar icon refers to which project.

For the same reason you may find it helpful to enable the *Show project directory in IDE title* checkbox too, to help you identify at a glance which IDE project is which.
You set your preferences for the size and position of the IDE windows in the *Window Positions* section. Clicking on one of the windows in the list shows its current settings. *Left* and *Top* designate the upper left corner of the window, *Width* and *Height* the size. You should bear the screen resolution in mind when you change these pixel values. You can give each window custom settings, or you might prefer to use the Lazarus presets using the *Use windowmanager* radiobutton.

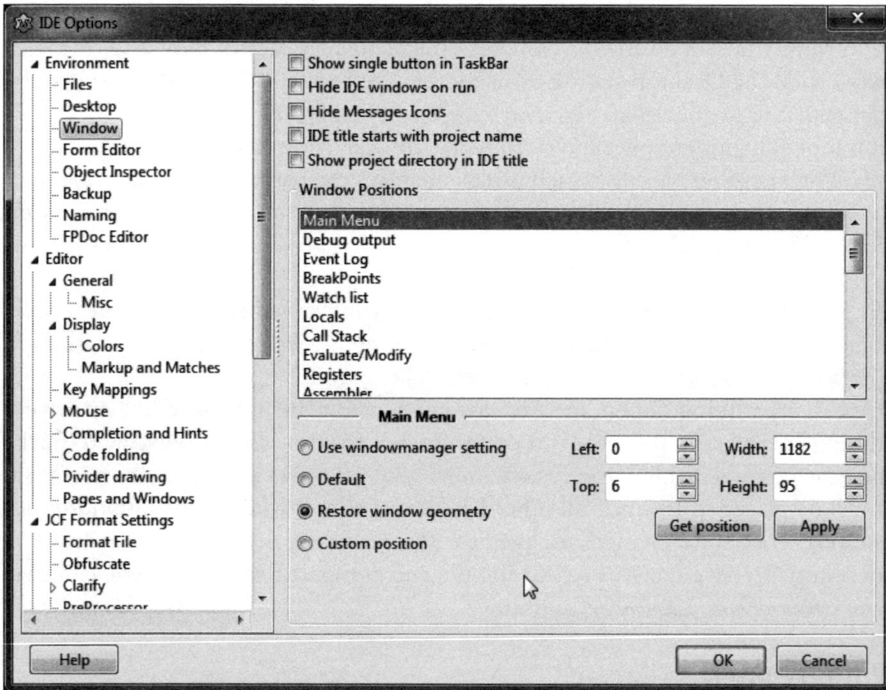

Figure 3.56: The Window page of the IDE Options dialog

The Form Editor page

The *Form Editor* page offers settings for the program windows you develop using the IDE. The *Grid* section offers the following options which all relate to using the Form Designer:

Show Grid shows a grid in each form to help with placing components that are dropped there. The grid is visible in all client areas that accept controls.

Show border spacing shows a rectangle around every control (which slows down the IDE slightly).

Snap to grid causes controls to jump to the nearest grid line when you move them or change their size.

Grid size X is the horizontal gridline spacing in pixels (*Grid size Y* is the vertical spacing). The *Colors* section lets you specify the colour of the various Form Designer items in the *Colors* list.

Grabber color is the colour of the eight little boxes used for changing the size controls when you select them.

Marker color is the colour of the four little boxes which are shown at the corner of every control included in a multiple selection.

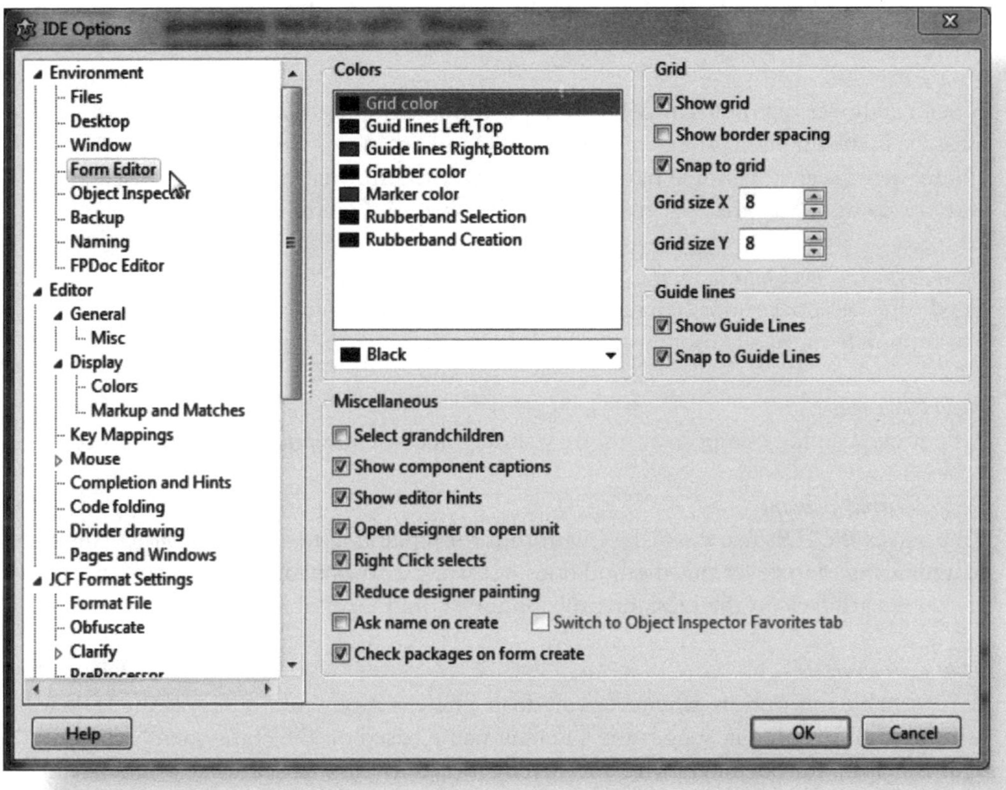

Figure 3.57: The Form Editor page of the IDE Options dialog

The *Rubberband* items in the *Colors* list refer to the 'rubberband' selection tool that appears in the Designer when you left-click on a form and drag the mouse. When you release the mouse button all elements within the rubber band are selected. Shift-clicking will add or remove controls from the selection. This is the *Rubberband Selection*.
The *Rubberband Creation* is a similar rubberband which is shown when you select a control from the Component Palette and – rather than dropping it with a single click on the form – you drag the mouse across the form holding the left button down. This creation rubberband can be coloured differently from the selection one. The *Miscellaneous* section contains several other settings which affect the Form Designer.

Select grandchildren:
When selecting components with the rubberband, by default you only select the children of the control on which the rubber band is drawn. Enabling this option will cause the child control's own child controls to be selected as well (for instance if you rubberband two *TPanels* each containing several *TButtons*).

Show component captions:
Components that are not seen at run time (such as dialog components) are represented on the form by a small icon. Enabling this option adds the name of the component below the icon (which like the icon is visible only at design time).

Show editor hints:
When you hover the mouse pointer over a component in the Form Designer a hint message is shown giving the component *Name* and position.
Components seen at runtime have a longer hint with information about their size, and (for components that can receive focus) their *TabStop* and *TabOrder*.

Open designer on open unit:
The Form Designer is opened automatically when the unit file is opened.
This option is especially useful for beginners, so it is activated by default.

Right Click selects:
A right-click on the component not only shows its context menu, but selects it too.

Reduce designer painting:
This makes the IDE use the fastest algorithm for repainting forms (*InvalidateRect* instead of redrawing). However this method does not work with all widgets in all widget-sets. If you see artefacts in the Designer, this option should be disabled.

Ask name on create:
If you enable this option, whenever you drop a new component on a form the IDE will ask you what to name it, suggesting a default name based on the component's class. This is helpful for beginners who are thereby forced to think about what would be an appropriate name. Good naming improves the consistency and readability of your code, especially for others. Experienced programmers may just find this functionality annoying.

Switch to Object Inspector Favorites tab:
This option works in conjunction with the previous option and is only available if the *Ask name on create* option is enabled. Enabling the *Switch to Object Inspector Favorites tab* option causes the IDE to activate the Object Inspector once you have entered (or accepted) the name of the new dropped component, with the focus set to the *Favorites* page.

Check packages on form create:
Enabling this option causes Lazarus to check whether all the packages needed for the component you are creating are installed. The *Guide lines* show which control the current selection is aligned to (if *Show Guide Lines* is enabled).

Snap to Guide Lines:
When moving a component (or changing its size) in the Form Designer, the movement will snap to the nearest guide line. The colours of the left and top guidelines can be set in the *Colors* section with the *Guide lines Left, Top* and likewise for the right and bottom aligned guidelines.

The Object Inspector page

This page lets you set how the Object Inspector looks and behaves. *Colors* lets you have the various listed parts of the Object Inspector drawn as you wish. If you don't want to set each item individually you can click on the *Use default Lazarus settings* button to set all colours at once, or you might prefer the Delphi defaults for which a further *Speed settings* button is provided. The main difference between the two settings is found in the additional colours offered in the Lazarus defaults.

The *Miscellaneous* section contains only the *Item height* setting which is the default height of each property row. Widget-set restrictions may prevent you changing the size of edit and combo boxes (for instance the Win32 widget-set does not allow changing the combobox height).

The *Options* section controls several Object Inspector behaviours:

Show hints shows hints when the mouse moves over a property.
Enabling *Auto show* ensures that the Object Inspector is always shown at start-up even when it was closed before the end of the previous session (normally window changes are saved and at the next start-up restored exactly as they were before).
You may wish to enable *Bold non default values* which **emboldens** all properties whose values differ from their defaults, so you can pick them out more easily.

Draw grid lines separates individual properties (and events) with dotted lines.

Show gutter draws a vertical separation line left of the property (or event) names (the gutter space is always drawn, whatever the setting of this option).

Show status bar shows a status bar at the base of the Object Inspector.

Show information box makes the Object Inspector taller by including an information panel below the property listing (visible whatever page is showing above) with information (sometimes detailed) about the selected property. This information comes from the XML help files written with *fpdoc*, and is becoming more extensive all the time as knowledgeable volunteers contribute to the Lazarus project.

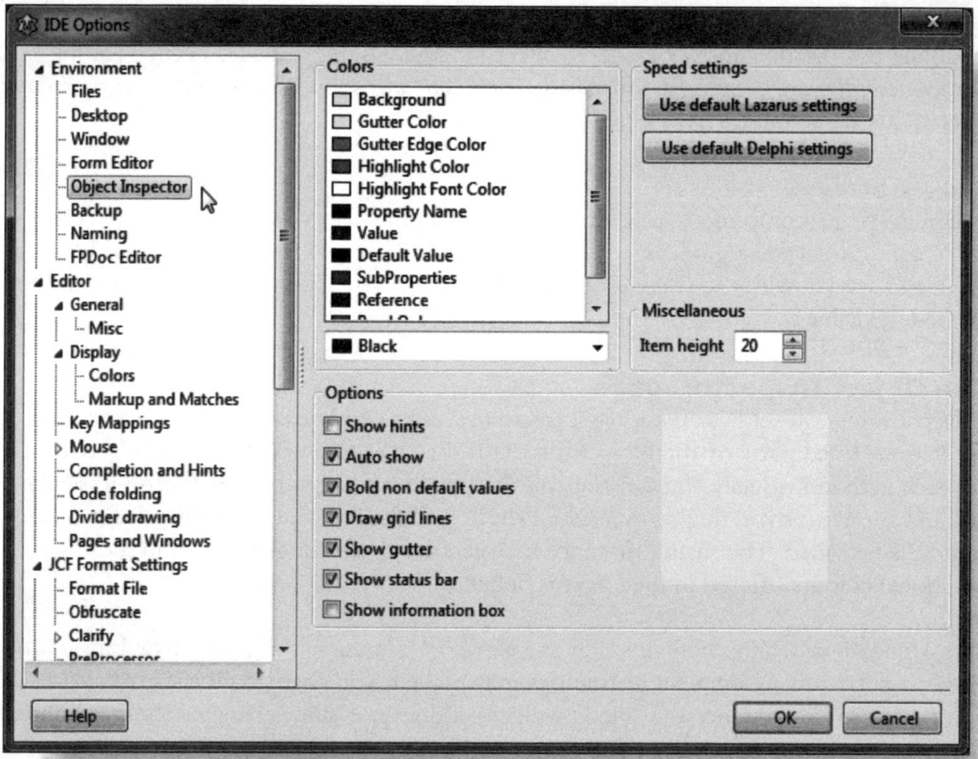

Figure 3.58: The Naming page of the IDE Options dialog

Note: Individual projects can define Pascal source code files with any extension. These are not overwritten by the IDE on the basis of the *Default pascal extension.*

Before compilation the IDE checks if there are ambiguous file names (for instance if there is a unit present twice in the unit path).
However, the compiler takes the first unit that it encounters. This is not always what the developer needs and can lead to extraordinary error messages, whose origin is hard to fathom. With *Ambiguous file action* a specific – and more helpful – action can be set for such occasions.

The *Save as* section is important for cross-platform developers. If you only program for a case-insensitive file system (like Windows) and don't share your code with others, you will be happy with the *No automatic renaming* option. Otherwise, source file names must be written correctly for case-sensitive platforms, and you must understand how the compiler searches for files whose names are identical save for the case of the characters. The compiler searches first for a unit name as written in the *uses* section, then for that name in all *lower*case, and then for that name in all *upper*case letters.

You can either ensure that all unit names are case-correct (not easy for Windows users), or you can instruct the IDE to save all new units automatically using lowercase names, or you can instruct the IDE to ask the user for a decision at every save.
The Editor shows unit names as they are written in the source code. The IDE always shows you the way the names were written originally in the *uses* clause.
Since Lazarus 0.9.28 a new section has been added where you can specify what has to be done with a unit reference when the unit is renamed. The references can be updated *Always*, *Never* or *Ask* the user. A general setting lets you instruct Lazarus to *Ask for a file name* whenever a new file is created.

The FPDoc Editor page

On this page you can set paths for the locations of FPDoc help files. These files, available in XML format, document both the LCL and the RTL, and are being continually revised, expanded and improved.

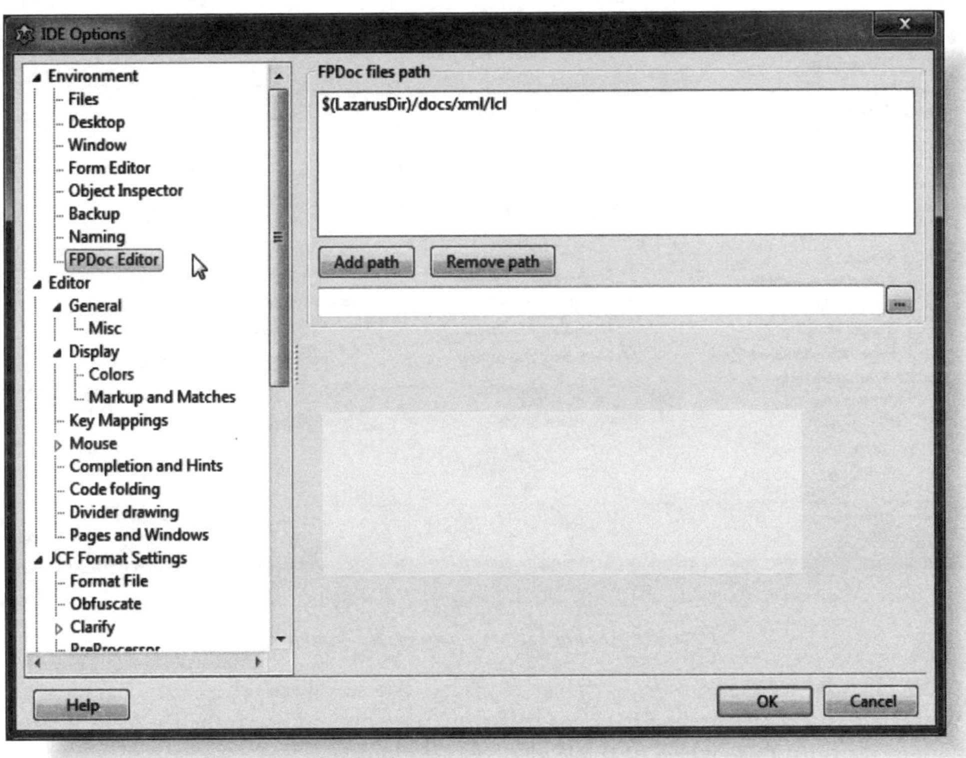

Figure 3.59: The FPDoc editor page of the IDE Options dialog

The Editor pages

You control the look and feel of Lazarus source code Editor on these pages, which offer a sometimes bewildering array of options for tweaking aspects of the Editor.

The General page

The *General* page controls the Editor's behaviour. The *Undo/Redo* settings control the reversing of (mistaken) actions. If you enable *Undo after save* the undo list persists through a file save, allowing you to reverse changes after saving the file. Enabling *Group Undo* collects consecutive changes of the same kind which are then reversed in one call to Undo, instead of having to individually reverse every small change. *Group undo* covers repeated actions too. You set the maximum number of undo actions at *Undo Limit.*

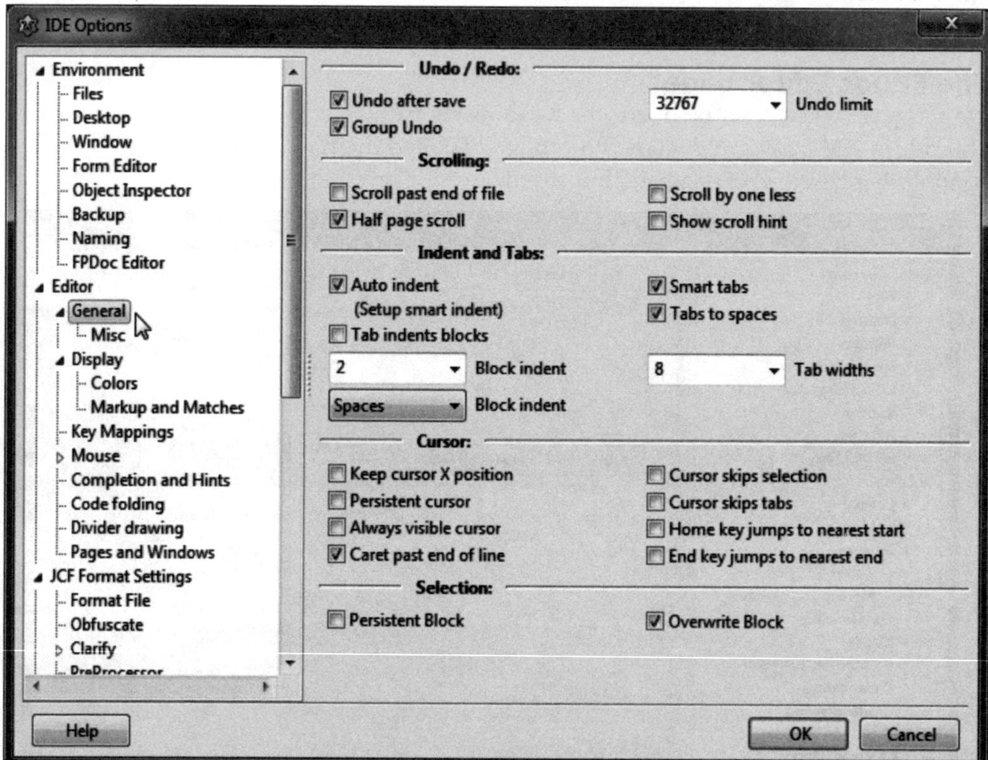

Figure 3.60: The General page of the Editor options

At the *Scrolling* settings, *Scroll past the end of file* lets you scroll past the EOF character. With *Half page scroll* scrolling happens half-page-wise up and down (half a page at a time) with either the mouse wheel or the [PgUp] and [PgDn] keys.

Scroll by one less scrolls one line less than a page-full.

Show scroll hint

If you enable *Show scroll hint* and use the mouse wheel to scroll an editor page, a small hint window appears in the top right showing the line number. After scrolling, the hint window automatically disappears after 1.5 seconds.

The settings for *Indent and Tabs* control the handling of indenting and tabs.
With *Auto indent* the cursor of a newly inserted line is indented to match the indentation of the line above. This improves the readability of your source code because parts belonging together are grouped visually at the same level.
Enabling *Tab indents blocks* lets you select a block of code and indent it all by pressing the [Tab] key. [Shift][Tab] will un-indent the same block.

Block indent sets how many characters the block is indented by (see *Edit → Indent selection*). The default is 2 spaces. The *Autoindent* combobox (mislabelled *Block indent* in some Lazarus versions) offers three ways of filling the space at the beginning of a new line: *Spaces* uses space characters for the fill.

Space/tab as prev line uses the same mix of spaces and tabs as the line above.

Position only merely positions the cursor correctly. Spaces are used to fill the indent if you type something.

Smart tabs affects use of the [Tab] key once you type past the start of a line, when a tab will result in the cursor being indented to the level of the next word in the line above. If the current line is longer than the line above, a longer previous line is searched for. If you enable *Tabs to spaces* then every tab you type in the Editor will be converted to the appropriate number of spaces. This only affects typing in the current line. If you want all the tabs in the file to be replaced by spaces, then select the entire text with [Ctrl][A] followed by *Edit → Tabs to spaces in selection* to start the conversion.

Tab widths defines the number of spaces a tab represents.
Cursor behaviour is controlled in the *Cursor* section.

Keep cursor X position keeps the horizontal position of the cursor when moving through the source code. So when scrolling this means that the cursor does not change – when it is located at the tenth character, for instance, it remains at the tenth character. Otherwise the cursor may jump to the beginning or ending of lines.

A *Persistent cursor* stays visible when scrolling.

An *Always visible cursor* continues to blink when the Editor loses the focus. This option is necessary for some systems, where the message focusing does not work properly.

Caret past the end of line allows the cursor to go past the last character of the line. Otherwise the cursor will move to the next line.
With *Cursor skip selection* the cursor jumps to the beginning of the selected text when the [←] key is pressed, and the [→] key moves the cursor to the end of the selected text.
With *Home key jumps to nearest start* pressing the [Home] key brings you to the beginning of the line, if it's closer by, and with *End key jumps to nearest end* the [End] key jumps towards the end of the line.

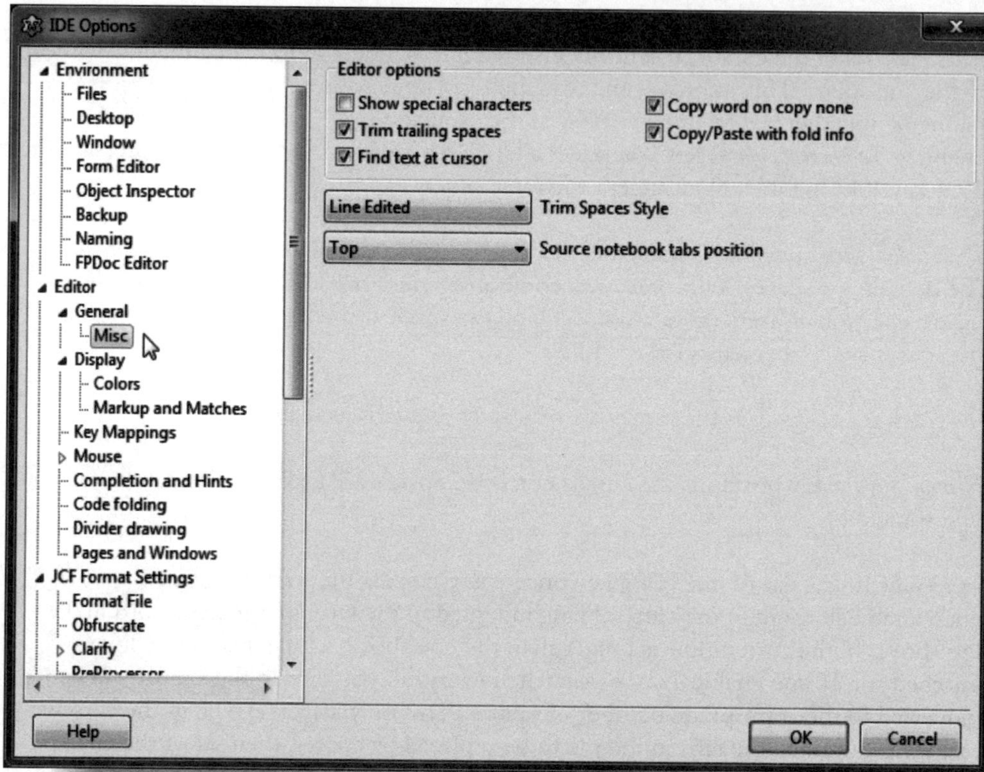

Figure 3.61: The Misc page in the Editor section of the IDE Options dialog

The Misc page

Some of the common Editor settings have been grouped together on a separate *Misc* page.

Show special characters shows spaces as dots (.) and invalid characters as question marks (?).

Trim trailing spaces removes spaces at the end of the line (this only works on edited lines). Enabling *Find text at cursor* means that the word at the cursor position is placed into the search field when a search function is called, saving you from having to type it.

Enabling *Copy word on copy none* means that if no text is selected when you call *Edit* → *Copy* ([Ctrl][C]) then the word at the cursor is placed on the clipboard. The same is true for *Edit* → *Cut* ([Ctrl][X]).

Enabling *Copy/Paste with fold info* instructs the IDE to remember if text copied within the IDE was folded when copied, and (if possible) to subsequently restore the folds on *Edit* → *Paste* ([Ctrl][V]).

Trim spaces style:
This combobox lets you set how aggressively spaces will be trimmed. SynEdit (the component on which the IDE Editor is based) allows you to enter 'uncommitted' spaces at the end of a line, so you can continue typing as usual. If SynEdit deems those spaces no longer needed it will trim them. In any of these cases spaces you type at the end of a line will not be saved in the file.

- *Leave Line*: This is the default, SynEdit will keep all spaces at the end of the current line. If the caret moves to another line, the spaces at the end are trimmed.
- *Line Edited*: As *Leave Line* but in addition SynEdit will remove any space to the right of the caret, if the line is edited. If you type spaces at the end of a line, they will be to the left of the caret and not affected.
- *Caret or Edit*: This is the most aggressive mode, like *Line Edited* but also trimming spaces to the right of the caret, if you move horizontally; so that cursor-left at the end of a line acts like the [BkSp] key.
- *Position Only*: No spaces or tabs are inserted past the end of line. Only the caret is moved (and forced past EOL). If text is typed, the gap is always filled with spaces. This means tabs are lost (converted to space). Hence autoindent "copy tabs" does not work in this mode, and because you are past the EOL, smart un-indent does not work in this mode either.

Source notebook tab positions:
This combobox lets you set the where tabs are placed when editing more than one file in the Editor, which then looks like a notebook with tabs for selecting each page or file. These tabs can be at the *Top* (the default), *Bottom*, *Left* or *Right* side of the Editor notebook.

The Display page

The *Display* page controls the Editor's appearance.
Enabling *Visible right margin* places a vertical line at the right edge of the Editor, representing the right margin. This is to help developers avoid excessively long lines (which makes source code difficult to read).

The *Right margin* combobox lets you change the position of the right margin from the default (80 characters to the right).
At the left side of the Editor is a grey edge, the gutter. On this additional information can be shown, like the line numbers. Disable *Visible gutter* if this is not to be shown.
If line numbers are to be shown, *Show line numbers* must be enabled.
If you don't need every single line to be numbered the numbering can be set to each n-th line. The separate settings for the edge are obviously effective only when the gutter is visible.

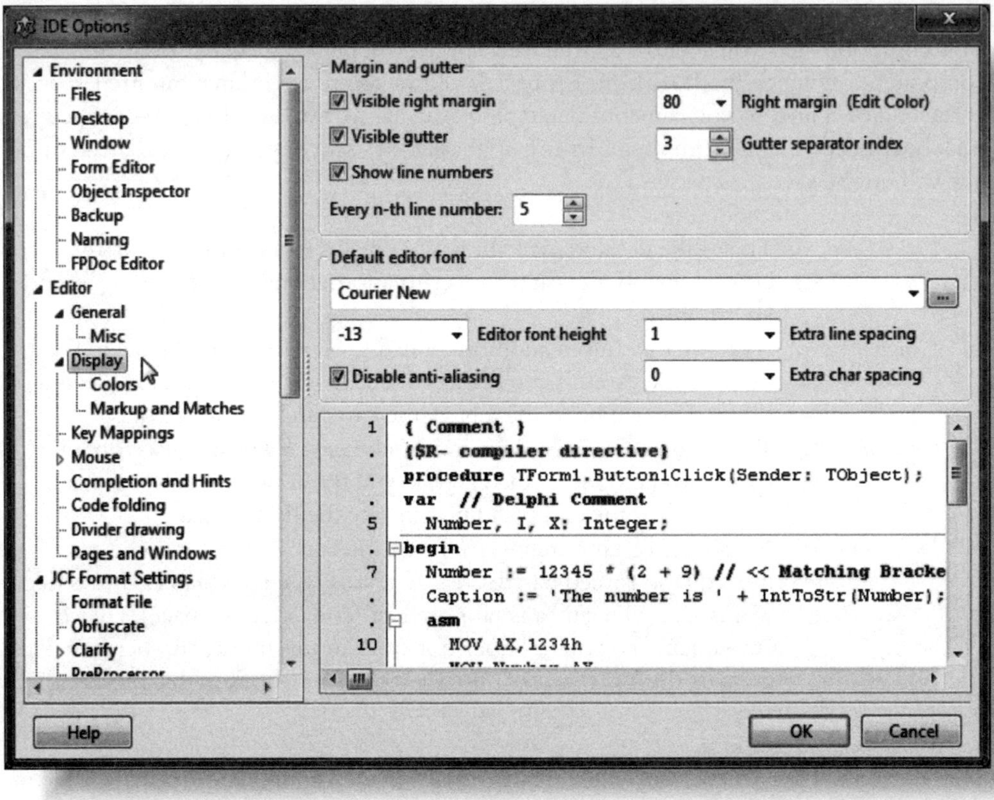

Figure 3.62: The Display page of the Editor section in the IDE Options dialog

The next section is where you can change settings for the font used by the Editor. It is possible to choose any installed font present on the computer, but depending on the operating system and the widget-set there are differences in the available fonts. Occasionally the appropriate font has to be installed first before the source code Editor display is useable.

You have to take care when using a widget-set that is not the operating system's standard. For instance the Linux KDE interface is based on Qt, but Lazarus is compiled with the default Gtk2 widget-set. In this case it may be that the operating system font settings have no effect on the source code Editor.

In any case a font with good readability is preferred: for instance the character 0 should distinguish itself clearly from the character O. The *Default editor font* is shown in a combobox. If you click the [...] button beside this a dialog opens where you can select a different font. The window below shows a preview of any changes you make.

The size of the font is set in the separate *Editor font height* field (negative values include line spacing in the value while positive values don't include this). The *Extra line spacing* allows you to add extra space (in pixels) between adjacent lines. The same is possible for characters with the *Extra char spacing* field.

Disable anti aliasing can be used to enhance the clarity of font display.

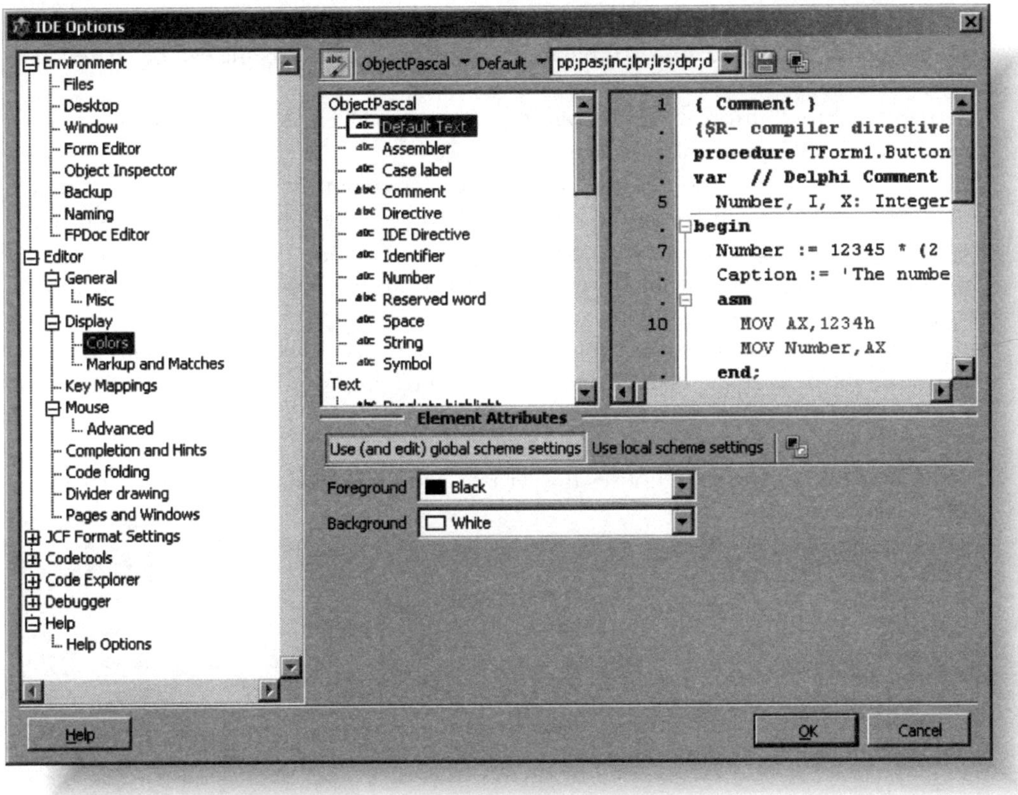

Figure 3.63: The Colors subpage in the Display section of the IDE Options dialog.

The Colors page

You set colour highlighting for the Editor on the *Colors* page.
At the top of the page the leftmost toolbutton (with a small *abc* icon) toggles syntax highlighting on and off for the current language.
The combobox beside it (*ObjectPascal* by default) lets you choose the colour scheme for each programming language you use, each of which has a predefined syntax highlighter.
The 'languages' available are:
Object Pascal (the default), HTML document, C++, XML document, Lazarus Form definition, Perl, Java, UNIX Shell Script, Python, PHP, SQL, Javascript, Diff file, MS-DOS batch language, and INI file.
The adjacent combobox offers several colour schemes: Default, Delphi, Pascal Classic, Twilight and Ocean.
It is advised to select the language first and then the colour scheme, and then set single elements.
The file extensions combobox lets you set the range of files which the syntax highlighting is applied to.

The export toolbutton beside it (bearing a floppy disc icon) lets you save your modified colour-scheme settings to an XML file so your custom colour-scheme can be shared with other users.
The rightmost toolbutton, *Set all elements to default,* resets all elements, according to the selected highlighting and colour scheme.
The *Element Attributes* section has two mutually exclusive buttons: either you *Use (and edit) global scheme settings* or you *Use local scheme settings.* The preview window shows the current highlighting of all elements for the current language. A click on one of the elements shows their settings in the fields below. An alternative is to click on an element of the text in the preview window.
If you aren't satisfied with your changes, the remaining *Set element to default* toolbutton will restore the default according to the selected highlighting and colour scheme.

The Markup and Matches page

The *Markup and Matches* page houses the settings previously found (pre version 0.9.29) under *Automatic features.*

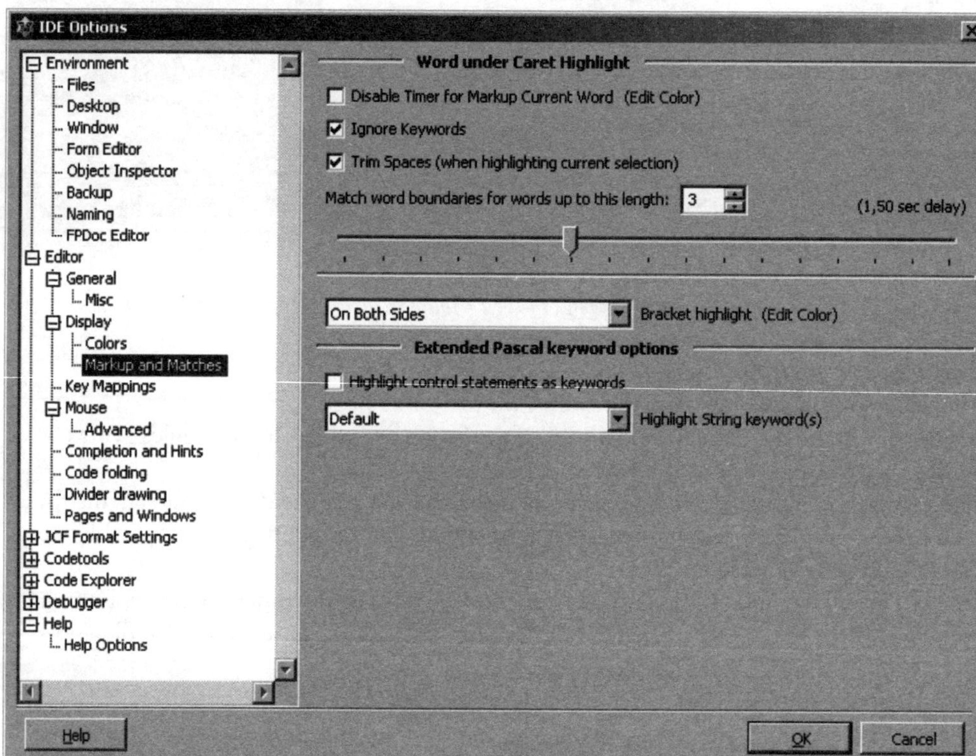

Figure 3.64: The Markup and Matches page in the Editor section of the IDE Options dialog

The *Markup and Matches* page controls functions which run automatically in the background such as highlighting and auto completion.

If the cursor pauses at a word in the Editor, this word together with all other instances of the word becomes highlighted. This gives you an automatic overview of where a certain variable appears in the source. You can set the length of delay before highlighting is shown with the trackbar which ranges from 0 (left) to 4 seconds (right).

Although the trackbar graduations do not have any time units, a label just above the rightmost end of the trackbar dynamically reports the time setting as the pointer thumb is altered.
Searching for the current word in very large files can take a noticeable time, during which you cannot do further editing. Consequently you can disable the timer using the *Disable Timer for Markup Current Word* checkbox. Highlighting then occurs after a certain idle time.

If you enable *Ignore Keywords* this will exclude keywords from highlighting. What counts as a keyword depends on the chosen syntax highlighter (Object Pascal by default).

The option *Trim spaces* regulates the removal of unnecessary spaces during highlighting. With *Match word boundaries for words up to this length* the highlighting is limited to words with less than the set number of characters, provided the original word itself is no longer. *Bracket highlight* is a useful facility to help keep track of where nested functions or procedures begin and end inside one another. It can be set to highlight brackets left of the cursor, right of the cursor, on both sides, or not at all.

Coloured links beside some of the settings give access to the corresponding item at the *Colors* page, where you can change the appearance of the item.
Highlight control statements as keywords does what it says.

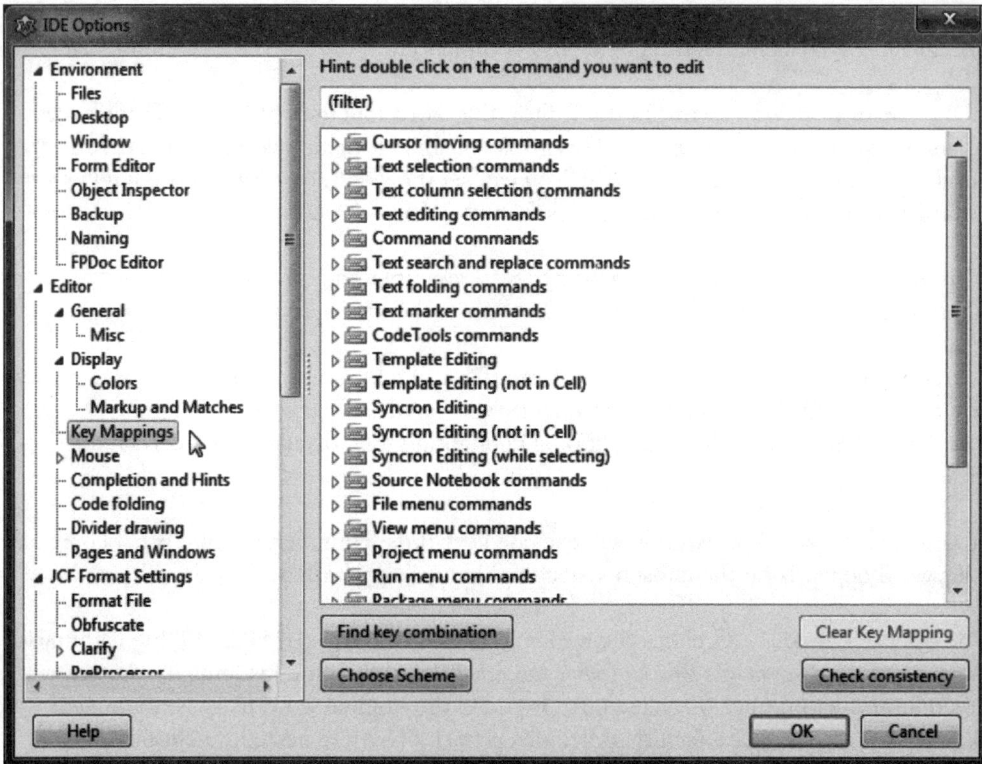

Figure 3.65: The Key Mappings page in the Editor section of the IDE Options dialog

The Key Mappings page

The *Key Mappings* page provides comprehensive options for setting Lazarus' key mappings. If you are familiar with a different IDE and are accustomed to its keyboard mapping, may wish to use this mapping for Lazarus too. Or you may be forced to change the mapping because the operating system or another important program grabs one or more desired key combinations already. Not being able to change the key mapping would possibly result in calling an operating system function instead of a Lazarus IDE function. While Lazarus has been developed as a cross-platform development environment, not every operating system exception can be allowed for.

The many Lazarus IDE commands are listed in the window in particular command groups. A click on the ► chevron (or + in some systems) icon in front of a group expands the node to show all the commands in that group.
In the *(filter)* field at the top you can search for a specific command name incrementally – for each character you type the search result is dynamically reduced.
If you prefer to search for a mapping the other way around, the *Find key combination* button is available. In this subsequent dialog a key combination can be typed manually or you can use the *Grab key* button.

With the *Grab key* button a dialog opens and you press the key combination you want. The combination is shown and after confirmation with OK, only the command mapped to this combination is shown (if a command has already been assigned to it). Lazarus has several default key mappings available that can be loaded with the *Choose scheme* button.

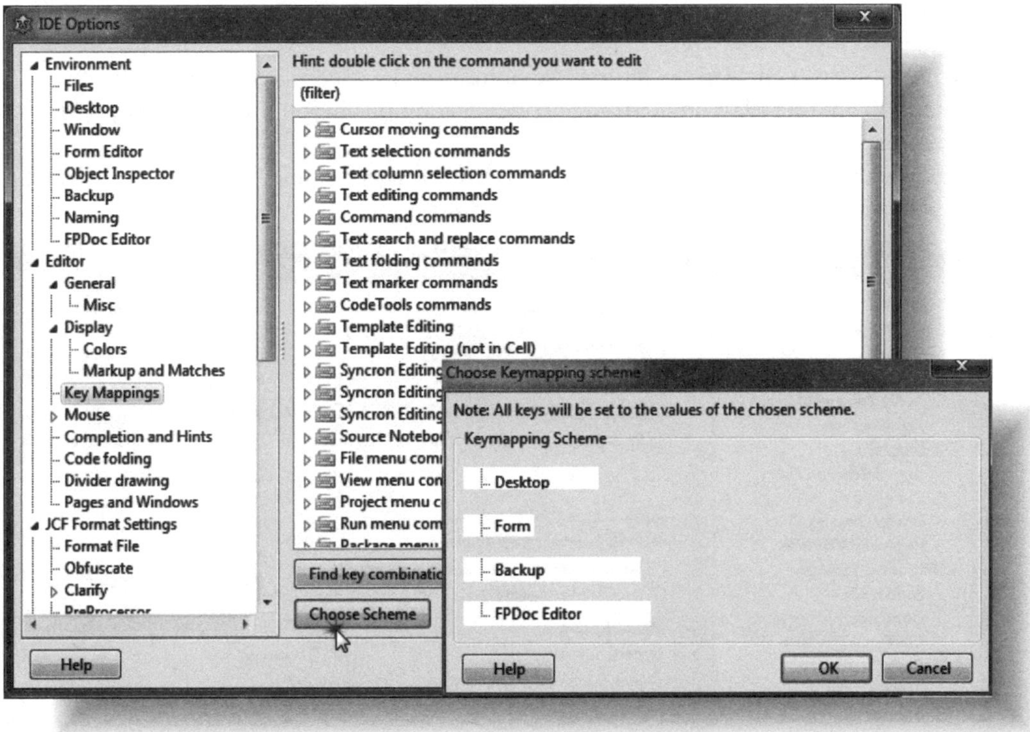

Figure 3.66: The dialog for choosing a key mapping scheme, invoked from the Key Mappings page.

Check consistency searches for keys used more than once and presents an appropriate message. A click on one of the commands with duplicated shortcut keys opens a dialog to change that shortcut key setting.

The Mouse page

Lazarus offers numerous options for customising the behaviour of the mouse in the Editor. The basic settings are found on the *Mouse* page (see Figure 3.67), and detailed settings are offered by the secondary page *Advanced*. Sometimes you find that the mouse cursor covers the source code position that you clicked on to edit. Either you can move the mouse away from it after clicking, or you can enable the *Hide mouse on typing* setting. Then while you type, the mouse cursor is not shown (though it reappears after keyboard inactivity).

In the *Gutter* section two options are available. When *Standard* is selected, those actions are executed when the mouse is clicked on the gutter. With *Extended* the action is executed when the mouse button is released after clicking it. This way marking can be done before the action is executed.

The *Text* section contains settings affecting the source code. The option *Alt-key sets column mode* lets you select column blocks with an [Alt] mouse combination, in the same way that the mouse alone can be dragged to select horizontal line blocks.
A right-click in the Editor normally opens a context menu. When additionally you want the cursor to be moved to the right-click position, *Right mouse button moves cursor* must be enabled.
With *Drag Selection* enabled the left mouse button can be used to move the current selection to another place in the source code. If additionally you press the [Ctrl] button, a copy is made.
Normally a double-click selects a word, a triple-click selects a line. To be able to select a line with a double click, *Double Click selects line* must be enabled.

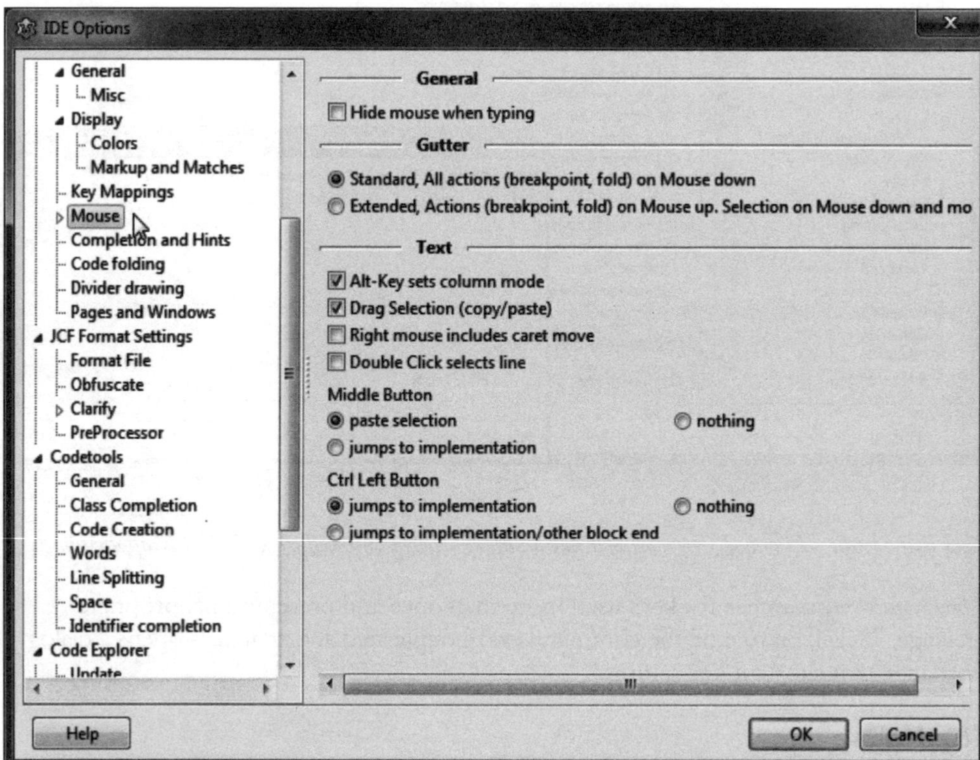

Figure 3.67: The Mouse page in the Display section of the IDE Options dialog

For a triple-button mouse the middle-click action can be assigned to one of three options:

- *Paste selection*: If a copy is active, it is pasted at the click position.
- *Jumps to implementation*: A jump is made to the location in the source code where the current method identifier is implemented (even when located in another unit).
- *Nothing*: No action.

You can set the action for the [Ctrl] left-click combination :

- *Jumps to implementation* :
  A jump is made to the location in the source code where the current method identifier is implemented (even when located in another unit)
- *Jumps to implementation/other block end* :
  When the cursor is not on an identifier but on a bracket or a begin or end, a jump is made to the corresponding bracket or word.
- *Nothing* :
  No action.

You save any changes both on this page and the Advanced page by clicking the *OK* button at the bottom of all the pages.

The Advanced page

The *Advanced* page (see Figure 3.68) lets you make numerous settings for specific mouse behaviour.
This page offers a way to avoid the Window Manager (or operating system) intercepting clicks, which otherwise would not be available to Lazarus.

However, it is rightly called an *Advanced* page, and many users will not have a need for it. Because Lazarus has to run on several operating systems, a general setting will not suffice (or would have to be limited just to the common ground between all operating systems).

You initiate settings in the middle treeview (to the right of the *Options* navigation treeview), by selecting the area of interest (say Text, as in the illustration).
The larger window then lists the possible mouse actions.

The *Change*, *Add* and *Delete* buttons above let you implement your desired changes.
The treeview shows that a click on 'normal' *Text* can trigger a different action from a click on *Selection* text. It is possible (in theory) to have distinct actions for the left, middle and right mouse button, just as for single, double, triple and quadruple clicks, but not every platform permits the use of every combination.
For instance on Windows a triple and quadruple click can be set only for the left mouse button.

An action should be set only when you are sure that the action will be correctly executed. After all a computer doesn't know if you wanted to execute a double-click followed by a single-click or whether a triple-click was meant.
Additionally the mouse clicks can be combined with the [Shift], [Ctrl] and [Alt] buttons. You can set a priority for overlapping or ambiguous clicks.

The configuration with the highest priority (the lowest number) is the preferred one.
The lower table shows the actions attached to the same button.
This helps you locate conflicts more quickly.
The settings can be saved to and loaded from a file.

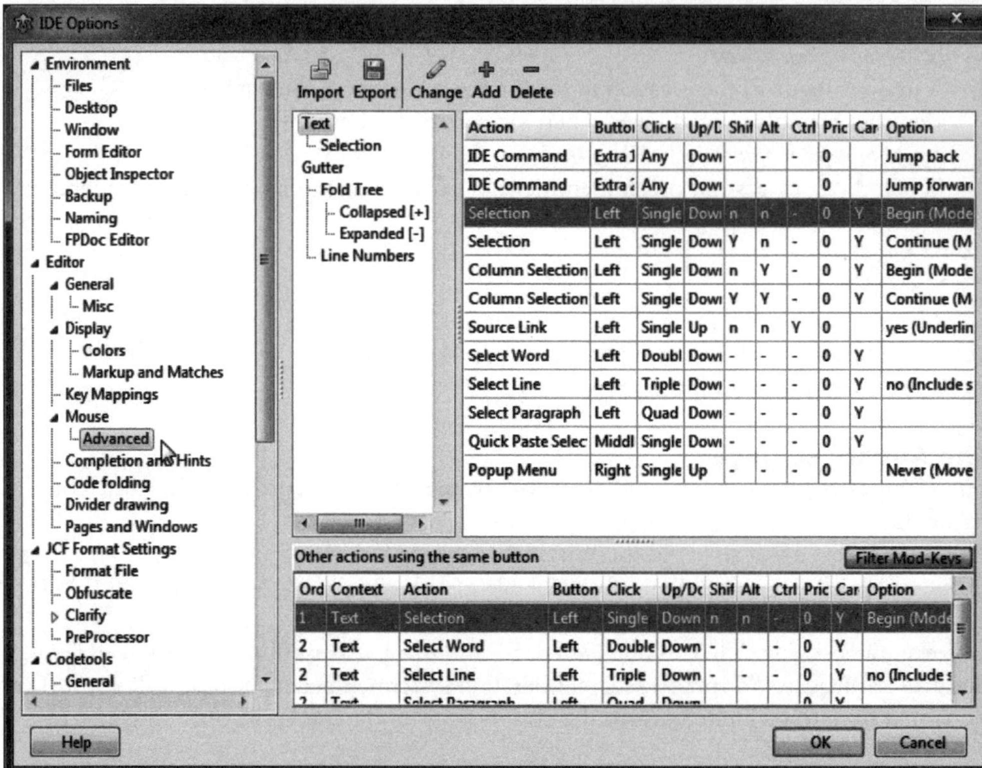

Figure 3.68: The Advanced page for Mouse settings in the Editor section of the IDE Options dialog

The Completion and Hints page

[The *Completion and Hints* page holds settings previously found under *Automatic features* (no longer existing) which were not relocated to the *Markup and Matches* page].

Like the *Markup and Matches* page the *Completion and Hints* page controls functions which run in the background automatically, for instance hinting and auto completion.

Auto remove empty methods is executed when saving a unit.
If the option is enabled and the main class (normally the form, for instance *TForm1*) contains published methods that have no assigned code (an empty `begin ... end` construct), these methods are removed.

When you enable the *Add close statement for Pascal blocks* option, the IDE automatically adds an *end;* when the user types *begin* and presses the [Enter] key.
Enabling *Show declaration hints* causes useful informational 'tooltip' hints to show.

Declaration hints give information about the declaration of an identifier if the cursor pauses on it (the delay before the hint appears is set in the trackbar below).

For instance if *Show declaration hints* is enabled, and the cursor pauses on *TForm*, the hint will show:

```
type TForm          TForm: class
c:\lazarus\lcl\forms.pp (691,3)
```

giving the type, the declaration statement, and the unit where the identifier is declared, and the line number and position of the declaration in that unit file.
Show value hints while debugging causes the IDE to try to evaluate the expression at the cursor in a tooltip. This works best for simple variables such as integers and booleans.
Sometimes filenames or paths are too long to fit within the control where they are displayed in the IDE.
To get the cut-off section to display in a tooltip (overwriting other components), set the *Show long line hints* combobox to a value other than *Never.*
The display options are *Extend right only*, *Extend some left* and *Extend far left.*
The delay before such long line hints are shown is set in the trackbar above the combobox.

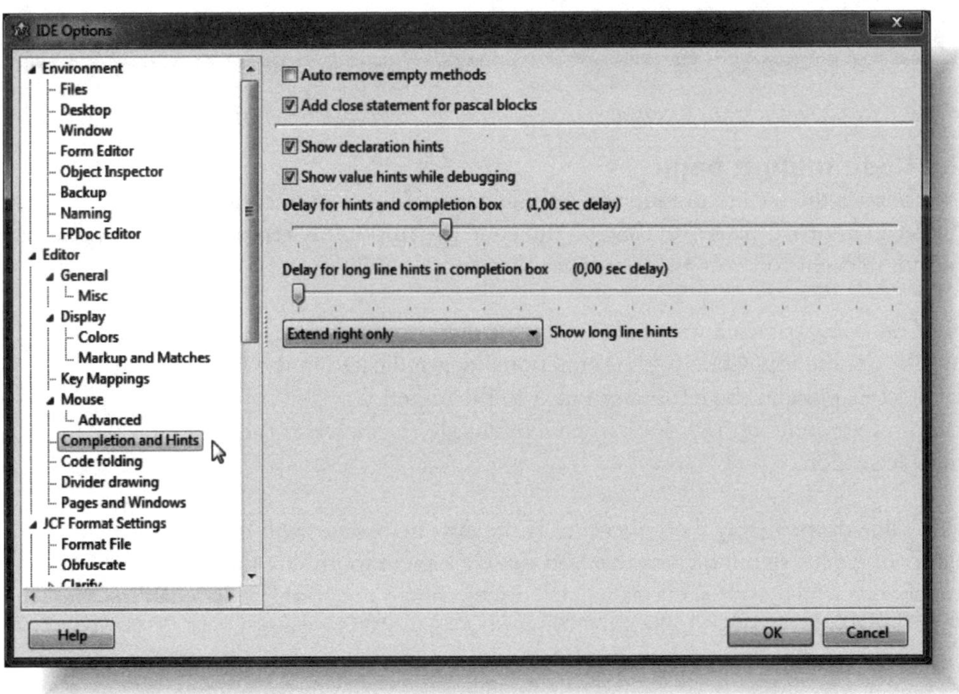

Figure 3.69: The Completion and Hints page in the Editor section of the IDE Options dialog

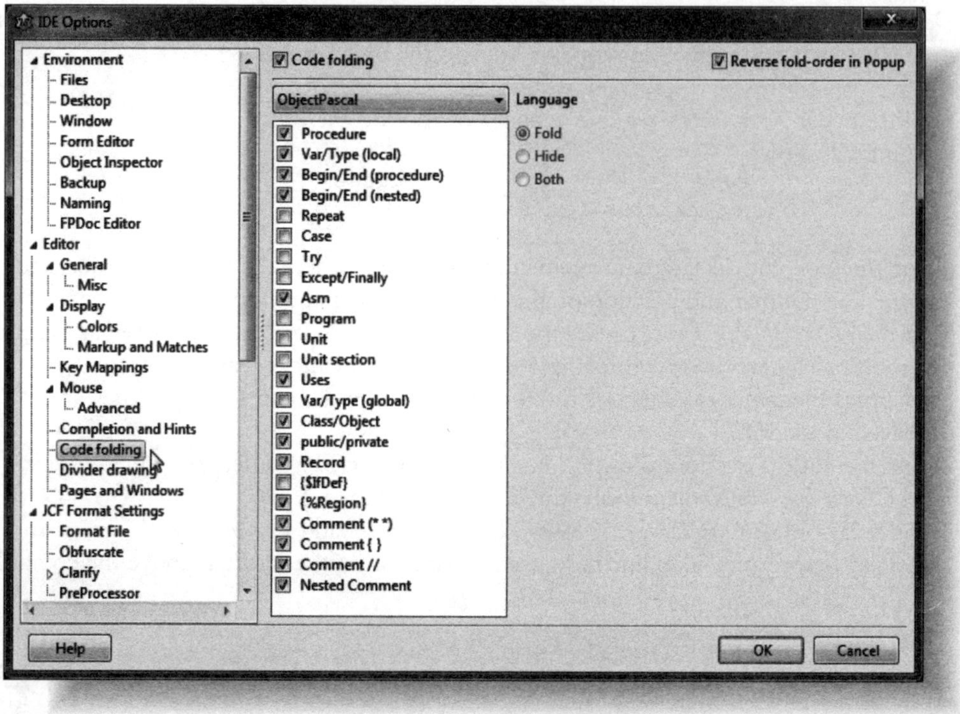

Figure 3.70: The Code folding page in the Editor section of the IDE Options dialog

The Code folding page

Code folding is the facility to hide and unhide parts of the source code, which can improve your overview of the code by temporarily removing parts of the code that not relevant for your focus at that moment.

The *Code folding* page allows you to enable or disable code folding using the *Code folding* checkbox at the top. Code folding functionality is indicated in the Editor by small grey [–] or [+] icons place in the left margin next to the gutter.
You can hide code in the Editor when a minus sign is shown at the beginning of the hideable section.

A grey line drops below the [–] icon to show how many lines will be hidden by clicking that icon. A plus sign indicates that you can click there to unhide that section.
You choose which code sections will be susceptible to code folding by enabling the checkbox for the corresponding section on the code folding page.

For instance, enabling the *Uses* checkbox will put a [–] icon in front of every *uses* statement in your code, so that each *uses* section can be folded (or unfolded) with a single click. The {%Region} directive allows you to define any arbitrary region to be folded (irrespective of the Pascal syntax it may or may not include).
If you find you gather too many hidden sections in a unit, it is advisable to think about splitting the unit into two or more units.

The Divider drawing page

The Editor has the ability to draw horizontal dividers between blocks of code to help a programmer to see at a glance where a block starts and ends.
You instruct the Editor about how you want this functionality to work on the *Divider drawing* page. You can define in detail what constitutes a 'block' for each language and block type.

Divider lines can be configured in detail too.
For example, if you click on *Procedure/Function* in the list of 'blocks' three control settings appear to the right of the list: *Draw divider level, Line color* and *Nested line color.*
You can choose to have a divider after every top-level procedure or function by setting the *Draw divider level* to 1. Or you can include nested functions up to a desired level (2 or more).

You can have dividers after the following logical breaks:

Unit Sections	i. e. implementation, interface, initialization.
Uses Clause	helpful if it becomes multi-line.
Var/Type	any var, type or const block at the top level (not in a procedure).
Var/Type (local):	any var, type or const block inside a procedure. The nesting level indicates how deeply the procedure is nested (since var blocks cannot nest themselves) .
Class/Struct:	class, record or object declarations. The nesting level is for records defined inside a class.
Class/Struct(local)	same as above if used inside a type declaration local to a procedure.
Procedure/Function	if you accept the default enabled setting for Use right margin colour, the faint line drawn matches the code folding line (if used).
Begin/End	includes case and repeat, but not try...except. The nesting is counted to the containing procedure.
Try/Except	identifies the final end; of a try-finally or try-except block from other end; statements.

Note: unfinished blocks (a `begin` with no `end`) can fool the highlighter, and single-line blocks are ignored.

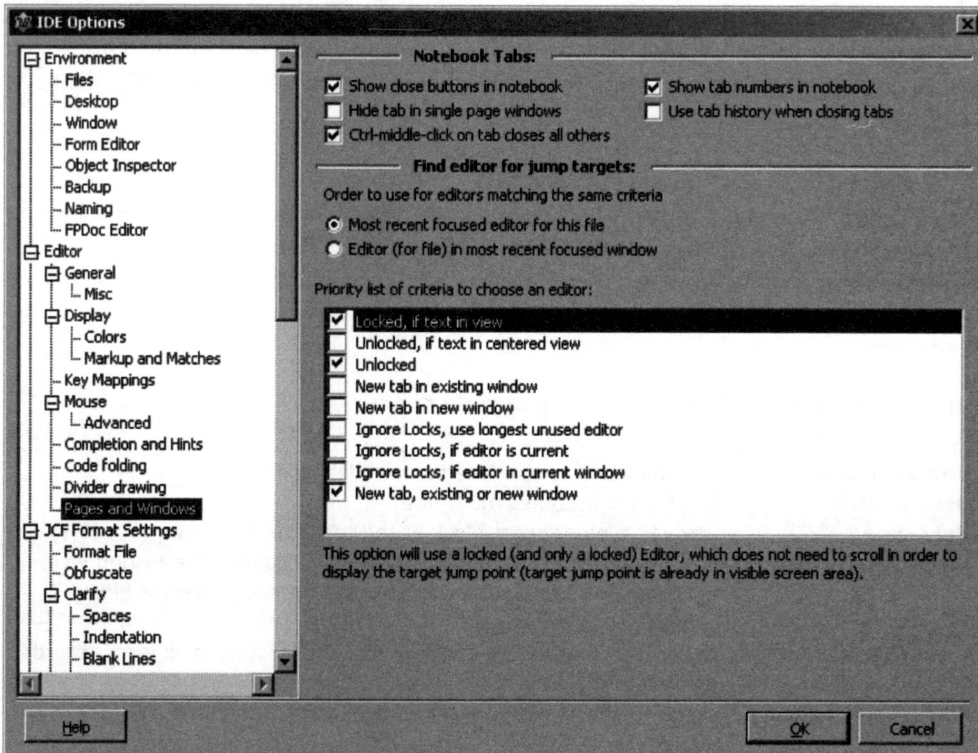

Figure 3.71: The Pages and Windows page in the Editor section of the IDE Options dialog

The Pages and Windows page

Pages and Windows is a relatively new page in the *Options* dialog which collects together several settings governing how the IDE works when you have more than one file open in the Editor.

Notebook Tabs section
The option *Show close buttons in notebook* places a close button [X] on each tab when enabled (this option does not work under Windows).
No tab is shown if you only have only one file open in the editor and you enable *Hide tab in single page window*. The name and modified status ("*") of the file is shown in the window's title.

Enabling *Ctrl-middle-click on tab closes all others*, closes all pages of the notebook, except the one clicked on, when you [Ctrl] click the *middle* mouse button on a tab.
Enabling the option *Show tab numbers in notebook* places a number on each tab showing the order in which the files were opened.

Use tab history when closing affects which of the remaining open files will be focused after the previous file is closed. Enabling this option gives the most recently active page the focus. Disabling this option gives focus to the page with the highest number.

Find editor for jump targets section
You can open several Editor windows for the same file in Lazarus.
Normal editor navigation, such as page up or down, simple find and replace, next occurrence of word and so on work as if the current window were the only Editor window open.
If you have more than one Editor window open for a file and none of them is focused (say because you have opened a search dialog) and you want to jump to a new location in the file which the search dialog has found for you, then which Editor window will you jump to?
The *Find editor for jump targets* section lets you set a preference for which duplicate file Editor window should be the target for the jump.

The setting affects the action when clicking on a find-in-files result, when clicking a compiler message, when jumping to a bookmark or history point, when jumping to a declaration (in another file, if the other file has more than one Editor) and so on.
In some cases it can also affect Codetools jumps (jumps to a declaration or between *interface* and *implementation*) within the same file.

For example, if you jump to the declaration in the interface, and the declaration is already shown in another Editor window of the same file, you may want to switch to the other Editor window. By default Lazarus will use the current Editor.
Or if you jump to a different file, it will use the most recently used Editor for that file.

Order to use for editors matching the same criteria
If, after evaluating the file window priorities, more than one Editor window can be used to display whatever code you requested to jump to, Lazarus will choose the Editor according to the radiobutton selected here.

- *Most recent focused editor for this file* (the default setting).
  Lazarus remembers when each Editor was last focused. It will re-focus the Editor that was most recently focused. This might be the currently active Editor, if the current Editor displays the requested file and matches the jump criteria.

- *Editor (for file) in most recent focused window.*
  With this setting Lazarus looks at the window that holds each Editor. It re-focuses the most recently focused window (including the current active window).

You can change how the target Editor for any of the above actions is to be found:

- When you jump to a code location that is already within the visible screen area of one of the Editors, but not showing in the editor you used most recently.
  The above default would take you to the last focused editor, which would have to scroll to reach your target. You may instead want Lazarus to use the Editor that is already at the correct location.

- When you have scrolled an Editor to an important location (say a complex data structure you need to keep referring to), and you do not want Lazarus to move that location out of view, i. e. you want Lazarus to always use another window as the jump target, and not disturb the one you have set up. In this case you can "lock" the page that you do not want to scroll, and force Lazarus to use another Editor.

In many cases the settings lead to the same result. But consider the following example :
The current active window has an Editor for file A, but it currently shows file B.

File A is also shown in another window and the Editor for A in the other window was used more recently than the one in the current window.
Then you select a find-in-files-result for file A.
With *Last editor focus* it will select the editor in the other window, with *Last window focus* it will select the editor in the current window.

Priority list of criteria to choose an editor
If Lazarus needs to find an editor in order to jump to the code you requested, then it will work down this priority list and use the first editor which matches the jump criteria.
If the criteria matches more than one editor, *Order for editors matching the same criteria* is applied.

- *Locked, if text in view*: Will check if any locked Editor already has the requested target in its visible screen area.

- *Unlocked, if text in centred view*: Similar to *Locked, if text in view*. The 'centred view' is the area of the text where a jump does not scroll the Editor. Depending on the size of your window, if you jump to the first or last few lines on the screen the Editor will scroll. However, currently some jumps force a reposition of the Editor, and will scroll anyway. This is a separate option, because a locked editor is always assumed to be intentionally located at its present position. An unlocked editor may just happen to be at the same location. Choosing this option is therefore more likely sometimes to unexpectedly change the window or Editor.

- *Unlocked* : Any unlocked Editor. Note that many of the other criteria (except those that explicitly say *locked only*), will also check for unlocked Editors themselves. Disabling this option often makes no difference.

- *New tab in existing window*: If no unlocked Editor is found, then open a new tab in an existing window. If there is no window that does not already have a locked Editor for this file, then no tab will be opened and the next criteria is evaluated.

- *New tab in new window*: If no unlocked Editor is found, then open a new tab in a new window, even if there are other windows in which this Editor could also have been opened. This will always work, so further criteria are never evaluated.

- *Ignore Locks, longest unused editor*: If no unlocked tab is found, then locks will be ignored. The Editor which has been unused (unfocused) for the longest time will be used. This will always work, so further criteria are never evaluated. The 'longest unfocused time' is always evaluated by the Editor's focus order (not the time the windows were focused).

- *Ignore Locks, if editor is current*: If no unlocked tab is found, and the current active Editor is an editor of the requested file, then the lock of the current active Editor is ignored and it is used. If the current active Editor displays another file, the next criterion will be used.

- *Ignore Locks, if editor in current window*: If no unlocked tab is found, and there is an Editor of the requested file in the current active window, then that Editor is used and its lock is ignored. If there is no Editor for the file in the current active window, the next criterion will be used.

- *New tab, existing or new window*: This is the default fallback behaviour and cannot be disabled (the checkbox is permanently checked). If no Editor was found, a new Editor page is opened, if possible in an existing window, otherwise in a new window.

About Page-Locking
Page locking functionality is accessed from the context menu of each Editor (the *Lock Page* menu item). Clicking on this menu item to enable it locks that Editor window, and puts a message in the status bar saying *Locked*.
It tells Lazarus that you want to freeze this Editor at its current location, and scrolling (both via mouse and via keyboard movement keys) is disabled until you unlock the page.
If a page is locked and you try to jump to a location in your code (bookmark, declaration, find in file results) then Lazarus will use another Editor (of the same file) to display the target location. Incremental search and simple search/replace are not considered jumps, and therefore relocate the Editor.

The JCF Format settings page

You will only see this page in the most recent versions of Lazarus.
Versions up to 0.9.28 did not install the JCF Format package by default (though you could install it manually) as the very latest versions do.
Since its integration into Lazarus is a work in progress, details of settings for this formatting tool are not covered here.

The Code Tools pages

The Lazarus IDE uses a purpose-written library called *Codetools* to analyse Pascal source code (whether Object Pascal, Delphi or Kylix). To find Pascal sources, search paths and compiler flags are needed when searching for $IFDEFs.

These values are defined by rules, the so-called *Define Templates*.
Codetools manages a series of values for every directory, and every unit in that directory shares the same values (Paths and Flags).
Therefore you should only place two packages or projects in the same directory when you want them to share the same settings.
Otherwise this directory-based system permits the use of an indefinite number of different sources at the same time (for instance, Free Pascal and Delphi source code, or code for two different Free Pascal versions).
The IDE doesn't have to be restarted and nothing has to be recompiled.
The compiler of course, can handle only one source type.

The General page

Additional Source search path for all projects gives lazy programmers the opportunity to organize a package, and gives programmers who don't want to share their package or project the ability to enter a global search path here.

The *Jumping (e. g. Method Jumping)* section
Adjust top line due to comment in front: When you jump from a method declaration to its implementation, the IDE attempts to position the source code in such a way that the first line shown in the Editor is the first line of the procedure. Normally comments in front of a procedure belong to the procedure. Enabling this setting ensures that after the jump the editor scrolls to show the comment too.
Center Cursor Line: When jumping from the procedure body to the declaration (in class or interface), the IDE will place the cursor at the centre of the target line.
Cursor beyond EOL: When the IDE jumps to a new position, it is permitted to jump to any position, even if this lies beyond the end of the line.
Skip forward class declarations: When enabled, jumps ignore any forward declarations altogether.
Recently Lazarus has offered a new way to set *indentation*, based on *example code*. You can accept the formatting in the provided example, or write your own differently formatted example which the IDE will parse to discover how you want indenting to operate.
This pattern will be copied for auto-indenting. You tell the IDE where to find your own formatted example at *Example file*.

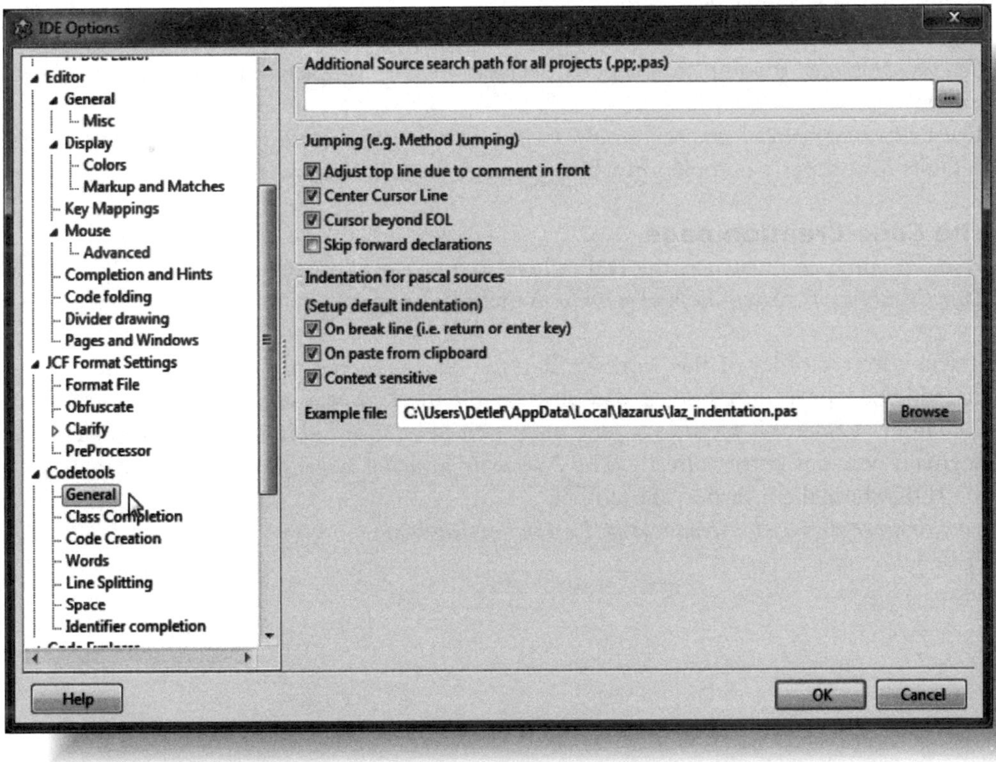

Figure 3.72: The General page in the CodeTools section of the IDE Options dialog

The Class Completion page

Settings for the way Codetools generates new source code are found on the two pages *Class Completion* and *Code Creation.*

Class part insert policy: new variables and methods can be inserted in the class declaration either *Alphabetically* or *Last* (at the end of the declaration).

Method insert policy: means where the method body is inserted in the implementation section, *Alphabetically*, *Last* (at the end of the other method implementations), or in *Class order* (following the order of method declarations in the *interface* section). When you want Codetools to group methods and properties separately during class completion, the setting *Mix methods and properties* should be disabled.
If the order is of no importance this option can stay enabled.

Header comment for class adds a header comment in front of the class declaration.
For instance, at the definition of *TForm1* the comment {*TForm1*} would be added.
Implementation comment for class adds the same comment as at the declaration before the first method in the *implementation* section.
The *Property completion* section offers the following options:
Complete properties: Incomplete property declarations are completed if you enable this setting.
The fields *Set property Variable, Variable prefix, Stored postfix, Write prefix,* and *Read prefix* are defaults for property completion which you can change if you wish.

The Code Creation page

Procedure insert policy instructs the IDE where to insert new procedure bodies:
Last (i.e. at end of source), In front of methods or *Behind methods.*

If you want the order of the procedures in the *interface* section to be followed when inserting new procedure bodies, you must enable the *Keep order of procedures* option.
Sometimes Codetools requires a dependent unit to be inserted in the uses clause, which normally contains entries already. The *New units are added to uses sections* setting instructs the IDE where the insertion should fall:
First, In front of related, Behind related, Last or *Alphabetically.*

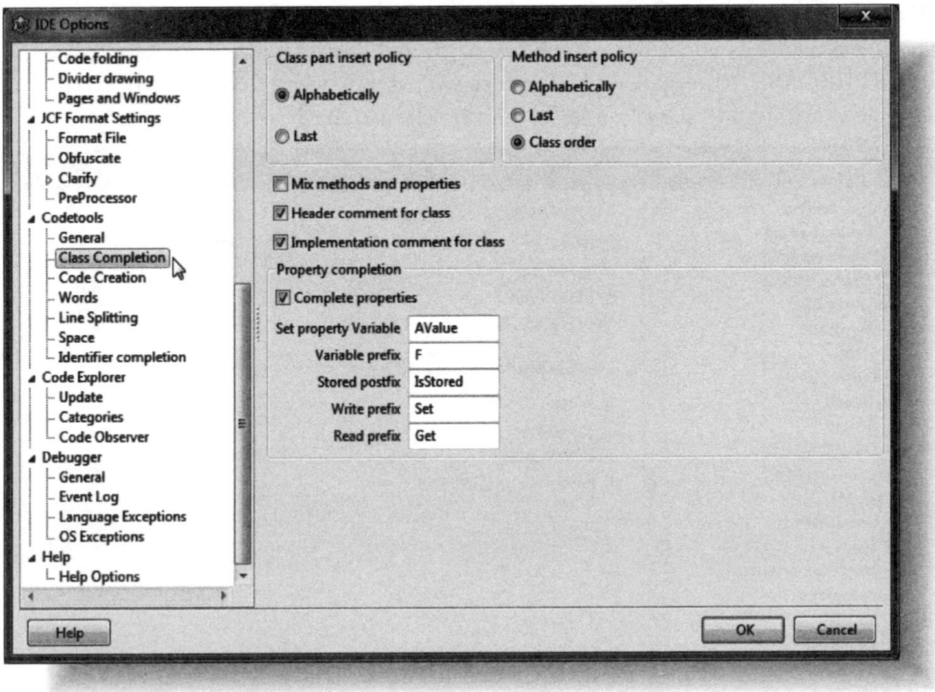

Figure 3.73: The Class Completion page in the CodeTools section of the IDE Options dialog

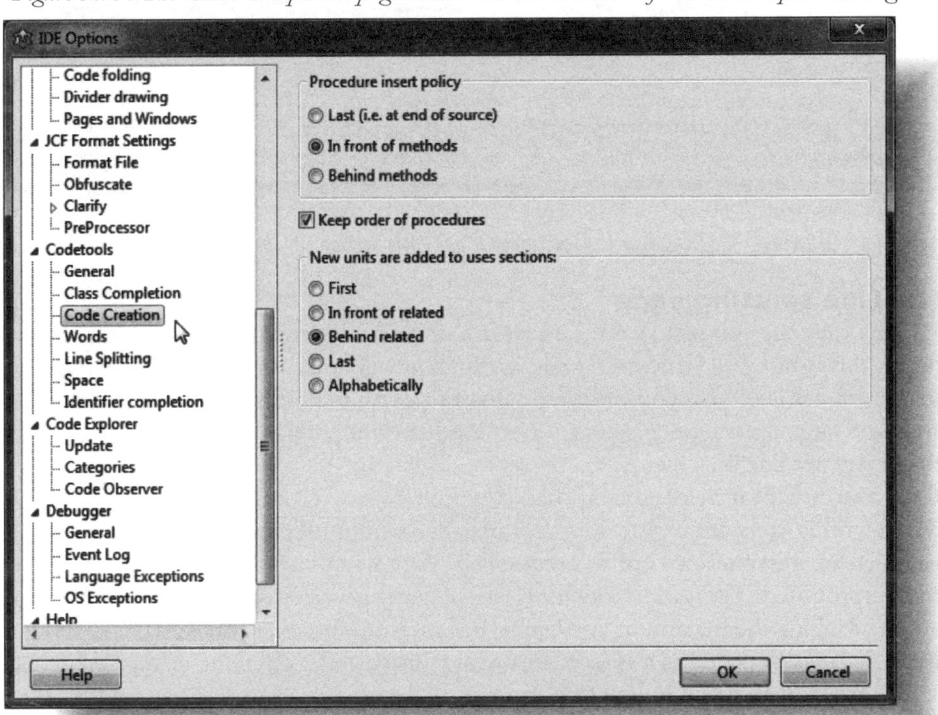

Figure 3.74: The Code Completion page in the CodeTools section of the IDE Options dialog

The Words page

The *Words* page lets you set how new keywords and new identifiers are written (in UPPERCASE, lowercase or Mixed case with the first letter capitalised).
If you don't want any automatic reformatting choose the *None* radiobutton.

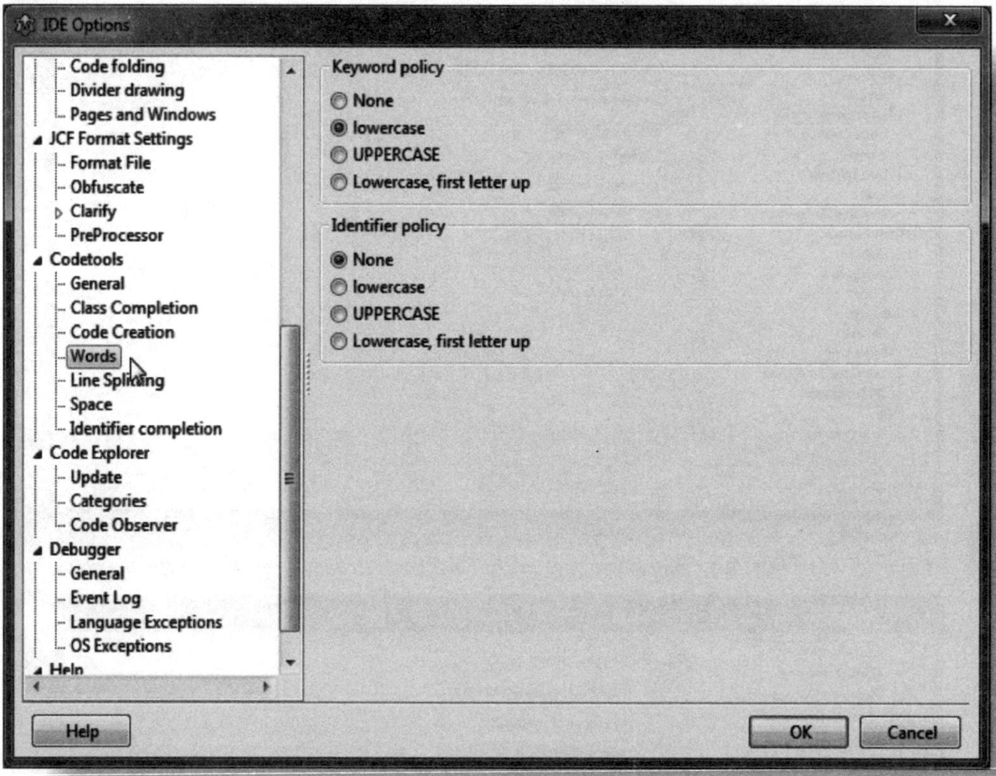

Figure 3.75: The Words page in the CodeTools section of the IDE Options dialog

The Line splitting page

Theoretically the complete source code of a unit could be written as a single line, but clearly this is not well structured code. Often you will limit yourself to a maximum of 80 characters per line. This convention originates from a period before the advent of the GUI and large (or multiple) screens. Text mode permitted a maximum of 25 lines of 80 characters per line onscreen.
The Lazarus Editor marks the 80 character limit with a vertical line.
When writing complex expressions (for instance with multiple nesting) it may be that the complete expression does not fit on one line. With wrapping, the readability should not be compromised. Therefore Codetools offers many possible options for wrapping lines, or for changing the maximum line length before wrapping is enforced.
The *Line Splitting* page has a *Preview* area which displays the effect of changes you make before they are saved with the *OK* button.

The Space page

You can improve the readability of your code by judicious insertion of spaces around new elements. The *Space* page offers numerous options for customising the automatic insertion of space characters as you type.
The *Preview* window displays the effect of enabling and disabling the many options.
If automatic features like this annoy you, simply disable all the options to turn the feature off altogether.
You need to take care if you combine these options with the JCF Format settings, as it is not clear what results if the two settings conflict.

The Identifier completion page

Various automatic Editor features can be enabled or disabled on the *Identifier completion* page. Pascal statements normally end with a semicolon, and enabling *Add semicolon* will insert the semicolon for you.
At the *Identifier completion* page you can set whether the CodeTools should add a semicolon.
The same goes for the := operator when assigning values and properties.
Add assignment operator := will insert it if enabled.

Identifier completion is operational only when *Automatically invoke after point* is enabled. After inserting a point (for instance with *Form1.*) a selection list appears with all available properties and methods for *Form1.*
As you type more characters the list becomes shorter.
If you choose an incorrect entry, just delete the inserted text including the point, and type a new point which will invoke identifier completion again.
If the identifier has several sections (for instance *Form1.Button1.Color*) you can invoke completion after typing each point. The *Add parameters brackets* option will enable automatic adding of brackets following parameters too.

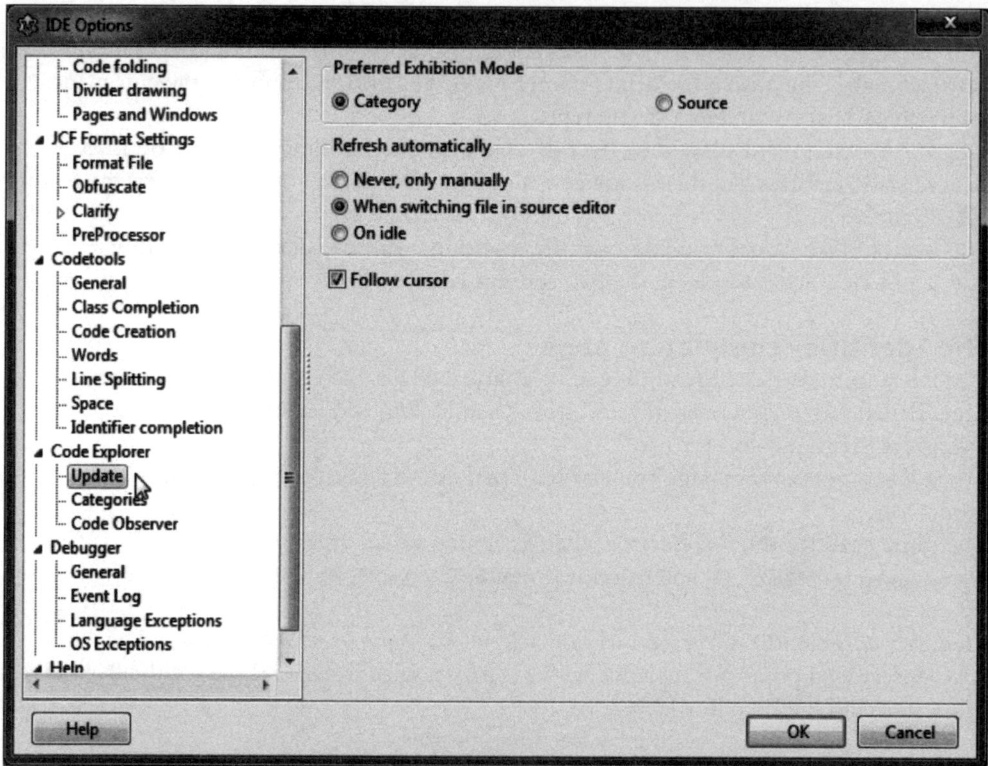

Figure 3.76: The Update page in the Code Explorer section of the IDE Options dialog

The Code Explorer pages

Since Lazarus 0.9.28 the settings for the *Code Explorer* have been integrated into the *IDE Options* dialog.

The Update page

In the *Preferred Exhibition Mode* section you set whether the Code Explorer listings are grouped by *Category* or shown in the order of the items in the *Source* code.
If you select *Category*, your category preferences can be set on the following page.
The trigger for automatic rescanning is set in the *Refresh automatically* option:
Never, only manually (i. e. only when you click the *Refresh* button),
When switching file in source editor, or *On idle.*

The Categories page

The *Categories* page shows the available categories (which only apply if *Category* is your *Preferred Exhibition Mode*). Enable all the categories you want to see in the Code Explorer. Sorting by category means by *Type*, *Variable*, and so on. The *Code Observer* category lists uncommon or hard to read code fragments. The detailed settings for this are found on the next page.

The Code Observer page

The *Code Observer* page lets you view the IDE's assessment of your code. If enabled it will make observations about suboptimal, unusual or difficult to read coding.
This page instructs the IDE on what observations you want it to make (should your code give rise to such observations). The Code Explorer lets you make a quick search from which perhaps some possible improvements will be evident to you.
The *Show observations about* section lets you determine which difficult to read or poorly coded sections you want pointed out. You can select entire categories to look out for (*Complexity , Empty constructs, Style, Other*), or just enable one or two individual items such as *Unnamed constants* or *Wrong indentation.*
Long procedures lists all procedures containing more lines than the *Line count of procedure treated as long* field will allow. The default is 50 lines. If you encounter such a procedure, it is advisable to split it with *Edit →Extract procedure.*
The option *Many parameters* lists all procedures that contain more parameters than the *Parameter count treated as many* field allows. The default is six parameters.
Many nested procedures lists all procedures that contain more nested sub-procedures than the *Nested procedures count treated as many* field allows.
The default is three sub-procedures.
Empty procedures lists all procedures that contain no code (comments and directives are ignored). Enabling this option on Linux would find this procedure:

```
begin
  {$IFDEF win32}write('Win32');{$ENDIF}
end;
```

Empty blocks looks for absence of code between *begin* and *end;* and between *repeat* and *until.*

Empty class sections looks for sections like *private, public* or *protected* that contain no code.

Unnamed constants looks for any constants (usually they will be numbers) that have no name assigned. In the field underneath you can enter unnamed constants that you want this search to ignore.

Unsorted visibility lists all unsorted class sections, for instance when a *private* section is placed after a *public* section.

Unsorted members lists all class variables, methods and properties that are not sorted alphabetically.

Wrong indentation produces a list of all lines with suspect indentation.

Published properties without default lists all properties that do not have a default value, such as:

```
Published
  Property Flag: Boolean read FFlag write SetFlag;
```

Since compiler version 2.2.4 such properties are treated as if they were defined with *nodefault*. The lower part of the *Code Observer* page has two *Ignore* fields containing several values (which can be removed) or added to with you own values. The *Ignored* values are not listed by the Code Observer even though they belong to a category being looked out for. *Ignore constants in next functions* is useful for instance to ignore frequently used SQL strings. If, for instance, `.ParamByName` is entered in the field, lines like

```
SQLQuery1.Params.ParamByName('FieldName').AsString := …
```

are not taken into account.

The Debugger page

The Debugger settings are discussed in detail near the end of this chapter.

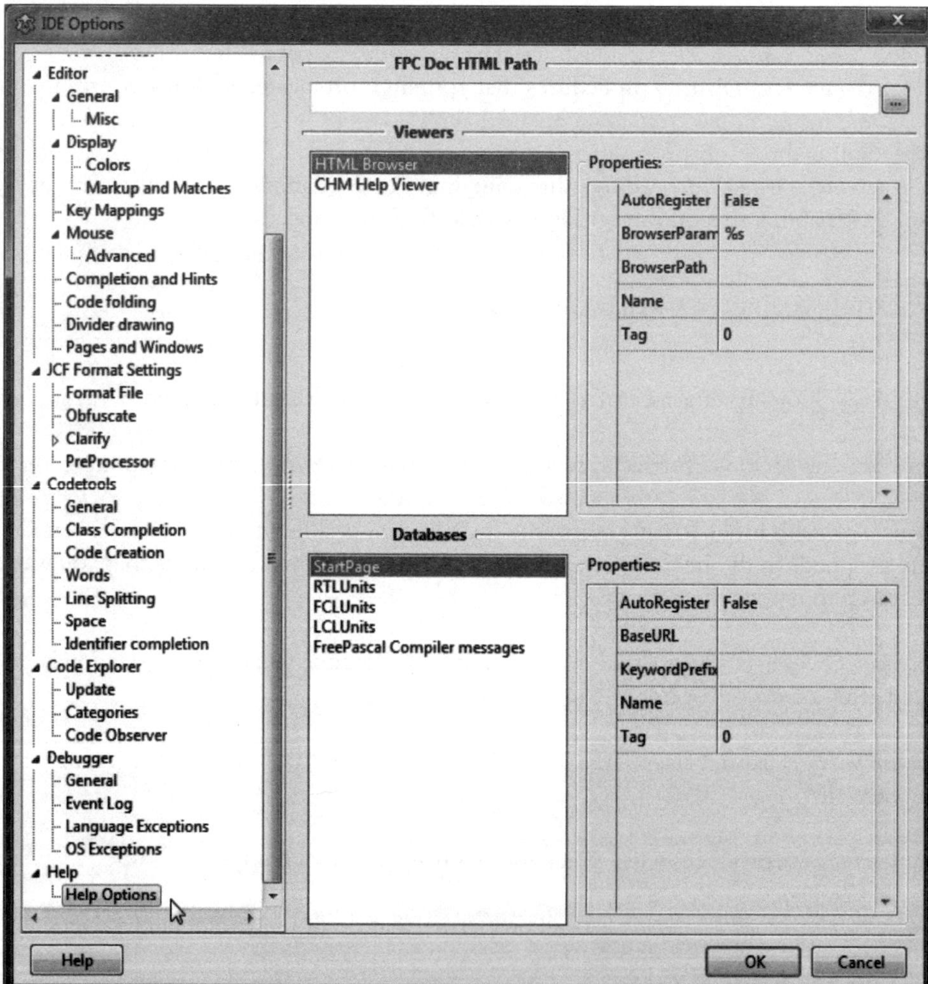

Figure 3.77: The Help Options page in the Help section of the IDE Options dialog

The Help page

The *Help* page lets you set the paths to the available online documentation (for instance for the FCL or the RTL), information which is accessed by pressing the [F1] key.

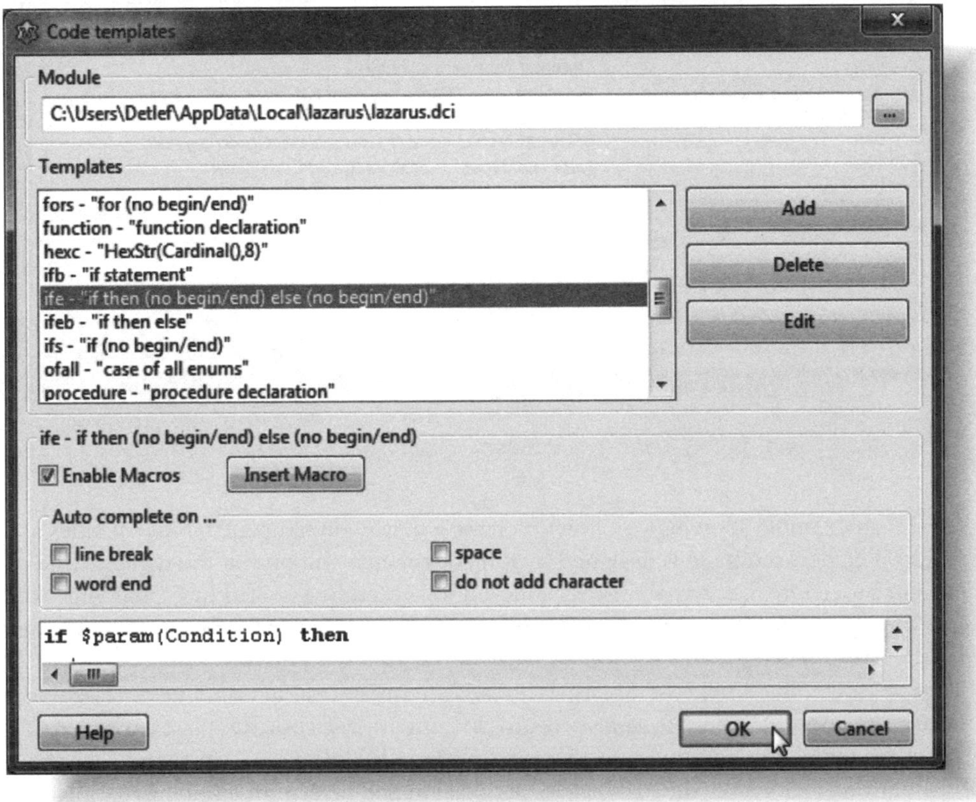

Figure 3.78: The dialog for managing the Code Templates.

The Environment → Code Templates menu option

Code Templates are sections of 'boilerplate' source code (for instance `if ... then ... else`) that can be inserted into your code without you needing to type them in manually.
They are easily invoked via a shortcut key combination.
[Ctrl] [J] calls a selection menu from which you click the desired item to insert the appropriate code. You can invoke the code template more quickly (avoiding the selection dialog) if you know the first few letters that identify the code template you want.
The example above can be invoked directly if you type *ife* and then press [Ctrl] [J].
Code templates can contain not only text but macros as well.
You can also add your own macros by creating a design time package and using the *macrointf.pas* file from the *IDEIntf* package.
The *Code templates* dialog accessed through *Environment* → *Code Templates* lets you *Edit* or *Delete* existing templates and *Add* new ones using the buttons provided. Several templates come installed with Lazarus. Clicking a template in the *Templates* list shows the template code in the field below.

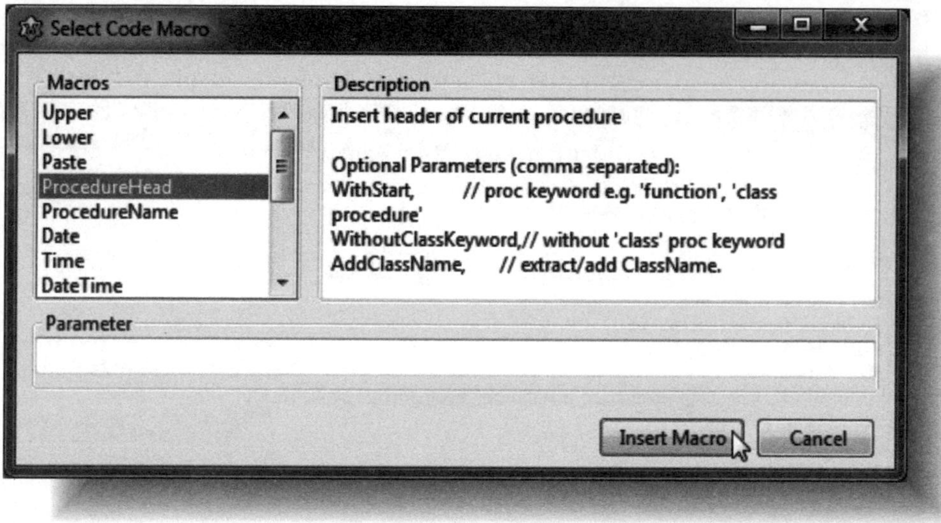

Figure 3.79: The dialog that helps you insert a macro in a Code Template

Here is an example showing you how to create a new code template which includes a macro. The new template is designed to add code which will output the name of the current procedure, i. e. writeln('ProcName'), and should be invoked by typing *wp* [Ctrl] [J]. Use the *Add* button to open the *Add code template* dialog which asks for two simple items.

Type *wp* in the *Token* field (if a there is already a template named *wp*, a new name would have to be chosen). The *Comment* serves to document your code template and does not affect the template operation. For this example type *WriteLn('ProcName')* and click the *Add* button. This closes the *Add code template* dialog and inserts an empty *wp* template in the *Templates* list. In the long field below, type the instruction WriteLn(,|);.
The vertical line '|' is the pipe character (next to the Z key on many keyboards) and represents the new cursor position.
Tick the *Enable Macros* checkbox.
Now place the cursor just after the first bracket and click the *Insert Macro* button.
In the *Select Code Macro* dialog which appears, all available macros are listed at the left.
Scroll until *ProcedureName* is visible and click it.
A description of its function appears in the *Description* field. For this example the *Parameter* field is left empty. Click the *Insert Macro* button and add ' ' to enclose the inserted macro.
The *Code Templates* dialog should now look similar to Figure 3.80.

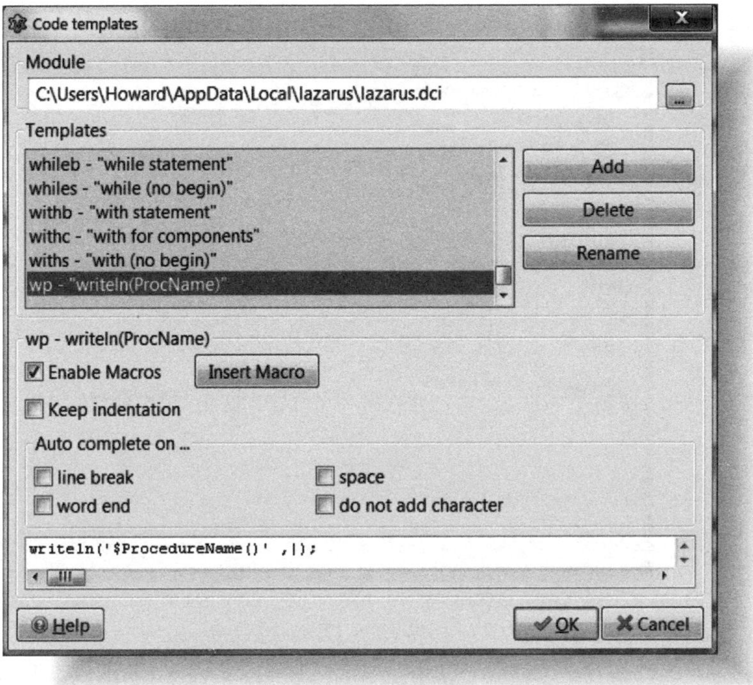

Figure 3.80: The Code templates dialog with the new wp template added

Click *OK* to close the *Code templates* dialog. Now test out the new template. In a method body type *wp*. For instance :

```
procedure TForm1.FormDestroy(Sender: TObject);
begin
  wp|
end;
```

The vertical line | symbolises the cursor here. Then press [Ctrl][J]. If you entered the template correctly the code is expanded to:

```
procedure TForm1.FormDestroy(Sender: TObject);
begin
  WriteLn('TForm1.FormDestroy', | );
end;
```

The Environment → CodeTools Defines Editor… menu option

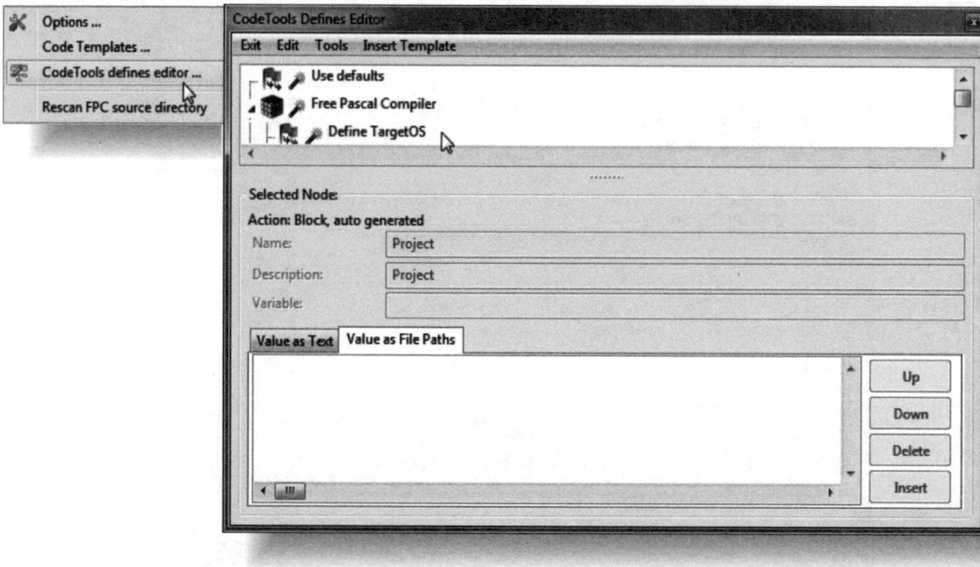

Figure 3.81: The CodeTools Defines Editor dialog

The *Environment → CodeTools Defines Editor…* menu opens a view of the Codetools settings. The values shown are only valid for the Codetools, and do *not* apply to the compiler. Search paths are set by *Environment → Options* settings, by compiler settings, by the Package Editor and by the Project Inspector.
The IDE automatically generates nodes for these values. The *CodeTools Defines Editor* dialog allows you to examine and edit the Define templates for each of these nodes.
All values and variables can contain macros. The dialog is a mini-application with its own menu (*Exit, Edit, Tools, Insert Template*).
After editing templates your changes are saved with *Exit → Save and Exit*, or if you want to reject the changes made use *Exit → Exit without Save.*
Either option closes the editor dialog.
The upper treeview (which can be expanded using the splitter handle just below it) initially shows nodes for:
Use defaults, Free Pascal Compiler, Free Pascal sources, Lazarus sources, Packages and *Projects.*
You begin by expanding a node and clicking on the item you are interested in. Its value (either as *Text* or as *File Path*) is shown in the lower read-only field.
In *Value as File Paths* the text value is split at the semicolons and every path is shown on a separate line.
The item's *Action, Name, Description* and *Variable* (if appropriate) are shown in the middle of the dialog in the *Selected Node* section.
The *Free Pascal Compiler, Free Pascal sources* and *Lazarus sources* nodes are automatically generated and cannot be edited in the dialog.

The *Edit* menu lets you *Move, Insert, Delete* or *Convert* a node.

Move node up moves the selected node ahead of its nearest upper sibling.
Move node down moves the selected node below the nearest lower sibling.
Move node one level up moves the node one level towards its parent.
Move node one level down makes the node a child of the previous sibling.
Insert node below creates a new node and inserts it below the selected node.
Insert node as child creates a new node and inserts it as child of the selected node.
Delete node removes the selected node.
Convert node changes the type of the node.

The following types are available for inserting when editing a node:

Define sets a flag / value for the current directory.
Define Recurse does the same as Define, but takes subdirectories into account as well. With *Undefine* the selected variable is removed from the current definition library.
Undefine Recurse does the same as Undefine, but again takes subdirectories into account as well.
Undefine All does the same as Define, but removes them all. This is helpful for directories that create their own environment (for instance the FPC sources).

The node type *Block* is only available with grouped nodes.
The node type *Directory* generates a valid node for a specific directory only.
The child-nodes are analysed only for the directory specified in *Value*.

With *If* the expression in *Value* is executed and when the result of the compiler is 1, the child nodes are executed.

The syntax is the same as for the compiler. For instance, when the variable *aVariable* is defined, *defined(aVariable)* returns 1, otherwise it returns 0.

With *IfDef,* if the variable is defined, the child-nodes are executed.
With *IfNDef,* if the variable is not defined, the child-nodes are executed.
ElseIf: If all previous *Ifs* return false, the *ElseIf*-node is executed. *ElseIf* is the same as *Else* and *If*.

Else: When all previous *Ifs* or *ElseIfs* return false, this node is executed.
A variable that was assigned an empty value ("") is still assigned. This means that *IFDEF Variable* still returns True. *Delete* eliminates a variable.

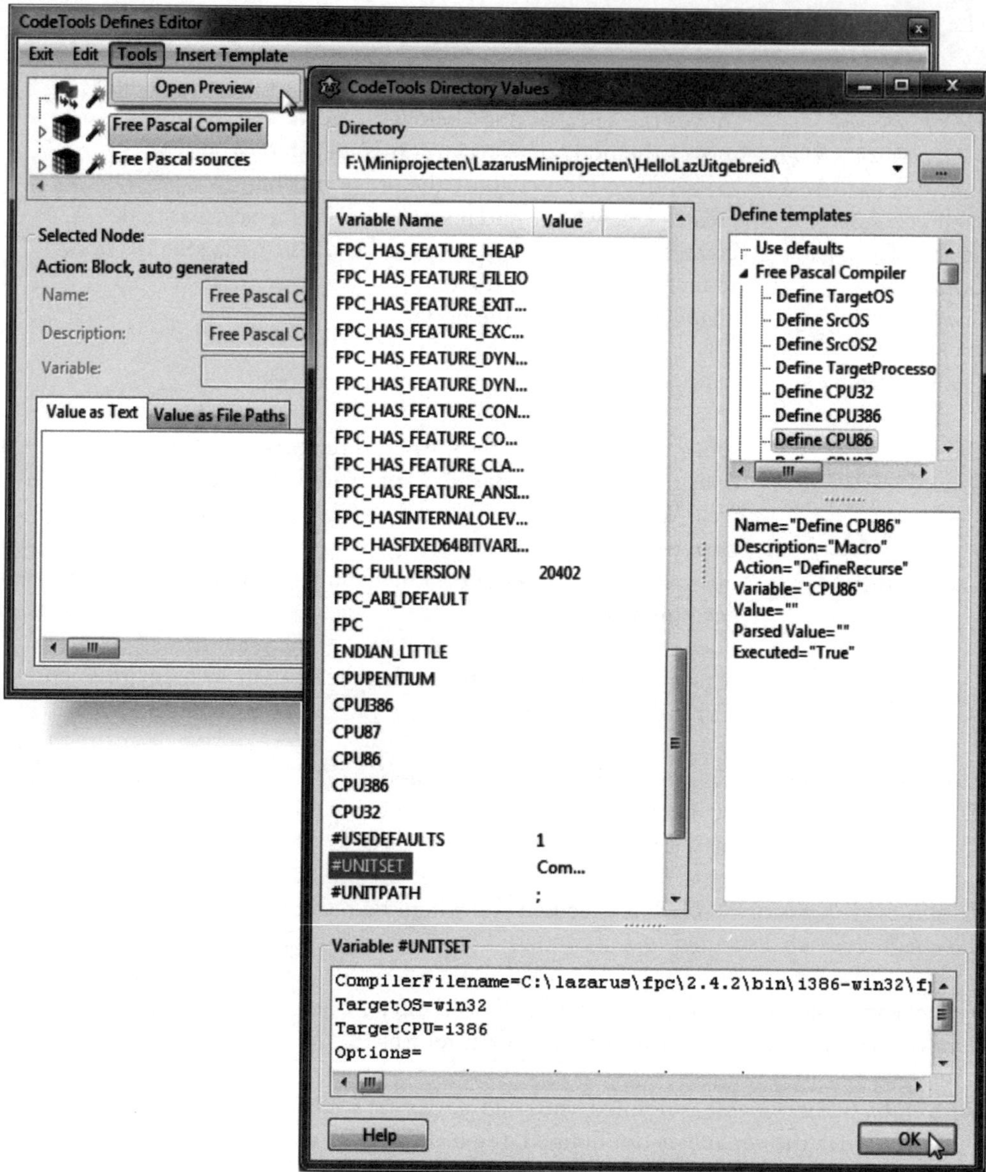

Figure 3.82: The CodeTools Directory Values dialog

The *Tools* menu has only one option, *Open Preview*, which opens the *CodeTools Directory Values* dialog from which further settings can be made. It can be closed again with *OK*, which then returns you to the *CodeTools Defines Editor* dialog.

The *Insert Template* menu creates a new node from the template you select and inserts it below the current node.

There are several templates available :
Free Pascal Project Template, Free Pascal Compiler Template, Free Pascal SVN Source Template, Lazarus Directory Template,
Delphi 5/6/7 Compiler Template, Delphi 5/6/7 Directory Template, Delphi 5/6/7 Project Template,

The *Environment → Rescan FPC source directory* menu option
Clicking *Rescan FPC source directory* refreshes the IDE's knowledge of the directory where the FPC source code is stored. Lazarus uses these files to generate the correct event handlers and when searching for class, procedure and variable declarations.
If you change the directory in the *Environment → Options* settings, it is automatically refreshed, to be sure that Lazarus uses the correct files. However, it can happen that a directory is changed without Lazarus noticing. In this case error messages arise, for instance with *Search → Find Declaration at cursor.* Then the FPC source code files settings in the environment options have to be checked or the FPC source code directory has to be refreshed.

31.11 The Window Menu

The *Window* menu lists all currently open windows. Using this menu is the most convenient way to change from one window to another, because not only are all the IDE windows listed, but also all the windows that belong to the current project.
Project windows are shown at the end of the list. The project windows are identified by the name that is set in the window's *Caption* property (such as *Form1* and so on).
When Lazarus is newly started, the *Window* menu normally contains the following entries: *Source Editor, Object Inspector, Messages* and *Form1*. You may quickly add further entries such as *Project Inspector, Code Browser Components*, further forms, and other windows, so the Window menu can get quite long. Clicking on any of the listed windows gives that window the focus and brings it to the foreground. Naturally the main window itself is not shown, because the Lazarus menu is located in this window and to view this menu the main window must already be in front.
With some widget-sets the individual Pascal code units opened in the Editor are listed (in addition to the forms).

3.1.12 The Help Menu

The *Help* menu contains three items. Recently the main focus for the Lazarus development team has been introducing new features and eradicating bugs. Consequently at the moment, the *Help* options do not yet meet the high standards that would be expected from a comprehensive development tool as sophisticated as Lazarus. On the list of improvements to make before version 1.0, *Help* is near the top of the list.

Figure 3.83: The Help menu

Online help opens a web page with Internet links to pages with fuller information about Lazarus and Free Pascal.
As an open source project, Lazarus lives on the contributions of its users. Part of your contribution might be to report bugs you find. When you click on the *Reporting a bug* menu option, a page is shown from the Lazarus Wiki (`http://wiki.lazarus.freepascal.org/How_do_I_create_a _bug_report`). This describes how to inform the Lazarus developers about the bug you have found. Naturally, this only works if you have a working internet connection. Since the project language is English, the Wiki page is also in English, but other languages are available, and at least some pages can be read in Afrikaans, Arabic, Bahasa, Chinese (simplified and traditional), Czech, Dutch, Finnish, French, German, Hungarian, Italian, Japanese, Korean, Persian, Polish, Portuguese, Romanian, Russian, Slovak, Spanish, Swedish, Ukrainian and Vietnamese.
About Lazarus shows some general information about Lazarus, including the version number and a list of the contributors. Details about the version number as well as the operating system make the allocation of the bug reports easier.
You can copy this information to the clipboard by right-clicking in the version information area, and then pasting it into your bug report.

3.2 Programming Tools available in the IDE

3.2.1 The Object Inspector

The Object Inspector is an important tool for visual programming. In simple cases, changes made through the Object Inspector can complete a program without the need to write any code!
How does Lazarus remember the changes you make in the Object Inspector, because nothing changes in the source code (`.pas` or `.pp` file)? The answer is that property changes are stored in the `.lfm` (short for **L**azarus **f**or**m**) file belonging to the form class. This is a text file, and you can easily edit it outside the Lazarus IDE.
However, to do that you need to understand what the individual items mean.
Because any changes made in the Object Inspector could also be coded manually in the source code, it's up to you to choose between an extensive `.lfm` or `.pas` file.
Normally the Object Inspector is found at the left side of the screen, directly beside the source Editor.
The appearance of the Object Inspector is influenced by the settings made at *Environment → Options → Environment → Object Inspector*. You can have an information box at the lower edge of the Object Inspector, which gives helpful information about the selected property or event.
The uppermost part of the Object Inspector lists all the current project's objects (forms, data modules and components). Clicking on one of the objects shows that object's properties and events in the grid below. This grid-like section has four tabs for the four pages: *Properties*, *Events*, *Favorites* and *Restricted*. Depending on the space available, you may not be able to see all four tabs at the same time without scrolling.
When showing there can be differences between the chosen widget-sets.

On the *Properties* page (see Figure 3.84) you can see all properties of the current object which were declared as published. Unpublished properties have to be changed in the source code, and their values are not shown in the Object Inspector. The two columns in the grid have no headings, but if they did they would be *Property name* and *Value.*

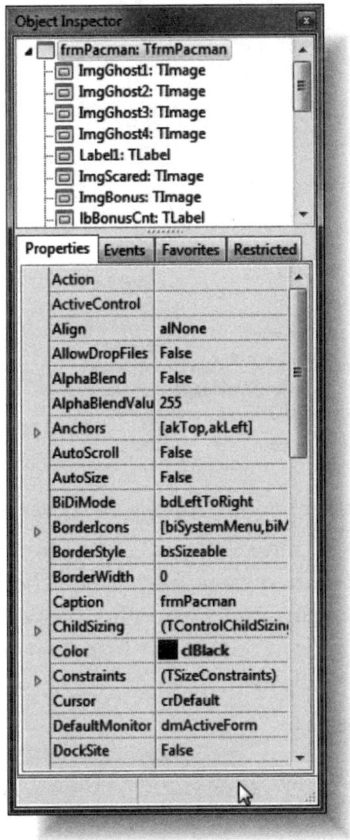

Figure 3.84: The Object Inspector

If the properties affect the visibility of a component, the changes you make in the Object Inspector are seen immediately in the form containing the component. Likewise, changes in the form are immediately shown in the Object Inspector. Sometimes a change in one property leads to a change in another property. For instance when changing the *Name* property of the form, the *Caption* property gets the same value. These dependencies need to be taken into account when multiple properties are changed at once.
To change a property you simply click on the particular value and edit it. Note that changes in the Object Inspector cannot be reversed by *Edit* → *Undo.* When in doubt you should remember the former value.
Some properties are allowed only a limited number of possible values. Such properties reveal their nature when clicking on the *Value* column – the field changes to a combobox. Boolean properties, for instance, having only the value *True* or *False* are such properties. In this case, a double-click on the value toggles it from *True* to *False* or vice versa.

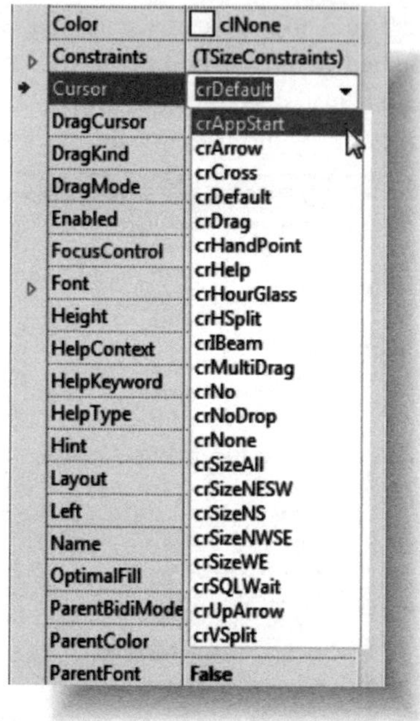

Figure 3.85: The Object Inspector showing the Cursor property's possible values

Naturally, the value can be overwritten manually, but for enumerations it is simpler and less error-prone to select the desired value from a list. There are also properties that do not contain a simple value, but for instance another property or a long string. You cannot then change the property directly in the Object Inspector. This is recognised by the provision of a button with an ellipsis [...].

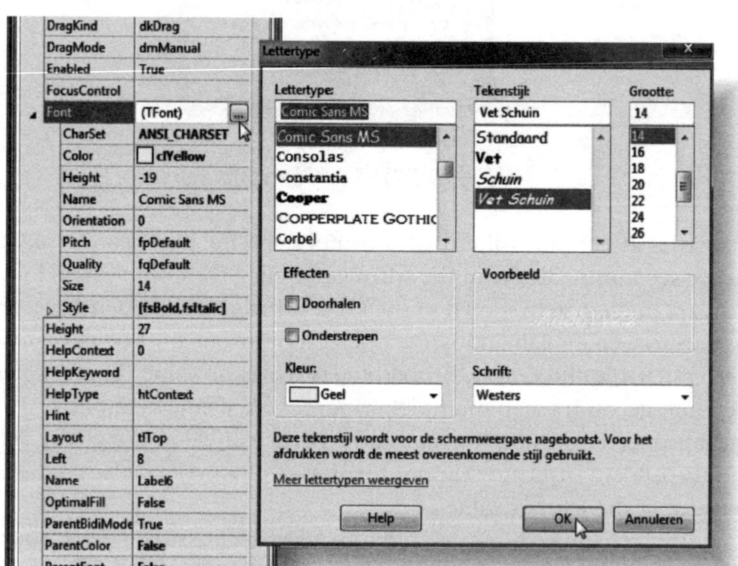

Figure 3.86: The Object Inspector with a [...] property showing a Font editor

To change the property, the […] button needs to be clicked. The editor that opens depends on the type of property that will be changed.

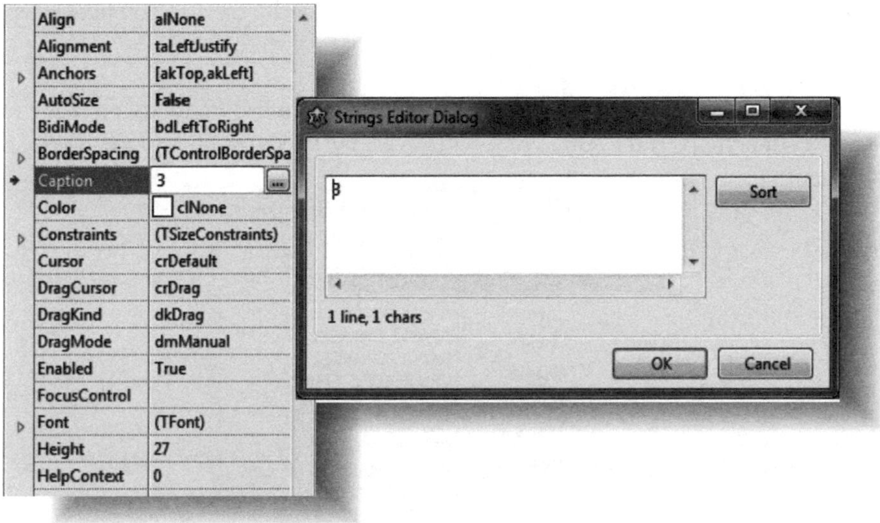

Figure 3.87: A Caption property being changed in a String Editor Dialog

With a click on *OK* the string you entered is accepted.
To keep the Object Inspector display from becoming overcrowded some properties are hidden. These properties can be recognised by the ► icon in front of the property. Depending on the widget-set, another character may be used rather than ►, for instance a + icon.

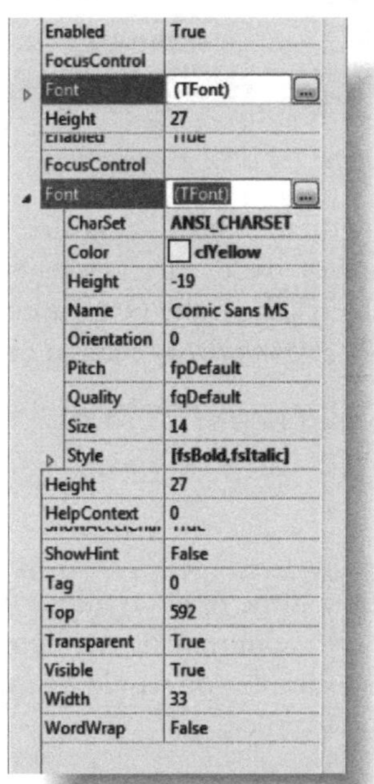

Figure 3.88: The Object Inspector showing a collapsed Font property overlaid with the same property expanded

A click on the ▶ (or +) sign makes the hidden properties visible. The hiding can be stretched out over several nested levels. After a click on the ▶ (or +) sign, it changes into a Δ (or –) sign, to show that the properties following can be collapsed. These properties are indented slightly to distinguish them graphically from the others.

The *Events* page lists all the object's event properties including those that already have procedures attached to an event. The events available vary from component to component

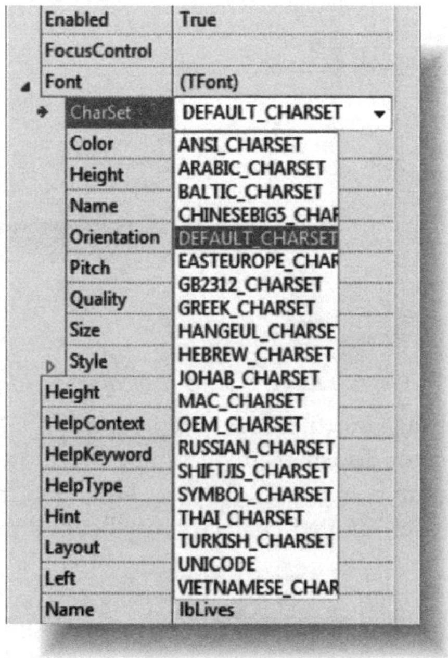

Figure 3.89: The Object Inspector showing editing of a collapsible property

Creating a new event procedure or attaching an existing procedure to an event can be done easily. Double-click on one of the events, and a new procedure body is created in the Editor. For instance a double-click on the *OnClose* event of *TForm1*, writes the following procedure body in the *implementation* section of the form unit:

```
procedure TForm1.FormClose(Sender:TObject; var CloseAction:TCloseAction);
begin

end;
```

Naturally, the method declaration at the *type* definition of *TForm1* is also created. You, the programmer, don't have to worry about making the right call and can focus instead on the content of the method. In this example you would be asking yourself:
"What has to happen when the form closes?"

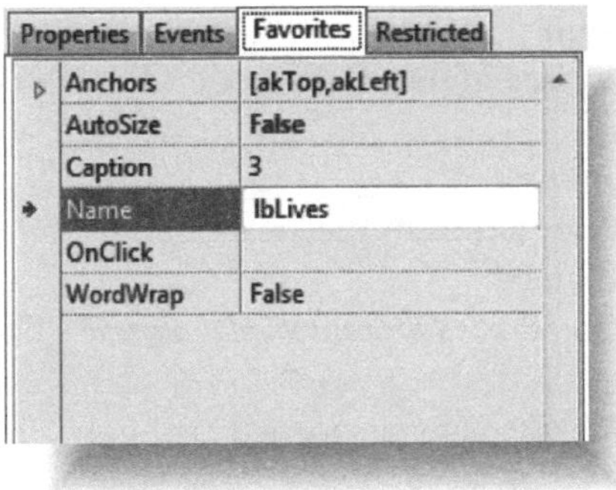

Figure 3.90: The Object Inspector's Favorites page

The *Favorites* page lists frequently chosen *Events* and *Properties* used in the past. When an item has to be changed again, the *Favorites* page often leads to the target more quickly than searching the *Properties* or *Events* pages.

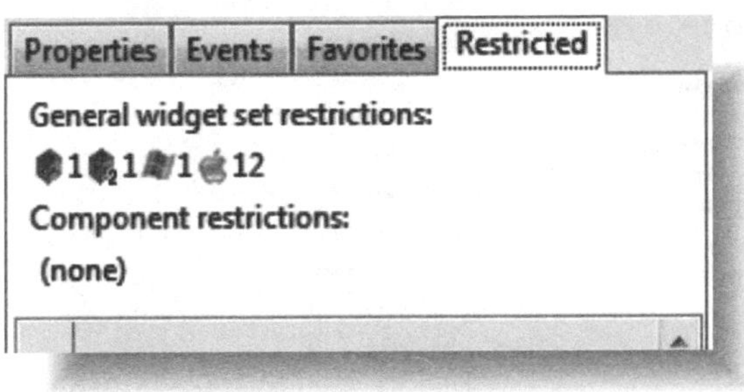

Figure 3.91: The Object Inspector's Restricted page

The *Restricted* page lists those properties that function differently (i. e. with differing limitations) with different widget-sets. In the chosen example, two properties are not available with Mac OS X. As Lazarus developers have no influence on the development of the various widget-sets, you can assume that, generally speaking, such restrictions will remain in the future.

3.2.2 The Source Code Editor

The Editor is the part of the IDE where source code files are edited. It is important that users of an editor find its functionality supportive and not distracting if they are to be productive (since editing is such a central task in software development). Lazarus offers various editing features designed to facilitate development, as well as countless settings that can be tweaked to suit your preferences.

The Editor is based on the *TSynEdit* components (which you can find on the *SynEdit* page of the Component Palette).

You can change Editor settings by right-clicking on the Editor to show the context menu, or via the menu at *Environment → Options... → Editor.*

The context menu options duplicate most of the options accessed via the main menu, so you can choose the most convenient access method for you.

The Editor's context menu

Find Declaration locates the place in the source code where the identifier at the cursor is defined.

Find offers four search options:

- *Procedure Jump*: The cursor jumps to the location in the interface section, where the current procedure is defined.
- *Find next word occurrence* and *Find previous word occurrence* : These are actually self -explanatory.
- *Find in files* : The *Find in files* dialog is opened taking the entry at the cursor as the search item.

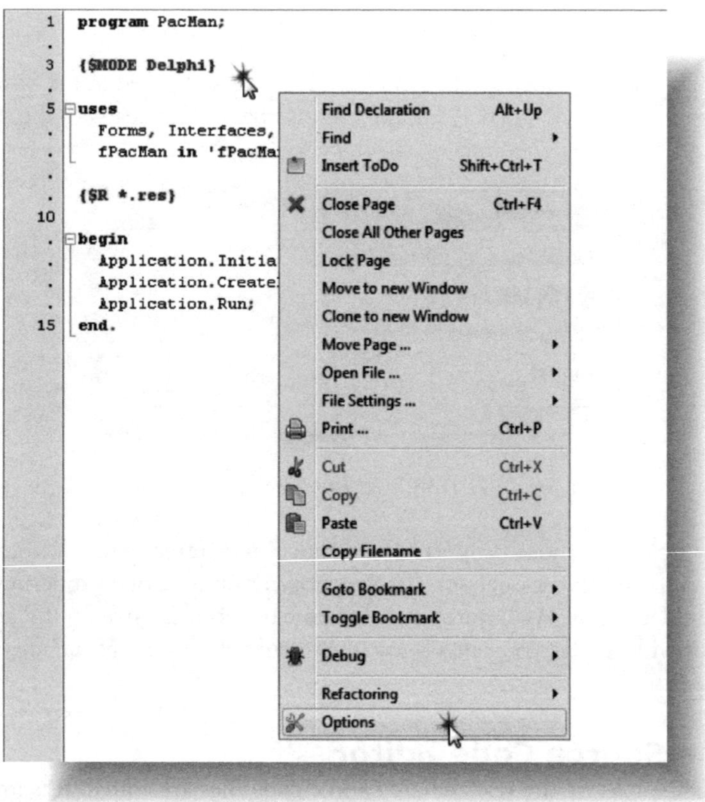

Figure 3.92: The Editor's context menu

With *Insert ToDo* a ToDo comment is inserted at the cursor position.
This comment marks the place in your source code where at some later time you want to do more work. Consider the situation where the code is changed to solve a problem with a dependency. Later on you change the dependency, and then that part of the source code has to be changed back. Inserting a ToDo comment helps you not to forget to remove that change.

In addition to inserting a ToDo comment in your code the *Insert ToDo* dialog comes up, asking for information. The *Text* is the actual content of the comment.

If different ToDos should have different priorities set, a *Priority* field is available (which accepts a simple integer to denote priority). Especially when several developers are working on the same source code, it makes sense to include the commenter's name (in the *Owner* field). You can also categorise the comment. A typical comment might look like this:

```
{ TODO 2 -oMichael -cGraphics : Adjust case statement for new compiler version
}
```

You can view all the *ToDo* comments belonging to your project at *View* → *ToDo List.*

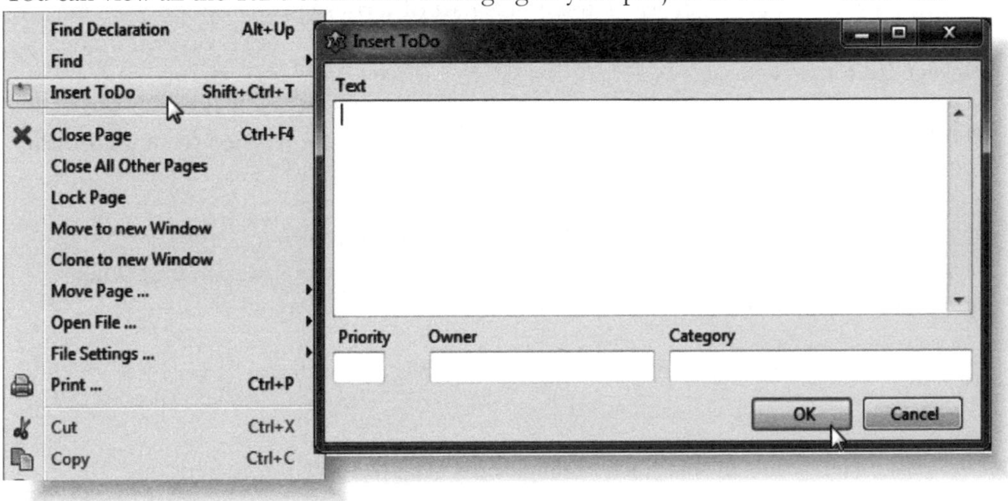

Figure 3.93: Inserting a ToDo comment via the Editor's context menu

Close Page removes the current unit from the Editor.
Close All Other Pages closes all pages of the Editor except the current unit. Both *Close* commands unclutter your workspace.
The following three options are only relevant when more than one file is open in the Editor at a time:
Lock Page, Move to New Window and *Clone to New Window.*
Lock Page tells Lazarus that you don't want this Editor to scroll away from its current position. If a page is locked and you try to jump to a new location in your code (say to a bookmark, a declaration, or the result of a find-in-file search) then Lazarus will open another Editor of the same file to display the target location. Note that incremental and simple search/replace operations are not considered 'jumps', and therefore scroll a 'locked' page.

With *Move to New Window* the opened source code file is moved to a newly opened Editor page. After this two Editor pages are available for the same file.
Clone to New Window works the same way only the file is cloned to a newly opened Editor window. After this another extra Editor window is available, which you can move around and resize without affecting the original Editor.
When several Editor windows are already open, extra options are available.
The file can be opened in a new or in an existing Editor.

If you have several pages open and you appreciate the order of the opened units, the current unit's tab can be moved left or right with the option *Move Page* until the desired position is reached. It is also possible to move the tab directly to the leftmost or rightmost position. If your tabs are arranged vertically, you will have to transpose 'leftmost' and 'rightmost' accordingly.

Open File opens more files. If the cursor is at a unit name in the uses section, this unit can be opened with *Open file at cursor*. If the unit is part of a package, the option *Open package <packagename>* is shown. With a click on it, the package file (`*.lpk`) is opened in the Package Editor.

The *File Settings* contain several settings that mostly can also be reached from the Editor *Options*:

Read Only: Provides the current unit with a write protection (or removes it).
Show Line Numbers: Shows (or hides) the line numbers. This can save you time when debugging since the compiler directs you to a line number on errors.

Unit Information: Shows the same four-page dialog that can be accessed via *View* → *Unit Information.*

Highlighter : Here you can set which highlighter is used to show the current unit (the default is Free Pascal).

Encoding : The character encoding (the default is UTF-8).
The character encoding is particularly important when the source code is to be shared and used on another computer as well.

Line ending: This lets you change the line ending from the default for your operating system to another type.
Changes in the file settings are normally effective after your next file save.
Further down the context menu is a command for printing either the entire file, or just the text selection. (You must have installed the *printers4lazide* package for printing to work).
There are also the usual commands for cutting, copying and pasting of information. For search calls and other purposes, the path to the current file can be placed on the clipboard with *Copy Filename.*
Naturally, functions to set and jump to bookmarks are available. These can also be found the main *Search* menu.

Debug offers six commands for the Debugger:

Toggle breakpoint,
Evaluate/Modify,
Add Watch at Cursor,
Inspect,
Run to Cursor
View Call Stack.

Once a breakpoint is set, a single click suffices to remove it again. The Debugger is considered in detail in chapter 3.2.5 The Debugger Settings.
With *Refactoring* some commands to edit and to improve the source code can be called : *Complete Code, Enclose Selection, Rename Identifier, Find Identifier Reference, Extract Procedure, Invert Assignment, Show abstract methods* (which shows abstract methods if any are found). *Show empty methods* shows a dialog to search for empty methods. *Show unused units* shows a dialog where you can easily remove unused units. An unused unit is a unit that is not used in the rest of the source code although it is listed in the *uses* section.

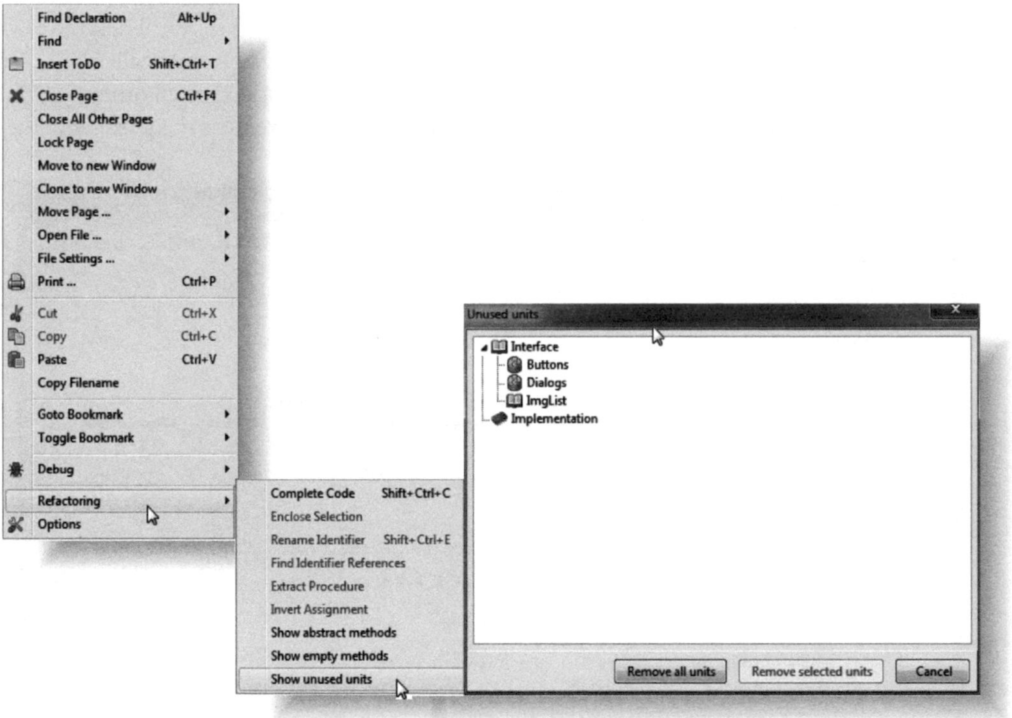

Figure 3.94: The dialog for removing unused units, accessed from the Editor context menu Refactoring option

Options calls the same dialog that is accessed via *Environment* → *Options…*→ *Editor.* Some functions of this dialog can be found at *File Settings*, among them for instance showing/hiding line numbers, or the choice of highlighter.
The options available for the Editor differ somewhat depending on the chosen widget set. However the differences are negligible and should not cause problems. Figure 3.95 shows an example.

The [X] button to close a page, at the right side of the page name, is not available on Windows (so enabling the option for it makes no difference on Windows). However, Windows users can still close pages with a shortcut key ([Ctrl] [F4]) or via the context menu.

The source Editor offers a very convenient option for quickly modifying many instances of an identifier at once called 'syncron' editing. Formerly your only way to do this was to *Search* for the identifier and replace it with *Replace.* If the source code is large and the identifier is frequently used, this can take some time. With this newer syncron method you mark the appropriate part of the text (this might be the entire source with [Ctrl] [A]). At the left edge of the Editor a small icon with a pen appears that you click on (or you press [Ctrl] [J]). The selection changes colour to indicate the syncron mode. Then the mouse or cursor is moved onto an instance of the identifier which automatically highlights every instance. All changes to that one identifier are applied to all other instances automatically. After a second click on the icon (or by pressing the [Esc] key) the syncron mode is abandoned.

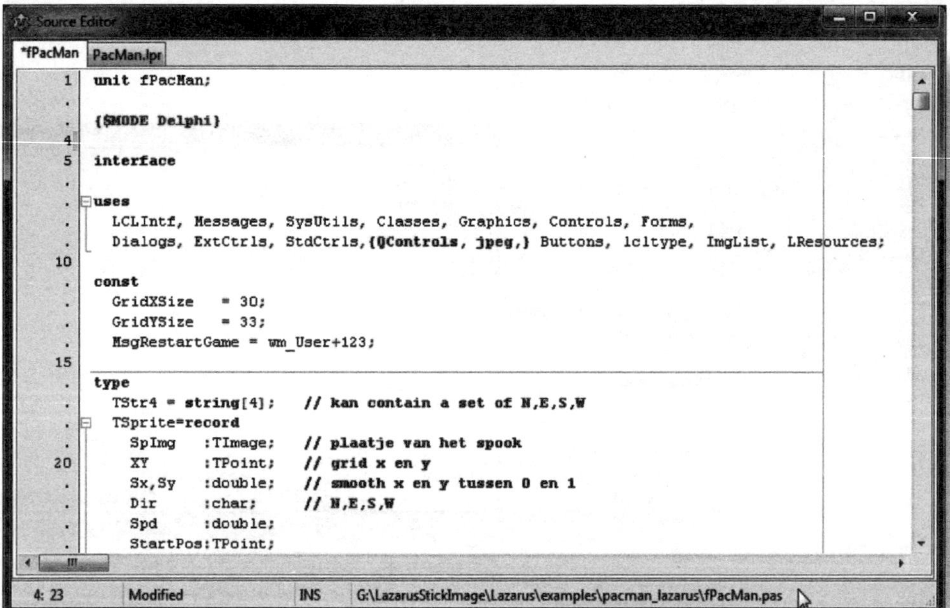

Figure 3.95: The source Editor on Windows

3.2.3 Code completion

Behind the *Edit → Complete Code* menu option are very powerful features of Lazarus that can save programmers a lot of typing. Several functions can be called depending on the cursor position in the Editor.

Class completion

If a class has been written and the methods and properties have been added, the *Class Completion* feature can add the method body, the property access methods and variables, and the private variables. As an example consider the following new class:

```
TExample = class(TObject)
 public
   constructor Create;
   destructor Destroy; override;
 end;
```

Now place the cursor somewhere in the class and press [Ctrl] [Shift] [C]. This generates the missing method bodies. Now the cursor is moved to the first of the method bodies and writing of the class code can begin. The implementation source code should look like this :

```
{ TExample }
constructor TExample.Create;
begin
      I ← the cursor will be placed here ready for you to enter code
end;

destructor TExample.Destroy;
begin
  inherited Destroy;
end;
```

Jumps can be made between a method's declaration and its body with [Ctrl] [Shift] [↑] and [Ctrl] [Shift] [↓].

Lazarus has also added the *inherited Destroy* command. This is always done when the keyword *override* is found in the class definition.

Now a method *DoSomething* is added :

```
TExample = class(TObject)
  public
    constructor Create;
      procedure DoSomething(i: integer);
    destructor Destroy; override;
  end;
```

If [Ctrl] [Shift] [C] is pressed now, the following is added by Lazarus :

```
procedure TExample.DoSomething(i: Integer);
begin
   I ← the cursor will be placed here ready for you to enter code
end;
```

The new method body is insert by Lazarus between *Create* and *Destroy*, in exactly the same order as in the class definition. This way the bodies keep the order laid down by the developer. The insert policy is defined in the menu at *Environment → Options…→ CodeTools → Code Creation.*

Variable declaration completion

If [Ctrl] [Shift] [C] is pressed when the cursor is located at an *identifier*, an *assignment* or a *parameter*, the local variable definition to an *Identifier := statement;* instruction is added. Assume the following procedure is found in the source code:

```
procedure TForm1.FormCreate(Sender: TObject);
begin
  i := 3;
end;
```

Now the cursor is placed on or directly behind the i and [Ctrl] [Shift] [C] is pressed. The source code will be changed to look like this:

```
procedure TForm1.FormCreate(Sender: TObject);
var
  i: Integer;
begin
  i := 3;
end;
```

The Codetools test if the identifier *i* is already declared. If not, the declaration *var i : Integer;* is added. The type of the identifier is guessed from the expression after the equal sign. Numbers like 3 default to *Integer.*
Another example :

```
type
  TWhere = (Behind, Middle, InFront);

procedure TForm1.FormCreate(Sender: TObject);
var
  a: array[TWhere] of Char;
begin
  for Where := Low(a) to Hi(a) do WriteLn(a[Where]);
end;
```

If the cursor is positioned on *Where* and [Ctrl] [Shift] [C] is pressed, you get:

```
procedure TForm1.FormCreate(Sender: TObject);
var
  a: array[TWhere] of Char;
  Where: TWhere;
begin
 for Where := Low(a) to Hi(a) do WriteLn(a[Where]);
end;
```

An example of parameter completion :

```
procedure TForm1.FormPaint(Sender: TObject);
begin
  with Canvas do begin
    Line(x1, y1, x2, y2);
  end;
end;
```

If the cursor is positioned on *x1* and [Ctrl] [Shift] [C] is pressed, the result is :

```
procedure TForm1.FormPaint(Sender: TObject);
var
  x1: integer;
begin
  with Canvas do begin
    Line(x1, y1, x2, y2);
  end;
end;
```

which is not complete, but has definitely saved you some typing.

Procedure call completion

Source code completion lets you generate new procedure from a procedure call. Assume an instruction *DoSomething(Width);* just has been written :

```
procedure SomeProcedure;
var
  Width: integer;
begin
  Width := 3;
  DoSomething(Width);
end;
```

Now the cursor is placed on *DoSomething* and [Ctrl] [Shift] [C] is pressed. The result adds code which looks like this:

```
procedure DoSomething(aWidth: LongInt);
begin

end;

procedure SomeProcedure;
var
  Width: integer;
begin
  Width := 3;
  DoSomething(Width);
end;
```

3.2.4 Message Composer

The Message Composer is a tool to help you generate message dialogs quickly and simply. If you program a dialog manually, you frequently get the parameters wrong or forget one. This is irritating, and looking up the dialog parameters takes time. The Message Composer has abolished that frustration.

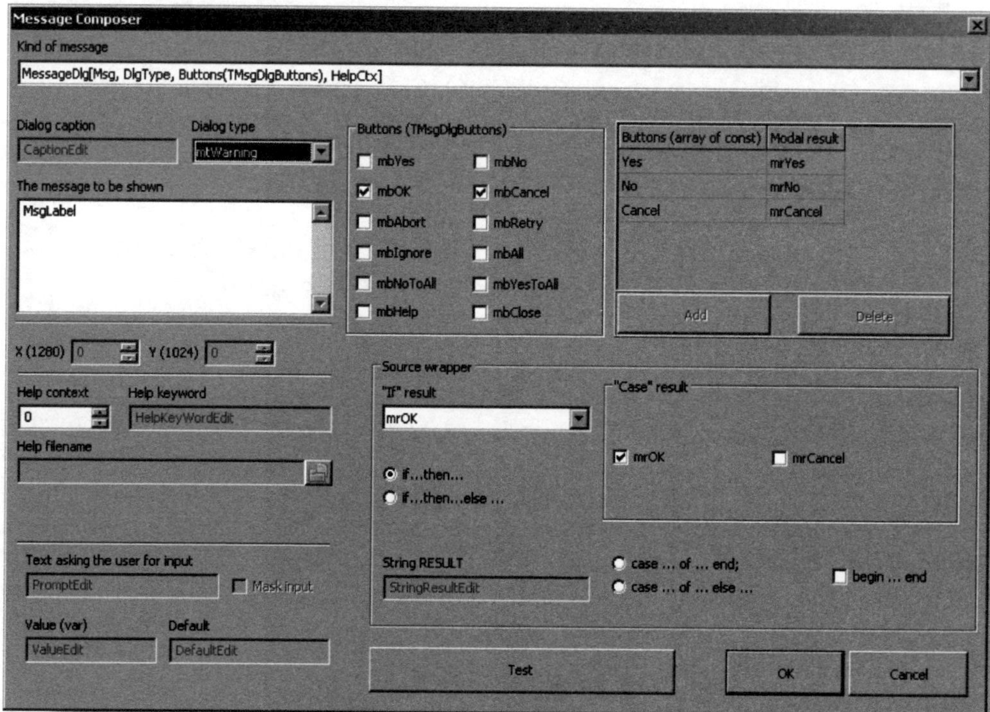

Figure 3.96: The Message Composer

For this tool to be available in the Lazarus IDE, the *messagecomposerpkg* package needs to be installed. If you have not yet installed it, go to *Package → Install/Uninstall packages….* In the dialog that results scroll through the *Do not install* list to locate *messagecomposerpkg*, and click on it. This enables the *Install selection button.*
Click this button, and then click the *Save and rebuild IDE* button. Clicking the *Continue* button in the confirmation dialog that ensues will add the package to a rebuilt IDE. You can then access the Message Composer via *Edit → Message Composer* or with the shortcut key [Ctrl] [M]. The new message dialog generated by this option is inserted in your Editor code at the cursor position.

The options available are mostly self-explanatory. Some fields only make sense when used with specific dialog types and so are disabled unless appropriate. The topmost combobox lets you select what type of dialog you want, followed by the message text to be displayed, and which buttons to be included, and (if desired) an entry for a help file. Clicking on the *Test* button gives you a previewed of the dialog you have just designed.

If it is not exactly what you wanted, a you can easily change a setting or two and preview the effect of your changes. Clicking the *OK* button closes the dialog and inserts the correctly generated code at the cursor. If you change your mind and do not want dialog code inserted, choose the *Cancel* button.
The example from Figure 3.96 (simply accepting default values everywhere) generates this code :

```
if MessageDlg('MsgLabel', mtWarning, [mbOK, mbCancel],0) = mrOK then
```

3.2.5 The Debugger Settings

By Marc Weustink

A serious development environment requires a debugger for investigating and removing any errors. Lazarus at the moment relies on the GNU debugger, *gdb*.
Because this is an external program, it does not offer identical functionality or reliability on all platforms. In the mid-term to long-term an internal Lazarus debugger will be developed, fully exploiting the potential of the IDE.

This section explains the various debugger settings. The Lazarus wiki and other documents referenced there explain how to use the debugger so there is no further usage explanation here.

The information generated by the Free Pascal compiler for gdb is all lowercase. When you are monitoring a variable you have to bear this in mind because normally Pascal uses capital as well as lowercase letters in variable names.
The GNU debugger gdb originates in the world of C programming, so is unaware of a *string* type. So Pascal strings are converted to a record with two fields: one contains the length, the other an array of characters.

Another limitation to be aware of relates to exception handling code which you write yourself. If you run a project within the IDE (in order to work with the debugger), the debugger interferes with your exception handling code. To be able to test such routines, you have to start the project outside the IDE.

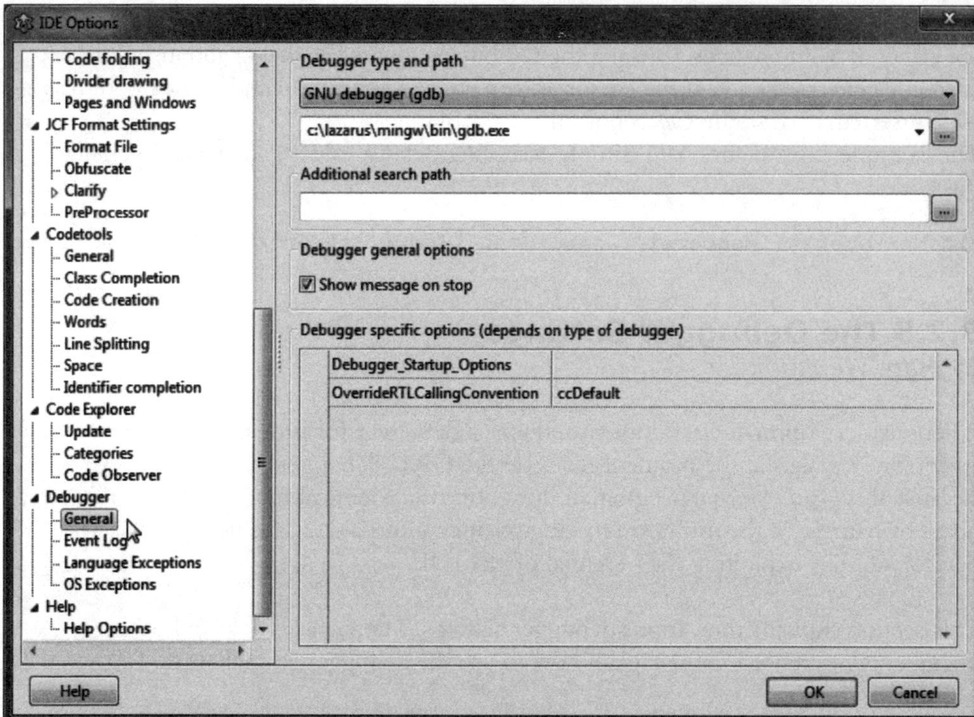

Figure 3.97: The General page of the Debugger section in the dialog accessed via Environment → Options…

The IDE's debugger configuration settings are found in the *Debugger* section of the *IDE Options* dialog accessed through the *Environment → Options…* menu. There are four pages of settings:
General, Event Log, Language Exceptions and *OS Exceptions.*

The General Page

The General page starts with a *Debugger type and path* section where you specify which debugger to work with and where it is found. For the moment this is gdb. The debugger type combobox has three options:

- *(none)*: No debugger is active. Clicking *Run → Run* runs the current program without a debugger.
- *GNU debugger*: The default setting. As gdb is external to Lazarus, the developer has to take care of the installation himself. With the Windows installer gdb is automatically installed in the *mingw* subdirectory of the Lazarus installation. On Unix gdb is usually available as a separate package. If gdb is installed before Lazarus, the IDE will recognise the path to gdb. If not, the path has to be entered manually.
- *GNU debugger through SSH (gdb)*: This is the setting for remote debugging. Over a SSH connection gdb can be executed on another computer. A SSH connection without password access is required for this.

You can enter more directories to be searched for source files where debugging information is stored by the executable in the *Additional search path* field.
This setting is valid for all projects.
If you want a message to be shown when the program stops, this can be set at *Debugger general options.*
Debugger specific options (depends on type of debugger). Since at present gdb is the only debugger used, only a few options are interesting. In cooperation with FPC there is particularly one option : *OverrideRTLCallingConvention.*
This is an internal flag which can be kept at the default *ccDefault.* To be able to handle software exceptions, Lazarus sets some internal stop points at places where these exceptions are triggered. When an executable file is compiled with complete debug information (and the RTL has also been compiled with complete debug information), you can retrieve the parameters passed to these exception routines. However, this is normally not the case, and that is why Lazarus has the internal possibility to test the Call Stack and Registers.
To interpret these arguments correctly, you need to understand the internal call conventions these routines need. Before FPC 1.9.x arguments were placed on the stack, whereas in more recent versions arguments are put in the registers. If the FPC version recognition routine gives the wrong result, then you have the opportunity to override the call convention here.

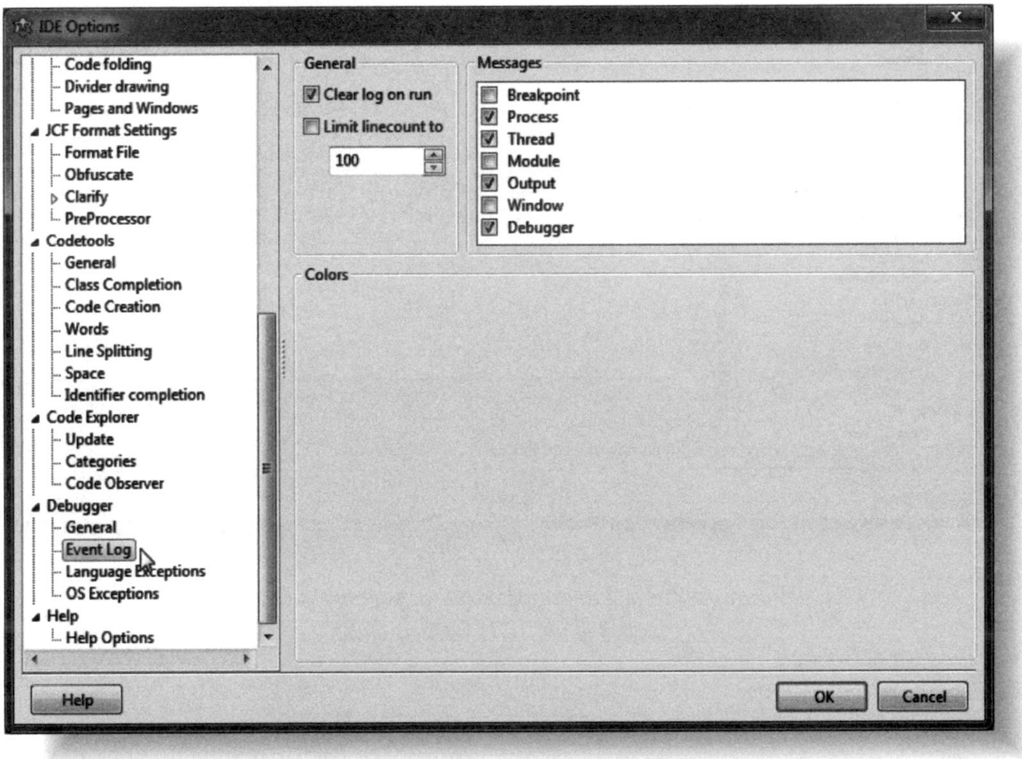

Figure 3.98: The Event Log page in the Debugger section of the dialog accessed via Environment→ Options…

The Event Log page

The *Event Log* page has only partial functionality at the moment, with basic features still being developed.
Eventually the IDE will have an *Event Log* window. Until then log information is shown in the *Debug output* window, accessed via *View → Debug windows → Debug output.*
Enabling the *Clear log on run* checkbox forces the log to be emptied whenever the program is started.
Enabling the *Limit line count to* checkbox makes the IDE keep no more than a maximum number of lines of debugger output. The maximum number is set in the spin edit field below the checkbox.
The *Messages* section is intended to let you define which messages are (and which messages are not) listed in the event log. Your version of Lazarus may have this feature, but it was not implemented at the time of writing.

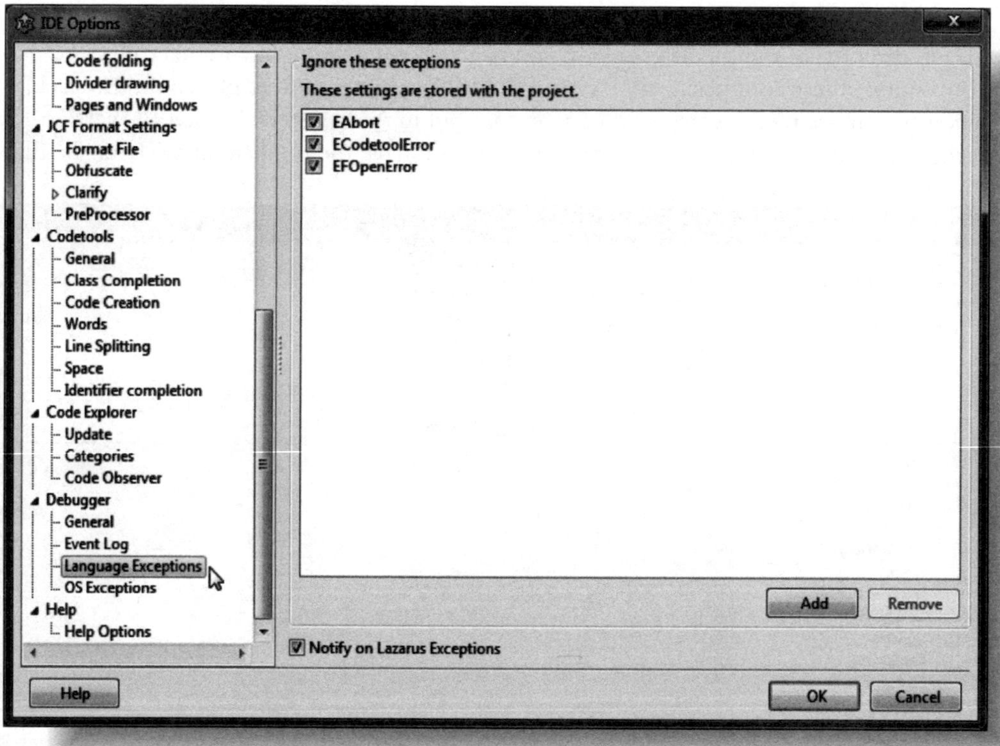

Figure 3.99: The Language Exceptions page in the Debugger section of the IDE Options dialog

The Language Exceptions page

The *Language Exceptions* page controls how exceptions are handled within the programming language. When a program cannot read a file, for instance,
an exception may be triggered. This page lets you choose whether the debugger should halt on such an exception. The debugger will ignore exceptions listed at *Ignore these exceptions.* You can add other exceptions using the *Add* button which presents a simple dialog where you type the name of the exception you want the debugger to ignore.
You might, for instance want the debugger to ignore the *EDivByZero* exception.
You can also select an ignored exception in the list and click the *Remove* button to remove this exception from the list, causing the debugger to halt if that exception is thrown.
If you don't want the debugger to halt at *any* exceptions, you need to disable the *Notify on Lazarus Exceptions* option as well.

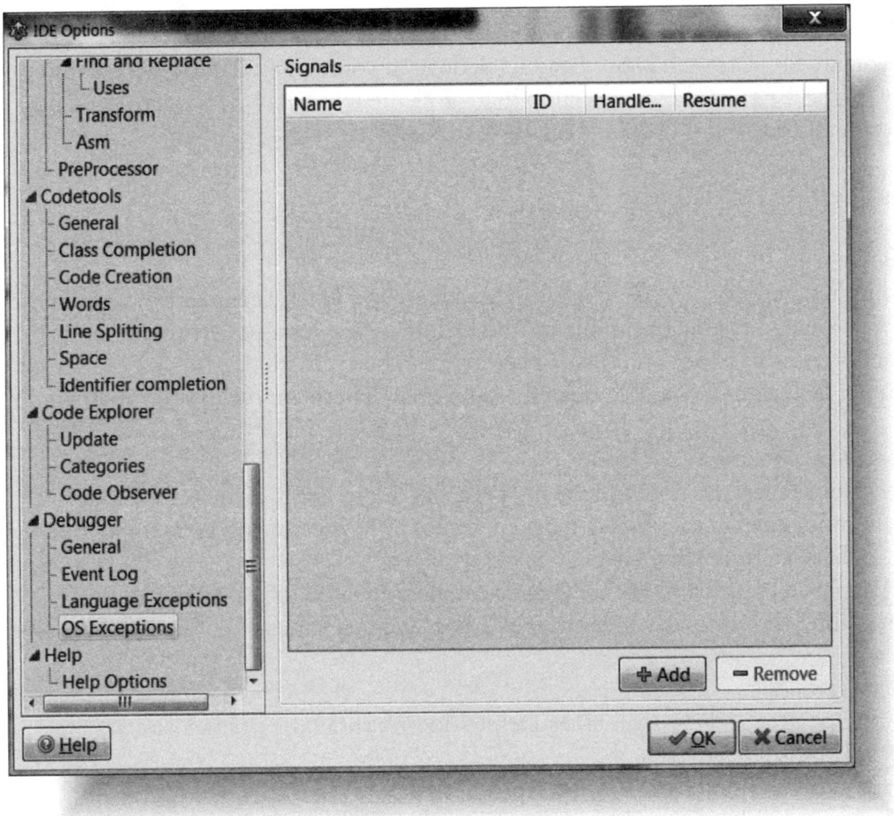

Figure 3.100: The OS Exceptions page in the Debugger section

The OS Exceptions page

The *OS Exceptions* page controls how exceptions which originate from the operating system are handled. The *Signals* section was not implemented at the time of writing. Here the intention is to define whether signals are handled by the debugger or by another program. For instance, if a division by zero is signalled by the operating system, then it is translated to an *EDivByZero* exception by the RTL. When the signal is handled by the debugger, the program stops before the RTL translates the message.
At the moment the debugger always stops on a signal.

There are eight different debug windows provided in the Lazarus IDE which are accessible via the *View → Debug windows* menu or through shortcut keys.
The various windows are *Watches, Breakpoints, Local variable, Registers, Call Stack, Assembler, Event Log, Debug output.*

If you are familiar with Delphi and its debugger, you may find gdb's behaviour frustrating. So the following section highlights the important debugger differences between Lazarus and Delphi (version 7) to forewarn you:

Local variables: No differences.

Watches:
Monitored expressions (Watches) can be edited, but Lazarus can only change the expression and enable or disable it. The Delphi debugger also lists functions as monitored expressions and the display style can be formatted. Also you can set a repeat counter in Delphi (a variable treated as an array). These are the disabled parts in Lazarus.

Formatting expressions:
Modify and *Inspect* are not implemented yet, but are in the Roadmap for Lazarus.
You cannot change the display types of values in Lazarus using format identifiers (as in the Watch/Display style).
In Delphi an expression like *somevalue,p* can be evaluated to show the value as a pointer or *somevalue,x* to show it as a hexadecimal value.

Showing variables:
For the pointer and class variables Delphi doesn't show the pointer or class type but only the address.
For Lazarus the value leads to the type.
In Lazarus the classes are shown sometimes as *TSomething* and sometimes as *^TSomething*.
This is a limitation of the debugger format in conjunction with gdb. The reason is that Pascal classes are mapped to C-classes which are equivalent to Pascal objects.
The dwarf3-debugger specification knows classes in Pascal style, and FPC is able to write them, but gdb cannot show them.
Dynamic arrays are shown only as pointers in Lazarus, while Delphi shows the contents.
This is determined by the debugger format since it is written as a pointer to a type according C, whereas dwarf3 knows dynamic arrays.

Breakpoints:
Setting and activating breakpoints is (almost) identical. In Lazarus only source code breakpoints are evaluated.
In Delphi, on the other hand, address, data and module load breakpoints are available. These are not implemented in Lazarus at the moment, but are in the Roadmap.
Breakpoints cannot be edited in Lazarus. This means that groups cannot be changed, activated or deactivated and that no other action than a halt is possible at a breakpoint. The functionality is available, and is only waiting for the appropriate dialog to be implemented.

Call Stack:
This is an extended version of the Delphi call stack. The length of the stack is limited, something that eases the debugging of deep recursive functions. Jumps can be executed both forwards and backwards.
The current scope can be changed. This means that variables of the calling procedure can be tested and considered.
The stack can be copied to the clipboard. Delphi can also do this but doesn't offer it in a menu or via a tool button. [Ctrl] [C] just does its job.

Debugger output:
Shows the internal status of the debugger.

Run → Stop:
Run →Stop will stop the debugging process. Sometimes stopping the debugging with [Ctrl] [F2] can lead to an unresponsive IDE. This means that the debugger is still running, while the debugged process has stopped already.
With Delphi the only option is to quit Delphi and restart it.
A similar situation arises with database applications. When an exception occurs during database access and the application is stopped by clicking the error message, the debugger may still continue running. To recover from the error and restart the application (to test if you have actually fixed the error), the debugger must first be stopped.

Threads / Module / CPU / FPU:
Not implemented yet, but these features are on the Roadmap.
If the debugger locates a problem, information about it can be shown in several windows. In Delphi, these are found at *View → Debug Windows.*
You can either open a window that you think will be needed before the debugging or at the first occurrence of an error.
A general point is that Object Pascal, with its strict typing of variables, will not call the debugger as often as is the case with many programming languages.
Various inconsistencies that otherwise would require the functionality of a debugger, are intercepted already by the compiler using Object Pascal.
The compiler's error messages are normally quite clear.

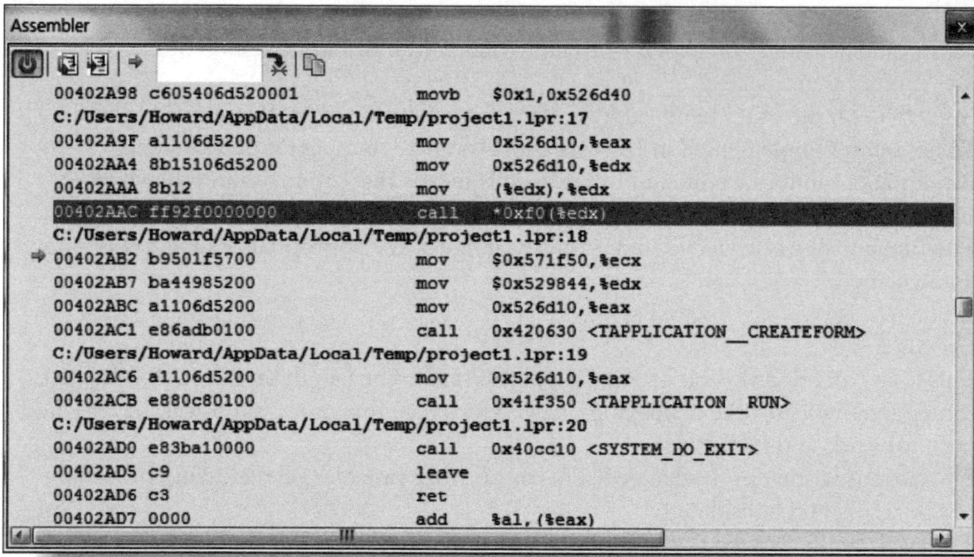

Figure 3.101: The Assembler window accessed via
View → Debug windows → Assembler

3.3 Recompiling the IDE

The IDE can regenerate itself. If you have downloaded the Lazarus source using the SVN repository, you will keep your copy of the sources up to date using an SVN update. You will then need to rebuild Lazarus before you can see the latest changes in functionality (the Lazarus SVN repository only contains the source code).
Another reason for rebuilding the IDE is to install packages. Lazarus only supports static packages at the moment, so the IDE has to be recompiled each time a new package is installed.
With an operating system having multiple widget-sets at its disposal, you might compile the IDE for another widget-set.

You need to bear in mind that Lazarus support is not equally good for all widget-sets. For instance the developers have spent a lot of time developing the Gtk widget-set, whereas for Cocoa on the Mac OS X development only began in earnest recently. Since Lazarus supports cross-compiling, you should choose the most stable widget-set for the IDE. You initiate this via *Tools → Build Lazarus with profile: xyz*.

After a confirmation dialog Lazarus is rebuilt according to the *xyz* setting. An error may halt the process. The most common reason for this is the presence of multiple versions of files. If this is the case the *Clean Up* option of the *Tools → Configure "Build Lazarus"* menu will help out.

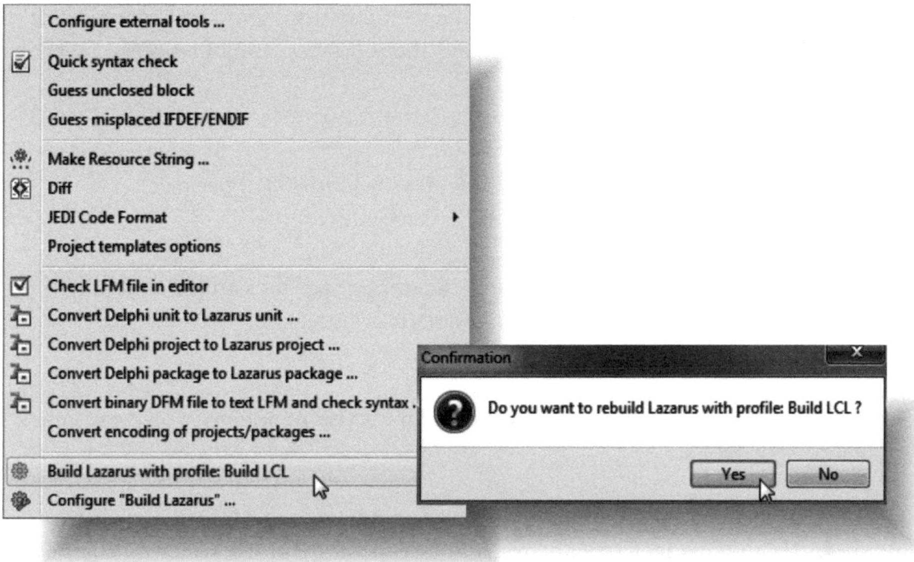

Figure 3.102: The confirmation dialog before rebuilding Lazarus after a call to Tools → Build Lazarus

You can configure several settings for a Lazarus rebuild. You access the settings in the *Configure "Build Lazarus"* dialog, accessed via *Tools → Configure "Build Lazarus"...*
This dialog contains predefined quick-build options but you can also configure all settings manually too.

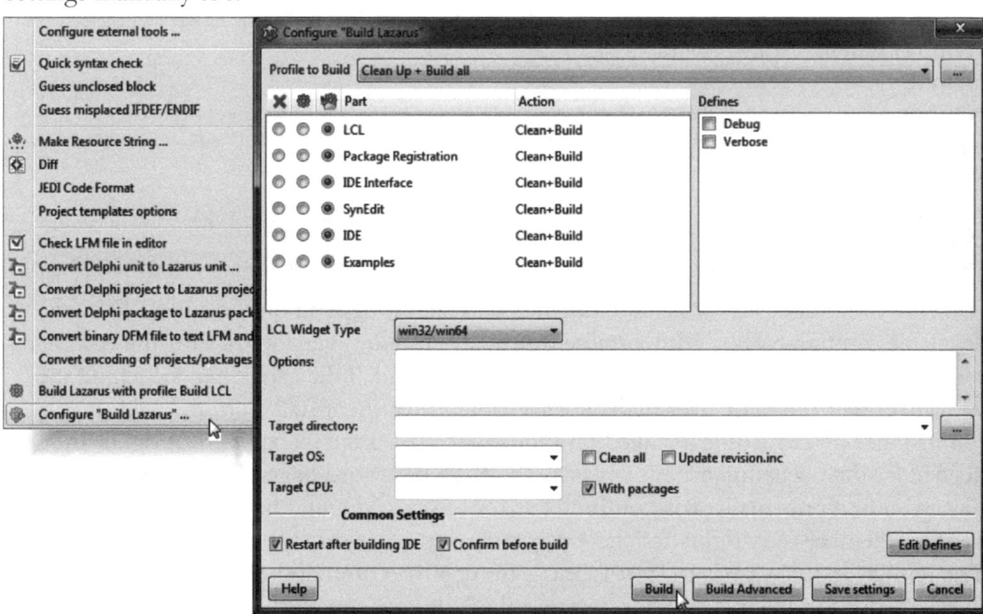

Figure 3.103 :The Configure "Build Lazarus" dialog accessed via Tools → Configure "Build Lazarus

The *Profile to build combobox* is designed for the inexperienced and offers some basic preset options. Pulling down the combobox displays the following combinations of what will be rebuilt, and how:

- *Build LCL*: Only the LCL is recompiled.
- *Build IDE with packages*: The IDE is rebuilt with all installed packages.
- *Build IDE without packages*: Only the IDE is rebuilt.
- *Build All*: recompiles everything.
- *Clean up + Build All*: Before rebuilding all unnecessary files are deleted – for instance the .ppu files, since they will be regenerated).
  Then everything is recompiled.

The [...] ellipsis button opens a dialog which enables you to add your own preset combinations to the list.

You set the widget-set for which the rebuild should be done at the *LCL widget type* combobox. Multiple widget-sets are available for most operating systems. You need to make sure that the necessary libraries are available for additional widget-sets. So, for instance, it makes no sense to select the Qt widget set on Windows without having the Qt-4 library available on the system. You must also bear in mind that not all widget-sets are at the same level of development. At the moment the following are available:

Widget-set	Current status in Lazarus
Gtk	Stated as stable but outdated
Gtk 2	Beta state, but the default on Linux and FreeBSD since Lazarus 0.98
Win32/Win64	Stated as stable
WinCE	Beta state
Carbon	Beta state
Qt	Alpha state
fpGUI	Experimental
NoGUI	Experimental
Cocoa	Experimental

Table 3.6: Available Widgetsets

Some of the widget-sets which are not stated as stable, depend on the latest FPC version (available through SVN). With a stable (normally an older) version of FPC the compiling can hang, perhaps because necessary files are not found. Take care when switching the widget-set that the same user rights are available as for the installation of Lazarus.
For instance, if Lazarus is installed on Linux with a package manager, root rights are needed (at the packet manager's start-up, the Root password has to be entered).
Since you don't normally work on Linux as root user, changing the widget-set will fail, because the necessary rights for the Lazarus directory are missing.
The remedy in this case is to start Lazarus though the command *sudo*. However this doesn't work for all Unix systems, because the X-host is not always free to use other accounts than the current one. Therefore the account that currently started the X-server has to execute the command *xhost* + in a console window, if the IDE cannot connect to the X-host.

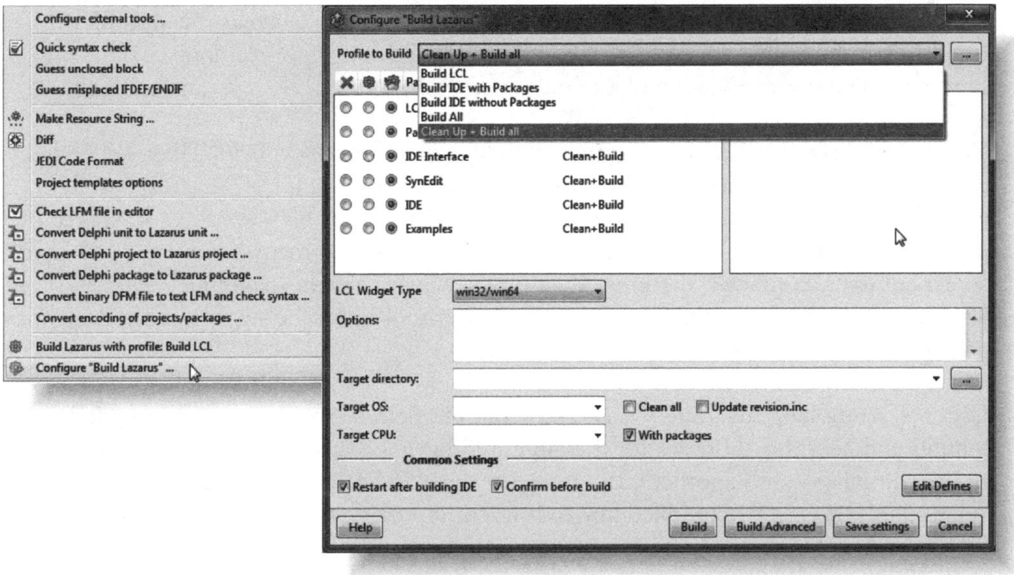

Figure 3.104: The Configure "Build Lazarus" dialog showing the five preset Profile to Build options

Lazarus comprises the following parts:

- The LCL: The Lazarus Component Library and the current widget-set. The LCL contains the visual components like TButton and TForm. The non-visual components are not part of the LCL but are provided by Free Pascal libraries (the FCL or RTL).
- Package registration: Contains the fundamental package unit, used by all Lazarus packages.
- IDE Interface: The IDEIntf package. Each runtime package which extends the IDE has to include this interface package.
- SynEdit: This is the source code editor component, needed by the IDE. It contains the visual component TSynEdit and the highlighters.
- CodeTools: A collection of tools for analyzing and editing source code.
- IDE: the rest of the IDE.
- Examples: The simpler demos are found in the examples directory. More complex demos and examples are in several subdirectories below examples.
- Starter: The application startlazarus which restarts the IDE when it is recompiled.

The parts are ordered. This means that when the LCL is to be rebuilt, all parts below it have to be rebuilt also. This can be controlled separately for each part with the radio buttons:
None (left column, no compilation), *Build* (middle column, compile it),
Clean + Build (right column, cleanup and compile it).
The *LCL Interface* only concerns the compiling of Lazarus (including the LCL), all other IDE features use the compiler settings in the project menu.

Enabling *Clean all* deletes all files not necessary for compiling (such as the .ppu files). Especially when you change the widget-set you should enable this option.
If the installed packages should be rebuilt in addition to the IDE you can enable this at *With packages.*
You are able to pass parameters to the compiler using the *Options* field. These are added to the command-line with the *OPT* compiler switch. For instance, if Lazarus is to be compiled for the Qt widget-set, up to revision 21913, parameter `-dUse_QT_45` has to be passed (with Qt-version 4.5). It is worth bearing in mind that many parameters still have an experimental character, therefore their efficacy is not always guaranteed.
The Lazarus component that is affected by the settings has to be set to *Clean* at the upper part, to have the changes enabled after compiling.

For cross-compiling the *Target OS* can be set in the field of that name. All compiled binutils and necessary libraries for the target OS have to be present.
If the compilation has another CPU as target, this CPU can be set at *Target CPU.*
When the IDE is to be compiled into a different directory, this directory can be set at *Target directory.* This setting affects only the IDE, not other parts of Lazarus.
If the Lazarus rebuild was successful, you can direct an automatic restart by enabling the *Restart after building IDE* checkbox. It is only after a restart that the changes are effective. If you need to study the compiler output messages this option has to be disabled. Normally it can stay activated.

With *Confirm before build* enabled, a confirmation is needed before starting.
When you click *Build,* the settings are saved and the rebuild is started. If the rebuild is to be done later on, you can save changed settings with the *Save settings* button. The *Cancel* button discards all changes and closes the dialog.
What options do you have, if a rebuild goes totally wrong and the IDE is not responding anymore?
You have to start a console, and go to the Lazarus directory. You can build a minimal IDE with the command-line *make clean all,* with which you can make a new start. (On Windows, Lazarus's *make.exe* has to be in front of all other make executables in the PATH environment variable). The packages that were installed previously are not available for the moment, but are marked for installation. A call to *Build Lazarus* includes the marked packages and incorporates them after a new start. If the problems were caused by the installation of a new package, normally de-installation of the package will solve this.

Chapter 4
Projects

by Felipe Monteiro de Carvalho

Lazarus is a development environment for writing any type of application in Pascal, not just GUI applications. Lazarus allows you to create many application types.

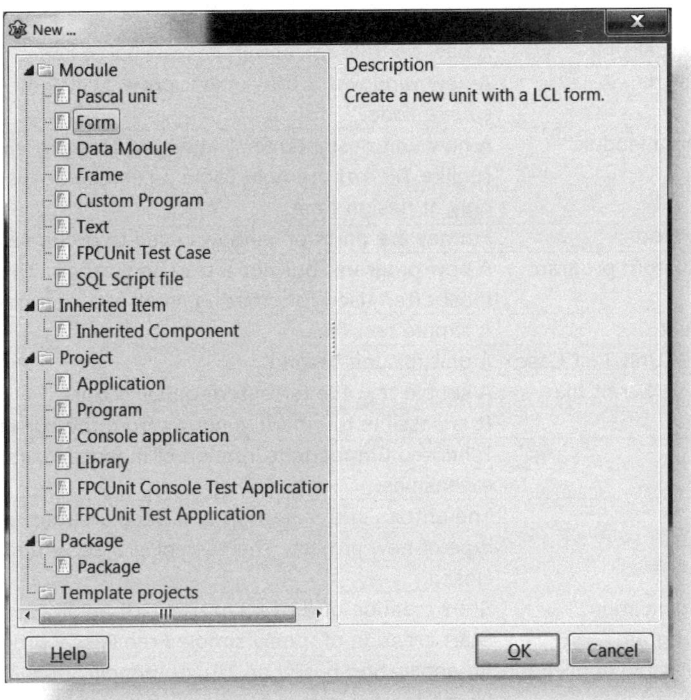

Figure 4.1: The File → New dialog

The Lazarus menu selection *File → New* presents you with a dialog where you can choose what type of project you want to develop from a wide range of possibilities. Table 4.1 shows the many possible project types that Lazarus offers. Moreover, this list can be extended with other project types by using additional packages – either packages included with Lazarus (but not installed by default) or packages you obtain from third parties.

Figure 4.1 shows the *New ...* dialog which you see after selecting *File → New* from the main menu with the default options offered in a fresh Lazarus installation. Here you can choose from the Module options (perhaps a new form or text file) or from the Project options (perhaps a new application or console program) or indeed any of numerous other possibilities which you can see illustrated above.

The *New* ... dialog's content appears to be fixed, but in fact it can be extended by using the so-called *Tools API*. This API allows programmers to extend any part of the IDE with the addition of new menu options, properties, and dialogs.
Such new functionality comes in the form of additional packages.
The *New* ... dialog shown in Figure 4.1 offers a structured way to make a selection from the file types and project types outlined in Table 4.1.

Category	Entry	Description
Module		This section includes both items that can be used to start a new project, and also items to add a file to the current project.
	Pascal Unit	A new text file to contain Pascal source code.
	Form	A new window for the current project, including its associated source code.
	Data Module	A new unit designed for containing controls which (unlike *TForm*) are not visible on screen at run time, only at design time.
	Frame	Frames are parts of windows used to group several controls.
	Custom program	A new program, but not a true application. This option is most often used for creating small test routines.
	Text	A simple text file.
	FPCUnit Test Case	A unit for unit testing.
	SQL Script file	A simple text file for entering SQL scripts.
Inherited		It is possible to inherit windows from the current application.
Item		Inherited ComponentCreation of inherited components for extensions.
Project		The entries in this section begin the creation of a specific type of new project. The current project is first automatically closed.
	Application	Start creation of a new Lazarus GUI application.
	Program	Start creation of a new simple Free Pascal program.
	Console application	An application based on TCustomApplication. The difference from Program is that Program offers fewer options compared to a console application managed by Lazarus.
	Library	Create a DLL (in Windows) or shared object (.so in Unix) rather than a full application. This makes functionality available to other programs in the form of a library.
	FPCUnit Console Test application	Create a new console application for unit testing.
	FPCUnit Test Application	Create a new GUI application for unit testing.
Package		Creates a new package as a set of units and components. The only entry is "Package".
	Package	Create a new package.
Template projects		This entry is empty. Because there are no sub-entries nothing can be selected. This is a container for extensions.

Table 4.1: The project types that you can start in a default Lazarus installation

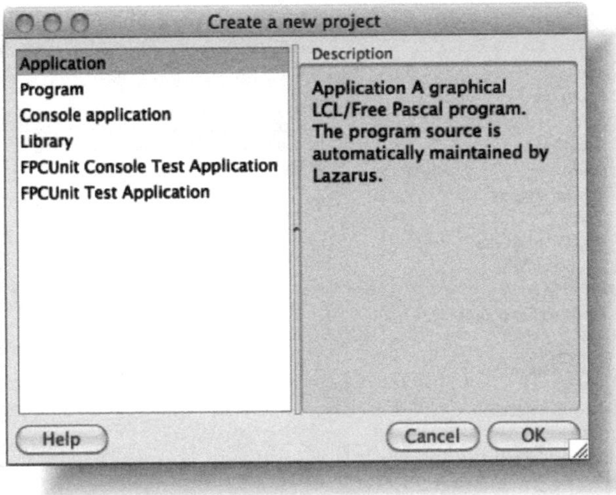

Figure 4.2: The Project → New Project dialog offers the same Project options as File → New

4.1 GUI Applications

Since their introduction in the 1980s, Graphical User Interfaces (GUIs) have gained full acceptance. Nowadays, it is really only system administrators who still work on the command-line. Platform-independent user interfaces are powered by platform-independent GUI libraries, some of which even support Unicode, enabling support for displayed text from many languages. Table 4.2 shows several modern GUI libraries available for programming with Pascal.

Library	Bindings to Pascal	Win32	Win64	Linux, BSD	Mac OS X native	WinCE
Lazarus LCL	Written in Pascal	✓	✓	✓	✓	✓
KOL-CE	Written in Pascal	✓	–	–	–	✓
fpGUI	Written in Pascal	✓	✓	✓	–	✓
MSEgui	Written in Pascal	✓	–	✓	–	–
Qt 4.5+	✓	✓	✓	✓	✓	✓
Delphi VCL	Written in Pascal	✓	–	–	–	–
Gtk+ 2.x	✓	✓	✓	✓	–	–

Table 4.2: Pascal GUI Libraries

Applications can be written with each of these (except Delphi's VCL) in Lazarus, but only LCL applications can be designed with Lazarus' GUI designer, Object Inspector and Component Palette. In this book, of course, we discuss working with the Lazarus Component Library (LCL).

To start working on a new GUI program based on this library, select *Application* in the *New …* dialog accessed from the *File → New* menu. A new main window named *Form1* will open, ready to accept components.

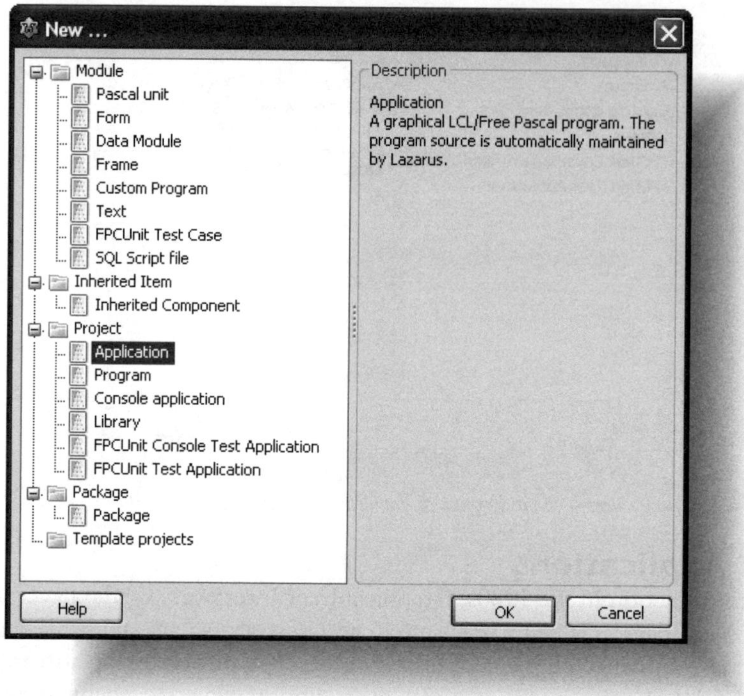

Figure 4.3: Creating a new GUI Application with File → New

When a new (GUI) *Application* is selected, all necessary files are created for you, and the Designer and Source Editor windows are opened. Any further Pascal unit you want can be added to the Editor as a new source window with *File → New Unit.*
Any additional forms required are added with *File → New Form* or via the dialog accessed via *File → New* with an appropriate choice under the Module heading.
If your application contains more than one window, the main window can be changed using the *Project → Project Options* menu to access the *Project Options* dialog.

The *Options for Project:project1* dialog has a heading *Project Options* which includes a *Forms* section where you can specify the main form (click on *Forms* to open the Forms page).
The first window created in the project file is always the main window.
(This is shown at the top of the *Auto-create forms*: listbox).
If the main window is closed, the GUI application is terminated.
For console applications, Lazarus just acts as a comfortable source code editor.
Whereas for *LCL* programs the integration of the IDE has much more to offer.
The Lazarus IDE automatically generates quite a lot of the source code your application needs. For instance, when a component is added to a form, the corresponding code unit is automatically added to the *uses* statement in the source code (if you have not already added it yourself). The form class definition is also managed automatically.
When you double-click an event (listed in the *Events* tab in the Object Inspector) the body of the event handler is automatically inserted in the source code.
Even the *END* corresponding to a *BEGIN* is automatically inserted
(though this is sometimes annoying – so you can switch this feature off).

A Lazarus project does not just consist of a single program file. Each project requires many different files. The main project file has the extension `.lpi` and is in XML format. This is normally used to open the project in the IDE. The main program loop is in the `.lpr` file (which corresponds to Delphi's `.dpr` file). You can also open the project by selecting this `.lpr` file in the Lazarus IDE.
Each project only has one file with the `.lpi` extension, and one file with the `.lpr` extension.
A Lazarus program contains many other files. An overview of these can be found in Table 4.3. Lazarus writes and controls the main project file (`.lpi`) using XML format. It should not be hand-edited – even though it is possible to do so. This file contains all the non-standard option settings for the project and the directory paths, which facilitates moving a project to another user's account or even to another operating system.
This rarely creates any problems. If (and only if) moving a project does create problems, the stored paths can be deleted from the `.lpi` file.

File	Description
Project1.ico	The main project icon in Windows icon format.
Project1.lpi	The main project file, normally used to open the project. It contains data about the files that belong to the project, and all other project-related information. The IDE settings can be stored in here, if they are not stored in a separate `.lps` file.
Project1.lpr	The source code of the main program. This is normal Pascal source code, saved with a special filename extension (analogous to Delphi's `.dpr` project file).
Project1.manifest	A Windows-specific file, which can be deployed along with the exe-file, though this is not mandatory. This file specifies that controls will be displayed in Windows XP's themed style. The file has no effect in Windows versions prior to Windows XP.
Project1.rc	A Windows resource file. This is a true source file (not a binary file as with Delphi's `.res` files). This resource information is compiled into the Windows exe-file together with the main program icon.
Form1.pas	Pascal source code for the *Form1* window. This contains the class definition and the source code of the main form unit. Other files with the .pas extension can contain other forms and other source code. Apart from the `.pas` extension, `.pp` is also allowed as an extension for Pascal source files. This is usually a better choice, as it prevents confusion with Delphi source files.
Form1.lfm	This file contains information about all the components in the *Form1* window that the source code refers to (analogous to Delphi's `.dfm` files).
Form1.lrs	A Lazarus resource file. This is automatically generated from the `.lfm` file.

Table 4.3: File types found in a typical Lazarus project

The following listing is a typical section from an .lpi file:

```
<?xml version = "1.0" ?>
<CONFIG>
  <ProjectOptions>
    <Version Value = "7" />
    <General>
    <Flags>
      <AlwaysBuild Value = "False" />
    </Flags>
  <SessionStorage Value = "InProjectDir" />
</CONFIG>
```

The lfm files also have a very simple structure. Their layout and syntax is very similar to those of .dfm files in Delphi:

```
object Form1: TForm1
  Left = 369
  Height = 240
  Top = 156
  Width = 320
  Caption = 'Form1'
  ClientHeight = 240
  ClientWidth = 320
  Menu = MainMenu1
  LCLVersion = '0.9.31'
  object Button1: TButton
    Left = 16
    Height = 25
    Top = 72
    Width = 75
    Caption = 'Button1'
    OnClick = Button1Click
    TabOrder = 0
  end
  object MainMenu1: TMainMenu
    left = 10
    top = 10
  end
end
```

.lrs files are the binary form of .lfm files and are only needed because versions 2.2.x of the Free Pascal compiler (and earlier versions) did not support binary resource files.

The IDE creates the .lrs files automatically, so they do not need to be stored with the source code, nor do they need to be included in any SVN, CVS or Git Repository for source code distribution. All that is needed is to list all the units in the Project Inspector. Versions 0.9.28 and above of the Lazarus IDE create the .lrs files in the same output folder where the .ppu files are created.

The files listed so far are needed if you distribute your source. For distribution of the executable, normally only the executable file (without extension for Unix or its equivalent, and with the .exe extension for the Windows version) has to be delivered.

Lazarus and the Free Pascal compiler create a large number of intermediate files during the compilation of a project. These files never have to be distributed and can even be deleted to save disk space. This includes all files with the extensions `.o, .ppu, .res, .or, .lrs, .rc` and, last but not least, `.compiled`. The compiler also creates a `.manifest` file, which is only needed when the program has to be used in Windows XP (or Vista or Windows 7) for showing the themed look of the controls on this platform. It is not needed for the appearance of the GUI, nor for the functionality of the program. The `.o` and `.or` files are object files written by the compiler. The `.rc` file is the source code of the resource file and the `.res` file is the result of compiling it.
Since Free Pascal 2.4 a project can contain either an `.rc` file, which is automatically compiled by Free Pascal, or a precompiled `.res` file.
To accomplish this, set the compiler directive *{$R MyResource.rc}*. In contrast with Delphi the `.ppu` file is not the binary of the compiled unit (in Lazarus the `.o` file is the binary). Rather it is an additional description file needed for the compiled unit. If there is no source code, both `.o` and `.ppu` files are necessary to compile a program using that unit.
Here is the initial code found in the form unit (named by default `unit1.pas`):

```
unit Unit1;
{$mode objfpc}{$H+}
interface

uses Classes, SysUtils, FileUtil, LResources, Forms, Controls,
                                            Graphics, Dialogs;


type
  TForm1 = class(TForm)
  private
{ private declarations }
  public
{ public declarations }
  end;
var Form1; TForm1;

implementation

initialization
{$I unit1.lrs}
end.
```

Development of a GUI application begins with this source code and an empty form window. The definition of the window class and the import of the necessary units have already been prepared. The program file (by default named `project1.lpr`) for a new GUI application automatically starts the prepared window. Usually this file does not need any manual changes:

```
program project1;
{$mode objfpc}{$H+}
uses
  {$IFDEF UNIX}{$IFDEF UseCThreads}
   cthreads,
  {$ENDIF}{$ENDIF}
   Interfaces, // this includes the LCL widgetset
   Forms, Unit1
  { you can add units after this };
{$R *.res}
begin
   Application.Initialize;
   Application.CreateForm(TForm1, Form1);
   Application.Run;
end.
```

4.2 Console Applications

The structure of a console application is a lot simpler than that of a GUI application. It basically contains no windows (as *TForms*), nor any other visual components. Of course console applications can contain non-visual components from the FCL. These are usually manually defined and initialized.
Lazarus can handle normal Free Pascal programs. In that case the basic operations are done in a version of the project file (`.lpr`) that is different from the one used for GUI applications.
All console applications communicate in a terminal window using standard Pascal input/output routines for reading and writing text. To communicate with a terminal window, text is written to it sequentially. User input is read as text, usually with [Enter] to signal completion of the input. Several external libraries can be used to write more complex text-based user interfaces.

Under Linux/Unix the preferred ones to use are *ncurses*, available from:
`http://www.freepascal.org/packages/ncurses.html`
(a C library with headers in the unit `ncurses`), and Free Vision, available from:
`http://wiki.freepascal.org/Free_Vision`
(derived from Turbo Vision from Turbo Pascal 6 and 7).
The latter uses the platform-independent Free Pascal units Mouse, Keyboard and Video. To tell the compiler we want to create a console application which needs input and output channels, we have to insert the (Delphi-compatible) compiler command *{$apptype console}* in the project file (with `.lpr` extension in Lazarus), which also contains the main body of the Pascal program with the keyword program.
A minimal console program looks like this:

```
program Consoledemo;

{$apptype console}

begin
  WriteLn('This is a console program');
end.
```

{$apptype console}* is used in this case where we otherwise would specify *{$apptype gui}. For GUI applications however, that directive is optional.
On non-Windows platforms compiling a program with the *{$apptype console}* directive will lead to a warning, telling us this compiler directive is not supported on that platform.
The directive instructs the compiler that a textmode console must be opened when the program is started under Windows. Also the correct font for the text mode is selected (this depends on the operating system) and the standard input and output channels for communication with the outside world are set up. Standard output is the text console, and standard input is the keyboard. Both of these can also be redirected, using the symbols “<” and “>”.
In Windows, if the *{$apptype console}* compiler directive has not been set when creating a console program, the first attempt to output data to the console with *Write* or *WriteLn* will result in the run time Error 103, and a corresponding exception will be thrown.
In Linux/Unix the console is always available.

The output will only be visible if the program has been started in a console window.
The line:

```
WriteLn('This is a console program');
```

which makes the Windows GUI application crash, is in Linux and Unix a very useful way to display error and information messages. To prevent problems with Windows compatibility, use *{$ifndef}* directives to prevent these output instructions from being compiled into the Windows version of the program:

```
{$ifndef Windows}
WriteLn
  ('This console writing issue only appears in Windows programs');
{$endif}
```

These examples show it is possible to create mixed mode console and GUI programs in Linux and Unix. But *{$apptype console}* can also be included in the project file for Windows GUI applications. In that case a console window will be opened in addition to the normal GUI window(s) when the program is started. When the application ends, this additional window will automatically be closed again. This option to automatically open a console window is not available in Unix.
Conclusion: a program on any platform can be designed to utilise a text console.

But this is not really the right way to do it. To start creation of a new console program in Lazarus, you should select *Console application* or *Program* in the dialog that opens after the *File* → *New* menu selection.

The choice Program results in the creation of a generic Free Pascal program. Either the source code in the `.lpr` file should include the directive *{$apptype console}*, or you should use the menu selection *Project* → *Project Options* to open the Options for project: xyz dialog box, and on the Linking page (one of the options under the Compiler Options heading) remove the tick from the checkbox Win32 gui Application (-WG).
Both methods have the same result and are only possible in Windows!

4.2.1 Managed Console Applications

A better alternative to the ultra-simple console program above is to select *Console pplication* from the dialog after choosing *File → New*. In this case Lazarus creates a more complex program structure. Programs based on this variation have an application class derived from *TCustomApplication*. The source code of the main program will not contain
a begin..end block, but a *DoRun* method defined in this class instead.
After selecting *Console application*, a *New console application* dialog will be opened to let you adjust the basic settings of the program template.
This allows setting the name of the application class (predefined as *TMyApplication*) and the application title (the default is *My Application*). It also allows you to specify whether the command line option -h (normally used for showing help text) will be supported. There is also a setting to specify whether any exception that occurs should halt the program execution (if not, only an error message will be displayed) and whether you want a constructor and destructor to be set up (each can be selected separately). The final option allows you to specify whether the program should report when it is called with an erroneous command line option.

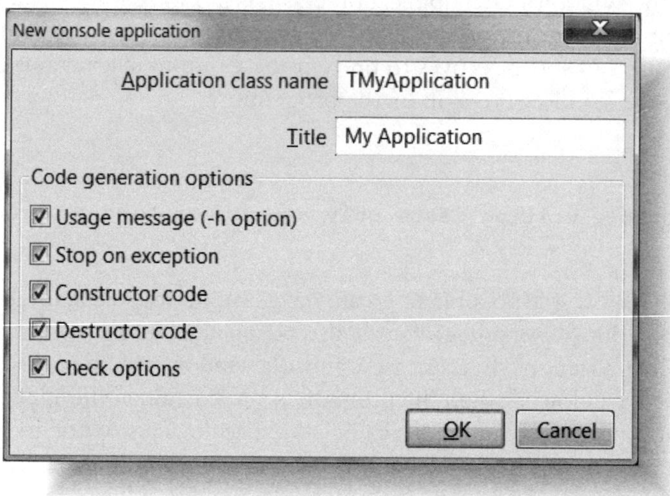

Figure 4.4: The New console application dialog

TCustomApplication (which is defined in the unit `CustApp`), is the base class for console applications. It has several helpful routines for evaluating parameters and showing help text, as shown in the listing on the next page. The following abbreviated class definition omits the private and protected methods and properties:

```
type TExceptionEvent = Procedure(Sender: TObject; E: Exception) of Object;

 TCustomApplication = Class(TComponent)
  Public
    constructor Create(AOwner: TComponent); override;
    destructor Destroy; override;
      // Some Delphi methods
    procedure HandleException(Sender: TObject); virtual;
    procedure Initialize; virtual;
    procedure Run;
    procedure ShowException(E: Exception);virtual;
    procedure Terminate; virtual;
      // Extra methods
    function FindOptionIndex(Const S : String;
                             Var Longopt : Boolean) : Integer;
    Function GetOptionValue(Const S : String) : String;
    Function GetOptionValue(Const C: Char; Const S : String) : String;
    Function HasOption(Const S : String) : Boolean;
    Function HasOption(Const C : Char; Const S : String) : Boolean;
    Function CheckOptions(Const ShortOptions : String;
                          Const Longopts : TStrings;
                          Opts,NonOpts : TStrings) : String;
    Function CheckOptions(Const ShortOptions : String;
                          Const Longopts : TStrings) : String;
    Function CheckOptions(Const ShortOptions : String;
                          Const LongOpts : Array of string) : String;
    Function CheckOptions(Const ShortOptions : String;
                          Const LongOpts : String) : String;
    Procedure GetEnvironmentList(List : TStrings;NamesOnly : Boolean);
    Procedure GetEnvironmentList(List : TStrings);
    Procedure Log(EventType : TEventType; const Msg : String); virtual;
      // Delphi properties
    property ExeName: string read GetExeName;
    property HelpFile: string read FHelpFile write FHelpFile;
    property Terminated: Boolean read FTerminated;
    property Title: string read FTitle write SetTitle;
    property OnException: TExceptionEvent read FOnException
                          write FOnException;
      // Extra properties
    Property ConsoleApplication : Boolean Read GetConsoleApplication;
    Property Location : String Read GetLocation;
    Property Params [Index : integer] : String Read GetParams;
    Property ParamCount : Integer Read GetParamCount;
    Property EnvironmentVariable[envName : String] : String
                          Read GetEnvironmentVar;
    Property OptionChar : Char Read FoptionChar Write FOptionChar;
    Property CaseSensitiveOptions : Boolean Read FCaseSensitiveOptions
                          Write FCaseSensitiveOptions;
    Property StopOnException : Boolean Read FStopOnException
                          Write FStopOnException;
  end;
```

The *CheckOptions* method checks which options were selected. This enables you to include very effective error and parameter handling in your application. In case of errors, useful messages can be given to the user. The method *HasOption* checks whether an option should be activated and allows you to react to its status.
Lazarus creates the following default structure for a console application:

```
program Project1;
{$mode objfpc}{$H+}
uses
  {$IFDEF UNIX}{$IFDEF UseCThreads}
  cthreads,
  {$ENDIF}{$ENDIF}
  Classes, SysUtils, CustApp
  { you can add units after this };
type
{ TMyApplication }
   TMyApplication = class(TCustomApplication)
   protected
     procedure DoRun; override;
   public
     constructor Create(TheOwner: TComponent); override;
     destructor Destroy; override;
     procedure WriteHelp; virtual;
   end;
{ TMyApplication }

procedure TMyApplication.DoRun;
  var  ErrorMsg: String;
begin
  // quick check parameters
  ErrorMsg:=CheckOptions('h','help');
  if ErrorMsg <> '' then
  begin
    ShowException(Exception.Create(ErrorMsg));
    Terminate;
    Exit;
  end;
  // parse parameters
  if HasOption('h','help') then
  begin
    WriteHelp;
    Terminate;
    Exit;
  end;

  { add your program here }

  // stop program loop
  Terminate;
end;
```

```
constructor TMyApplication.Create(TheOwner: TComponent);
begin
  inherited Create(TheOwner);
  StopOnException:=True;
end;

destructor TMyApplication.Destroy;
begin
  inherited Destroy;
end;

procedure TMyApplication.WriteHelp;
begin
 { add your help code here }
  writeln('Usage: ',ExeName,' -h');
end;

var  Application: TMyApplication;

{$R *.res}

begin
  Application:=TMyApplication.Create(nil);
  Application.Title:='My Application';
  Application.Run;
  Application.Free;
end.
```

Communication with terminals should use standard ANSI strings with the local system character set. More information about the channels of console applications can be found in chapter 8.2.1.

4.3 DLLs And Shared Objects

Every program has a main routine. In the C language, for instance, this is called main() and it takes as parameters the number and contents of the command line parameters. Normally this main() function in C has an int type, which means it supplies a return value. The return value of the main() function will be the return value of the program. Conventionally a return value of 0 implies normal successful completion of the program. An Object Pascal program does not have a routine named main() explicitly, but internally it does have such a routine of course. It is the main body of the program in the project file (with extension `lpr` in Lazarus). The sequence

```
begin
  Application.Initialize;
  Application.CreateForm(TForm1, Form1);
  Application.Run;
end.
```

corresponds directly to the main() function in C. The return value of the application is automatically predefined as zero, but can be changed for instance with Halt(1).

The *TApplication* object is not the application – in Lazarus the meaning of *TApplication* differs from that in Delphi. This is discussed later in this section.
A Lazarus program always begins with program *ProgramName*; in the project file. Definition of the main program is mandatory. Libraries, beginning library *LibaryName*; can be the basis for reusable source code and for programming involving multiple programming languages. There are two types of libraries: *dynamic* and *static*. Static libraries are linked into the application when it is compiled, whereas dynamic libraries can either be loaded at run time as needed, or linked statically into the application. However they are always located in a separate file from the main executable, with the extension `.so` (Linux/Unixes), `.dll` (Windows) or `.dylib` (Mac OS X Unix Library).

4.3.1 Dynamic Libraries

When creating a dynamic library, the main project file has to include the keyword *library* instead of *program*. Also, the names of all functions and procedures to export have to be listed (comma separated) as exports of the main project file.
A library does not have a main program, but it may include initialization code.
For all functions to be imported or exported from a library, the calling conventions have to be specified, unless it is an internal library (to be used only in Lazarus itself).
In that case the predefined convention applies for both import and export.
The predefined convention involves passing parameters in the CPU registers, as far as free registers are available. Not all CPU registers can be used, because some of them are reserved for specific uses. This depends on the processor being used. Function return values are passed in the accumulator (the first processor register) if they fit into it.
Calls to methods (of objects or classes) have an additional, invisible parameter: *Self*.
It is located at the far left of the call to the method (and is therefore passed to the method last). When the procedure or function ends, it will clean up the stack.

Modifier	Parameter order	Stack cleaned by	Alignment	Saved Registers
register	Left to Right	Function	Default	None
cdecl	Right to Left	Caller	GCC-Alignment	GCC-Registers
interrupt	Right to Left	Function	Default	All Registers
pascal	Left to Right	Function	Default	None
safecall	Right to Left	Function	Default	GCC-Registers
stdcall	Right to Left	Function	GCC-Alignment	GCC-Registers
oldfpccall	Right to Left	Caller	Default	None
mwpascal	Right to Left	Caller	GCC-Alignment	GCC-Registers

Table 4.4: Free Pascal calling conventions and their effect in x86 processors (applies to Lazarus also)

Other calling conventions are available for linking with external object files and libraries. These are outlined in Table 4.4. The first column lists the possible modifiers you can specify in declaring a procedure. The second column gives the order in which parameters are put on the stack. The third column specifies whether the caller or the function is responsible for cleaning up the stack. The alignment column holds information about the alignment of the parameter in the stack space. The fifth column tells us which registers (if any) are saved in the initial code of the subroutine.

Further information on the available calling conventions is published in the Programmer's Manual for Free Pascal (by Michaël Van Canneyt: Free Pascal 2, published by C&L Verlag, ISBN 978-3-936546-53-8). It is important to note that the same rules should be applied for export and import. The following listing shows a dynamic library which exports a procedure called SwitchNumbers:

```
library numbers;
{$mode delphi}
  procedure SwitchNumbers(var A, B: Integer); // exported procedure
    var C: Integer;
  begin
    C := B;
    B := A;
    A := C;
  end;

  exports     // export definition
  SwitchNumbers;     // Case-sensitive!
end.
```

Because no specific calling convention is indicated, this library can only be used internally within a Free Pascal program. A library can export a large number of procedures and functions and the routines exported do not have to be defined in the project file.
For compatibility reasons it is advisable not to export object oriented routines (i.e. methods), because this will make import into other programming languages complicated. If you do import object oriented routines, you will have to make provision for the Self parameter mentioned earlier. Besides that you will have to make sure the routine is imported in exactly the same way as it was specified in the *exports* block.
Export and import are case-sensitive.

The program *callnumbers* calls this library:

```
program callnumbers;
{$apptype console}
{$mode delphi}

// static import of the procedure from the library, loaded into memory during
// the initialization of the program

  procedure SwitchNumbers(var A, B: integer); external 'numbers';
// the main program
    var  A, B: integer;
  begin
    A := 5;
    B := 10;
    WriteLn('Original data: A:',A, ' B: ',B);
    SwitchNumbers(A, B);
    Writeln('Values after the call to SwitchNumbers: A:',A, ' B:',B);
end.
```

In this example the dynamic library – not the routine called – was statically linked into the program. As a result of this the program will not be able to start if the library is missing – it will halt with an error message. We can prevent this from happening by loading the library only when it is actually needed. This does make the call more complicated. First we have to load the required library with the *LoadLibrary* function call. When this function is called with the name of the library it will search for it and (if found) return a handle to it:

```
function LoadLibrary(Name: AnsiString): TLibHandle;
```

The next step is to use:

```
function GetProcedureAddress(Lib: TLibHandle; ProcName: AnsiString):
                                                              Pointer;
```

to get a pointer to the location where the symbol *ProcName* is stored, that is the name of the procedure or function. The function needs the handle provided earlier by *LoadLibrary.*

GetProcedureAddress gives a pointer to the location of the symbol *ProcName* in the dynamically loaded library the handle *Lib* refers to. If the symbol is not found or the handle is invalid, the function will return NIL. In Windows, only procedures and functions that have been explicitly exported can be examined in this way. In Unix-like environments, this can be used to inquire about any exported symbol.

```
function FreeLibrary(Lib: TLibHandle): Boolean;
```

The three functions mentioned here are part of the Free Pascal standard library and are located in the `dynlibs` unit, which needs to be included in your application's *uses* statement. When the program ends (or when the routine is no longer needed), the library has to be removed from memory again with FreeLibrary. This function returns True if unloading was successful.

To use dynamic loading our little program would look like this:

```
program callnumbers;
{$apptype console}
{$mode delphi}
uses   dynlibs;          // LoadLibrary, GetProcedureAddress and FreeLibrary
  type TSwitchNumbers = procedure(var A, B: Integer); cdecl; // External
  var  SwitchNumbers: TSwitchNumbers; // External procedure variable       procedure type
       A, B: Integer;
       H   : TLibHandle;
begin
  H := LoadLibrary('numbers');                // Loads the library
  if H = 0 then begin                         // if it wasn't found then abort
    WriteLn('The library "numbers" wasn''t found!');
    Halt(1);
  end;
  // Searches for a procedure by its name
  SwitchNumbers := GetProcedureAddress(H, 'SwitchNumbers');
  if @SwitchNumbers = 0 then begin      // if the procedure wasn't found
    WriteLn('The procedure SwitchNumbers wasn''t found in the library
      "numbers"!');
    FreeLibrary(H);                           // Release the library and quit
    Halt(2);
  end;
  // After loading the library the program code can start:
  A :=  5;
  B := 10;
  WriteLn('Original values: A: ', A, ' B: ', B);
  SwitchNumbers(A, B);
  WriteLn('Are changed after calling SwitchNumbers
          to: A: ', A, ' B: ', B);
  // Needs a WriteLn('Press [Enter] to exit');
  // ReadLn; to avoid the output scrolling away too fast to be seen under Windows

  FreeLibrary(H);                             // Release the library
end.
```

Of course using dynamic run time loading is not a sensible thing to do in a little command-line program like this, but it can have great advantages in larger programs. In that case external functionality which is not available at run time might for instance just gray out a single menu, but not prevent use of the rest of the program. This is especially useful for filters.

Libraries basically export functions which can be used by other programs. It is a lot more practical to provide functions that are often needed in the form of a library than to have to repeat them in every application that happens to need them. But libraries come at a price, as we have seen in our example. If an application needs a new library, there is a possibility it cannot be found and the program cannot function. It can also decrease the portability, if the library is only available for specific operating systems. And it makes developing the application more difficult. In general we can say: The more complex a function is, the greater the advantage in implementing it as a library.

A disadvantage of dynamic linking is that it slows down program execution if the libraries are not often needed. And we need to keep track of library versions to ensure compatibility between our application and the linked code. This is because libraries tend to grow over time and this can affect their interfaces with the outside world. Adding new properties does not pose a problem, but removing an exported method or changing a parameter can render the library incompatible with applications based on its old API. For this reason, every dynamic library should have a version number. Dynamic libraries are called Dynamic Link Libraries in Windows. In Linux they are called Shared Objects. The functionality is the same, only the name is different.

Operating System	Prefix for dynamic libraries	Extentions for dynamic libraries	Extentions for compiled static libraries
Linux, FreeBSD, etc.	lib	.so	.a
Mac OS X (Unix Library)	lib	.dylib	.a
Mac OS X Framework	lib	.framework (actually a folder where the Mac OS X UNIX libraries are placed)	Frameworks only apply to dynamic libraries
Windows and WinCE	–	.dll	.lib, .a

Table 4.5: File name extensions of static and dynamic libraries on various platforms

The version number is particularly important in Unix-like operating systems, because these only allow loading of a library once. It is therefore not possible to use more than one version of a library with the same name.
In Linux, FreeBSD and similar systems, you must always name your dynamic library like this:

```
<packagename>.so.<version>
```

for instance: `libz.so.1` or `libz.so.1.2.2`
The version does not have to be specified, but I recommend that you do.
In MacOS X the library should be named:

```
<packagename>.<version>.dylib
```

Unix will look for a library in the path found in `LD_LIBRARY_PATH`, then in `/lib`, then in `/usr/lib` and finally in the path of `/etc/ld.so.conf`.

Windows will look for a library first in the current directory and in the directory where the executable is located, then in the system directory and then in the locations found in the environment variable PATH. It can therefore function without being influenced by the global configuration of the machine where it has to run.

There is a disadvantage to this system. If there are multiple copies of a library available on the hard disk of the system and it is not available in the application directory, the first library that matches in the search path will be used.
That may be a defective or outdated version!

We can see the negative effects of this behaviour in Free Pascal itself. If we install the compiler, with or without Lazarus, and we include the binary directory of the compiler in the system search path, several other programs may stop working.
This is because some of the programs distributed with Free Pascal make use of the Cygnus-DLL `cygwin.dll`. The library distributed with the compiler may or may not be compatible with other programs based on this POSIX compatibility library. If they are not, they will stop working, and the error messages produced will not give a clue to the real cause of the problem.

If the program and the library are both written in Pascal, it is usually sufficient to copy the function declaration from the library into the source code of the program and mark it as *extern*. If the library is to be used in co-operation with other programming languages or for general use, then the calling conventions will have to be taken into consideration.

The default setting is *register* (see Table 4.4), which results in maximum calling speed. Most C and C++ compilers (except C++ Builder) do not understand this way of passing parameters, so the calling method has to be specified along with the calls.
Under Unix/Linux and Windows CE (and partially under Windows) the definition of *cdecl* is useful. However, Windows mostly uses *stdcall.*

On Unix-systems, the created file has to be prefixed with lib and moved into `/usr/local/lib` and then the linker has to be provided with a directive to be able to find it before the program can be built. In Lazarus this option is available via the *Project → Project Options...* menu.
In the resulting *Options dialog* select the *Linking* page and tick the *Pass Options To The Linker (Delimiter is Space)* checkbox under *Options: (-k)* for passing additional settings to the linker. Fill in the option field below with

```
-lnumber   (or in general  -l<packagename>).
```

Under MacOS X use the following instruction in a terminal window to move the generated library to the right location:

```
sudo mv numbers.dylib /usr/local/lib/libnumbers.dylib
```

Under Unix the library has to be available both during linking and during execution of the program. Under Windows the dynamic library needs to be present only when the program is run.

4.3.2 Libraries in MacOS X

The way MacOS X handles libraries needs some extra attention. First of all we have to indicate where the library will be located on the system during building.
This is handled with the linker option

```
-install_name <path>
```

Second we need to specify a compatibility version. This is the lowest version number with which the library is compatible. The linker option *-compatibility_version* handles this. For instance if we build library version 4.5.6 which is fully compatible with its predecessors 4.5.x (but not with versions before that) the compatibility version can be set to 4.5. This enables programs which have been compiled with older versions of the library to link to this file without problems. If the version is omitted, no version checking will take place. The library version is indicated with:

```
-install_name <path>
```

Another special case in handling libraries on MacOS X are the so-called *frameworks*. These are packages which contain one or more libraries. Frameworks are directory structures with binary library files, include files, resources and sub-frameworks in subdirectories, identified in the following format:

```
Version/<version number>, Version/version number/Header,
  Version/<version number/Resources and Frameworks.
```

The main advantage of frameworks is that they provide an easy way for you to organize a group of related libraries, resources and headers. They are a quasi-installation method. Frameworks can be easily de-installed, by simply dragging the installation directory to the recycle bin. If the library were packed into a MacOS X package, uninstalling would not be that easy, because MacOS X does have a package installer, but there is no corresponding uninstaller. Frameworks are therefore a very convenient solution for managing libraries.

The basic Unix-libraries are to be found in `/usr/lib`, together with other Unix-derived files, ready to be referenced by Unix programs after compilation. However all visual and Macintosh oriented libraries like Carbon and Cocoa (including their non-visual parts) are organized as frameworks. Frameworks developed by Apple are located in the directory `/System/Library/Frameworks`, while other frameworks (including, of course, the ones we create ourselves) have to be stored in `/Library/Frameworks`. However it is not sufficient to put the binary files and the include and resource files that belong to the library into the version directory. Additionally dynamic links from the main directory of the framework have to be made. The version directory is not involved for most libraries.
Usually it is sufficient to create a directory for version A and put the files into it. The library binary files should not have the usual prefixes and suffixes for MacOS X, nor should they have an extension.

Frameworks are installed by simply dragging their directory to `/Library/Frameworks`. Normally the program installers take care of this. Such installers should be available in the disk image of an application.

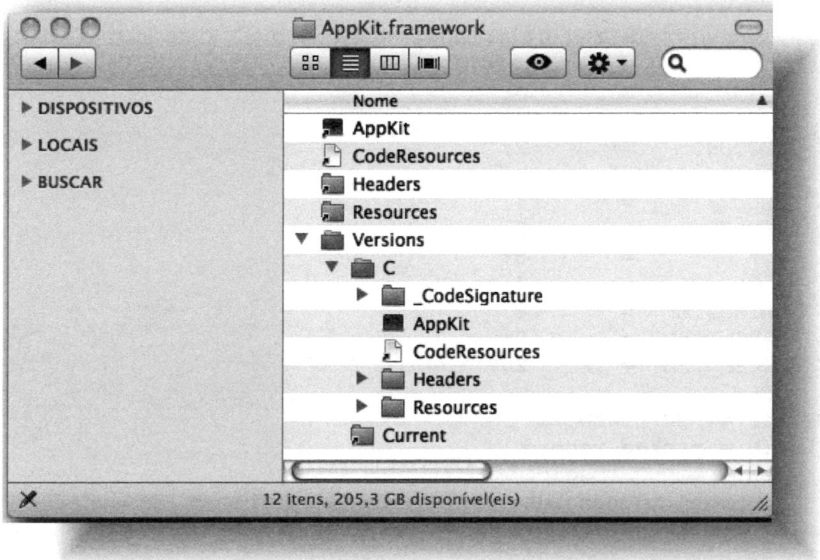

Figure 4.5: The structure of a Framework in MacOS X

4.3.3 Control Panel applications for Windows

Windows Control Panel is a program that takes all the files with extension `.cpl` in the Windows system directory together and displays them if needed. The Windows system directory is named SYSTEM in Windows 9x and system32 in NT-versions.
This behaviour is quite common in Windows.
The program `rundll.exe` which comes with Windows can also be used to load other DLLs into memory.

So the Applets for the Windows Control Panel are simply DLLs. They need to export a function named CPlApplet. (**In this exact spelling!**) Certain constants and types are also needed. The applet can only work if various additional resources have been defined precisely.
First the resources: An icon (with ID 1000) has to be available in the resource file, together with a name for the applet (with ID 1000) and an information string (with ID 1001). In the `.rc` file it must look like this:

```
STRINGTABLE
1000, "CPL-Example"
1001, "Example of a Control Panel Applet"
1000 ICON "the binary Icon definition as a hexdump"     ...
```

More convenient than working with such `.rc` files is creating resources in `.res` format with a resource editor such as the free XN Resource Editor. All control panel applications are based on the following definitions:

```
const
  WM_CPL_LAUNCH    = (WM_USER+1000);
  WM_CPL_LAUNCHED  = (WM_USER+1001);
  CPL_DYNAMIC_RES  =      0;
  CPL_INIT         =      1;
  CPL_GETCOUNT     =      2;
  CPL_INQUIRE      =      3;
  CPL_SELECT       =      4;
  CPL_DBLCLK       =      5;
  CPL_STOP         =      6;
  CPL_EXIT         =      7;
  CPL_NEWINQUIRE   =      8;
  CPL_STARTWPARMS  =      9;
  CPL_SETUP        =      200;
type
  PCPLInfo = ^TCPLInfo;
  TCPLInfo = packed record
    idIcon:         Longint;
    idName:         Longint;
    idInfo:         Longint;
    lData:          Longint;
  end;
  TNewCPLInfo = packed record
    dwSize :        DWord;
    dwFlags:        DWord;
    dwHelpContext:  DWord;
    lData:          Longlnt;
    hIcon:          HICON;
    szName:         array[0..31]  of AnsiChar;
    szlnfo:         array[0..63]  of AnsiChar;
    szHelpFile:     array[0..127] of AnsiChar;
  end;
```

These entries can be found in a similar form in Delphi version 3 or higher in a file named `cpl.pas`, which can be used in Lazarus as well. It is also possible to enter these definitions into a new Lazarus project file.

To do that create a new library under *File → New*.

The most important element of the library is the function *CPlApplet* we mentioned before. This has to be exported. This function has to respond to requests from the Control Panel. Communication goes in the form of messages as usual under Windows. Therefore the function header is quite complex. The message passing convention has to be specified as *StdCall*:

```
function CPlApplet(hwndCPL: THandle; uMsg: Cardinal;
      const lParam1: Longint; var lParam2: Longint): Longint; Stdcall;
```

The variable hwndCPL is used to pass the handle of our window to Control Panel.

This handle is only needed if the applet window has to be used as a "child" of the Control Panel window. Parameter *uMsg* is essential. Because an extension for Control Panel exports only this function, the tasks to be performed have to be determined by examining the message type. Depending on the message in *uMsg* the parameters *lParam1* and *lParam2* can have different functions. *lParam2* usually contains a pointer by which a whole set of information is transferred to the applet.
Applets are implemented in several steps. Control Panel will call the applet several times, once for each step. Each call will carry a different message in *uMsg*. The steps occur in the following sequence:

`CPL_INIT` **(=1)**

When Control Panel is started, all `.cpl` files in the system directory will be loaded *(LoadLibrary)* and first initialized. So the *CPlApplet* function will be called with this message for each of them (for each `.cpl` file). This gives the applets a chance to do their initialization (acquiring a module handle and initializing variables that will be needed later on). The other parameters are not used in this step. The return value of the function has to be non-zero to signal successful initialization.

`CPL_GETCOUNT` **(=2)**

A Control Panel extension may contain more than one applet (and so have more than one icon in the Control Panel window). This message, which follows immediately after CPL INIT, is used to return the number of applets in this `.cpl` file.
The other parameters are not used.

`CPL_INQUIRE` **(=3)**

This is the third message transferred at the start of Control Panel. This requests some information about the applet (symbol and name). *lParam1* contains information about the number of applets being asked about (the count starts at 0). *lParam2* contains a pointer to a data structure of type *TCPLInfo*, where the data has to be stored. The function result has to be zero to signal successful completion. The information record is defined as an integer in Delphi. Under Lazarus it is better to use a *LongInt*, because integers are sometimes defined as entries of only 16 bits in Free Pascal.

```
tagCPLINFO = packed record
    idIcon: Longint;   // icon resource id
    idName: Longint;   // name string resource id
    idInfo: Longint;   // info string res. id
    lData : Longint;   // user defined data
  end;
TCPLInfo = packed record
```

The field *idIcon* contains the identification number of the icon defined by the resource, which has to be displayed in the Control Panel. *idName* refers to the string resource, which contains the name to be displayed below the icon.

The Control Panel window has a status line showing additional information about the currently activated symbol. The field *idInfo* refers to a string resource which contains this information. *lData* is an *integer variable* that can be used freely. It will re-appear in the message CPL_DBLCLK. So the actual information is not directly transmitted, all that is transferred is a number of references to resources in the `.cpl` library. Control Panel is responsible for getting the actual data.

`CPL_NEWINQUIRE` **(=3)**

This message is sent together with CPL_INQUIRE. It has the same function, but the returned data structure (type *TNewCPLInfo*) is larger. CPL_NEWINQUIRE is a relic from the Windows 3 era. The Win32 API documentation advises to use CPL_INQUIRE because this is "cacheable" (which gives better performance). So all that is needed is to return a non-zero return value for this message, which will be ignored by Control Panel. The messages CPL_INQUIRE and CPL_NEWINQUIRE both occur at the start of Control Panel and at the moment an applet is activated (see message CPL_DBLCLK).

`CPL_SELECT` **(=4)**

This message is another relic from the past. It is not transmitted in Win32, so we don't need to discuss it.

`CPL_DBLCLK` **(=5)**

CPlApplet is called with this message when the user activates the applet in Control Panel by double-clicking its symbol. A modal dialog now has to be created for the user to interact with the applet. *lParam1* contains the number of the applet (counting starts at 0). *lParam2* contains the user defined data value passed in the field *lData* in *TCPLInfo* (see message CPL_INQUIRE). Return 0 as result to signal successful completion. Applets have to be prepared for this message to arrive more than once. As long as the modal dialog is open, the message will not be sent to the applet, even when the user double clicks its icon again.

`CPL_STOP` **(=6)**

We are getting near the end now. The message is sent by Control Panel to the `.cpl` extension to signify closing of the applet (the modal dialog) was detected. lParam1 and lParam2 contain the number of the applet and the value of *lData*, just as for CPL_DBLCLK. The function result can simply be zero, to acknowledge arrival of the message.

`CPL_EXIT` **(=7)**

This message appears after an applet has been closed. The parameters are not used. The function result should be zero. Implementation of these interactions have been available in Delphi for some years now. This can only partially be transferred to Lazarus.

The main difference is that the application object is always available in Delphi, while it has to be explicitly declared in Lazarus.

Here is the source code for a complete Control Panel applet:

```
library Bspl;
{$mode Delphi}{$H+}

uses    Interfaces, // this includes the LCL widgetset
        Forms, Unit1, LResources, Dialogs, Windows
{ you can add units after this };
($IFDEF WINDOWS}($R bspl.rc}{$ENDIF}
($R CPLDATAI.RES}    // External resource with Icon, Name and text information
                     // here it integrates the data which would go in a Unit

const WM CPL LAUNCH    = (WM_USER+1000);
      WM_CPL_LAUNCHED  = (WM_USER+1001);
      CPL_DYNAMIC_RES  = 0;
      CPL_INIT         = 1;
      CPL_GETCOUNT     = 2;
      CPL_INQUIRE      = 3;
      CPL_SELECT       = 4;
      CPL_DBLCLK       = 5;
      CPL_STOP         = 6;
      CPL_EXIT         = 7;
      CPL_NEWINQUIRE   = 8;
      CPL_STARTWPARMS  = 9;
      CPL_SETUP        = 200;

type PCPLInfo = ^TCPLInfo;
     TCPLInfo = packed record
       idIcon : Longint;
       idName : LongInt;
       idInfo : Longint;
       lData  : Longint;
     end;
     TNewCPLInfo = packed record
       dwSize          :    DWord;
       dwFlags         :    DWord;
       dwHelpContext   :    DWord;
       lData           :    Longint;
       hIcon           :    HICON;
       szName          :    array[0..31]  of AnsiChar;
       szInfo          :    array[0..63]  of AnsiChar;
       szHelpFile      :    array[0..127] of AnsiChar;
     end;
```

```
function CPlApplet(hwndCPL: THandle; uMsg: Cardinal;
     const lParam1: Longint; var lParam2: Longint): Longint; Stdcall;
         // The exported system control function
  var CPLInfo: TCPLInfo absolute lParam2;
      AppInitcalled: Boolean;
begin
  Result := 1;
  AppInitcalled := False;
  case uMsg of                            // handling of uMsg
    CPL_INIT: Result := 1;                // initialization
    CPL_GETCOUNT: Result := 1;            // number of applets in this example
    CPL_INQUIRE: begin                    // query for icon, name and info
      if lParam1 = 0 then
      begin                               // only interested in this applet
        with CPLInfo do
        begin
          idIcon := 1000;   // ResourceID of the Icon in CPLDATAI.RES
          idName := 1000;   // ResourceID of the Name in CPLDATAI.RES
          idInfo := 1001;   // ResourceID of the text info in CPLDATAI.RES
          lData  := 1234;   // freely definable value
        end;
        Result := 0;
      end
      else
        Result := 1; // error (nonexistent applet)
    end;
    CPL_NEWINQUIRE: Result := 1;          // this message will be ignored
    CPL_DBLCLK:
    begin                                 // start applet
      if lParam1 = 0 then
      begin                               // only interested in this applet
        if not AppInitCalled then
        begin
          Application.Initialize;         // vital for Lazarus!
          AppInitCalled := True;          // only initialize once
        end;
        if Form1 = NIL then
          Form1 := TForm1.Create(Application); // Lazarus and Delphi
        Application.UpdateMainform(Form1);      // Lazarus specific
        Form1.ShowModal;      // Show is not enough
        Form1.Free;           // free the window
        Form1 := NIL;         // and set it to NIL
        Result := 0;
      end else Result:=1;   // error (nonexistent applet)
    end;
    CPL_STOP: Result := 0; // window has been closed
    CPL_EXIT: Result := 0; // DLL is released
  end; // Case
end;

exports
CPlApplet;
end.
```

For a Control Panel module containing only one applet, this is all that is needed. The difference with Delphi is very clear. What can be done with

```
CPL_DBLCLK: begin   // start applet
              if lParam1 = 0 then
              begin
                Form1 := TForm1.Create(Application);
                Form1.ShowModal;
                Form1.Free;
                Result := 0;
              end
              else Result := 1;
            end;
```

in Delphi takes a lot more effort in Lazarus, as can be seen in the listing above. The result however is the same: As soon as the applet is called, the main window Form1 will open. If more than one applet has to be implemented, some of the code becomes more complex. First CPL_GETCOUNT and CPL_INQUIRE:

```
CPL_GETCOUNT : Result := 2;      // here we now have two applets
CPL_INQUIRE  : begin             // query for icon, name and info
                 if lParam1 = 0 then
                 begin           // first applet
                   with CPLInfo do
                   begin
                     idIcon := 1000;   // Icon resource ID
                     idName := 1000;   // Name resource ID
                     idInfo := 1001;   // text information resource ID
                     lData  := 1234;   // freely definable value
                   end;
                   Result := 0; //
                 end
                 else
                   if lParam1= 1 then
                   begin // second applet
                     with CPLInfo do
                     begin
                       idIcon := 2000;   // icon resource ID
                       idName := 2000;   // name resource ID
                       idInfo := 2001;   // text information resource ID
                       lData  := 4321;   // freely definable value
                     end;
                     Result:= 0;
                   end
                   else Result := 1;     // error – missing applet
               end;
```

This can of course be extended as required. As can be seen in the example, the identifiers for the resources are simple to define.

The block for the actual call to invoke the applets can be doubled in a similar way:

```
CPL_DBLCLK: begin   // start applet
              if lParaml = 0 then
              begin  // first applet
                if not AppInitCalled then
                begin
                  Application.Initialize;   // vital for Lazarus!
                  ApplnitCalled := True;    // only initialize once
                end;
                if Forml = NIL then
                  Forml := TForml.Create(Application); // Lazarus and Delphi
                Application.UpdateMainform(Forml);     // Lazarus specific
                Forml.ShowModal; // Show is not enough
                Forml.Free;       // free the window
                Forml := NIL;     // ... and set it to NIL
                Result := 0;
              end    // first applet

              else
                if lParaml = 1 then
                begin  // second applet
                  if not AppInitCalled then
                  begin
                    Application.Initialize;   // important in Lazarus!
                    AppInitcalled := true     // only initialize once
                  end;
                  if Form2 = NIL then          // Lazarus and Delphi
                    Form2 := TFor21.Create(Application);
                  Application.UpdateMainform(Form2); // Lazarus specific
                  Form2.ShowModal;    // Show is not enough
                  Form2.Free;         // free the window
                  Form2 := NIL;       // ... and set it to NIL
                  Result := 0;
                end    // second applet

                else
                  Result := 1; // error – not available applet
            end;    // start applet
```

Control Panel *applets* are problematic in two ways. The first problem is development of the *applet* itself: The DLL cannot be started and tested in Lazarus. For that reason we need two projects: One of them is used to open the window(s) from a program in the normal way. The main window is then transferred into the library project. This project also gets the correct target name and the extension `.cpl` in the IDE. To do this go to *Project → Project Options* and under the *Compiler Options* heading choose Paths and enter the desired name in the Target file name (-o): edit box (for instance `my_first_applet.cpl`). The second problem is trickier: Windows partially blocks Control Panel applets.
They can be started with a double click in the current directory, but then they are not called from the Control Panel.

But if we copy them to `C:\Windows\System32` you then cannot delete them again, because they become locked by Windows, and we wish there were an uninstallating procedure for them. We can easily write an uninstalling routine ourselves. This consists of a batch file in any directory, for instance `C:\Programs` with any name.
This `rmfile.bat` contains only the line

```
@del C:\WINDOWS\system32\My_First_Applet.cpl
```

(or whatever the name of the file is). This file is entered into the registry with RegEdit with RunOnce. To do this, open RegEdit and search for RunOnce. Then enter a new sequence of characters, for instance rmfile, with the value `C:\Programs\rmfile.bat`.
This will instruct Windows to delete the CPL file at startup, that is, before it has become active. By selecting RunOnce we ensure that this happens only one time.
Of course it is better to use proper installers to enter such system files into the operating system and remove them again. As long as we are dealing with small programs, a self-created .inf file would suffice.

4.4 Unit Testing

A framework for performing unit tests is an integral part of FPC and Lazarus. Unit testing has been established as a reliable method for testing object oriented code. The implementation of FPCUnit is directly derived from the test framework JUnit, which was written in Java. The philosophy behind the method of unit testing is that along with each function in their code, programmers write test routines which can test and prove their correct operation (or otherwise).

The *File* → *New* dialog contains three elements needed for unit testing. These are all that is needed:

- **FPCUnit Test Case** This adds a new test case to the group. This may involve creating and registering several FPC unit test classes in your test application. When the application is running it will show an onscreen window, displaying all tests listed in a tree structure. This is also used to display the test results.

- **FPCUnit Console Test Application** This is for building a new test application without a graphical user interface (GUI), so testing has to be initiated from the command-line. If you start the application with the command-line option -help further information is displayed. Test results will be displayed on the console.

- **FPCUnit Test Application** This is similar to the Console Test Application, but instead creates a test project which has a GUI rather than a command-line interface.

The following example shows how to test if part of the compiler's arithmetic works correctly. A test is considered successful if the routine *Fail* has not been called:

```
unit TestArithmetic;
{$mode objfpc}{$H+}
interface

uses  Classes, SysUtils, fpcunit, testutils, testregistry;
type  TMyTest= class(TTestCase)
        published
        procedure TestHookUp;
      end;

implementation

procedure TMyTest.TestHookUp;
  var  x: Integer;
begin
  x := 2 + 2;
  if x <> 4 then
    Fail('The compiler''s arithmetic doesn''t work!');
end;

initialization
  RegisterTest(TMyTest);
end.
```

4.5 Packages

A Lazarus package is a set of units and components. It can either be the basis for other projects or packages that need its functionality, or it can be a plugin, for instance a package which adds a new menu option to the Lazarus IDE.

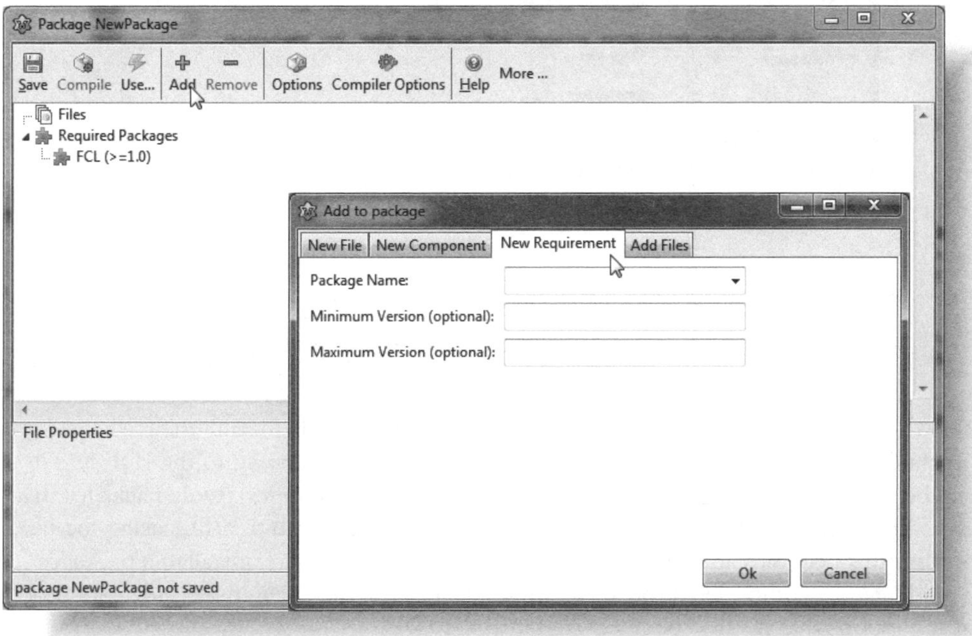

Figure 4.6: Adding a new dependency to a project

Currently the Free Pascal compiler only supports statically linked packages, not dynamically linked ones. This means Lazarus packages have to be linked into the executable file of the project. (Dynamic packages would make it possible to store the package as a separate library as is possible in Delphi).
The only unpleasant side effect of this limitation of the compiler is that the Lazarus IDE has to be recompiled every time a new package is installed, whether it adds to the functionality of the IDE or not, and whether or not new components will be added to the component palette.
The more packages have been pre-compiled, the faster this goes.
For that reason it is not a good idea to execute a make clean in the Lazarus directory.

Free Pascal developers are working on dynamic packages, but a stable cross-platform solution has not emerged at the time of writing.

Packages may need other packages, and projects need packages anyway.
The dependencies between a project and a package are added to the Required Packages section in the Package Editor or in the Project Inspector. It is possible to specify versions as well. There is provision for setting minimum and maximum compatible versions.
It is also possible to leave out the version information. In that case any version of the specified package will be accepted.

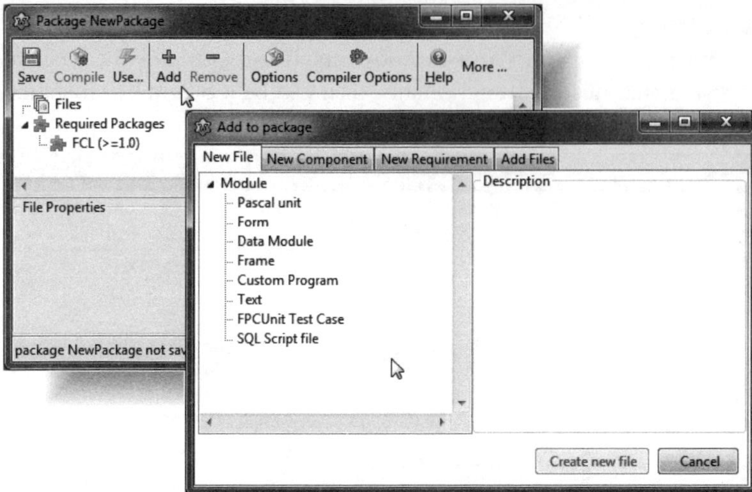

Figure 4.7: The Package Editor

The Package Editor contains a *Compile* button to compile and "install" the package. "Installing" in this case means the package will thereafter be known to the IDE and it will be recompiled (along with all the previously installed packages). Only packages that are needed for the development process should be installed into the IDE using the *Use...* button (this becomes an *Install* button with some packages). Such installable packages would include: components for the Component Palette; menu extensions; dialogs, and other options that need to be integrated into the IDE.

If a package is only intended to be part of a project, it should not be installed. That would be no use, since installing it in the IDE does not make it accessible to the project. Such a package should be added as a dependency in the Project Inspector. To do that, click the *Required Packages* node in the Project Inspector's tree structure and press the button with the plus sign. You can add your project's new package dependency in the resulting dialog, indicating minimum and maximum versions as required.

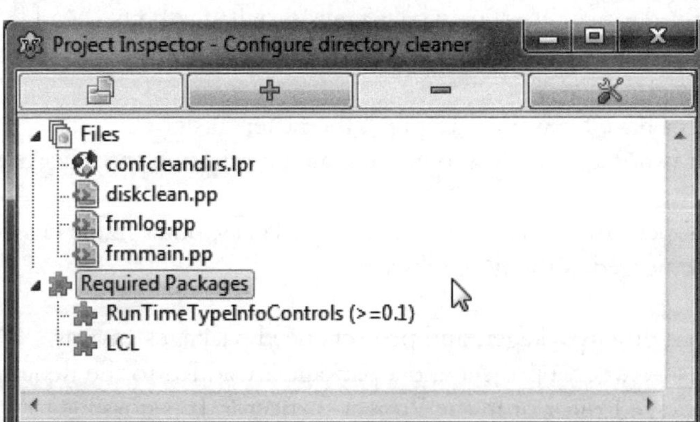

Figure 4.8: The Project Inspector

You create a new package with the menu selection *Package → New Package* or with *File → New → Package*. This will open the Package Editor for adding new files to the package. Lazarus packages usually contain Pascal source code, but any kind of file such as images or resources can be added as well. The package system helps you to organize these files.
Every Lazarus package is associated with a file with extension `.lpk`.
This is the most important file in the package. To open the Package Editor for a package you can simply load its `lpk` file into Lazarus. Every package has a name and a version. The name of the package has to be the same as the name of the `.lpk` file (without the extension).
The IDE automatically creates a main source file `PackageName.pas` and adds the uses clause for all Pascal source files in the project and also adds source code for registering the units in the IDE.
This source file should never be edited manually, as all necessary configurations have already been set by selecting the files in the Package Editor. Clicking the checkbox *Package Unit* has added the uses clause and registered the units. This establishes registration in the uses clause in the main package file and in the IDE.
Here is an example of a main unit in a package:

```
//This file was automatically created by Lazarus. Do not edit!
//This source is only used to compile and install
//the package GTKOpenGL 1.0.

unit GTKOpenGL;
interface
uses GTKGLArea, GTKGLArea_Int, NVGL, NVGLX, LazarusPackageIntf;

implementation
procedure Register;
begin
  RegisterUnit('GTKGLArea', @GTKGLArea.Register);
end;

initialization
  RegisterPackage('GTKOpenGL', @Register)
end.
```

The directory containing the `lpk` file is called the *package directory*, and all path specifications should be relative to this directory. This means the package structure can reside in any location in the file system. It is theoretically possible to specify absolute paths, but this should not be done, as it goes against the philosophy of the package system.

Two types of search paths for packages are possible in the Package Editor:

- the paths in the Compiler Options dialog (used when compiling the package)
- the paths on the Usage page (tab) of the Options dialog which are needed by packages and projects that want to make use of this package

In general the *Compiler Options* path will point to the directories where the package *sources* are located, whereas the *Usage* paths point to the directory where the *compiled units* are stored. Most of the time you will not have to worry about the paths, nor change them manually. If a unit which is not in the package path is added to a package, the IDE will notice this and ask whether this path should be added to the compiler settings path. As all compilation results are stored in the same location for binaries, no matter where the source is located, there is no reason to change the location for those.

The preset output directory is set in the package directory as `lib/$(TargetCPU)-$(TargetOS)/` and this should not be changed.
A list of packages opened in the development environment is maintained in the file `packagelinks.xml`. This file is located in the configuration directory of the IDE. It is updated with every install and uninstall. It will not be deleted when Lazarus is uninstalled. This is something to keep in mind when installing again, as the old settings will remain. If you don't want that to happen, you will need to delete the user's local Lazarus configuration directory.

If the IDE cannot find a package, load the lpk file in the IDE. All you need to do is to make the file known to the IDE by opening it. This name-based system has the consequence that package names have to be unique. No two packages with the same name can be installed in the same IDE. Therefore it is important to choose the names as clearly and consistently as possible. FCL, LCL and SynEdit are special base packages which form part of the IDE and are started automatically. They are read-only and do not have an `.lpk` file. As a result of that they cannot be removed or altered.
Lazarus saves a state file for each package it compiles with the name *PackageName.compiled* which stores the options used to build the package, and whether it should be rebuilt when these options change. Here is an example of such a `.compiled` file for a package:

```
<?xml version="1.0"?>
<CONFIG>
  <Compiler Value="/usr/bin/ppc386" Date="781388725"/>
  <Params Value=" -Rintel -S2cgi -CD -Ch8000000 -OG1p1
    -Tlinux -gl -vewnhi -l -Fu../../../lcl/units
    -Fu../../../lcl/units/gtk -Fu../../../packager/units
    -Fu. -FElib/ gtkopengl.pas"/>
</CONFIG>
```

The IDE will check all the dependencies before compiling a package. It will rebuild those as well if necessary and if their configuration allows it. Then the main package source file with the package units in the uses clause and registration code will be written. Only then will Free Pascal compile the package. Compiled units will be written to the output directory, and a status file by the name of *PackageName.compiled* with the options in effect during compilation will be written. Only in the situation where these options have been changed will the package will need to be regenerated.

4.5.1 Adding components

Packages are used to add new components to the Component Palette in the **IDE**. To do this, open the package to which you want to add the component (or create a new package). Then go to the Package Editor and press the [+] button. In the *Add to package* dialog which appears select the *New Component* tab. Then choose the *Ancestor Type* (class) from the combobox of that name, and enter the *New class name* of the new component and choose the *Palette Page* for the new component.
This will add a new file to the package for the new component, and installing the package will add this component to the IDE.

4.5.2 Registering components

To make a component appear on the Component Palette, it has to be registered.
The component needs a registration procedure for this (just as in Delphi). You normally locate the registration procedure in the same unit file as the component source code.
The procedure has to be declared in the interface part of the unit and it must have the name *Register*, and its implementation must call the procedure *RegisterComponents* whose declaration is as follows:

```
procedure RegisterComponents(const Page: String;
                            ComponentClasses: array of TComponentClass);
```

This declaration can be found in the Free Pascal file `cregist.inc` and it is included as a procedure pointer in `classesh.inc`. This file is added by the Free Pascal standard unit *classes*. This registration procedure needs to be used to register every component in the unit. The same goes for registering a new property editor or component editor for the new component. A property editor is used for editing values in one of the rows of the Object Inspector, and a component editor is used to manipulate the component in the Form Designer. The procedures for these are *RegisterPropertyEditor* and *RegisterComponentEditor* (which are not part of Free Pascal, but belong to Lazarus).

RegisterComponentEditor is defined in `ComponentEditors.pas`:

```
procedure RegisterComponentEditor(ComponentClass: TComponentClass;
                                  ComponentEditor: TComponentEditorClass);
function GetComponentEditor(Component: TComponent;
     const Designer: TComponentEditorDesigner): TBaseComponentEditor;
```

RegisterPropertyEditor can be found in the `propedits.pp` unit:

```
procedure RegisterPropertyEditor(PropertyType: PtypeInfo;
           PersistentClass: TClass; const PropertyName: ShortString;
                                    EditorClass: TPropertyEditorClass);
```

4.5.2 Registering components

To register a component you adapt its unit's code as follows. First the registration procedure is declared in the *interface*:

```
procedure Register;
```

Then, in the *implementation* part of the *Register* procedure the real work is done:

```
procedure Register;
begin
  RegisterComponents('OpenGL', [TOpenGLControl]);
  RegisterComponentEditor(TOpenGLControl, TOpenGLControlEditor);
end;
```

The component will only appear in the IDE when it is added to a package, which can be installed in the IDE. The unit containing the 'register' procedure must be marked in the package as "register unit". This can be done by selecting the file in the package editor and setting the 'register unit' checkbox.

4.5.3 Property Editors

Property Editors offer custom dialogs to edit component properties in the Object Inspector. Standard properties (such as strings, string lists and enumerated types) have existing editors already provided by Lazarus, but if a new component has special properties, a custom dialog will be needed to configure it. Every Property Editor is a class based on *TPropertyEditor* (or one of its descendants), which implements certain methods of the base class. All property editors need to be registered in the IDE with the function *RegisterPropertyEditor* from the unit *PropEdits*. The naming convention is to name a property editor as the class name of the property, followed by *PropertyEditor*. For instance the property editor for the property *TField* is named *TFieldPropertyEditor*.

```
 TPropertyEditor = class
  public
    function  AllEqual: Boolean; Virtual;
    function  AutoFill: Boolean; Virtual;
    procedure Edit; Virtual;        // Activated by double-clicking the
                                    // property value
    procedure ShowValue; Virtual;   // Activated by control-clicking the
                                    // property value
    function  GetAttributes: TPropertyAttributes; Virtual;
    function  GetEditLimit: Integer; Virtual;
    function  GetName: ShortString; Virtual;
    procedure GetProperties(Proc: TGetPropEditProc); Virtual;
    function  GetHint(HintType: TPropEditHint; x, y:integer): String;
                                                              Virtual;
    function  GetDefaultValue: AnsiString; Virtual;
    procedure GetValues(Proc: TGetStrProc); Virtual;
    procedure SetValue(const NewValue: AnsiString); Virtual;
    procedure UpdateSubProperties; Virtual;
    function  SubPropertiesNeedsUpdate: Boolean; Virtual;
    function  IsDefaultValue: Boolean; Virtual;
    function  IsNotDefaultValue: Boolean; Virtual;
    // ... shortened
end;
```

TPropertyEditor has a number of methods, the most important of which are listed in Table 4.8.

Property	Description
GetValue	To get a string which displays the current value of the property in the object inspector.
Edit	Is called when the [...] button is pressed or the property is double-clicked. Usually this brings up a dialog.
GetAttributes	Information for the object inspector about how to display the property. See Table 4.9 below about *TPropertyAttributes* for more information.
GetValues	Called when *paValueList* is returned in *GetAttributes*. Fills the list of values in the drop down list of the property. For example, the standard *TEnumPropertyEditor* for enumerated types will pass every element in the enumeration.
GetEditLimit	Returns the largest number of characters the user is allowed to enter for the value in the object inspector. The default limit is 255.
GetProperties	Returns the subproperties of an expandable property. By default no sub-properties are assumed, except for descendants of *TClassPropertyEditor*, which passes all published properties of the class as subproperties, and descendants of *TSetPropertyEditor*, which passes all elements of the set as subproperties.

Table 4.6: The most important methods of TPropertyEditor

4.5.3 Property Editors

TPropertyAttributes is an important class to understand in writing a new Property Editor. Its main fields are shown below.

Property	Description
paValueList	The property can be edited like an enumerated list. The names inside the list are the ones returned by the *GetValues* method. In this case there won't be an ellipsis [...] edit button but rather a drop-down arrow to show the complete list of values.
paSortList	The list returned by *GetValues* should be sorted before use.
paPickList	Used together with *paValueList* to indicate that the user cannot insert arbitrary text but must choose one of the options from the dropdown list.
paSub-Properties	Used for classes and record types to make the item expandable to change properties inside it. The *GetProperties* method will return the list of attributes to be shown.
paDynamic-SubProps	Indicates that the editor's sub properties can change. If this occurs, the Object Inspector must read them again through a call to *UpdateListPropertyEditors*.
paDialog	Indicates that the Edit method will bring up a dialog. This will cause the ellipsis [...] button to be displayed to the right of the property in the Object Inspector.
paMultiSelect	Allows the property to be displayed when more than one component is selected. Some properties are not appropriate for multi-selection, for example the Name property.
paAutoUpdate	Causes the *SetValue* method to be called for each change made in the editor, rather than only after pressing [Enter]. This is used for properties such as Caption whose visible text is updated continuously as the user types.
paReadOnly	The value is not allowed to change through use of the Object Inspector editor or by selecting a combo box item in lists. The value can be changed however if *paDialog* is active and the dialog allows this.
paRevertable	Allows the property to be reset to its original value.
paFullWidth-Name	Tells the Object Inspector that the value does not need to be displayed and so the name should be rendered using the full width of the Object Inspector.
paVolatile-SubProperties	Any change to the property requires that the Object Inspector reloads the entire list of *subproperty* values.
paDisable-SubProperties	All sub-properties are read-only.
paReference	Used in conjunction with *paSubProperties* so that the properties of the object referred to in the value of this property are displayed in the sub-properties. This is used in properties which hold a reference to other controls. For example in *TDataSource* the property *DataSet* is expandable when set to a valid *DataSet* and its subproperties are the properties from the selected *DataSet*.
paNotNestable	Indicates that the property cannot be shown in the list of expanded subproperties because it references another property which references itself, which would generate an endless loop of nested properties. For example: class A might have a property of class B which itself has a property of class A.

Table 4.7: The fields of TPropertyAttributes

Tfont provides a good example of a property editor in use.

Simply descending from *TClassPropertyEditor* is enough to be able to use its basic functionality. Continuing the *TFont* example: inheriting from *TClassPropertyEditor* already offers part of the desired behaviour so that the *TFontPropertyEditor* class only needs to implement showing the dialog in the Edit method, and setting the editor's attributes in *GetAttributes*:

```
 TFontPropertyEditor = class(TClassPropertyEditor)
public
  procedure Edit; Override;
  function  GetAttributes: TPropertyAttributes; Override;
end;

procedure TFontPropertyEditor.Edit;
  var  FontDialog: TFontDialog;
begin
  FontDialog := TFontDialog.Create(NIL);
  try
    FontDialog.Font    := TFont(GetObjectValue(TFont));
    FontDialog.Options := FontDialog.Options + [fdShowHelp,
                                               fdForceFontExist];
    if FontDialog.Execute then SetPtrValue(FontDialog.Font);
  finally
    FontDialog.Free;
  end;
end;

function TFontPropertyEditor.GetAttributes: TPropertyAttributes;
begin
  Result := [paMultiSelect, paSubProperties, paDialog, paReadOnly];
end;
```

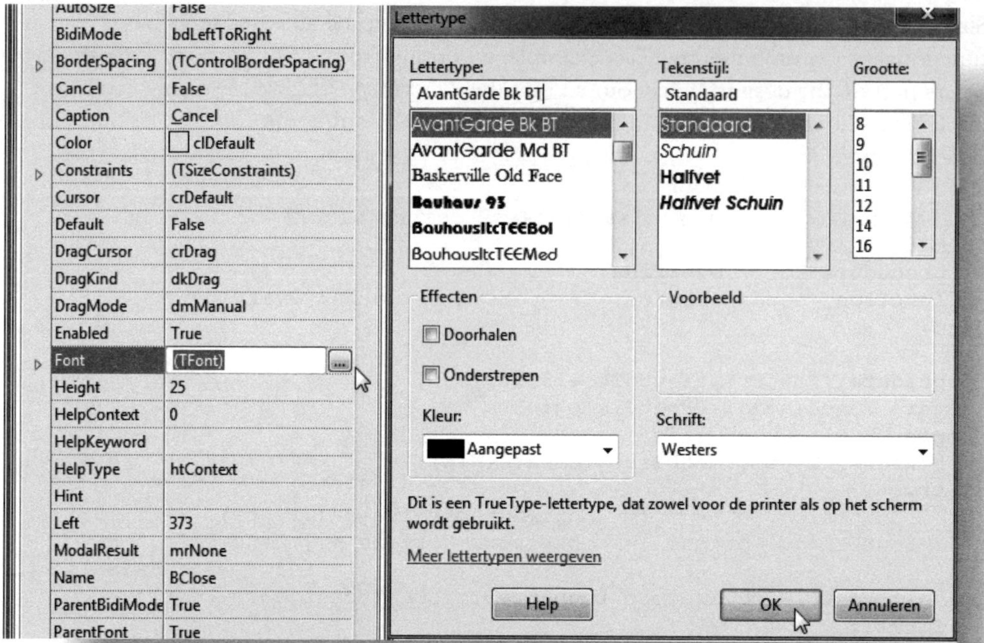

Figure 4.9: Pressing the TFont property's [...] button opens its property editor.

This property editor handles operating system fonts.

Property editors are particularly useful for changing *class properties* in a component (such as the *TFont* class pictured above). Classes tend to have fields in many different formats. These more complex properties cannot be changed in a normal input field such as you would use for editing a string or a numerical value.

The Object Inspector convention for making class property editors available is to permanently show the name of the class in parentheses and provide an ellipsis [...] button which opens a dialog where you can edit the properties of the class. This display behaviour with the accompanying button (but not the dialog itself) is implemented by a standard property editor named *TClassPropertyEditor*, from which you can derive specific editors for your own classes:

```
TClassPropertyEditor = class(TPropertyEditor)
public
  constructor Create(Hook: TPropertyEditorHook; APropCount: Integer);
                                                           Override;
  function GetAttributes: TPropertyAttributes; Override;
  procedure GetProperties(Proc: TGetPropEditProc); Override;
  function GetValue: AnsiString; Override;
  property SubPropsTypeFilter: TTypeKinds read FSubPropsTypeFilter
                                          write SetSubPropsTypeFilter
                                        default tkAny;
end;
```

4.5.4 Component editors

Component editors handle the processing of right-clicks and double-clicks in the Form Designer. Each component editor is a class, which is derived from *TBaseComponentEditor* (usually through its descendant *TComponentEditor*) and your descendant has to implement the methods of the base class. Component editors have to be registered in the Register procedure using the function *RegisterComponentEditor* (found in the `ComponentEditor` unit). The convention for naming component editors is to use '*ComponentEditor*' prefixed with the class name the editor is designed for. So the component editor for the *TStringGrid* component is called *TStringGridComponentEditor*.

```
TBaseComponentEditor = class
protected
public
  constructor Create(AComponent: TComponent;
                     ADesigner: TComponentEditorDesigner); Virtual;
  procedure Edit; Virtual; Abstract;
  procedure ExecuteVerb(Index: Integer); Virtual; Abstract;
  function  GetVerb(Index: Integer): String; Virtual; Abstract;
  function  GetVerbCount: Integer; Virtual; Abstract;
  procedure PrepareItem(Index: Integer; const AnItem: TMenuItem);
                                                  Virtual; Abstract;
  procedure Copy; Virtual; Abstract;
  function  IsInInlined: Boolean; Virtual; Abstract;
  function  GetComponent: TComponent; Virtual; Abstract;
  function  GetDesigner: TComponentEditorDesigner; Virtual; Abstract;
  function  GetHook(out Hook: TPropertyEditorHook): Boolean;
                                                      Virtual; Abstract;
  procedure Modified; Virtual; Abstract;
end;
```

The most important method in a component editor is always called Edit. It is called when the component is double-clicked in the Form Editor. When a component's context menu is called by right-clicking, the menu is built using the methods *GetVerbCount* and *GetVerb*. When one of the 'verbs' is clicked ('verb' refers to menu entries in this instance), the method *ExecuteVerb* is activated.

There is a pre-defined component editor named *TDefaultEditor*, which implements *Edit* in a way that searches the properties of the components to find the best way to edit them. The method picks an event for this, adds a prepared section of source code in the source code window and puts the cursor there, ready for you to complete the code.

Another important *TBaseComponentEditor* method is *ExecuteVerb(Index)*. This executes an additional menu entry like a keyboard shortcut or hotkey when the popup menu is right clicked. *GetVerb* gives the names of all such additional popup menu entries.

The component editor is responsible for putting the menu entries together in the right way. In particular it handles the correct assignment of shortcuts with '&' and the menu separators, which are special entries whose *Caption* is a minus sign '-'. *GetVerbCount* gives the number of entries to be added to the popup menu.

The index of the routines *GetVerb* and *ExecuteVerb* is zero-based, so it counts from 0 to *GetVerbCount* - 1. The method *PrepareItem* is called for every verb after creation of its menu entry. At this stage further modification of the menu is possible, for instance insertion of submenus or check boxes. Entries can even be hidden here, by setting their *Visible* property to *False*.
The last method worth mentioning is *Copy*, which you call to copy a component to temporary storage. Component data used internally in Lazarus is always added and cannot be changed. The *Copy* method is designed for transferring a component to another application via the clipboard, without affecting Lazarus' own component insertion functionality.

TCheckListBox has a simple but interesting component editor, which creates a dialog for editing its contents. It is much more convenient to inherit from *TBaseComponentEditor* than to implement all methods from scratch. This is what *TCheckListBoxEditor* does. Its base class already has empty implementations for most methods and some pre-filled ones for many more. The actual editing is done by calling *ExecuteVerb(0)*, so the first menu entry executes the same action as a double click. This is normal component editor behaviour. It makes it unnecessary to implement *Edit* separately.
The basic action on double-clicking and for the first popup menu entry is often presentation of a dialog window. And *TCheckListBox* is no exception:

```
TCheckListBoxComponentEditor = class(TComponentEditor)
protected
  procedure DoShowEditor;
public
  procedure ExecuteVerb(Index: Integer); override;
  function GetVerb(Index: Integer): string; override;
  function GetVerbCount: Integer; override;
end;

procedure TCheckListBoxComponentEditor.DoShowEditor;
  var  Dlg: TCheckListBoxEditorDlg;
begin
  Dlg := TCheckListBoxEditorDlg.Create(nil);
  try
    if GetComponent is TCheckListBox then
    begin
      Dlg.aCheck := TCheckListBox(GetComponent);
      if not HasHook then exit;
      AssignCheckList(Dlg.FCheck, Dlg.aCheck);
      //ShowEditor
      if Dlg.ShowModal=mrOK then
      begin
        AssignCheckList(Dlg.aCheck, Dlg.FCheck);
        Modified;
      end;
      if Dlg.Modified then Modified;
    end;
  finally Dlg.Free;
  end;
end;
```

```
procedure TCheckListBoxComponentEditor.ExecuteVerb(Index: Integer);
begin
  DoShowEditor;
end;

function TCheckListBoxComponentEditor.GetVerb(Index: Integer): string;
begin
  Result:=clbCheckListBoxEditor+'...';
end;

function TCheckListBoxComponentEditor.GetVerbCount: Integer;
begin
  Result:=1;
end;
```

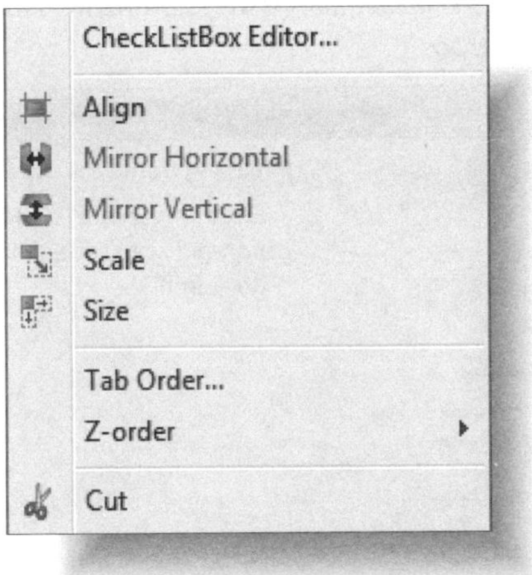

Figure 4.10: The popup menu for TCheckListBox

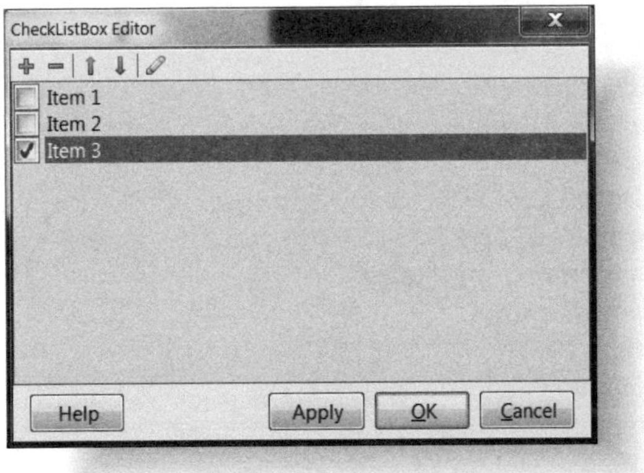

Figure 4.11 Double-clicking a TCheckListBox in the Form Designer produces this editor dialog

4.6 Services and Daemons

Unix *daemons* and Windows *services* are programs that have no direct interaction with the user. Such applications have different names in each operating system. Examples of daemons would be **http** and **ftp** servers. Because they do not directly communicate with the user, they close their *stdin*, *stdout* and *stderr* channels at startup. Lazarus documentation refers to all such programs as daemons, using it as a term which covers all platforms.

To create platform-independent daemons in Lazarus, use the package *lazdaemon*. Before we can start developing a daemon, we first have to install this package via *Package* → *Open package file (.lpk)*, or by directly opening the file `Lazarus/components/daemon/lazdaemon.lpk` This package will install some new components and menu entries in the IDE. Once it is installed, the *File* → *New* dialog will show a new entry *Daemon (service) applications* with sub entries *Daemon (service) application*, *Daemon Module* and *Daemon mapper*.

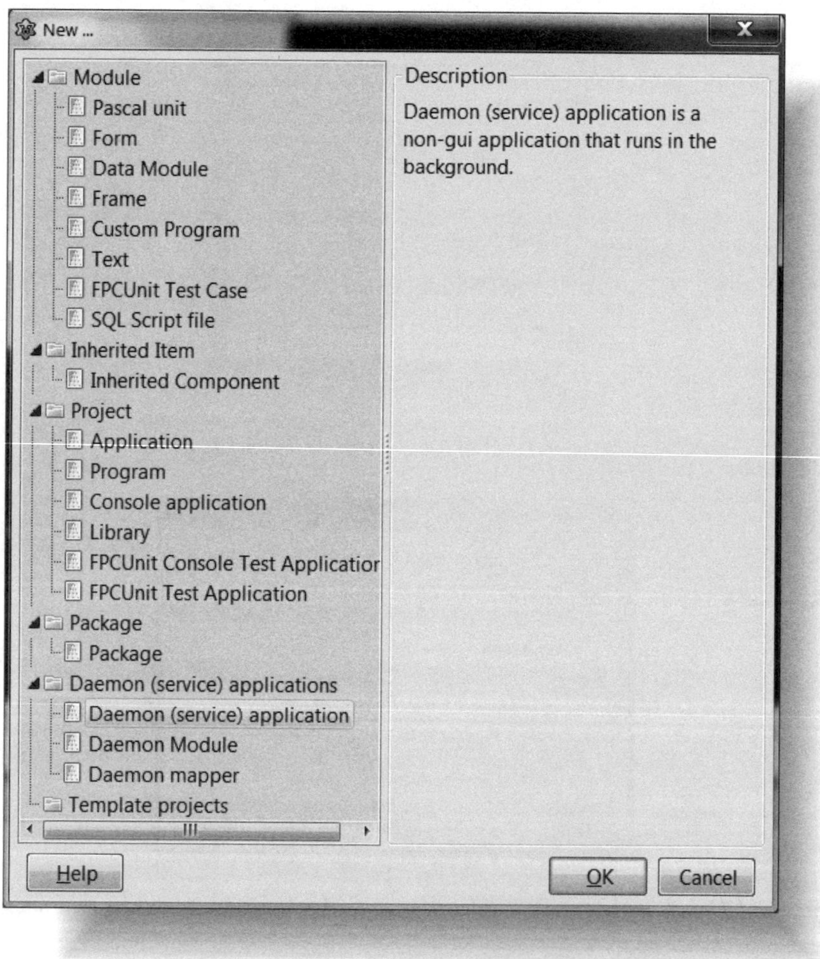

Figure 4.12: The new entries for daemons in the New… dialog

Entry	Function
Daemon (service) application	This entry creates a new daemon program and automatically registers a *TDaemon* and a *TDaemonMapper* instance for it.
	Registration procedures will be added automatically for the daemon and daemon mapper classes.
Daemon Module	Creates a new *TDaemon* instance.
Daemon mapper	Creates a new *TDaemonMapper* instance. This option is rarely used, because each daemon program can have only one mapper and one is automatically added whenever a new daemon application is created. Registering a second will cause an error.

Table 4.8: The daemon entries in the File → New ... dialog

Class	Description
TCustomDaemon	This is a *TDataModule* descendant that does all the work. There can be several *TCustomDaemon* classes and/or instances running at the same time and in the same process in the case of a multi-threaded daemon.
TCustomDaemon Application	This is a *TCustomApplication* descendant which creates *TCustomDaemons*. This does not need any change. It runs in Windows until it receives the Stop call or in Linux until it receives the TERM signal. See the chapter section 10.2 POSIX Signals and Exceptions.
TDaemonMapper	This component handles the service registration. Each instance needs one entry in the property *DaemonDefs*.

Table 4.9: The Lazarus daemon classes

Under Linux daemons are normally started by a script in `/etc/init.d/service`. This script is handed a parameter as needed, e.g. start, stop or pause.
Under BSD this is handled in a different way. Here they are loaded via the RC mechanism, either through a script in `/etc/rc.d/` or in `/usr/local/etc.d/` and an entry in `/etc/rc.conf`, or alternatively by a definition in `/etc/rc.local`. The administrator decides which method is used. In both cases the services are not able to contact the user and their configuration can only be set through files in `/etc` or (under BSD) `/usr/local/etc`. Under Windows many services will put an icon in the system tray, as the Apache HTTP server does, for instance. Another way to control services under Windows is through Control Panel applets.

The system tray icon is very useful anyway. This lets you start and stop the service, and may also allow you to alter its configuration or give access to help information. When creating daemons in Lazarus you use these options by putting a *TTrayIcon* component into a window. *TTrayIcon* is found on the Additional tab of the Component Palette. Implementation of services needs to be handled with care. Since Windows Vista, daemons are no longer allowed to interact directly with the desktop. So the daemon and the controlling program have to be in separate executable files. It is also important to register daemons before Windows is started. Daemons based on the Lazarus class *TCustomDaemonApplication* can do this by starting the program with a command line option -i. They can be un-registered by calling them with -u. Normally this call with -i is performed by the installation program, the call with -u is done by the de-installer. After installation the service can be started by calling the program with -r.

Chapter 5
Target Platforms

By Felipe Monteiro de Carvalho

Lazarus programs can be compiled to run on three major computer platforms: Windows, Linux/Unix, and MacOS X. That is fewer platforms than the Free Pascal compiler is able to target. The reason for this is that appropriate compiler capability is not the only condition that must be met before you can create a Lazarus program for a new platform.

The following three conditions have to be fulfilled before you can install and use Lazarus on any platform:

- A current Free Pascal compiler for the *target platform* must be available. At the moment these are available for Windows 32, Windows 64, Windows CE, MacOS X, Linux, FreeBSD and OS/2 (and eComStation) and (to a certain extent) for Solaris.
- A current Free Pascal compiler for the *target CPU* must be available. At the moment these are available for x86, x86_64, PowerPC, PowerPC64 and Arm (ARM4-instruction set only – the THUMB instruction set is not supported).
- There must be a *GUI library* available for the operating system platform. Currently fully supported are Windows, Windows CE and MacOS X, and also the Linux/Unix widget-set Gtk versions 1 and 2, and the platform-independent Qt 4 (Unix, MacOS, Windows).

This third requirement is the reason it is not possible to create OS/2 programs with Lazarus. A Free Pascal compiler for x86-OS/2 exists, but there is no support for the OS/2 presentation manager and for eComStation. In theory it should be possible to install Lazarus under XFree86/2 and create OS/2 programs for X. Nobody has tried this yet, but all the requirements can be met: there is a compiler and there is a port of Gtk version 2.

There are huge differences between the four basic platforms Win32/64, WinCE, MacOS and Linux/FreeBSD/Solaris. For that reason it is important if you want to create applications to run on multiple platforms (or if you intend to port software from one platform to another) to get acquainted with the details of using Lazarus on each of these platforms before making a start. That way you can investigate beforehand what problems you might encounter, and so make the right choices when designing software to run on all the desired platforms without problems. With some experience you can then develop software completely on one platform, and simply recompile your program to make it available on additional platforms.

This chapter gives a general overview of this theme, explaining the main features of the different operating systems, and also shows you how to make use of the native APIs if necessary (although you should normally avoid doing this if you are trying to create portable software).

At first sight it would seem very easy to make sure programs developed with Lazarus will run on all platforms. If you use only libraries that exist on all target platforms, and if you use only calls to the Free Pascal RTL and FCL and to the Lazarus LCL – your programs will work on all supported platforms, in theory, without change. *In theory* because there are still many operating system differences to keep in mind. If everything is done in the right way the RTL, FCL and LCL will hide or minimise these differences, but we may also have to work around them (and if the need arises we may have to correct code manually).

It gets more difficult if we need functionality that is not provided by Lazarus's libraries. It that case we will be forced to find another library that does offer such functionality on multiple platforms (hopefully on all of them), or we will have to work with the low-level APIs of each operating system to implement a solution for each platform ourselves.
In these cases we will have to use *conditional compilation.*
When we do that, parts of the source code for the different operating systems will need to be separated. Free Pascal offers the sequence of commands

$ ifdef condition ... $else ... $endif to facilitate this.

However, having to interlace source code for different operating systems in large routines in this way is not ideal. A cleaner solution is to provide separate source files, each offering a solution for one of the platforms. A good way to handle this in Free Pascal and Lazarus is to make use of the meta-command *$include filename.inc* to include these parts of the code into the source. A common convention is to create one subdirectory per platform and put all platform-specific code in the appropriate subdirectory.
Anything between the conditional commands *$ifdef* and *$endif* will be used only if the condition given after *$ifdef* is True. This applies to the include statements too.
We can include a file for just one operating system with a one-line construction in the code.

```
{$ifdef Linux}   {$include linux.inc}   {$endif}
{$ifdef Win32}   {$include win32.inc}   {$endif}   // ... etc.
```

A more elegant way is to use macros in search paths. If we include $(TargetOS) in the search path for include files, we can simply use:

```
{$include unit1.inc}
```

In that case the include file for Win32 might be located in: Win32/unit1.inc
while the include file for Linux could be found in: `Linux/unit1.inc`
In this way all Linux-specific files can be stored together in one directory.
Macros can also be used for unit search paths.

If platform-dependent source code is organised into functions and methods in separate files in a structured way, the reuseability of the routines is guaranteed. *$ifdef* commands can also be nested.
More about compiler switches and conditional compilation can be found in Chapter 5.3, starting on page 732, in Michael Van Cannëyt's *Free Pascal 2 Handbook*.
The most important compiler defines have been summarized in Table 5.1 (compiler and CPU specific) and Table 5.2 (operating system specific).

Define	Description
FPC	The current compiler is Free Pascal
VER2	Free Pascal, Version 2.x.x
VER2_0	Free Pascal, Version 2.0.x
VER2_2	Free Pascal, Version 2.2.x
VER2_4	Free Pascal, Version 2.4.x
ENDIAN_LITTLE	The target processor is little endian (x68, Alpha, ARM)
ENDIAN_BIG	The target processor is big endian (PowerPC)
CPUI386, CPU386, CPU86, CPU87	The target processor is x86 compatible
CPUPOWERPC	The target processor is a PowerPC
CPUARM	The target processor is ARM
CPUX86_64	The target processor is ARM64 or Intel 64-bit
CPU32	The target processor is a 32-bit CPU
CPU64	The target processor is a 64-bit CPU

Table 5.1: Commonly used CPU defines known to the Free Pascal compiler

The Free Pascal and Lazarus libraries are very powerful and support almost any functionality an application program might need. For each individual project you should consider carefully whether it is really necessary to use the platform's low-level routines. And of course you may have to be modest or selective, particularly when it comes to the GUI of the latest version of an operating system.

It is not feasible to transfer each and every newly introduced gimmick to other platforms. Also avoid using platform-specific help functions. If you include platform-specific help on one platform, you will be forced to implement it yourself (as far as it is possible) on the other platforms.

Define	Operating System
LINUX, UNIX	Linux
FREEBSD, BSD, UNIX	FreeBSD
SUNOS, SOLARIS, UNIX	Solaris
WIN32, MSWINDOWS, WINDOWS	32-bit Windows
WIN64, MSWINDOWS, WINDOWS	64-bit Windows
WINCE, WINDOWS	Windows CE, Windows Mobile etc.
BSD, DARWIN, UNIX	MacOS X

Table 5.2: The most frequently used target operating system defines used with FPC

The following partial listing shows how to use some of these compiler defines in your source code. This section of code was implemented for Windows and Unix and requests the login name of the current user. The source code makes use of *$ifdef* directives.
The platform-dependent code was separated into reuseable functions. Note that the *uses* clause also uses *ifdefs* to refer to the *Windows* unit under Windows. It is always a good idea to carefully document platform-dependent code, particularly to explain why it is needed. This is very important, as porting will often be done by programmers other than the original author, and because a new version of an operating system might change the rules in an unexpected way in future.

```
uses   SysUtils, {$ifdef Windows}Windows{$endif}
                 {$ifdef UNIX}LCLProc{$endif} ;
{ function GetCurrentUserName: String;
  Returns the current user name.
  The resulting string is utf-8 encoded.
  Supported platforms: Windows NT, WinCE, UNIX }

function GetCurrentUserName: String;
{$ifdef Windows}
var
  WideBuffer: array[0..255] of WideChar;
  BufferSize: Cardinal;
begin
  BufferSize := 256;
  Windows.GetUserNameW(WideBuffer, BufferSize);
  Result := UTF8Encode(WideBuffer);
{$endif}
{$ifdef UNIX}
var
  Buffer: String;
begin
  Buffer := GetEnvironmentVariableUTF8('USERNAME');
  if Buffer = '' then
    Buffer := GetEnvironmentVariableUTF8('USER');
  Result := Buffer;
{$endif}
end;
```

5.1 Platform Specifics

Different platforms use different separators in the directory path. The separator that is valid on the current platform is always available in the constant *PathDelim* within Lazarus. In portable code you should not use "/"or "\", but use this constant instead. This is illustrated by the following example:

```
// Only valid for Windows:
MyPath := BaseDir + '\extradir';
// Platform-independent form:
MyPath := BaseDir + PathDelim + 'extradir';
// Or:
MyPath := SetDirSeparators(BaseDir + '\extradir');
```

Of course platform-specific constants are not always wrong. They can be useful, for instance, if information has to be sent to another computer. But usually using the above-mentioned constants is the way to go. Don't overuse *PathDelim* however. If data is transferred over **FTP** the Unix separator is always used, not matter what operating system is used! Each platform also has its own convention for the end-of-line character(s) in text files. Free Pascal offers the constant LineEnding as an alternative to the platform-specific value.

Constant	Use
AllFilesMask	Inserts the correct mask to use when searching for all files inside a folder. In UNIX and similar platforms this is * and in DOS and Windows *.*
LineEnding	The new line marker. The common values are #10 (UNIX, BeOS, Amiga), #13#10 (Windows, DOS, SymbianOS, PalmOS, OS/2, internet protocols such as HTTP, FTP, SMTP, etc.) and #13 (Mac).
LFNSupport	Long filename support. False only in DOS, which supports filenames only in the 8.3 format.
DirectorySeparator	Separates directory names in a path, the same as PathDelim.
DriveSeparator	Separates the drive from the rest of the path. Only DOS, Windows and OS/2 have the concept of drive separators.
PathDelim	See DirectorySeparator
PathSeparator	Separates multiple paths when a list of paths needs to be given. This is usually ";" Note the difference from DirectorySeparator and PathDelim.
maxExitCode	Maximum value of a process exit code.
MaxPathLen	Maximum length that a path can have, including the filename.
FileNameCase-Sensitive	Indicates if the operating system supports case-sensitive filenames. Note that this also depends on the file system being accessed. For example, a FAT partition will remain case-insensitive, even if accessed from a UNIX.
UnusedHandle	Indicates an invalid Pascal file handle.
StdInputHandle	The Pascal file handle for the standard input.
StdOutputHandle	The Pascal file handle for the standard output.
StdErrorHandle	The Pascal file handle for the standard error.
CtrlZMarksEOF	A boolean value, indicating whether the character #26 marks he end-of-file (an old DOS convention).

Table 5.3: Operating-system-independent constants in Free Pascal

Table 5.3 gives an overview of the constants Free Pascal provides to mask the differences in handling input and output in the various operating systems.
When creating platform-independent software, we must always remember to think in multiple layers. Lazarus supports the main platforms Windows, MacOS X and Linux/Unix. In ideal cases a single program source can simply be recompiled successfully for each of these platforms. However, these three platforms are not really the full range of supported platforms. These are:

- Windows 32 and Windows 64 up to Windows 7
- Windows CE
- MacOS X with Carbon
  (development with visual components is not possible yet for Cocoa)
- Linux and FreeBSD 32-bit and 64-bit on Intel (i386, amd64)
- Free Pascal programs based on the RTL and FCL only are also available on other platforms like DOS and OS/2. There is no Lazarus and LCL for these.

There is a great difference even between software development for 32-bit Windows and 64-bit Windows. How much greater the differences encountered in software development for all the platforms supported by Lazarus or even more so for Free Pascal. Normally 64-bit operating systems support 32-bit program as well. The reverse is not the case. Of course 32-bit programs will be able to address only 2 gigabytes of memory on 64-bit systems.

5.1.1 The Windows 32/64 API

Windows is still the dominant operating system on desktop PCs (often incorrectly associated only with Windows 32, whereas most of what we state here applies equally to Windows 64).
Hence Windows is nearly always one of the target platforms in platform-independent programming projects. Windows uses the backslash "\" as its path separator. Batch files (with extensions `.bat` and `.cmd`) can be used to automate tasks with a DOS-like syntax. Drive letters are used to refer to disk drives. For instance, `C:\Windows` refers to the Windows directory located on drive C.
Every drive has a drive letter. Normally A and B are reserved for floppy disk drives and C refers to the main hard disk. D and higher can refer to extra hard disks, network drives, CDROMs, DVD drives, pen drives etc. The file name extension usually indicates the type of the file and indicates whether a file can be executed. Files with the extension `.exe` are executables, `.bat` refers to batch files, and libraries usually have the extension `.dll`. There are however many more extensions for executable files. For instance `.scr` is the extension for a screen saver, and `.cpl` files are Control Panel applets, which are really special DLLs with a specific calling procedure.

Directory and file names are not case-sensitive under Windows (`c:\windows` is the same as `C:\WINDOWS`). While a program is being executed, Windows blocks the `.exe` and all DLLs in use against write access. When a program opens a file, that file is also blocked for access, unless specific options are set.

5.1.1 The Windows 32/64 API

The native low-level API in Windows is the Windows API. Because Windows has a monolithic design, this API is very large and it offers a great number of functions.
The many base libraries are the same in almost all Windows versions. New releases always have new features, but features rarely disappear. There are however some APIs and functionalities that are only available on specific versions of Windows.
Unicode support, for instance, is only available in the NT series.
Microsoft currently supports only versions starting from Windows XP. Many new libraries have only become available with the introduction of Windows Vista.
It is a good idea to check the operating system version, before using any of the newer features. The main API routines are declared in the unit *Windows* in the Free Pascal RTL. Additional APIs can be found in other units, see Table 5.4.

API NAme	Unit(s)	Description
Shell	shellapi shfolder shlobj	Organizes virtual objects, like remote printers, the Desktop or the Recycle Bin into a hierarchical namespace. Main routines: *ShellExecute*, *SHGetPathFromIDList*, *SHGetSpecialFolderLocation*. Main Interface: *IShellLink*.
Common Controls	commctrl	Standard Windows controls, like the toolbar, imagelist, listview, treeview, button, edit, listbox, combobox, etc.
Common Dialogs	commdlg	Open, Save and Print dialogs.
COM	activex comconst comobj	A mechanism for exporting/importing classes between different programming languages. Those classes are passed as interfaces and have a unique identifier called a GUID. Main routines: *CreateComObject*, *CoInitialize*, *CoUninitialize*.
Multimedia	mmsystem	Used to play and record wav and midi sounds. Main routine: *PlaySound*
Richedit	richedit	The Windows Richedit control
-	winver	Simplifies verifying the Windows version. Main routine: *CheckWin32Version*
Other libraries	flatsb imagehlp wininet	Other less frequently used APIs.

Table 5.4: The Windows API and the Free Pascal units containing its most important constituents.

To read the documentation on a specific function, go to Google and enter site:msdn.microsoft.com<function name> into the search box.
This will open the corresponding page in the Microsoft Developer Network.
There is however also offline documentation to the Windows API, for instance as a help file included with Delphi.
Once it is clear what API to use and how it works, you can use the Lazarus IDE to see how the routine has been declared in Pascal.
To do that, type the name of the routine into your source code, right click it and select *Find Declaration* from the context menu that pops up.

For this to work the unit that contains the function declaration has to be named in the uses clause of the current unit. Alternatively you can enter the name of the unit into the source, followed by a dot (for instance "shellapi.") and wait a moment. This will give you a list of all the routines in that unit. The list can be shortened by entering the first character of the routine name. You can see from this that it is worth learning the names of a few key units (see Table 5.4)!
In the next example, we will see calls to the Windows API, as in this special case we will call routines that are not available in the platform-independent Pascal library. The program creates a hotkey shortcut to `C:\Windows\Calc.exe` (the Windows calculator) on the current user's desktop. To do this an *IShellLink* COM object has to be created with *CreateComObject.* After that, the necessary information about the shortcut is entered and *SHGetSpecialFolderLocation* gives the location of the current user's Desktop folder. *IShellLink.Save* is called to save the shortcut to the hard disk.

```
(*======================================================================= *)
(*                          createshortcut.lpr                               *)
(*          Creates a link to the Windows calculator in the desktop          *)
(* ===================================================================== *)
program createshortcut;
  {$ifdef fpc}
    {$mode delphi}
  {$endif}
uses SysUtils, Windows, ShlObj, ActiveX, ComObj;
  var IObject    : IUnknown;
      ISLink     : IShellLink;
      IPFile     : IPersistFile;
      PIDL       : PItemIDList;
      InFolder   : array[0..MAX_PATH] of Char;
      TargetName: String;
      LinkName   : WideString;
begin
  CoInitialize(NIL);
  TargetName := 'c:\windows\calc.exe';    // In the system encoding!
 (* Creates an instance from IShellLink *)
  IObject := CreateComObject(CLSID_ShellLink);
  ISLink  := IObject as IShellLink;
  IPFile  := IObject as IPersistFile;
  ISLink.SetPath(PChar(TargetName));
  ISLink.SetWorkingDirectory(PChar(ExtractFilePath(TargetName)));

 (* Locates the Desktop folder *)
  SHGetSpecialFolderLocation(0, CSIDL_DESKTOPDIRECTORY, PIDL);
  SHGetPathFromIDList(PIDL, InFolder);
  LinkName := InFolder + '\Link created with Free Pascal.lnk';

 (* Creates the link *)
  IPFile.Save(PWChar(LinkName), False);
  CoUninitialize;
end.
```

The Windows-specific code requires some explanation. Strings are always passed in null-terminated format as is usual in C programs. Null-terminated means the length of the string is found by searching for the first *#0* character.
ANSI strings are also null-terminated, so they can be simply and efficiently converted in PChars.
This trick is also used in *IShellLink.SetPath* and in *IShellLink.SetWorkingDirectory*. When a string is to be acquired from the Windows API, memory has to be allocated first.
To do that, it is possible to set the correct length of an ANSI string with *SetLength* or to get memory with *GetMem*.
GetMem storage space always has to be released with *FreeMem* again. The Windows API does none of that for you.

The example shows a third way of reserving memory: by declaring a local array (*InFolder*).
Most Windows API functions also require the size of the memory chunk as a parameter.
For *SHGetPathFromList* the string has to be of size MAX_PATH.

The Unicode coding in Unicode-capable functions in the Windows API is UTF16.
In this encoding each character can be two or four bytes wide. The Pascal types Widestring and Widechar support this.
For historical reasons widestrings are not reference-counted under Windows (in contrast to ansistrings). A typecast to and from *PWChar* does work however, as can be seen from the call to *IPersistFile.Save*.
When allocating memory for widestrings with *GetMem*, please note that *GetMem* counts the size in bytes, not in characters, so the number of characters has to be multiplied by two.
As the LCL expects all strings as UTF-8, the UTF16 widestrings have to be converted with UTF8Decode and UTF8Encode.

Figure 5.1 shows Windows XP's directory structure. Some folders like *Program Files* and *Documents and Settings* may have different names, depending on the country for which the Windows version was released.
The English *Program Files* is called *Programme* in the German version, and *Documents and Settings* is called *Dokumente und Einstellungen*. Starting with Windows Vista things have changed compared to Windows XP, so many system directories have changed names in Vista/Win7.

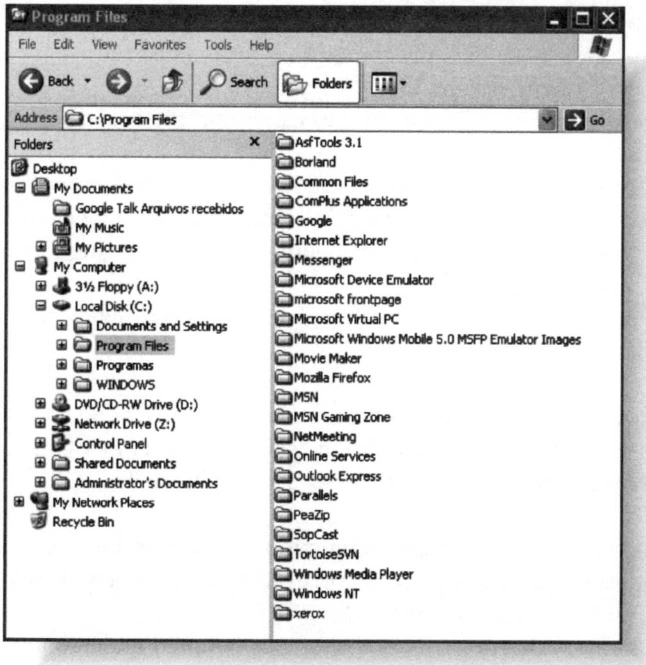

Figure 5.1: Windows XP's directory structure

Because of the different names of operating-system-dependent directories these paths never ever be hard-coded in your software, and that is also the reason for using *SHGetSpecialFolderLocation* in the example.

Directory/CSID	English Win XP	German Win XP	Vista/Windows 7
Desktop folder CSIDL_DESKTOP_ DIRECTORY	C:\Documents and Settings\Username\ Desktop	C:\Dokumente und Einstellungen\ Username\Desktop	C:\Users\Username\ Desktop
User-specific configuration files CSIDL_LOCAL_ APPDATA	C:\Documents and Settings\Username\ Local Settings\ Application Data	C:\Dokumente und Einstellungen\ Username\Lokale Einstellungen\ Anwendungsdaten	C:\Users\ Username\ AppData\Local
Applications CSIDL_PROGRAM_ FILES	C:\Program Files	C:\Programme	C:\Program Files (x86)
Contents of the "Start Menu" CSIDL_PROGRAMS	C:\Documents and Settings\Username\ Start Menu\Programs menu\Program	C:\Dokumente und Einstellungen\ Username\Start Programs	C:\Users\Username\ AppData\Roaming\ Microsoft\StartMenu\
Windows operating system folder CSIDL_WINDOWS	C:\Windows	C:\Windows	C:\Windows

Table 5.5: The special Windows directories and their names in various Windows versions and locales. There are other constants, such as CSIDL_MYDOCUMENTS for the user's local documents, and each new Windows version might also add new directories.

The values shown in Table 5.5 for your current operating system can easily be acquired in a small Lazarus program. All that is needed for this program is to put a memo field onto an empty form and assign an OnCreate event for the window with the Object Inspector.

```
uses
  Windows, LCLProc, ShlObj;

procedure TForm1.FormCreate(Sender: TObject);
  var PIDL  : PItemIDList;
      Folder: array[0..MAX_PATH] of Char;
begin
  SHGetSpecialFolderLocation(0, CSIDL_DESKTOPDIRECTORY, PIDL);
  SHGetPathFromIDList(PIDL, Folder);
  Memo1.Lines.Add('Desktop: ' + SysToUTF8(Folder));
  SHGetSpecialFolderLocation(0, CSIDL_LOCAL_APPDATA, PIDL);
  SHGetPathFromIDList(PIDL, Folder);
  Memo1.Lines.Add('Application data for the current user: ' +
                                                    SysToUTF8(Folder));
  SHGetSpecialFolderLocation(0, CSIDL_MYDOCUMENTS , PIDL);
  SHGetPathFromIDList(PIDL, Folder);
  Memo1.Lines.Add('User documents: '+ SysToUTF8(Folder));
  SHGetSpecialFolderLocation(0, CSIDL_PROGRAM_FILES, PIDL);
  SHGetPathFromIDList(PIDL, Folder);
  Memo1.Lines.Add('Program files: ' + SysToUTF8(Folder));
  SHGetSpecialFolderLocation(0, CSIDL_PROGRAMS, PIDL);
  SHGetPathFromIDList(PIDL, Folder);
  Memo1.Lines.Add('Start menu: '+ SysToUTF8(Folder));
  SHGetSpecialFolderLocation(0, CSIDL_WINDOWS, PIDL);
  SHGetPathFromIDList(PIDL, Folder);
  Memo1.Lines.Add('Windows Folder: ' + SysToUTF8(Folder));
end;
```

In the uses clause of the unit you should specify the units `Windows, LCLProc` and `ShlObj`. The program will run in the Windows emulator Wine as well. Then it will show the values for the Windows version currently being emulated in Wine.

5.1.2 Windows CE, a special case

Since Lazarus version 0.9.24 you have been able to develop native Windows CE applications in Pascal. Windows CE (WinCE) is a very flexible operating system which is being used in many appliances – initially it was mainly used in automotive applications, but now it is found on PDAs (PocketPC), smartphones (Windows Mobile) and handheld computers (TabletPC). The operating system is the same in all these cases, but there are great differences in the resources available on this great variety of hardware.
Some appliances do not have a GUI, others have a limited GUI with a touchscreen, some very simple phones have a GUI without a touchscreen, while the GUI for a TabletPC is very much like the GUI in a standard PC. These many differences must be taken into account when creating programs to run on Windows CE.

The Lazarus Component Library offers several mechanisms to aid in writing Windows CE applications or in porting existing applications to or from Windows CE.

5.1.2 Windows CE, a special case

In contrast to other platform-independent development environments – like Java's J2ME for Mobiles, for instance – which have completely different APIs for mobile and desktop applications, with the LCL we are always using the same API. In this case we just have to use switches to control the behaviour on mobile platforms. In this section we will cover these switches and other details specific to Windows CE.

The Windows CE API is similar to the normal Win32 API and many interfaces are identical. As the main properties of both operating systems are the same, we will concentrate here on the differences between them. The first difference is that Windows CE uses only Unicode text strings. The Ansi APIs are outdated.

As in the desktop version the main APIs are in the unit `Windows`, and the additional APIs are in separate libraries. The main APIs in Windows CE and Windows may be the same, but the special APIs are sometimes very different. Also their availability may vary from device to device, depending on its complexity.

API NAme	Unit	Description
AYG Shell	aygshell	Miscellaneous shell routines from the agyshell.dll library. Many versions of this library can be downloaded from `http://hpcmonex.net/izemize.htm` Main routines: *SHRecognizeGesture*, *SHFindMenuBar*, *SHCreateMenuBar*
Bluetooth	bt_api, bthapi, bthutil	Bluetooth client/server API.
Synchronization	cesync	ActiveSync synchronization modules for Windows CE.
Common Controls	commctrl	Standard Windows controls like the toolbar, imagelist, listview, treeview, button, edit, listbox, combobox, etc.
Common Dialogs	commdlg	Open, Save and Print dialogs.
Control Panel	cpl	Control panel extension DLL definitions.
GPS	gpsapi	GPS Intermediate Driver API.
OLE	oleauto	Declarations for oleaut32 WinCE API.
Phone API	phone, tapi	The telephone API.
PIM	pim	Manages PIM data (contacts, calendar, tasks and notes).
Shell	shellapi	Organizes virtual objects, like remote printers, the Desktop or the Recycle Bin into a hierarchical namespace. Main routines: *SHGetSpecialFolderLocation*, *SHGetPathFromIDList*
Notification LED	nled	Notification LED API. Unlike other system LEDS, this one can be ON or blinking even when the device is powered down. Requires hardware support.
SMS	sms	For sending/receiving SMS messages.

Table 5.6: The units that expose Windows CE APIs in Free Pascal

Prerequisites and preparations

Before you can begin development of a Windows CE application, some preparations have to be made. For testing the Lazarus programs you will either need hardware running WinCE, or you will need a device emulator installed on your development PC.
Microsoft specifies Windows XP SP2 or Windows Server 2003 is needed to be able to install the emulator.
Four files need to be downloaded:
The Pocket-PC-Emulator Standalone Device Emulator 1.0 with Windows Mobile OS Images from Microsoft can be downloaded from:

1. `http://www.microsoft.com/downloads/details.aspx?FamilyId C62D54A5-183A-4A1E-A7E2-CC500ED1F19A&displaylang=en`

First the file *V1Emulator.zip* (the actual emulator) has to be extracted and installed. This file is valid for Windows 2000 and for Windows XP. We cannot give a description of all the installation details here, as this is subject to changes with each update of the emulator Microsoft releases. You also need to download the file `efp.msi` from the same website, but do not install it yet (see later). Under Windows Vista and beyond we cannot install version 1 of the emulator; version 3 is required there. (In Windows XP/2003 we are free to use either version 1 or version 3.) The German version 3 of the file `vs_emulator.exe` (Win32) or `vs_emulator_x64_vista.exe` is available on the Microsoft server on the page Microsoft Device Emulator 3.0 - Eigenständige Version at:

2. `http://www. microsoft.com/downloads/details.aspx? displaylang=de&FamilylD = a6f6adaf-12e3-4b2fa394-356e2c2fb114`

There is an error on the website where it states that the Virtual Machine Network Driver needs to be installed and the link given for that does not work. Instead we need to download Virtual PC.
The emulator is officially declared suitable for Windows XP SP2 and beyond only.
The reason for that is not the emulator itself, but Virtual PC 2007, which is needed as well. If you want to work with the old Windows 2000, that is possible too.
Virtual PC 2004 SP1 has the drivers too and it will also be accepted by efp.msi, which we will install in the next step. This program is still available for download from Microsoft. The download can be found at:

3. `http://www.microsoft.com/germany/windows/virtualpc/default.mspx`

or alternatively you can search with Google for Virtual PC 2004 to find it.
If you work with Windows XP or Vista, you will need to install Virtual PC 2007, which is also available for free. Download it from:

4. `http://www.microsoft.com/downloads/details.aspx?FamilyID=04d26402-3199-48a3-afa2-2dc0b40a73b6&DisplayLang=en`

and install it. Both emulators will be installed with all required drivers included.

Now you can install the file efp.msi (the emulator image) you downloaded from the first website. Important: This file also has to be installed under Vista. To get it, after downloading version 3.0 of the emulator, switch to version 1.0 on the website.
Now you should have a fully functioning PocketPC emulator, ready for development of applications in combination with Lazarus. To enable information exchange you will also have to install ActiveSync on the host PC. This can be found at:

```
http://www.microsoft.com/downloads/activesync
```

Download version 4.2 (or higher) of ActiveSync and install it. The file you need for version 4.2 is *setup.exe*, for 4.5 it is `setup.msi`. You can skip the configuration settings. Please note that ActiveSync is not compatible with Windows Vista/7. These later Windows need the Windows Mobile Device Center, which offers the same functionality.
Now a shared folder for the emulator has to be set up. In the emulator menu *File → Configure* a directory for data exchange on the host has to be selected.
This will be the location for Lazarus to deposit the executable images for running on WinCE. The directory defined as Shared Folder on the host will be available in the emulator explorer (*Menu Start → Programs*) as Storage Card.
There you will find the executable files, which can be started by double clicking.

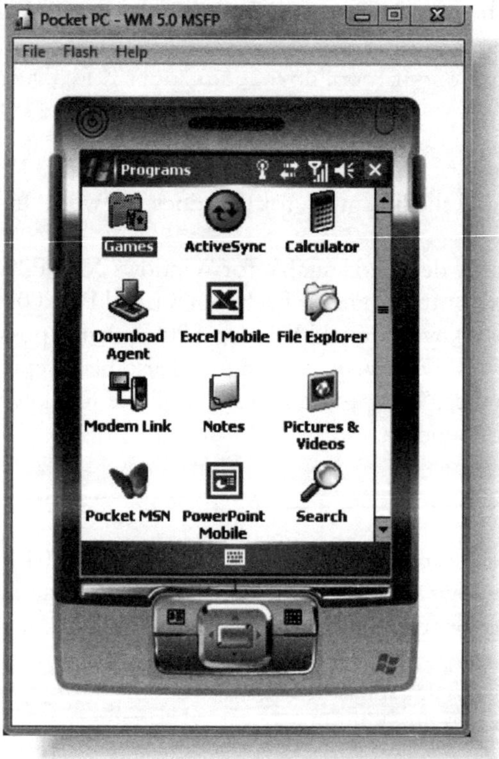

Figure 5.2 The Microsoft Pocket PC Emulator 5.0

5.1.2 Windows CE, a special case

To use a Lazarus application in the emulator, it is executed directly. To do that go to the Windows program menu *Windows Mobile Emulator Images → PocketPC*. It is also possible to use the gdb debugger through ActiveSync from the command line. The emulator or the device must be connected to ActiveSync for that to work. Then the Windows command line can be opened and pointed to arm-wince-Target. The command

```
gdb --tui C:\MyProgram\MyWinceAp\MyApp.exe
```

will call the GUI of gdb. To start the application you just need to type the letter r and confirm it by pressing [Enter]. `gdb` will then copy the executable file to the device in the `\gdb` directory and execute it.

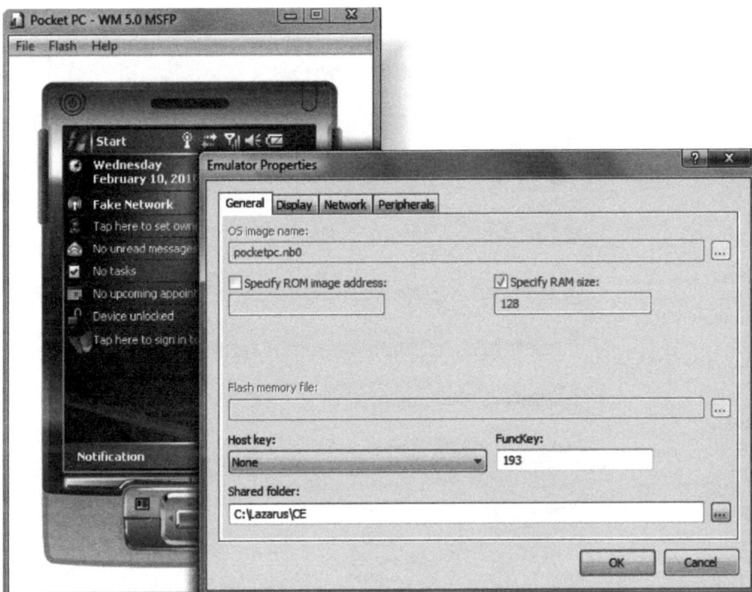

Figure 5.3: The configuration dialog in the Pocket PC emulator

No we can start to set up the development environment. There is more than one way to set up a Lazarus build environment for Windows CE applications. Either through the stable Addon Installer, or through the Snapshot Addon Installer, or through manually putting the Windows CE LCL interface into LCL with Subversion. The simplest way is to use the stable Addon Installer. To do this, first install the regular 32 bit Windows version of Lazarus in the suggested directory (usually `C:\Lazarus`). This version (and also the next archive which we will need) is most easily acquired from the linked list on the main website: `www.lazarus.freepascal.org`

With version 0.98.2 you will get along with installation of `Lazarus-0.9.28.2-fpc-2.2.4-win32.exe` also the `Lazarus-0.9.28.2-fpc-2.2.4-cross-arm-wince-win32.exe`. The compiler will then be able to write both target types: Win32 and WinCE ARM. There is also currently (depending on the way versions are built) an Addon archive for Win64.

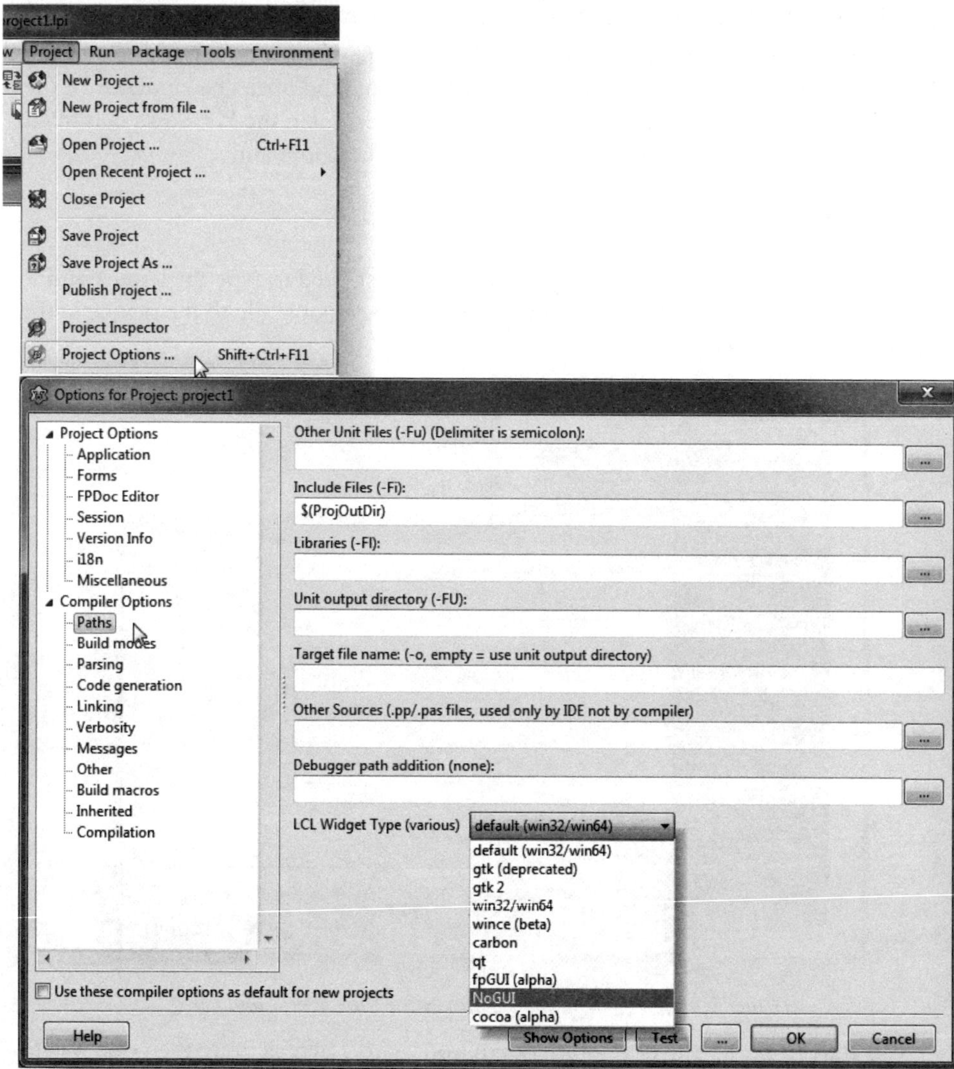

Figure 5.4: The Paths page in the Project Options dialog where you set the Widget Type

You can see whether you are dealing with the full version or with the Addon by the size of the installation archive, and by the *-cross-* in the file name.
After this installation Lazarus is able to compile ARM WinCE applications.

In the newly installed Lazarus IDE go to *Project →Project Options* and click on *Paths* in the treeview on the left. Then specify the compiler options in the *Paths* page (see Figure 5.4) by clicking on the combobox labelled *LCL Widget Type (various)*, and selecting the *WinCE (beta)* option from the dropdown list.
In the same dialog click on the *Code generation* node and specify the target platform (see Figure 5.5).

Next you can check the compiler settings. To do that, press the [Test] button at the bottom of the dialog (see Figure 5.6). The procedure to handle a current developer version is exactly the same as discussed above. These can be found in the link list on `www.lazarus.freepascal.org` under Daily Snapshots.

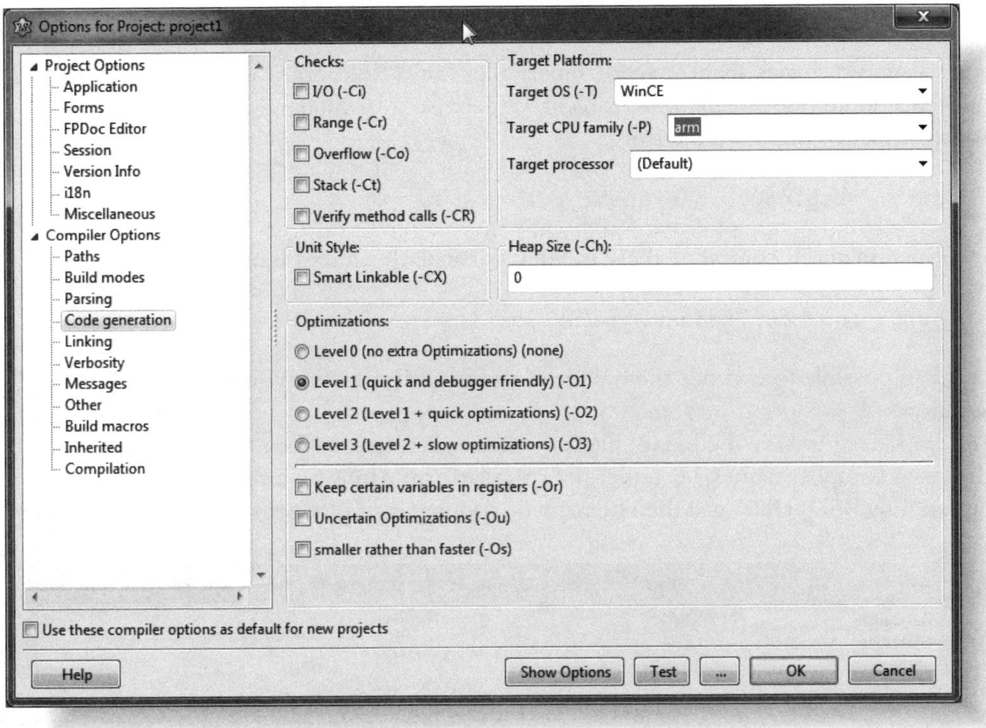

Figure 5.5: The Code generation page where you set the Target OS and Target CPU

You should not mix these versions (stable and developer version) of the archive and the compiler. It is however possible to install both of them in separate working directories.

The Lazarus cross compiler version only installs the additional binary units. It is equally important to install the GNU **binutils** for Windows CE on ARM processors (see Figure 5.8). The binutils include the assembler (`as`), the linker (`ld`), the debug information stripper (`strip`), the resource compiler (`windres`), the debugger (`gdb`) and the archiver (`ar`). Without these no program can be compiled. They are target platform dependent and they are needed for working with the native operating system (in the short name version) and for performing the cross compilation (in the version with target prefix in the name).

Cross compilation with Free Pascal is not the subject of this book on Lazarus and it is quite complex with Lazarus to build up a correct tool chain. (The *tool chain* is the sequence of programs needed to do the full translation process including compiling and linking). For Lazarus the tools needed are the Free Pascal compiler, the resource compiler, the assembler and the linker.

Strip is not essential, but very useful, because removing the symbols can shrink the program to as little as ten percent of its original size.
There are two ways to get a stable tool chain for Windows CE on Windows.
At:

```
ftp://ftp.freepascal/pub/fpc/contrib/cross
```

and its subdirectories a whole set of binary files is available. Some of these are quite old, but that should not usually be a problem. Otherwise you will have to download the source code for binutils 2.2.0 from:

```
http://ftp.gnu.org/binutils/
```

Information about compiling these utilities, particularly under Linux can be found at:

```
http://sources.redhat.com/binutils/
```

It is also possible to compile them under Cygwin with the MingW compiler under Windows.
It is important to save the binary files not only under their native names, but also under the cross compiler names, i.e. under the cpu platform name. So a file called "`as`" for the target "FreeBSD/i386" will then be named – on any host platform – `i386-freebsd-as`.

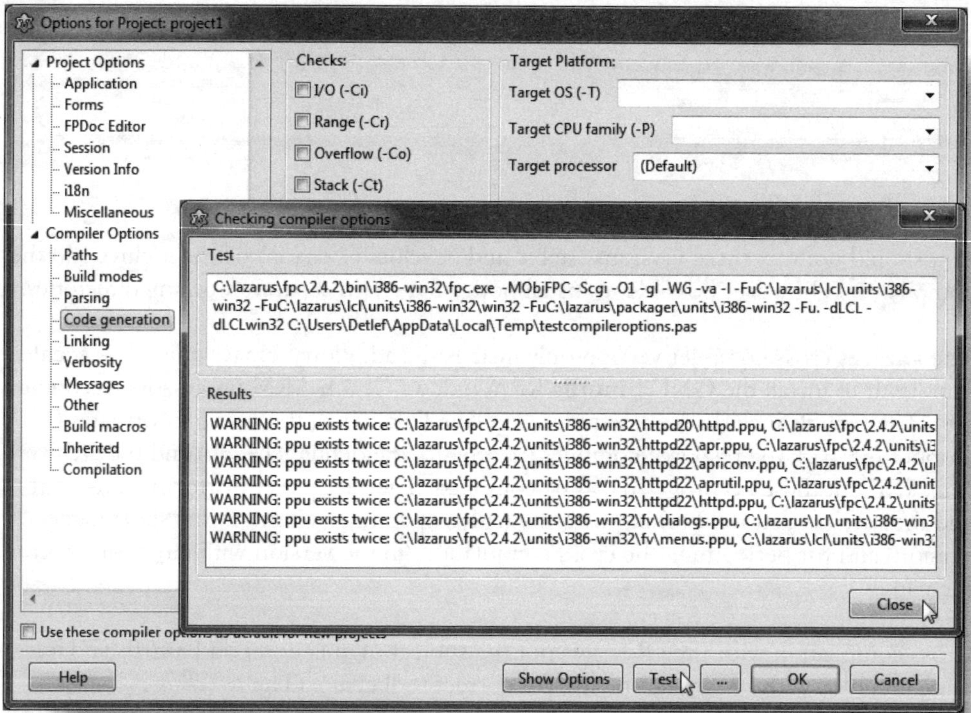

Figure 5.6 The compiler test

Figure 5.7 The Microsoft Pocket PC Emulator 5.0

Apart from these files you will also need the files from RTL, FCL and LCL for successful cross compilation, i.e. the units from Free Pascal itself plus those from Lazarus. This will increase the size of the Lazarus installation substantially. So it is worth considering the usefulness of cross compiling for a platform for which Lazarus is available. It may be more efficient to just install Lazarus on both platforms separately. The compiler is free anyway!

The LCL for Windows CE

As mentioned earlier, Windows CE is not the same as Windows. All forms of the operating system have different functionality. Lazarus categorizes this in a property of its global Application object (defined in the Forms unit). The ApplicationType property of this global object will force the LCL into a particular mode. The possible values that Application.ApplicationType can take are listed in Table 5.7.

5.1.2 Windows CE, a special case

As mentioned earlier, Windows CE is not the same as Windows. All forms of the operating system have different functionality. Lazarus categorizes this in a property of its global Application object (defined in the Forms unit). The *ApplicationType property* of this global object will force the LCL into a particular mode. The possible values that *Application.ApplicationType* can take are listed in Table 5.7. The application type *atKeyPadDevice* used to be called *atSmartphone* until Lazarus 0.9.28 and there was also a functional type *atHandheld.* The latter was removed in 0.9.29 and *atSmartphone* was renamed to *atKeyPadDevice,* as this type was not related to the telephone functionality at all, and the name assigned by Microsoft caused confusion. PDAs usually have more buttons than smartphones, so they are better described by *atPDA. atKeyPadDevice* describes devices like bar code scanners with very limited input and output capabilities.

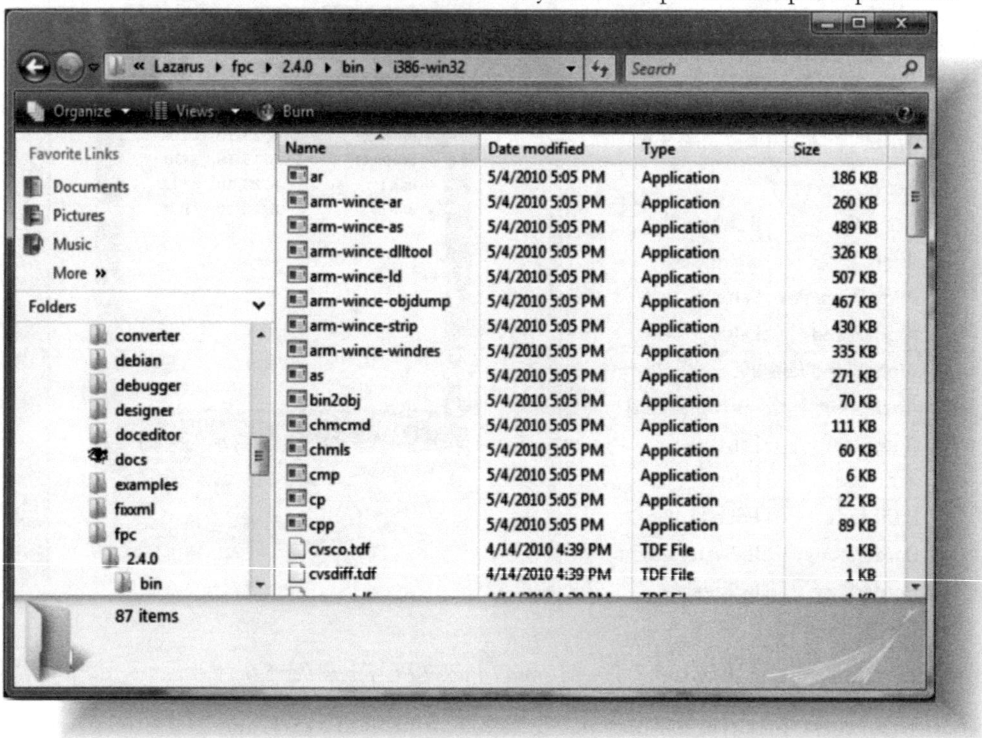

Figure 5.8: Looking at Free Pascal, which comes with Lazarus, you can see cross compilation for Windows CE is possible. Apart from the normal binutils, binutils for target "arm wince" can be included as well.

The most important function of *ApplicationType* in the WinCE interface is control of the creation of windows. As the screen of a PDA or smartphone is too small for most forms, moveable windows are not needed. Most values of *BorderStyle* will result in the window size being ignored and the window will be shown full screen.

The application type can be changed to be able to support different device types, but this change has to be done before *Application.Initialize*. Changing later can be done for instance after closing the window or when re-opening it. Normally *ApplicationType* will be set to *atDefault* and the *LCL* will try to guess the correct value.

Version	Description
atDefault	In the call to *Application.Initialize*, present in all LCL applications, if *Application.ApplicationType* is set to *atDefault*, then Lazarus will try to detect automatically to which application type the hardware corresponds, and it will change *ApplicationType* to the detected mode.
atPDA	A PDA or Smartphone with a touch screen and a small screen. Forms are usually maximized to occupy the whole work area, and custom positioning and sizing is ignored. Windows CE in default resolution will always have a Width of 240 pixels, and the Height can change from device to device, but 320 pixels is a good guess. In some devices it is possible to specify a bigger size if the screen supports it.
atSmartphone, atKeyPadDevice	Simple phones and some GPS devices and Bar-code scanners. Devices of this type are very limited and have a small screen, lacking a touch screen or other pointing device. The very limited navigation capabilities mean that the application must be simplified as much as possible. Under WindowsCE for example only 2 top level menus are possible and most forms will be automatically maximized by Lazarus to fill the entire small screen available.
atDesktop	The application mode for hardware with a large screen and a pointing device. This is used both for desktop computers, as well as for notebooks and for tablet PCs. Windows CE tablets run in this mode, which works very similarly to the Win32 Lazarus interface.

Table 5.7 Application types possible in the LCL

Application Type	Border style	Behavior	Window state	Caption bar
atDesktop	Any	As in desktop Windows.	As in desktop Windows.	As in desktop Windows.
atPDA, atKeyPadDevice	bsDialog	Accepts custom sizing. The X, Y position is ignored and always set to be the top-left corner, but taking into account the existence of an eventual Taskbar on the top.	Not applicable.	Separate title bar with an (ok) close button
atPDA, atKeyPadDevice	bsNone	Allows full control of the size and position.	Not applicable.	Doesn't exist
atPDA, atKeyPadDevice	bsSizable, bsSingle, bsToolWin, bsSize-ToolWin	Rejects custom size and position and is always set to fill the entire work area excluding the menu. The definition of Work Area already excludes the Taskbar	Not applicable.	Merged into the taskbar with an (ok) close button

Table 5.8: How ApplicationType controls the behaviour of windows in Windows CE

```
program MyProgram;
uses  Forms, Interfaces, MyUnit,
begin
  Application.ApplicationType := atSmartphone;
  Application.Initialize;
  Application.CreateForm(TMainWindow, vMainWindow);
  Application.Run;
end.
```

Another hot item in the LCL for WinCE are the buttons available in the title bar.
There is no pre-defined close button under WinCE, but there is an (X) button to *minimize* the window. Because the button has an "X" (and similar buttons in desktop applications *close* the window) many application developers are led to believe that (X) is a button to close the form (window). To prevent this wrong assumption, the LCL WinCE interface shows (by default) an (ok) button to close windows instead of the (X) button for minimizing.
This default behavior can, however, be changed by using the *WinCETitlePolicy* property of *WinCEWidgetset.* Although setting non-default values for the *WinCETitlePolicy* property can change this default window behaviour, developers should be very careful with any option that allows an (X) button, since a click on (X) in the main window will *not* close the application.
As a developer you are responsible for warning the user when a second instance of your program is started and for offering them an option to view the original and close the new one. Otherwise the device's memory will fill up with useless duplicate instances of your program, started because the user did not realise he or she had only minimised the previous instance.

Value	Description
tpAlwaysUseOKButton	The default which gives all forms an (ok) close button.
tpOKButtonOnlyOnDialogs	All forms will have (X) minimize buttons except forms with the *bsDialog* borderstyle, which will still have an (ok) close button.
tpControlWithBorderIcons	If *biMinimize* is included in the form's BorderIcons, then an (X) minimize button will be shown, otherwise an (ok) button is shown.

Table 5.9: Possible values of the property WinCEWidgetset.WinCETitlePolicy

Figure 5.9: Caption bar of a form with an (X) minimize button

Figure 5.10: Caption bar of a form with an (ok) close button

Here is an example of how to change the default caption bar button setting.
The attribute has to be changed before calling *Application.Initialize*.
Changing it later has no effect.

```
program mywinceapp;
uses  Forms, Interfaces, MyUnit,{$ifdef WinCE} WinCEInt;{$endif}
begin
{$ifdef WinCE}
  WinCEWidgetset.WinCETitlePolicy := tpOKButtonOnlyOnDialogs;
{$endif}
  Application.Initialize;
  Application.CreateForm(TMainWindow, vMainWindow);
  Application.Run;
end;
```

5.1.3 Linux, FreeBSD and other Unix-systems

Linux, FreeBSD, Solaris and many other Unix systems have great similarities, so they can all be discussed together. A normal Linux program will usually run without changes by just recompiling on FreeBSD as well, and the same goes for the other Unix variants.
This only works if no system-specific tricks like direct calls to the kernel or device names in `/dev` have been used. All Unix systems use "/" as separator in directory paths, just like Internet URLs. Scripts for automation are called shell scripts and may have a `.sh` extension. One of the big differences between Windows and Unix is that the file name extension does not indicate the file type. Under Windows this is a usual way to recognize documents. Unix executable files have no extension. Libraries have an .so extension.
By contrast with Windows, Unix file names are case-sensitive. An exception to this is when foreign file systems (such as those in FAT or NTFS format) are accessed from Unix.

Category	User access rights	Description
/	Read	Root directory.
/home	Read	Holds one folder for each user, named after the user's account. This will be the user's document folder.
/media and /mnt	Read/Write	Where devices such as CD-ROMs, DVDs, pendrives, etc. are located. This location's name changes depending on the Linux distribution.
/etc	Read	For global configuration data.
/proc	Read	A virtual directory which contains virtual files with information about the Linux kernel, such as IRQs (interrupt numbers), I/O ports, running processes, etc.
/root	–	The home directory for the root user.
/tmp	Read/Write	A global location for temporary files.
/usr	Read	Holds program data and resource files.
/usr/bin	Read	Holds globally accessible executables installed by third-party software.
/usr/share	Read	Programs should create a sub directory here with their read-only resource files.
/usr/share/man	Read	Manual pages (console-based help system).

Table 5.10: The most important directories in a typical Linux system

The hierarchy of directories in Unix is very different from that in Windows. There are no drive letters and all drives are part of the same hierarchy. To add a drive to the system, it has to be mounted in a directory. All files on that disk are then addressed as if they resided in that directory. The concept of a "file" is extended compared to Windows, as devices like sound cards are also addressed as if they were files. The speakers are addressed with write commands.

Directories are also files in Unix with the result that there are files for which the size cannot be determined or for which the modification date is not a valid concept.

This is important to know when you create programs that search the file system.

In contrast with Windows, files are usually not locked for access. Consequently executable programs can be updated while they are running, and files can be opened by any number of programs simultaneously.

Symbolic links (or symlinks) are also used to a much greater extent than under Windows. A symbolic link is a file which points to another file. If a link is opened for reading, it is in fact the link's target which is opened. Directories can also be symbolic links.

The concept of symbolic links is used by the FPC compiler in a smart way. Under Linux the file /usr/bin/ppc386 (which appears to be the Free Pascal Compiler for the i386) is really only a link to the real compiler. This is located in the directory /usr/lib/fpc/<Compilerversion>/. This makes it possible to install and use multiple versions of Free Pascal in parallel, without having to duplicate the complete installation. You can switch compiler version by simply changing the link.

Linux/Unix also supports hard links, which makes it possible for a file on a drive to be represented to the outside world under more than one name. Unlike symbolic links, hard links cannot cross mount point boundaries. The FileUtil unit provides a function *ProgramDirectory* which resolves links. Table 5.10 lists the Linux file system directories which are the most important ones for developers.

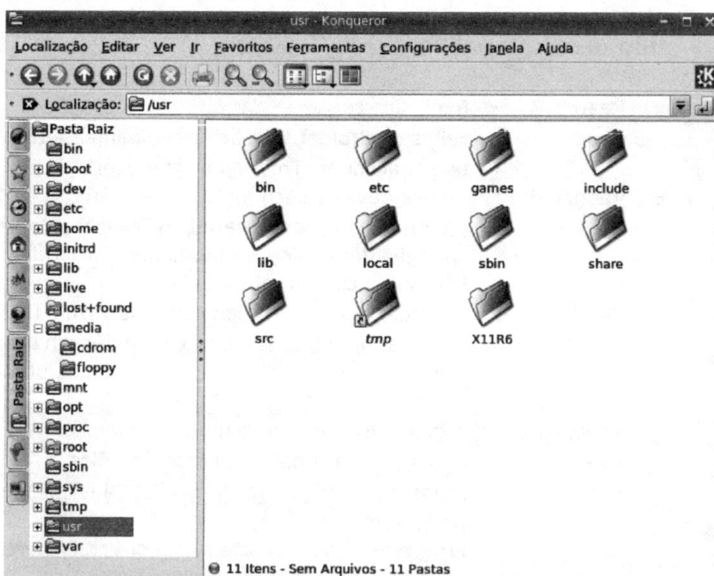

Figure 5.11: The directory structure in Mandriva Linux. It may be slightly different in other distributions (or even distribution versions) but most of it is fixed for reasons of Unix compatibility.

The directory hierarchy in FreeBSD is slightly different from that in Linux. `/proc` is optional here and may contain other data too. The most important installation path for programs is not `/usr`, but `/usr/local`. But Linux also has some exceptions to the directories shown in Table 5.10. An important additional path in some distributions is `/opt`, which is used for installing optional program packages.

The free Unix distributions feature several GUIs, the most important of which are KDE 3, KDE 4, Gnome 2 and Xfce 4. Gnome 2 and Xfce 4 are mainly based on the GUI toolkit Gtk 2, which was originally developed for Gimp. KDE 3 is based on Qt3 and KDE 4 on Qt 4. Qt was created by Trolltech, which is now a branch of Nokia. Programs based on one of the toolkits will also run if the user has selected another GUI, but the necessary libraries do have to be installed. Lazarus offers a choice between Gtk 1, Gtk 2 and Qt 4. And the IDE itself can even use a different toolkit than the program being developed. Lazarus is pre-configured to use the old Gtk version 1 up to version 0.9.26. Starting with version 0.9.28 Gtk 2 is used.
You are advised not to link against the old Gtk 1 any more, as it is no longer automatically installed with many distributions. The user would then have to manually install it later. A current theme will also not be installed, so it will look weird (however, a theme can be delivered along with Lazarus). Gtk 1 also does not support Unicode, so only the current system language will be possible. For Qt 4 an additional library has to be installed, because Qt is written in C++, and the FPC is not able to address that directly. Gtk 2 applications will work without a problem.

It is important to install the toolkit a program is based on, not just on the development PC, but on the target system as well. Table 5.11 shows the minimum requirements for each of the toolkits.

Lazarus	Min.FPC	Gtk	Qt 4	Win32	Carbon
0.9.24	2.2.0	Gtk 1.18+	Qt 4.2+	Windows 98+	Mac OS X 10.4+
0.9.26	2.2.2	Gtk 1.18+	Qt 4.3+	Windows 98+	Mac OS X 10.4+
0.9.28	2.2.4	Gtk 2.6+	Qt 4.5+	Windows 98+	Mac OS X 10.4+
0.9.29 (under development)	2.4.0	Gtk 2.6+	Qt 4.5+	Windows 98+	Mac OS X 10.4+

Table 5.11: Minimum required versions of FPC and the toolkits required for Lazarus

Qt 4 basics

Qt is an object oriented API. To be able to use such an API from another programming language, it has to be exported in a procedural format. A library exporting all the methods, constructors, destructors, fields and properties in a procedural way has to be written for it. The calling convention has to be such that it can be handled by both compilers. For a library such as Qt, compiled with the platform-independent GCC, the cdecl calling convention is a solution.
The Qt library makes objects from one language (C++) into opaque types for the other (Pascal). This means the objects will only by addressed through the functions offered by the interface library.

It is important to know that all methods possess a hidden parameter *Self*. When a method is called, the compiler automatically provides a pointer to an instance of the method class. This hidden parameter has to be taken into account when the API is flattened into its procedural form.

For example, consider the following C++ header from the file `gmainwindow.h` in the Qt toolkit:

```
class Q_GUI_EXPORT QMainWindow : public QWidget {
public:
explicit QMainWindow ( QWidget *parent = 0,
                       Qt::WindowFlags flags = 0 );
~QMainWindow ();
QWidget *centralWidget () const;
void setCentralWidget ( QWidget *widget );
};
```

This declares a class *QMainWindow* with four methods: a contructor; a destructor, and a *setter/getter* pair for the *centralWidget* property. These four methods can be flattened in the following way (which you can find in the file `gmainwindow.hb`).

```
C_EXPORT QMainWindowH QMainWindow_create(QWidgetH parent,
                                            unsigned int flags);
C_EXPORT void QMainWindow_destroy(QMainWindowH handle);
C_EXPORT QWidgetH QMainWindow_centralWidget(QMainWindowH handle);
C_EXPORT void QMainWindow_setCentralWidget(QMainWindowH handle,
                                              QWidgetH widget);
```

We will also need a C++ interface file. In this case it is called `gmainwindow.cppb`:

```
QMainWindowH QMainWindow_create(QWidgetH parent, unsigned int flags){
  return (QMainWindowH) new QMainWindow((QWidget*)parent,
                                         (Qt::WindowFlags)flags);
}
void QMainWindow_destroy(QMainWindowH handle) {
  delete (QMainWindow *)handle;
}
QWidgetH QMainWindow_centralWidget(QMainWindowH handle) {
  return (QWidgetH)((QMainWindow *)handle)->centralWidget();
}
void QMainWindow_setCentralWidget(QMainWindowH handle,
                                  QWidgetH widget) {
  ((QMainWindow *)handle)->setCentralWidget((QWidget*)widget); }
```

This will be imported into a Pascal program by a transformed form of the header, for which we will also need an interface file `gt4.pas`:

```
function QMainWindow_create(parent: QWidgetH = NIL;
                      flags: QtWindowFlags = 0): QMainWindowH; cdecl;
                           external QtIntf name 'QMainWindow_create';
procedure QMainWindow_destroy(handle: QMainWindowH); cdecl;
                          external QtIntf name 'QMainWindow_destroy';
function QMainWindow_centralWidget(handle: QMainWindowH): QWidgetH;
             cdecl; external QtIntf name 'QmainWindow_centralWidget';
procedure QMainWindow_setCentralWidget(handle: QMainWindowH; widget:
QWidgetH); cdecl; external QtIntf name'QmainWindow_setCentralWidget';
```

But we cannot directly use C++ objects from Object Pascal or use Pascal constructs for creating and releasing classes in the same way as we can call the methods. Because of the flattening of the C++ structures our own software will have to make much more use of the procedural variant of the API bindings discussed above.
Such procedural code might look like the following:

```
program qttest;
uses qt4;
  var  MyMainWindow: QMainWindowH;
       MyLabel     : QLabelH;
       w           : WideString;
begin
  QApplication_Create(@argc, argv);

  w := 'FPC/Qt4 Hello world';
  MyMainWindow := QMainWindow_create;

  MyLabel := QLabel_create;
  QLabel_setText(MyLabel, @w);

  QMainWindow_setCentralWidget(MyMainWindow, MyLabel);
  QWidget_resize(MyMainWindow, 400, 200);
  QWidget_Show(MyMainWindow);

  QApplication_Exec;
end.
```

Clearly we cannot write large programs like this.

Figure 5.12: A small example of Pascal using Qt4

If procedural access to the API is successful, the object orientation could be restored by adding another layer on top of the procedural bindings. This would make using the API easier, although it is not absolutely necessary. It would, however, greatly improve development efficiency for small to medium-sized programs, and it would aid in code management.
For large applications it would be useful to create our own, completely object oriented wrapper around the procedural API, which better suits our needs. This has been done with the Qt 4 interface for Lazarus. More information can be found in the files

`lazarus/lcl/interfaces/qt/qtobjects.pas` and
`lazarus/lcl/interfaces/qt/qtwidgets.pas` in any Lazarus installation.

One of the differences between C++ and Object Pascal that may lead to problems occurs with multiple inheritance in C++. Object Pascal has no concept of multiple inheritance, so special measures are called for. It is important to know that each class has a table with the addresses of its virtual methods, the so-called Virtual Method Table (VMT). In Object Pascal each class has exactly one such table. In C++ a class that inherits from more than one other class, can have more than one VMT. To be able to address from Pascal a class with multiple ancestors, the Self pointer in a normal flattened method of the procedural interface has to point to the right method table.
An example in Qt 4 is *QWidget*, which inherits from *QObject* and from *QPaintDevice*.
If we have a pointer to a *QWidget* and we want to pass it on to a function which expects a *QPaintDevice*, a typecast will be needed. However, this special type of typecast is a C++ language construct and it is not available in Object Pascal. So we need a helper function, which has to be implemented additionally in the bindings. Here is the implementation of *QWidget_to_QPaintDevice*:

```
QPaintDeviceH QWidget_to_QPaintDevice(QWidgetH handle) {
  return (QPaintDeviceH) (QPaintDevice *)(QWidget *)handle; }
```

The typecast *(QPaintDevice* *) changes the pointer in *(QWidget* *) to make it point to another VMT for the same class.
To be able to access Qt 4 from Pascal, Qt 4 needs to be installed. In Linux and in BSD this can be done with the packet management tools in the operating system or distribution. For Windows and MacOS X it can be downloaded from
`http://qt.nokia.com/downloads#lgpl`
To execute programs with the precompiled QT4 Pascal library only the (smaller) framework needs to be downloaded. Besides that the interface DLL is needed. The Win32 and the Windows CE versions can be found in the Lazarus SVN repository as the file
`http://svn.freepascal.org/svn/lazarus/binaries/i386-win32/qt/libqt4intf.dll`
but it can also be installed along with the Win32 version of Lazarus if required. The source code and further information about the DLL is available on the original site for FPC QT bindings on
`http://users.telenet.be/Jan.Van.hijfte/qtforfpc/fpcqt4.html`
To compile this C++ binding library yourself, you will need to download the complete framework and the Qt source code.

5.1.4 The MacOS X APIs

MacOS X, which normally runs only on Apple hardware, is a real Unix operating system. Therefore, most of what we discussed about Linux is valid here too. Due to this similarity with other Unix systems, Unix console applications will usually run without change on MacOS X.

GUI applications however are a different matter. MacOS X has its own conventions for these. The MacOS X installation DVD does include X11, so that Linux applications do run after recompiling, but they often have problems interacting with native MacOS X software and with the system. This approach is therefore only valid for small or in-house applications. For commercial software a full port to the native platform will be necessary.

The first peculiarity about MacOS X is what we have to develop. Instead of providing an installer as in Windows, or a hierarchical package as in Linux, the whole GUI program will have to be made available in the form of a so-called "Application Bundle", which is really a directory structure containing all the data the application needs.

The user can install this on the system in any location he chooses. Under MacOS X Lazarus will independently determine whether software being developed already has a bundle. If it has not, Lazarus will create one.

You also need to keep in mind another entity typically found only in MacOS X – the framework. A framework is a special, packed library, which you can link into your Pascal program source either with the Free Pascal command line instruction:

```
-k-framework -k<Frameworkname>
```

or by using the compiler directive: *{$R Linkframework <Frameworkname>}*

There are several frameworks, some of which also have sub-frameworks.

The most important ones are *Carbon*, *Cocoa* and *OpenGL*.

The Carbon framework contains the basic C APIs of the Mac operating system and is located in the unit *MacOSAll* in Free Pascal starting from version 2.2.2 (and in the unit *FPCMacOSAll* in older versions of the compiler).

Cocoa is the newer Objective C API and is compiled with Carbon. The Cocoa framework consists of three smaller frameworks: Foundation, Appkit and CoreData. They are accessed by adding a unit with the name of the framework to the uses clause in your program. The units contain type definitions, Objective C classes, and some exported routines.

Framework	Description
Foundation	Base non-visual classes, like *NSObject*, *NSString*, *NSAutoreleasePool*, etc.
Appkit	Classes for the development of GUI software, like *NSApplication*, *NSWindow*, *NSView*, *NSButton*, etc.
CoreData	Provides infrastructure for graph management, undo and redo, and object persistence (saving objects to and fetching objects from a persistent store, such as a file on disk).

Table 5.12: The Cocoa sub-frameworks

To develop Cocoa programs in Pascal, the current version of the PasCocoa project and the sub-frameworks need to be downloaded from:

`http://wiki.lazarus.freepascal.org/PasCocoa`

Each sub-framework has a separate unit of the same name, see Table 5.13.

Define	Description
CoreFoundation	Fundamental data types and essential services which are useful for both Carbon and Cocoa.
CarbonSound	Older sound API, which was also the base for QuickTime Audio. Has been deprecated as of Mac OS X 10.5 and Apple recommends that CoreAudio be used instead, or QuickTime Audio if versions prior to Mac OS X 10.5 need to be supported.
CommonPanels	Supports Color picking and Font dialogs. The most important functions are *PickColor*, *FPShowHideFontPanel* and *SetFontInfoForSelection*. Not supported in 64-bit.
Help	Provides an API to the Apple help system. For cross-platform applications it's better to use a cross-platform help system.
HIToolbox	A new Carbon user interface API introduced in Mac OS X 10.2. Its main types are HIObject, HIToolbox and HIView. Not supported in 64-bit.
HTMLRendering	An HTML rendering library. Is deprecated as of Mac OS X 10.4 and the Web Kit Objective-C API is recommended by Apple instead.
ImageCapture	An API to communicate with image capture devices such as cameras and scanners. Its most important functions are: *ICAGetDeviceList*, *ICACopyObjectPropertiesDictionary*, *ICARegisteForEventNotification*, *ICAOpenSession*, *ICAObjectDownLoadFile* and *ICACloseSession*.
Ink	An API for special interaction with tablets and stylus. For most uses the standard mouse routines are enough.
NavigationServices	An API for standard dialogs, such as Open File, Save File, Open Directory, Set Audio Volume, etc.
OpenScripting	An Apple-specific interprocess communication mechanism (IPC). For cross-platform applications it is better to use a cross-platform IPC, like sockets, pipes, or the simpleipc unit from Free Pascal.
Print	Used by Carbon applications to display a user interface for printing. rovides a page setup dialog, a print dialog and a printing status dialog. Needs to be used together with CorePrinting to do the actual printing. Not available in 64-bit.
SecurityHI	Provides security-related dialogs. Not available in 64-bit.
SpeechRecognition	An interface to the Speech Recognition Manager.

Table 5.13: Carbon sub-frameworks

With FPC 2.5.1 the compiler introduced direct access to Objective C classes. That has opened the way for creating a real Cocoa widget-set for Lazarus. With the stable FPC 2.4.0 however, this is not yet possible, so we will only cover the PasCocoa project here. All sub-frameworks are accessed by adding the unit *MacOSAll* to the *uses* clause in your project and to your working units.
MacOS X up to 10.6 uses HFS as file system, which has some differences compared to Linux and BSD file systems. First of all it is not case sensitive, resembling Windows. However, this can be configured and on some OS-X servers that has already been done. Secondly, OS X uses normalized UTF-8 for file names. An a-umlaut can be encoded in different ways in Unicode (and the ext2+ file system in Linux will distinguish between them). HFS normalizes all a-umlauts to one encoding. So for comparing file names, it is best to always use the *FileUtil* function *CompareFilenames*.

Directory	User access	Description
/	Read	Root directory.
/Users	Read	Holds one folder for each user, with the same name as the user. This will be the user's document folder.
/Applications	Read	Native applications should be installed here, by dragging their application bundle to this directory.
/Library	Read	Holds data files and frameworks provided by third-party developers.
/System/Library	Read	Holds Apple data files and frameworks.
/Developer	Read	Is created when the developer tools are installed and contains applications, tools, documentation, and other resources for developing Mac OS X software. The original C and Objective-C headers for Apple libraries are located in `/Developer/SDKs`.
/tmp	Read/Write	A global location for temporary files.
/usr	Read	Reserved for Apple Unix software, except for the /usr/local directory.
/usr/lib	Read	The location of Unix dynamic link libraries.
/usr/local/bin	Read	The location for normal user executable Unix files for general access.
/usr/local/share	Read	Unix applications should create subdirectories here for storing their read-only resource files.

Table 5.14: The most important directories in MacOS X

MacOS X directories have a dual nature. It is a Unix file system, but that is not visible to the normal user. For instance the standard directories like `/usr` are not visible in the Finder (the Mac file manager). These directories can be accessed in the terminal.
It is where Unix applications are installed.

The names of the Mac standard folders are displayed unlocalized (in English) on the command line – so their names are fixed – but in the Finder they are displayed in the system language. Table 5.14 shows the most important directories in MacOS X.

Figure 5.13: The Finder in MacOS X. Note that system directories like /usr and /tmp are not displayed, and folder names are localized, although they have to be referred to by English names in the terminal and in source code.

Older MacOS X versions

Applications compiled under MacOS X without additional options are only guaranteed to work under the current main version and higher main versions. So if, for instance, we compile a program under MacOS X 10.5.6, we can only be sure it will run under MacOS X 10.5.x or higher. The reason for this odd behaviour lies with the SDKs which are versioned against the main operating system version and therefore are directly linked against the current version. Fortunately the Apple development tools are usually delivered with the SDK for at least the previous operating system version. You can link against this older SDK by going to the *Project → Project Options* dialog and clicking on *Other* (one of the nodes below *Compiler Options*), then entering in the *Custom options* memo the following directives for the linker:

```
k-macosx version min -klO.4
XR/Developer/SDKs/MacOSX10.4u.sdk/
```

It is also possible to enter another minimum version, or a path to a different SDK here.

The Cocoa framework

Binding Object Pascal applications with the Cocoa API has only been possible since 2007. The bridge between Objective C and Object Pascal is called PasCocoa.
Because Objective C has a C library containing all necessary functions for creating classes, registering methods and their export, it was possible to shift this bridge, which does not need external libraries or the overhead of additional libraries for the Objective C code. This is possible since both programs – the one written in Pascal and the one written in Objective C – call functions in the same library.

In OS X terminology a framework is a library packaged in a special way. The Free Pascal compiler has to be pointed to it with an additional command-line parameter.
The switch to use is -k-framework -k<framework_name>. The framework consists of three smaller frameworks named *Foundation*, *Appkit* and *CoreData* (see Table 5.12).
These three sub-frameworks can be accessed by adding a unit with the same name as the framework to the uses clause of your program.
The units contain type definitions, Objective C classes and exported routines. Cocoa is often used together with the Carbon C APIs, which are located in the unit *MacOSAll* since Free Pascal 2.2.2 (and in older versions in the unit *FPCMacOSAll*).
When linking the application with the command line directive *-k-framework -kcocoa -k-lobjc* (or entering the same in the *Options: (-k)* edit field on the *Linking* page of the *Project Options* dialog) it can be directly linked to Cocoa. The availability of the libraries is never a problem: Cocoa is available in all MacOS X versions.

In Cocoa all class, data type and procedure names begin with "NS" indicating they all stem from NextSTEP. Most of the calls in the framework are also derived from the base class *NSObject* in the sub-framework Foundation, like the Object Pascal classes, which are usually derived from *TObject*. Objective C differs from Pascal in its lack of properties. Instead of properties it provides getter/setter pairs.
If you find definitions of *CFStringRef* instead of the expected *NSString* in example Pascal source code, this is because alias definitions of the Carbon types have been declared in *PasCocoa* for convenience.

The most important Cocoa classes

We can only give a short overview here of the most important base Cocoa classes with their most important methods. With the help of a search engine you will find all the details about these classes in the Apple documentation. You can limit the search to the Apple developer's site by including *site:developer.apple.com NSApplication* in your Google search string.

Cocoa item	Description
NSObject	The basic object in the Cocoa hierarchy. Many methods easing the work of Pascal developers have been added to this.
Constructor Create;	Creates a new Pascal class and also a new Objective C class linked to it.
Constructor CreateWithHandle (aHandle: objc.id);	Does not create a new Objective C object, but uses the one indicated in the parameter instead.
Property Handle: objc.id;	The Objective C object.
Procedure AddMethods;	Is overridden during subclassing to register methods for calling by ObjectiveC.
Procedure AddMethod(aName, aParameters: String; aPointer: Pointer);	Registers a method.
Function CreateClassDefinition(const name, superclassName: String): Boolean;	Registers a class in the Objective C runtime.
Class NSAutoreleasePool	Each thread used by PasCocoa should create an NSAutoreleasePool before addressing other Objective C calls. The object has to be destroyed at the end of the thread.
Class NSResponder	Implements the Cocoa event system.
Class NSApplication	Represents the application. Returns the common application object.
Constructor sharedApplication;	This must be used to initialize the global variable NSApp.
Procedure run;	Jumps into the event loop, which will only be ended when the application closes.
Procedure terminate;	Ends the program.
Class NSView	The base class for adding child control elements.
Procedure addSubview(_aView: objc.id {NSView});	Adds a child element to it.

Table 5.15 Selected PasCocoa classes and methods Part 1.

Cocoa item	Description
Class NSControl	An abstract class offering three basic GUI functions: drawing on the screen; reacting to user input; and sending action notices.
Constructor initWithFrame(_frameRect: NSRect);	Creates a new instance of the control element, initially with the size _frameRect.
Procedure setStringValue(_aString: CFStringRef);	Getter and setter methods for the data the control element contains. In an
Procedure setIntValue(anInt: Integer); **Function** stringValue: CFStringRef; **Function** intValue: Integer;	*NSTextField* for instance, this is the string shown on the screen.
Class NSWindow	The screen window. This window class has not been derived from *NSView* and can herefore not receive any child elements directly. The associated *NSView* will be set via contentView. That is where the control elements can be added.
Procedure orderFrontRegardless;	Sets the window uppermost in the Z-order.
Function contentView: objc.id {NSView};	Returns the *NSView* associated with the window.
Constructor initWithContentRect styleMask backing defer(**_contentRect**: NSRect; windowStyle: LongWord; **_bufferingType**: NSBackingStoreType; _flag: LongBool) ;	Creates a new NSWindow object. **_contentRect** is the position on the screen, windowStyle can be either *NSBorderlessWindowMask* or a combination of other window style constants ORed together. **_bufferingType** should be *NSBackingStoreBuffered* and deferCreation should be LongBool(NO).
Function title: CFStringRef; **Procedure setTitle(aString: CFStringRef);**	The getter/setter for the window title.
Class NSButton	A button control element.
Class NSTextField	The control element for showing text in a window.

Table 5.15 Selected PasCocoa classes and methods. Continuation: part 2

Cocoa requires a whole lot of programming techniques to make Objective C and Pascal code work together. These include: creating instances of the Cocoa classes; calling class methods; calling exported functions; subclassing a Cocoa class; and overwriting methods of derived classes.

Instantiating Cocoa classes

If an instance of a class is derived, its methods can be called until the class is destroyed again. To create a class in Objective C memory has to be reserved first, then the class can be initialized. In Pascal both these steps are handled together in the constructor. To make the bridging Pascal conform to this all PasCocoa constructors have therefore been changed into Pascal constructors.
Besides that, you cannot exchange references to Pascal objects with Objective C objects. However, when one of these is available, the other can always be acquired. Each Pascal object that corresponds to an Objective C object has a property *Handle* representing a link to the corresponding object. And conversely *NSObject.CreateWithHandle* enables us to query an Objective C object for the corresponding Pascal object.
The following code shows how a typical Objective C source should be converted into Pascal to create an *NSAutoreleasePool.* First, here is the Objective C code:

```
#import <Cocoa/Cocoa.h>

int main(int argc, char *argv[]) {
   // Create the pool object
   NSAutoreleasePool* pool=[[NSAutoreleasePool alloc] init];

   // Call release method from object pool
   [pool release];
}
```

And here is the equivalent Object Pascal version:

```
program MyPasCocoaApp;
uses Foundation;
  var  pool: NSAutoreleasePool;
begin
  pool := NSAutoreleasePool.Create;
  pool.Free;
end.
```

Class methods and procedure export

Class methods are called just as in normal Object Pascal code. The following example calls the class method *sharedApplication* from *NSApplication.* This routine will return the global application variable. Keep in mind that *NSApp* should not be defined as this variable has already been defined in the unit *AppKit.* However it is not initialized at program startup.

```
uses AppKit;
begin
  NSApp := NSApplication.sharedApplication;
  // ... further code here
```

Objective C is a superset of C, so all procedural code in Objective C is also C source code. Procedures are called in the same way as in C and they can be used from Pascal in the same way as C routines with the appropriate declarations.
To understand how a Cocoa class can be used by subclassing, and how to override a method, we will now analyse an example application. Simple subclassing is not complicated. We can simply declare a Pascal class and specify any Cocoa class we want as the parent object. Code written in Objective C cannot access the method declared here. For Objective C to recognize its own methods they have to be declared in a specific syntax and then registered. Only then will the layout of its own methods fit the real Objective C methods.

```
TMyController = class(NSObject)
  public
  // Additional binding functions
  constructor Create; Override;
  procedure AddMethods; Override;
  // Objective C methods
  class procedure doShowStatusitem(_self: objc.id; cmd: SEL;
                                   sender: objc.id); CDecl; Static;
  class procedure doHideStatusitem(_self: objc.id; cmd: SEL;
                                   sender: objc.id); CDecl; Static;
  class Procedure doClose(_self: objc.id; cmd: SEL; sender: objc.id);
                                 CDecl; Static;
  class function applicationShouldTerminateAfterLastWindowClosed(
          _self: objc.id; cmd: SEL; theApplication: objc.id): Cbool;
                                                       CDecl; Static;
end;
```

In this example declaration *doShowStatusitem*, *doHideStatusitem* and *doClose* are Pascal methods, which are prepared for access from Objective C. This is needed, for example, for event callbacks in a button. *applicationShouldTerminateAfterLastWindowClosed* implements a handler for a signal from *NSApplication*. Please note the methods have to be class methods. This means access to the Self reference from Pascal is not possible. However there is another *_self* available. This identifier offers an Objective C class and a Pascal class. To reach the Pascal class, we can, for instance, use a global variable and get a Pascal class returned in objc.id by calling *NSObject.CreateWithHandle*.

The next section of source code shows the correct implementation of *TMyController.AddMethods*. This procedure will register the methods. It will also show the constructor *TMyController.Create*. It will register the current class as a new Objective C class, before the deferred constructor is called, which will in turn call *AddMethods*.

Finally we will give the source for a complete Cocoa application, written in Free Pascal. This example program creates a window and shows a control element of type *NSTextField* with the text "Hello Cocoa!" in it.

The first call in the program is *NSAutoreleasePool.Create.* This has to be called in every thread in the program and before all other Cocoa routines. It creates a normal storage manager for Cocoa objects. Then the global variable *NSApp* is initialized by *NSApplication.sharedApplication*, which completes the program initialization. The next step is to create the program window with *NSWindow.initWithContentRect* and to set its title with *NSWindow.setTitle.* Then the text field is initialized with *NSTextField.initWithFrame* in a similar way.

Because windows in Cocoa are descendants of *NSView*, which allows child control elements, the NSView of the windows is set with *NSWindow.contentView.*
This method returns an Objective C class, which is converted for the call with *NSView.CreateWithHandle* (MainWindow.contentView).

Once we have the *NSView* of the window, we can insert the text field with *NSView.addSubview(TextField).* The next step is to point to the main window with *NSWindow.orderFrontRegardless* and finally to call *NSApp.run* to get the program into the event loop until the application is ended.

The easiest way to compile the program is to load the lpi project file and to have the program generated from within Lazarus. PasCocoa is packed into a Lazarus package, which sets the correct paths. Figure 5.14 shows what this program will look like onscreen.

```
{'v@:@' adds methods to the class.
  Notes on the parameter strings:
  The first parameter is the result (v = void), followed by self and _cmd (@ id = and: = SEL)
  and at the end of "sender"(@ = id)}

procedure TMyController.AddMethods;
begin
  AddMethod(Str doShowStatusItem, 'v@:@', Pointer(doShowStatusitem));
  AddMethod(Str doHideStatusitem, 'v@:@', Pointer(doHideStatusitem));
  AddMethod(Str doClose, 'v@:@', Pointer(doClose));
  AddMethod(Str applicationShouldTerminateAfterLastWindowClosed,
    'v@:@',Pointer(applicationShouldTerminateAfterLastWindowClosed));
end;

constructor TMyController.Create;
  var  fileName: CFStringRef;
begin
    // The class registered before the NSObject constructor is registered
    // in the Objective-C run-time
  if not CreateClassDefinition(ClassNameO, Str_NSObject)
    then WriteLn('Failed to create objc class');
  Inherited Create;
end;
```

The method *AddMethods* has to call *NSObject.AddMethod* for each method to be registered and pass a string with the parameter of the method. This string is assembled from four parts. The first part is the code for the type of the return value of the function, the second stands for _self as identification of the class, the third stands for _cmd, the selector of the class (that is an internal Objective C identifier), and the last one for the parameter free. The substring for _self should always just be @ to mark an Objective C class and the one for _cmd should always be a colon, the symbol for a selector. Table 5.16 shows the most common values, a complete list is available at:

`http://wiki.lazarus.freepascal.org/PasCocoa#Type_Encodings.`

Substring	Pascaltype	Unit	Description
v	-	-	Indicates the absence of the parameter
b	cbool	ctypes	C-compatible Boolean type
@	id	objc	An Objective C class instance
:	SEL	objc	Objective C selector
i	cint	ctypes	C-compatible integer
I	cuint	ctypes	C-compatible unsigned integer
?	Pointer	-	A generic pointer

Table 5.16: Registering Cocoa data types in Free Pascal

GetAppConfigDir(True)	C:\Documents and Settings\All Users\Application Data\configtest\
GetAppConfigDir(False)	C:\Documents and Settings\Username\Local Settings\Application Data\configtest\
GetAppConfigFile(True)	C:\Documents and Settings\All Users\Application Data\configtest\configtest.cfg
GetAppConfigFile(False)	C:\Documents and Settings\Username\Local Settings\Application Data\configtest\configtest.cfg

And this is the information for the German version of the operating system:

GetAppConfigDir(True)	C:\Dokumente und Einstellungen\All Users\Anwendungsdaten\configtest\
GetAppConfigDir(False)	C:\Dokumente und Einstellungen\Username\Lokale Einstellungen\Anwendungsdaten\configtest\
GetAppConfigFile(True)	C:\Dokumente und Einstellungen\All Users\Anwendungsdaten\sysfolder\configtest.cfg
GetAppConfigFile(False)	C:\Dokumente und Einstellungen\Username\Lokale Einstellungen\Anwendungsdaten\sysfolder\configtest.cfg

When the function is called with True, it will report the directory where the global configuration is stored under Windows. The local configuration is stored in the directory of the current user account.

In Vista with FPC 2.2.4, things look quite different. In this case there is also no difference depending on the system locale. Starting with Vista, Microsoft fools the user into thinking local file names are being used, just as is common practice in Apple's MacOS X.

GetAppConfigDir(True)	C:\ProgramData\configtest\
GetAppConfigDir(False)	C:\Users\martin\AppData\Local\configtest\
GetAppConfigFile(True)	C:\ProgramData\configtest\configtest.cfg
GetAppConfigFile(False)	C:\Users\martin\AppData\Local\configtest\configtest.cfg

5.1.4 The MacOS X APIs

```
program simplewindow;
{$ifdef fpc}{$mode delphi}{$endif}
uses
{$ifdef ver2_2 0}
   FPCMacOSAll,
{$else}
   MacOSAll,
{$endif}
   objc, ctypes, AppKit, Foundation;

const
   Str_Window_Title = 'Pascal Cocoa Example';
   Str_Window_Message = 'NSTextField Control';
var
   //classes
   pool   : NSAutoreleasePool;
   MainWindow: NSWindow;
   MainWindowView: NSView;
   TextField : NSTextField;
   CFTitle, CFMessage: CFStringRef;        (* strings *)
   MainWindowRect, TextFieldRect: NSRect; (* sizes *)

begin
   // Creates an autorelease pool for that thread (Each thread must have one).
   pool := NSAutoreleasePool.Create;
   // Creates the application object NSApp
   NSApp := NSApplication.sharedApplication;

   // creates a simple window
   MainWindowRect.origin.x                   := 300.0;
   MainWindowRect.origin.y                   := 300.0;
   MainWindowRect.size.width                 := 300.0;
   MainWindowRect.size.height                := 100.0;
   MainWindow := NSWindow.initWithContentRect_styleMask_backing
      defer(MainWindowRect,
   NSTitledWindowMask OR NSClosableWindowMask OR NSMiniaturizableWindowMask OR
      NSResizableWindowMask, NSBackingStoreBuffered, LongBool(NO));
   // initialize the window title
   CFTitle := CFStringCreateWithPascalString(NIL, Str Window Title,
      kCFStringEncodingUTF8);
   MainWindow.setTitle(CFTitle);
   // Adds a string to the NSTextField
   CFMessage := CFStringCreateWithPascalString(NIL, Str_Window_Message,
      kCFStringEncodingUTF8);
   TextFieldRect.origin.x                    := 50.0;
   TextFieldRect.origin.y                    := 50.0;
   TextFieldRect.size.width                  := 200.0;
   TextFieldRect.size.height                 := 25.0;
   TextField := NSTextField.initWithFrame(TextFieldRect);
   TextField.setBordered(LongBool(NO));
   TextField.setDrawsBackground(LongBool(NO));
   TextField.setStringValue(CFMessage);
   MainWindowView := NSView.CreateWithHardle(MainWindow.contentView);
   MainWindowView.addSubview(TextField.Handle);
   MainWindow.orderFrontRegardless;          // window to bring forward
   NSApp.run;                                // places the program in the event loop
   pool.Free;                                // autorelease thread pool is freed
end.
```

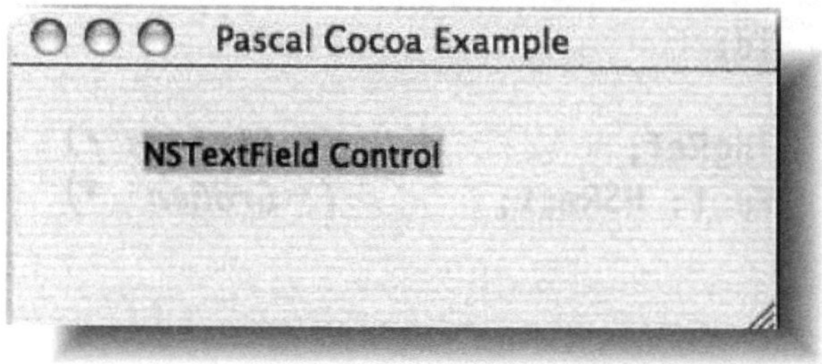

Figure 5.14: The simple Cocoa example program :ontbreekt

The greatest disadvantage for Pascal programmers is that almost all available programming examples are written in Objective C, so they have to be converted into Pascal before they can be used. Besides that, most Pascal programmers are uncomfortable at first with the need to register the methods used. Since the Spring of 2010 the development version 2.5.1 of Free Pascal offers native support for Cocoa. This is called *Objective Pascal* and it makes working with Cocoa a lot easier. However, it does have the same disadvantage as PasCocoa: you cannot use the LCL component framework. So this is all still at an experimental stage.

5.1.5 32-bit and 64-bit

Platform independent programming does not stop with different operating systems and architectures. There are also some subtleties to keep in mind if we want to be sure an application will work on both 32 and 64-bit processors, and if we want to port applications from a 32 to a 64-bit system.
A common misconception amongst developers is that the size of a pointer is always the same, normally 4 bytes. This may be true on most 32 bit systems, but on 64 bit processors it is 8 bytes. And this means it is not possible to typecast pointers to integers. To make developers' lives easier, Free Pascal provides two integer types which are guaranteed to have the same size as pointers. These are called *PtrInt* and *PtrUInt*. PtrInt is a signed 32 bit integer on 32-bit platforms and a signed 64-bit integer on 64-bit platforms. PtrUInt is a similar unsigned integer.
The following example code will only work on 32-bit platforms:

```
function ObjectToInteger(AObject: TObject): Cardinal;
begin
  Result := Cardinal(AObject);
end;
```

And here is a version, corrected to work on 64-bit platforms as well:

```
function ObjectToInteger(AObject: TObject): PtrUInt;
begin
  Result := PtrUInt(AObject);
end;
```

5.1.5 32-bit and 64-bit

The integer type is four bytes in size, even on 64-bit systems.
Consequently, the compiler may create record and class variables with unused space in them, because this alignment allows the processor to access the data more quickly. The attribute packed can be used to avoid this.

```
type
  TFixedSizeRecord = packed record // no gaps between variables
    i: Integer;
    j: Integer;
  end;
```

This record always has a size of 8 bytes.

To write 64-bit compatible code you can also use the following *ifdef* construction:

```
{$ifdef CPU64}
   // 64-Bit-Code
{$else}
   // 32-Bit-Code
{$endif}
```

5.2 Configuration Files

Each program that needs to save its current status between successive sessions has to be able to save its configuration. Configuration files are the best way to save session data about a program. Such session information can either be global (applying to all users on the system) or it can be user-specific. Platform-independent programs will also require a configuration file to know where to save the application's resource files.

The unit *SysUtils* has special routines for discovering the correct storage location for configuration files. With *GetAppConfigDir* and *GetAppConfigFile* we can retrieve the storage directory or even the complete file name of the configuration file.

```
function GetAppConfigDir(Global: Boolean): String;
function GetAppConfigFile(Global: Boolean): String;
function GetAppConfigFile(Global: Boolean; SubDir: Boolean): String;
```

Both functions have a single parameter Global. If this is True, the global configuration file name will be returned, otherwise the configuration file name for the current user's account is returned. Where the actual location is depends on the operating system, and is not important to the developer nor to the end user.

But for debugging purposes or for manually checking the contents of the file it may be useful to know the storage location of the configuration file. Therefore the following tables show the actual location of the configuration files on several operating systems. The following information applies to Windows XP with FPC 2.2.4 (English version first). The program used to get this information is called *configtest.*

The new directory structure in Windows 6.x (as Vista and Windows 7 are known internally at Microsoft) is basically different from the one in Windows 5.x (Windows 2000 and XP). Of course it is always possible Microsoft will decide to change this again in future Windows versions. This makes it even more important to use routines like *GetAppConfigDir* (or to use equivalents from the Windows API) and never to use hard-coded paths. Microsoft has made changes in this area in the past several times as well, as can be seen when we run the program under Windows 98 SE (internally known as Windows 3.98). This does not have user accounts like the Windows NT line and the paths turn out to be as follows:..

GetAppConfigDir(True)	C:\WINDOWS\All Users\Application Data\CONFIGTEST\
GetAppConfigDir(False)	C:\WINDOWS\Local Settings\Application Data\CONFIGTEST\
GetAppConfigFile(True)	C:\WINDOWS\Local Settings\Application Data\CONFIGTEST\
GetAppConfigFile(False)	C:\WINDOWS\Local Settings\Application data\configtest\ Configtest.cfg

The main difference between Windows XP and Windows 98 is that local configuration files are only stored separately per user in XP. Windows 98 does not know this concept. The results on German and English language PCs turned out to be the same in this case. In Linux everything looks very different, of course. Here is an example with Debian GNU/Linux 5 and FPC 2.2.4. FreeBSD gives the same results:

GetAppConfigDir(True)	/etc/configtest/
GetAppConfigDir(False)	/home/Username/.config/
GetAppConfigFile(True)	/etc/configtest.cfg
GetAppConfigFile(False)	/home/Username/.config/configtest.cfg

In Linux and FreeBSD the global configuration files are stored in an application-specific subdirectory in /etc and local configurations are stored in a hidden directory in the home directory of the current user, which is usually `/home/$USER/`, but might be anywhere else. Directory names with a leading dot are hidden under Linux. To be able to save the file, we first have to use the Pascal command *MkDir* to create the local directory indicated by *GetAppConfigDir*. Only after doing that will saving be possible.

In MacOS X 10.4 the home directories are normally located under `/Users`, so with FPC 2.2.4 we see the following result:

GetAppConfigDir(True)	/etc
GetAppConfigDir(False)	/Users/Username/.config/configtest
GetAppConfigFile(True)	/etc/configtest.cfg
GetAppConfigFile(False)	/Users/Username/.config/configtest.cfg

The test project to acquire this information can either be the following simple command-line program:

```
program configtest;
{$apptype Console}
uses SysUtils;
begin
  WriteLn('GetAppConfigDir(True):    ', GetAppConfigDir(True));
  WriteLn('GetAppConfigDir(False):   ', GetAppConfigDir(False));
  WriteLn('GetAppConfigFile(True):   ', GetAppConfigFile(True));
  WriteLn('GetAppConfigFile(False):  ', GetAppConfigFile(False));
end.
```

Or it can be a small GUI program, which is actually just as easy to write. In this case we use a *TMemo* field as the output widget. In the window's *FormCreate* event we insert the following lines:

```
procedure TForm1.FormCreate(Sender: TObject);
begin
  Memo1.Lines.Add('GetAppConfigDir(True):    ' +
                                       GetAppConfigDirUTF8(True));
  Memo1.Lines.Add('GetAppConfigDir(False):   ' +
                                      GetAppConfigDirUTF8(False));
  Memo1.Lines.Add('GetAppConfigFile(True):   ' +
                               SysToUTF8(GetAppConfigFile(True)));
  Memo1.Lines.Add('GetAppConfigFile(False):  ' +
                              SysToUTF8(GetAppConfigFile(False)));
end;
```

The advantage of this GUI program is hat it does not have to open a console window to display the result, so it can easily be studied in the development environment itself. The result of both programs is of course identical.

5.3 Resource Files

Resource files are used to store read-only external data, which is necessary for executing the program. It is impossible to write any useful program which lacks resources. Examples of such resources are pictures, audio data, XML files, database files, help files etc. The location to save this information has to be carefully considered because it differs between operating systems. Some operating systems – Linux for example – even need a path that is configured depending on the distribution used. The example unit we will show in this section takes these kinds of details into account.

Most programs are executed without administrator (or root) privileges. That is why programs need to have all their data in locations that can be read by any user. Write access is not always needed. Configuration files however, need to be stored in locations where both reading and writing is allowed.

MacOS X is an exception amongst Unix systems, because it works with application bundles containing both the software and the data for an application. This means resource files need to be part of the bundle. If the bundle is moved, the application still needs to keep functioning. The correct location for the bundle can be retrieved with API calls from *Core* and *Foundation.*

Operating System	Best location for resource files
Windows, Windows CE	The same directory as the executable, or one of its subdirectories.
Mac OS X	Inside the application bundle.
FreeBSD resource	`/usr/local/share/app_name` In FreeBSD the directory `/usr/share` shouldn't be used for files.
Other UNIXes (Linux, Solaris, etc.)	In a fixed, but configurable, location. Usually either `/usr/share/app_name` or `/opt/app_name` `/usr/share /app_name` or `/opt/app_name`.

Table 5.17: Recommended resource file storage locations

The following example shows a solution for Windows, where the data files are stored in the same location as the executable program (or in a directory based on that like `MyDirectory + 'data' + PathDelim + 'myfile.dat'`). In Unix systems they are stored in a directory specified in a configuration file. Just in case there is no configuration file or it does not contain this information a constant `/usr/share/myapp/` is used as a default directory. As discussed in the previous section, the path to the configuration file is acquired through the *GetAppConfigFile* function of the Free Pascal RTL.

The following complete unit can be used in your own programs after changing the program name from *myApp*:

```
unit appsettings;

interface

{$ifdef fpc}
  {$mode delphi}{$H+}
{$endif}
uses
{$Iifdef MSWindows}
  Windows,
{$endif}
{$ifdef Darwin}
  MacOSAll,
{$endif}
  Classes, SysUtils, Forms, IniFiles, constants;

type
  { TConfigurations }
  TConfigurations = class(TObject)
  private
     ConfigFilePath: String;
     MyDirectory: String;
  public
     constructor Create;
     destructor Destroy; Override;
     function GetResourcesDir: string;
     procedure ReadFromFile(Sender: TObject);
     procedure Save(Sender: TObject);
  end;

var
  vConfigurations: TConfigurations;

implementation

const
  DefaultDirectory  = '/usr/share/myapp/';
  SectionGeneral    = 'General';
  SectionUnix       = 'UNIX';
  IdentMyDirectory  = 'MyDirectory';
  BundleResourcesDirectory = '/Contents/Resources/';

{ TConfigurations }
constructor TConfigurations.Create;
begin
  ConfigFilePath := GetAppConfigDirUTF8(False)  + 'myapp.ini';
  ReadFromFile(NIL);
end;

destructor TConfigurations.Destroy;
begin
  Save(NIL);
  inherited Destroy;
end;
```

```
function TConfigurations.GetResourcesDir: string;
{$ifdef Darwin}
var
  pathRef: CFURLRef;
  pathCFStr: CFStringRef;
  pathStr: shortstring;
{$endif}
begin
{$ifdef UNIX}
{$ifdef Darwin}
  pathRef := CFBundleCopyBundleURL(CFBundleGetMainBundle());
  pathCFStr := CFURLCopyFileSystemPath(pathRef,
     kCFURLPOSIXPathStyle);
  CFStringGetPascalString(pathCFStr, @pathStr,
     255,FStringGetSystemEncoding());
  CFRelease(pathRef);
  CFRelease(pathCFStr);

  Result := pathStr + BundleResourcesDirectory;
{$else}
  if MyDirectory  = '' then Result := DefaultDirectory
     else Result := MyDirectory;
{$endif}
{$endif}

{$ifdef Windows}
  Result := ExtractFilePath(Application.EXEName);
{$endif}
end;

procedure TConfigurations.Save(Sender: TObject);
var
  MyFile: TIniFile;
begin
  MyFile := TIniFile.Create(UTF8ToSys(ConfigFilePath));
  try
     MyFile.WriteString(SectionUnix, IdentMyDirectory, MyDirectory);
  finally
     MyFile.Free;
  end;
end;

procedure TConfigurations.ReadFromFile(Sender: TObject);
var
  MyFile: TIniFile;
begin
  MyFile := TIniFile.Create(ConfigFilePath);
  try
     // Here other configurations can be read
     MyDirectory := MyFile.ReadString(SectionUnix, IdentMyDirectory,
        '');
  finally
     MyFile.Free;
  end;
end;
```

```
initialization
   vConfigurations := TConfigurations.Create;

finalization
   FreeAndNil(vConfigurations);
end.
```

Here is an example code snippet which uses a routine from this unit:

```
   // ...
   bmp := TBitmap.Create
   try
      bmp.LoadFromFile(vConfigurations.GetResourcesDir() +
          'MyBitmap.bmp');
   finally
      bmp.Free;
   end;
```

More Windows-like than working with `.ini` files is reading and writing the data from and to the registry. Free Pascal offers special routines for this in the unit *Registry*. When you use the registry, you should be very careful not to leave any garbage behind when your program is removed from the system. That is why it should make use of a proper installation program based on the Nullsoft Installation System (NSIS), see:

`http://nsis.sourceforge.net/Main_Page`

or InnoSetup, see:

`http://www.jrsoftware.org/isinfo.php`

As the registry is only available under Windows all calls to the routines and also the link to the unit *Registry* itself should be located in conditional compilation sections {*$ifdef MSWindows*}, whereas `.ini` files are truly cross-platform.

Chapter 6
The class libraries

by Michael Van Canneyt

Developing programs in Lazarus uses Object Oriented Programming (OOP). Whenever you design an application's GUI, or its business objects, or some other interaction with the Operating System (OS), you will always be using classes or objects. The entire gamut of classes available for you to use is organized in three distinct groups or layers:

- **RTL**
  The Free Pascal Run Time Library. This contains all the functions which you need for interaction with the OS. It contains both platform-specific and platform-independent units. Generally, the routines you find in the RTL units are not object oriented, but procedural.

- **FCL**
  The Free Pascal Free Component Library. This is a set of all-purpose crossplatform classes and components: components for image handling, process management, database access, web programming. In contrast to Delphi's VCL, the classes in Lazarus are strictly divided between a set of non-visual components, and a set of visual classes. The FCL contains only non-visual classes.

- **LCL**
  The Lazarus Component Library. This is the GUI layer of Lazarus which contains all Lazarus' visual code. The components in this layer abstract the underlying widget set. Consequently the same set of components can be used on all platforms, and it is the aim of the Lazarus team to make sure they work identically on all supported platforms.

The first two layers are part of Free Pascal, the compiler underlying Lazarus. Classes and routines in those layers can be used without Lazarus, by using the command-line compiler or another Free Pascal IDE (for instance MSEide, or fpGUI). The third layer, the *LCL*, is specific to Lazarus and how it defines *GUI programming*. One of Lazarus' goals is to encapsulate all supported widget sets in a set of components (the LCL) in such a way that another widget set can be used simply by recompiling the program using a different set of widget set units.

The following widget sets are supported:

- The Win32/win64 API.
- The Windows CE and Windows Mobile API, which is a reduced form of the Win32/win64 API.
- The platform-independent QT 4 widget set. It can be used on Windows, Linux/Unix, MacOS X and is supported well by Lazarus.
- The older GTK1 widget set. Until version 0.9.26 this was the default widget set in Lazarus on Linux/Unix, and hence is supported well.
- The newer GTK2 widget set. As of version 0.9.28 this is the default widget set in Lazarus on Linux/Unix, and hence is also well supported.
- Carbon on MacOS X.
- Free Pascal can access the Cocoa layer of MacOS X and the iPhone. The *LCL* currently does not support this widget set, so Cocoa programs must be written manually.
- *fpGUI* is an alternate widget set for Free Pascal. An *LCL* layer that builds on top of *fpGUI* is planned.

Lazarus supports the Win32/Win64 and GTK1/GTK2 and Qt layers best of all (currently at the beta-stage). The other widget sets are alpha-stage components.

The division between *RTL, FCL* and *LCL,* as well as the distinction between the various widget sets is largely academic and of little practical importance for the end-user application developer.
The distinction between visual classes and non-visual components is more relevant. The visual classes or components are actual GUI elements: forms, buttons, checkboxes, edit components, menus – anything that the user sees is a visual class. In Lazarus, all visual classes descend from *TControl* (defined in the *LCL),* and they are discussed below. Most of the components found on the Lazarus IDE's Component Palette are visual components.

By contrast, the non-visual classes or components are classes that are not visible to the application user. They fall into one of two categories: components or non-components. The components are classes that can be dropped from the component palette onto a Lazarus form. They are then represented by a small icon on the form, so they can be selected by the programmer and subsequently manipulated through the IDE's Object Inspector. The non-component classes are classes that the programmer constructs manually in code to perform a required task.

Since all visual controls descend from *TControl,* which is the base class defined in the *LCL,* all *RTL* and *FCL* classes are – by definition – non-visual. Nevertheless, there are a lot of component classes in the FCL which can be dropped on a Lazarus form. The database components are a good example of non-visual components defined in the FCL.

Visual components also fall into one of two categories: 'normal' components, and their DB-aware counterparts, which are descendants of normal components, enhanced with the ability to connect to the data in a database.

This means that they can show the contents of a field in a database table; and when the user manipulates the control (for instance editing a text field) the DB-aware control knows how to communicate these changes to the database. In the case of a DBedit, the database field's value will be set to the newly entered text. The DB-aware controls are grouped together on their own component palette tab named Data Controls.
They are mainly quite simple GUI controls.

6.1 The RTL (Free Pascal Run Time Library)

The classes in the RTL are the most basic classes of all: they are located in the Classes unit and form the basis of everything else. Actually this unit contains very few classes, and of course they are non-visual. Most routines in the System, SysUtils, Strings units (and many others) are strictly procedural and are not important for understanding the classes discussed here. You can find a complete reference to the RTL in the book Free Pascal 2 by Michaël Van Canneyt, ISBN 978-3-936546-53-8, published by C&L.

The base classes of the RTL are:

- **TPersistent**
  This class is used as a base class for everything that uses RTTI (Run Time Type Information). If a class needs to be manipulated in Lazarus' Object Inspector, then it must descend from TPersistent.

- **TComponent**
  This class descends from *TPersistent,* adding the concepts (explained below) of name, ownership and streaming to *TPersistent.* If a class needs to be manipulated in Lazarus' Form Designer, then it must descend from TComponent.

- **TStream**
  This class is used to define input/output, or more generally, for moving data around in memory or on disk. Two important descendants are TFileStream (representing data on disk) and TMemoryStream (representing data in memory).

- **TCollection**
  Together with its companion class *TCollectionItem* (a *TPersistent* descendant), this class is used to manage collections of identically structured items, such as columns in a grid, actions in an actionlist and many others.

- **TList**
  A general list class used to manage lists of other classes.

- **TStrings**
  A class designed to manage and manipulate a list of strings. This is an abstract class, which has an all-purpose descendant *TStringList.*

These six classes form the basis of all programming done in Lazarus, and are shown in their class hierarchy in Figure 6.1:

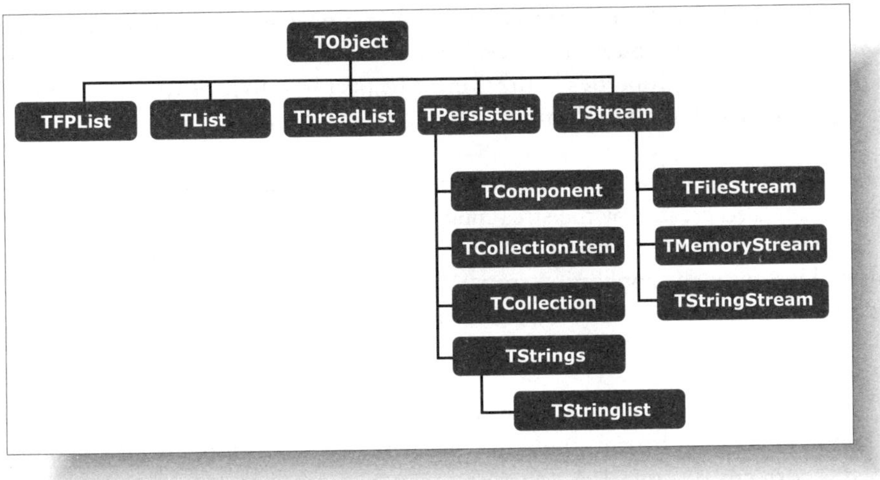

Figure 6.1: The basic Lazarus class hierarchy

6.1.1 Streaming and RTTI

The Classes unit also defines a streaming system. The streaming system is designed so all published properties of the components on a form in the Lazarus IDE can be saved to a stream (usually a file, the `.lfm` file). The published properties are the properties that can be manipulated in the Object Inspector. This file then contains enough information to restore all the properties at run-time, so the form can be reconstructed from the stream data. The same happens, of course, when Lazarus opens a form file from disk.

Because the streaming system is defined in the Classes unit, it is available to all programmers needing to store the state of any object. All they need to do is descend their object from TComponent, and use the streaming system to save the object's current state. The data in the stream can then be saved to disk (perhaps in a database), to be retrieved when the object's state needs to be restored.

The streaming system relies on the presence of published properties. For any property that is declared in a class's Published section, the compiler generates metadata: *Run Time Type Information* (RTTI). This information can be used to get or set the value of a published property (this system is called Introspection in .NET and Java). The RTTI is used by the streaming system to write all published properties to a stream (usually the `.lfm` file), and subsequently to reconstruct the form at run time from the data in the stream.

Because RTTI is stored in the application executable, it takes a lot of disk and memory space, perhaps unnecessarily. This is why classes do not automatically have the ability to publish properties. Classes must be compiled with a special compiler switch *{$M+}*, to enable the use of published properties for that class and all its descendants.
Using published properties in a class that was not compiled with this switch results in a compiler error.

The *TPersistent* class has been compiled with this compiler switch, so all descendants of *TPersistent* are able to use published properties. Since the Lazarus IDE uses RTTI to manipulate published properties in the Object Inspector, it follows that any class which must be manipulated in the IDE, must descend from *TPersistent*.

When a *TForm* instance is created at run time, all controls (including non-visual controls) it contains are also created by the streaming system, and they exist as instances of the corresponding class in memory. When the form is no longer needed (for instance when the user closes it, or the application stops), the form instance is destroyed and removed from memory. Obviously, all components on the form must then also be destroyed, or memory leaks would ensue.

The *TComponent* class was introduced to make this happen transparently – so no programmer designing a form would have to worry about ensuring that each component he used is correctly destroyed. A *TComponent* can own other *TComponents* (its children). When the owner *TComponent* is removed from memory, it will automatically remove from memory all the other components that it owns, and only then will it remove itself from memory.

TForm and *TDatamodule* (an invisible container for non-visual components) both descend from *TComponent*. All controls that are dropped on them are also descendants of *TComponent*, and are automatically registered as owned by the *TForm* (or *TDatamodule)* instance. So when the form (or datamodule) is closed and removed from memory, all the controls they own are also automatically removed from memory. The same is true for any non-visual components that are dropped on the form.

This automatic memory management feature is the reason that any object you drop on a form in the Lazarus IDE must be a descendant of *TComponent*. It is also the reason why the streaming system only allows streaming of *TComponent* descendants, since any class instances created automatically by the streaming system must also be disposed of automatically.

6.1.2 TComponent and the naming of class instances

All components have a Name property. The Name property is declared in *TComponent,* which also defines the numerical Tag property:

```
TComponent = class(TPersistent,IUnknown,IInterfaceComponentReference)
private
...
public
...
published
  property Name: TComponentName read FName write SetName stored False;
  property Tag: Longint read FTag write FTag default 0;
end;
```

This immediately explains why the form's Name is restricted to valid Pascal identifiers. Since the form declaration is also parsed and compiled by the compiler, the names of all components dropped on the form must be valid Object Pascal identifiers.

The streaming system ensures that the Button1 field in the form's declaration actually contains the *TButton* instance with name 'Button1' because the Name property of a component is treated specially.

When the streaming system is recreating the form at run time, it creates a *TButton* instance and sets its Name to 'Button1'. After that, it also checks the RTTI information of the *TForm1* class, and it looks for a field of type *TButton* and name 'Button1'. It then sets the field's value to the *TButton* instance it just created. This is possible, because all components dropped on the form are declared as fields in a published section of the form (the first section of any *TPersistent* class is Published by default).

All this, of course, happens transparently. The really important thing is that as soon as you drop a component on a form and give it a Name, it can be accessed in the form's code using the same name, because it is declared as a field of the form.

6.2 The FCL (Free Component Library)

The Free Component Library contains many classes which can be used by the Lazarus programmer, and which are also available to Object Pascal programmers who don't use the Lazarus IDE.

General classes

All classes in the *FCL* are non-visual classes. Many – if not most – classes in the *FCL* are not components (meaning they cannot be dropped on a *TForm),* but must be created and destroyed by the programmer. Rather they are utility classes designed to deal with various general programming tasks which are not immediately GUI-related. The following table (not exhaustive) contains a list of selected classes – none of them components – showing the units in which they are implemented.

6.1.2 TComponent and the Naming of class instances

There are two important restrictions on the *Name* property:

1. It must be a valid Pascal identifier. This means that you cannot type just anything in the name field of the Object Inspector.
2. It must be unique: *TComponent* ensures that each child that it owns has a unique name. A component cannot own two children with the same name.

The exception to this rule is that the component *Name* property can be left empty when creating components at runtime.

Why these two restrictions? The reason is quite simple, and lies in the *TForm* declaration. When a new form is created, and a component is dropped on it (say a *TButton* control, by default named Button1) the Lazarus IDE creates the following code in the form's Pascal file:

```
TForm1 = Class(TForm)
  Button1 : TButton
Private
// private declarations go here
Public
// public declarations go here.
end;
```

As can be seen, the form is declared as a descendant of class *TForm*, and the button dropped on the form is declared as a field of type *TButton*, with the name of the field equal to the name of the button component. When the name of the component is changed, the IDE will automatically change the name of the field in the form declaration.

Having the button component available as a field in the form's declaration is very convenient since it allows you to write:

```
begin
  Button1.Caption := 'Press me';
end;
```

If this were not so, then you would have to write code to find the button among the form's child components, like this:

```
  Var B : TButton;
begin
  B := FindComponent('Button1') as TButton;
  B.Caption := 'Press me';
end;
```

– which is obviously more cumbersome.

Each component dropped on the form is declared as a field in the form's class declaration. This explains why all children of a *TComponent* must have a unique name: since the form instance owns all components dropped on it which are all defined as fields, and since each form field must have a unique name, the children of a *TComponent* (in this case a *TForm)* must have a unique name.

Class	Unit	Used for
TASCII85DecoderStream	ascii85	Decoding data encoded in ASCII85 format.
TASCII85EncoderStream	ascii85	Encoding data to ASCII85 format.
TAVLTree	avl_tree	An AVL tree implementation.
TBase64EncodingStream	base64	Encoding data in Base64 (mime) format.
TBase64DecodingStream	base64	Decoding data from Base64 (mime) format.
TBlowFishEncryptStream	blowfish	Encrypting data using the blowfish cypher.
TBlowFishDeCryptStream	blowfish	Decrypting data using the blowfish cypher.
TFPObjectList	contnrs	A list of objects (the TFPList mentioned earlier is a list of pointers).
TObjectList	contnrs	A list of objects with list change notifications.
TComponentList	contnrs	A list of TComponents.
TClassList	contnrs	A list of TClass class pointers.
TStack	contnrs	A stack of pointers.
TObjectStack	contnrs	A stack of objects.
TQueue	contnrs	A queue of pointers.
TObjectQueue	contnrs	A queue of objects.
TFPHashList	contnrs	A hash list with pointers as data.
TFPHashObjectList	contnrs	A hash list with objects as data.
TFPStringHashTable	contnrs	A hash list with strings as data.
TFPObjectHashTable	contnrs	A hash list with objects as data.
TBucketList	contnrs	A bucket implementation with pointer data.
TObjectBucketList	contnrs	A bucket implementation with object data.
TIDEAEncryptStream	idea	A stream for encoding data in IDEA format.
TIDEADeCryptStream	idea	A stream for decoding data in IDEA format.
THashedStringList	inifiles	A TStrings descendant that maintains a hash list for fast lookups.
TIniFile	inifiles	A class for managing `.ini` files.
TIOStream	iostream	A stream representing standard input/output file descriptors.
TTarArchive	libtar	A class to read data from tar archives.
TTarWriter	libtar	A class to create tar archives.
TPropsStorage	rttiutils	A class for easy access to RTTI information and storing all published information of a class in an `.ini` file.
TSimpleEvent	syncobjs	A class for event synchronization between threads.
TCriticalSection	syncobjs	A class for critical sections.
TXMLDocument	dom	A class for manipulating XML documents.
TXMLWriter	xmlwrite	A class for writing XML files.
TXMLReader	xmlread	A class for reading XML files.
TRegistry	registry	A class for accessing the Windows registry (or an emulation on other platforms).
TInputPipeStream	pipes	The input end of a pipe.
TOutputPipeStream	pipes	The output end of a pipe.

Table 6.1: classes of the fcl

Non-visual components

The FCL also implements some non-visual classes which are *TComponent* descendants, and which are therefore available on the Lazarus component palette:

Class	Unit	Purpose
TProcess	process	To execute and control other applications.
TSimpleIPCClient	simpleipc	A simple (one-way) inter-process-communication IPC client.
TSimpleIPCServers	impleipc	A simple (one-way) inter-process-communication IPC server.
TEventLog	eventlog	Gives access to the system log service.

Table 6.2: Non visual components of the FCL

DB classes

Many of the components provided by the FCL are database connection components. They constitute a large category of their own and are therefore listed separately. These classes are discussed in the chapter on creating database connections. Most of them appear on the component palette's Data Access and SQLDB tabs. A summarizing overview can be found in the following table:

Component	Unit	Purpose
TDatasource	db	Connect GUI elements to databases.
TSDFDataset	sdf	Handle CSV files.
TFixedFormatDataset	sdf	Handle fixed-length formatted text files.
TParadox	paradox	Handle Paradox files.
TDBF	dbf	Handle dBase (`.dbf`) files.
TMemDataset	memdataset	Handle in-memory data.
TSQLQuery	sqldb	Any SQL-database dataset.
TSQLTransaction	sqldb	Transaction control for SQL-based databases.
TSQLScript	sqlscript	Execute multiple SQL statements.
TPQConnection	pqconnection	Handle connections to PostgreSQL.
TIBConnection	ibconnection	Handle connections to Firebird/Interbase.
TOracleConnection	oracleconnection	Handle connections to Oracle.
TMySQL40Connection	mysql40connection	Handle connections to MySQL 4.0.
TMySQL41Connection	mysql41Connection	Handle connections to MySQL 4.1.
TMySQL50Connection	mysql50connection	Handle connections to MySQL 5.0.
TODBCConnection	odbcconnection	Handle connections to any database using ODBC.
TSQLLite3Connection	sqliteconnection	Handle connections to SQLite 3.0 databases.

Table 6.3: Database components

6.3 The LCL (Lazarus Component Library)

The LCL contains a great number of classes, so the complete class tree takes several A3 sheets to print. However, at the top of the tree are five fundamental classes, which are present in every Lazarus GUI application. These classes are shown in the following Figure:

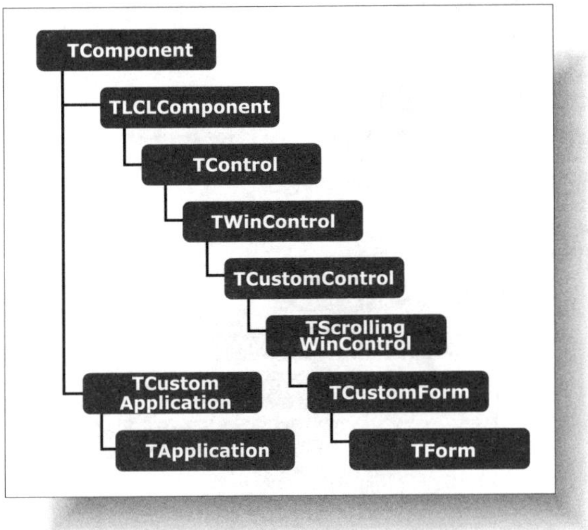

Figure 6.2: The base classes of the LCL

The main classes in this diagram are

TLCLComponent – All components in the LCL descend indirectly from this class. (see also Figure 6.4)

Tcontrol – All visual components in the LCL descend from this class. (see also Figure 6.4)

TWinControl – All visual controls which have a window handle descend from this class. (see also Figure 6.5)

TForm – The ancestor class for all forms designed in the editor.

TApplication – The global GUI application object.

The other components in the diagram introduce minor functionalities, which don't help in understanding GUI programming in Lazarus (these components group sets of functionalities so as to facilitate the work of the Lazarus LCL maintainers).

Console applications are commonly programmed according to a top-down model. The program flow is quite clear, because there is a clear beginning and ending to all code and procedures. Typically, console program flow looks like this:

```
begin
  InitializeData;
  If Option1 then
    DoTask1
  else if Option2 then
   DoTask2;
  FinalizeData;
end.
```

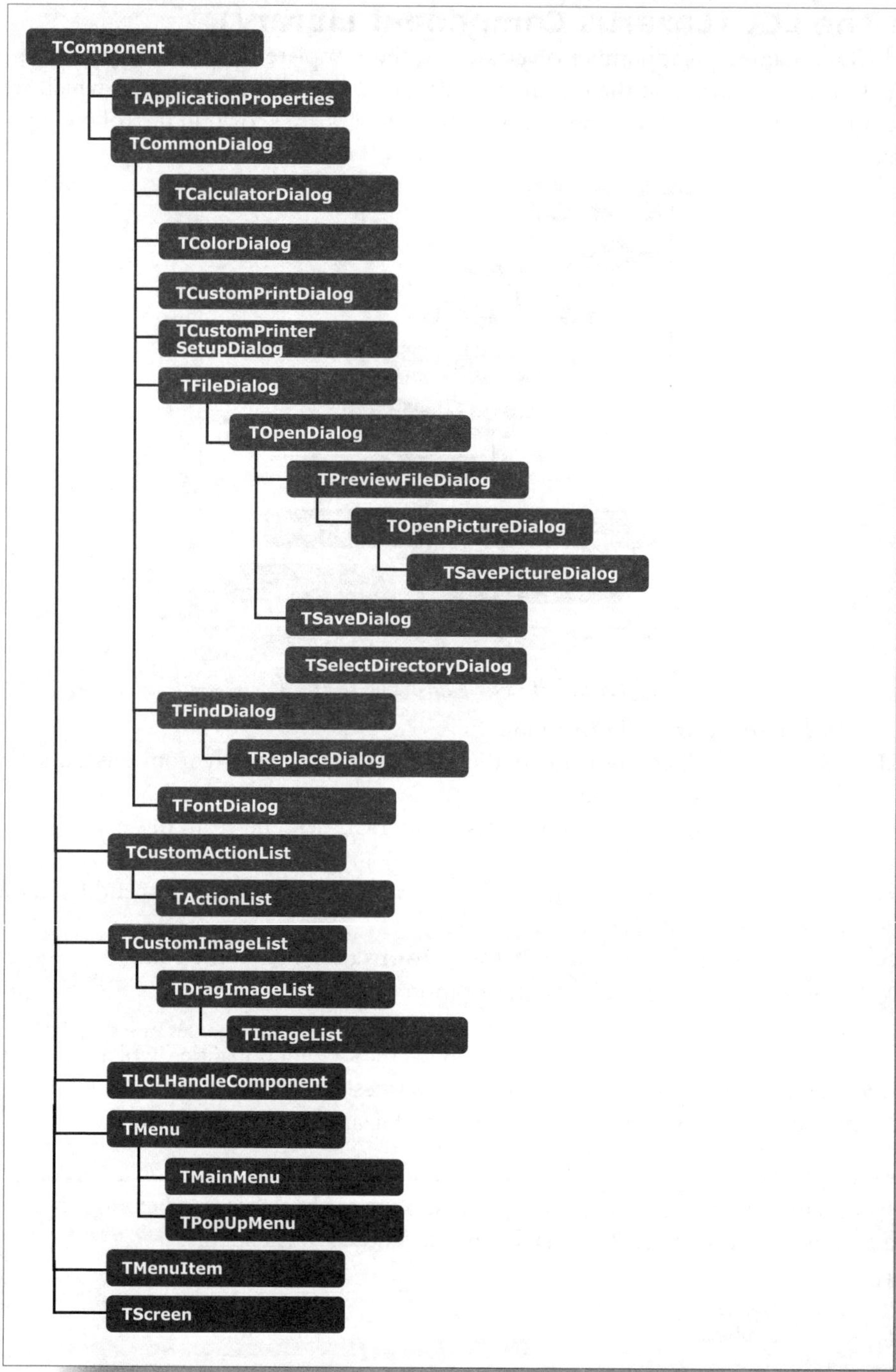

Figure 6.3: TLCLComponent and it's child components

Depending on the task that must be executed (*Option1 or Option2*), an appropriate subroutine is run. Standard Pascal is well suited to this kind of programming, and Object Pascal no less.
GUI programs are handled in a completely different way. The actions in the program are completely user-controlled, and the user determines which part of the program is activated by clicking with the mouse on the various controls that make up the application. The user actions are communicated to the program by the windowing system. The windowing system delivers messages to the program using a mechanism which depends on the GUI system – Windows works differently from X-Windows in this regard.

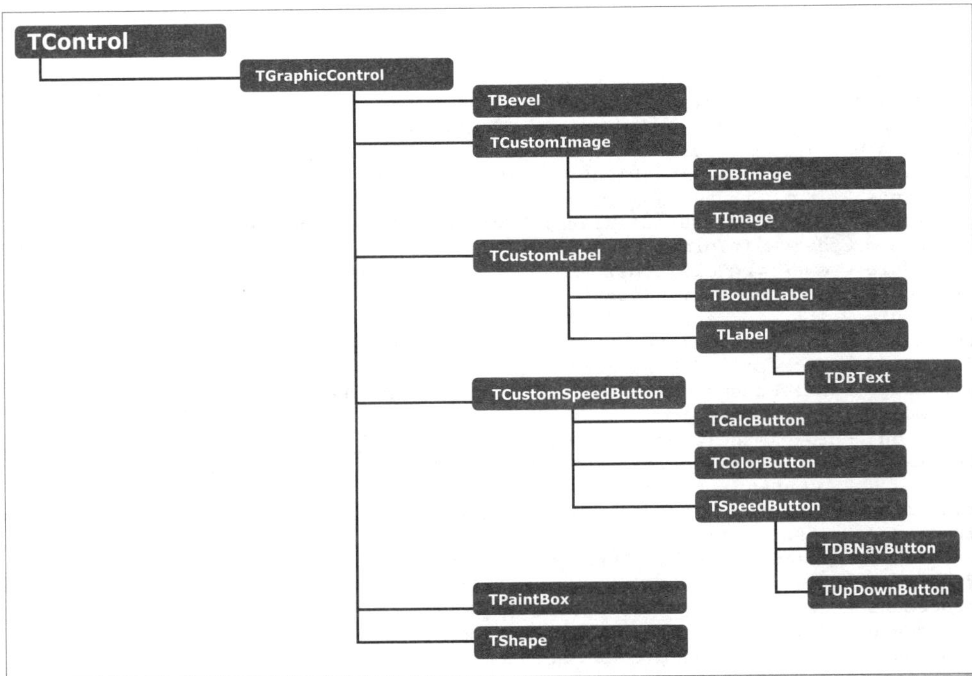

Figure 6.4: TControl and its descendants

6.3.1 The Application Object

To explain how a GUI program works in Lazarus, let us look at a typical Lazarus program file. When a new project is started, the Lazarus IDE creates – in addition to an XML configuration file with the `.lpi` extension – a file with the extension `.lpr` (short for Lazarus PRogram). This is a Pascal program file which looks like this:

```
program Project1;
uses
  Interfaces, Forms, Unit1, LResources; // Minimum needed for a GUI program.
begin
  Application.Initialize; // Initialize the LCL
  Application.CreateForm(TForm1, Form1); // Create the first (main) form
  Application.Run; // Run the message queue.
end.
```

6.3.1 The Application Object

To see the program file for a Lazarus program, open the Project Inspector (under the *Project* menu) and double-click the `project1.lpr` file.

As can be seen, all logic is handled by an Application object instance. This is an instance of the *TApplication* class, which takes care of the main application logic. It creates windows and runs the message loop. There are three main methods which are called by Lazarus: Initialize, CreateForm and Run. They are explained in the following sections. The full declaration of *TApplication* looks like this:

```
TApplication = class(TCustomApplication)
private
// all private variables
public
 constructor Create(AOwner: TComponent); override;
 destructor  Destroy; override;
 procedure ControlDestroyed(AControl: TControl);
 function  BigIconHandle: HIcon;
 function  SmallIconHandle: HIcon;
 procedure BringToFront;
 procedure CreateForm(InstanceClass: TComponentClass; out Reference);
 procedure UpdateMainForm(AForm: TForm);
 procedure QueueAsyncCall(const AMethod: TDataEvent; Data: PtrInt);
 procedure RemoveAsyncCalls(const AnObject: TObject);
 procedure ReleaseComponent(AComponent: TComponent);
 function  ExecuteAction(ExeAction: TBasicAction): Boolean; override;
 function  UpdateAction(TheAction: TBasicAction): Boolean; override;
 procedure HandleException(Sender: TObject); override;
 procedure HandleMessage;
 function  HelpCommand(Command: Word; Data: PtrInt): Boolean;
 function  HelpContext(Sender: TObject; const Position: TPoint;
              Context: THelpContext): Boolean;
 function  HelpContext(Context: THelpContext): Boolean;
 function  HelpKeyword(Sender: TObject; const Position: TPoint;
              const Keyword: String): Boolean;
 function  HelpKeyword(const Keyword: String): Boolean;
 procedure ShowHelpForObject(Sender: TObject);
 procedure RemoveStayOnTop(const ASystemTopAlso: Boolean = False);
 procedure RestoreStayOnTop(const ASystemTopAlso: Boolean = False);
 function  IsWaiting: boolean;
 procedure CancelHint;
 procedure HideHint;
 procedure HintMouseMessage(Control : TControl; var AMessage: TLMessage);
 procedure Initialize; override;
 function  MessageBox(Text, Caption: PChar; Flags: Longint): Integer;
 procedure Minimize;
 procedure ModalStarted;
 procedure ModalFinished;
 procedure Restore;
 procedure Notification(AComponent: TComponent; Operation: TOperation);
              override;
 procedure ProcessMessages;
 procedure Idle(Wait: Boolean);
 procedure Run;
 procedure ShowException(E: Exception); override;
 procedure Terminate; override;
 procedure DisableIdleHandler;
 procedure EnableIdleHandler;
 procedure NotifyUserInputHandler(Msg: Cardinal);
```

```
 procedure NotifyKeyDownBeforeHandler(Sender: Tobject; var Key: Word;
       Shift: TShiftState);
 procedure NotifyKeyDownHandler(Sender: TObject; var Key: Word; Shift: TShiftState);
 procedure ControlKeyDown(Sender: TObject; var Key: Word; Shift: TShiftState);
 procedure ControlKeyUp(Sender: TObject; var Key: Word; Shift: TShiftState);
 procedure AddOnIdleHandler(Handler: TIdleEvent; AsFirst: Boolean=True);
 procedure RemoveOnIdleHandler(Handler: TIdleEvent);
 procedure AddOnIdleEndHandler(Handler: TNotifyEvent; AsFirst: Boolean=True);
 procedure RemoveOnIdleEndHandler(Handler: TNotifyEvent);
 procedure AddOnUserInputHandler(Handler: TOnUserInputEvent;
       AsFirst: Boolean=True);
 procedure RemoveOnUserInputHandler(Handler: TOnUserInputEvent);
 procedure AddOnKeyDownBeforeHandler(Handler: TKeyEvent;
       AsFirst: Boolean=True);
 procedure RemoveOnKeyDownBeforeHandler(Handler: TKeyEvent);
 procedure AddOnKeyDownHandler(Handler: TKeyEvent; AsFirst: Boolean=True);
 procedure RemoveOnKeyDownHandler(Handler: TKeyEvent);
 procedure AddOnActivateHandler(Handler: TNotifyEvent; AsFirst: Boolean=True);
 procedure RemoveOnActivateHandler(Handler: TNotifyEvent);
 procedure AddOnDeactivateHandler(Handler: TNotifyEvent; AsFirst: Boolean=True);
 procedure RemoveOnDeactivateHandler(Handler: TNotifyEvent);
 procedure AddOnExceptionHandler(Handler: TExceptionEvent; AsFirst: Boolean=True);
 procedure RemoveOnExceptionHandler(Handler: TExceptionEvent);
 procedure AddOnEndSessionHandler(Handler: TNotifyEvent; AsFirst: Boolean=True);
 procedure RemoveOnEndSessionHandler(Handler: TNotifyEvent);
 procedure AddOnQueryEndSessionHandler(Handler: TQueryEndSessionEvent;
       AsFirst: Boolean=True);
 procedure RemoveOnQueryEndSessionHandler(Handler: TQueryEndSessionEvent);
 procedure AddOnMinimizeHandler(Handler: TNotifyEvent; AsFirst: Boolean=True);
 procedure RemoveOnMinimizeHandler(Handler: TNotifyEvent);
 procedure AddOnModalBeginHandler(Handler: TNotifyEvent; AsFirst: Boolean=True);
 procedure RemoveOnModalBeginHandler(Handler: TNotifyEvent);
 procedure AddOnModalEndHandler(Handler: TNotifyEvent; AsFirst: Boolean=True);
 procedure RemoveOnModalEndHandler(Handler: TNotifyEvent);
 procedure AddOnRestoreHandler(Handler: TNotifyEvent; AsFirst: Boolean=True);
 procedure RemoveOnRestoreHandler(Handler: TNotifyEvent);
 procedure AddOnDropFilesHandler(Handler: TDropFilesEvent; AsFirst: Boolean=True);
 procedure RemoveOnDropFilesHandler(Handler: TDropFilesEvent);
 procedure AddOnHelpHandler(Handler: THelpEvent; AsFirst: Boolean=True);
 procedure RemoveOnHelpHandler(Handler: THelpEvent);
 procedure AddOnHintHandler(Handler: TNotifyEvent; AsFirst: Boolean=True);
 procedure RemoveOnHintHandler(Handler: TNotifyEvent);
 procedure AddOnShowHintHandler(Handler: TShowHintEvent; AsFirst: Boolean=True);
 procedure RemoveOnShowHintHandler(Handler: TShowHintEvent);
 procedure RemoveAllHandlersOfObject(AnObject: TObject); virtual;
 procedure DoBeforeMouseMessage(CurMouseControl: TControl);
 function  IsShortcut(var Message: TLMKey): boolean;
 procedure IntfQueryEndSession(var Cancel : Boolean);
 procedure IntfEndSession;
 procedure IntfAppActivate;
 procedure IntfAppDeactivate;
 procedure IntfAppMinimize;
 procedure IntfAppRestore;
 procedure IntfDropFiles(const FileNames: Array of String);
 procedure IntfThemeOptionChange(AThemeServices: TThemeServices;
      AOption: TThemeOption);
 function  IsRTLLang(ALang: String): Boolean;
 function  Direction(ALang: String): TBiDiMode;

public
 procedure DoArrowKey(AControl: TWinControl; var Key: Word; Shift: TShiftState);
 procedure DoEscapeKey(AControl: TWinControl; var Key: Word; Shift: TShiftState);
```

```
 procedure DoReturnKey(AControl: TWinControl; var Key: Word; Shift: TShiftState);
 procedure DoTabKey(AControl: TWinControl; var Key: Word; Shift: TShiftState);
 property Active: boolean read GetActive;
 property ApplicationType : TApplicationType read FApplicationType write
        FApplicationType;
 property BidiMode: TBiDiMode read FBidiMode write SetBidiMode;
 property CaptureExceptions: boolean read FCaptureExceptions
        write SetCaptureExceptions;
 property FindGlobalComponentEnabled: boolean read FFindGlobalComponentEnabled
        write FFindGlobalComponentEnabled;
 property Flags: TApplicationFlags read FFlags write SetFlags;

 //property HelpSystem : IHelpSystem read FHelpSystem;

 property Hint: string read FHint write SetHint;
 property HintColor: TColor read FHintColor write SetHintColor;
 property HintHidePause: Integer read FHintHidePause write FHintHidePause;
 property HintHidePausePerChar: Integer read FHintHidePausePerChar write
        FHintHidePausePerChar;
 property HintPause: Integer read FHintPause write FHintPause;
 property HintShortCuts: Boolean read FHintShortCuts write FHintShortCuts;
 property HintShortPause: Integer read FHintShortPause write FHintShortPause;
 property Icon: TIcon read FIcon write SetIcon;
 property Navigation: TApplicationNavigationOptions read FNavigation write
        SetNavigation;
 property MainForm: TForm read FMainForm;
 property ModalLevel: Integer read FModalLevel;
 property MouseControl: TControl read FMouseControl;
 property TaskBarBehavior: TTaskBarBehavior read FTaskBarBehavior write
        SetTaskBarBehavior;
 property OnActionExecute: TActionEvent read FOnActionExecute write
        FOnActionExecute;
 property OnActionUpdate: TActionEvent read FOnActionUpdate write
        FOnActionUpdate;
 property OnActivate: TNotifyEvent read FOnActivate write FOnActivate;
 property OnDeactivate: TNotifyEvent read FOnDeactivate write FOnDeactivate;
 property OnIdle: TIdleEvent read FOnIdle write FOnIdle;
 property OnIdleEnd: TNotifyEvent read FOnIdleEnd write FOnIdleEnd;
 property OnEndSession: TNotifyEvent read FOnEndSession write FOnEndSession;
 property OnQueryEndSession: TQueryEndSessionEvent read FOnQueryEndSession
        write FOnQueryEndSession;
 property OnMinimize: TNotifyEvent read FOnMinimize write FOnMinimize;
 property OnModalBegin: TNotifyEvent read FOnModalBegin write FOnModalBegin;
 property OnModalEnd: TNotifyEvent read FOnModalEnd write FOnModalEnd;
 property OnRestore: TNotifyEvent read FOnRestore write FOnRestore;
 property OnDropFiles: TDropFilesEvent read FOnDropFiles write FOnDropFiles;
 property OnHelp: THelpEvent read FOnHelp write FOnHelp;
 property OnHint: TNotifyEvent read FOnHint write FOnHint;
 property OnShortcut: TShortcutEvent read FOnShortcut write FOnShortcut;
 property OnShowHint: TShowHintEvent read FOnShowHint write FOnShowHint;
 property OnUserInput: TOnUserInputEvent read FOnUserInput write FOnUserInput;
 property OnDestroy: TNotifyEvent read FOnDestroy write FOnDestroy;
 property ShowButtonGlyphs: TApplicationShowGlyphs read FShowButtonGlyphs
        write SetShowButtonGlyphs default sbgAlways;
 property ShowMenuGlyphs: TApplicationShowGlyphs read FShowMenuGlyphs
        write SetShowMenuGlyphs default sbgAlways;
 property ShowHint: Boolean read FShowHint write SetShowHint;
 property ShowMainForm: Boolean read FShowMainForm write FShowMainForm
        default True;
 property Title: String read GetTitle write SetTitle;
end;
```

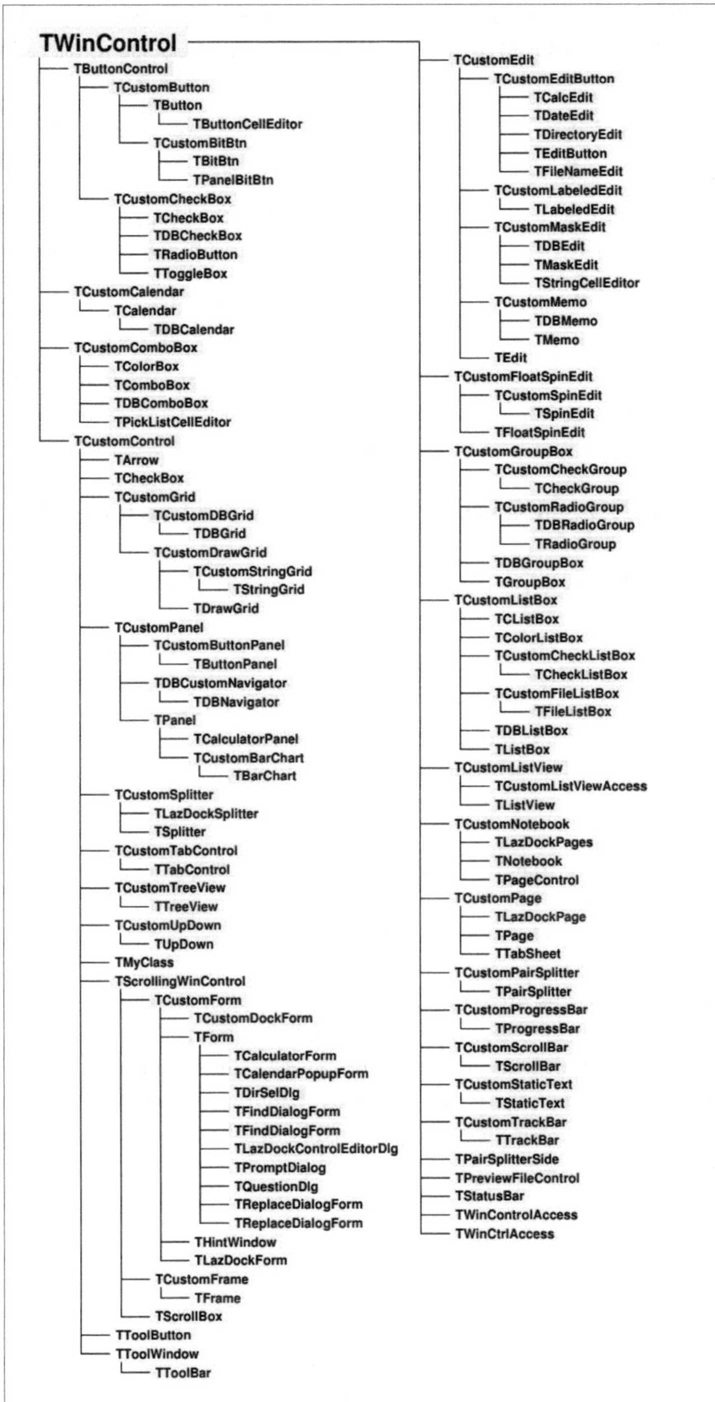

Figure 6.5: TWinControl and its descendants

It is defined in the Forms unit, together with many other types needed for the *TApplication* class. One of these types is worth mentioning, because it indicates the application type:

```
TApplicationType = (atDefault, atDesktop, atPDA, atKeyPadDevice );
```

Initialization

As you develop a program, further lines of code will probably appear automatically in the program file (`.lpr`) as a *TApplication* property is set, or additional forms are added with CreateForm calls.

In the Initialize method, the *LCL* is set up for proper use. Various checks are made and various resources are loaded. It is of little practical interest, but must always be called so the other methods of *TApplication* will do their job properly. To skip this initialization step would cause errors when the program runs.

After initializing the *LCL*, the application object creates the main form using the CreateForm method:

```
Application.CreateForm(TForm1, Form1);
```

This method instantiates a form of class *TForm1,* and stores a reference to it in the variable Form1.
Both the class *TForm1* and the variable Form1 are created in the unit unit1 by the IDE. After the instance is created its various properties are set, and it is filled with controls as specified in the form file. The form is not shown yet, it just exists in memory and is still hidden from the user.

If you have designed more than one form, several CreateForm statements will be inserted in the program file. Then when the program starts, all these forms will be created but remain hidden. The main form is always the first form created in this way.

You can control which forms are (and which are not) automatically created at program startup. In the Project Options dialog, the Form tab can be used to specify which forms you want to be auto-created. Forms that are not created automatically must still be created manually, of course, before they are used. Failure to create them before use would result in a run time error, because the form variable associated with that form's class would be invalid.

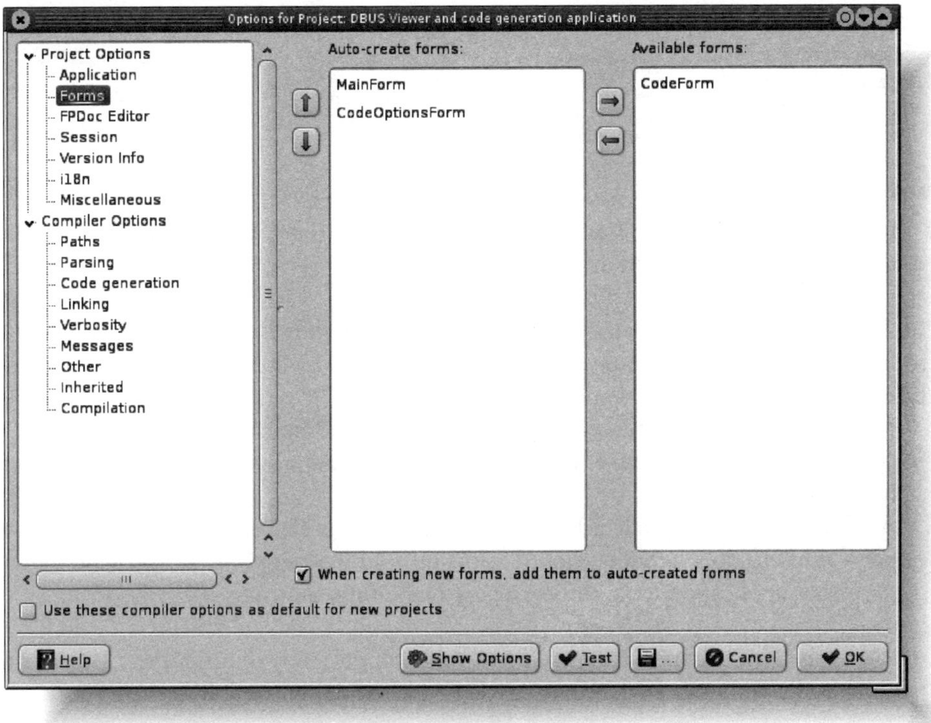

Figure 6.6: Automatically created forms versus available forms

Once all forms have been created, the Run method is called which performs three tasks:

- It shows the main form. The main form is always the first form created.
- It runs the message loop.
- After the last form closes (normally this is the main form), the Run method exits, after which the program ends.

The message loop is actually the main part of the program. It is implemented differently for each widget set (or GUI system), but in essence it is a loop which checks if a message is available, and if so, it sends it to the appropriate window or control where it will be handled by the *LCL*.

As soon as the main window is closed (explicitly in program code or by a user action) the message loop stops and the Run method ends. After that, the Application object is freed, as well as any secondary forms that were still open.

Programming application logic in events

The application's Run method runs the message loop. This is done in the ProcessMessages method of the *TApplication* object.

Essentially the Run method looks like this:

```
procedure TApplication.Run;
begin
  ShowMainForm;
  while not Terminated do
    ProcessMessages;
end;
```

If the main form of the application is closed, it sets the *Terminated* variable to *True*. This terminates the main loop and exits the *Run* procedure.

The *ProcessMessages* call checks with the windowing system if there is a message for the program, and if so, dispatches it to the control for which the message is destined. The receiving control then has two options:

1. It can fully handle the message. For instance, a paint message is handled by the control itself. It will know what to do with this message since each control knows how to draw itself.
2. Additional action is needed. For instance, a button is clicked. The button does not know what to do when it is clicked – it is up to the programmer to provide the necessary application logic to be executed when the button is clicked.

Of course the first situation is not relevant to the application programmer. The second situation – where additional action is needed – is covered in the following section.

Using event handlers: properties of procedural type

Technically, an event is a variable or property of procedural type and if the variable is set, the procedure it points to will be executed. The basic procedural type used throughout the *LCL* is *TNotifyEvent:*

```
TNotifyEvent = Procedure(Sender : TObject) of object;
```

It is a method pointer, because all event handlers are implemented as methods of the form class. *TNotifyEvent* has a single parameter: Sender. When an event handler is called, Sender will contain a pointer to the instance that triggered the event. It is of type *TObject,* so that it can be used for any component.

Luckily it is not necessary to create event handlers and connect them to the necessary variables or properties because the IDE does all this automatically.
The Object Inspector's Events tab lists all possible published events for the currently selected component, as shown in Figure 6.7:

Figure 6.7: The Events tab in the Object Inspector

When selecting an event from the list, you have two options:
Your first option would be to select an existing event handler. For example, three buttons can have the same event handler connected to their *OnClick* event. The handler can distinguish which button fired the event through the *Sender* argument:

```
TMainForm = class(TForm)
  Button1: TButton;
  Button2: TButton;
  Button3: TButton;
procedure ButtonClick(Sender: TObject);
private
{ private declarations }
public
{ public declarations }
end;

  Var MainForm : TMainForm;

implementation

{ TMainForm }

procedure TMainForm.ButtonClick(Sender: TObject);
// The same event handler used for all 3 buttons.
begin
  ShowMessage('Button "'+(Sender as TButton).Name+ '" was clicked.');
end;
```

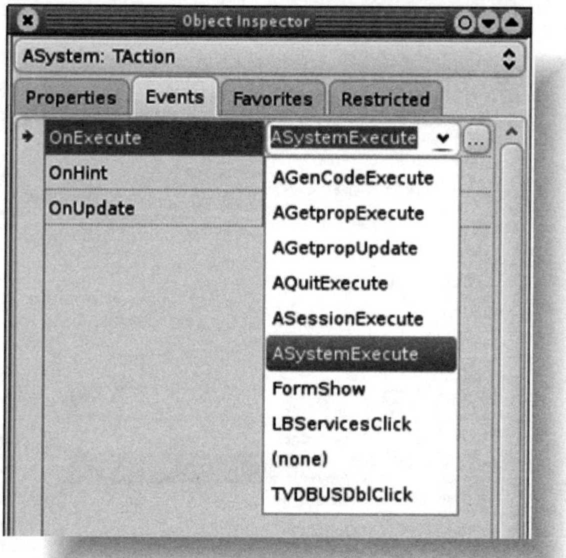

Figure 6.8: Selecting an event handler in the Object Inspector

Your other option is to create a new event handler. Simply clicking the ellipsis button will create a new event handler with a Lazarus-suggested name – which is the name of the component, followed by the event name. You can avoid this auto-naming by typing the name you would prefer first, and only then click the ellipsis button.

As with component names, the event handler names are used for methods of the form, and so they must be valid Pascal identifiers.

Suppose a button called BPress is dropped on the form, and you enter the name ShowHello in the button's OnClick event. Pressing the ellipsis button changes the unit's code to the following:

```
TMainForm = class(TForm)
  BPress: TButton;
  procedure ShowHello(Sender: TObject);
private
  { private declarations }
public
  { public declarations }
end;

  var MainForm: TMainForm;

implementation
{ TMainForm }

procedure TMainForm.ShowHello(Sender: TObject);
begin

end;
```

An empty method is created, ready to be filled with your code.

The method handler is inserted automatically in the first section of the form declaration. This section is reserved for Published methods and fields, and is the only section that the *Form Designer* and *Object Inspector* will use. Moving a method out of this section will make it unavailable to the Object Inspector. Conversely, moving a private method to the Published section of the form declaration makes it available in the *Object Inspector*.

The reason for the exclusive use of the Published section is that the streaming system uses the information in the form file to look up the method in the *RTTI* (*Run Time Type Information*) generated for the form. The *RTTI* is only generated for published sections, so only published methods are usable.
As soon as the method has been created, it can be filled with application logic. The code you enter will obviously depend on the purpose of the event in your application.

Events of components and controls
Each control has its own message event handlers, corresponding to the various messages it can receive from the windowing system. The component reference chapter lists which events each component supports.

But not all event handlers are called as a result of a message sent by the GUI system. Separate from user actions, there is also a need for clearly identified moments in the program. In the console example above, there were two calls to initialize and finalize data. How can this be done in a GUI application, where the program flow is directed by the user ?

The answer is to introduce events that are not directly related to user-triggered events, but events which are dictated by application logic. For instance there is a clearly defined point at which the application creates a form. Likewise, when the form is destroyed. Here are two clearly identifiable moments, which are guaranteed to happen only once in the lifetime of a form. The creation of the form is the recommended moment to allocate resources (for instance to create stringlists, and other objects) that will be needed throughout the form's lifetime. The destruction of the form is the recommended moment to free the resources that were allocated when the form was created.
So the form's *OnCreate* event is triggered when a form is instantiated, and its *OnDestroy* event is triggered when this instance is destroyed again: the perfect moments to allocate and deallocate resources.

The *OnCloseQuery* event is triggered when a form is closed. It can be used to prevent the form from closing, for instance if data still needs to be saved.
The *OnPaint* event, exposed by many controls, can be used to do custom drawing.
This event is triggered by the GUI system, when it decides that a control needs to be redrawn on screen.
There are many more events, all of them triggered at different points. It's outside the scope of this chapter to discuss them all. Most of them have self-explanatory names, so you should be able to surmise what their function is.

Working with TApplication

TApplication is a descendant of *TComponent,* and all forms that the Application instance creates are owned by the *TApplication* instance. Thus when the Application instance is freed (which happens automatically), any forms which the user has not closed will be closed and freed as well.

The Application object has several properties and events which can be used to control its behaviour. These events and properties can be set in code, or you can drop a *TApplicationProperties* component (found on the component palette's *Additional tab)* on your form, and its properties can be set through the Object Inspector. The component will then automatically set the properties and events of the global Application object. Its available events and properties are listed in the table below.

Property	Purpose
CaptureExceptions	Should exceptions be handled in the main loop?
Helpfile	The standard help file for the application.
Hint	The current hint.
HintColor	The Color of the hint window.
HintHidePause	The number of milliseconds the hint is visible.
HintPause	The number of milliseconds before the hint appears.
HintShortCuts	Should shortcuts be displayed in hints?
HintShortPause	The number of milliseconds before a shortcut hint appears.
ShowButtonGlyphs	Should standard glyphs be shown on buttons?
ShowHint	Should hints be shown?
ShowMainForm	Should the main form be shown explicitly?
ShowMenuGlyphs	Should glyphs be shown on menus?
Title	The application title.

Table 6.4: The GUI properties of TApplication

Event	Triggered when
OnDropFiles	A user drops files on an any window in the application.
OnEndSession	The windowing system is shutting down the application(Windows only).
OnException	An exception occurs which must be shown.
OnHelp	Help is requested.
OnHint	A hint must be shown.
OnIdle	The application goes idle (there are no more messages to process).
OnIdleEnd	All idle actions have been processed.
OnMinimize	The application is minimized.
OnQueryEndSession	The windowing system asks permission to shut down the application.
OnRestore	The application is restored.
OnShowHint	A hint is shown.
OnUserInput	A user-action message is received (a click or a keystroke).

Table 6.5: Events of TApplication

In addition to this, the Application object has methods to process the command-line, and to determine the location of the application executable. These options and methods are not available through the *TApplicationProperties* component, so you can only make use of them via code. They are listed in the two tables below.

Method	Purpose
FindOptionIndex	Get the location of a command-line option
GetOptionValue	Get the value of a command-line option (as in -o Value)
HasOption	Check if an option was specified on the command-line
CheckOptions	Check if all options on the command-line are valid
GetEnvironmentList	Return the list of environment variables

Table 6.6: Methods of TApplication

Property	Purpose
ConsoleApplication	True if the application is a console application.
Location	Directory of the application binary.
Params	Indexed access to the command-line options.
ParamCount	Number of command-line options.
EnvironmentVariable	Value of environment variables.
OptionChar	Character used for command line switches (usually '-').
CaseSensitiveOptions	Should command-line options be checked observing case?
StopOnException	Should the application halt when an exception is caught?

Table 6.7: Properties of TApplication

The following code snippet demonstrates typical use of the command-line option processing, where the location of a configuration file can be specified on the command-line with

`-c /path/to/file` or
`--config=/path/to/file`

and if not specified, the `'settings.ini'` file in the application directory is used. The main form checks this when it is created and then reads various settings:

```
procedure TMainForm.FormCreate(Sender: TObject);
  Var ConfigFileName : string;
begin
  // Ensure case insensitive treatment of command-line options
  Application.CaseSensitiveOptions := False;
  // if the name of a configuration file was specified, save it.
  If Application.HasOption('c','config') then
    ConfigFileName := Application.GetOptionValue('c','config')
  else
   // If no configuration file is given, use fallback location
    ConfigFileName:=Application.Location + 'settings.ini';
  ReadSettings(Configfilename); // actually read the configuration file.
end;
```

6.3.2 Windows

All visible windows of your application descend from *TForm* which makes *TForm* one of the most important *TWinControl* descendants. It is discussed in great detail in the following section, but its main properties are listed in the table below:

Property	Purpose
ActiveControl	The control that has focus when the form is shown initially.
AllowDropFiles	Can files be dropped on this form?
AutoScroll	Should the form display scrollbars when the content is too big for the form?
BorderIcons	Sets which border icons to display.
Caption	The window title.
DefaultMonitor	Which monitor should the form initially appear on?
Font	Default font for child controls.
FormStyle	Form style (dialog, sizeable etc.).
HorzScrollbar	Horizontal scrollbar settings.
Icon	The icon shown in the window title.
KeyPreview	Should keystrokes be sent to the form prior to sending them to the focused control ?
Menu	Which *TMainMenu* instance should act as the form's menu?
PixelsPerInch	The screen resolution.
Position	The form's initial position.
SessionProperties	Which component properties should be saved across form sessions?
ShowInTaskBar	How should the form be shown in the task bar?
VertScrollbar	Vertical scrollbar settings.
WindowState	The initial window state.

Table 6.8: Properties of TForm

The events which *TForm* introduces are listed in the table below:

Event	Triggered when
OnActivate	The form is activated (i.e. gets focus).
OnClose	The form is closed (made invisible).
OnCloseQuery	Confirmation is needed if the form can be closed.
OnCreate	The form instance is created.
OnDeactivate	The form is deactivated (i.e. loses focus).
OnDestroy	The form instance is destroyed.
OnDropFiles	The user drops files on the form.
OnHide	The form is made invisible.
OnShortCut	A shortcut key is pressed.
OnShow	The form is made visible.
OnWindowStateChange	The *WindowState* property changes.

Table 6.9: Events of TForm

6.3.2 Windows

Instances of *TForm* are – like normal windows in a GUI program – containers for all other elements in the program. By contrast with the other GUI elements of a program, a new form is always a new class, a descendant of *TForm. (TForm* is the only class for which this approach is used). This means that an application doesn't show a *TForm* instance, but always a descendant (such as *TForm1).*
For all other controls, the standard class itself is instantiated. For instance when you create a new button, an instance of *TButton* is initialized. Normally, the application programmer is not confronted with this difference: the Lazarus IDE takes care of all the details, creating the declaration of the *TForm* descendant in the form file where it also creates a variable with the same name as the form. Each form is created in a separate unit. It is not possible to create more than one form per unit. The name of the unit can be different from the form name, although Lazarus allocates a default name for each form and unit:

```
unit Unit1; // Proposed unit name
   {$mode objfpc}{$H+} // Compiler mode
interface

uses
   Classes, SysUtils, FileUtil, LResources, Forms, Controls,
   Graphics, Dialogs;

type
   TForm1 = class(TForm)  // Proposed name for the first form in the application.
     private
     { private declarations }
     public
     { public declarations }
   end;

   var Form1: TForm1; // Global Form variable to access the form instance.

implementation

initialization
   {$I Unit1.lrs} // Resource file for the form.
end.
```

Many programmers tend to name the unit `'frm'`, followed by the name of the form (e.g. `'frmMain'`), but this is not obligatory.

Since all GUI applications have at least one window, when the Lazarus IDE creates a new GUI application, it automatically defines the first form of the application – its declaration is shown in the previous section. This first form is by default called *TForm1,* but it can of course be renamed. Indeed it is good practice to rename the form class more descriptively (*TMainForm* for instance, for the main form).

The first form in the application plays a special role: it is the main form. It is special in the sense that the *LCL* will show this form automatically – all other forms must be shown manually, in code, which will be shown next. The first window is also special in the sense that when it is closed, the application will terminate – even if other windows are still visible. After the main window has closed, the *LCL* closes any other windows by freeing their form instances.

6.3.3 Working with TForm

Windows are manipulated manually through using *TForm's* methods: they can be created, displayed, activated, hidden, closed and destroyed. *TForm* also offers other form manipulation methods as well. Since *TForm* is a descendant of *TCustomForm,* you should search this class's methods when looking for a method that does some other window-related task you need. Most of the methods available also have corresponding events. For instance, the *OnShow* event is associated with the Show method.

Showing a window

The main window is shown automatically by the *LCL,* whereas all other windows must be shown manually via program code. When a window is shown, the *OnShow* event is triggered. In this event, you can perform any needed initialization – for instance setting the window's Caption, specifying a particular position for the window, or setting the focus to a specific window control. The following code shows a second window, and attempts to set the active control:

```
procedure TForm1.ButtonClick(Sender : TObject);
begin
  With Form2 do
  begin
    ActiveControl := Button1; // This will have no effect – see the following event handler
    Show;
  end;
end;
```

In the FormShow event of the second form, the active control is also set:

```
TForm2.FormShow(Sender : TObject);
begin
  Caption := 'Window opened at ' + FormatDateTime('c',Now);
  ActiveControl := Button2; // overrides any previous setting.
end;
```

There are two different methods in *TForm* to display a window: modal display and non-modal display. Modal windows block all other windows until they are closed again. If several non-modal windows are shown, the user can switch between the various windows. The designer windows of the Lazarus IDE are non-modal windows.

When the Lazarus IDE starts, many windows are visible at once. Yet only one window is the main window: the window with the menu and component palette. All other windows are started manually.

6.3.3 Working with TForm

To show a non-modal window you must use the Show method. To obtain the same effect as we find in the Lazarus IDE, you can do the following:

1. Create a new application. The IDE will create a main form, called Form1.
2. Through the File menu, create a second form. It will be called Form2, and will be in a unit called `unit2`.
3. In the *OnShow* event of the main form (Form1), create an *OnShow* event handler. Once the *OnShow* event handler is created, it can be used to show Form2, like this:

```
implementation

uses unit2;
{ TForm1 }

procedure TForm1.FormShow(Sender: TObject);
begin
  Form2.Show;
end;
```

In order for this to work, the unit `unit2` had to be included in the uses list of `unit1`: failure to add this will result in a compiler error, saying that it does not know Form2.

Secondly, the second form must also be auto-created by the IDE, or the Form2 variable: if this is not done, then the Form2 variable will not be initialized with an instance of the *TForm2* class.

As an alternative to the Show method, the form's Visible property may set to True, which has the same effect as calling Show:

```
procedure TForm1.FormShow(Sender: TObject);
begin
  Form2.Visible := True;
end;
```

The two statements are equivalent.

The example in the previous section shows two forms at once. The user can work in both windows at once, because they are visible simultaneously. This is often how you want it. It should be noted that in the code to show the second window:

```
procedure TForm1.FormShow(Sender: TObject);
begin
  Form2.Show;
end;
```

the call to *Show* returns immediately. After the second form is shown, the event handler of the first form exits, and the program control flow is returned to the program's main event loop which will continue dispatching events as they occur.
This is a common use of windows.

There are many situations in which you need to show an additional window requesting user input, and the program should not continue until the user has provided the necessary input. This input may be quite simple – clicking a button in acknowledgement of a message, or it may be actual typed input – the user may be asked his name, for instance.

For these kinds of situations TForm provides a variation on the *Show* method called *ShowModal,* which is a function, declared as follows:

```
Function ShowModal: Integer;
```

The *ShowModal* shows the form, and then runs the message loop, until the user closes the window somehow. It then returns an integer (representing a status code).
To demonstrate the *ShowModal* call, the program presented in the previous section can be modified as follows:

```
procedure TForm1.FormShow(Sender: TObject);
begin
  Form2.ShowModal;
end;
```

If you run the program, you will find that you can do nothing in the main form until you somehow close Form2.

In forms designed as dialogs which will be shown with *ShowModal,* it is possible to return a status code which will be the result of the *ShowModal function.* The status can be set through the *ModalResult* property of *TForm.* As soon as the property is written, the form will close itself.

Often, an *OK* button is placed on a form through which the user indicates that he or she has provided all data, and wants to close the form.
The *OnClick* handler of the *OK* button can be coded as follows:

```
procedure TForm2.Button1Click(Sender: TObject);
begin
  ModalResult := mrOK;
end;
```

As soon as this code is executed, the form will close, and the *ShowModal* call that was used to show it, will return with a return value of *mrOK.* Any value can be used as a return value, but the following constants are predefined and commonly used in system dialogs (the mr prefix stands for *ModalResult).* The predefined values you can assign to *ModalResult* are shown in the following table:

Value	Meaning
mrNone	No result, returned when user has clicked the Close button on the window border.
mrOK	Response of an OK button
mrCancel	Response of a Cancel button
mrAbort	Response of an Abort button
mrRetry	Response of a Retry button
mrYes	Response of a Yes button
mrNo	Response of a No button
mrAll	Response of an All button
mrNoToAll	Response of a 'No to All' button
mrYesToAll	Response of a 'Yes to All' button

Table 6.10: Allowed values for the ModalResult property

Closing a window

The Close method

A window can be closed in one of several ways – either via code, or by the user if the user clicks the close button in the window border's system menu. Each graphical system has its own way to let the user to close a window, and usually a shortcut key is offered for this purpose. Under Windows, this is the [Alt]+[F4] key combination, or [Ctrl]+[Alt]+X. These key events cannot be intercepted, they are converted directly by the window system to a close message which is handled by the application's message loop in Application.Run. The end result is that the form will be closed by the *LCL*.

To close a window in code, the *close method* can be used. It sends a *close message* to the window as well, and the LCL will handle it from there. The second form in the previous example could be closed by letting the user click on the window. To program this behaviour, insert the following code in the *OnClick* event handler of Form2:

```
procedure TForm2.FormClick(Sender: TObject);
begin
  Close;
end;
```

This closes the form as soon as the user clicks on it with the mouse. The following code is an equivalent way of closing the window:

```
procedure TForm2.FormClick(Sender: TObject);
begin
  Visible:= False;
end;
```

Irrespective of the way the window is closed (through code or through system events), closing the window will result in the triggering of the *OnClose* event.

6.3.3 Working with TForm

There are circumstances in which a form should not be closed. For instance, in a form that requires user input, the form should not be closed until all required data is entered correctly. You might wish to disable the use of the Close button on the window border, and require that the user closes the form only by means of other buttons you provide.

To make it possible to control the closing of a form, an *OnCloseQuery* event is provided which is triggered when a close message arrives. It looks like this:

```
procedure TForm2.FormCloseQuery(Sender: TObject; var CanClose: boolean)
begin

end;
```

Note the *CanClose* variable which is set to True by default. If, for some reason, the form should not be closed yet, then you can set the *CanClose* variable to False. In which case the form will not be closed, but remain visible. The following code prevents a window from being closed at all.

```
procedure TForm2.FormCloseQuery(Sender: TObject; var CanClose: boolean)
begin
  CanClose := False;
end;
```

Note that the *OnCloseQuery* handler is always called, even when the Close method is used. The only way to close the above window, is to free the form instance:

```
Form2.Free;
```

In that case, the window is not really 'closed', but simply removed from memory.

If no *OnCloseQuery* event was set, or it was set but returned True in the CanClose variable, the form can then be closed. When a form is closed, there are several possibilities:

1. The form must simply be made invisible, but should stay in memory
2. The form should be minimised
3. The form should be removed from memory.

For instance, when an auxiliary window is closed, it may be desirable to keep it in memory, and simply make it visible when it is required the next time.

The *LCL* provides an event where you can make the decision: the *OnClose* event. It looks like this:

```
procedure TForm2.FormClose(Sender: TObject; var CloseAction: TCloseAction);
begin
  // Code here what must happen with the form instance when the form is closed
end;
```

The CloseAction parameter of the *OnClose* event handler determines what happens to the form when it is closed. It can be set to any of the following values:

- **caNone** The default action is executed.
  What this action is depends on the kind of form.
- **caHide** The form is simply hidden (made invisible). This is the default action for most forms which are not the main form.
- **caMinimize** The form is minimized.
- **caFree** The form is destroyed and removed from memory. This is the default action for the main form.

If the form was the default form instance created by Lazarus, it is inadvisable to use the *caFree* result: after the form is destroyed, the reference to the form in the global variable is no longer valid.

Note that the *OnClose* event can also be used to perform any housekeeping tasks, such as hiding additional windows or cleaning up particular resources.

Hiding a window

Sometimes it is not necessary to actually close a window and remove it from memory. It can be sufficient to make it *invisible:* it will be hidden. This can be done with the *Hide method,* or alternatively, by setting the *Visible* property to False. As soon as this is done, the form will be hidden. To show a hidden form, it is sufficient to call the *Show method*, or alternatively to set *Visible* to True.

When a form is hidden, the *OnHide* event handler is triggered. This can be used to take additional actions when a form is hidden.
Let us demonstrate this with a program that shows or hides two windows simultaneously. The first step is creating a new project with three forms: Form1, Form2, Form3.
In the *OnClick* handler of Form1, the following code is executed:

```
procedure TForm1.FormClick(Sender: TObject);
begin
  Form2.Visible := Not Form2.Visible;
end;
```

This will make *Form2* visible if it was invisible, and *vice versa.*

The *OnShow* and *OnHide* events of the second form are filled with the following code:

```
procedure TForm2.FormShow(Sender: TObject);
begin
  Form3.Show;
end;

procedure TForm2.FormHide(Sender: TObject);
begin
  Form3.Close;
end;
```

As soon as Form2 is shown, so is Form3. And likewise when Form2 is hidden, so is Form3.

Switching between windows

Sometimes a window is hidden behind other windows – something which happens quite a lot in the Lazarus IDE when you are working on a project with many windows.
To bring a window to the top, and make it the active window, you can use the *BringToFront* method as follows:

```
procedure TForm2.FormShow(Sender: TObject);
begin
  Form3.Show; // ensure the window is visible
  Form3.BringToFront; // Make it the active window
end;
```

The first line makes sure that Form3 is visible, and the second makes Form3 the topmost window of the application. In the section on enumerating windows, a more elaborate example of *BringToFont* is given.

When the user switches between windows, the focus shifts from one window to another: the newly focused window becomes the application's active window. It is possible to react to this by implementing an *OnActivate* event handler. The following code changes the window title according to whether it is the active window or not:

```
procedure TMainForm.FormActivate(Sender: TObject);
begin
  Caption := FSavedCaption + ' (Active)';
end;
```

The *FSavedCaption* variable is initialized when the form is created:

```
procedure TMainForm.FormCreate(Sender: TObject);
begin
  FSavedCaption := Caption;
end;
```

Similar to the *OnActivate* event (triggered when the form becomes active) the *OnDeActivate* event is triggered when the form loses the focus.
The following event handler changes the form's *Caption* to signal this event:

```
procedure TMainForm.FormDeactivate(Sender: TObject);
begin
  Caption := FSavedCaption + ' (Inactive)';
end;
```

6.3.4 The properties of TForm

Like any control, the position of a form is determined by its Top and Left properties. The position is always relative to the screen's top left corner, which has coordinates 0,0 except for *MDI* windows (`FormStyle=fsMDIChild`), where the position is relative to the MDI parent window's origin.

Note that window managers on X-Windows or the OS itself (Mac OS or Windows) may shift the origin of the screen to display a taskbar; there is no way to circumvent this from within the program.

Likewise, the size of a window is determined by the *Width* and *Height* properties. The size does not include the window decorations (borders).
By default, when a form is initially shown, the *Top, Left, Width* and *Height* properties are set from the values in the Object Inspector. They can, however, be changed programmatically at runtime. The following code shrinks the form every time you click on it, while keeping its position centred around its middle:

```
procedure TMainForm.FormClick(Sender: TObject);
begin
  // Increase top, left
  Top := Top +10;
  Left := left + 10;
  Width := Width -20; // 20: 10 left, 10 right.
  Height := Height -20; // 20: 10 top, 10 bottom.
end;
```

Doing this will cause flickering (a lot of flicker if the form contains many controls) because the form changes position and shape four times per click. There is a faster way of setting a form's position and size, using its bounding rectangle property *BoundsRect:*

```
procedure TMainForm.FormClick(Sender: TObject);
  Var R : TRect;
begin
  // Get the current boundsrect
  R := BoundsRect;
  { InflateRect 'inflates' the rectangle with the indicated sizes, keeping its centre unchanged }
  InflateRect(R,-10,-10);
  // Apply the new size in 1 call !
  BoundsRect := R;
end;
```

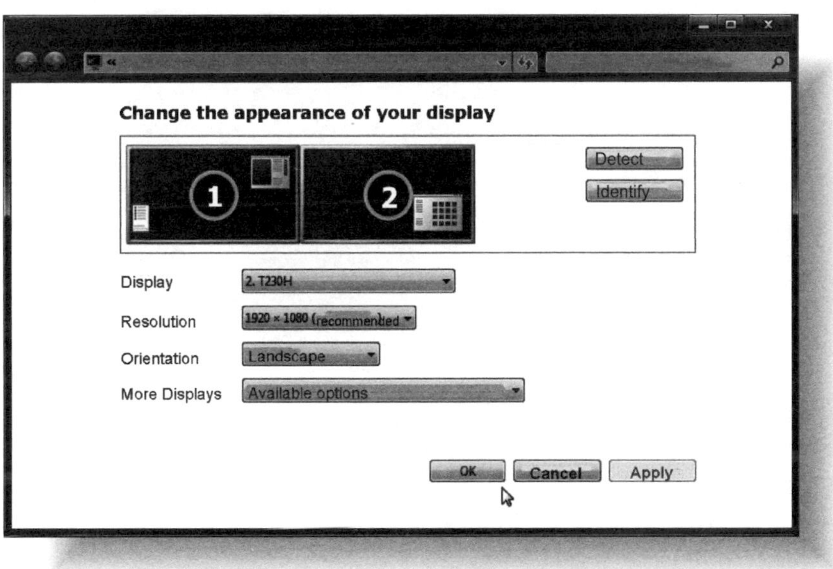

Figure 6.9: With this monitor setting, a form with position equal to poDesktopCenter will be shown cut off at the right edge of the second monitor

6.3.4 The properties of TForm

TRect is a record that describes a rectangle with the locations of its Top, Left, Bottom and Right sides. The second example above causes much less flicker, as the new size is applied just once per click.

By default a form's initial position and size are set to the values of Top, Left, Width and Height. However, the *Position* property can be used to change this.
It can have the following values:

Value	Effect
poDefault	Allow the window manager to position and size the form.
poDefaultPosOnly	Allow the window manager to position the form, using its designed size.
poDefaultSizeOnly	Allow the window manager to size the form, using its designed position.
poDesigned	The forms position and size are as designed.
poDesktopCenter	Position centred on the desktop (=all monitors), size as designed. If the user has several monitors, they form a single desktop and the form may be shown partially on several monitors (see Figure 6.9).
poMainFormCenter	Position centred on the main form, size as designed.
poOwnerFormCenter	Position centred on the owner form, size as designed.
poScreenCenter	Position centred on the current monitor, size as designed.

Table 6.11: Constant for TForm.position

The effect of the *Position* property can be demonstrated easily with a small program which offers a single window which can be duplicated at the press of a button.
The Position of the new window can be chosen using a *radiogroup,* as can as the Owner of the new form – this can be the current form, or the Application instance.
The program has three methods:

```
// BClose button can be used to close the current form.
procedure TMainForm.BCloseClick(Sender: TObject);
begin
  Close;
end;

// BDuplicate button can be used to duplicate the main form
procedure TMainForm.BDuplicateClick(Sender: TObject);
Var C : TComponent;
    F : TMainForm;
begin
   // Decide who is the owner for the new form
   If (RGOwner.ItemIndex=0) then
     C := Self
   else
     C := Application;
   // Create a new form instance with the chosen owner
   F := TMainForm.Create(C);
   { Set the position property based on the value in the RGPosition radiogroup }
   F.Position := TPosition(RGPosition.ItemIndex);
   // Now show the form in the chosen position.
   F.Show;
end;
```

{ *In the OnShow event handler, we display the value of the 'Position' property in the form's caption* }

```
procedure TMainForm.FormShow(Sender: TObject);
  Var S : String;
begin
   // GetEnumName returns the name of the Position property; requires 'uses typinfo;'
   S := GetEnumName(TypeInfo(TPosition),Ord(Position));
   // Set the caption
   Caption := 'Form placed using position : ' + S;
end;
```

Border properties

There are four properties controlling how the window border is drawn and how it behaves: *Caption*, *BorderWidth*, *BorderStyle* and *BorderIcons.*

The most obvious property is the *Caption*, the title of the window, which is also used to identify the window in the taskbar's window list. By default, the *Caption* is set to the form's name, which is usually not very informative, so you should change this. It can be set in the Object Inspector, or it can be set at run time – the window title will be updated immediately. Note that on Unix windowing systems, the window manager may append a number to the title if the same window title is used more than once. See Figure 6.11.

The result of this small program is shown in the following Figure:

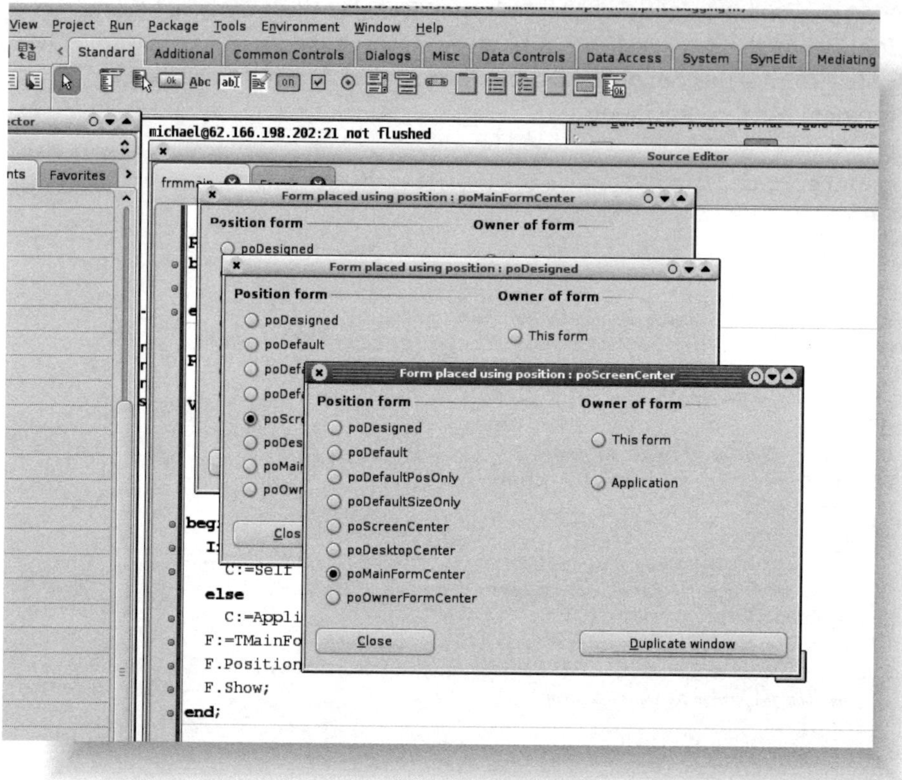

Figure 6.10: Various forms with different Position property settings

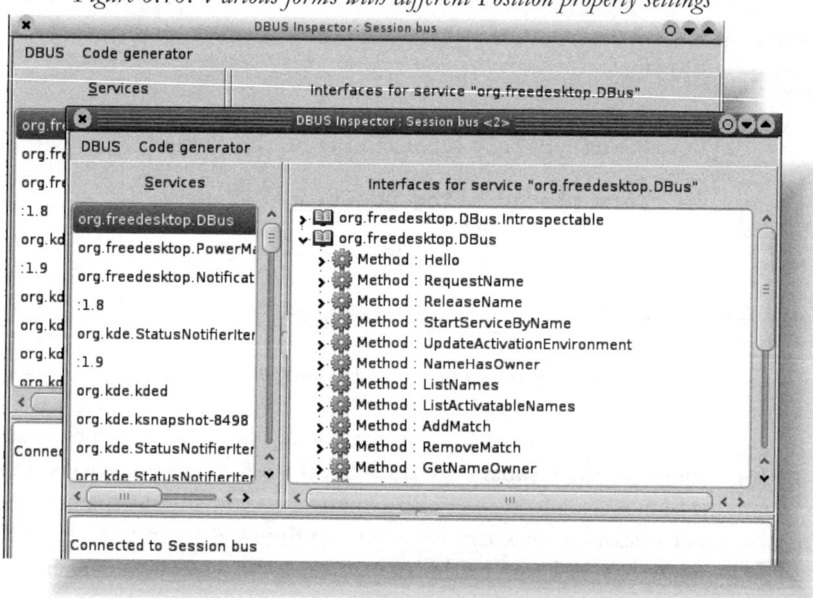

Figure 6.11: Windows with the same number are numbered

The *BorderIcons* property (of type *TBorderIcons*) determines which icons are drawn in the title bar. It is a set type which can contain combinations of the following values:

Value	Effect
biSystemMenu	A button which shows a small menu with window operations.
biMinimize	A button for minimizing the window.
biMaximize	A button for maximizing (and restoring) the window.
biHelp	A button which activates the help function.

Table 6.12: Available title bar buttons for LCL applications.

These values apply to the Windows operating system, and window managers on Unix or Mac OS may or may not honour this property. For instance the KDE window manager on Linux does not honour this property at all.

The *BorderWidth* property specifies the window's border width. The border width is applied inwards, but does not affect the *ClientRect* property of the window: the *ClientRect* is a rectangle that specifies the space available for components inside the window, but the *BorderWidth* needs to be subtracted from all this.

To demonstrate this, drop a memo on a form, and set its *Align* property to *alClient,* which means that it will always try to fill all available space in the form (there is more about this in the Managing Layout section).
Set the *OnShow* and *OnResize* events of the main form (called *MainForm*) to the following procedure, which will display the form's *ClientRect* values, as well as the memo's *BoundsRect* values, in the form's Caption:

```
procedure TMainForm.ShowSizes(Sender: TObject);
  Var S1,S2 : String;
begin
  With ClientRect do
    S1 := Format('(%d,%d) - (%d,%d)',[Left,Top,Right,Bottom]);
  With Memo.BoundsRect do
    S2 := Format('(%d,%d) - (%d,%d)',[Left,Top,Right,Bottom]);
  Caption := Format('%s - %d : %s',[S1,BorderWidth,S2]);
end;
```

The program should, when run, resemble the following:

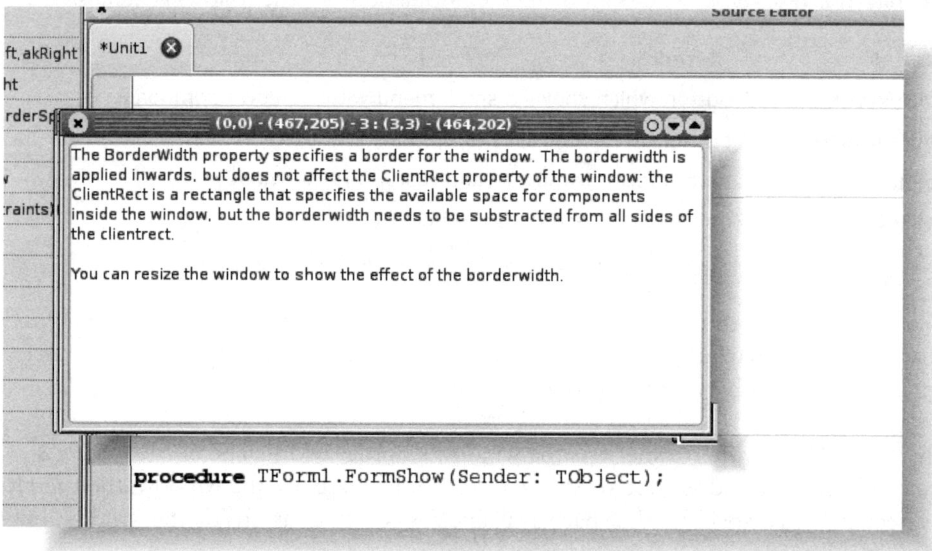

Figure 6.12: Effect of the BorderWidth property

The most important property, however, is the *BorderStyle* property.
It is an enumerated value, and can have one of the following values:

Value	Meaning
bsNone	The window has no border at all and is not sizable.
bsSingle	The window has a single border, and is not sizable.
bsSizeable	The window has a single border, and is sizable.
bsDialog	The window has a 'dialog' border, and is not sizable.
bsToolWindow	The window has a 'toolwindow' border (a very small border) and is not sizable.
bsSizeToolWin	The window has a 'toolwindow' border (a very small border) and is sizable.

Table 6.13: The borderStyle propery determines the window type

Tool windows have a smaller title bar than regular windows, and additionally, they do not appear in the window list in MS-Windows. Dialog windows are shown in the window list. Non-sizeable windows lack minimize and maximize buttons. On Unix-like platforms, the behaviour depends on the window manager. For instance, the KDE window manager does not respect most of the above properties.

The FormStyle property

The *FormStyle* property of *TForm* determines the kind of window that is created. It has the following possible values:

Value	Meaning
fsNormal	A normal window. Most windows are of this type.
fsStayOnTop	A window that tries to stay on top of all other windows.
fsSplash	A window that is used during program startup. It behaves like a normal window.
fsMDIChild	A MDI child window. This works only in the Windows and Qt widget sets.
fsMDIForm	A MDI parent window. This works only in the Windows and Qt widget sets.

Table 6.14: Possible values for the FormStyle property

A form with style *fsMDIForm* serves as a parent window for windows with style *fsMDIChild*. The child windows cannot leave the parent window, but can be moved about in it, and can be maximized or minimized in the parent window.
This works only if the Qt or Windows widget set is used for the *LCL: GTK* and *Carbon* have no concept of MDI windows.
The *fsStayOnTop* window style is used for little windows that stay on top of other windows, such as small tool windows. It is possible for an application to create more than one window with the *fsStayOnTop* style.

Minimizing and Maximizing: WindowState

In most operating systems, the user has a way of making the window cover the whole desktop: maximizing the window. This operation is performed by the operating system window manager. The converse is also possible: minimizing the window – in this state, the window will only be visible as an icon in the taskbar or task list (if the OS provides such a feature).

The current state of the window is available through the WindowState property. It can have the values indicated in the following table:

WindowState	Meaning
wsMinimized	The window is minimized (iconized).
wsNormal	The window is its usual size.
wsMaximized	The window is maximized.

Table 6.15: Possible values for the WindowState property

It should be noted that Unix window managers do not provide a *wsMaximized* state: the window is simply resized to cover the whole desktop, but is in no other way distinguished from the normal state. The *OnWindowStateChange* event is triggered when the form changes state, and it can be used to react to changes of window state.

You can also write to the *WindowState* property. The following code cycles the window between normal, maximized and minimized states when it is double-clicked, changing the Caption to display the current state.

```
procedure TMainForm.FormDblClick(Sender: TObject);
begin
  if WindowState = wsNormal then
    WindowState := wsMaximized
  else if WindowState = wsMaximized then
    WindowState := wsMinimized;
end;

procedure TMainForm.FormWindowStateChange(Sender: TObject);
begin
   Caption := GetEnumName(TypeInfo(TWindowState),Ord(WindowState));
end;
```

Showing multiple instances of the same window

By default, The Lazarus IDE creates all designed forms at program startup, and because of this, statements like these work without problems:

```
procedure TForm1.FormClick(Sender: TObject);
begin
  Form2.Visible := Not Form2.Visible;
end;
```

This code assumes that the variable Form2 contains a reference to *TForm2,* which is True for all windows that are automatically created by the Lazarus IDE.

For forms that are not automatically created, the form variable does exist, but contains Nil. Where that is True (Form2 was not *auto-created*) the code above would crash the program with an "Access Violation" error message.

For forms that are not automatically created, the programmer must create the form himself. Since a form is a class like any other this can be done quite simply:

```
procedure TForm1.FormClick(Sender: TObject);
begin
 // If Form2 does not exist yet, create it:
  If (Form2 = Nil) then
    Form2 := TForm2.Create(Application);
  Form2.Visible := Not Form2.Visible;
end
```

In this code, the statement

```
Form2 := TForm2.Create(Application);
```

is largely equivalent to the statement that the IDE generates in the program file if Form2 is created automatically:

```
Application.CreateForm(TForm2,Form2);
```

The difference is that this latter command keeps a reference to the first form created, and sets this as the main form so that the *TApplication.Run* method then knows which form to show.

Dynamically creating windows

Sometimes it is necessary to create multiple instances of the same form, each showing different data. For instance, in an invoicing application, it may be desirable to view the details of two invoices at once to compare them visually, or you might wish to compare the contact details of two clients. E-mail program such as Outlook or Thunderbird, allow multiple e-mails to be viewed or composed simultaneously.

Whether a form is created automatically by the IDE with a statement like

```
Application.CreateForm(TForm2,Form2)
```

or the form is created manually by the programmer like this:

```
Form2 := TForm2.Create(Application);
```

the result is that Form2 points to an instance of *TForm2*. Since only there is only ever one Form2 variable, and a variable can contain only one reference to a form instance, it follows that it is not possible to automatically create two instances of *TForm2*.

To create multiple instances of a single form, the form must be created manually:

```
Form2 := TForm2.Create(Application);
Form2.Show;
```

This will create and show an instance of *TForm2,* and store a reference to it in the Form2 variable. Repeating this statement a number of times, will create a number of *TForm2* instances, but only the last created instance will be stored in the Form2 variable.

Note that the Owner is set to the Application instance. As a consequence, the *LCL* will change the Name property of the form instances: they will not have the same *Name* property as when designed.
Instead, the *Name* property will be set to the designed name altered by appending an integer to it (so Form2_2, Form2_3 and so on).

The *LCL* does not offer any built-in way to keep track of the created instances (however see section 2.9). So if you need to refer to a list of forms you have created you must set this up manually, for instance by using a *TStringList* instance.

The following small program creates a second form each time the main form is double-clicked, and keeps a reference to all instances.

```
TForm1 = class(TForm)
  procedure FormCreate(Sender: TObject);
  procedure FormDblClick(Sender: TObject);
  procedure FormDestroy(Sender: TObject);
  procedure RemoveForm(Sender: TObject);
 private
 { private declarations }
 public
 { public declarations }
  FForms:TStringList;
  Delta : Integer;
end;

  var Form1: TForm1;

implementation
{ TForm1 }

uses secondform; // Secondform contains the definition of TForm2

procedure TForm1.FormCreate(Sender: TObject);
begin
  Fforms := TStringList.Create; // create a stringlist to store form instances.
end;

procedure TForm1.FormDestroy(Sender: TObject);
begin
  FreeAndNil(FForms); // Free the stringlist in which form instances are stored.
end;

procedure TForm1.FormDblClick(Sender: TObject);
begin
  Form2 := TForm2.Create(Application); // Create a form instance
  Form2.OnDestroy := @RemoveForm; // Attach a hook so we are notified when it is destroyed
  Form2.Top := Form2.Top+Delta; // Move the form a bit so they don't all appear on top of each other.
  Form2.Left := Form2.Left+Delta;
  Form2.Show; // Show it
  FForms.AddObject(Form2.Name,Form2); // Add the form name and instance to the form list.
  Inc(Delta,30); // increase the position delta
end;

procedure TForm1.RemoveForm(Sender: TObject);
  Var I : Integer;
begin
  I := FForms.IndexOfObject(Sender); // this is called whenever a Form2 instance is destroyed.
  If (I <> -1) then
  begin
    // Found it in the list, so display a message in caption
    Caption := 'Deleted instance ' + FForms[i];
    FForms.Delete(I); // and remove it from the list.
  end;
end;
```

Note the *RemoveForm* event handler: when a created form instance is destroyed, the reference to the instance must be removed from the list of forms. Care should be taken that the Form2 instance is actually freed when it is closed: the *CloseAction* parameter of its *OnClose* event handler should be set to caFree, as in the following code:

```
procedure TForm2.FormClose(Sender: TObject; var CloseAction: TCloseAction);
begin
  CloseAction := caFree;
end;
```

By default, a modal form is just hidden when it is closed, so this event handler should always be coded when keeping a list of forms. The result of this procedure after creating some windows and deleting one, is shown in Figure 6.13:

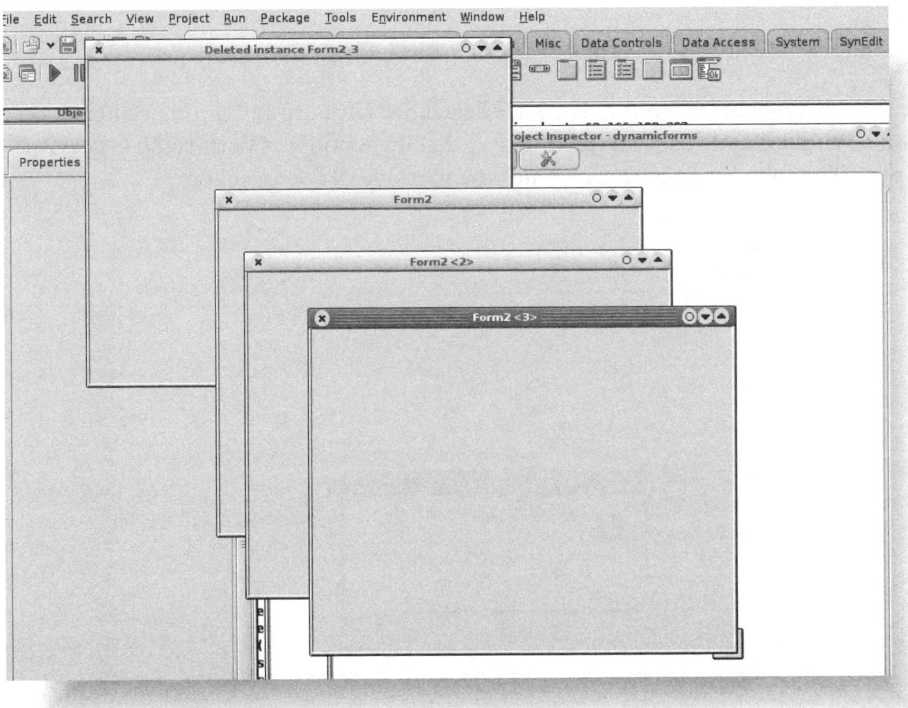

Figure 6.13: Manually creating multiple windows

6.3.5 Special windows

The programmer does not have to design every form, but can take advantage of ready-made simple forms available in the *LCL*. There are a couple of simple forms that are created dynamically by Lazarus, and whose functionality is wrapped in a couple of simple functions. Basically, there are two kinds of simple forms provided:

- A simple form showing a message and an icon. The user can only close this form.
- Or a variation on the above showing a message and an icon and a set of standard buttons.
- A simple form where a user can input a typed value (or cancel the dialog).

There is no need to design such simple forms since the *LCL* offers them ready-made. They are discussed in the following paragraphs.
The operating system also provides ready-made dialogs: file and directory selection dialogs; printer selection and setup dialogs; search and replace dialogs. They are complex and have many options: too many to be contained in simple functions. Consequently they are available as components which can be dropped on a form, and their options have been wrapped in properties. These dialog components are discussed in the component reference chapter.

ShowMessage

ShowMessage is the *LCL's* simplest ready-made window. It shows a message, and an *OK* button to close the dialog. Its declaration is very simple:

```
Procedure ShowMessage(Const aMsg : String);
```

The function returns when the user has clicked the *OK* button. No other interaction is possible, and it is only use is to tell the user that an action was performed successfully (or not). The following Figure illustrates the message dialog in action:

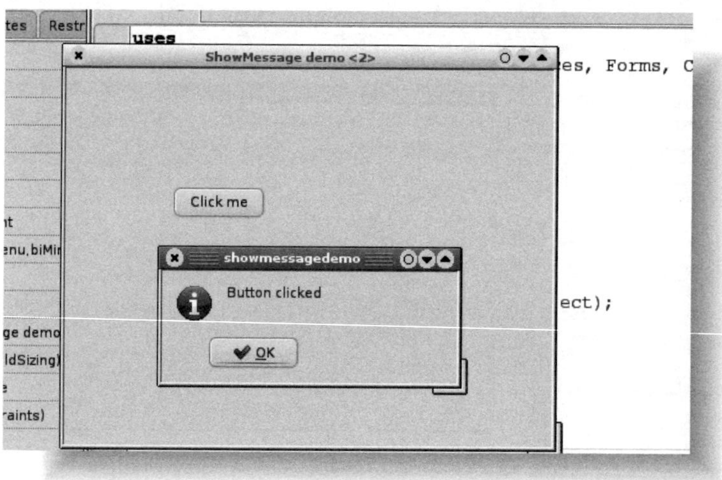

Figure 6.14: A message dialog

There are two slight variations on *ShowMessage:*

```
procedure ShowMessageFmt(const aMsg: string; Params: array of const);
procedure ShowMessagePos(const aMsg: string; X, Y: Integer);
```

ShowMessageFmt first formats the message using the provided arguments, just like the standard Format call, and then it behaves just like *ShowMessage.*
The second procedure positions the message dialog at the particular coordinates (X,Y).

MessageDlg

Sometimes it is necessary to request a user response – a simple *Yes* or *No,* maybe with an additional *Retry* or *Cancel.* The *ShowMessage* call is not suitable for this, so a slightly more extended function is provided called *MessageDlg.* It is defined as follows:

```
function MessageDlg(const aMsg: string; DlgType: TMsgDlgType;
  Buttons: TMsgDlgButtons; HelpCtx: Longint): Integer;
```

This call shows a dialog window with an icon, a text string (as specified in *aMsg*) and one or more buttons. The icon is one of several predefined icons, selected through the *DlgType* parameter. The possible values for this parameter are listed in the table below:

Constant	Function
mtInformation	A dialog giving information.
mtConfirmation	A dialog requesting confirmation.
mtWarning	A dialog warning about potentially dangerous action(s).
mtError	A dialog reporting an error situation.
mtCustom	A custom dialog with an information icon and the program name in the title bar.

Table 16 Possible message dialog types (values of the DlgType parameter)

Which button or buttons are shown in the dialog, is determined by the third parameter:
Buttons
This is a set parameter, which also determines the possible function return values.
The return value is one of the possible values for *ModalResult* because the dialog is shown modally, and must be closed before the program logic can continue.
The possible return values are listed in the following table.

Constant	Function and Button value
mrYes	When the button (caption: Yes) was pressed.
mrNo	When the button (caption: No) was pressed.
mrOK	When the button (caption: OK) was pressed.
mrCancel	When the button (caption: Cancel) was pressed.
mrAbort	When the button (caption: Abort) was pressed.
mrRetry	When the button (caption: Retry) was pressed.
mrIgnore	When the button (caption: Ignore) was pressed.
mrAll	When the button (caption: All) was pressed.
mrYesToAll	When the button (caption: Yes to all) was pressed.
mrNoToAll	When the button (caption: No to all) was pressed.
mrNone	When the dialog is not closed using a button, but when the user closed the window directly for instance by using the system menu.

Table 6.17: Return values of the MessageDlg function

The HelpCtx parameter can be used to provide a help context. The following screenshot shows the *MessageDlg* function in action:

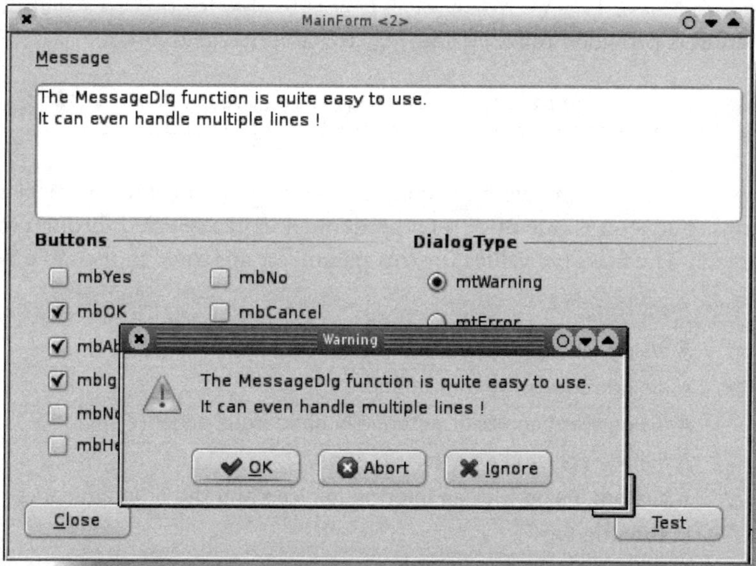

Figure 6.15: The standard MessageDlg function in action

Again, several adaptations of the basic *MessageDlg* function are provided offering slightly different functionalities:

```
function MessageDlg(const aCaption, aMsg: string; DlgType: TMsgDlgType;
  Buttons: TMsgDlgButtons; HelpCtx: Longint): Integer;

function MessageDlg(const aCaption, aMsg: string; DlgType: TMsgDlgType;
  Buttons: TMsgDlgButtons; HelpCtx: Longint; DefaultButton: TMsgDlgBtn):
  Integer;

function MessageDlg(const aCaption, aMsg: string; DlgType: TMsgDlgType;
  Buttons: TMsgDlgButtons; const HelpKeyword: string): Integer;
```

The first one allows you to specify a caption for the dialog (*aCaption*), and the second one allows you to specify which of the buttons should be the default button (if the Yes button is present, it is default in the regular variant). The third variant allows you to specify a help keyword instead of a help context.

The following two variants of the *MessageDlg* function allow you to specify the precise position (X,Y) to place the dialog:

```
function MessageDlgPos(const aMsg: string; DlgType: TMsgDlgType;
  Buttons: TMsgDlgButtons; HelpCtx: Longint; X, Y: Integer): Integer;

function MessageDlgPosHelp(const aMsg: string; DlgType: TMsgDlgType;
  Buttons: TMsgDlgButtons; HelpCtx: Longint; X, Y: Integer;
                           const HelpFileName: string): Integer;
```

In the second variant, the name of the help file to use can also be specified.

QuestionDlg

Research shows that users read a question that pops up in a rather superficial way, and tend to click Yes without actually thinking what they are saying Yes to. Consequently, it is often better not to provide the user with Yes and No buttons, but to rephrase your question, and provide appropriate answers to your question as captions for the close buttons themselves. You often see dialogs similar to this one:

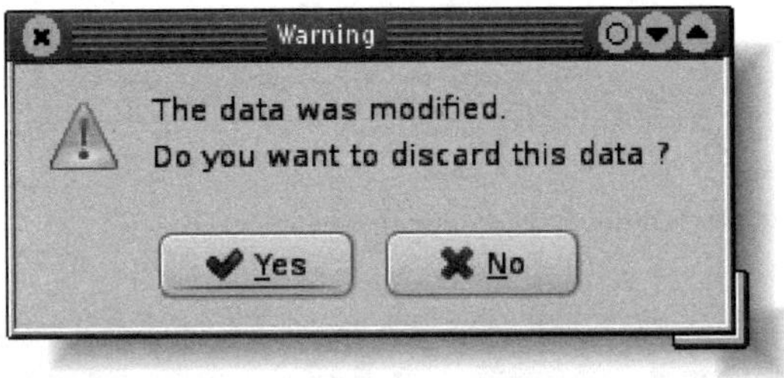

Figure 6.16: Misguided use of the MessageDlg function

The user clicks Yes out of habit without thinking, and loses his data! The *QuestionDlg function* allows you to offer an improved dialog. The function is defined as follows:

```
function QuestionDlg(const aCaption, aMsg:string; DlgType: TMsgDlgType;
  Buttons: array of const; HelpCtx: Longint): TModalResult;

function QuestionDlg(const aCaption, aMsg:string; DlgType: TMsgDlgType;
  Buttons: array of const; const HelpKeyword: string): TModalResult;
```

Just as in the *MessageDlg* function, the first three arguments are the *caption, message* and *icon* for the dialog. The Buttons array, however, is different: *Buttons* is an array of *TModalResult* values mixed with string values. For each *TModalResult* value, a button is created.
If the *TModalResult* value is followed by a string value, that string will be used as the caption for the button instead of the default caption associated with the *TModalResult* value.

For example, the following array:

```
[mrNo,'Discard data', mrYes,'Keep data', mrCancel]
```

shows three buttons:

- The first button has the caption Discard data and the dialog returns *mrNo* when it is pushed.
- The second button has the caption Keep data and the dialog returns *mrYes* when it is pushed.
- The last button has the caption Cancel and the dialog returns *mrCancel* when it is pushed.

In action, it could look something like this:

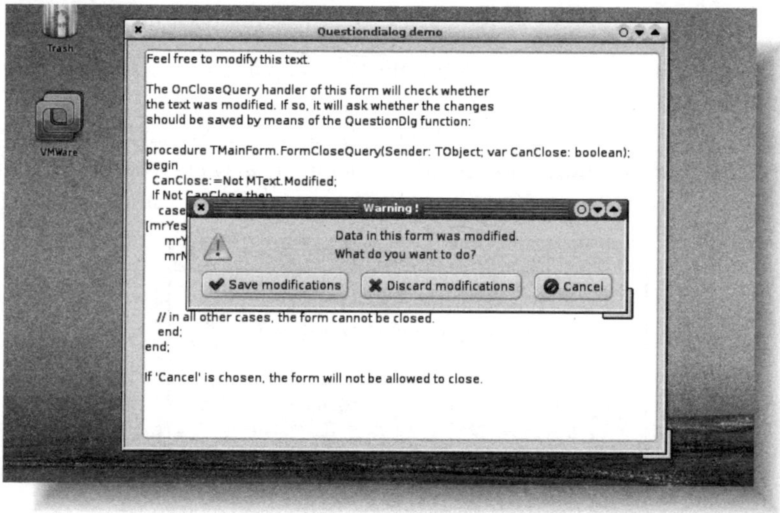

Figure 6.17: Better confirmation dialogs with the QuestionDlg function

The following code is used to produce this warning dialog:

```
Resourcestring
  SWarning = 'Warning !'; // Some messages
  SDataModified = 'Data in this form was modified.'+sLinebreak+
    'What do you want to do?';
  SDiscard = 'Discard modifications';
  SKeep = 'Save modifications';

procedure TMainForm.FormCloseQuery(Sender: TObject; var CanClose: boolea
begin
  CanClose := Not MText.Modified; // If nothing was modified, we can close.
  If Not CanClose then // Ask the user what to do
    case QuestionDlg(SWarning,SDataModified,mtWarning,
      [mrYes,sKeep,mrNo,SDiscard,mrCancel],0) of
      mrYes : Canclose := True;
      mrNo  : begin
                CanClose := True;
                // Save Data
              end;
    // in all other cases, the form cannot be closed.
    end;
end;
```

InputQuery

The standard dialogs considered so far have not allowed the user to provide a value; they presented the user with a button to click on, but no way to type anything. Nevertheless, you often need to ask the user for a value: a name, a number – anything. The InputQuery function allows exactly that:

```
function InputQuery(const ACaption, APrompt : String;
      var Value : String) : Boolean;
```

InputQuery pops up a window with caption ACaption in which the user can type a short answer (a default answer can be provided in AValue). The window has an *OK* and *Cancel* button, and can display a short message (APrompt). The function will return the value typed by the user in AValue and returns the result True if the user closed the function with the OK button, or False otherwise.
The following code asks the user to change the caption of the form, offering the current value of the caption as a starting default:

```
Resourcestring
  STitleChange = 'Change window caption';
  SEnterNewTitle = 'Enter the new value for the window title:';

procedure TMainForm.Button1Click(Sender: TObject);
  Var S: String;
begin
  S := Caption;
  if InputQuery(STitleChange,SEnterNewTitle,True,S) then Caption := S;
end;
```

The result of this code is shown below:

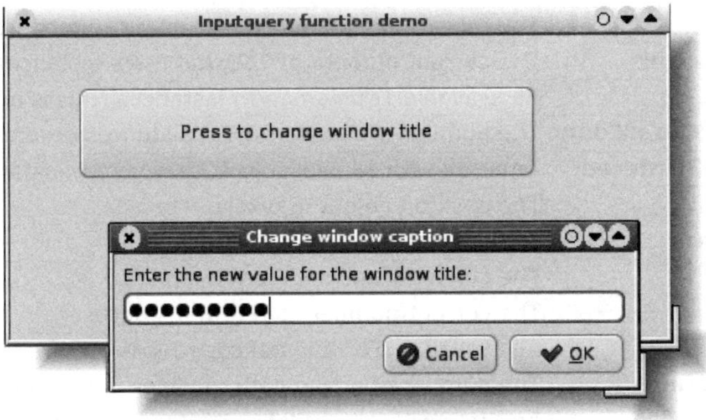

Figure 6.18: An example of using the InputQuery function

Sometimes, you will be asking for a password.
Therefore, a variant of the *InputQuery* is provided:

```
function InputQuery(const ACaption, APrompt : String; MaskInput : Boolean;
 var Value : String) : Boolean;
```

If the MaskInput value is True then the typed value will be masked (only a password character like **'*'** will be shown).
If you do not care which button the user pressed to close the dialog, then the following variants can be used:

```
function InputBox(const ACaption, APrompt, ADefault : String) : String;
function PasswordBox(const ACaption, APrompt : String) : String;
```

The first function returns ADefault if the user cancelled the dialog, and the second always starts with an empty password, and returns an empty string if the user cancelled the dialog.

6.3.6 The window environment

TScreen

Paralleling its *TApplication* instance, Lazarus maintains a global *TScreen* instance which is available through the *Screen* variable. It contains information about the current desktop, and consists mainly of a large number of properties that give all kinds of information about the current desktop environment, such as the size, the current cursor and so on. It also contains information about the current form instances of the application: each form – when instantiated – registers itself with the global screen instance, no matter whether it was created by the global application instance or manually in code. All the properties of the *TScreen* class are listed in the following table:

Property	Provides information about
ActiveControl	The currently active *TWincontrol* instance.
ActiveCustomForm	The currently active *TCustomForm* instance.
ActiveForm	The currently active *TForm* instance.
Cursor	The current cursor.
Cursors	The registered cursors (this is an array property).
CustomFormCount	The current number of *TCustomForm* instances.
CustomForms	All available *TCustomForm* instances (this is an array property).
CustomFormZOrderCount	The number of *TCustomForm* instances ordered by ZOrder.
CustomFormsZOrdered	An array with all available *TCustomForm* instances, in ZOrder.
DesktopHeight	The desktop height in pixels.
DesktopWidth	The desktop width in pixels.
FocusedForm	The currently active *TForm* instance.
FormCount	The current number of *TForm* instances.
Forms	All available *TForm* instances (this is an array property).
DataModuleCount	The number of active data modules in the application.
DataModules	An array with all available *TDatamodule* instances.
HintFont	The font commonly used for hints in the system.
IconFont	The font commonly used for icons in the system.
MenuFont	The font commonly used for menus in the system.
SystemFont	The default text font.
Fonts	A *TStrings* instance with the names of all installed fonts.
Height	The screen's height.
MonitorCount	The number of monitors.
Monitors	An array of all available monitors.
PixelsPerInch	The screen's DPI (Dots Per Inch).
PrimaryMonitor	Primary Monitor data.
Width	The screen's width.

Table 6.18: Properties of Tscreen

The *TScreen* instance has only two events:

Event	Triggered when
OnActiveControlChange	The focused control changes.
OnActiveFormChange	The active (focused) form changes.

Table 6.19: Events of TScreen

A typical use for the Screen instance is to create a list of your application's windows, from which you can populate a Window menu. This can be used to activate one of the windows. The following code shows how this can be done:

```
procedure TMainForm.RefreshWindowList(List: TStrings);
  Var I : Integer;
      F : TForm;
begin
  List.Clear;
  For I:= 0 to Screen.FormCount - 1 do
  begin
    F := Screen.Forms[i];
    List.AddObject(F.Caption,F)
  end;
end;


procedure TMainForm.MWindowsClick(Sender: TObject);
  Var I : Integer;
      MI : TMenuItem;
begin
  MWindows.Clear;
  RefreshWindowList(FForms);
  For I:= 0 to FForms.Count - 1 do
  begin
    MI := TMenuItem.Create(Self);
    MI.Caption := FForms[i];
    MI.OnClick := @RaiseWindow;
    MI.Tag := I;
    MWindows.Add(MI);
  end;
end;


procedure TMainForm.RaiseWindow(Sender : Tobject);
  Var I : integer;
      F : TForm;
begin
  I := (Sender as TMenuItem).Tag;
  F := TForm(FForms.Objects[I]);
  F.SetFocus;
end;
```

The result of this code can be seen in the following Figure:

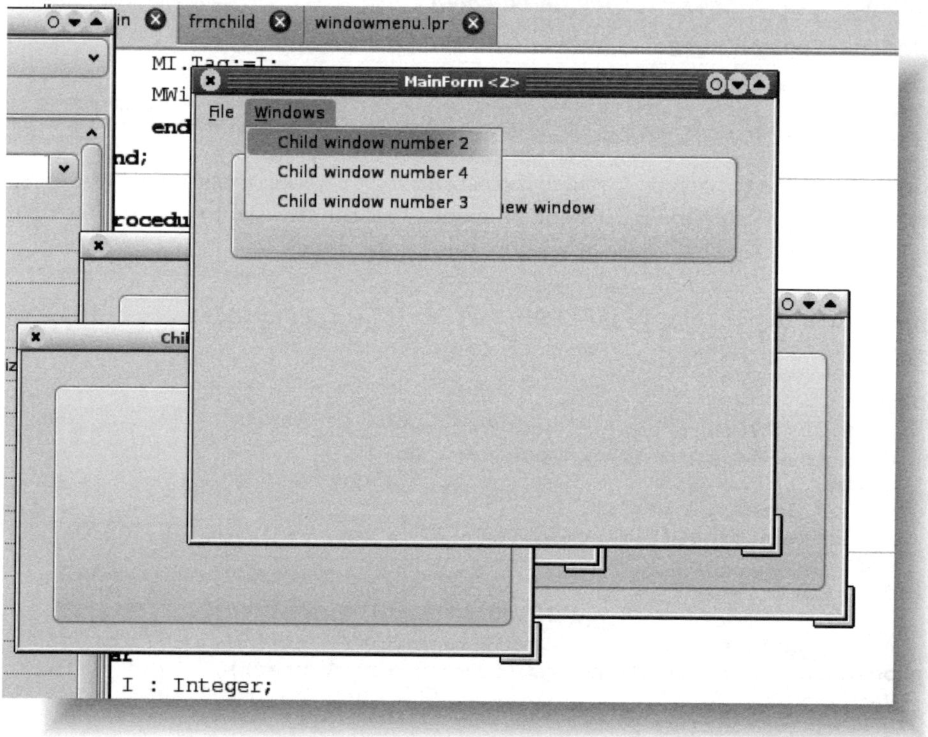

Figure 6.19: The Window menu in action

6.3.7 Adding content to a form: Controls

Obviously, programs with empty windows are not very exciting: they need to be filled with controls (also known as widgets). Controls are visual *TComponent* descendants, in other words they are visible on the form or window when the user runs the application. All controls used in a GUI application descend from *TControl* or *TWinControl*. The difference between these two classes is explained in the following sections, but first we look at the process of adding controls to a form in the IDE.

Handling controls

Adding a control

Adding a control to a form is quite easy: locate the control you want to place on the form in one of the component palette tabs of the Lazarus main window and click its icon. The toolbutton will remain depressed, to indicate that a control is being added.
Then click on the form. This places the control with its top left corner where click occurred (the Top and Left properties will be set to the coordinates of the mouse click location). The control appears on the form at a default size, and is selected.
You can change its properties in the Object Inspector immediately,
or you can resize and reposition it on the form using the mouse.

The control is given a default name – the class name (with the initial 'T' removed) followed by a number. (If in the Form Editor tab of the *Environment→Options* dialog the option Ask name on create has been ticked then a Choose Name dialog will pop up at this point where you can accept the default name or type a different name).
For instance if a label (of class *TLabel*, on the component palette's Standard tab) is dropped on an empty form, its default Name will be Label1.
A second label dropped immediately afterwards will be named Label2 (see Figure 6.20).

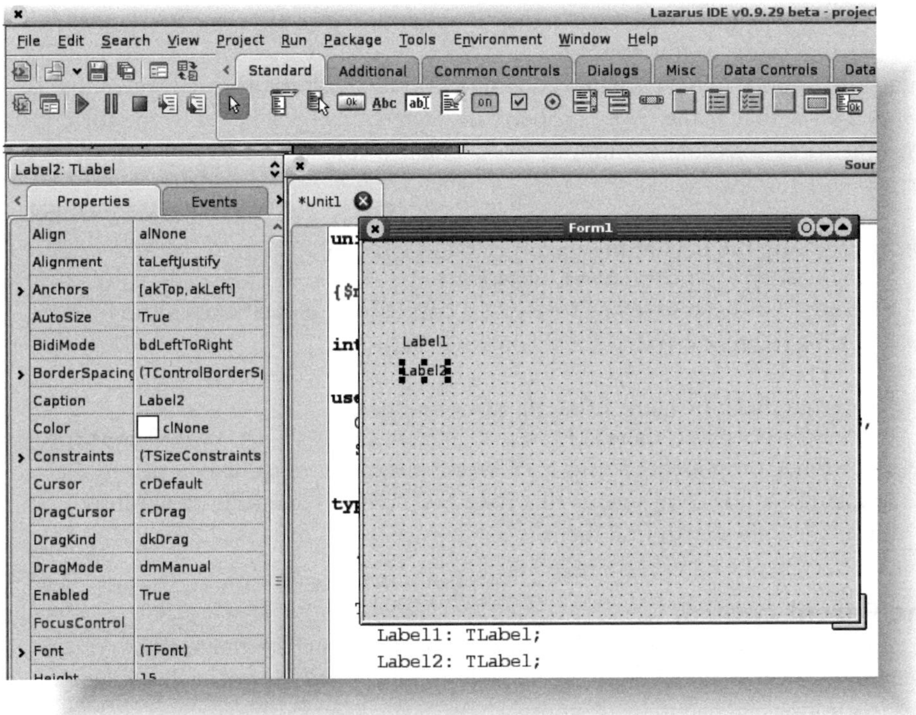

Figure 6.20: Adding controls to a form in the IDE

Lazarus changes the form's class definition whenever a control is dropped on a form by adding each control as a field to the form's class definition.
In the previous example with two added labels, the form class would look like this:

```
{ TForm1 }

 TForm1 = class(TForm)
   Label1: TLabel;
   Label2: TLabel;
  private
   { private declarations }
  public
   { public declarations }
 end;
```

Note that the field name in the class definition is the actual name of the control.
You can change the control's name by editing its *Name* property in the Object Inspector. Because the control is defined as a field in the form class, the *Name* has to be a valid Pascal identifier (i.e. it must start with a letter or underscore, and consist only of letters and numerical characters. Spaces are not allowed). It also follows that each control must be named uniquely.

As soon as you change the control's *Name* in the Object Inspector, the *Name* is also automatically changed in the form's class definition, and in any code in the form's methods that refers to this control.
The form instance (which is a descendant of *TComponent)* owns each control that is dropped on it: that is, the *Owner* property of each control will be set to the form instance when the form is created at runtime. Consequently, you can access any control on the form in either of two ways:

1. By accessing the field in the form's class declaration:
   ```
   Label1.Caption := 'Some caption';
   ```
   This is by far the easiest way to access a control: the name fields in the form contain a reference to the actual control instance.

2. By looking for it by name using FindComponent():
   ```
   (FindComponent('Label1') as TLabel).Caption := 'Some caption';
   ```
   Since FindComponent returns a *TComponent* result, it must be typecast to the proper class. For components that have been created manually at runtime, this is the only way to find them.

The Parent control

As explained in the previous section, all controls are owned by the form.
This simply means that when the form is destroyed, all its controls will also be destroyed. This is a non-visual hierarchy of controls: the owner–owned hierarchy.

There is a second hierarchy on a form, namely the parent–child hierarchy. It is a visual hierarchy. Controls can be dropped not only on a form, but also on other controls.
For instance you could drop a button on a panel. Doing so will make the panel the parent of the button. The panel doesn't own the button, but it does affect the button because the position of a child control (as determined by its Top and Left properties) is always relative to its parent control.

As a consequence, when a parent control is moved, all its children move too.
When a parent is made invisible, all its children become invisible.
The parent also restricts the size of its children – if the child control's dimensions exceed its parent's dimensions, it will be clipped.
Not every control can act as a parent to other controls – only certain controls accept child controls. For instance, you can't drop a control on a button – not even an image or a label.

6.3.7 Adding content to a form: Controls

As soon as a control is dropped on a form or one of the controls of the form, the control's *Parent* property is set. It is not possible to drag the control to another parent: you can only drag the control within the bounds of its parent. To change the control's parent, the control must be cut (to the clipboard) and pasted into the new parent control. The same is true for the form which acts as the parent for each control that is dropped on it. Moving a control from one form to another has to be done with cut and paste.

Cut and Paste of objects can be tricky, specially on some operating systems. If you are working on such a system, it is possible to manually edit the form definition. To do this you use the View source `(.lfm)` context menu of the Form Designer, which shows the form's definition as text. The definition clearly shows the parent–child hierarchy, and is often easier to manipulate these lines of code than attempt cut and paste in the visual Form Designer. An example form definition follows:

```
object Form1: TForm1
  Left = 250
  Height = 240
  Top = 250
  Width = 320
  Caption = 'Form1'
  ClientHeight = 240
  ClientWidth = 320
  LCLVersion = '0.9.29'
  object Button1: TButton
    Left = 28
    Height = 25
    Top = 27
    Width = 75
    Caption = 'Button1'
    TabOrder = 0
  end
  object Button2: TButton
    Left = 29
    Height = 25
    Top = 66
    Width = 75
    Caption = 'Button2'
    TabOrder = 1
  end
  object Panel1: TPanel
    Left = 29
    Height = 50
    Top = 112
    Width = 170
    Caption = 'Panel1'
    TabOrder = 2
  end
end
```

If you drag the Panel1 code section (marked grey) so it appears before the definition of the *Button1* control, then the buttons automatically become child controls of the panel. The reverse procedure is also possible.
When manipulating the form definition like this, the positions of the buttons will of course no longer remain as they were: if the parent changes, the position - which is measured relative to the parent, will also change. The positions can be corrected in the text, or visually by switching back to the Form Designer mode. To do that you must close the form source `(.lfm)` window and restore the Form Designer from the View menu, using the Toggle form/unit view item, or by using the default shortcut [F12].
Manipulating the `.lfm` manually is not without risks and I recommend that you create a backup of all the form's files `(.pas` and `.lfm)` before you edit the `.lfm` directly.

Initial control size
When you drop a control on a form with a simple click, it is given a default size – what size depends on the particular control's defaults. However, it is possible to click-and-drag when dropping a new control on a form. By not letting the mouse button go, but rather dragging the mouse, you can design the initial outline of the control at the size you want.

However some controls do not allow their size to be set. For instance a main menu's size is determined by the number of menu items, and the main menu always aligns itself with the top edge of the form, under the title bar.

Adding multiple instances of a control
As soon as you drop a control on a form, the component palette toolbar button that you used to add the control will be de-selected. So if you want to add the same control again, you have to click the button on the toolbar again. This behaviour is intentional, since most of the time subsequent clicks on the form will be to resize or reposition the newly dropped control.
There are two ways in which you can add multiple instances of a control without having to select it in the component palette each time:

1. Keep the [Shift] key depressed when you click the form. Then every click (with [Shift] still pressed) will add a new instance of the selected control to the form.

2. Press the [Shift] key when you click the toolbar button. Then each click on the form adds a new instance of the selected control to the form, and there is no need to keep the [Shift] key down.

If you use the second method, once your duplicated controls are all placed, you can turn off the selection of that toolbar button either by clicking it, or by clicking the selection arrow found at the far left of each tab in the component palette. This will restore normal operation.

Setting properties of multiple controls

When a control is selected, you can examine and set its various properties in the Object Inspector. When the samc property needs be set for several controls (for instance to right-justify all your labels' text alignment) this can be tedious work.
Fortunately, it is possible to select multiple controls at once. You click on them each in turn while keeping the [Shift] key depressed, and then set their property.
The Object Inspector will show only properties that the selected controls share in common, and if you change any of these common properties the new value will be set for all the selected controls.
Some properties do not allow this multiple setting technique. There is no general rule to say which properties do not allow this, but typically it happens for properties that have a special property editor.

Deleting a control

To delete a control, you select it and press the [Delete] key. The control will be deleted, and its field will be removed from the form's class definition. If the control was used in your code, that code will have to be adjusted manually.
To delete several controls at once, they can be selected by Shift-clicking them, and pressing [Delete], when all the controls you selected will be deleted.
If you press the [Shift] key while you delete them, the controls are copied to the clipboard prior to deleting, so they can be pasted somewhere else (to a different parent control, for instance).

TControl and TWinControl

All visual components descend from *TControl* and some also descend from *TWinControl* (which is itself a descendant of *TControl). TWinControl* introduces some important additional properties. Informed handling of controls requires that you understand the difference between *TControl* and *TWinControl* and know from which of these two classes the control you are using descends.

TControl

TControl is the base class for all visual components, so all visual elements – including the form class itself – descend from *TControl.* You never actually use the *TControl* class, only one of its descendants. *TControl* introduces all functionality that a GUI element needs:

- It provides a position and size, and the necessary logic to change these depending on changes in the form's layout.
- It can specify a cursor.
- It provides for the handling of mouse events.
- It provides basic drag-and-drop or docking functionality.
- It provides the means of drawing the control on a form.

All this functionality is introduced (but not necessarily exposed to the Object Inspector) in *TControl*. Note that the handling of keystrokes is missing from this list.
Other limitations of a direct *TControl* class descendant include:

- It cannot contain child controls.
- It must always be placed on a windowed control (more about this below).
- It cannot receive focus. This is related to the lack of keystroke handling, because keystrokes are sent to the currently focused control. Since a direct *TControl* descendant cannot receive focus, it cannot handle keystrokes.
- It has no canvas to draw on. A direct *TControl* descendant must draw itself on its parent control.

The main properties for this class are shown in the table below.
Their names are largely self-explanatory:

Property	Purpose and description
Left	The zero-based horizontal position relative to the parent control, with 0 the leftmost position.
Top	The zero-based vertical position relative to the parent control, with 0 the topmost position.
Width	The width of the control.
Height	The height of the control.
Cursor	The shape of the cursor as it moves over the control.
Align	How the control should align itself on its parent control.
DragCursor	The cursor to use when something is dragged on the control.
DragKind	What kind of dragging operates: drag-and-drop or docking.
DragMode	Who handles the drag-and-drop.
ParentColor	Should the control use the same Color as its parent control?
ParentFont	Should the control use the same Font as its parent control?
ParentHint	Should the ShowHint property be the same as for the parent control?
Text	The text shown in the control (if there is any text to be shown).
Constraints	The size constraints for the control (minimum and maximum dimensions).
BorderSpacing	The space between the borders of the control and any surrounding controls.
PopupMenu	A reference to the popup menu shown when the control is right-clicked.

Table 6.20: Important TControl properties

Not all properties in the above table are available under all circumstances and there are controls which do not expose all these properties to the IDE's Object Inspector.
The *TControl* class also has a number of events related to the functionality it offers:

Event	Triggered when
OnContextPopup	the popupmenu is shown
OnClick	a single mouse click occurs
OnDblClick	a double mouse click occurs
OnTripleClick	a triple mouse click occurs
OnQuadClick	a quadruple mouse click occurs
OnDragDrop	a drag and drop operation starts
OnDragOver	an object is dragged over the control
OnEndDock	a docking operation ends
OnEndDrag	the user drops the object on the control
OnMouseDown	a mouse button is pressed
OnMouseUp	a mouse button is released
OnMouseMove	the mouse is moving over the control
OnMouseEnter	the mouse enters the bounding rectangle of the control
OnMouseLeave	the mouse leaves the bounding rectangle of the control
OnMouseWheel	the user scrolls the mouse wheel
OnMouseWheelDown	the user presses the mouse wheel
OnMouseWheelUp	the user releases the mouse wheel
OnStartDock	a docking operation starts
OnStartDrag	a dragging operation starts
OnEditingDone	an editing operation ends

Table 6.21: Available TControl events

Again, not all *TControl* descendants publish all these events in the Object Inspector.

TWinControl

TWinControl is a *TControl* descendant which supplies functionality missing from *TControl.*

- Other controls can be dropped on a *TWinControl* (although not all *TWinControl* descendants allow this).
- A *TWinControl* can receive focus, meaning that it can become the active control on the form.
- Because it can receive focus, a *TWinControl* can handle keystrokes. As long as it has the focus, all keystrokes are sent to this control.
- A *TWinControl* has its own canvas.

Because of this extra functionality *TWinControl* uses more system resources than a regular *TControl.* The extra possibilities are exposed through extra properties and events, shown in the following tables.

Property	Used for
BorderStyle	setting the style of border (normally only supported by *TForm*)
BorderWidth	setting the width of the border
ChildSizing	determining how to resize and layout the child controls on this control
DockSite	determining whether other controls be docked on this control
DoubleBuffered	knowing if the control's display is double-buffered
TabOrder	setting the tab order of the control
TabStop	determining whether the [Tab] key skips past or stops on this control
UseDockManager	determining whether the docking manager should be used for this control, or whether docking is handled manually

Table 6.22: TWinControl properties, not available in TControl

Event	Used
OnAlignPosition	for repositioning the control
OnDockDrop	when a control is docked on this control
OnDockOver	when a user is dragging a control over this control in order to dock it
OnEnter	when the control receives focus
OnExit	when the control loses focus
OnKeyDown	when the user presses any key on the keyboard
OnKeyPress	when a regular (alphanumerical) key is pressed
OnKeyUp	when the user releases any key on the keyboard
OnUnDock	when a control is undocked
OnUTF8KeyPress	when a regular key is pressed, and the key is converted to UTF-8

Table 6.23: TWinControl events, not available in TControl

TWinControl has some descendants *(TCustomControl* and *TScrollingWinControl)* which are mostly internal to the *LCL* and which do not contain end-user functionality.
Most controls in the *LCL* descend from *TWinControl.* There are very few controls that descend directly from *TControl (TLabel* being a notable exception).

An overview of available controls

Which controls should you use? This depends on two factors: what your application should look like, and what the user should be able to do – the actions your application expects of the user. From these considerations you can select particular categories of controls (independently from considering the controls' class hierarchy, or which component palette tab to look on).
The following sections give an overview of the *LCL* controls available to you, grouped by the function or task they should perform, rather than by their class hierarchy or which tab on the component palette they occupy. The component palette's layout is determined more by historical factors than by design considerations, and it is not always the most helpful arrangement of the available controls. The following list is not complete – a complete control reference is presented in the next chapter – but it gives a rough indication of what controls are available to achieve particular tasks.

Controls for initiating user tasks

When the user wants to accomplish certain tasks (such as setting bold text, opening a file, adding a control to a form in a Designer), he expects to be able to click somewhere to initiate this action.
Often, that click is enough to complete the action, but most of the time, that click is just the first of a series of actions needed to complete the task. There are various controls that initiate a task. The following table lists them:

Control	Tab	Description
TButton	Standard	A simple button showing a Caption.
TBitBtn	Additional	A simple button showing a Caption and an image.
TSpeedButton	Additional	A button with Caption and image, which does not get focus.
TToolBar & TToolButton	Common controls	A row of buttons, each with an image and Caption.
TMenu	Standard	A complete menu structure, shown at the top of the form.
TPopupMenu	Standard	A menu structure which can be invoked with a right-click.

Table 6.24: Controls to start a task

Displaying simple items to the user

Many controls are designed just to show something to the user who is passive at that moment – they are not controls designed to help the user perform an operation. However the user can click on them with the mouse, and this can be used to code additional effects or actions, if they are needed.

Control	Tab	Description
TLabel	Standard	A simple text phrase without any mark-up.
TImage	Additional	A simple image-display control.
TShape	Additional	Provides display of several simple geometrical shapes.
TPaintBox	Additional	Allows drawing of more complicated shapes.
TBarChart	Misc	For displaying histograms (bar graphs).
TCalendar	Misc	For displaying a date in a calendar.
TProgressBar	Common Controls	To show progress during a time-consuming Operation.
TPopupNotifier	Common Controls	For showing additional information when a user lets the mouse hover over a control.
Tbevel	Standard	To group elements visually.

Table 6.25: Controls displaying status and simple shapes

Offering simple user choices

Often, you need to present the user with a simple choice to which the answer is Yes or No (Do or Don't). Or you may need to offer a longer list of predefined options to the user, who is expected to choose one or more of them. If the option list is long, you have to decide whether it should always be visible, or whether the user will first have to click to see the complete list.

Control	Tab	Function
TCheckBox	Standard	A simple yes/no choice.
TRadioButton	Standard	A simple yes/no choice, usually used in groups where only one option can be selected.
TRadioGroup	Standard	A group of radiobuttons where only one can be selected.
TCheckGroup	Standard	A group of checkboxes where multiple items can be selected.
TComboBox	Standard	The user can select one of a set of choices. Each choice is a string. The list of choices is shown in a drop-down list. Only the selected item is visible.
TListBox	Standard	The user can select one or more from a set of choices. Each choice is a string. The list of choices is always visible.

Table 6.26: Controls offering a choice

Getting simple user input

Sometimes, the user needs to enter information that goes beyond a simple Yes/No or selecting among a list of predefined values. For instance, the user may be required to type his name, or provide a filename under which data will be saved.

Control	Tab	Function
TEdit	Standard	Single line text entry.
TMemo	Standard	Multiple line text entry.
TSpinEdit	Misc	Entry of a numerical value with up/down buttons to increase or decrease the value.
TButtonEdit	Misc	Single line text entry with a button to perform an additional action.
TOpenFileDialog	Dialogs	Selecting a filename for reading a file.
TSaveFileDialog	Dialogs	Selecting a filename for writing a file.
TColorDialog	Dialogs	Selecting a colour.
TPrinterDialog	Dialogs	Selecting a printer.TFontDialogDialogsSelecting a font.

Table 6.27: Input controls

Complex controls

The controls presented so far are relatively simple controls, which show or request a single piece of information. There are also more complex controls which show more than one kind of information or which divide the screen into distinct parts to group or arrange information.

Control	Tab	Function
TPageControl	Common Controls	To divide the display area into multiple sheets.
TTreeView	Common Controls	To display a tree-like structure.
TListView	Common Controls	To display a list structure where each item in the list consists of more than one datum.
TStringGrid	Additional	To display a grid filled with string items.

Table 6.28: Complex controls

6.3.8 Layout and design

Layout is an important issue when designing a GUI program. There are many things to consider when designing the layout of an application:

- Screen resolutions and font sizes may vary.
- Themes may change font and button sizes.
- The user may decide to resize the window (the form).
- In an internationalized application, the text displayed will vary in size, so some controls may need to be shifted or resized to accommodate the translated text's new size.

Any of these considerations may necessitate resizing and moving the controls on the form. Obviously, it is possible to do all this resizing and positioning manually. This can be a daunting task, which fortunately is taken care of by the *LCL*, provided certain properties are set correctly.

Some widget sets take care of sizing and positioning issues by using layouting objects: the GTK and Qt widget sets work like this. Microsoft Windows provides no layouts, using fixed positions and sizes. The *Lazarus Component Library (LCL),* modelled on Delphi's VCL, also uses a fixed position and size approach, namely that by default a control does not change position or size. However this behaviour can be modified using several published properties which can be set in the Object Inspector in the Lazarus IDE. The main published properties that determine position and size are the following:

Property	Description
Top, Left	These properties determine the control's position. They are always given relative to the parent control's client-area top-left corner, and are measured in pixels.
Width, Height	These properties determine the control's size in pixels. They must be positive, and can be larger than the boundaries the parent control allows for. What happens if such oversize values are set depends on the parent control.
Align	This property can be used to align the control along one of the borders of the parent control. The default value alNone disables this feature.
Anchors	This property aligns some of the borders of the control with the borders of the parent control (by default), or aligns it with the borders of any other control on the form. When the parent control is resized, or the linked control is moved or resized, the current control's anchors cause it to be moved or resized as well.
AutoSize	This property tells the control to resize itself so that all its contents fit within it.
OnResize	This event can be used to take action when the control is resized. You use this to do manual resizing if the other properties are not flexible enough to do the resizing. For instance, in the case of a grid, this event can be used to rescale the columns so that they always take up the full width of the grid.
BorderSpacing	This is the amount of space (in pixels) that will separate the control from the other controls it is anchored to.
Constraints	This determines the minimum and maximum size a control may have when resizing.

Table 6.29: The most important layout properties of TConttol

The following public properties also can be used in code:
BoundsRect is a *TRect* record which defines the contours of the control. It can be used to set the *Top, Left, Width* and *Height* in one call, instead of four separate calls.
ClientRect is the area available for child controls. It does not include the border of the control. For a form with a main menu, the *ClientRect* starts just below the menu.
AnchorSides. These properties determine the controls that the current control is anchored to.

Manual resizing
Doing manual resizing is a tedious task, but sometimes there is no other way.
Manual resizing can be demonstrated easily using a simple form containing a memo, which we want to always keep its borders at the same distance from the form's borders (i.e. it grows and shrinks with the form). Its Close button should always stay in the lower-right corner of the form, and it should keep its designed size.
It looks like Figure 6.21.

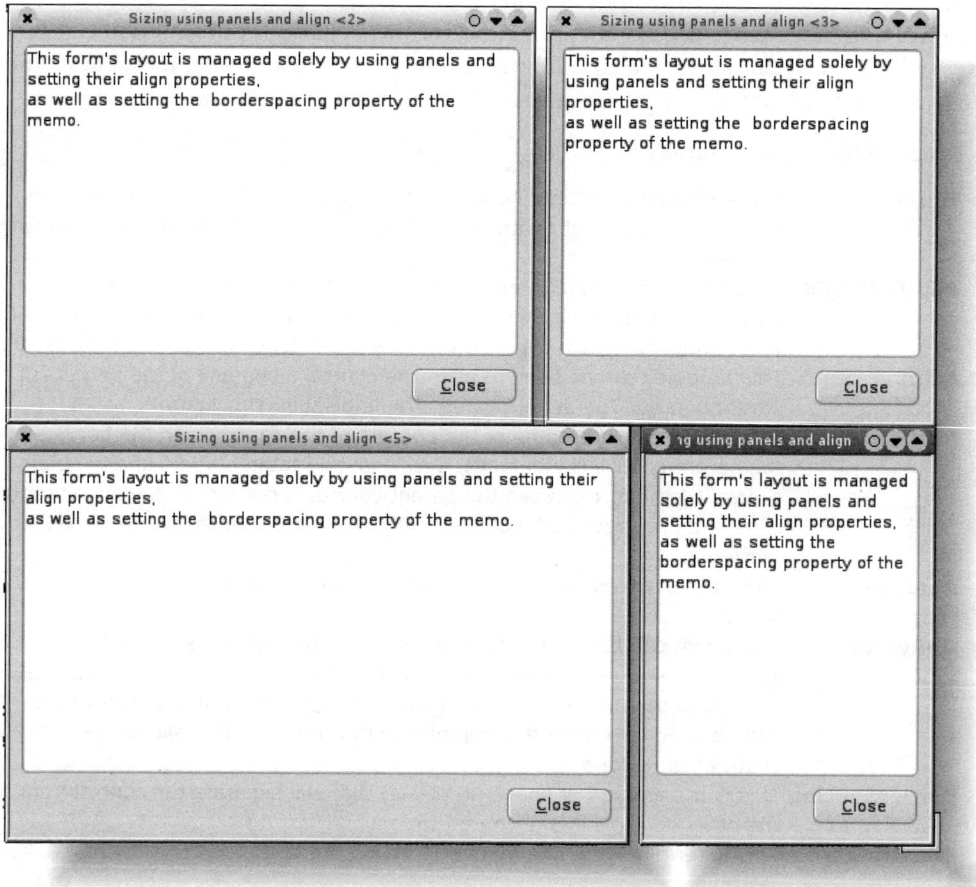

Figure 6.21: Manual sizing, 4 instances of the same window with different sizes

To achieve this layout manually, it's necessary to determine the offsets for the button position relative to the lower and right borders of the form, and the offsets of the memo's right and lower sides relative to the form's lower right border.
These distances are determined in the *OnCreate* event of the form:

```
procedure TMainForm.FormCreate(Sender: Tobject);
begin
  MHDiff := ClientHeight-MSize.Height;
  MWDiff := ClientWidth-MSize.Width;
  BTOff := ClientHeight-BCLose.Top;
  BLOff := ClientWidth-BClose.Left;
end;
```

The button is called BClose, the memo is called MSize. *ClientWidth* and *ClientHeight* are the width and height of the form, available to controls within the form. The four variables *MHDiff*, *MWDiff*, *BTOff* and *BLOff* can now be used in the form's *OnResize* event:

```
procedure TMainForm.FormResize(Sender: Tobject);
begin
  Msize.Height := ClientHeight-MHDiff;
  Msize.Width := ClientWidth-MWDiff;
  Bclose.Top := ClientHeight-BTOff;
  Bclose.Left := ClientWidth-BLoff;
end;
```

As you can see, it's not so hard to do this. But obviously if there are a lot of controls on the form, the code will get much more complicated and be tedious to maintain. Fortunately, there are other ways of doing this.

Sizing using Align

The *Align* property is useful for resizing as well as aligning. It's limited in its scope, but can be used in many cases, and you can often arrange quite complex layouts using only this property. The *Align* property can have the following values:

Constant	Function
alNone	No alignment is done. The control keeps its designed position.
alTop	The control is always glued to the top edge of its parent. This means that its height remains constant, but its width follows the width of the parent control.
alBottom	The control is always glued to the bottom edge of its parent. This means that its height remains constant, but its width follows the width of the parent control.
alLeft	The control is always glued to the left edge of its parent. The width property is kept constant, but its height follows the height of the parent control.
alRight	The control is always glued to the right edge of its parent. The width property is kept constant, but its height follows the height of the parent control.
alClient	The control resizes to fill the space available in its parent.
alCustom	[*Unused currently*]

Table 6.30: Available Alignment values

Note that several controls can have e.g. their *Align* property set to *alTop* simultaneously. Where this happens the first control is glued to the top edge of the parent control, the second is glued to the first control's bottom: they are stacked up to the top edge of the parent control.

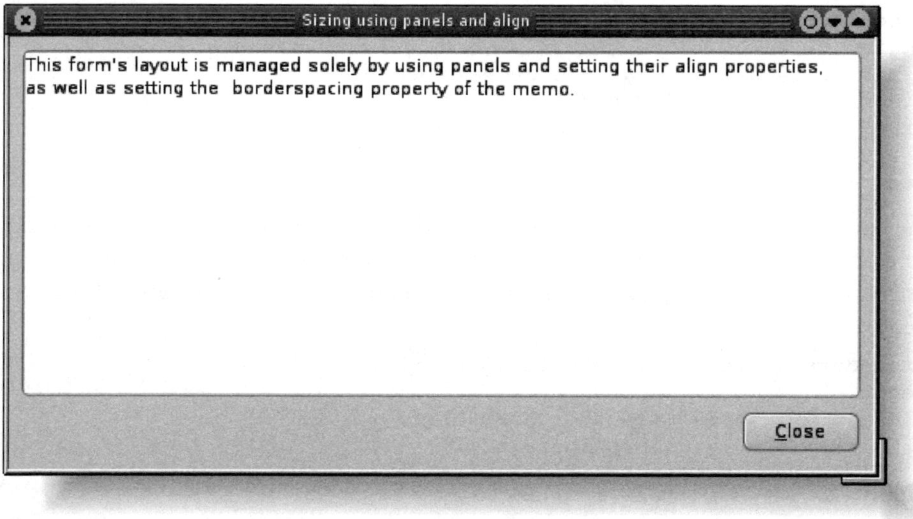

Figure 6.22: The AlignSize project

The Figure above shows a memo which grows or shrinks as the form grows and shrinks, and the button remains positioned in the bottom-right corner. You can create this form in the Designer as follows:

- Add a panel PButtons. Set *Align* to *alBottom*. Set *BevelInner* and *BevelOuter* to *bvNone*.
- Drop a second panel, PClose onto PButtons, setting its *Align* property to *alRight* and setting *BevelInner* and *BevelOuter* to *bvNone*.
- On the PClose panel, drop the BClose button.
- Add a Msize memo to the form, with its *Align* property set to *alClient*, and *BorderSpacing.Around* set to 8.
- Resize PClose and BClose so the Close button is right-aligned with the memo.

Now, when you resize the form it behaves identically to the earlier form where layouting was coded manually. Layouting using this technique is quick and easy, but it also has some drawbacks: *TPanel* is a windowed control so it takes extra resources; and since it can receive focus, it disturbs the tab order of the other controls (unless you set its *TabStop* to False), so it should be used sparingly. Luckily, the *LCL* provides other means to make the form resize correctly.

Sizing with anchors

Anchors are a powerful mechanism for automatic control resizing. To the anchor concept present in Delphi's VCL, Lazarus adds additional anchor functionality. *LCL* anchors can anchor controls not only to their parent, but also to neighbouring controls.
Anchoring is done through the *Anchors* property, which is a set with the following possible values:

akTop The control's top edge remains at the same distance from the parent control's top edge.

akLeft The control's left edge remains at the same distance from the parent control's left edge.

akRight The control's right edge remains at the same distance from the parent control's right edge.
If needed, the control is resized horizontally to achieve this.

akBottom The control's bottom edge remains at the same distance from the parent control's bottom edge. If needed, the control is resized vertically to achieve this.

The default Anchors set is `[akTop,akLeft]` which means that the control simply keeps its current position and size. Setting a TEdit's Anchors property to `[akTop,akLeft,akRight]` will make it keep its position, but it will grow and shrink so it always keeps the same distance from the form's right edge.
The earlier example with the memo and button can be reworked using only the controls' Anchors properties. It is sufficient to set the memo's anchors to `[akTop,akLeft,akRight,akBottom]` this ensures that all edges of the memo keep the same distance from the corresponding edges of the form. The button's *Anchors* property is set to `[akRight,akBottom]`, which ensures that it remains at the same position relative to the bottom-right corner of the form.

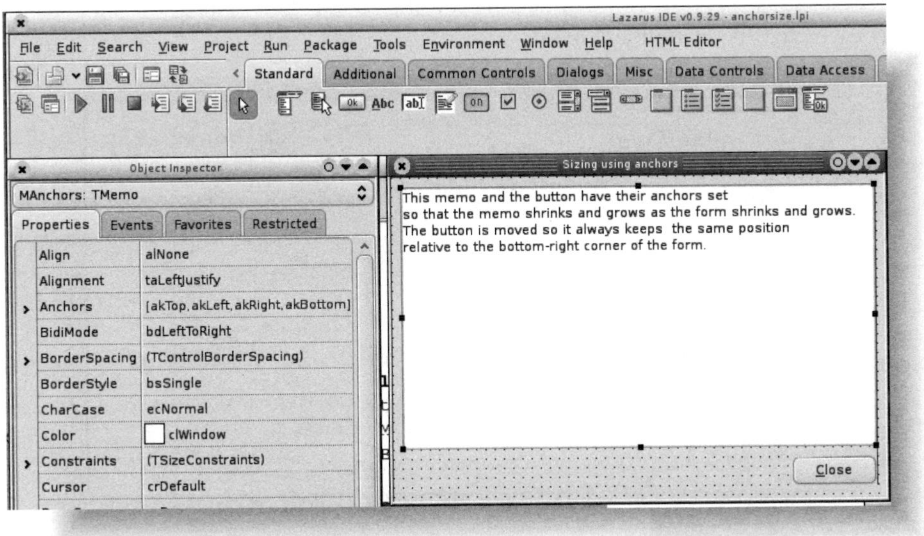

Figure 6.23: Anchor settings keeping a memo aligned correctly

6.3.8 Layout and design

Lazarus offers additional possibilities using anchors. It is possible to anchor controls to each other, specifying the separation distance between the controls. This is handy for more complex layouts. Imagine an edit control with a label beside it. The label may change size as its caption changes (for example when it is translated). The edit control should then be repositioned, so it keeps the same distance from its label.
This is demonstrated in the 'anchors' project which contains a label and two edits, one of which is at the same top position as the label, as you can see in Figure 6.24.

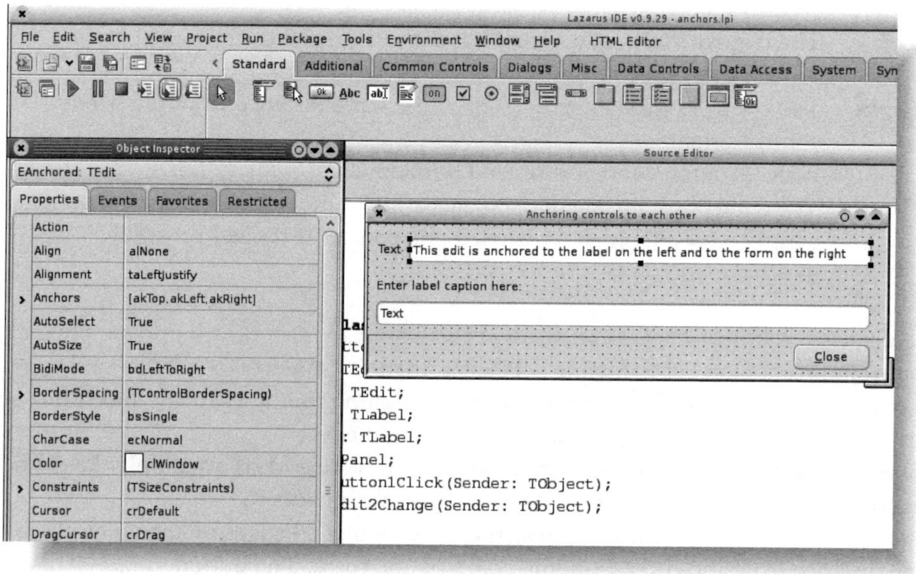

Figure 6.24: Anchoring one control to another

The text in the second edit is copied in the *OnChange* event to the label's Caption.
The first edit's *Anchors* property can be edited using the property editor of the *Anchors* property, which looks like Figure 6.25:

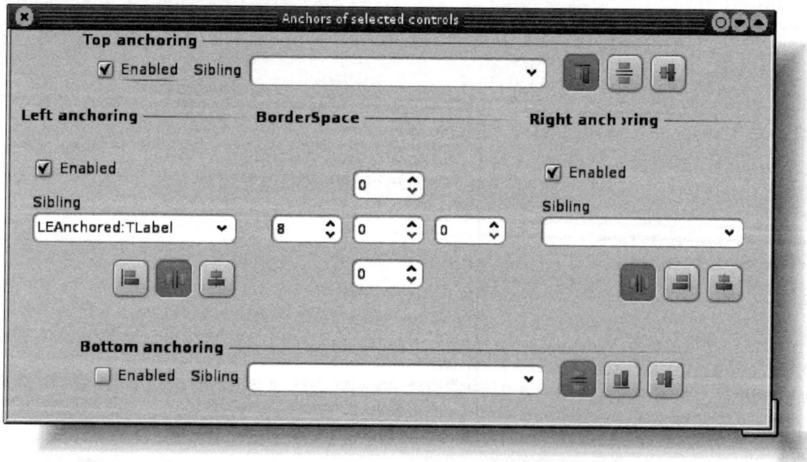

Figure 6.25: The Anchors editor

As can be seen in the screenshot, the top, left and right anchors have been set.
The top and right anchors have no sibling set. This means that they are anchored to the parent control, in this case the form. The left anchor has the sibling control set to the *LEAnchored* label. The middle *speedbutton* is depressed, which means that the edit control is anchored to the right side of the label. It could also have been anchored to its left side, or to its centre.
When you close the dialog and run the project you can see the effect of these anchor settings by typing in the second edit below which changes the label's caption.
Since the label's *Autosize* property is set to True, the label will change its size, and the first edit control is resized to keep the same separation from the label. The right edge of the edit remains at a constant distance from the form's border.
It should be clear that this mechanism allows for some very complex layouting to be set up. Nearly all situations can be catered for with this mechanism.
Besides the *Anchors* property, the dialog also sets the *BorderSpacing* property.
This property specifies the separation from other controls, plus an overall distance to be kept. Additionally, the *AnchorSides* property is set. This is an unpublished property, and cannot be manipulated in the Object Inspector. *AnchorSides* maintains the links to the neighbouring controls (the siblings of Figure 6.25) and the anchor 'sides' (represented by the three speedbuttons).

Layouting using ChildSizing

Although the *LCL* primarily uses a fixed-position layouting strategy, it does offer a way to arrange controls in a grid-like fashion, keeping the controls in the cells of a grid which resizes as the control is resized. This is accomplished using the *ChildSizing* property of some controls. This property is of type *TControlChildSizing*, a *TPersistent* descendant, which has two main properties. The first is *Layout*. This determines how the controls are positioned in the grid. It can take the following values:

Value	Effect
cclNone	Which means no rearranging is done: the controls are left at their designed location. This is the default, and amounts to no sizing at all.
cclLeftToRightThenTopToBottom	Which means that the controls are grouped in horizontal lines, starting at the left, filling the lines, and then continuing on the next line once that line is full.
cclTopToBottomThenLeftToRight	Which does the same as the previous value except the lines run from top to bottom.

Table 6.31: Available layout values

The second property of *TControlChildSizing* is *ControlsPerLine* which is the number of controls that are grouped per line.

The controls are grouped with space between them. The amount of space between the controls is controlled by the following four integer properties:

Value	Effect
LeftRightSpacing	The amount of space between the first control on a line and the left border.
TopBottomSpacing	The amount of space between the first control and the top border.
HorizontalSpacing	The amount of horizontal space between the controls.
VerticalSpacing	The amount of vertical space between the controls. When the control is resized, it can be told to resize or to reposition the controls it contains. The behaviour is controlled by the following four properties:
EnlargeHorizontal	What to do in the horizontal direction when the control is enlarged.
EnlargeVertical	What to do in the vertical direction when the control is enlarged.
ShrinkHorizontal	What to do in the horizontal direction, when the controls becomes too small to contain their contents.
ShrinkVertical	What to do in the vertical direction, when the controls becomes too small to contain their contents.

Table 6.32: Available ChildSizing values

These four properties are of the same type: *TChildControlResizeStyle*. This enumeration type has the following four values:

Value	Effect
crsAnchorAligning	This just maintains the controls' positions and sizes (as in Delphi).
crsScaleChilds	This will scale child controls, and keeps the amount of space between the children constant.
crsHomogenousChildGrowth	This will enlarge each child control equally so each child gets the same number of pixels added to its dimensions.
crsHomogenousSpaceGrowth	This will enlarge the space between child controls equally so each space has the same number of pixels added.

Table 6.33: Available TChildControlResizeStyle values

Note that this mechanism does not make use of any underlying widget set properties. The resizing and repositioning is done completely by the *LCL*, and hence is available on all supported platforms, even if the underlying widget set does not support it natively.

User controlled layout with splitters

The layout control explained in the previous sections is geared only towards the user changing the size of the containing form on which controls are positioned.
What if the user wants to change the relative sizes of the controls?

For instance, in an email-reading application the list of emails and the details of each email are often displayed in the same window. The user can resize the list and the details of the mail by dragging the divider between the two controls – this divider is known as a *splitter*.

6.3.8 Layout and design

Lazarus offers two kinds of splitters:

- *TSplitter:* This splitter 'sticks' to one of the controls on the form, and can be used to resize this control. The remaining controls should be able to resize themselves (usually by having their Align property set to alClient).
- *TPairSplitter:* This control acts as a panel divided into two sub-panels, joined by a simple *TSplitter* component. You can drop controls onto the two panels, and moving the TPairSplitter's central 'grip' will resize the two sub-panels, and the controls they contain.

The *TSplitter* component should always be used with two adjacent controls of which one has its *Align* property set to *alClient.* The other control should have its *Align* property set to one of *alTop, alBottom, alLeft* or *alRight.*

The *TSplitter* control should have its own *Align* property set to the same value as the second control. As a result, it will stick to one of the borders of that control, and when the user drags the splitter, the control will be resized. Since the first control has its *Align* property set to *alClient,* it will resize and take up the remaining space.

This can be demonstrated in a window of an email reading application:
Such a window contains a listbox, aligned left, and a *splitter* (SPDemo) which is also aligned left. The rest of the window is occupied by a memo which has its *Align* property set to *alClient.* The listbox would represent a list of emails, and the memo could display the contents of the currently selected email.

The *splitter* control has some properties that control its appearance and behaviour. They are listed in the following table:

Property	Description
AutoSnap	If set to True, then the splitter will hide the control if its size becomes smaller than MinSize. If not, MinSize becomes the minimum allowed size of the control so the splitter will not make it smaller than MinSize.
Beveled	Controls whether the splitter has a bevelled or flat appearance.
MinSize	The minimum size of the control that is being resized: the splitter will not make the control smaller than this size. If AutoSnap is True, then MinSize marks the size at which the splitter completely hides the diminishing control.
ResizeStyle	Controls how the splitter control is drawn while the user is dragging it.

Table 6.34: TSplitter properties

The email-reading application could have a menu to allow the user to change the position of the list of mails (in the listbox) and the memo with the contents of the currently selected mail. Assuming a menu item has the value of a *TAlign* value in its *Tag* property, then the following *OnClick* handler would change the location of memo and listbox:

```
procedure TMainForm.MIAlignClick(Sender: TObject);
  Const H = [alLeft,alRight];
  Var OA,Al : TAlign;
begin
  al := TAlign((Sender as TMenuItem).Tag);
  OA := SPDemo.Align;
  LBMails.Align := al;
  SPDemo.Align := al;
  If (OA in H)<>(al in H) then
   if al in H then
     LBMails.Width := SPDemo.MinSize + 1
   else
     LBMails.Height := SPDemo.MinSize + 1;
end;
```

The new value for the *Align* property is stored in the *Tag* property of the menu items. The first task is to retrieve this value, together with the current value.
Then the listbox's and the splitter's *Align* property is set to the new value.

Now, if the orientation of the splitter switches from e.g. horizontal to vertical, the control must be resized. If the alignment was *alLeft*, then switching it to e.g. *alTop* will let the listbox take up all space: the reason is that its height is equal to the whole height of the form: changing the orientation of the splitter will not change the height, but will set the width to the width of the form: as a result, the listbox will occupy the whole form! So the height must be set to something reasonable. This is done in the second part of the routine: the height is set to the minimum size + 1 (to visualize the problem, simply disable the code in the second half of the routine by commenting it out).
The email-reading application could be constructed with a *TPairSplitter* component, by dropping the *listbox* and *memo* component each in one of the panels of the *pairsplitter component,* setting their *Align* property to *alClient.*
The menu item to change the orientation of the window would then be much simpler:

```
procedure TMainForm.SplitterTypeClick(Sender: TObject);
begin
  PSDemo.SplitterType := TPairSplitterType((Sender as TMenuItem).Tag);
end;
```

The *Tag* property is used once again to specify the value for the *SplitterType* property.
In this example, the orientation can be changed without any additional code.

The demo program also contains the complex layout, created with *TPairSplitter* controls. This layout is established without the need for additional *TPanel* controls, as was needed when using simple *TSplitter* controls.

6.3.9 Actions

Any program should help the user by providing feedback about what the user can or cannot do at any moment. Providing this feedback could mean that a button should be enabled or disabled, an image on a button might be changed, or the action of a button might be changed depending on data entered by the user.
For example, the Login button in a login dialog should not be enabled before a user name has been entered, and – if a password is required – a password has been entered too. Likewise, a Save button should not be active until there is something to save: a document has been modified or some similar prerequisite condition is fulfilled.
In an event-driven application, this necessary feedback is usually provided by updating the status of the various *GUI* elements when user input changes something onscreen.

Through the appropriate event handlers, the status of a button can be set. If a lot of data (or controls) need to be monitored for changes, this can quickly become a great number of event handlers to write and maintain. Furthermore, the event handlers will most likely also be used for other things besides updating the status of other controls.
With *TActions,* the logic of checking controls and updating the state of other controls can be separated from other programming tasks. The *state* of an action is *checked* (or updated) continuously when the application is idle, i.e. when the user is not doing anything. This avoids the need for event handlers in each control that has to be checked for its state. Instead one event handler now checks all controls at regular intervals.

Most applications provide several means of performing the same task: saving a document can be done using a menu entry or by using a button on a toolbar.
Ideally, the menu-item and the toolbar button show the same image, the same hint, and are enabled or disabled at the same time, and quite a lot of properties or event handlers will be duplicated – although the event handlers can be shared.
Here also, actions provide a way to centralize the code. In an actionlist, all possible actions that can be performed by the user are gathered and managed.
For instance a 'Save' action, an 'Open' action, and so on. The actions can then be associated with several GUI elements: menus, toolbuttons, normal buttons or checkbuttons. As soon as the user activates one of the GUI elements, the action is executed: for some predefined actions, the action is performed by the *LCL*: for example the standard *TCutAction* will cut the current selection and copy it to the clipboard.
For other actions (the standard *TAction),* a user-defined event is called.
By using actions, the programmer is forced to define clearly what he wants the user actions for a given form to be, apart from the GUI elements that might execute this action. By grouping such actions in an *actionlist*, the programmer has an organised list of well-defined actions. With some extra coding, the user can be presented with a means of customizing how he wants his actions presented to him – how the menu is composed; how the toolbars are laid out; and even what shortcuts can be used to execute his actions.

Actionlists
Actions are *non-visible* components. They are organized in *TActionLists,* which are just design-time containers. Actions have a series of properties, which correspond to properties often found in visual controls:

Property	Meaning
Caption	The text displayed on the control.
Checked	For menus, toolbar-buttons or speedbuttons and checkboxes: whether the item appears checked.
Enabled	If the control is enabled or not.
GroupIndex	For menu items, checkbuttons or radiobuttons: the group.
HelpContext, HelpKeyword and HelpType	The various help possibilities.
Hint	The hint displayed in the tooltip.
ImageIndex	The ImageIndex in the imagelist associated with the control (or actionlist).
ShortCut, SecondaryShortCuts	Shortcut keys associated with the action. The action can be executed. using one of the shortcuts.
Visible	Is the control visible or not?
OnHint	An event handler to retrieve the hint for the control.
OnExecute	This handler is executed when the action is activated and needs to execute itself.
OnUpdate	This handler is executed in the idle loop of the application: it can be used to update the status of the action depending on the current state of the form.

Table 6.35 Properties of the TAction Class

As soon as an action is associated with a control – such a control is called a client of the action – the relevant properties are copied to the control. If any of the properties has changed, the change is instantly propagated to the client controls.

At least the following controls can be action clients: *TForm, TButton, TCheckBox, TRadioButton, TToolButton, TSpeedButton, TMenuItem:* all have an *Action* property.
As soon as this property is set, the control is a client of the action. In all cases, as soon as the control is clicked, the corresponding action is executed, which means its *OnExecute* event is executed. Some standard actions perform various well-defined actions (copy/cut to clipboard, and so on), and do not need an event handler, although one can be specified.

When an action is executed, the following chain of events takes place:
1. The actionlist of which the action is part is asked to handle the action.
2. If the actionlist does not handle the action, the application is asked to handle the action.
3. If the application does not handle the action, the action tries to execute itself – typically this means it executes its *OnExecute* event.

By default, an action disables itself if it cannot execute itself, so if no *OnExecute* event is set it is disabled.

Creating new actions

By default, a new action is of type *TAction* and it is an all-purpose action: its specific functionality is provided through event handlers such as *OnUpdate* and *OnExecute.* You can, however, make use of various predefined action classes which execute well-defined procedures.

Lazarus provides many predefined *TAction* classes inluding:

Group	Effect
Editing	Mostly actions which interact with an edit control: Cut, Copy and Paste the selection, Select the entire text, Undo and Delete.
Help	Actions to invoke a help system.
Dialog	Actions to open font and colour dialogs.
File	Actions designed for a file menu, such as Open and Save.
Database	Actions acting on a *TDataset* instance (or a *TDatasource*): navigation commands, Edit, Post, Cancel and Delete. For all other actions, either a standard *TAction* can be used, or you can program your own action class and register it in the IDE.

Table 6.36: Standard action classes in Lazarus

Programming a custom action is very easy. You need to override just three methods. To demonstrate this, a simple action which clears an edit control will be programmed:

```
TClearAction = Class(TAction)
Public
  function  HandlesTarget(Target: TObject): Boolean; override;
  procedure UpdateTarget(Target: TObject); override;
  procedure ExecuteTarget(Target: TObject); override;
end;
```

The first method to be programmed is the *HandlesTarget method.* When updating or executing an action, the target of the action is first determined. This is done by passing a series of controls to the *HandlesTarget method.* The following controls are passed:

1. The currently focused control.
2. The current form.
3. All visible controls on the form.

As soon as an appropriate target is found, the search stops. After a target is found, the *UpdateTarget* or *ExecuteTarget* method is executed. When updating, if no valid target is found, the action is disabled if the *DisableIfNoHandler* property is True (which is the default value for *Taction).*

So, for the *TClearAction,* the *HandlesTarget* should check whether the target is a custom edit, and whether it has focus. This can be done with the following code:

```
function TClearAction.HandlesTarget(Target: TObject): Boolean;
begin
 Result := (Target is TCustomEdit) and (TCustomEdit(Target).Focused)
end;
```

If no target is found, the action will be disabled. If a target is found, it is still possible to give feedback to the user. In the case of the clear action, the edit control should contain some text. If no text is present, the action should be disabled:

```
procedure TClearAction.UpdateTarget(Target: TObject);
begin
 Enabled:=(TCustomEdit(Target).Text<>'')
end;
```

Lastly, when the action is executed, the ExecuteTarget method is called, which should clear the edit control. This can be done as follows:

```
procedure TClearAction.ExecuteTarget(Target: TObject);
begin
 If (Target is TCustomEdit) then
  (Target as TCustomEdit).Clear;
end;
```

The check to see whether Target is really a *TCustomEdit* is normally not needed, since HandlesTarget should have verified this before the Execute method is called.
To register the action in the IDE, a call to RegisterActions can be inserted in the Lazarus package. This should look like the following call:

```
RegisterActions('Edit',[TClearAction],Nil);
```

The first parameter is the category in the Action List Editor. The second is a list of action classes you want to register (just one in the above example), and the last parameter is a resource component which can contain resources such as images, associated with the classes. This will not be discussed in this article. Instead, the demo program will create the action at runtime.
In the example program, several buttons are dropped on a form, as well as a speedbutton, an edit and a memo control. In the *OnCreate* handler of the form, the action is created:

```
procedure TMainForm.FormCreate(Sender: TObject);
begin
  Aclear := TClearAction.Create(Self);
  AClear.Caption := '&Clear';
  AClear.ActionList := ALTest;
  SBClear.Action := AClear;
end;
```

The action is assigned to the speedbutton *SBClear*. The reason for making it a speedbutton (and not a regular button) is that a speedbutton does not receive focus when it is clicked. If it were a regular button, the action would never be executed: at the moment of the click, the *HandleTarget* would always return False, since the button would have focus, and therefore the action would never be executed.
When the demo application is run, it should look like Figure 6.26.

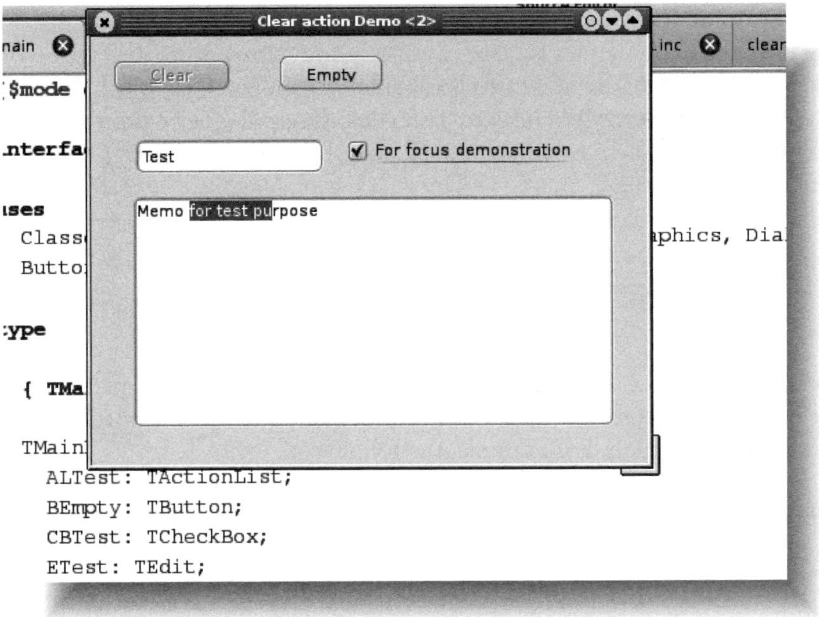

Figure 6.26: The custom action at work

The button is enabled only when the focus is on the edit or memo control, and contains text.

6.3.10 Drag and drop

Drag and Drop of objects and files is common practice in a GUI environment. Obviously, Lazarus needs to support drag and drop completely. Before explaining how to implement drag and drop, it is necessary to make a distinction between two kinds of drag and drop.

The first kind is when the user drags and drops an object within the application. For instance, dragging selected text to a new location; or dragging items from one list to another.
This kind of drag and drop must be explicitly enabled and programmed.

The second kind is when a user drops files on an application from a filemanager – with the intention that the application should open the dropped files. This kind of drag and drop is also supported, but is handled differently when compared to the first kind. Both sorts are treated below.

Drag and Drop of files

Handling drag and drop of files is quite easy. Only two *TForm* properties are involved. Firstly you must indicate that the form is capable of handling files, which is done using the *AllowDropFiles* property. When set to True, this allows files to be dropped on the form. (When dragging files, the cursor will change shape to indicate this). Once the files have been dropped on the form, the *OnDropFiles* event is invoked. It creates an event handler like this:

```
procedure TMainForm.FormDropFiles(Sender: TObject; const FileNames:
      array of String);
begin
end;
```

The *FileNames* parameter is an array of strings, which contains the full pathnames of the files that were dropped on the form. What is to be done with the dropped filenames depends on the application. For example, the following:

```
procedure TMainForm.FormDropFiles(Sender: TObject; const FileNames:
      array of String);
  Var I : Integer;
begin
  // High(Filenames) is the last element in the open array.
  For I:= 0 to High(FileNames) do
  begin
    NewEditor(FileNames[i]);
  end;
end;
```

In the above code, the *FileNames* array is traversed, and for each file, a new editor is opened. That is all there is to drag and drop of files.

Drag and Drop of objects

Lazarus also provides for drag and drop of objects, and it is not much harder to program than file drag and drop. Slightly more properties are involved, though:

Event/property	Use
DragMode	If set to *dmAutomatic*, then a drag and drop operation is started as soon as the user drags the mouse over the control. If set to *dmManual*, then a drag and drop operation must be started with *StartDrag*.
OnStartDrag	The event called when a drag and drop operation is started.
OnDragOver	The event called when something is dragged over the control. It should be used to indicate whether the item can be dropped on this control.
OnDragDrop	The event called when something is dropped on the control.
DragCursor	The cursor to use when dragging.
DragKind	Should be set to *dkDrag* (since *dkDock* is an entirely different operation).

Table 6.37: Events and Properties used in Drag and Drop

6.3.10 Drag and drop

To demonstrate these properties and events, a small application can be designed This technique is often used for selection of a couple of values from a list of possibilities. Moving the items between the listboxes can be done using buttons, or alternatively by using drag and drop. The listbox items can also be re-ordered, again using drag and drop.

The two listboxes are named *LBLeft* and *LBRight.* Both have their *DragMode* property set to True.

For this simple example, the listboxes do not need an *OnStartDrag* event.
The *OnDragOver* event of the *LBLeft* listbox should be coded as follows:

```
procedure TMainForm.LBLeftDragOver(Sender, Source: TObject; X, Y:
  Integer; State: TDragState; var Accept: Boolean);
begin
  Accept := (Source=LBLeft) or (Source=LBRight);
end;
```

The Sender parameter is the control that triggered the event *(LBLeft* in this case).
By default, the Source parameter is the control that initiated the drag and drop operation. The X,Y parameters can be used to determine exactly where over the Sender control the mouse is moving.

The above code tells the *LCL* that a drop on the *LBLeft* listbox is allowed if the drag was started by the *LBLeft* or *LBRight* list.

The same code is made for the *LBRight* listbox:

```
procedure TMainForm.LBRightDragOver(Sender, Source: TObject; X, Y:
  Integer; State: TDragState; var Accept: Boolean);
begin
  Accept := (Source = LBLeft) or (Source = LBRight);
end;
```

6.3.10 Drag and drop

When the items are dropped on the *LBLeft* or *LBRight* listboxes, the *OnDragDrop* event for these controls executes. The handlers are coded as follows:

```
procedure TMainForm.LBLeftDragDrop(Sender, Source: TObject; X, Y: Integer);
  Var LBFrom,LBTO : TListBox;
begin
  // Convert source and target
  LBFrom := (Source as TListBox);
  LBTo := (Sender as TListBox);
  If (LBTo = LBFrom) then
    MoveItemsToIndex(LBTo,LBTo.GetIndexAtXY(X,Y))
  else
    MoveItemsToListBox(LBTo,LBFrom,LBTo.GetIndexAtXY(X,Y));
end;

procedure TMainForm.LBRightDragDrop(Sender, Source: TObject; X, Y:Integer);
  Var LBFrom,LBTO : TListBox;
begin
  // Convert source and target
  LBFrom := (Source as TListBox);
  LBTo := (Sender as TListBox);
  // Do what is necessary
  If (LBTo = LBFrom) then
    MoveItemsToIndex(LBTo,LBTo.GetIndexAtXY(X,Y))
  else
    MoveItemsToListBox(LBTo,LBFrom,LBTo.GetIndexAtXY(X,Y));
end;
```

First, the source and target are determined. If the source and target are the same, it means the user is re-ordering the items in a listbox. If the source and target are different, the user is moving items from one listbox to another. The moving of the items from one location to the other is handled in the two following procedures:

```
procedure TMainForm.MoveItemsToIndex(LB : TListBox; Newindex : Integer);
  Var  L : TStringList; I : Integer;
begin
  LB.Items.BeginUpdate; // reduce flicker during multiple operations.
  try
    // Temporary list for the selected objects.
    L:=TStringList.Create;
    try
      For I := LB.Count - 1 downto 0 do
        If LB.Selected[I] then
        begin
          // Save in temporary list
          L.AddObject(LB.Items[i],LB.Items.Objects[i]);
          // Delete in source
          LB.Items.Delete(I);
          // Correct index
          If I <= NewIndex then
            Dec(NewIndex);
        end;
      For I := 0 to L.Count - 1 do
        LB.Items.InsertObject(NewIndex,L[i],L.Objects[i]);
    finally
      L.Free; // free temporary list.
    end;
  finally
    LB.Items.EndUpdate; // Tell control it's time to update.
  end;
end;

procedure TMainForm.MoveItemsToListBox(LBTo,LBFrom : TListBox; Newinde:Integer);
  Var  I : integer;
begin
  // Add per default at the start.
  If NewIndex = -1 then
    NewIndex := 0;
  // Reduce flicker
  LBFrom.Items.BeginUpdate;
  try
    LBTo.Items.BeginUpdate;
    try
      // The items from source are processed in reverse order
      // So they appear in correct order in the target list.
      For I := LBFrom.Count - 1 downto 0 do
        If LBFrom.Selected[I] then
        begin
        LBTo.Items.InsertObject(Newindex,LBFrom.Items[i],LBFrom.Items.Objects[i]);
        LBFrom.Items.Delete(I);
        end;
    finally
      LBTo.Items.EndUpdate;
    end;
  finally
    LBFrom.Items.EndUpdate;
  end;
end;
```

To complete the program, the listboxes are filled with some dummy items in the *OnCreate* event of the form:

```
procedure TMainForm.FormCreate(Sender: TObject);
  Var I : Integer;
begin
 For I:= 1 to 10 do
  LBleft.Items.add('Item numbered ' + IntToStr(i));
 For I:= Ord('A') to Ord('J') do
  LBRight.Items.add('Item labeled ' + Char(i));
end;
```

As you can see, the handling of the drag and drop can be done with quite simple code. The difficult routines are the routines that do the actual moving of the lines.
The screenshot below shows the program in action:

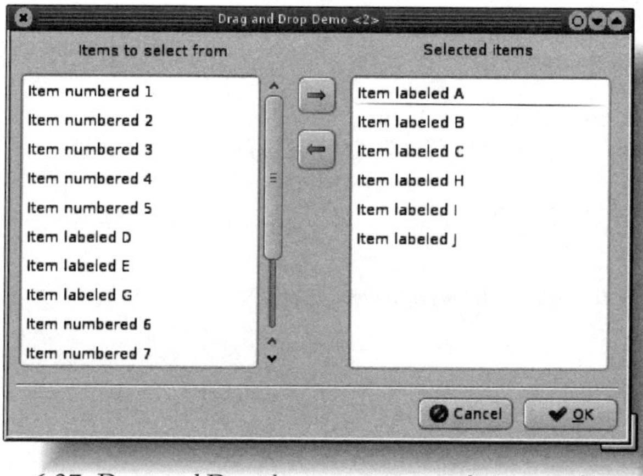

Figure 6.27: Drag and Drop between two controls in a single window

Creating custom drag objects

In the above code, the listbox checked whether a drop operation was allowed by checking the Source parameter directly. If the Source was the listbox control itself or the other listbox control on the form, the drop was allowed. If there are more than two source controls to allow, then this checking code will quickly grow. Also, what if the source control is located on another form? How can this be checked?
The drag and drop operation is represented internally in the *LCL* using a *TDragObject* class. This class is not used overtly, nor is it visible in the simple examples of the previous section, where its operation happens in the background. To address the more complex scenarios mentioned above, the *LCL* allows the programmer to create a custom *TDragObject* when the drag operation is started. This object is then used for the Source parameter of the *OnDragOver* and *OnDragDrop* events, instead of the control that started the drag operation.
To demonstrate this, the simple example can be changed slightly:
the main form of the application will contain only a listbox together with three buttons to create.

From each of these secondary forms, the user will be able to drag items to the listbox on the main form. In such a setup, the main form does not have a direct way to check where a drag operation was initiated.
The main form will be called *TMainForm,* and the secondary forms *TListboxForm, TMemoForm* and *TListviewForm.* The three buttons on the main form simply create new instances of the appropriate secondary form:

```
procedure TMainForm.BListBoxWindowClick(Sender: TObject);
begin
  With TListBoxForm.Create(Self) do Show;
end;

procedure TMainForm.BMemoWindowClick(Sender: TObject);
begin
  With TMemoForm.Create(Self) do Show;
end;

procedure TMainForm.BShowListviewClick(Sender: TObject);
begin
  With TListViewForm.Create(Self) do Show;
end;
```

Each of the forms, when created, first sets the caption of the form to a unique text (the number of times the form was created) so the user can identify each new form. Then it populates the control it has, with various items.
For *TMemoForm*, the code looks like the following:

```
procedure TMemoForm.FormCreate(Sender: TObject);
begin
  Inc(ThisFormCount);
  Caption := 'Memo form number ' + IntToStr(ThisFormCount);
  PopulateList(MText.Lines);
end;
```

MText is the memo control dropped on *TMemoForm.* The PopulateList call is implemented in the dragdroplist unit, and it simply adds a random number of items to a stringlist:

```
  Var Loffset : Integer;

Procedure PopulateList(List : TStrings);
  Var I,M : Integer;
begin
  M := 15 + Random(10);
  For I := 1 to M do
    List.Add('Item no '+ IntToStr(I + LOffset));
  Loffset := Loffset + M;
end;

procedure TListBoxForm.FormCreate(Sender: TObject);
begin
  Inc(ThisFormCount);
  Caption := 'Listbox form number ' + IntToStr(ThisFormCount);
  PopulateList(LBItems.Items);
end;
```

Similar code is executed for the *TListboxForm* and *TListviewForm:*

```
procedure TListviewForm.FormCreate(Sender: TObject);
  Var L : Tstrings;
      I : Integer;
begin
   Inc(ThisFormCount);
   Caption := 'Listview form number ' + IntToStr(ThisFormCount);
   L := TStringList.Create;
   try
     PopulateList(L);
     For I := 0 to L.Count-1 do
       LVItems.Items.Add.Caption := L[i];
   finally
     L.Free;
   end;
end;
```

Now, the *TMemo, TListView* or *TListBox* controls need somehow to communicate to the main form's listbox control which items are being dragged.
Therefore, we create a descendant of *TDragObjectEx* to contain the dragged items:

```
TStringsDragObject = Class(TDragObjectEx)
private
  FItems: Tstrings;
  procedure SetItems(const AValue: Tstrings);
Public
  Constructor Create(AControl : TControl); override;
  Destructor Destroy; override;
  property Items : Tstrings Read FItems Write SetItems;
end;
```

The class descends from *TDragObjectEx,* because then the *LCL* will automatically free this object when the drag and drop operation finishes.
The methods do nothing spectacular:

```
procedure TStringsDragObject.SetItems(const AValue: Tstrings);
begin
  if Fitems = AValue then exit;
  FItems.Assign(AValue);
end;

constructor TStringsDragObject.Create(AControl : TControl);
begin
  inherited Create(AControl);
  Fitems := TStringList.Create;
end;

destructor TStringsDragObject.Destroy;
begin
  FreeAndNil(FItems);
  inherited Destroy;
end;
```

Most of this is memory management: making sure the list of items is correctly filled and freed when the object is destroyed.
This object can now be created in the *OnStartDrag* object of the *listview*, *listbox* and *memo* controls of the secondary forms. For the ListBoxForm, the following code is needed:

```
procedure TListBoxForm.LBItemsStartDrag(Sender: TObject;
                                  var DragObject: TDragObject);
  Var SDO : TStringsDragObject;
      I : Integer;
begin
  SDO := TStringsDragObject.Create(LBItems);
  For I := 0 to LBItems.Count - 1 do
    If LBItems.Selected[i] then
      SDO.Items.Add(LBItems.Items[i]);
  DragObject := SDO;
end;
```

The *TStringDragObject* class is created, and its *Items* property is filled with the selected items from the listbox, and finally it is returned in the *DragObject* parameter.
The code for *TMemoForm* is even simpler:

```
procedure TMemoForm.MTextStartDrag(Sender: TObject;
                              var DragObject: TDragObject);
Var SDO : TStringsDragObject;
begin
  SDO := TStringsDragObject.Create(MText);
  SDO.Items.Text := MText.SelText;
  DragObject := SDO;
end;
```

The code for *TListViewForm* is closer to that of the *TListboxForm's* handler:

```
procedure TListviewForm.LVItemsStartDrag(Sender: TObject;
                                  var DragObject: TDragObject);
  Var SDO : TStringsDragObject;
      I : Integer;
begin
  SDO := TStringsDragObject.Create(LVItems);
  For I := 0 to LVItems.Items.Count - 1 do
    If LVItems.Items[i].Selected then
      SDO.Items.Add(LVItems.Items[i].Caption);
  DragObject := SDO;
end;
```

Everything is now ready for dropping the items on the main form's listbox.
The *OnDragOver* event of the main listbox should look like this:

```
procedure TMainForm.LBMainDragOver(Sender, Source: Tobject;
            X, Y: Integer; State: TDragState; var Accept: Boolean);
begin
  Accept := Source is TStringsDragObject;
end;
```

The main form's listbox will only accept a drop if the source is a *TStringsDragObject* instance. If the drop is accepted, then the following code will be executed if the user drops the items:

```
procedure TMainForm.LBMainDragDrop(Sender, Source: TObject; X, Y: Integer);
  Var I,L : Integer;
      SDO : TStringsDragObject;
begin
  L := LBMain.GetIndexAtY(Y);
  If L = -1 then
  begin
    L := LBMain.Count-1;
    If L = -1 then
      L := 0;
  end;
  SDO := Source as TStringsDragObject;
  For I := SDO.Items.Count-1 downto 0 do
    LBMain.Items.Insert(L,SDO.Items[i]);
end;
```

First the location of the drop is calculated (with some safety checks) and then all items from the *TStringDragObject* are copied over to the listbox.

The application can be seen at work in Figure 6.28:

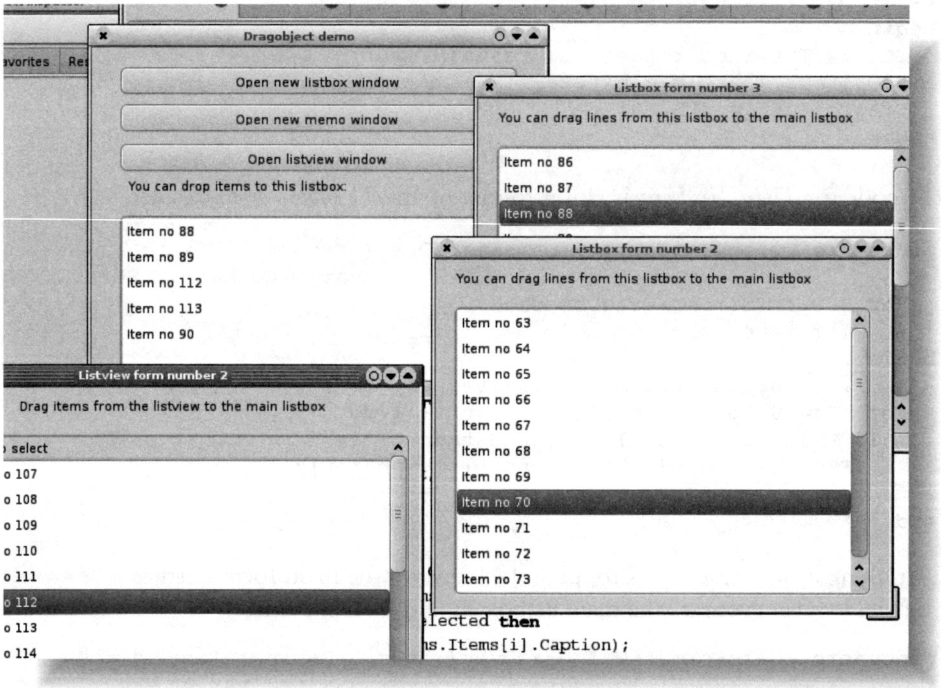

Figure 6.28: Drag and Drop between different windows in an application.

6.3.10 Drag and drop

To conclude the description of drag and drop operations, it is instructive to have a look at the drag and drop structures as they are defined in the Controls unit:

```
{ TDragObject }

TDragObject = class;

TDragKind = (dkDrag, dkDock);
TDragMode = (dmManual , dmAutomatic);
TDragState = (dsDragEnter, dsDragLeave, dsDragMove);
TDragMessage = (dmDragEnter, dmDragLeave, dmDragMove, dmDragDrop,
dmDragCancel,dmFindTarget);

TDragOverEvent = procedure(Sender, Source: TObject;
                           X,Y: Integer; State: TDragState;
                           var Accept: Boolean) of object;
TDragDropEvent = procedure(Sender, Source: TObject; X,Y: Integer) of object;
TStartDragEvent = procedure(Sender: TObject;
                           var DragObject: TDragObject) of object;
TEndDragEvent = procedure(Sender, Target: TObject; X,Y: Integer) of object;

TDragObject = class

private
public
  constructor Create(AControl: TControl); virtual;
  constructor AutoCreate(AControl: TControl);
  procedure HideDragImage; virtual;
  procedure ShowDragImage; virtual;
  property AlwaysShowDragImages: Boolean read FAlwaysShowDragImages
                                        write FAlwaysShowDragImages;
  property AutoCreated: Boolean read FAutoCreated;
  property AutoFree: Boolean read FAutoFree;
  property Control: TControl read FControl write FControl; // the dragged control
  property DragPos: TPoint read FDragPos write FDragPos;
  property DragTarget: TControl read FDragTarget write FDragTarget;
  property DragTargetPos: TPoint read FDragTargetPos write FDragTargetPos;
  property Dropped: Boolean read FDropped;
end;

TDragObjectClass = class of TDragObject;

{ TDragObjectEx }

TDragObjectEx = class(TDragObject)
public
  constructor Create(AControl: TControl); override;
end;
```

6.3.11 Drag-and-Dock

Once an application's controls have docking functionality, users can move well-defined parts of the user interface to new positions where they will remain anchored (or some parts can be closed, removing them from the interface). How the control is anchored at its new location depends on the kind of control that was moved.
Lazarus' support for drag-and-dock is similar to its support for drag-and-drop, but instead of dragging the contents of a control (such as dragging an item from a *listview* to drop it on a *treeview),* the control itself is dragged across the screen in order to be docked elsewhere. Since the techniques of drag-and-dock and drag-and-drop are similar, the preparations and starting point for programming them are also similar.

Automated Drag-and-Dock

Two properties are responsible for making a control dockable: *DragKind* and *DragMode.* The former is set to *dkDrop* by default, and for docking functionality should be set to *dkDock,* to indicate that when a drag operation starts, the control must be dragged instead of the control contents. (It is possible to provide for both drag-dropping and drag-docking, which will be explained later). *DragMode* should be set to *dmAutomatic.* This means that the LCL will automatically start a drag operation as soon as it sees that the mouse is being dragged following a click.
Using the object inspector, the above-mentioned properties can be set for a toolbar control. When the application with the toolbar runs, you will find that the toolbar can now be dragged off the main form. After the floating window where the toolbar resides has been closed, the user subsequently finds himself without any toolbar buttons.
This is a typical pitfall in programming such applications, and the problem can be easily remedied with a popup menu, or a View menu item in the main menu, in which the toolbar can be shown or hidden. Here is an event handler for such a menu item:

```
procedure TForm1.MenuItemShowToolbarClick(Sender: TObject);
begin
  TSampleToolbar.Parent:=Self;
  TSampleToolbar.Visible:=True;
end;
```

Clicking the menu item after the floating toolbar window has been closed will place the toolbar on the top of the window again. In a real application, that menu item would be disabled as long as the toolbar is visible, of course.
Docking a control is no more complicated than ripping it off the window, but it needs additional preparation. To allow docking of a control to another control, the other control must be marked as a docking site. Docking to many *TWinControl* descendants is possible, but by default controls are not dock sites. To allow docking of other controls, the target control's *DockSite* property must be set to True.
The main form itself should not be made a dock site. This would allow the user to drop a control toolbar anywhere on the form, which is most likely not the intention.
Usual locations for a toolbar are along the edges of the main window. To provide for this, four panels must be placed on the form, and aligned along the edges of the form. The *Docksite* properties of each must be set to True, and – equally important – their *AutoSize* properties must also be set to True.

This ensures the panels' size will adapt to the size of the control docked to them. Note that setting *Autosize* to True in the Lazarus object inspector causes the panels to disappear (in contrast to Delphi). This behaviour is normal in Lazarus. However to keep the panels from disappearing in the Designer, leave the *AutoSize* property set to False, and set it to True in the *OnCreate* event of the form:

```
procedure TForm1.FormCreate(Sender: TObject);
begin
 PTop.AutoSize:=True;
 PBottom.AutoSize:=True;
 PLeft.AutoSize:=True;
 PRight.AutoSize:=True;
end;
```

After these preparations, the toolbar can be dragged from one edge of the form to another. The toolbar's *Align* property must be set to match the alignment of the panel on which it is dropped. This can be done in the *OnDockDrop* event, which is executed when the control is docked on another control:

```
procedure TForm1.SetDocksiteSize(Sender: TObject;
 Source: TDragDockObject;  X,Y: Integer);

Var
 C : TControl;
begin
 C:=(Sender as TControl);
 if Source.Control is TToolbar then
 Source.Control.Align:=C.Align
 else
 Source.Control.Align:=alNone
end;
```

Other controls have their *Align* property set to *alNone,* so that they keep their natural size. Note the Source parameter to this event: it is of type *TDragDockObject,*
and describes the drag and dock operation. It has many properties, of which the following are the relevant ones for docking operations (see the listing in Table 6.38). Figure 6.29 shows the extended example.

The control which is dragged.

Property	Description
DragPos	The starting point of the drag operation.
DragTarget	The target control over which we are currently dragging.
Dockrect	A rectangle indicating the area where the control will be docked if the mouse is released.
DropAlign	The alignment to use when docking the control relative to *DropOnControl.*
DropOnControl	A control already docked to the dock site, relative to which the dragged control will be docked.
Floating	Can be used to determine whether the control is currently floating onscreen.

Table 6.38: The most important properties of TDragDockObject for docking

Figure 6.29: Toolbar docked at the bottom

When experimenting with the example dock site implementation, you will notice an annoying side-effect of the *Autosize* property: the docking rectangle (which is usually formed by the contours of the dock site), has zero width or height.
This is because the dock site has no *width* or *height* – depending on which form edge the dock site is aligned to. This annoying behaviour can be remedied manually in the *OnDockOver* event:

```
procedure TForm1.PTopDockOver(Sender: TObject;
 Source: TDragDockObject;
 X,Y: Integer;
 State: TDragState;
 var Accept: Boolean);

Var
 R : TRect;
 C : TControl;
begin
 R:=Source.DockRect;
 C:=Sender as TControl;
 If (R.Bottom-R.Top)<=1 then
 Case C.Align of
 alTop : R.Bottom:=R.Bottom+Source.Control.Height;
 alBottom: R.Top:=R.Top-Source.Control.Height;
 end
 else If (R.Right-R.Left)<=1 then
 Case C.Align of
 alLeft : R.Right:=R.Right+Source.Control.Width;
 alRight : R.Left:=R.Left-Source.Control.Width;
 end;
 Source.DockRect:=R;
end
```

The *DockRect* property of the Source object can be modified to provide feedback to the user over the area where the control will be docked. The above code simply increases the rectangle so it has a non-zero size.
When the toolbar is dragged, it has the width of the form, hence the rectangle will be increased to the size of the form when hovering over the left or right edges.
To demonstrate the effect of the above code better, a panel is dropped on the form, and made draggable by setting its *DragKind* and *DragMode* properties. When dragging the panel over one of the left or right edges, a rectangle is drawn as in figure 6.30.

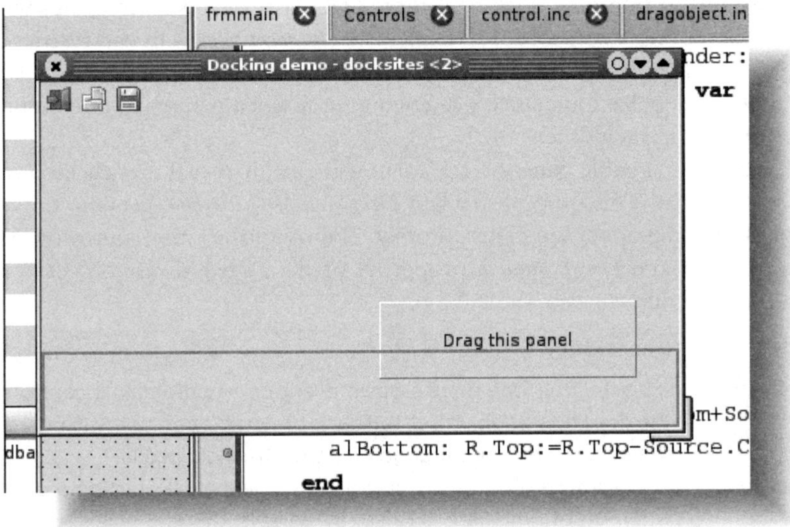

Figure 6.30: Adjusting the size of the DockRect

More detailed feedback can be given and the docking mechanism can be fine-tuned, so that the mouse must be at least 10 pixels inside the docking zone before the docking feedback is triggered (the 10-pixel value is hardcoded). This zone can be increased or decreased or even set to zero. Additionally, a dock site can be prevented from accepting panel controls. You do this in the *OnGetSiteInfo* event. This event is triggered as the control is being dragged. For the panels along the edges of the form, the event can be implemented as follows:

```
procedure TForm1.PLeftGetSiteInfo(Sender: TObject; DockClient: TControl;
 var InfluenceRect: TRect;  MousePos: TPoint;
 var CanDock: Boolean);
begin
 CanDock:=DockClient is TToolbar;
 If CanDock then
 Case (Sender as TControl).Align of
   alLeft,alRight : InflateRect(InfluenceRect,20,0);
   alBottom,alTop : InflateRect(InfluenceRect,0,20);
 end;
end
```

The *CanDock* parameter can be used to indicate that the dock site will accept the control being dragged. The *InfluenceRect* is the bounding rectangle of the dock site, increased by ten pixels. The code above adds another twenty pixels to this. If the *CanDock* parameter is True (its value on entry) and the control is dragged within the *InfluenceRect,* the docking rectangle will be shown.
Even if the *CanDock* parameter is true, and the docking rectangle is shown, it is still possible to reject the docking of the control in the *OnDockOver* event, since setting the Accept parameter of that event to False will cause the docking to be rejected.
You can use this to fine-tune docking. Where *OnGetSiteInfo* merely indicates whether a dock site is accepting a control for docking, the *OnDockOver* event can restrict the docking to certain areas of the dock site. If you work with Delphi as well as Lazarus you will recognize this behaviour, since you encounter it when you try to dock multiple tool windows on top of each other.
Playing with the draggable panel on the form will quickly reveal that clicking on the panel will cause it to float. This is because when *DragMode* is set to *dmAutomatic* the *MouseDown* event starts the drag operation. This automatic behaviour is rather annoying. You can use the *DragThreshold* and *DragImmediate* properties of the global Mouse object to remedy this automatic behaviour (see also Table 6.39).

Property	Description
DragImmediate	If set to True, the mouse-down event on any draggable control will start the drag operation. If set to False, the drag operation will only start after the mouse has been dragged for DragTreshold pixels.
DragTreshold	The distance the user must drag a mouse before starting a drag operation when DragImmediate is False. By default, this is 5 pixels.

Table 6.39: Mouse properties used in dragging

To make the panel clickable again, the following code must be placed in the form's OnCreate event:

```
procedure TForm1.FormCreate(Sender: TObject);
begin
 Mouse.DragImmediate:=False;
 Mouse.DragThreshold:=50;
end;
```

Manual Drag-and-Dock

Automatic drag-and-dock is easily programmed, but you quickly encounter its limitations. There is another mechanism by which a control can be made clickable, without tinkering with the *Mouse* object. This mechanism requires more work, but is also more powerful. To use the second mechanism, the *DragMode* property must be set to *dmManual,* which indicates that drag operations will be started manually using the *BeginDrag* method of *TControl.* This method is declared like this:

```
procedure BeginDrag(Immediate: Boolean;
                    Threshold: Integer = -1);
```

When invoked and *Immediate* is True, this method will start a drag operation.
If *Immediate* is False, then the drag operation will start after the mouse has been dragged for *Threshold* pixels. if *Threshold* is -1, then the value of Mouse.DragThreshold is used.
This method can now be used to initiate the drag operation in the *OnMouseDown* event of the panel:

```
procedure TForm1.Panel1MouseDown(Sender: TObject;
 Button: TMouseButton;
 Shift: TShiftState;
 X, Y: Integer);
begin
 If (Button=mbLeft) and (ssCtrl in Shift) then
 Panel1.BeginDrag(False,10);
end;
```

This is not very different from the case when `DragMode=dmAutomatic`.
It is therefore only worth using this method when you want to switch between a drag-and-drop operation and a drag-and-dock operation.
The following code starts a drag-and-dock operation if the [Ctrl] key is pressed while the mouse is dragged. If the [Ctrl] key is not pressed, then a drag-and-drop operation is started:

```
procedure TForm1.Panel1MouseDown(Sender: TObject;
 Button: TMouseButton;
 Shift: TShiftState;
 X, Y: Integer);
begin
 If (Button=mbLeft) then
 begin
 if (ssCtrl in Shift) then
 Panel1.DragKind:=dkDock
 else
 Panel1.DragKind:=dkDrag;
 Panel1.BeginDrag(False,10);
 end;
end;
```

Obviously, for a panel there is not much to drag and drop, but code such as the above can provide useful functionality in grids, listboxes, listviews and treeviews where the user can simply drag and drop items, or can drag and dock the control itself using the [Ctrl] key.
So far we have seen how a control can be dragged out of its form using the mouse.
We can also code this operation manually using the ManualFloat method which is declared thus:

```
function ManualFloat(TheScreenRect: TRect;
                     KeepDockSiteSize: Boolean): Boolean;
```

The *TheScreenRect* parameter is the bounding rectangle - relative to the screen - for the control when it is floating. The optional *KeepDockSiteSize* parameter determines whether the size of the current dock site should be retained (the default) or not.
You can use this method, for instance, in a panel's double-click event:

```
procedure TForm1.Panel1DblClick(Sender: TObject);

Var
  R : TRect;

begin
  R:=Panel1.BoundsRect;
  R.TopLeft:=ClientToScreen(R.TopLeft);
  R.Right:=R.Left+Panel1.Width;
  R.Bottom:=R.Top+Panel1.Height;
  Panel1.ManualFloat(R);
end;
```

Most of this code serves to calculate the size and position of the bounding rectangle for the panel, relative to the screen.
Similar to manual floating of a control, it is also possible to dock a control via code. Controls have the ManualDock method for this purpose:

```
function ManualDock(NewDockSite: TWinControl;
                    DropControl: TControl = nil;
                    ControlSide: TAlign = alNone;
                    KeepDockSiteSize: Boolean = true): Boolean;
```

The *NewDockSite* parameter contains the target docking control, and is the only required parameter of this call. The *DropControl* and *ControlSide* parameters are optional, and are used when the docking site already has some controls docked to it. These two parameters can then be used to specify the relative position of the docked control. *DropControl* is the control relative to which the new control will be placed, and *ControlSide* determines where exactly the control will be docked. These parameters correspond to the *DropOnControl* and *DropAlign* properties of the *TDragDockObject* described earlier.
Finally, the *KeepDockSiteSize* parameter can be used to specify whether the target docking control will be resized or not. By default, it will retain the size it had prior to the docking operation.

When a toolbar is made draggable, its initial location is lost as soon as it is dragged away by the user. To prevent this, the top of the form can be made into a dock zone by means of a panel aligned to the top. The toolbar can then be dropped unaligned somewhere on the form, and in the form's *OnCreate* event it is docked to the panel. This creates a default initial situation which can later be restored. In the example, Toolbar1 is the dockable toolbar, *PTop* the panel at the top edge of the form:

```
Toolbar1.ManualDock(PTop);
```

There is another good reason for manually docking the toolbar. Each docking control has an event *OnUndock*. This event is triggered when a drag-and-dock operation starts: it is triggered from the *TWinControl* dock site where the control is currently docked. It can be used for instance to prevent a drag-and-dock operation, as in the following example:

```
procedure TForm1.PTopUnDock(Sender: TObject;
 Client: TControl;
 NewTarget: TWinControl;
 var Allow: Boolean);
begin
 Allow:=(NewTarget<>PBottom)
end;
```

The *Allow* parameter tells the LCL whether the undock operation is allowed or not, *NewTarget* is the new dock site on which the user wants to dock the control. Note that this event is only triggered when the user actually drops the control somewhere, i.e. when the drag & dock operation is finished, and the LCL attempts to dock the control.
In the previous example, the toolbar was initially not docked. Thus, no *OnUnDock* event is triggered when it is docked for the first time. Manually docking it in the top panel will make sure that the *OnUnDock* event is also triggered when the toolbar is docked for the first time.
When a control is docked somewhere, the *OnEndDock* event is triggered. This can be used for example to provide some feedback to the user:

```
procedure TForm1Toolbar1EndDock(Sender, Target: TObject;
 X, Y: Integer);
begin
 Caption:='Toolbar docked on '+TComponent(Target).Name;
end;
```

You can of course also save the new dock location in an .ini file and restore it with *ManualDock* when the program is run again.

The DockManager

With the techniques described so far, only one control at a time is allowed at a dock site, and the LCL just places the new docked control on top of any existing ones at the dock site. As a result the last control dropped will be the only visible one.
When a *TWinControl* is a dock site, and a control is docked on it, the position of the latter is controlled by the *Dockmanager* – an instance of the abstract *TDockManager* class.
This behaviour can be disabled by setting *UseDockManager* to False.
When no *Dockmanager* is used, the docked control is simply made a child control of the dock site.
If the *UseDockManager* property is True – the default for all controls except *TForm* – then, as soon as a control is docked, a dock manager instance is created if none existed before. By default, the actual class of the dock manager instance is determined by the global variable *DefaultDockManagerClass* in the controls unit:

```
var
DefaultDockManagerClass: TDockManagerClass;
```

The standard dock manager implementation (in class *TDockTree)* does not contain any logic for repositioning of controls on a dock site. Some descendants of *TControl* such as *TPageControl* implement their own dock manager class to provide customized behaviour. The dock manager used by *TPageControl* will dock each dropped control on a new page of the page control. This can easily be seen by creating a form with 2 dockable panels on it and a *TPageControl* instance which is a dock site. After docking both panels on the dock form, a situation like that in Figure 6.31 will be created: The original form as in the designer is also visible, to show the difference.

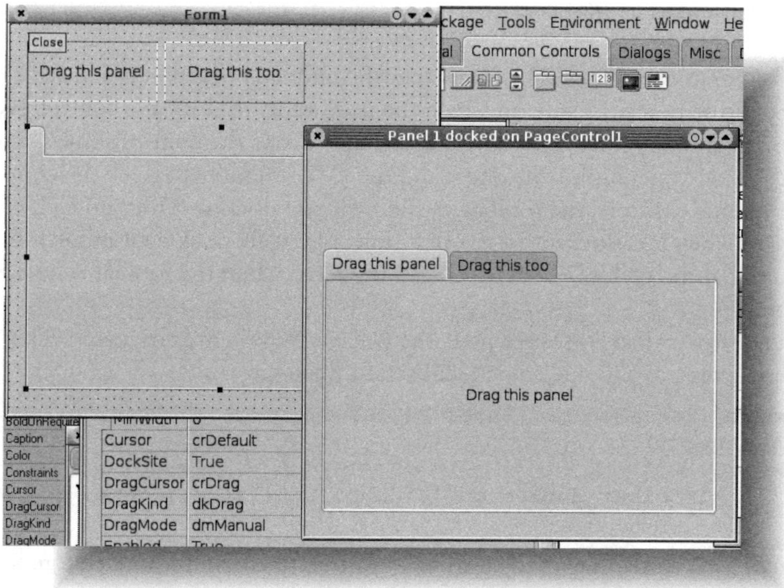

Figure 6.31: The dockmanager of TPageControl

The standard docking class does not do anything special with the controls docked on a dock site. However, the ldocktree unit implements an extended dock manager class. It is automatically installed as the *DefaultDockManagerClass* and offers a lot more functionality.

It is possible of course to install other docking managers. The `examples/dockmanager directory` in the Lazarus source tree contains an implementation of a docking manager that implements several other effects, and it comes with demonstration programs which can be compiled with different compiler directives, to show the differences.
It also contains an example which adds support for docking to the Lazarus IDE itself.
If you use docking – and it is an essential functionality required for building modern user interfaces – you should definitely look at these examples, from which you will be able to learn a lot about docking and implementing dock managers

6.4 An introduction to the component palette

The component palette is located in the main window of the Lazarus IDE, just below the menu bar, and to the right of the array of speedbuttons. Every component compiled into the IDE is represented by an icon somewhere on the palette.
Precisely which components are present depends on the Lazarus installation and operating system.
If Lazarus was recompiled using the command 'make clean all', then the component palette will only contain the components that are defined in the *LCL* itself.
No components other than those of the *LCL* will be installed. Some versions of Lazarus contain slightly different groups of *LCL* components, because some components do not work on all platforms. For instance, the SQLDB package contains some components that do not function under 64-bit Windows.
To make it easier to manage the large number of available components, the component palette is divided into a series of tabs. The rest of this chapter considers each of these tabs in turn. If you have installed a package with additional components, they may appear on one of the existing tabs, or you may see an additional new tab where that package's components appear.
The position of the tabs may change. The default tabs (as defined by the *LCL* – Standard to SynEdit) have fixed positions. Additional tabs (appearing as new packages are installed) may be ordered in various ways, depending on the order the packages were installed. Currently, it is not possible to change the order of the tabs in the component palette.

Using the component palette is quite easy: you click on the component you need, and then click a second time on the form where you want to place that component.
The component is always placed at the position where the mouse click occurred.
If you want to drop several instances of a component onto a form, press the [Shift] key when you click the component's icon on the component palette.
Each subsequent click on a form then creates further copies of the component on the form.
Alternatively, you can click a component's icon to select it as normal, and then keep the Shift key pressed down when you click on the form. As long as the Shift key remains down, more and more copies of the component can be dropped onto the form with successive mouse clicks.
For non-visual components, it doesn't matter where you place them on the form, and the image representing the component is visible only in the designer (*not at run-time*).
So it is best to place non-visual components where they don't interfere with the designing of the form.

As soon as a component is selected on the component palette, its icon will appear depressed. The 'selected' status will return to normal as soon as the component is dropped on a form. On the other hand, if you pressed Shift when selecting the component, then its status will return to normal (*i.e. unselected*) only when you click on the arrow icon (which is always the leftmost symbol on each tab of the component palette).

6.4 An introduction to the component palette.

The Lazarus component palette is designed to behave as much like the Delphi component palette as possible. Many Lazarus developers also work in Delphi, and keeping similar components at the same palette positions as in Delphi makes it easier to work in both environments.
This has caused some inconsistencies in the naming of components and tabs because some components are present in Lazarus only in an attempt to be Delphi-compatible. Having said that, not all Delphi's standard components have been duplicated in Lazarus. However (with possible exceptions resulting from commercial license restrictions, and Delphi-component dependency on the Windows API), it should be possible to port missing components to Lazarus. Right-clicking on a component icon displays a context menu shown in Figure 6.29.

Figure 6.32 The component palette's context menu

The first popup menu entry opens the package which registered that component on the component palette in the package manager. If you are only interested in the unit where that particular component is declared, then choose the second menu option.
The third menu option opens a search dialog (shown in Figure 6.30) which lets you search for a component by typing its name. A similar dialog can be found on the main menu under *View → Components.*

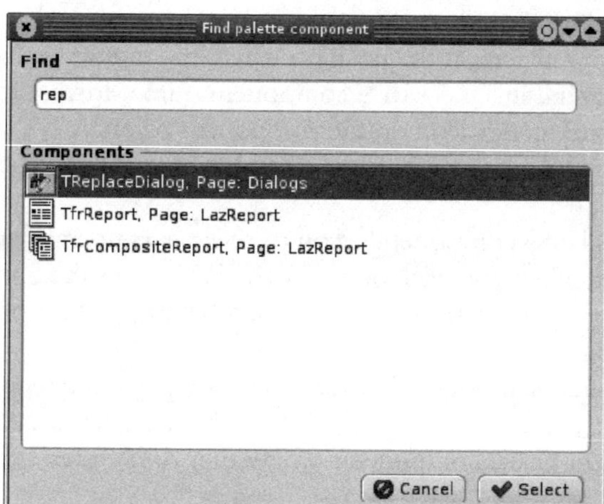

Figure 6.33: The component search dialog

Lazarus currently comes with over a hundred pre-installed components. More than half of those are visual components which descend from *TControl.* These controls form the user interface of your application, and are responsible for the way users will interact with your application. As you design the ways users can interact with your software, you have to decide whether users will initiate actions using toolbar buttons or though menus.

Standards for good user interface design have developed over the years.
Following such guidelines will help to make your users feel at home with your program. Consequently, you need to know how to make correct use of the many controls available to you. The first step is to become familiar yourself with the controls available to you.
It can seem strange at first sight that many controls are available in three flavours.
You can have a normal control, or the same control in a data-aware version, or the same control with *RTTI* capabilities (RTTI – Run-Time Type Information).

This chapter discusses the normal controls. The other two versions of each control function exactly the same, but also have the additional functionality of being able to fetch (or store) information from (or to) a database, or some object's published property.
If you are new to the concept of components and know little about the various controls' capabilities, you will be glad to know that Lazarus comes installed with more than 50 example applications, which demonstrate how nearly all the available controls can be used. The example programs can be compiled along with the Lazarus IDE.
You can also compile the examples using makefiles that the Lazarus team have provided. To examine an example's code it is easiest, of course, to load that example project in the IDE and study its source code in the editor.
All visual controls descend from *TControl*. This means that they all share many basic properties such as Position and Size, or the Anchors property and the OnResize event. As well as these common properties, visual controls have a number of other properties that control their behaviour which are listed in Table 6.40.

Property	Description
Color	The background colour of the control.
Cursor	The shape of the mouse cursor when the mouse is over the control.
Enabled	If set to False, the control will neither receive any events, nor will it receive focus. Depending on the kind of control, it will be usually be displayed in a different colour, indicating it is not available ('grayed out').
Font	The font used to display any text (if applicable to that control).
Hint	A hint that can be shown in a small popup window as the mouse moves over the control. This is also known as a tooltip.
ShowHint	If set to True, the hint will pop up when the mouse is over the control. If False, no hint will be shown.
ParentColor	If set to True, the Color property of the control is always equal to the Color roperty of the control's parent.
ParentFont	If set to True, then the Font property is always equal to the parent control's Font (similar to ParentColor). You can use this to quickly reset a font.
ParentShowHint	If set to True (the default), the value of ShowHint is always the same as the ShowHint property of the control's parent. This means that setting the ShowHint property of a form to True will enable hints for all the form's controls.

Table 6.40: Properties that visual controls share in common

Visual controls also share the events listed in Table 6.41. These events can be used to respond to mouse movement and mouse events. The *OnMouseDown* and *OnMouseUp* events are more fine-grained events than the *OnClick* and *OnDblClick* events.
A control may receive an *OnMouseDown* event, but not an *OnMouseUp* event, in which case no *OnClick* event would be generated. This can happen if the user presses the mouse button on one control, moves the mouse to another control, and only then releases the mouse button – a typical 'drag & drop' operation.

Events	Description
OnClick	Triggered when the user clicks the control with the left mouse button.
OnDblClick	Triggered when the user double-clicks the control with the left mouse button.
OnMouseEnter	Triggered when the mouse crosses the boundary of the control from outside it and starts moving over the control.
OnMouseLeave	Triggered when the mouse crosses the boundary of the control from inside it, moving away from the control.
OnMouseMove	Triggered when the mouse moves over the control.
OnMouseDown	Triggered when a mouse button is pressed while the mouse is over the control.
OnMouseUp	Triggered when a mouse button which has been depressed is released while the mouse is over the control.

Table 6.41: Events that visual controls share in common

In the sections that follow, the various basic controls which Lazarus provides are introduced. For each control I explain both the properties specific to that control, and how they are intended to be used. The components are covered in tab sequence (according to the tab they appear on), and for each tab the most important components are discussed first.

6.4.1 The Standard Tab

The **Standard** tab on the component palette (Figure 6.31) contains the LCL's simplest controls which are always installed in the IDE. Table 6.42 lists the controls on this tab.

Figure 6.34: The component palette's Standard tab

Components	Description
TMainMenu	Is a component which contains a form's main menu – the menu bar at the top of a (main) form.
TPopupMenu	Is a component which contains a popup (context-sensitive) menu in an application. Each control can have its own popup menu.
TButton	Is a simple clickable button with a text Caption. The user presses the button with a mouse click to perform an action.
TLabel	This control simply displays text (its Caption). The text can be single-line, or multi-line. One of the characters in the Caption can function as a hotkey, and pressing this hotkey will set the focus to a designated *TWinControl* (specified in the FocusControl property). The character key acting as a hotkey should be preceded by an ampersand (&), and it will then be displayed underlined.
TEdit	Allows the user to enter a single line of text. The text can be limited in length, and can be masked with a password character (so the text is not displayed onscreen – the password characters are shown instead).
TMemo	Allows the user to enter more than one line of text. The memo will automatically display scrollbars if need be. The text is displayed in a uniform font – no enhancements to the formatting are possible.
TToggleBox	Is similar to a TButton, but once clicked it remains depressed until the user clicks it again.
TCheckBox	Displays a box with a checkmark, accompanied by a short label (its Caption). By clicking the box a user can toggle the checkmark on and off. Several checkboxes can be placed next to each other. Each one can be checked or unchecked independently. Their principal use is for letting users set (or unset) program options.
TRadioButton	Is similar to a *TCheckBox*, but differs in that if several radiobuttons appear on a control, only one of the radiobuttons can be selected at a time. Checking one radiobutton unchecks all the others. This is useful for letting the user select one option from several mutually exclusive options.

Table 6.42: Controls found on the Standard tab (part 1)

Components	Description
TListBox	Displays a number of strings, and allows the user to select one or more of the strings. The strings can be drawn in a variety of styles (depending on the listbox's Style).
TComboBox	Like a *TEdit*, a combobox allows the user to enter text, but offers a list of possibilities to choose from. You can limit the possible entries to one of the pre-defined items, or to allow the user to enter text which is not yet in the list. The list of items is shown when the user clicks a 'dropdown' button, but it can also be made a permanently visible list.
TScrollBar	Is a bar with a small handle (the 'thumb') which can be dragged along the bar. The altered thumb position is then used to position other controls.
TGroupBox	A groupbox is used to group a set of controls together. It draws a bevel around the controls and puts a Caption in the bevel. This is a purely cosmetic control.
TRadioGroup	A radiogroup is actually a combination of a groupbox and a set of radiobuttons. For each line in the Items property, a corresponding radiobutton is displayed in the group. The ItemIndex property determines which one of the radiobuttons is checked.
TCheckGroup	Similar to the radiogroup, the checkgroup displays a series of checkboxes. The Checked array determines which of the items is checked.
TPanel	Is similar to a label, but includes an enclosing border, and can contain other controls. Panels are often used as containers to group other controls, and are very handy to force certain layout designs. It's also often used as the ancestor of other drawn controls since it provides a canvas to draw on.
TFrame	This is a container for other controls, much like a form, but must be dropped on a form.
TActionList	A list of actions, which can be coupled to other controls.

Table 6.42: Controls found on the Standard tab (Continuation)

Main and Popup menus

Most, if not all, applications have a menu bar at the top of the main window. It is used to select and perform any of the actions that your application offers. Two of the menus that appear in almost every application menu are File, with file-related actions, and Edit, with actions such as *Cut, Copy, Paste, Undo* and similar.

At various locations in an application, a local menu can also be used – by clicking with the right mouse button, a menu pops up at the mouse location, from which you can choose a menu action. Many edit controls use popup menus to offer the Select all, Cut, Copy, Paste and Undo actions.

Lazarus encapsulates these menus in two components: *TMainMenu* for the top menu, and *TPopupMenu* for a local menu. They both appear on the component palette's Standard tab. Both components have an Items property, defined as follows:

```
Property Items: TMenuItem;
```

The *TMenuItem* class represents a single item in a menu. The *TMenuItem* class has a pair of properties allowing construction of a submenu:

```
Property Count: Integer;
Property Items[Index: Integer]: TMenuItem;
```

The Count property represents the number of items in the submenu, and the Items property provides indexed access to each of these items.
Since the Items property is also of type *TMenuItem,* this allows you to build a tree-like structure of submenus: the items of each *TMenuItem* instance represent the items in the submenu.
The *TMenuItem* class has a number of properties that determine how it looks and behaves. The three main properties are *Caption*, *Shortcut* and the *OnClick* event.
The Caption property contains the text displayed on the menu. The Caption can contain a shortcut key. The character preceded by an ampersand character (&) will act as the shortcut key for that menu item, when the menu is visible. For example, a caption of '&File' in a top-level menu will make 'F' the shortcut key for the menu, and it will be activated when `Alt-F` (or `Alt-f`) is pressed. In a submenu, simply pressing the letter F (or f) will activate it. It will be displayed as 'File' in the menu.
If the Caption property is set to '-' (a dash), that menu item will appear as a separator in the menu.
The Shortcut property sets a shortcut key for the menu. The shortcut key can be used to execute the menu item's action even if the menu item is not visible. For example '`Ctrl-S`' is often used to activate the Save menu. In the menu display, the shortcut key will be shown right-aligned at the end of the menu item's Caption.
The *OnClick* event is triggered when the menu item is activated, either by clicking it or by using its shortcut key, and the Sender parameter of the event handler is the menu item.
The following is an example of an *OnClick* handler:

```
procedure TMainForm.DoMenuClick(Sender: TObject);
begin
  With (Sender as TMenuItem) do
    ShowMessage('Menu item with caption "'+ Caption + '" was chosen');
end;
```

Most menu items use only these three properties. However, there are additional properties that can be used to alter the behaviour and appearance of the menu item which are listed in Table 6.43.

Property	Description
Checked	If this boolean property is set to True, the menu item will have a check-mark in front of it. By default, the Checked property is False, and it must be set manually in code when the menu item is clicked.
AutoCheck	If this boolean property is set, then clicking the menu item will set or unset the Checked property: There is no need to set or unset the checked property in the OnClick event handler. The event handler is still called of course, after the checked property was altered.
RadioButton	If this boolean property is set, then all menu items that appear in the same group will act as a set of radio buttons - checking one item will uncheck all other items in the group.

Table 6.43: Further menu item properties

The 'group' of menu items (affected by the *RadioButton property*) is determined by the *GroupIndex property*: *GroupIndex* should be a number larger than zero.
Multiple groups can exist within the same submenu, in which case all menu items with the same *GroupIndex* value belong to the same group.
Lastly, the *ImageIndex* property can be used to display an image in front of the menu item. When set to a value other than -1, the image will be taken from the images in a *TImageList* component (which can be found on the component palette's Common tab).
For the images to be displayed, the Images property of the *TMainMenu* or *TPopupMenu* must be set to the imagelist whose images are to be used.
In theory, the images in that list can have any size, but in practice a size of 16x16 pixels produces the best results.
All these properties can be managed through the Lazarus menu editor. The menu editor can be invoked by double-clicking the *TMainMenu* or *TPopupMenu* instance, or by invoking it from the Items property in the object inspector.
As can be seen in Figure 6.32, the menu editor is intuitive in its use: the menu is constructed as it will appear in the program. A popup menu shows what actions are available, and using the popup menu an entire menu can be designed as it should appear in the final program (see Figure 6.33)

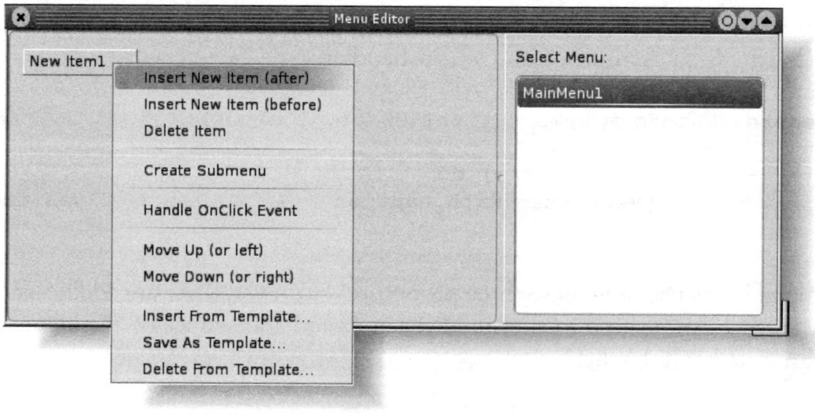

Figure 6.35: The menu editor

Once a menu item is added to the menu, it can be selected and its properties can be set in the object inspector. As a shortcut, the *OnClick* event handler can be created straight from the menu editor's popup menu. If several menus have been dropped on a form, the menu editor will show all available menus in a list at the right. This allows you to manage all your menus at once without leaving the menu editor.

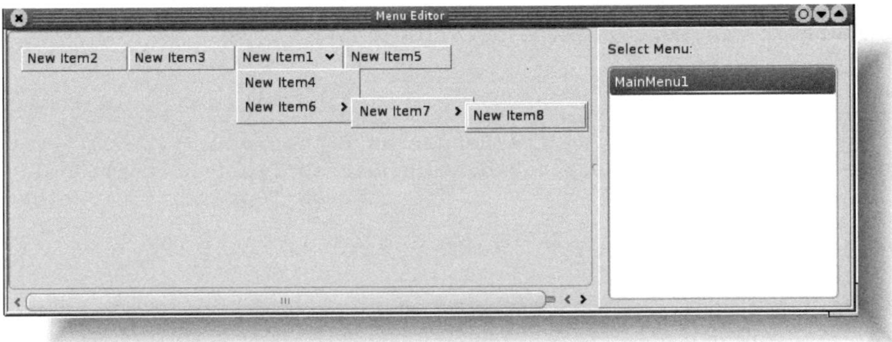

Figure 6.36: A menu at design time

To show the main menu, the MainMenu property of the form must be set: the form will show the menu in this property. When you drop the first *TMainMenu* component on a form, the property is automatically set to this instance. Immediately, the menu will appear at the top of the form, and it can be browsed using the mouse – it will behave as it would at runtime (see Figure 6.34).

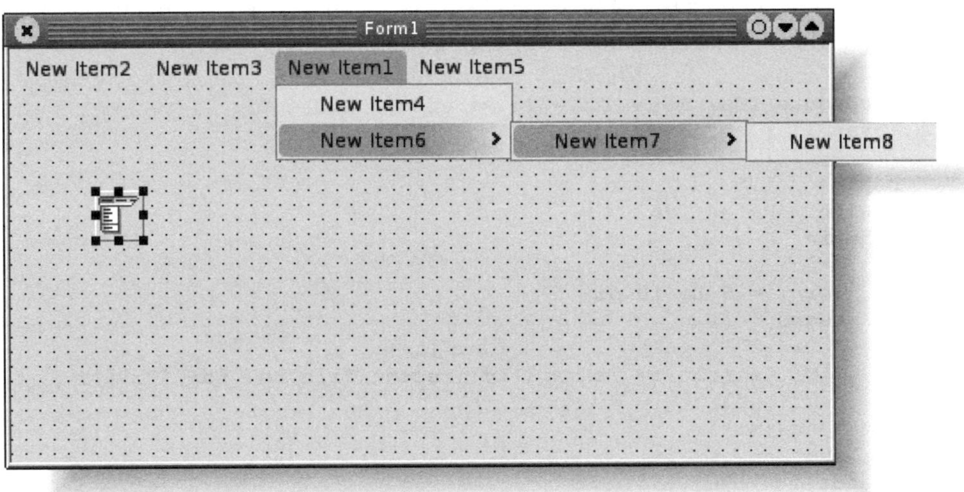

Figure 6.37: A newly designed menu as it looks in the form designer

To show a popup menu when right-clicking a control, the PopupMenu property of that control must be set to the *TPopupMenu* instance that you want shown. The popup menu will then be shown at the spot where the user clicked with the right mouse button.

The popup menu can also be shown programmatically using the Popup method. It needs the coordinates of the position where the menu should be shown (the coordinates are screen coordinates, not coordinates relative to the form). The coordinates can be calculated from the mouse position at the moment of the click, or you could show the popup at a fixed position:

```
Procedure TForm1.MenuClick(Sender: TObject);
  Var X, y : Integer;
begin
// calculate position
  x := Left + PanelLeft.Width+(Sender as TSpeedButton).Left;
  y := Top + TitleBar.Height.Width+(Sender as TSpeedButton).Top+
                                  (Sender as TSpeedButton).Height;
// Show menu:
  if (Sender = BPrg) then
    PMPrg.Popup(X,Y)
  else
    PMHelp.Popup(X,Y);
end;
```

There are situations in which it is not possible to create the whole menu structure at design-time, in the Lazarus IDE. For example, many programs have a Recent Files menu. Such a menu has to be created at run-time, and its menu items have to be inserted in the menu structure in code.
The following code fragment shows how to create such a menu entry. It should be implemented in the *OnClick* handler of the File menu. It populates the Recent Files menu item (*MIRecent*) with a dummy list of files, as follows:

```
procedure TMainForm.MFileClick(Sender: TObject);
  Var I  : integer;
      MI : TMenuItem;
begin
  With MIRecent do
  begin
    Clear;
    For I:= 0 to 10 do
    begin
      MI := TMenuItem.Create(Self);
      MI.Caption := Format('%d: recent file no. %d',[I,I]);
      MI.OnClick := @DoMenuClick;
      Add(MI);
    end;
  end;
end;
```

First, all existing menu items are removed with the Clear method. The MIRecent menu items' submenu is then filled in a loop: each item is created (using the form as the owner of the item) and stored in a local variable (*MI*). The Caption and *OnClick properties* are set up, and finally the *TMenuItem.Add()* method is used to add the menu item to the MIRecent submenu.

Buttons

The Button control *(TButton)* and its companion control BitButton *(TBitBtn)* are simple button controls. They display a simple Caption (and in the case of a BitButton, additionally an image) and the user can click on them. The text is specified in the Caption property, and can contain an accelerator character which can be used to activate the button.
To make construction of standardized dialog forms easier, some additional button properties are provided, which are shown in Table 6.44. Combining these properties makes it easy to construct standardized dialogs which close themselves when the user presses Escape or Return. The former should discard any changes made in the dialog, the latter should save all changes.

Property	Description
Cancel	The button acts as the Cancel button on the form: pressing the Escape key will activate the button, usually to close the dialog without saving changes.
Default	The button acts as the default button of the form (usually the OK button). It will be activated if the user presses the Enter or Return on the keyboard.
ModalResult	If this is set to any value other than mrNone, then clicking the button will set the ModalResult property of the form on which the button is located, and this automatically closes the form if it is shown modal. Note that the OnClick handler is still executed: it can be used to perform saving of data if needed. As soon as the handler finishes execution, the form is closed.

Table 6.44: TButton and TBitBtn properties useful in constructing dialog forms

The *TBitBtn* control has additional properties controlling its layout which are listed in Table 6.45. Both buttons are windowed controls, which means they can receive focus. If a button is specified in the FocusControl property of a label, then pressing the accelerator character of the label will focus the button, but will not cause the *OnClick* event to be fired. The accelerator character in the button's Caption, by contrast, will trigger its *OnClick* event.

Property	Description
Glyph	The image to show on the button if the Kind property is *bkCustom.KindBy* default this is *bkCustom*, meaning that a custom image and caption can be specified. If this is set to any of the other values (*bkOK, bkCancel, bkHelp, bkYes, bkNo, bkClose, bkAbort, bkRetry, bkIgnore, bkAll, bkNoToAll, bkYesToAll*), default values for the *Glyph, Caption* and *ModalResult* properties are filled in.
Layout	Determines the location of the glyph relative to the caption. It can have one of the following values: *blGlyphBottom, blGlyphLeft, blGlyphRight* and *blGlyphTop*, with obvious meanings.
Margin	This is the number of pixels between the button border and the image on the button. Setting it to -1 will centre the text and image on the button.
NumGlyphs	This is the number of images in the *Glyph* bitmap. The first will be used as the standard image, the second as the image when the button is disabled.
Spacing	This is the number of pixels between the caption and the image on the button.

Table 6.45: TBitBtn's display properties

The Lazarus distribution contains an example program (`../examples/bitbutton.lpi`) which demonstrates the properties of *TBitBtn.* It is shown in Figure 6.35. (The regular button currently has no Lazarus demonstration program).

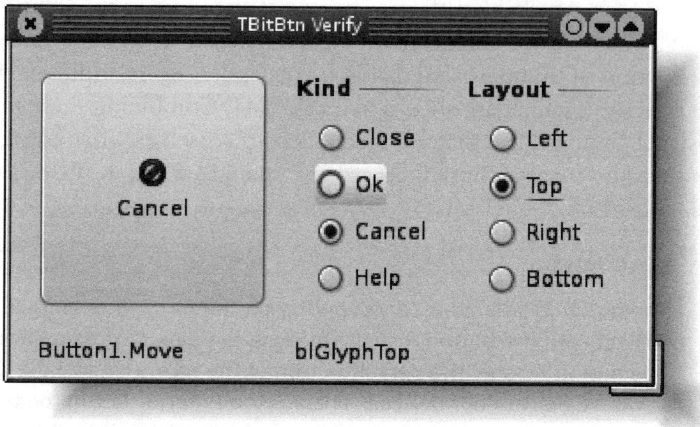

Figure 6.38: The Lazarus TBitBtn example program

The Label control

The label control (the *TLabel class*) can be used to show text in a single font and colour. Its main use is to label other controls such as edits, memos and so on.
It introduces the properties listed in Table 6.46.

Property	Description
Alignment	Is the horizontal alignment which determines whether the label's text is left-aligned, right-aligned or centred. The effect of this property is masked when *Autosize* is *True*.
Autosize	Determines whether the label resizes itself so it is big enough to display all of its *Caption*. If it is set to *False*, and the *Caption* is too long, the displayed text is truncated.
Caption	The text displayed by the label. If a character in the text is preceded by an ampersand (&), then it will appear underlined, and will function as an accelerator character – pressing *Alt* and that character key simultaneously will shift focus to the control specified in *FocusControl*. This behaviour can be disabled with the *ShowAccelChar* property. To actually display a single ampersand, two consecutive ampersands must be entered (&&).
FocusControl	The control which will receive focus when the accelerator key is pressed. This must be a *TWinControl* descendant, i.e. a control which can actually receive focus.

Table 6.46: TLabel properties (part 1)

Property	Description
Layout	Governs the vertical alignment, determining whether the text is aligned to the top, bottom or is centred. Again, if the property *Autosize* is True, setting Layout has no visible effect.
ShowAccelChar	Determines whether the ampersand (&) character in the *Caption* denotes an accelerator key.
Transparent	If *True*, the background is not coloured prior to drawing the label, i. e., the *Color* property is ignored.
WordWrap	If *True*, a *Caption* which is too long for the label's width will be wrapped, i. e. text which does not fit on a single line will be broken into several lines. This property has no effect if *Autosize* is True. Note that hard linefeeds in the caption will still be respected if *WordWrap* is True.

Table 6.46 TLabel properties (Continuation)

Text entry controls

The most common input action for a user is probably typing text into a field. This is done using either the *TEdit* or the *TMemo* controls. The difference between the two controls is that the former can only contain a single line of text, and the latter can handle more than one line of text. Both are descendants of *TCustomEdit.* There are a number of other descendants of *TCustomEdit* including *TSpinEdit* and *TFloatSpinEdit* for editing numerical values. The *TEditButton* class shows a small speedbutton to the right of the edit control. This button can be used for instance to open a dialog for further input – the controls *TFileNameEdit, TDirectoryEdit, TDateEdit* and *TCalcEdit* are a series of descendants of this control which provide ready-made functionality for the button. They all open a dialog which allows you to select or calculate a text value. The hierarchy of edit controls is shown in Figure 6.36.

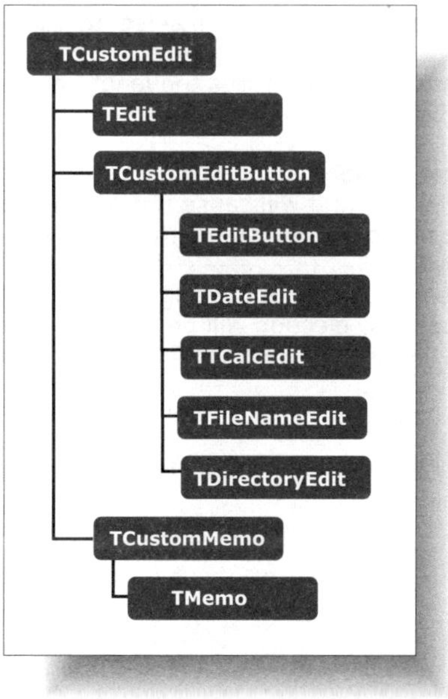

Figure 6.39: The hierarchy of edit controls

The main properties of the *TEdit* control are listed in Table 6.47.

Property	Description
AutoSelect	If set to *True*, the entire text in the edit control will be selected when the control receives focus. This means that as soon as the user types in the edit control, previous text (*if any*) will be completely overwritten with the newly typed text. If set to *False* (*the default*) then newly typed text will simply be inserted at the cursor position.
CharCase	Determines the case of typed text: *ecNormal* does not alter the case of any typed letters; *ecLowercase* forces all typing to lowercase; *ecUppercase* forces all typing to uppercase.
EchoMode	Determines how typed characters are shown in the edit control. *emNormal* means they are shown exactly as they are typed by the user. A value of *emNone* means the user is typing blind: no characters are echoed to the screen. Lastly, *emPassword* means that the password character is substituted for all characters which the user types in the box.
MaxLength	If set to a value larger than zero, this value will be used as the maximum number of characters the user can enter. Once the maximum length is reached, any further characters typed by the user are discarded (*this includes copy and paste actions*).
PasswordChar	If *EchoMode* is set to *emPassword* then all letters in the *Text* property will be substituted by this character prior to displaying the text. Note that the *Text* property retains its original value (i.e. what the user typed). This property affects the display, not the *Text* value.
ReadOnly	If set to *True*, the edit control is read-only. This means the user cannot type anything in the control. The difference from setting the *Enabled* property to *False* is that the control is still active, and can still receive the focus. For example the user can select text in a read-only control.
SelLength	This run-time property returns the length of the selection in characters. It can also be set programmatically.
SelStart	This run-time property returns the position of the start of the selected text. It can also be set, and will cause the cursor to move. Note that the position is a zero-based index of characters in the *Text* string.
SelText	This is the selected text in the edit control. It can be both retrieved and set. Any previous selection will be replaced by the new value of this property, regardless of whether the control is in insert or overwrite mode.
Text	This is the actual text displayed in the control.

Table 6.47: The main properties of TEdit

The main events of *TEdit* are listed in Table 6.48.

Events	Description
OnChange	Fired whenever the text is changed in the edit field. For instance it is fired for each character typed.
OnKeyPress	Is fired whenever a key is pressed. This event can be used to disable certain keys when typing in the control.
OnEditingDone	Is fired when the user has finished editing the contents in the edit control. Currently, two different actions will trigger this event: the focus leaves the control, or pressing the *Enter* key. Using this event to check for changes is preferred if a time-consuming check must be done because this event is fired less often than the *OnChange* event.

Table 6.48: TEdit's principal events

The selected text in an edit control can be cleared with a single method call: *ClearSelection*. The entire text of the control can be cleared with *TEdit's Clear method.*

The following table lists the properties of the *TEditButton* class and its descendants.

Property	Description
ButtonWidth	The width of the speedbutton. The height is always equal to the height of the edit control.
ButtonOnlyWhenFocused	If set to *True*, the speedbutton is only visible when the edit control has focus.
DirectInput	If set to *True*, the user can type a value in the edit control. If it is set to *False*, the only way to enter something in the edit control is by clicking the speedbutton, which gives you more control over which values can be entered.
Flat	If set to *True*, the speedbutton has a flat look.
Glyph	Contains the image shown in the button.
NumGlyphs	The number of images in the glyph.
OnButtonClick	The event triggered when a user clicks the speedbutton.

Table 6.49: Properties of TEditButton

The *TMemo* control has the same function as the *TEdit* control, but allows entry of more than one line of text – the number of lines allowed is almost unlimited.
The control can display scrollbars if the length of the lines is too long, or if the number of lines is too big to fit in the display space. Because of these features, the *TMemo* control has several different properties from the *TEdit* control.
The main property is *Lines:* the lines of text that are displayed in the control which are contained in a *TStrings* instance. Any changes to this stringlist are immediately displayed in the control.

It is important in this regard to understand the difference between a line in the Lines property and the lines actually displayed in the memo control. The memo control will start a new line for each string in the *Lines* property, but if a line is too big to fit, the memo control may wrap this line visually over several lines. Technically, considering the entire text of a *TStrings* instance, the memo control always starts a new line whenever it encounters a CR/LF pair or LF or CR characters.
(the actual character so identified depends on the operating system.)

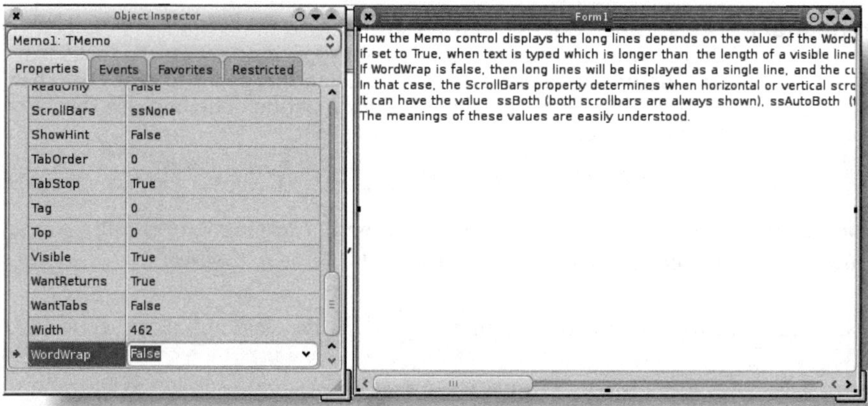

Figure 6.40: A memo control without wordwrap

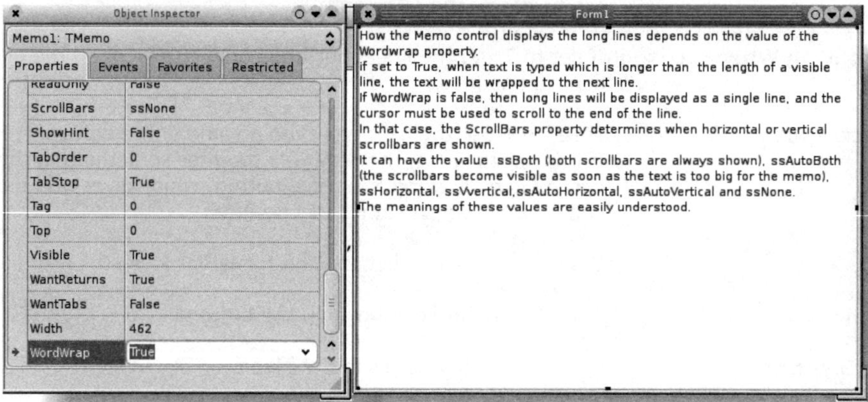

Figure 6.41: A memo control with wordwrap

How a Memo control displays any long lines depends on the value of the *Wordwrap* property. If True, then text which is longer than the length of a visible line will be wrapped to the next line. If *WordWrap* is False, then long lines will be displayed as a single line, and the cursor must be used to scroll to the end of the line. In that case, the ScrollBars property determines when horizontal or vertical scrollbars are shown. It can have the value *ssBoth* (both scrollbars are always shown), *ssAutoBoth* (the scrollbars become visible as soon as the text is too big for the memo), *ssHorizontal, ssVertical, ssAutoHorizontal, ssAutoVertical* and *ssNone.* The meanings of these values are self-explanatory.

If you want to give users the ability to insert tab characters using the Tab key, then you must set the *WantTabs* property to True, in which case the Tab key is used by the memo control to insert and display a tab character. The normal behaviour (when this value is False) is to interpret use of the Tab key as a signal from the user to move the focus to the next control.
Having the contents of the *TMemo* control as a *TStringList* instance means that the contents can be easily loaded from a file:

```
If OpenDialog1.Execute then
  Memo1.Lines.LoadFromFile(OpenDialog1.FileName)
```

Likewise, the contents can be saved to file:

```
If SaveDialog1.Execute then
  Memo1.Lines.SaveToFile(SaveDialog1.FileName);
```

Nothing could be simpler!
The *ReadOnly, SelText, SelStart* and *SelLength* properties function as in the *TEdit* control, which is not really very convenient since the position origin is relative to the first character of the first line in the control. Likewise, the *Clear* and *ClearSelection* methods of *TMemo* do the same as the methods in *TEdit.*
When filling a memo with text, the *Lines* property is updated. Depending on the operating system, this operation can be very slow, since the addition or modification of each line can cause the control to repaint itself, which will cause a lot of flicker on the screen. However, a way is provided to avoid this through a call to *BeginUpdate* at the start of the filling routine, and a call to *EndUpdate* at the end of the filling routine. Both are methods of the Lines property of the memo. The effect of this is that the memo will only update its display once, at the *EndUpdate* call. A typical routine named *FillMemo()* looks like this:

```
procedure TMainForm.FillMemo(B: Boolean);
  Const LineCount = 50000;
  Var I: Integer; Start: TDateTime; S: String;
begin
  Start := Now;
  With MTest.Lines do begin
    If B then BeginUpdate;
    try
      Clear;
      For I := 1 to LineCount do Add('This is line ' + IntToStr(I));
    Finally
      If B then EndUpdate;
    end;
    S := FormatDateTime('hh:nn:ss.zzz',Now-Start);
    S := Format(SFillTime,[LineCount,S]);
    ShowMessage(S);
  end;
end;
```

At the end of the routine, the time it took to fill the memo with 50,000 lines is displayed. With some widget sets, the difference between the optimized routine using *BeginUpdate/EndUpdate* and the unoptimized routine lacking these calls is not great. However with other widget sets the difference can be very noticeable.
I recommend therefore that you always surround heavy modifications of the *Lines* property with calls to *BeginUpdate* and *EndUpdate*. This is best done inside a *Try...Finally* block to avoid errors (*lockup*) if an exception were to be thrown.

The ToggleBox control

The ToggleBox control (*TToggleBox*) looks like a regular button control, but behaves like a checkbox: it remains 'checked' (depressed) when the user clicks it. To 'uncheck' it, you must click it again. It has the same properties and behaviour (including the OnChange and OnClick handlers) as a checkbox control which is considered next.

The CheckBox control

The checkbox control (*TCheckBox*) is similar to the Button control in the sense that it is clickable. Its *OnClick* event is triggered when the check mark is toggled by clicking it (*or pressing the space bar*) if the checkbox has focus. The fact that both the *TCheckBox* and *TButton* classes descend from the *TButtonControl* class, accounts for this similarity.
Use checkboxes whenever your user needs to enable or disable program options. Several checkboxes are needed to set multiple options.
TCheckBox shares with *TButton* the common *Caption* and *OnClick* properties. Additionally the checkbox has some special properties which determine its behaviour and appearance, listed in Table 6.50.

Property	Description
Autosize	As for the *TLabel* control, *AutoSize* determines whether the checkbox adjusts its width to accommodate the size of the *Caption* (*True*), or whether it keeps a fixed size (*False*).
AllowGrayed	Determines whether the checkbox can appear in the grayed state.
Checked	Determines whether a checkmark appears in the control.
State	The state is one of *cbUnchecked*, *cbChecked* or *cbGrayed*.
UseOnChange	Determines what happens if the *Checked* property is changed in code. Normally, when the checked property changes (*due to a user action or in code*), both an *OnClick* event and an *OnChange* are triggered. If the *UseOnChange* property is set to *True*, only an *OnChange* event is triggered when the *Checked* property is changed in code (behaviour that is compatible with Delphi).

Table 6.50: Special TCheckBox properties

The most important properties of the checkbox are *Checked* and *State*. Usually, you work with *Checked* which determines whether a check mark is displayed at first or not, and the user can change the setting of the property by clicking it. The third status *cbGrayed* can also be established by the user if the property *AllowGrayed is True*
(by default it is False).

When the checkbox is in the *cbUnchecked* state, and the user clicks it, then it jumps to the checked state, and a second click will set the status to *cbUnchecked.* The order in which the state changes depends on the used widget set when using the GTK2 widget set it functions as follows:
If the state is *cbGrayed,* and *Checked* equals False, then the first click will enable the checkbox, and the second one will show the check mark. The *State* property can therefore be interpreted as "Nothing has yet been chosen, but this is the default setting". This is extremely useful for the data-aware checkbox control, when the value of a field is *Null.* Note that the *cbGrayed* state is not the same as the 'disabled' state obtained by setting Enabled to False. A disabled checkbox can have any *State* but it cannot be changed by the user.

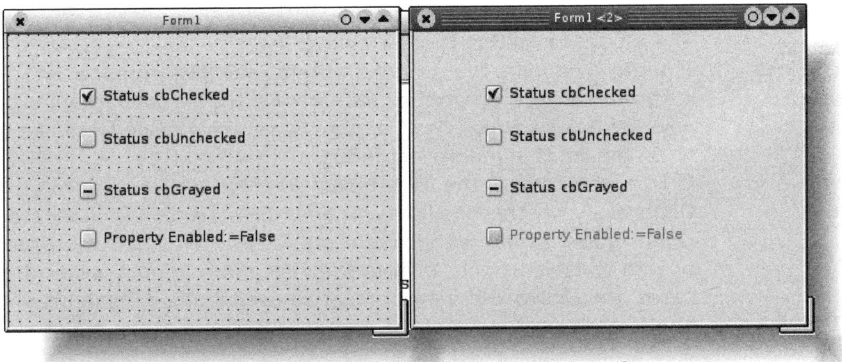

Figure 6.42: Three TCheckBox states in the Designer and at run time

The RadioButton control

The RadioButton control *(TRadioButton)* is similar to a checkbox and has the same properties as the Checkbox. The difference from a checkbox is that only one radiobutton can be checked at a time. Checking one radiobutton will clear all other radiobuttons in the same group. Therefore a radiobutton should be used to let a user choose between mutually exclusive options. If several options can be valid simultaneously, a series of checkboxes must be used.
Radiobuttons belong to the same group if they have the same parent control. This parent control can be any containing control: a form, a panel, a groupbox. Only the immediate parent is taken into account.

The Listbox control

Listboxes can be used to select one or more items from a list. The list of options is always visible in a *TListBox* control. The function of this control (to select one or more items from a list) is similar to that of the radiogroup or checkgroup. However, the radiogroup or checkgroup are not scrollable, which makes them unsuitable for large lists, whereas a listbox shows as many items as possible, while also allowing you to scroll through the complete list if the full list takes up more space than the listbox.
A combobox is similar to a listbox. Both controls keep their list of items as a stringlist (a *TStrings* instance), and both controls have support for custom drawing of the items, so it's possible to display the items graphically in a more attractive way.

The listbox is the simpler of the two controls. It simply shows the list of items, and the user can select one of the items by clicking on it. Listbox behaviour is controlled by the properties listed in Table 6.51

Property	Description
ExtendedSelect	If set to *True* (the default) then extended selection mechanisms become available when the control is in multiselect mode: Ctrl-click then adds a single item to a selection, and Shift-click adds several neighbouring items. If set to False, items must be selected (or deselected) by double-clicking them.
IntegralHeight	If *True*, an item won't be drawn unless it fits completely in the listbox.
ItemIndex	The index of the selected item in the list provided the list is not in multiselect mode. This is a run-time property. The index is zero-based.
ItemHeight	The height of an item (in pixels).
Items	The list of strings that is shown in the list.
MultiSelect	If set to *True* more than one item can be selected from the list.
Selected	A boolean array property: for each item in the list, the array indicates whether it is selected (*True*) or not (*False*). This property can be used only when the list is in multiselect mode.
Sorted	If *True*, the items in the list are kept sorted.
Style	Determines whether the listbox is an ordinary listbox (*lbStandard*), an owner-drawn listbox with fixed height for the items (*lbOwnerDrawFixed*) or with variable height (*lbOwnerDrawVariable*). In both owner-drawn cases, the *OnDrawItem* event must be used to draw the items in the list.
TopIndex	The (zero-based) index of the item that is shown at the top of the list.

Table 6.51: Important Listbox properties

Depending on the setting of *MultiSelect*, it is possible to select either several or just one item from the list. If *MultiSelect* is False, then the *ItemIndex* property indicates which item is selected. If *MultiSelect* is True, then you have to traverse all the items in order to determine which ones are selected. The following code snippet shows how to remove the selected items from the listbox, irrespective of the setting of MultiSelect:

```
  Var I : Integer;
begin
  With ListBox1 do
    if MultiSelect then
    begin
      For I := Items.Count-1 downto 0 do
        If Selected[i] then Items.Delete(I);
    end
    else Items.Delete(ItemIndex);
end;
```

Note that the list is traversed in reverse order.

The suggestion made for optimizing use of the memo control when adding a lot of items to its stringlist is also valid for listboxes.
When executing a long list of changes to the Items property, it is best to enclose this operation within a pair of *BeginUpdate* – *EndUpdate* statements.

The Combobox control

The *TComboBox* control can be used for the same purposes as a listbox. It differs from a *TListbox* control in that the full list of items to select from is hidden by design. It can be shown using a button, which causes the list to drop down. As a result, the *TCombobox* control uses less screen space than a listbox or a radiogroup. Additionally, an item which is not present in the list of items can be entered in the combobox by simply typing its name in the control's edit field. The combobox then acts like a normal edit control except that it also has a list of predefined values from which the text can quickly be set, much like a history list. This behaviour is customizable. The *TComboBox* control has many properties controlling its behaviour. The properties are listed in Table 6.52. The items in the list are specified in the *Items* property, which is of type *TStrings*, on which any stringlist operation is possible.

Property	Description
ArrowKeys-TraverseList	If ArrowKeysTraverseList is *True*, using the Up and Down arrow keys while the control has focus will select the previous or next item in the list. If *False*, the mouse must be used to select an item.
AutoComplete	If set to *True*, when typing text in the control, the text will be completed with the first matching item. A match is found when the item starts with the same characters as the already typed text. Much like 'incremental search' kind of behaviour.
AutoComplete-Text	Can be used to fine-tune the autocomplete option. It is a set property with various self-explanatory values. Including the first item in the set (*cbactEnabled*) is equivalent to setting the *AutoComplete* property.
AutoDropDown	If set to *True*, then the list will be made visible as soon as a character is typed in the combobox.
AutoSelect	Is the same as for the *TEdit* control – if set to True, the entire displayed text is selected when the combobox gets the focus.
CharCase	As for the *TEdit* control it determines the case of the typed characters (*uppercase, lowercase,* or *unchanged*).
DropDownCount	Determines how many items are shown when the dropdown list is shown. If there are more items in the list than the value set here, scrollbars will be shown to allow scrolling through the list.
ItemHeight	The height of the items in the *list.ItemIndex* the index of the currently selected item. It can also be set programmatically. It only has meaning if the style is one of the *ownerdraw* styles or *csDropDownList*.
ItemWidth	The width of the dropdown list in pixels.
MaxLength	The maximum length of text that can be shown. Note that if the text of an item in the list is longer than the value specified here, the text will be clipped.
Sorted	Determines whether the items in the list appear sorted.
Style	Used to specify the style of the combobox. The *Style* property can have several values, listed in Table 6.53.

Table 6.52: TComboBox properties

Styles	Description
csDropDown	The user can enter text freely, and can use the list to set the text to a predefined value. Newly entered text is not automatically added to the list.
csDropDownList	The user can only select a value which appears in the list.
csOwnerDrawFixed	Like *csDropDownList*, but the items are drawn in the *OnDrawItem* event, with fixed heights.
csOwnerDrawVariable	Like *csDropDownList*, but the items are drawn in the *OnDrawItem* event, with variable heights.
csSimple	On Windows, this gives the combobox the appearance of an edit control with a listbox under it (i.e. the list is always visible). Other than that the control acts like a *csDropDown* combobox. On other platforms, this value equals the *csDropDown* style.

Table 6.53: Styles available to a combobox

The ScrollBar control

Many controls are able to display scrollbars automatically when needed. Such controls include forms, memos, grids and listboxes. However, this may not always be enough to provide for all situations. Therefore, the *TScrollBar* control is available separately, to add a scrollbar at any position – for instance in conjunction with a paintbox.
The main properties are the *Kind* property, which determines the orientation of the scrollbar, and the *Position* property, which determines the position of the scrollbar, and which can vary between the values in the Min and Max properties.
To react to any changes made by the user, the *OnChange* event can be used.

The GroupBox control

The groupbox control *(TGroupBox)* shares some properties with a bevel and a panel. It draws a frame, and displays a caption in the top left corner of the frame. Like the panel, it can contain controls, and can receive focus. It is commonly used to group controls, providing a title for the group. The title can have an accelerator character, which can be used to set the focus to the groupbox.
The groupbox control has no additional distinguishing properties. Setting the Caption and the *ChildSizing* property should be all the customization that is needed after the control is positioned on the form.

The RadioGroup control

The radiogroup control *(TRadioGroup)* is a combined control: it is simply a groupbox which contains a number of radiobuttons. The captions of the radiobuttons are determined by the *Items* property. Which radiobutton in the group is selected is determined by the *ItemIndex* property.
Two properties determine the layout of the radiogroup, and they are listed in Table 6.54.
Reacting to changes made by the user can be done as in the *TRadioButton* control: the *OnClick* event is triggered whenever the user makes a change.

Property	Description
AutoSize	Determines whether the options are evenly distributed down the side of the control. If *False*, the options are just placed one after the other, with no space between them. If *AutoSize* is True (the default) then enough whitespace is put between the radiobuttons to fill the complete groupbox.
ColumnLayout	If there is more than one column of radiobuttons this property determines the direction of fill – across the columns, or vertically column by column.
Columns	The number of columns in the radiogroup.

Table 6.54: TRadioGroup properties

The CheckGroup control

The checkgroup control *(TCheckGroup)* is similar to the radiogroup control. Instead of radiobuttons, checkboxes are used, which means that the user might check none of the checkboxes, or just one, or several, or all of them. For this scenario, an *ItemIndex* property no longer makes sense. Instead use the *Checked* array property to discover which of the items are checked. The *CheckEnabled* array property can be used to enable or disable particular checkboxes (by default, each item is enabled). Neither array is published, so you have to access them in code rather than through the Object Inspector.

The Panel control

The panel control *(TPanel)* is similar to a *TLabel* control in that it displays a *Caption.* However being a windowed control, it has more extensive capabilities. Other controls can be dropped on it (no controls can be dropped on a label). The fact you can drop other controls on a panel can be very useful for grouping components, or to achieve particular layout effects. Additionally, the panel can draw a border around itself and can be used as a tab stop.

TPanel shares many of *TLabel's* properties, but has additional properties controlling the two bevels which make up the panel's border. *BevelInner* controls the appearance of the inner bevel; *BevelOuter* controls the appearance of the outer bevel; and *BevelWidth* controls the width of the bevels. The *BevelInner* and *BevelOuter* properties can have the values *bvNone, bvLowered, bvRaised* and *bvSpace,* with obvious meanings.

Because a *TPanel* is a windowed control other controls can be dropped on it.
It also means that a panel can receive focus, and participate in the tab order of the form. This behaviour is controlled by the *TabStop* property: if it is set to True, then the panel can be focused when the user presses the Tab key. By default, it is set to False.

Frames

A frame is a container for other controls, just like *TForm.* Frames must be created by selecting *Frame* from the *File → New* dialog. You design them just as you would a form: indeed, they are defined in the unit *Forms,* and descend from *TCustomFrame.*

When you choose *File → New…Frame* from the IDE's New dialog it creates a new unit populated with a *TFrame* descendant, just as it does for a new form:

```
TFrame1 = Class(TFrame)
  BitBtn1 : TBitBtn;
  SubFrame : TFrame2;
 private
   { private declarations }
 public
   { public declarations }
end;
```

Once a frame has been created, it can be dropped on a form by choosing the frame icon from the Standard tab on the component palette. The IDE then pops up a dialog showing all frames defined in your application; and after selecting one, an instance of that frame can be dropped on a form (or on a suitable windowed control, such as a panel). Frames are quite helpful for achieving a consistent look when precisely the same set of controls must be shown at more than one place in an application.

Action lists

The ActionList component is a container for *TAction* components. Actions are discussed in detail in section 6.3.9.

6.4.2 The Additional Tab

Figure 6.43: The component palette's Additional tab

The Bitbutton control

The bitbutton control *(TBitBtn)* is a button which can additionally display a glyph (*this is entirely optional*). It has all the properties of a regular *TButton*. The use of such a glyph is highly operating system dependent. While it is common practice on Windows, it is definitely not the rule on Mac OS X.

Name	Description
TBitBtnLike	*TButton* but with the additional display of an icon.
TSpeedButton	A non-windowed button with an icon.
TStaticText	A label with the look and feel of an edit.
TImage	Has the built-in functionality needed to display an image.
TShape	For drawing a simple geometrical shape.
TBevel	For drawing bevels.
TPaintBox	Lets you draw arbitrary graphics.
TNotebook	Similar to *TPageControl*, included for compatibility only.
TLabeledEdit	A *TLabel* and *TEdit* combined in a single control.
TSplitter	A control allowing users to resize parts of a form.
TTrayIcon	To display an icon in the system tray.
TMaskEdit	A *TEdit* descendant which offers a mask for controlling keyed input.
TCheckListBox	A *TListbox* which displays a checkbox alongside each item.
TScrollBox	A container for displaying other controls in a scrollable area.
TApplication-Properties	A component for setting *TApplication* properties or reacting to application-wide events.
TStringGrid	A descendant of *TDrawGrid* which displays strings.
TDrawGrid	A grid which is completely drawn using event handlers.
TPairSplitter	An extended *Tsplitter*.
TColorBox	A *TComboBox* descendant for selecting a colour.
TColorListbox	A *TListBox* descendant for displaying and selecting colours.

Table 6.55: Controls on the Additional tab

The SpeedButton control

Through an array of speedbuttons on a simple panel, it is possible to provide quick access to important or often-needed functions. In contrast to the other types of button, the speedbutton is not a windowed control. You can't therefore activate it with the Tab key, because it cannot get focus. Speedbuttons can be used when a toolbar control would be over engineered for the intended use, for instance when only a couple of buttons are needed. Where many buttons are required, the *TToolbar* component (discussed later in this chapter) is better suited – especially when the intention is to create a complete toolbar under the main menu which duplicates the functions of the main menu.
In that case all actions can be synchronized through a *TActionList* component. If only a few speedbuttons are needed then *TSpeedButton* is better suited. The images directory under the Lazarus directory provides a large number of images which you can use for your speedbuttons.

The Static text control

This is a special version of the *TLabel* control, which has the characteristics of a *TPanel,* using its own canvas to draw on, whereas the *TLabel* control uses its parent's canvas to draw on. *TStaticText* differs from a *TPanel* in having a *FocusControl property,* and if the accelerator key is pressed, the specified focus control gets the focus.

The Labeled edit control

TLabeledEdit is a special version of the *TEdit* control, which has a *TLabel* associated with it. The position of the *EditLabel* relative to the edit control can be controlled with the *LabelPosition* property, and the distance from the edit control can be set using the *LabelSpacing* property.
Other than that, this control behaves like a regular *TEdit* control.

The Image control

This control can be used to display an image. The Picture property determines what image should be shown. The *Stretch property* allows resizing of the bitmap so it fits the *TImage* dimensions. It works together with the *Proportional* property, which tells the *TImage* control not to distort the image when it resizes it. The *Center* property allows you to display smaller bitmaps in the centre of the control. The *TImage* control can read most popular image formats by default, such as PNG, BMP, JPG and XPM.
Other image types can be added by including the imagesforlazarus package in the IDE. This adds TARGA, PNM and TIFF support.

The Shape control

The *TShape* control displays a simple geometrical figure. Its *Shape* property can be used to choose between a (rounded) rectangle, circle, diamond, ellipse or (rounded) square.
The drawing can be controlled through the *Pen* property, and the way the shape is filled is controlled with the *Brush* property.

The Bevel control

The bevel control *(TBevel)* is visually related to the panel control: it shows a border, or part of a border, but without any caption. The 'inside' of the bevel is empty, and no controls can be dropped on it. It's a control which simply draws a frame along its borders. It can be put around other controls to group them visually (just like a panel). Unlike a panel, *TBevel* is not a windowed control. Therefore it does not participate in the tab order of the form. The controls inside it are part of the tab order of the control on which the bevel is located (usually, the form).

Two properties control a bevel's appearance: *Shape* this can be a box (*bsBox*), *frame* (*bsFrame*) or any of the four edges of the bounding rectangle (*bsTopLine etc.*).
The *Style* property can have either the value *bsLowered* or *bsRaised* which determines whether the lines look engraved or embossed.

The Paintbox control

The paintbox control *TPaintBox* can be used when the shape control or image control is not enough, or whenever something must be painted that other regular controls do not provide. It has no particular properties other than the ones specifying its dimensions and how it should respond to resizing and positioning on the form.
All painting should be done in the control's *OnPaint* event.

The Tray icon

The *TTrayIcon* control is not quite like any other control, in the sense that it is not displayed on the form where it was placed. Rather, it shows itself in the desktop tray bar. The *Icon* property can be used to set the icon which should be displayed in the tray bar (*system tray*). The *PopupMenu* property can be set to a *TPopupMenu* instance which will be shown when the icon is clicked. Note that the tray icon is shown only during the lifetime of the form on which it is placed: as soon as the form is destroyed, the icon is removed from the system tray. However, the tray icon remains visible if the form is merely hidden (and not destroyed).

The Masked Edit control

This is a *TEdit* descendant which allows you to set an edit mask as a result of which anything typed in this control must fit the specified mask, or it will be rejected.
You would apply such a mask to control entry of dates, phone numbers, bank account numbers or other data which needs to conform to a specific format. The format of the data to be entered is specified in the *EditMask* property. To create a mask, click on the ellipsis button [...] in the Object Inspector alongside the *EditMask* property.
The editor which pops up allows you to test the mask you have entered to ensure it does what you want.

The Scrollbox

The scrollbox is a small control which does not offer any functionality other than providing room for other controls dropped on it, and making sure that there are scrollbars visible whenever the space taken by the controls is larger than the scrollbox itself, so the controls can always be scrolled into view.

The Grid controls

To present a large amount of data in tabular form you will usually use a grid. This shows a series of rows and columns, possibly with a title column and/or row. Users can scroll through the data both horizontally and vertically, if there is more data than will fit on the screen. Optionally, users can edit the data in the grid cells.
Lazarus provides three flavours of grid components:

- **TDrawGrid** Here all cells of the grid must be painted by the programmer. This grid component has no storage for data associated with the cells.
- **TStringGrid** This grid has the ability to associate a string with each cell in the grid, and it knows how to display the strings.
- **TDBGrid** is a special data-aware grid. It knows how to display the data from a *TDataset* descendant.

All three grids descend from *TCustomGrid*, and most of their functionality is implemented in this common ancestor.

Property	Description
AlternateColor	If the *AlternateColor* property is set to a colour different from the *Color* property, then the grid will be shown with alternating row colours: one row is painted with the *Color* property's colour, and the next row with the *AlternateColor*.
AutoAdvance	When the contents of a cell is edited, and the user hits the Enter or Tab keys, this property determines which cell is selected next. By default (*aaRight*) this is the next cell in the current row, until the end of the row is reached. Setting this to *aaNone* disables the automatic advance.
AutoEdit	Clicking on a cell will put it in edit mode. The main difference with the *goAlwaysShowEditor* option is that with the latter, the cells are always in edit mode. *AutoEdit* puts a cell in edit mode if it is clicked. If neither *AutoEdit* nor *goAlwaysShowEditor* are *True*, two clicks are needed to put a cell in edit mode: the first to select the cell, and the second to put it in edit mode.
AutoFillColumns	If set to *True* then the columns are automatically resized so they always fill the complete width of the grid. All columns are resized evenly, but this can be arranged differently using properties which are detailed below.
ExtendedSelect	Allows you to select multiple cells even if the grid is editable. In Delphi, range selections are not possible for editable grids.
Flat	If set to *True*, the fixed cells will be drawn using a flat look. (This property may disappear to be replaced with an extra TitleStyle option).
HeaderHotZones	Determines which fixed cells respond to hottracking.
HeaderPushZones	Determines which fixed cells respond to pushing.
TitleStyle	Determines how the fixed cells are drawn. Can be one of *tsLazarus*, *tsNative* or *tsDefault*. For *tsLazarus*, a flat look is used, and the Flat property is ignored.
UseXORFeatures	If this property is set to *True*, then the focus rectangle will be drawn using an XOR pen, so it will be visible no matter what the background Color is.
Options	Set property with Delphi-compatible options, extended with some extra possibilities. The values are listed in table 6.55.

Table 6.56: Common grid properties

Values	Description
goFixedVertLine	Draw vertical lines between fixed cells.
goFixedHorzLine	Draw horizontal lines between fixed cells.
goVertLine	Draw vertical lines between normal cells.
goHorzLine	Draw horizontal lines between normal cells.
goRangeSelect	Allow selection of a range of cells.
goDrawFocusSelected	Draw a rectangle around the focused cell.
goRowSizing	Allow the user to change the height of individual rows.
goColSizing	Allow the user to change the width of individual columns.
goRowMoving	Allow the user to move rows.
goColMoving	Allow the user to move columns.
goEditing	Allow editing of cell contents.
goTabs	Allow the user to move to the next cell by using the Tab key.
goRowSelect	Always select a complete row.
goAlwaysShowEditor	The selected cell is always editable immediately.
goThumbTracking	Correctly calculate the position from the scrollbar thumb.
goColSpanning	This option allows text to cover adjacent cells, as in Excel. When a cell is painted, the text rectangle is extended to span as many columns as needed to show the cell text fully.
goDblClickAutoSize	This option enables a spreadsheet feature: double-clicking the border between two column header cells will auto-size the column to the left. The column width will be changed so its width matches the widest text entry in the column. The *goColSizing* option must be *True* for this option to take effect.
goFixedRowNumbering	If enabled, the row number is shown in the first fixed column.
goHeaderHotTracking	If enabled, the header cell over which the mouse pointer is currently positioned will be shown in a different colour. The cells for which the hot-tracking is enabled can be specified in the *HeaderHotZones* property.
goHeaderPushedLook	If enabled, clicking a header cell will look like a depressed button once clicked. The fixed cells for which this is enabled can be specified in the *HeaderPushZones* property.
goRelaxedRowSelect	If this property is specified, then the currently selected cell is drawn inverted to the rest of the selected row.
goScrollKeepVisible	If this property is specified, the selected cell remains at the same position relative to the top of the grid when scrolling with the scrollbar. By default the selected cell will scroll along with the other cells.
goSmoothScroll	If this option is not set, then the grid is scrolled cell-by-cell, i.e. he top row always shows a complete cell. If the option is set, then the grid is scrolled on a pixel-by-pixel basis. Obviously, this option only has effect if goThumbTracking is specified.

Table 6.57: Common grid options

The *TStringGrid* component is the easiest and least complex grid component, therefore it will be used to explore the properties of Lazarus grids.
The basic properties of the grid are the rows and columns. In the *TStringGrid* and *TDrawGrid* controls, the number of rows is determined by the *RowCount* property: this is the number of rows that will be shown in the grid. The number of columns is determined by the *ColCount* property. Setting these properties will determine the size of the grid, which can be changed at any time.
The first rows or columns can be used as title columns or rows. If the grid is very large, and the user scrolls through the rows or columns, these columns or rows do not scroll, but stay fixed and visible all the time. The number of fixed columns is determined by the *FixedCols* property, and the number of fixed rows is controlled by the *FixedRows* property. Both properties default to 1, and they can never be equal to or larger than the number of columns or rows, respectively.
The data in a *TStringGrid* is kept in the *Cells* property. This is a 2-dimensional array property of strings, declared as

```
Property Cells[ACol, ARow: Integer]: string;
```

The *Acol, ARow* indexes range from 0 to *ColCount-1* and *RowCount-1*, respectively.
To display data in the grid, all that is needed is to set the *Cells* property to the string that should be displayed in the cell. This can be done in code as follows:

```
  Var I : Integer;
begin
  GDays.Cells[0,0] := 'Year';
  For I := 1 to 12 do
    Gdays.Cells[i,0] := ShortMonthNames[I];
```

This code will fill the first row of the grid with the names of the months, and the first column with the 'Year' string.

The following lines will enumerate the years in the first column of the rows:

```
  Var I,R : Integer;
begin
  R := 1;
  For I := 2010 downto 1951 do
  begin
    GDays.Cells[0,R] := IntToStr(I);
    Inc(R);
  end;
end;
```

The rest of the cells could be filled with random data, for instance the number of rainy days in the month of that year:

```
  Var I,R : Integer;
begin
  For I := 1 to 12 do
    For R := 1 to 60 do
      GDays.Cells[I,R] := IntToStr(Random(MonthDays[False,i]));
end;
```

The rows and columns can also be set in a single assignment statement, by assigning a *TStrings* instance to them. For instance, if *Titles* is a stringlist with the titles to be displayed in the first (fixed) row, then the following statement sets the titles:

```
Titles.Add('Year');
For I := 1 to 12 do
  Titles.Add(ShortMonthNames[I]);
Gdays.Rows[0] := Titles;
```

Similarly, the first column can be set with the years:

```
Titles.Clear;
Titles.Add('Year');
For I := 2010 downto 1951 do
  Titles.Add(IntToStr(I));
Gdays.Cols[0] := Titles;
```

The effect is the same as the routine above.

The grid has a plethora of options for configuring its behaviour. The first one to examine is the *Options* property, a set of options which can be turned on or off, and which are explained in Table 6.57. Other than those options, the *DefaultColWidth* and *DefaultRowHeight* are used to determine the grid's appearance. They determine the standard width and height of the cells in the grid. By default the rows and columns all have the same standard height and width.
The *goDblClickAutoSize* option only works for columns which are not fixed columns. Luckily, the grid has a method which allows you to automatically resize a column. The following code will resize all columns in the grid so they fit the size of their contents:

```
  Var I : integer;
begin
  For I := 0 to SGDemo.FixedCols-1 do
    SGDemo.AutoSizeColumn(i);
end;
```

The *AutoSizeColumns* method (note the 's' at the end) of the grid auto-sizes all columns in the grid.
As well as having extra properties compared to a Delphi *TStringGrid*, a Lazarus *TStringGrid* can be edited at design time. You can set the strings in a grid using the component editor (available from the designer popup menu when right-clicking the grid component) which is shown in Figure 6.41.

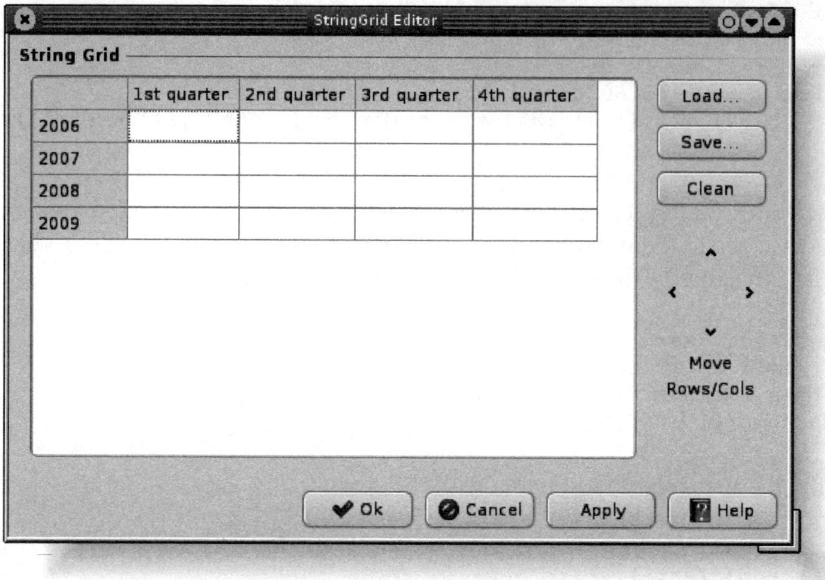

Figure 6.44 The TStringGrid editor

Columns

Perhaps the biggest difference from Delphi's *TStringGrid* is that the Lazarus implementation provides a *Columns* property: a collection of *TGridColumn* items which describe the properties of a column in the grid, similar to the *Columns* property in a *TDBGrid*. The property is mutually exclusive with the *ColCount* property: as soon as columns are used, the *ColCount* property can no longer be set.
The *Columns* property describes only the non-fixed columns. That is, if there are 2 fixed columns (*FixedColCount=2*) and 3 *Columns*, then the grid will display 5 columns.
The *Columns.Enabled* property determines whether columns are in use. The following code transforms a grid without column definitions to a grid using columns:

```
  Var I,ACount : Integer;
begin
  ACount := SGDemo.ColCount-SGDemo.FixedColCount;
  SGDemo.Columns.Clear;
  For I := 1 to ACount do
    With TGridColumn(SGDemo.Columns.Add) do
      Title.Caption := 'Column ' + IntToStr(i);
end;
```

Figure 6.42 shows a simple grid with 3 fixed rows and a fixed column, which could represent monthly sales figures.

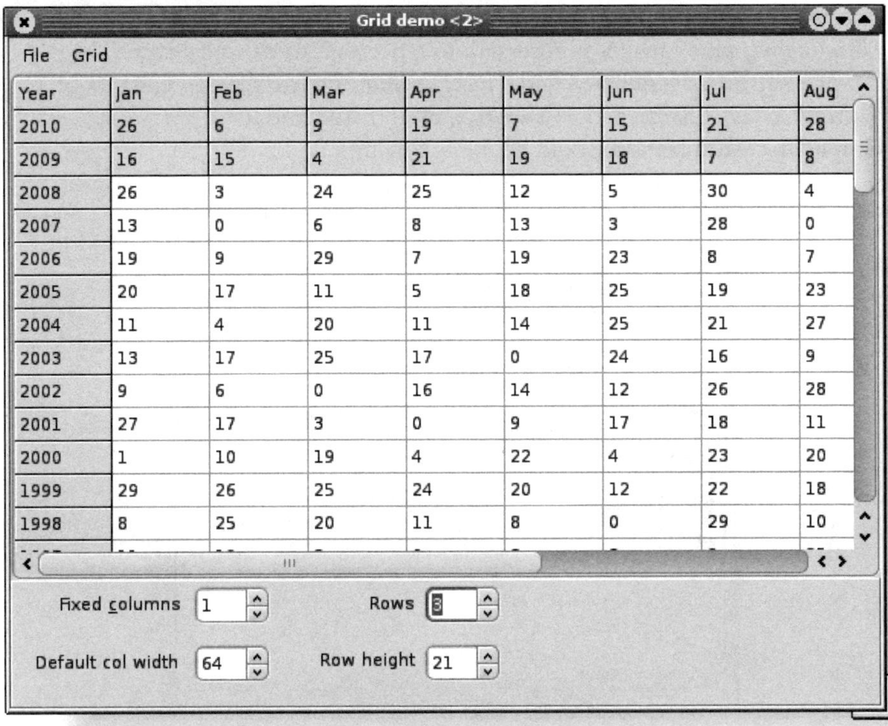

Figure 6.45: A string grid showing sales figures

Editing

The Lazarus *TStringGrid* does not use the *TInPlaceEditor* class as the Delphi grid does. Instead, it uses a *TButton*, *TMaskEdit* or *TComboBox* control directly.
Which of these controls is used in a cell is controlled by the *ButtonStyle* property of *TGridColumn*: the style to be used can be set per column in the grid.
The appearance of the edit controls cannot be set by properties of the grid. Instead, the *OnSelectEditor* event allows you to customize the editor when it is about to be displayed. The following is an example of an *OnSelectEditor* event handler:

```
procedure TMainForm.DoSelectEditor(Sender: TObject;
                                   aCol, aRow: Integer;
  var Editor: TWinControl);
begin
  If Editor is TStringCellEditor then
    CustomizeEdit(aCol,ARow,Editor as TStringCellEditor)
  else
    if Editor is TButtonCellEditor then
      CustomizeButton(aCol,ARow,Editor as TButtonCellEditor)
    else
      if Editor is TPickListCellEditor then
        CustomizePickList(aCol,ARow,Editor as TPickListCellEditor);
end;
```

Since the actual editor can be one of several different classes, the Editor argument is of type *TWinControl*, which makes it necessary to typecast it to its actual type. The *TStringCellEditor*, *TButtonCellEditor* and *TPickListCellEditor* are the descendants of *TCustomMaskedEdit*, *TButton* and *TComboBox*, used by the grid.
An example of customization would be the following …

```
procedure TMainForm.CustomizeEdit(Acol,ARow : Integer;
                                  Editor : TStringCellEditor);
begin
  Editor.PasswordChar := '*';
  Editor.MaxLength := 5;
end;
```

…which has the effect shown in Figure 6.43.

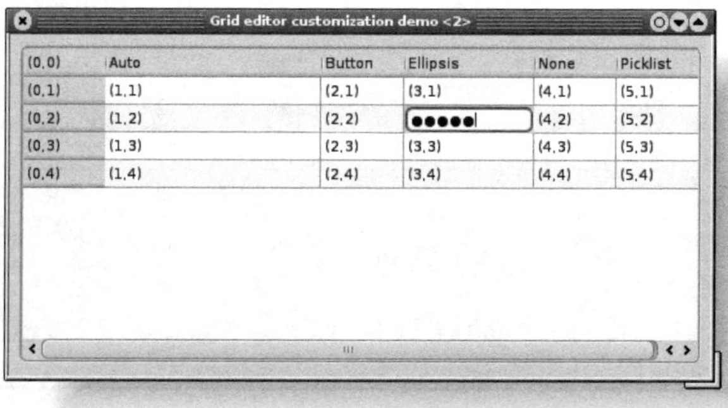

Figure 6.46: A user-defined editor

The ColorBox control

The *TColorBox* control is a descendant of *TComboBox* which allows you to select a colour from a list of pre-defined system colours (the number of items in the list is determined by its Palette property). Each colour is shown as a name with a small square in front of it, coloured appropriately. The selected colour is available in the *Selection* property – it can be both read and set. As with the *TColorListbox* (see next section), the displayed colours are available in the *Colors* array property.

Name	Description
TTrackbar	Trackbar to set an integer value.
TProgressBar	Progress indicator.
TTreeview	Tree-like structure with icons and text.
TlistView	Structure to represent a list in several modes.
TstatusBar	Status indication.
Ttoolbar	A button bar.
TUpdown	A pair of arrows to increase/decrease a value.
TPageControl	A control to organise a set of tab sheets
TTabControl	A set of tabs.
THeaderControl	A set of headers for columns.
TimageList	A component to keep a set of images in a memory efficient way.
TPopupNotifier	A component to show a tooltip.

Tabel 6.58: Components on the Common Controls tab (part 1)

Name	Description
TColorButton	TButton descendant that allows to select a color.
TSpinEdit	Edit with arrows to select, increase/decrease an integer value.
TFloatSpinEdit	Edit with arrows to select, increase/decrease a float value.
TArrow	Draws an arrow in the form of a triangle.
TCalendar	Calendar control to select a date.
TEditButton	Edit control with a button attached to it.
TFileNameEdit	Edit control with a button that pops up a dialog to select a filename.
TDirectoryEdit	Edit control with a button that pops up a dialog to select a directory.
TDateEdit	Edit control with a button to select a date from a popup calendar.
TCalcEdit	Edit control with a button to show a small calculator.
TFileListBox	Listbox to select a file from a list of files in a directory.
TFilterCombobox	Combobox to select a filter.
TXMLPropStorage	Component to store published property values in an XML file.
TINIPropStorage	Component to store published property values in an .INI file.
TBarChart	Component to show a bar chart (histogram).
TButtonPanel	Panel to show standard buttons in a dialog, in accordance with OS guidelines.
TShellTreeView	TreeView to show a directory structure.
TShellListView	Listview to show the contents of a directory.
TIDEDialogLayout	StorageLayout storage container for IDE dialogs.

Tabel 6.58: Components on the Common Controls tab (Continuation)

The ColorListbox control

The *TColorListbox* control is a descendant of *TListbox* which allows you to select a set of colours from a list of pre-defined system colours (the number of items in the list is determined by the *Palette* property). Each colour is shown as a name with a small square in front of it, coloured appropriately. The displayed colours are available in the *Colors* array property – this is useful for determining which colours are selected when the listbox allows selection of multiple colours. If only a single colour can be selected, the selected colour is available in the *Selection* property – it can be both read and set. The *Style* property can be used to enable certain colour groups, and to determine whether the user is allowed to define custom colours.

The CheckListBox control

The *MultiSelect* property of a *TListBox* determines whether a user can select more than one item in the listbox. From a user's point of view, it may be preferable to have a checkbox next to the items he wants to select, such as in a *TCheckGroup* control.
The *TCheckListBox* is a descendant of *TListBox* which shows all its items with a checkbox in front of it. The state of each checkbox can be verified using the *Checked* array property. The following code shows all selected items in a checklistbox in a message.

```
procedure TMainForm.BShowClick(Sender: TObject);
  Var I : Integer;
      S : String;
begin
  S := SCheckedItems;
  For I := 0 to LBTest.Items.Count-1 do
    If LBTest.Checked[i] then
      S := S + sLinebreak+LBTest.Items[i];
  ShowMessage(S);
end;
```

It simply loops over all items, and saves the ones that are checked. **Note** that the *TCheckListBox* still has the *MultiSelect* property, and the *Selected* array present in its ancestor *TListbox*. The *Checked* and *Selected* properties are independent of each other and can both be used.

6.4.3 The Common controls tab

Figure 6.47 The component palette's Common Controls tab

The Trackbar

The *TTrackBar* control can be used to let the user specify an integral number by means of a slider which he can slide to the selected value. The slider can be oriented vertically or horizontally, depending on the value of the *Orientation* property. The selected value is available through the *Position* property, which can vary between the values of the *Min* and *Max* properties. The *ScalePos* property can be used to set the location of the scale: below or above the slider. The OnChange event can be used to take action when the user changes the selected value.

The Progressbar

The progressbar in many ways resembles the *TTrackBar* control. But where the *TTrackBar* is used to let the user set a value, the *TProgressBar* is used to report to the user what proportion of a lengthy operation has been completed – the user cannot set the position.

Like the *TTrackbar* control, the progressbar shows – graphically – the value of the *Position* property, which is located between the Min and Max properties.
The *Orientation* property determines the orientation of the progressbar. If the *Smooth* property is set to False, then the progress bar uses small blocks to indicate the position. If it is set to *True*, a solid bar is drawn. If a solid bar is used, the *BarShowText* property indicates whether the position should be written as text as well. Finally, the *Style* property can be used to make the progress bar act as a normal progress bar, or as a marquee – in which case it acts as a small block which moves continuously from left to right and *vice versa.*

The Treeview control

Often an application needs to display a hierarchical structure: the directory structure of the local hard disk; the structure of a book (a help file); the structure of an XML file; threads in a mailing list discussion or newsgroup. Such structures are commonly shown in a tree. The *TTreeView* component is designed for such uses, and displays a tree structure on screen. The user can select a part of the tree, or even change the names of the items in the tree.Each of the branches or leaves in the tree is represented by a *TTreeNode* instance. The *TTreeNode* instance defines how the node is shown onscreen:

- The text associated with the node.
- The image shown in front of the node.
- An additional state image for the node, shown next to the normal image.

Additionally, arbitrary data can be associated with each *TTreeNode* instance: for example, it could point to the XML element of the XML document that is being shown.
The main properties of the *TTreeView* are described in Table 6.59.

Property	Description
AutoExpand	Should the tree nodes automatically expand when the user double-clicks them?
DefaultItemHeight	The default height of the items in the tree.
ExpandSignColor	The colour of the expand sign in front of a node.
ExpandSignType	The kind of expand sign used, this is one of *tvestArrow* (a small arrow), *tvestPlusMinus* (a plus and minus sign) or *tvestTheme* (the sign used by the operating system theme).
Indent	The indent width (in pixels) for each new level of nodes.
Images	The imagelist containing the images shown in the treenode.
Items	The list of *TTreeNode* instances (items) shown in the tree.
Options	A list of options describing the behaviour of the tree (see table below)
ReadOnly	If set to *True*, the nodes' captions cannot be changed by the user.
RightClickSelect	If set to *True*, then right-clicking an item automatically selects it.
RowSelect	Should the whole current line be shown as selected when selecting an item?
SelectionColor	The colour of a selected node.
ShowButtons	If set to *False*, the expand/collapse sign will not be drawn in front of the nodes that can be collapsed or expanded.
ShowLines	Should lines be drawn between the various nodes or not?
ShowRoot	Should the tree display a root node (a top node) from which all nodes descend?
SortType	How tree nodes are sorted. It takes one of these values: *stNone, stText, stData* or *stBoth*.
StateImages	The imagelist used for the state icons in front of the nodes.
TreeLineColor	The colour of the line connecting the tree node items.
TreeLinePenstyle	The style of the line connecting the tree node items.

Table 6.59: TTreeView's principal properties

A treeview's *Options* property is a set of options, many of which correspond to a regular property of the *TTreeview* component. The possible values are listed in Table 6.60.

Option	Description
tvoAllowMultiselect	Allow multiple nodes to be selected (using Ctrl-click).
tvoAutoExpand	Same as the *AutoExpand* property.
tvoAutoInsertMark	Automatically insert mark.
tvoAutoItemHeight	Automatically determine the item height from the image height.
tvoHideSelection	Hide the selection when the tree does not have focus.
tvoHotTrack	Scrolling the tree happens synchronously.
tvoReadOnly	Same as the *ReadOnly* property.
tvoRightClickSelect	Same as the *RightClickSelect* property.
tvoRowSelect	Same as the *RowSelect* property.
tvoShowButtons	Same as the *ShowButtons* property.
tvoShowLines	Same as the *ShowLines* property.
tvoShowRoot	Same as the *ShowRoot* property.
tvoShowSeparators	Show separator lines between nodes.
tvoToolTips	Same as the *ShowHint* property.
tvoNoDoubleClickExpand	Double click will not expand or collapse the clicked node.

Table 6.60: Possible values for TTreeView's Options property

The node items (of class *TTreeNode*) have various properties which control their appearance:

Property	Description
Caption	The displayed text.
Expanded	Determines whether the node is expanded or not.
ImageIndex	The index of the image to show when the node is displayed normally.
OverlayIndex	The index of an image which will be displayed on top of the normal image.
SelectedIndex	The index of the image to show when the node is selected.
StateIndex	The index for the node's state image.
Data	A pointer to whatever data should be associated with the tree node.

Table 6.61: Important TTreeNode properties

The *ImageIndex* and *SelectedIndex* images are taken from the imagelist pointed to by the treeview's *Images* property. The *StateIndex* is an image index into the imagelist pointed to by the treeview's *StateImages* property.
If StateImage is set, a second image will be shown next to the image indicated by ImageIndex.

Filling a tree with elements

There are two ways to fill a treeview with nodes. Firstly you can fill the tree with nodes at design time. The *Items* property editor allows you to design a tree completely in the **IDE**. The *New Item* and *New SubItem* buttons allow you to create new items at the current level or at a lower level, respectively. The three image indexes can be specified for each node, and as soon as the *Apply* button is pressed, the *TTreeView* instance is updated.
Alternatively you can fill a tree with treenodes in code, using the methods of the *TTreeNodes* class. The basic method to use when filling the tree is the *AddChild* method:

```
function AddChild(ParentNode: TTreeNode; S: string): TTreeNode;
```

This method will add a child node below *ParentNode* with caption *S*, and returns the newly created child node. If *ParentNode* is *Nil*, then the node will be added at the top level of the tree.

There are several variants on the *AddChild* method which offer slightly different functionality:

```
function AddChildFirst(ParentNode: TTreeNode; S: string): TTreeNode;
function AddChildObject(ParentNode: TTreeNode; S: string; Data:
                                                  Pointer): TTreeNode;
function AddChildObjectFirst(ParentNode: TTreeNode; S: string; Data:
                                                  Pointer): TTreeNode;
```

AddChildFirst will add the new node as the first child node (the default is to add a node at the end).

AddChildObject and *AddChildObjectFirst* perform the same task, but allow you to specify the *Data* pointer for the newly created node. The following call adds a new node at the same level as the *SiblingNode* node:

```
function Add(SiblingNode: TTreeNode; S: string): TTreeNode;
```

The node will be added as the last node. Paralleling the *AddChild* method, there are several *SiblingNode* variant methods that allow you to specify the *Data* pointer, and which add the new node as the first node:

```
function AddObject(SiblingNode: TTreeNode; S: string; Data: Pointer):
                                                            TTreeNode;
function AddFirst(SiblingNode: TTreeNode; S: string): TTreeNode;
function AddObjectFirst(SiblingNode: TTreeNode; S: string; Data:
                                                  Pointer): TTreeNode;
```

The following code sample demonstrates how to fill a treeview with the contents of a directory tree:

```
Function TMainForm.ShowDirectory(Const ADir: String; TV: TTreeView;
                                 ParentNode: TTreeNode): Integer;
  Var I,II: Integer;
         N: TTreeNode;
         L: TStringList;
         D: String;
begin
  L := TStringList.Create;
  try
    Result := GetSubDirectories(ADir,L);
    if result > 0 then
    begin
      TV.Items.BeginUpdate;
      try
        For I := 0 to L.Count-1 do
        begin
          D := L[i];
          N := TV.Items.AddChild(ParentNode,D);
          D := IncludeTrailingPathDelimiter(ADir) + D;
          if ShowDirectory(D,TV,N) > 0 then
            II := 1
          else
            II := 0;
          N.ImageIndex := II;
          N.SelectedIndex := II;
        end;
      finally
      TV.Items.EndUpdate;
    end;
  end;
  finally
    L.free;
  end;
end;
```

The *BeginUpdate* and *EndUpdate* methods of the *TTreeNodes* class are used to optimize the filling of the tree, because the tree repaints itself whenever a node is added. If (as in the example above), many nodes are added at once, this causes a lot of flicker, and would considerably slow down the redrawing. The *BeginUpdate* and *EndUpdate* prevent this. After a call to *BeginUpdate*, repainting of the tree is deferred until *EndUpdate* is called. If *BeginUpdate* is called more than once, then *EndUpdate* should be called an equal number of times.
The sample code above uses a recursive technique to show all subdirectories below the given directory in nodes below the *ParentNode* node. It returns the number of subdirectories. This number is used to change the image shown for each directory node. If the directory contains subdirectories of its own, another image is shown for the node. **Note** that the *SelectedIndex* is set to the same value as the *ImageIndex* property: failing to do so would make the image disappear when the node is clicked.
The result can be seen in Figure 6.45.

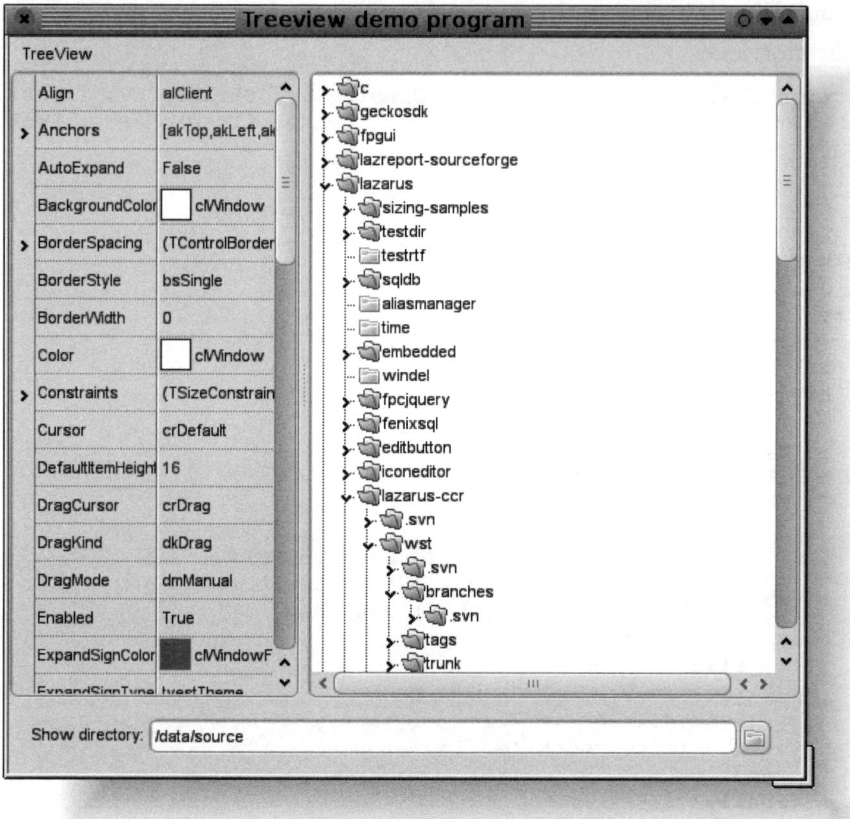

Figure 6.48: A treeview demo with directories

Traversing the tree

Sometimes it is necessary to traverse all nodes of the tree – for instance to check if a file or directory has changed or disappeared, or to collect data from each node.
The *TTreeNode* class has various methods to do this. The methods are based on traversing the child nodes and the nodes on the same level as the current node:

```
function GetFirstChild: TTreeNode;
function GetNextSibling: TTreeNode;
```

The first child is the first node below the current node, while the next sibling is the next node at the same level. There are some variants on this call:

```
function GetLastChild: TTreeNode;
function GetLastSibling: TTreeNode;
```

They return the last child node of the current node, or the last node at the same level as the current node. There are several more variants of these functions, but those given are the main methods you will use.
The following sample code uses these methods to traverse the directory tree shown in the treeview, and to update each node with some statistics about the directory it represents:

```
procedure TMainForm.ShowDirectoryStatistics(ADir: String;
                                N: TTreeNode; Var D,F: Integer);
  Var ND,NF : Integer;
       NDir : String;
begin
  While N <> Nil do
  begin
    NDir := ADir + N.Text;
    GetDirStats(NDir,ND,NF);
    N.Text := Format('%s (Files: %d, Dirs: %d)',[N.Text,NF,ND]);
    D := D + ND;
    F := F + NF;
    ShowDirectoryStatistics(NDir,N.GetFirstChild,D,F);
    N := N.GetNextSibling;
  end;
end;
```

The parent node can be used to determine the full directory path to the current node:

```
Function TMainForm.GetPath(Node: TTreeNode): String;
begin
  Result := '';
  While (Node <> Nil) do
  begin
    If (Result <> '') then
      Result := '/' + Result;
    Result := Node.Text + Result;
    Node := Node.Parent;
  end;
  Result := DEShow.Directory + Result;
end;
```

This can be used to update the form's caption as soon as a node is selected. When the node selection changes, the **OnSelectionChange** event of the treeview is triggered:

```
procedure TMainForm.TVDirsSelectionChanged(Sender: TObject);
  Var S : String;
begin
  S := GetPath(TVDirs.Selected);
  Caption := Format('%s : %s',[SCaption,S]);
end;
```

As can be seen, the *Selected* property of the treeview is used to retrieve the selected node. The *Selected* property can also be used to set the selected node in the treeview.
More than one node can be selected if *tvoAllowMultiselect* is specified in the *Options* property. Each node has a boolean property *MultiSelected*, which is set to *True* when a node is selected using multi-select. The full list of selected nodes can be constructed by examining all nodes:

```
  Var I : Integer; Dirs : TStringList;
begin
  Dirs := TStringList.Create;
  Try
    For I := 0 to TVDirs.Items.Count - 1 do
      if TVDirs.Items[i].MultiSelected then
        Dirs.Add(GetPath(TVDirs.Items[i]));
    ShowMessage(SSelectedDirs + Dirs.Text);
  Finally
    Dirs.Free;
  end;
end;
```

The *Items* property contains all nodes (irrespective of their position in the tree) and by checking their *MultiSelected* property, the list of selected nodes – or the directory they represent – can be constructed. The result of this action is shown in Figure 6.46.

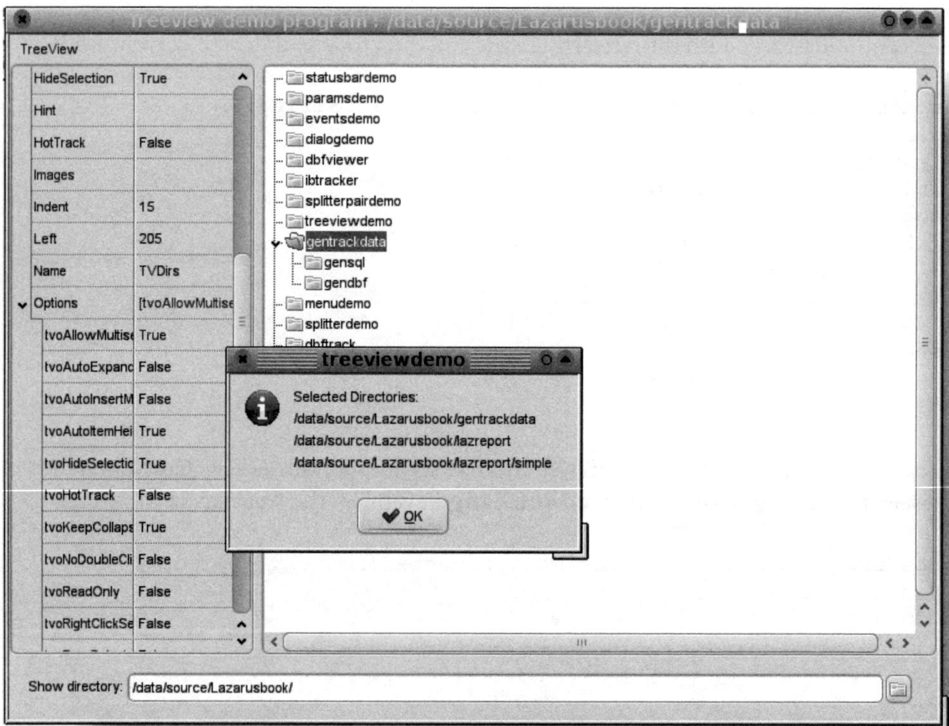

Figure 6.49: More than one directory selected in a treeview

It is possible to prevent the user from changing the currently selected node. Use the *OnChanging* event for this. It has a parameter *AllowChange* which can be set to *False*. If set to *False*, the currently selected node stays selected, even though another node was clicked:

```
procedure TMainForm.TVDirsChanging(Sender: TObject; Node: TTreeNode;
                                   var AllowChange: Boolean);
begin
  AllowChange := CheckAllowChangetGetPath(Node));
end;
```

The method *AllowChangeDir* should somehow decide whether it is allowed to change to the selected directory. The same can be done for editing a treeview. When it is not read-only (its *ReadOnly* property is set to *False*, the default), the user can edit the text of the nodes by clicking them a second time when they are selected. At that moment, the *OnEditing* event will be triggered, which has an *AllowEdit* parameter: when this is set to *False* in the handler, then the treeview will not start editing the node. If it is set to *True* (the value when the handler is called), then the treeview will start editing the node. The following event handler will allow you to edit only nodes which are leaf nodes, i.e. nodes that have no child nodes of their own:

```
procedure TMainForm.TVDirsEditing(Sender: TObject; Node: TTreeNode;
                                              var AllowEdit: Boolean);
begin
  AllowEdit := (Node.GetFirstChild = Nil);
end;
```

Once the user has edited the node, the *OnEdited* event is called, and is passed the node which was being edited, as well as the new value for the text of the node. This can be used to perform an action, such as a confirmation:

```
procedure TMainForm.TVDirsEdited(Sender: TObject; Node: TTreeNode;
                                                      var S: string );
  Var OldDir, NewDir, Msg: String;
begin
  OldDir := GetPath(Node);
  NewDir := ExtractFilePath(OldDir) + S;
  MSg := Format(SRenameDir,[OldDir,NewDir]);
  If Not ((mrYes = MessageDLG(Msg,mtConfirmation, [mbYes,mbNo],0))
     and RenameFile(OldDir,NewDir)) then
    S := Node.Text;
end;
```

This will ask for confirmation: should the directory actually be renamed? If not, or the rename was not successful, then the newly entered value will be reset to the value of the node text prior to the editing operation.

The ListView

A companion to the *Treeview* component is the *Listview* control. It has its origins in the Windows File Explorer, which used the listview to display the contents of a directory, where the treeview was used to display the directory tree. Generally, it can be used to show a list of items, where each item has a name, an icon and possibly a set of other attributes (called subitems). The original Windows Explorer provided four view-modes to view the contents of a directory (in the latest versions, more modes are available). Each of these modes listed differing details of the files in the directory that was shown. These four view modes are encountered in the possible values for the *ViewStyle* property of the Listview control: *vsIcon* (showing large icons); *vsSmallIcon* (showing small icons); *vsList* (a simple list), and *vsReport* (a detailed report).

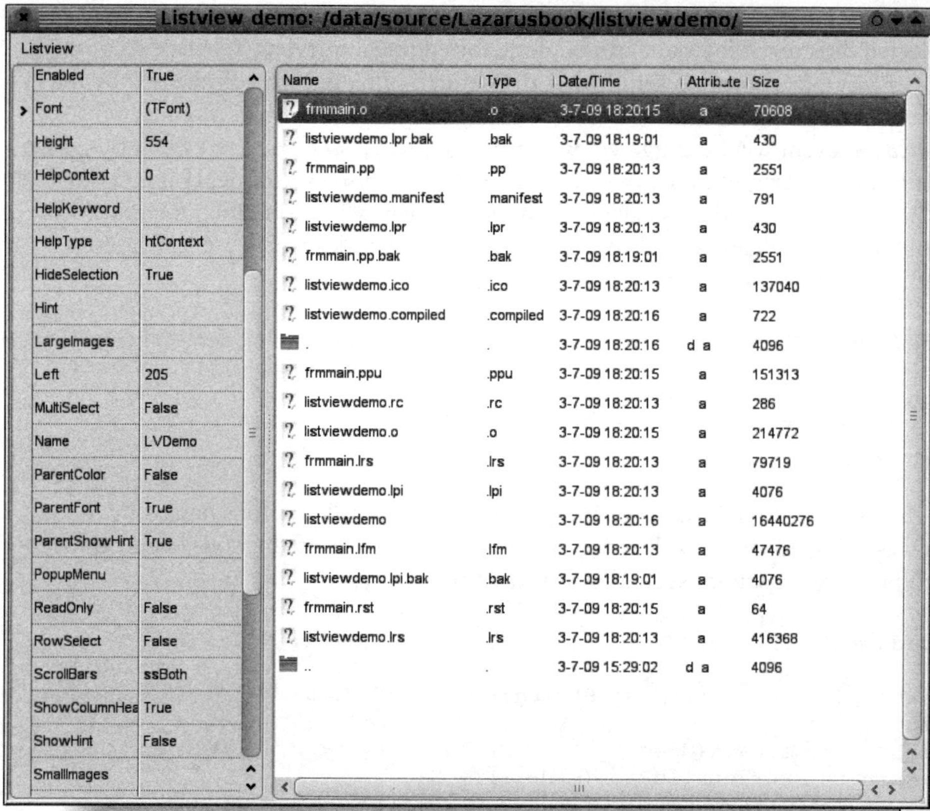

Figure 6.50: A TListView control showing the contents of a directory

To use a listview control, you need two classes: The *TListView* control and the *TListItem* class. The *TListItem* class represents an item that can be shown in the list. The main properties of *TListItem* are listed in Table 6.62.

Property	Description
Caption	The text associated with the item (usually the filename).
ImageIndex	The index of an image in an imagelist.
SubItems	An array of strings, which are shown in separate columns when the mode is *vsList* or *vsReport*.
Data	Can be used to store a pointer to arbitrary data.
Checked	If the Listview has its *Checkboxes* property set to *True*, then this property indicates whether the checkbox for this item is checked.

Table 6.62 TListItem's principal properties

These properties more or less speak for themselves.
The *TListView* control has many more properties.

Property	Description
CheckBoxes	Should a checkbox be shown in front of every item, so it can be selected?
ColumnClick	When set to *True*, the column headers are clickable, and when clicked the *OnColumnClick* event will be triggered.
Columns	A collection of column definitions. When the list is in *vsList* or *vsReport* mode, this property defines which columns are actually visible in the listview. If none are defined, only the icon and Caption of the list items will be shown.
HideSelection	If set to *True*, then the selection will not be shown highlighted when the listview does not have focus.
Items	The list of items (each of type *TListItem*) to be shown in the listview.
LargeImages	The list of images to use when the *ViewStyle* is *vsIcon*. The listitem's *ImageIndex* property is an index into this list.
MultiSelect	If set to *True*, multiple items can be selected in the list.
RowSelect	If set to *True*, the whole line is shown as selected in the details or report view. If *False*, then only the caption is shown as selected.
ShowColumn Header	Should the column headers be shown in report view?
SmallImages	The list of images that must be used when the ViewStyle is *vsSmallIcon*. The listitem's *ImageIndex* property is an index into this list.
SortColumn	The number of the column to sort on.
SortType	The sorting method to use. This can be one of *stText*, *stData*, *stBoth* or *stNone*.
StateImages	The imagelist referenced by the StateIndex property.
ViewStyle	The view style to use.

Table 6.63 Principal properties of TListView

The *Items* property of a listview can be set up using its property editor. This property editor allows you to set up the *Items* list with an intuitive and easy interface, as shown in Figure 6.48. You can use it to set up all aspects of the list.

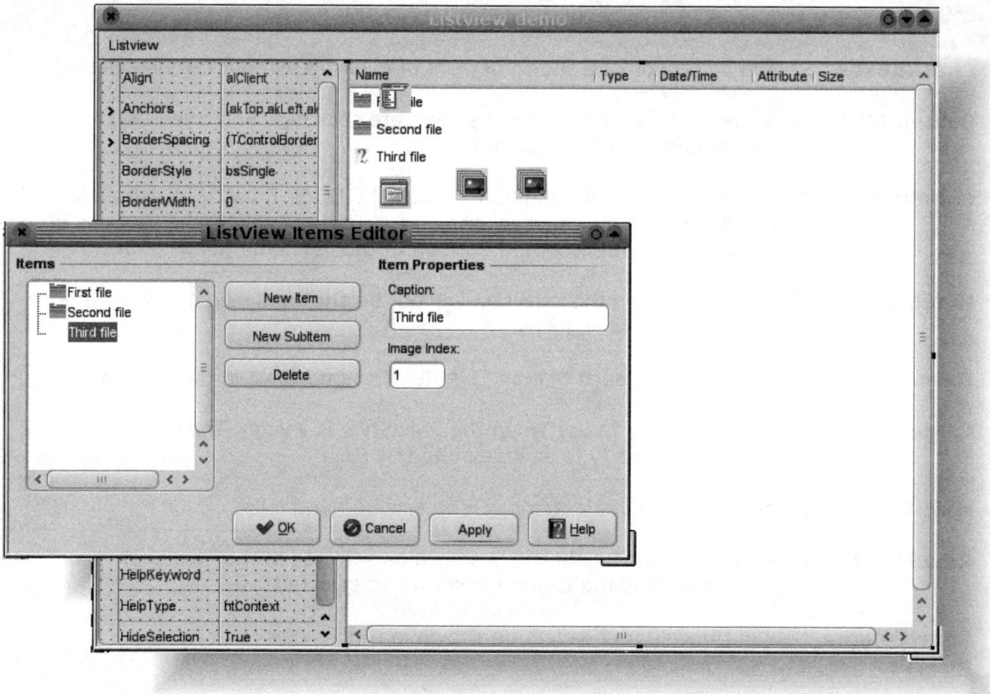

Figure 6.51: The Listview editor in the Lazarus IDE

In practice, the *Items* property will usually be set up in code: the *Items* property contains the necessary methods for this. Since the list structure of a listview is more straightforward than the tree structure of a treeview, its interface is simpler:

```
function  Add: TListItem;
procedure AddItem(AItem: TListItem);
function  Insert(const AIndex: Integer): TListItem;
procedure InsertItem(AItem: TListItem; const AIndex: Integer);
```

The *Add* call creates a new item and adds it to the list. The newly created item is returned. The *AddItem* call will add an existing item to the list. The two *Insert* calls do the same, only they insert the items at a particular position in the list. Deleting items can be done using the *Delete* or *Clear* calls:

```
procedure Clear;
procedure Delete(const AIndex: Integer);
```

If a lot of updating is to be done, it is good practice to enclose the updating operation in a pair of *BeginUpdate*, *EndUpdate* calls:

```
procedure BeginUpdate;
procedure EndUpdate;
```

They prevent the listview from redrawing itself every time an item is added or deleted. You can examine the items of a listview using its simple list-like interface:

```
property Count: Integer;
property Item[const AIndex: Integer]: TListItem;
```

Finally, it is possible to search the list using the following three calls:

```
function FindCaption(StartIndex: Integer; Value: string;
                     Partial, Inclusive, Wrap: Boolean;
                     PartStart: Boolean = True): TListItem;
function FindData (const AData: Pointer): TListItem;
function IndexOf  (const AItem: TListItem): Integer;
```

The first call *FindCaption* searches for an item with a caption that equals *Value*, where the search is started at item *StartIndex* (if *Inclusive* is *True*), or at the next item if *Inclusive* is *False*. The *Partial* parameter specifies that the caption may be matched partially, while *Wrap* wraps the search around and starts anew at the beginning of the list. If the *PartStart* parameter is *True* then a partial match is considered a match only if the match starts at character position 1 of the *Caption*.
The *FindData* call searches for an item with *Data* pointer equal to *AData*, and finally *IndexOf* returns the index of the given listitem.

The following code sample shows the contents of a directory. For each file, it shows the name, extension, last modification date and file size and finally the file attributes. This means that five columns are needed to show the directory contents in list or report view style. These columns can be defined using the *Columns* property editor, assigning more or less appropriate widths and captions to each of them.

```
procedure TMainForm.ShowDirectory(ADir: String);
Var Info: TSearchRec;
begin
  Caption := Format(SCaption,[ADir]);
  ADir := IncludeTrailingPathDelimiter(ADir);
  With LVDemo.Items do
  begin
    BeginUpdate;
    try
      Clear;
      if FindFirst(ADir + AllFilesMask,faAnyFile,Info) = 0 then
        try
          Repeat AddFile(Info);
          Until (FindNext(Info) <> 0) ;
        finally
          FindClose(Info);
        end;
    finally
      EndUpdate;
    end;
  end;
end;
```

Note the use of the *BeginUpdate/EndUpdate* pair. The actual adding of the items to the listview happens in the *AddFile* call:

```
Function TMainForm.AddFile(Const Info: TSearchRec): TListItem;
begin
  Result := LVDemo.Items.Add;
  Result.Caption := Info.Name;
  LVDemo.ColumnClick;
  Result.ImageIndex := Ord((Info.Attr and faDirectory) = 0);
  With Result.SubItems do
  begin
    Add(ExtractFileExt(Info.Name));
    Add(DateTimeToStr(FileDateToDateTime(Info.Time)));
    Add(AttrToStr(Info.Attr));
    Add(IntToStr(Info.Size));
  end;
end;
```

The *SubItems* property is of type *TStrings,* so filling it just means converting the various file properties to suitable strings and adding them to the *SubItems* list. The ListView has two imagelists associated with it, one for the small icons view, and one for the icons view. Each imagelist contains two icons: one for a directory, one for a normal file (in a real-world application, the kind of image would of course be determined by the file type: its extension).

The Statusbar

A status bar is often put at the bottom of a form to display status information, such as the current position of the cursor in text, or the insert or overwrite mode of the editor, or additional hints. Dropping a status bar on a form will automatically place it at the bottom of the form. As with the toolbar component, this is just a default location: a status bar can be set at any location in the form by setting the *Align* property to *alNone*, and then setting the position and size properties.
There are few properties of interest in a statusbar, which are shown in Table 6.64.
The most interesting is probably *SimplePanel*: If this is set to *True* then the statusbar acts as a single panel, displaying the value of the *SimpleText* property. If set to *False*, the panels as defined in the Panels property are shown; these panels must be defined in the panel editor (a simple collection), and the text of each panel can be set through indexed access to the panel, and setting its *Text* property as shown below.

Property	Description
Panels	A collection of panels (of type *TStatusPanel*),which are shown on the status bar. Each panel can contain a short text string, specified in its *Text* property. The panels can be edited by double-clicking the statusbar in the designer. This shows the panel editor. It is depicted in Figure 6.49.
AutoHint	If set to *True* then the hint property of the current control will be shown in the first panel of the status bar, regardless of whether the *ShowHint* property for this control is set or not. By default it is set to *False*.
SimpleText	The text shown on the panel if *SimplePanel* is set to *True*.
SizeGrip	This property determines whether a window size grip is shown at the right-bottom corner of the status bar. It can be used to resize the window.

Table 6.64: Properties of a TStatusBar

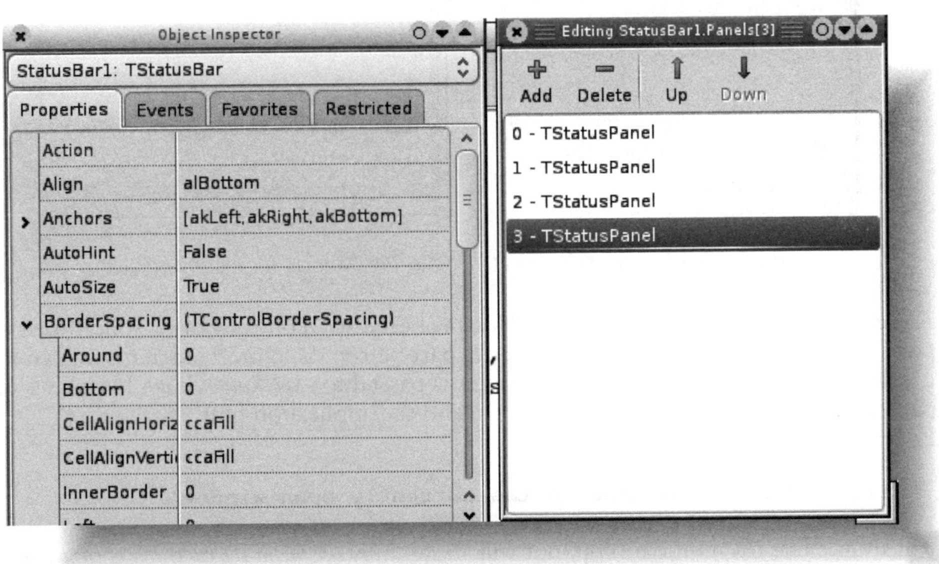

Figure 6.52: The status bar editor in the IDE

Often, panels are used to provide hints and tips about the currently active control or window in the application. Each control has a *Hint* property, and this property can be used to display information in the status bar. The *OnHint* event handler of the global *Application* object can be used to display a hint in the status bar. This event handler is called by the LCL whenever the mouse hovers over a control with a hint: the *Application.Hint* property then contains the hint of the control. It is shown as follows:

```
procedure TMainForm.DoApplicationHint(Sender: TObject);
begin
  SBMain.Panels[1].Text := Application.Hint;
end;
```

As can be seen, the *Text* property of the second panel (panels are numbered starting with zero) is set to the application hint.

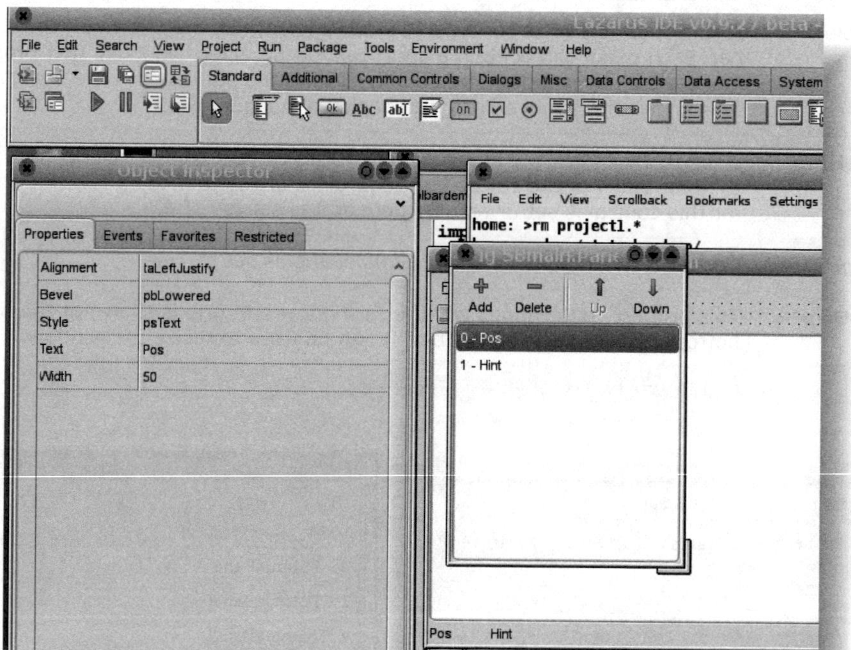

Figure 6.53: The properties of a status bar panel in the object inspector

A nice feature of the **LCL** is that the *Hint* property of a control can be split into two parts, separated by a | (pipe) character: the part before the pipe character is shown in the tooltip balloon. The part after the character is passed to *Application.Hint*. If there is only 1 part, it is used for both the tooltip balloon and the application hint.
For example the following hint:

```
'Save file|Save the file in the currently open window'
```

will show *"Save file"* in the tooltip, but will show *"Save the file in the currently open window"* in the status bar.

The toolbar

In addition to a menu, most applications sport a toolbar: a series of buttons (each with an icon) located below the main menu bar, which provides quick access to some of the most-used actions (which you can normally also find somewhere in the menu). Usually a button image is identical with the image for the same action displayed in the menu. When dropped on a form, a toolbar will automatically align itself to the top edge of the window. To change this, alter the *Align* property from its default value *alTop* to any of the other alignment values. Like any other control, the toolbar can be positioned anywhere on a form, but the default is simply to align it at the top of the window.
To add a button to the toolbar, the toolbar can be clicked with the right mouse button, and the *New button* item can be chosen from the context menu, as shown in Figure 6.51 below. A new button is then added to the toolbar.

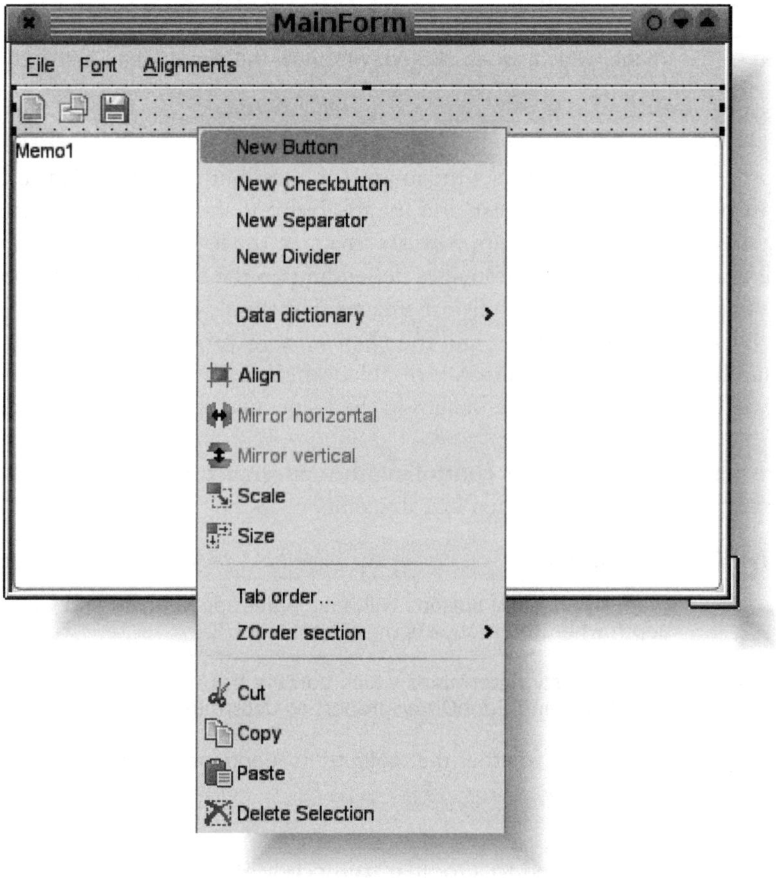

Figure 6.54: The IDE context menu for a toolbar

The button can adopt one of five styles, listed in Table 6.65

Style	Description
tbsButton	This toolbutton acts as a regular speedbutton.
tbsCheck	A button with this style acts as a checkbox, i.e. it remains down when pressed.
tbsSeparator	This is not actually a button that can be clicked, but an empty space between buttons.
tbsDivider	Similar to *tbsSeparator*, it resembles empty space and is used to separate buttons. The main difference from *tbsSeparator* is that it has a different visual look: its function is exactly the same.
tbsDropDown	A button with this style can be associated through its *DropDownMenu* property with a *TPopupMenu* instance. The button will show a small arrow image, which, when clicked, will show the popupmenu below the button.

Table 6.65: Possible Styles for a TToolbarButton

Just as for a menu, to be able to set the image for a toolbutton, the toolbar must have its Images property set to an imagelist, and the toolbuttons should have their *ImageIndex* property set to the index of the appropriate image in the list.
The toolbar can display different images depending on the state of the button: the *HotImages* property specifies a list of images that should be used when the mouse cursor is over one of the buttons, and the *DisabledImages* property can contain the images that should be shown when a button is disabled: the *ImageIndex* property of the toolbar buttons will be used to locate the images in the respective imagelists.

There are many more properties controlling the appearance and behaviour of a toolbar. The most important ones are listed in Table 6.66.

Property	Description
Flat	If set to *True* the buttons will have a flat appearance, and will only take on depth when the mouse is over them.
EdgeBorders	This property determines which borders have a bevelled look. The *EdgeInner* and *EdgeOuter* properties determine the shape of the bevel.
ShowCaptions	Determines whether the toolbuttons' *Captions* are shown.

Table 6.66 Principal properties of TToolBar

Toolbuttons can also be added to a toolbar using code. The method called *CreateExtraButtons* shown below demonstrates how this can be done. It starts by calculating the first free position on the toolbar. Since the toolbuttons are just controls on the toolbar, this means that a small loop over the toolbar's *Controls array* property is sufficient to determine the first free position: it is simply the position of the rightmost button plus the width of that button.

```
procedure TMainForm.CreateExtraButtons;
  Var I,P : Integer;
        C : TControl;
        B : TToolbutton;
begin
  P := 0;
 // Calculate width of existing buttons. TBMain is the TToolbar instance
  For I := 0 to TBMain.ControlCount-1 do
  begin
    C := TBMain.Controls[i];
    If C.Left + C.Width > P then
    P := C.Left + C.Width;
  end;
 // Now create the new buttons starting at position P
  For I := 1 to 4 do
  begin
    B := TToolButton.Create(Self);
    B.Name := 'TBExtra' + IntToStr(i);
 // This places the toolbutton on the toolbar:
    B.Parent := TBMain;
    B.Left := P;
    B.Width :=TBMain.ButtonWidth; // Standard width
    B.ImageIndex := 4 + I;
    B.Caption := 'B' + IntToStr(i);
 // Eventhandler, executed when button is clicked
    B.OnClick := @ButtonClick;
    B.Tag := -1;
 // Go to next position.
    P := P + B.Width;
  end;
end;
```

Buttons can be added to the toolbar by simply creating them and setting the toolbar as the new toolbutton's parent. The rest of the code is simply setting all properties in code, just as if you were setting them in the Object Inspector.

The UpDown control

TUpDown consists of a pair of arrow buttons that can be used to let the user increase or decrease an integral value. The orientation of the arrows can be set with the *Orientation* property. It keeps track of the value through its *Position* property, which can vary between the values of the *Min* and *Max* properties. The value of the *Increment* property determines how much the *Position* is increased when the user clicks the up or down arrows. It can be associated with any control on the form by means of its *Associate* property, meaning that it will always align itself to this control. The *AlignButton* property determines which side of the associated control it aligns itself to.

The Pages control

The *TPageControl* control can be used to create tab sheets. For each tab sheet (a control of class *TTabSheet*) a tab is shown with a *Caption*. When the user clicks the tab, the associated sheet is also shown displaying any controls that tab sheet contains.

This is useful when there is more information to be shown than will fit on a form (the information can then be spread over multiple tab sheets). For example each tab sheet could be used to show information about a single document. As more documents are opened, more tab sheets can be added to the *TPageControl.* Most internet browsers nowadays use tab sheets to hold different web pages which can be shown one at a time by clicking on the appropriate tab.

To add pages, the popup menu in the form designer must be used. It can also be used to switch the active page to the next or previous page in the list. The active tab sheet can also be set using the *ActivePage* property or the *ActivePageIndex* property: the former contains the actual *TTabSheet* instance, the latter simply the index number of the tab sheet.
The *OnChange* event is called when the user changes the active tab (the *ActivePage* property will already contain the new tab). Before the *OnChange* event handler is executed, the *OnChanging* event handler can be used to prevent the user from actually changing the tab.

The Tabs control

The *TTabControl* control is similar to the *TPageControl.* It differs from the *TPageControl,* in that it just displays a list of tabs: no sheets are shown. The list of tabs to display is a simple stringlist, each line in the list will be used to create a tab.
It is up to the programmer to do something when the user clicks on a tab.

The Header control

The *THeaderControl* can be used to display some form of column header.
The *Sections* property is a collection of headers to display. For each *THeaderSection* an *ImageIndex*, *Text*, *text Alignment*, *Width*, *MinWidth* and *MaxWidth* can be specified. The user can always resize all columns. If the *DragReorder* property of the *THeaderControl* is set to *True*, the user can reorder the columns in the headercontrol as well, by dragging them. Several events are provided so you can respond to resizing or dragging of the headers.

The Popup notifier

The *TPopupNotifier* control is not a control per se – rather it is used to display a notification popup (like a tooltip, but larger), showing a notification message, for instance in conjunction with the *TTrayIcon* control. The popup can have a *Title* and a *Text* as well as a small *Icon*, and can be shown with the *ShowAtPos(X,Y)* method, where the *X* and *Y* coordinates are screen coordinates. It contains a small 'close' button, so the user can close the notification (or a timer can be used to close it automatically after a given period).

6.4.4 The Dialogs Tab

Figure 6.55: The component palette's Dialogs tab

The LCL uses the native operating system's dialogs. It does not create its own dialogs. The advantage of this is that the user is presented with familiar dialogs, and will be able to use them instinctively.

There are a lot of standard dialogs in an operating system, most notably the file and directory selection dialogs. The LCL encapsulates these dialogs in a set of dialog components. The dialogs available are shown in Table 6.67.
Each of these dialogs has a particular set of properties that controls the visual appearance and the particular possibilities offered to the end user. All of them descend from the *TCommonDialog* component, which has the following public interface:

```
TCommonDialog = Class(TLCLComponent)
  function Execute: boolean; virtual;
  procedure Close; virtual;
published
  property OnClose: TNotifyEvent;
  property OnCanClose: TCloseQueryEvent;
  property OnShow: TNotifyEvent;
  property HelpContext: THelpContext;
  property Width: integer;
  property Height: integer;
  property Title: string;
end;
```

The meaning of the properties and events should be clear, with *Title* being perhaps the most useful. The most important method is the function:

```
Function Execute: Boolean;
```

This function shows the dialog to the user. It returns when the user closes the dialog. It returns *True* if the dialog was closed appropriately, or *False* if the user cancelled the dialog.

6.4.4 The Dialogs Tab

Component	Description
TOpenDialog	A dialog to select a file from disk.
TSaveDialog	A dialog to enter a filename to save data to.
TSelectDirectoryDialog	A dialog to select an existing directory.
TColorDialog	A dialog to select a colour.
TFontDialog	A dialog to select a font.
TFindDialog	A dialog to enter a search term.
TReplaceDialog	A dialog to enter search and replace terms.
TOpenPictureDialog	A dialog to select a picture file from disk. It shows a preview of the pictures.
TSavePictureDialog	A dialog to specify a filename to save a picture in. It shows a preview of the existing pictures.
TCalendarDialog	A dialog to show a calendar, allowing the user to select a date.
TCalculatorDialog	A dialog to show a calculator. The user can perform a calculation whose result is returned.
TPrinterSetupDialog	A printer setup dialog is shown, allowing the user to set various properties of the printer.
TPrintDialog	A print dialog is shown, allowing the user to specify which printer to use, the number of pages to print, and other printing details.
TPageSetupDialog	A dialog is shown in which the printer page settings can be manipulated.

Table 6.67: Lazarus' dialog components found on the Dialogs tab

When the result of a dialog Execute method is *True* the properties of the dialog are changed to reflect the choices the user has made. The relevant properties for the various dialog components are listed in the following table:

Component	Properties
TOpenDialog	Filename
TSaveDialog	Filename
TSelectDirectoryDialog	Filename
TColorDialog	Color
TFontDialog	Font
TFindDialog	FindText
TReplaceDialog	FindText, ReplaceText
TOpenPictureDialog	FileName
TSavePictureDialog	FileName
TCalendarDialog	Date
TCalculatorDialog	Value
TPrinterSetupDialog	None. The selected printer is set in the Printers unit.
TPrintDialog	Copies, FromPage, ToPage, PrintRange, Collate
TPageSetupDialog	None. The page settings are set in the Printers unit.

Table 6.68: Dialog properties where user choices are saved when the dialog is closed

The typical use of a *TOpenDialog* component would be in the *OnClick* handler of a *File→ Open* menu item, which might look something like this:

```
Procedure TMainForm.FileOpen(Sender: TObject);
begin
  If OpenDialog1.Execute then
    OpenFile(OpenDialog1.FileName);
end;
```

This will present the user with an 'Open file' dialog, and if the user has selected a file, the *OpenFile()* method (which must be implemented by the programmer) will be called to actually open the file, using the *FileName* property of the *OpenDialog1* component – this property contains the actually chosen file.
Note that the *FileName* property can be set prior to showing the dialog. It will then be suggested as a default filename (and it will also set the initially shown directory).
A typical situation in *Open* and *Save* dialogs is the selection of a file format. This happens through a combobox in the dialog itself. The contents of this combobox is determined by the *Filter* property. The *Filter* property contains one or more file masks for file extensions. When one of the masks is selected, the file dialog will list only files that correspond to the selected mask.
The *Filters* property is constructed through a series of *FileDescription | SearchMask* items. The text prior to the pipe (|) symbol is displayed in the combobox, and the second part is used to filter files. It is possible to specify multiple file masks, in which case they must be separated by semicolons (;). If multiple masks must be specified, they must also be separated by the pipe (|) symbol. The simplest mask is the following:

```
OpenDialog1.Filter := 'All files|' + AllFilesMask;
```

The **AllFilesMask** constant is defined in the system unit: for Windows, it contains '*.*', which means all files. On Unix-like operating systems, it contains '*', because '*.*' will not show all files.
A combined filter to show two types of files can be constructed as follows:

```
OpenDialog1.Filter := 'Firebird and Interbase databases|*.gdb; *.fdb';
```

If the search dialog must show only one type of file at a time, then the *Filter* property should be constructed as follows:

```
OpenDialog1.Filter:=
                 'Firebird databases|*.fdb|Interbase Databases|*.gdb';
```

It can be useful to show the file extension in the file description:

```
OpenDialog1.Filter:='GIF images (*.gif)|*.gif'
   +'JPEG images (*.jpg/*.jpeg)|*.jpg;*.jpeg|'
   +'Tagged Image Format (*.tif/*.tiff)|*.tif;*.tiff'
   +'All files|' + AllFilesMask;
```

The *FilterIndex* property can be used to select the default file filter format. In contrast to most other **LCL** lists, the FilterIndex index is 1-based. It can be set prior to opening the dialog, and will be set to the user-selected filter when the dialog is closed.
Constructing a filter like this can be quite cumbersome, but the Lazarus **IDE** offers a filter construction dialog which makes the task much easier. It is shown in Figure 6.53.

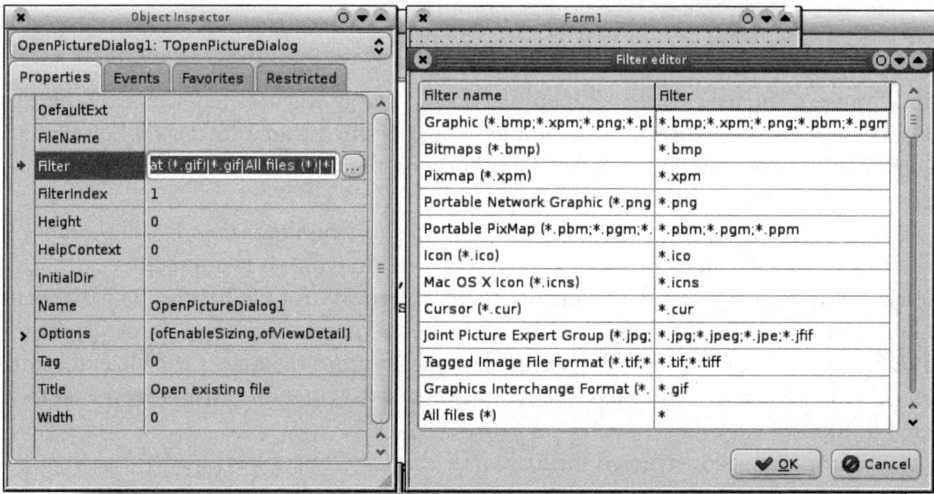

Figure 6.56: Lazarus' Filter construction dialog for filenames

The *TFileOpenDialog* has a lot of options which are shown in Table 6.69. One of the important options is *ofAllowMultiselect*, which tells the dialog that it should allow selection of more than one file. In that case, the selected files are available through the *Files property* (of type *TStrings*) as soon as the user has closed the dialog: one file per item in the list. The opening of a file must then be treated in a loop:

```
  Var I : Integer;
begin
  With OpenDialog1 do
   If Execute then
     For I := 0 to Files.Count-1 do
       OpenFile(Files[i]);
end;
```

The *OpenFile* method must of course be implemented by the programmer.

Option	Description
ofAllowMultiselect	More than one file can be selected (open dialogs only).
ofAutoPreview	Always show a preview of the selected file if the widget set or OS allow it.
ofCreatePrompt	If a non-existing file is selected, the user is prompted with the question whether the file should be created.
ofDontAddToRecent	Do not add the selected file to the 'Recent files' list.
ofEnableIncludeNotify	Not implemented in Lazarus.
ofEnableSizing	Allow sizing of the file select dial.
ogfExtensionDifferent	Allow user to select a file with a different extension.
ofFileMustExist	The selected file must exist on disk.
ofForce	Always show hidden files.
ofHideReadOnly	Do not show read-only files.
ofNoChangeDir	Do not allow the user to change the directory set in InitialDir.
ofNoDereferenceLinks	Do not resolve symbolic links.
ofNoLongNames	Only on windows: only show filenames in 8.3 format.
ofNoNetworkButton	Windows only: disable the networks button.
ofNoReadOnlyReturn	Do not allow the user to select a read-only file.
ofNoTestFileCreate	Do not create a test file to test for write permission in the directory.
ofNoValidate	Not implemented in Lazarus.
ofOldStyleDialog	Not implemented in Lazarus
ofOverwritePrompt	If the user selects an existing file, show an overwrite warning dialog.
ofPathMustExist	The directory of the selected file must exist. Only used when the user does not select a file, but types the name in the file selection dialog.
ofReadOnly	Only on windows: enables the 'Read-Only' checkbox in the dialog.
ofShareAware	Only on windows: Show an error if the user selects a file that is already opened in another application.
ofShowHelp	Show the 'Help' button in the dialog.
ofViewDetail	Show the files in 'detailed' view.

Tabel 6.69: TFileOpenDialog options.

Name	Description
TColorButton	TButton descendant that allows to select a color.
TSpinEdit	Edit with arrows to select, increase/decrease an integer value.
TFloatSpinEdit	Edit with arrows to select, increase/decrease a float value.
TArrow	Draws an arrow in the form of a triangle.
TCalendar	Calendar control to select a date.
TEditButton	Edit control with a button attached to it.
TFileNameEdit	Edit control with a button that pops up a dialog to select a filename.
TDirectoryEdit	Edit control with a button that pops up a dialog to select a directory.
TDateEdit	Edit control with a button to select a date from a popup calendar.
TCalcEdit	Edit control with a button to show a small calculator.
TFileListBox	Listbox to select a file from a list of files in a directory.
TFilterCombobox	Combobox to select a filter.
TXMLPropStorage	Component to store published property values in an XML file.
TINIPropStorage	Component to store published property values in an .INI file.
TBarChart	Component to show a bar chart. (histogram).
TButtonPanel	Panel to show standard buttons in a dialog, in accordance with OS guidelines.
TShellTreeView	TreeView to show a directory structure.
TShellListView	Listview to show the contents of a directory.
TIDEDialog-LayoutStorage	Layout storage container for IDE dialogs.

Table 6.70: Components on the 'Misc' tab of the component palette

6.4.5 The Misc Tab

Figure 6.57: The component palette's Misc tab

The Misc tab contains – the name says it all – miscellaneous components. Most of them have some specialized functionality, and they are all briefly discussed below.

Specialized edit controls

The *TEdit* and *TMemo* controls are the basic editing controls. However, there are several other edit controls, all descending from the *TCustomEditButton* control. This control is an ordinary edit control, but has a *speedbutton* control attached to it, which can be clicked. In the controls delivered with Lazarus, the button is used to pop up a dialog. The result of the dialog (in some form) is then stored as the edit text. The *TEditButton* control is a *TCustomEditButton* descendant which simply publishes the newly introduced properties and events. These properties are listed in Table 6.71.

Property	Description
ButtonWidth	The width of the speedbutton. The height is always equal to the height of the edit control.
ButtonOnly-WhenFocused	If set to *True*, the speedbutton is only visible when the edit control has focus.
DirectInput	If set to *True*, the user can type a value in the edit control. If it is set to *False*, the only way to enter something in the edit control is by clicking the speedbutton, which gives more control over the entered values.
Flat	If set to *True*, the speedbutton has a flat look.
Glyph	Contains the image shown in the button.
NumGlyphs	The number of images in the glyph.
OnButtonClick	The event triggered when the user clicks the speedbutton.

Table 6.71: TEditButton properties

The *OnButtonClick* event will normally be used to pop up a dialog asking for user input, and then filling the text of the edit control with some value based on that user input:

```
procedure TMainForm.ETestButtonClick(Sender: TObject);
  Var S: String;
begin
  S := ETest.Text;
  If InputQuery(SPromptCaption,SPrompt,S) then
    ETest.Text := S;
end;
```

The *InputQuery* call is a standard call in the LCL, declared as follows:

```
Function InputQuery(Const ACaption, APrompt: String;
                                Var AValue: String): Boolean;
```

It shows a dialog with caption *ACaption* and prompts the user with message *APrompt* to enter a string. The string is returned in *AValue*. If *AValue* is not empty when the function is called, it is set as the default value. The function returns *True* if the user ended the dialog with the OK button, it returns *False* otherwise.
Several controls descend from *TCustomEditButton*, and they are listed in Table 6.72.

Control	Description
TFileNameEdit	The dialog popped up is one of the filename dialogs. When the dialog is closed, the selected filename is set as the text of the edit control. The control has some extra properties which control the kind of dialog that is shown, plus all the common properties of the file dialogs. It has an extra event *OnAcceptFileName*, which can be used to verify and possibly change the selected filename.
TDirectoryEdit	The dialog popped up is the directory selection dialog. When the dialog is closed, the selected directory is set as the text of the edit control. The control has some extra properties which control the appearance of the directory dialog.
TDateEdit	When the speedbutton is clicked, a small calendar pops up, and the user can select a date. The selected date is set as the text of the edit control.
TCalcEdit	When the speedbutton is clicked, a small calculator pops up, and the user can perform a calculation. The calculated value is set as the text of the edit control.

Table 6.72: LCL controls which descend from TCustomEditButton

Two edit controls do not appear on the class hierarchy chart: *TSpinEdit* and *TFloatSpinEdit*. These controls are useful for editing an integer or floating-point value. They have up and down arrows attached to them, which can be used to increment or decrement the value shown in the edit control. They are not in the above list because they do not descend from *TCustomEdit*. Instead, they descend directly from *TWinControl*. Nevertheless, these controls have roughly the same properties as a *TCustomEdit control*, and have some extra properties which control their appearance. These properties are listed in Table 6.73.

Property	Description
Decimals	The number of decimal places shown in the control - this property is only present in the *TFloatSpinEdit* control.
Increment	The amount by which the value shown in the control is incremented or decremented when one of the up/down arrows is clicked.
MaxValue	The maximum value that can be shown in the control.
MinValue	The minimum value that can be shown in the control.

Table 6.73: Selected properties of TSpinEdit and TFloatSpinEdit

The ColorButton

TColorButton is a simple button that displays a coloured rectangle. Clicking the button pops up a colour-selection dialog allowing the user to select a colour. The selected colour is available through the *ButtonColor* property of the button. By default, a *TColorDialog* with default properties is used to select the colour. If more fine-grained control is needed, then the *ColorDialog* property can be used to specify a (suitably configured) *TColorDialog* control which will be used to let the user select a colour: this customised dialog will then be used to allow the user to select a colour.

The Arrow control

TArrow can be used to draw an arrow that looks like the arrows used in scrollbars or *TUpDown* controls. The arrow can be clicked, which triggers an *OnClick* event.
The direction of the arrow can be set using the *ArrowType* property and its appearance can be modified using the *ShadowType* property, which can be used to give the arrow a 3-D look.

The Calendar control

The *TCalendar* control is a simple calendar control which can be dropped on a form – it is the same calendar as is used in the *TCalendarEdit* popup. The selected date can be set or retrieved through the *Date* property. Several calendar options (such as whether to start with Mondays, whether to show week numbers, and so on) can be set using the *DisplaySettings* property.

The File Listbox control

Another descendant of the *TListBox* control is the *TFileListBox*, which is used to show a list of files from a directory, allowing the user to select one or more files.
Three properties determine which list of files is shown, and they are listed in Table 6.74. The selected file is available through the *FileName* property which contains the name of the currently selected file. The *UpdateFileList* method can be used to update the list of files. It is called automatically when one of the properties shown below is changed.

Property	Description
Directory	The directory from which files should be shown. The current Lazarus version does not publish this property, so it should be set at run-time.
FileType	The attributes which a file needs in order to be shown in the listbox. The values correspond to the values used in the FindFirst and FindNext calls found in the `SysUtils` unit.
Mask	A file mask specification, as used in FindFirst call of the SysUtils unit. Do not specify a path here.

Table 6.74: Commonly used properties of TFileListbox

The FilterCombobox

TFilterCombobox is a simple *TComboBox* descendant, which allows you to select a filter from a list of filters. The *Filters* property can be set to a string containing a list of filename masks, just as for the *TOpenDialog* or *TSaveDialog* components. The user is shown the descriptions of the filters to choose from, and the file mask corresponding to the selected filter can be retrieved with the *Mask* property.

The BarChart

TBarChart can be used to create simple bar charts (histograms) from any kind of numerical data. The *Bars* property is a collection of bars which will be shown. Each item in this collection can specify a *Caption*, *Value* and *Color*, which will be used to draw the bar in the chart. The *Depth* property controls the visual depth of the bars, and the *LabelPosition* determines where the bars' captions will be shown.

The Button panel

TButtonPanel is a panel which contains standardized versions of four buttons: it can display an *OK*, *Cancel*, *Close* and *Help* button, and it does this in accordance with the GUI design rules for the platform it is running on. The buttons will be displayed in the correct order, with the correct icons to match their function. This can be used in dialog forms to create a uniform look which follows the GUI design rules.

6.4.6 The Data Controls Tab

The *Data Controls* tab contains visual controls for the displaying and editing of data in a database: they communicate with a dataset component, and therefore can be used with any database for which a *TDataset* descendant is available. These controls are descendants of the controls available on other component palette tabs, and do not introduce any new functionality beyond being able to take their content from a data source. Database access is discussed in depth in chapter 12.

Figure 6.58 The controls on the component palette's Data Controls tab

6.4.7 The Data Access Tab

The *Data Access* tab contains components that allow you to access data in a database. They form the connection between the database and the controls that allow you to actually display and edit the data. These controls are available from the *Data Controls* tab. The *Data Access* tab contains components that give access to flat-file databases which are listed in Table 6.75. Other data sources can be installed, but are located on different tabs.

Figure 6.59: The components on the Data Access tab of the component palette

Name	Description	Package
TDatasource	Connects visual controls to a dataset.	FCL
TSDFDataset	A dataset for CSV (comma-separated values) files.	SDFLaz
TFixedFormatDataset	A dataset for fixed-width text files.	SDFLaz
TMemDataset	A dataset that has no file, but keeps data in memory.	MemdsLaz
TDBF	Adataset that handles dBase and Foxpro files.	DBFLaz
TParadox	A dataset which reads Paradox files.	lazparadox

Table 6.75: The components on the Data Access tab

6.4.8 The System Tab

Figure 6.60: Components on the 'System' tab of the component palette

The *System* tab on the component palette offers mostly non-visual components that serve a variety of purposes, and offer an abstracted programming interface for some parts of the operating system. The components are listed in Table 6.76.

Property	Description
TTimer	A component which triggers events at regular intervals.
TIdleTimer	A component that triggers events when the application goes idle.
TLazComponentQueue	A component to read (or write) components from (or to) a stream.
THTMLHelpDatabase	A component to manage online help in HTML files.
THTMLBrowserHelpViewer	A component to show help using a HTML browser.
TAsyncProcess	A component for executing other programs, non-blocking.
TProcessUTF8	Like *TProcess*, but with UTF-8 support.
TProcess	A component for executing other programs, blocking.
TSimpleIPCClient	A component for sending messages to a *TSimpleIPCServer.*
TSimpleIPCServer	A component to receive messages from client applications.
TXMLConfig	A component for saving configuration data, similar to *TIniFile*.
TEventLog	A component to write to the system log.

Table 6.76: The components available on the System tab

6.4.9 The Synedit tab

Figure 6.61: Components on the 'Synedit' tab of the component palette

The *SynEdit* tab contains the components from the *SynEdit* package, which contains two visual controls *TSynEdit* and *TSynMemo* which can be used to add syntax highlighting to an editor. They work just like the more familiar *TMemo* component, but offer some additional options controlling the appearance of the editor. All the other *SynEdit* components are non-visual components which either add syntax highlighting rules to the *TSynEdit* or *TSynMemo* control, or offer additional functionality such as export to HTML, autocompletion or macro recording. The Lazarus IDE itself uses this tab's components to provide its source editor's functionality. All these components are listed in Table 6.77.

Name	Description
TSynEdit	The actual editor.
TSynAutocomplete	Autocompletion support for *TSynEdit*.
TSynExporterHTML	Component to export highlighted source as HTML.
TSynMacroRecorder	Macro recording capabilities for the editor.
TSynMemo	Similar to *TSynEdit*, but offering a *TMemo* interface.
TSynPasSyn	Pascal syntax rules.
TSynFreePascal	SynPascal syntax rules, with support for Free Pascal enhancements.
TSynCppSyn	C++ syntax rules.
TSynJavaSyn	Java syntax rules.
TSynPerlSyn	Perl syntax rules.
TSynHTMLsyn	HTML syntax rules.
TSynXMLSyn	XML syntax rules.
TSynLFMSyn	LFM (Lazarus Form) syntax rules.
TSynUnixShell-ScriptSyn	Unix shell script syntax rules.
TSynCssSyn	CSS data syntax rules.
TSynPHPSyn	PHP syntax rules.
TSynTexSyn	TeX syntax rules.
TSynSQL	Syn SQL syntax rules.
TSynPython	SynPython syntax rules.
TSynVBSyn	Visual Basic syntax rules.
TSynAny	SynUser-Defined syntax rules, configurable in the IDE.
TSynMulti	SynUser-defined syntax rules, loadable from file.

Table 6.77: The components available on the component palette's SynEdit tab

Chapter 7: Porting Delphi components

by Michael Van Canneyt and Mattias Gärtner

When you need to port a Delphi application to Lazarus, you will often encounter the need to port not only Delphi VCL components but a variety of third-party Delphi components, all of which have to be converted to work under Lazarus in a cross-platform way. For most non-visual components, the conversion work required is not very complicated. However, when you port visual components from a Windows-only development environment (Delphi) to the new platforms accessible through Lazarus you will have to undertake considerably more work, particularly for visual components that make direct calls to the Windows API (as most Delphi visual components do). All those calls to the Windows API in the code you encounter will have to be replaced with platform-independent equivalents. To do that, you have to know how Lazarus components are built.

7.1 The Architecture of Lazarus Components

The LCL offers many components, with very different capabilities. You can use these to develop applications quickly and easily. In addition to the components shipped with Lazarus, there are many third-party components available which extend the functionalities of the basic Lazarus components. This chapter explains the basic building blocks of the LCL, and gives an overview of the whole process of developing custom components. This knowledge should make it possible for you to understand how to port third-party components to Lazarus successfully.

The LCL is based on two sets of hierarchical class trees, which are tightly coupled to each other. One of these sets of classes is the platform-independent part – the components on the component palette (such as *TButton)* belong to this set, and this set is Delphi compatible. The second set of classes is the so-called widget-set or, more precisely, the Lazarus interface to the native widget-set. A widget-set is a native library, for example GTK on Linux, or the WinAPI on Windows. The interface between the platform-independent LCL (*TButton*, for example) to the GTK native button (called gtk_button) is called the LCL interface.

Each LCL interface is named after the underlying widget-set to which it binds.

For this reason, the concepts of the widget-set and the LCL interface are often used as synonyms.

Not all LCL components have a counterpart in the widget-set, and often custom components are simply build on top of the platform-independent part of the LCL.

Consequently the platform-independent part will be described first.

The relation between the various classes is depicted in Figure 7.1.

The various parts of a Lazarus application are shown. The arrows indicate for each part with which other parts it communicates. The as can be seen, only the LCL Classes communicate with the widget-set classes. This means that the widget set classes can be replaced with another widget set, and the application will function without any code changes.

7.1.1 The LCL's platform-independent layer

All LCL components descend from the *TLCLComponent* class, which descends from the *TComponent* class. *TComponent* is defined in the FCL (the Free Pascal Component Library) and it provides two important features. Firstly, *TComponent* inherits from *TPersistent* the ability to define published properties which lets the compiler generate code to allow the properties to be read and set at runtime in a generic way. This is what allows the Object Inspector to display and manipulate a component's published properties.
The second important feature provided by *TComponent* is its ability to stream its published properties to a stream, of which the `.lfm` file is an example. This works because all components have a Name property and can be nested; and this enables you to drop, say, a *TButton* on a *TForm* instance in the Form Designer. *TComponent's* streaming capabilities are very powerful, allowing both inheritance and nesting – something which is supported visually in the Lazarus IDE. This double functionality built in to *TComponent* is also the reason why most third-party components are *TComponent* descendants.
You can find an example showing how easy it is to save a component with all its children to a stream (and how they can be read again from this stream) in the Lazarus source tree in the directory `examples/componentstreaming`.

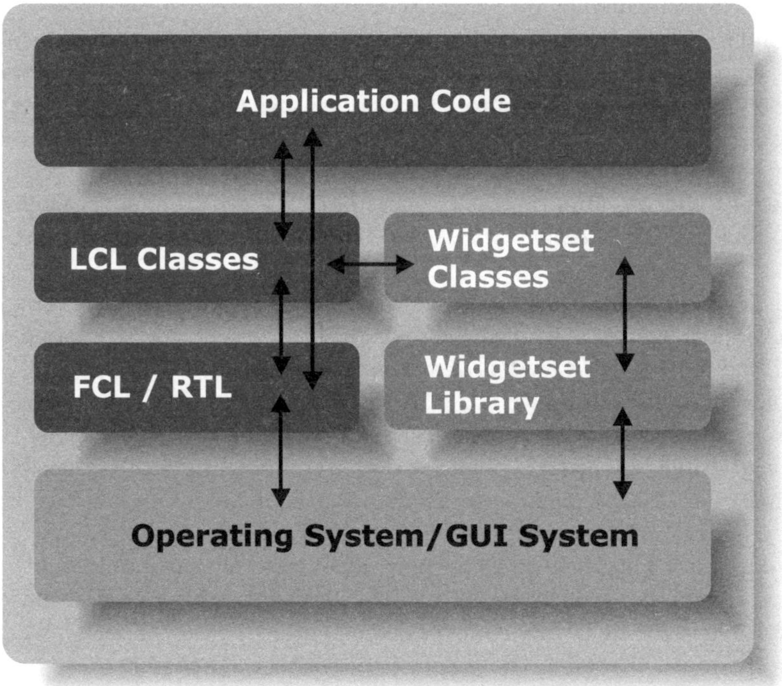

Figure 7.1: The relation between the various classes

7.1.1 The LCL's platform-independent layer

The LCL begins with the *TLCLComponent* class, which introduces an LCLRefCount property, and a WidgetSetClass property. The latter forms the link between the component and the widget-set interface – more about this later. All LCL components that appear on the component palette descend from *TLCLComponent,* and fall into one of three groups.

The first group are the dialog components, for example *TOpenDialog,* which you would use to select a file. The dialog components descend from *TCommonDialog. TOpenDialog* is implemented completely by the underlying widget-set and so *TOpenDialog* depends on the operating system, and for instance on Windows, users will immediately recognise its Windows-style icons and buttons. Whereas on Mac OS X a Mac user will be presented with the Mac dialog he is accustomed to see. Both are using exactly the same *TOpenDialog* component. When a new version of the operating system is released, the program does not have to be recompiled. The dialog will follow the current version standards since it is created by the operating system. By contrast, *TFindDialog* – used for text searches – is a simple dialog window. *TFindDialog* looks the same on all operating systems.
Someone who needs to write a new dialog should check the *TFindDialog* code. Whereas, a *TOpenDialog* cannot be changed, since it depends on the widget-set and its capabilities.

The second component group comprises the menus: *TMenu, TPopupMenu* and *TMenuItem.* These are also implemented by the widget-sets.
The third and largest group descends from the *TControl* class. *TControl* defines many properties – including the Top, Left, Width and Height properties which determine the position and dimensions of the control. Basic events such as mouse and key events, painting and the focus handling are also defined in *TControl.* Despite these properties and events, few controls descend directly from *TControl.* Two classes descend directly from *TControl* each of which is important as an ancestor of its own component family: *TGraphicControl* and *TWinControl.*

First of all *TGraphicControl.* This class enhances *TControl* with the *OnPaint* event, but does not have a window handle of its own. This means that it has no corresponding widget-set control, and the *TGraphicControl* is drawn completely by the LCL.
For example, *TSpeedButton* is drawn in a platform-independent way. The absence of a handle also means that no other controls can be dropped on a *TGraphicControl.*
TGraphicControl is the best starting point for simple components such as clickable symbols, images or visual separators which do not need the focus, or any keyboard input.
TWinControl is a powerful descendant of *TControl. TWinControl* can have child controls, and is provided with a handle for this purpose: the handle is needed for direct communication with the widget-set. *TWinControl* has many specialized descendants, all publicly available in the LCL. Few controls descend directly from *TWinControl,* though a notable exception is *TOpenGLControl,* which implements a 3D context.
When implementing a complex control, the best class to descend it from is a *TWinControl* descendant, the *TCustomControl* class. This class can show scrollbars, has a canvas to paint on and has an OnPaint event.

TCustomControls draw themselves and therefore appear the same on all platforms. Examples include *TTreeView*, *TSynEdit* (The control used in the Lazarus source editor) and *TOIPropertyGrid* (the Object Inspector grid).
Their scrollbars are drawn by the widget-set, and their position and size are controlled by *TCustomControl.*
TScrollingWinControl enhances *TCustomControl* by managing the scrollbar *HorzScrollbar* and *VertScrollbar* automatically. It can serve as the basis for components that allow child controls to be dropped on them – other than that, it offers the same functionality as *TCustomControl.*

All the components discussed above share the requirement that they must be embedded in a *TWinControl* – an instance of a suitable containing control is available through the Parent property of *TControl.* Controls that are freely movable windows (not needing a parent control) need to take as their base class *TCustomForm,* (a *TScrollingWinControl* descendant) which serves as the base class for all such components. Some properties change their meaning in this class: a window does not simply have a position, it also has a *Monitor, BorderIcons* and *WindowState* – it can be maximized and minimized.
Many widget-sets (WinCE is one of several) put additional limitations on these properties.
Finally, *TForm* is the *TCustomForm* descendant used by the IDE as the base class for all windows. Every window created by the IDE is a descendant of *TForm* – and is therefore in itself a new component class (i.e. new forms are not created as *TForms*, but as *TForm* descendants).
Looking at the LCL component hierarchy, you will notice that almost all classes in the component palette are descendants of a class that starts with the name *TCustom.*
For example, the declaration of *TTreeView* consists only of a published block: the actual implementation is in *TCustomTreeView.* The reason for this is that a property's visibility can be raised in a descendant, but never lowered.
If a property – for example, Left – is defined as Public, then it can no longer by made Protected or Private in a descendant class, and it must be supported, even if it would make no sense. For this reason, almost all LCL classes are implemented as *TCustom* classes with very few Public and Published properties: the end classes such as *TTreeView* simply make Public or Published any properties required to have a higher visibility.
If you wanted to create a treeview with some unavailable properties, you merely need to make it descend from *TCustomTreeView,* with none of the unavailable properties made Public or Published.

7.1.2 Platform dependent layer

As described above, the LCL includes a hierarchy of classes which parallel the usual LCL classes. As well as the *TCustomButton* class, there is an equivalent *TWSButton*.
This is an abstract base class for the LCL interface which contains only abstract class methods.
And just as *TCustomButton* descends from *TButtonControl,* so *TWSButton* descends from *TWSButtonControl.* The WS-classes are implemented in each LCL interface.
For example, the LCL Win32 interface defines a class *TWin32WSButton,* implementing the *TWSButton* functionality for the MS-Windows platform. *TCustomButton* has the *WidgetSetClass,* and this has the value *TWin32WSButton* on the Windows platform.
Although this sounds complicated, it allows *TCustomButton* to call the LCL interface in a straightforward manner:

```
procedure TCustomButton.WSSetDefault;
begin
  // Default only tells us if button was set to Default at design time
  // At runtime, Active actually shows us if the button is the default button.
  If HandleAllocated then
  TWSButtonClass(WidgetSetClass).SetDefault(Self,FActive)
end;
```

The *HandleAllocated* function tests whether a handle (used to access the widget-set) is available and calls the LCL interface. It does not matter which widget-set was used to compile the program.
Writing custom widget-set classes was one of the most difficult challenges facing the LCL developers. If you look, for example, at the *TOpenGLControl* you will see that it extends both class hierarchies and contains implementations for four widget-sets. The control is implemented in the package `components/opengl/lazopenglcontext.lpk`.

7.2 The Component model

Delphi applications are ported to Lazarus for several reasons.
Perhaps the way CodeGear-Embarcadero developed Delphi after version 7 is reason enough – the installation or enabling of .NET to write native applications does seem strange. Maybe the application needs to run on 64-bit Windows (at the time of writing this is not possible with Delphi), or perhaps Linux and MacOS X are target platforms.

Lazarus offers assistance in various ways to make it possible to port applications without too much hassle, but the best first step in porting to new platforms is still to examine your application's design carefully.
A necessary step is to check whether third-party components have been employed.
In order to do this, you have to know what constitutes a Delphi component and how Delphi components differ from Lazarus components. It is also important to know whether the component's source code is available, because Delphi components that are only available in binary form (whether as a `.DCU` file or a `.DCP` package) are not usable in Lazarus.

7.2.1 Components in Delphi

We can categorise Delphi components in various ways. A rough major distinction can be drawn between *visual* and *non-visual* Delphi components. Both can be descendants from a base class but implementing completely new functionality; or they could be very advanced components that extend components in the existing VCL class library.
In the latter case, you should check whether similar functionality is not already provided by an existing LCL component.
Another type of Delphi component are those which wrap Windows API functionality. Good examples of such wrappers are the *RichEdit* component, and also the *TSerial* and *TPrinter* components from the German journal *Toolbox*. These components are easily to port to Lazarus, but will function only on Windows.
A third component category, rather than being low-level wrappers around the Windows API, are components which offer an interface to Windows OLE objects: ActiveX wrappers. Typical examples are the Internet-Explorer module, or the Adobe Acrobat reader component, and the various wrappers around Microsoft Office modules such as Word and Excel. Lazarus – with its goal of platform-independence – does not offer a way to port these controls, since they are bound to the Windows platform.
These considerations lead to multi-layered categories of Delphi component portability:

- The simplest components to port are those which provide VCL extensions.
  Even though VCL and LCL are very similar, the VCL focus on Windows sometimes makes porting difficult. Nevertheless, these components are usually portable to other platforms.
- For other visual Delphi components, deeply rooted in Windows, the porting process is near-impossible, and it is usually easier to rewrite them from the ground up in a cross-platform way.
- Windows API-wrapper components are usually portable, but will generally only run on Windows.
- ActiveX controls are not portable, and should not be attempted.

7.2.2 Differences in architecture

When you start porting from Delphi to Lazarus, you should be aware of two aspects of the component:

1. What belongs to a component in Delphi.
2. Which part of this is actually needed.

A component in Delphi is always implemented in a `.pas` source file. Prior to Delphi 2009 this file was always in Windows ANSI format, and it must be converted to UTF-8 encoding in Lazarus. Associated with the `.pas` source file there may be one or more resource files, usually created with the Borland Resource Workshop. These files have the extension `.res` or `.dcr` (which stands for Delphi Component Resource).
A `.dcr` file normally contains the icon representing the component on the component palette, but can also contain other information. The icon in the `.dcr` file is not a Windows icon, but a Windows bitmap of size 24x24, using 2, 16 or 256 colours.

The bitmap's name should be the uppercase name of the component. You often see the statement **{$R *.dcr}**in the source file. Typically Delphi's Image Editor would have been the tool used to create the component's image.
Delphi supports creation of packages. A package is a special kind of DLL, in which component information is stored. The advantage of Delphi packages is that the component library does not need to be recompiled to be used in the Delphi IDE (although in Delphi versions 1 and 2 this was still required). Components are not linked statically in Delphi's IDE – in contrast to Lazarus – but are loaded dynamically using Delphi packages. Delphi packages are therefore not equivalent to Lazarus packages.
The above addresses question 2 at the beginning of this section: you definitely need a component's source file to be able to port it to Lazarus – even if it will only be used under Windows. In addition, you also need the image for the component palette as an image file. Last but not least, the `.res` file must be checked for any strings which, if present, will have to be extracted.
The Pascal source file for a Delphi Windows component does not differ essentially from its Lazarus counterpart: the Pascal language is virtually identical. By contrast, the resource binding differs substantially between the two components.

Converting the resources

As indicated earlier, Delphi uses a bitmap in the `.dcr` file to represent a component on the component palette. Assuming that the component is not a prehistoric 16-bit component, a 32-bit resource file has to be located and converted. One way is to load it in the Delphi Image Editor. Although this program cannot export a bitmap (as the Resource Workshop can) it can edit bitmaps. The edited bitmap can then be copied to the clipboard and pasted into another application such as Microsoft Paint. It can then be saved as a `.BMP` bitmap file.
Another possibility is to use the free XN resource editor which you can download from:

```
http://www.wilsonc.demon.co.uk/delphi2006.htm
```

This program can read `.DCR` files and extract (one at a time) parts such as images or strings.
Once you have a component bitmap, it must be embedded in the Lazarus counterpart to the `.dcr` file which is the `.lrs` file. The Lazarus resource compiler **lazres** can be used to do this. It is distributed in source code form with Lazarus, and must be compiled from the sources available in the tools directory below the Lazarus installation directory.
If the PATH environment variable does not contain the Free Pascal compiler binary directory – advisable under Windows, since the `cygwin1.dll` in it can conflict with other cygwin applications – then the lazres tool must be compiled using complete pathnames for the binaries.
Assuming that Lazarus is installed in `c:\lazarus`, and the compiler is Free Pascal 2.4.2, then lazres can be compiled from a command prompt window with the following commands:

```
> cd \lazarus\tools
> \lazarus\fpc\2.4.2\bin\i386-win32\make
> \lazarus\fpc\2.4.2\bin\i386-win32\strip *.exe
```

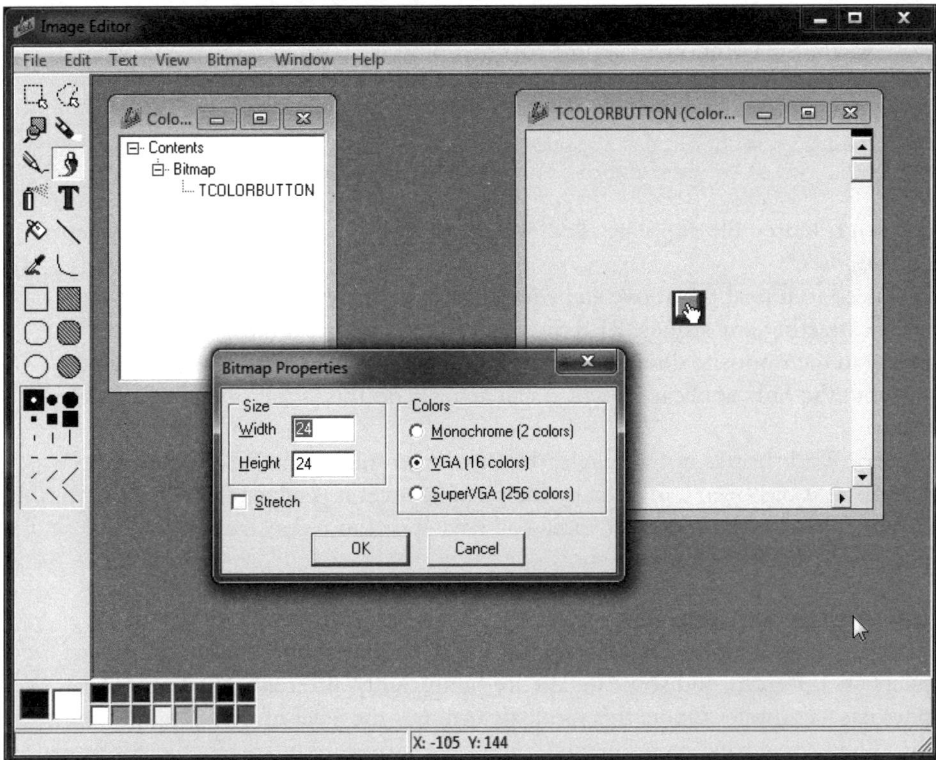

Figure 7.2: Delphi 7 delivered a special program for editing dcr resources - the Image Editor

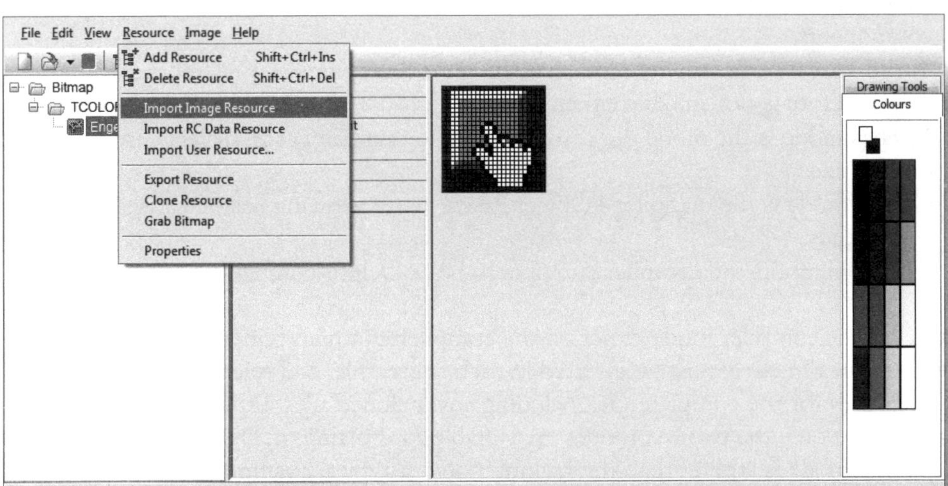

Figure 7.3: The XN Resource Editor of Colin Wilson is freeware and handles a lot of fileformats

Once you have done this, `lazres.exe` can be used to create a resource file in the directory where the component source files are located. Assuming the component sources are in `c:\lazarus\components\fabprocess`,
then the following commands

```
> cd \lazarus\components\fabprocess
> \lazarus\tools\lazres fabproc.lrs tfabprocess.xpm
```

will create a resource file `fabproc.lrs`, which will contain an icon for a component named *'tfabprocess'*.
You will need to repeat the above steps for all images in the `.dcr` file,
as well as extracting any strings. RES files are created from `.RC` files,
so moving in the opposite direction – decompilation of a `.res` to a `.rc` – is also possible, but the only application which can actually do this is the Borland Resource Workshop.
If Resource Workshop is not available, then the `.res` file can be inserted into the Lazarus file as it has been compiled by Delphi. However it is generally better to insert the `.rc` source file with the $R directive (if you have it or can reconstruct it), since then it is compiled using the FPC resource tools.

Preparing the source file

Free Pascal orients itself to Delphi, and not the other way round. Despite this, the compilers are different, and some details are significantly different. The Free Pascal compiler has a compiler mode: this mode determines the level of compatibility with Delphi. When converting components, you have to take care to specify the appropriate compiler mode you want to work under:

- Plain FPC; the default mode. Classes, exceptions, threads or other Delphi features are not allowed. Obviously, this mode is not very suitable for porting Delphi components.
- Turbo-Pascal compatibility mode has the same limitations as FPC mode, and therefore is not suitable either.
- Macpas mode is the mode the compiler uses to compile Pascal dialects used on the Mac.
- Objfpc mode is the compiler's Object Pascal mode allowing use of classes and threads.
- In Delphi mode, the compiler attempts to be as Delphi-compatible as possible.

You select the compiler mode either on the compiler command-line or through a directive. The directive must be inserted in each source file, and selects the mode the compiler uses for the complete file, including any included files. From the list above, it is clear that only the two last modes are suitable for porting of Delphi components. The objfpc mode is stricter than the Delphi mode. A typical example is that in objfpc mode, no method parameter names may be used as property names. This can be illustrated with the following example, which compiles in Delphi, but not in FPC:

```
TmyComponent = Class(TComponent)
 FValue: integer;
 Procedure SetOtherValue(AValue : Integer);
 Property AValue : Integer Read FValue Write FValue; // Syntax error in FPC
end;
```

In the implementation of *SetOtherValue*, the identifier *AValue* is ambiguous: does it signify the parameter or the property name? Therefore, in objfpc mode, a 'Duplicate identifier Error' is issued when encountering such code. In Delphi mode, the Delphi rules are followed: the parameter *AValue* takes precedence over the property *AValue*.
The Lazarus team itself always uses objfpc mode, so it is used everywhere in the LCL and is a requirement for the inclusion of packages in the LCL repository.
To set the compiler mode for a unit to Delphi mode, the following lines must be inserted before the line containing the *unit* keyword:

```
{$ifdef  FPC}
{$mode delphi}
{$endif}
```

The *IFDEF* ensures that the Delphi compiler can still compile the units. It does not understand the {*$mode* ...}directive and gives an error on encountering it. When specifying objfpc mode, the *$ifdef* directive makes no sense, since Delphi cannot compile code written in objfpc mode anyway, so the following is sufficient when selecting objfpc mode: {*$mode objfpc*}
If code must be used under both compilers, Delphi mode is the only option. For code that needs to work only under FPC, objfpc mode is a better choice.
The next task in preparing source code to be ported is to check the case of the units named in the *uses* clause of the component source file. Pascal is a case-insensitive language, but all Unix-like operating systems use a case-sensitive file system. So when code is ported to Unix, the case of the unit names becomes important: the compiler must be able to match each unit name to the correct unit file. There are two ways to ensure this happens:

1. The unit name is made to match the case of the unit filename. The compiler searches for a unit name first with the exact filename as it appears in the uses clause.
2. All files are saved using all-lowercase-letter filenames. If the compiler doesn't find a unit file spelled exactly like the *uses* clause name, then it searches for the unit file using filenames which are entirely lowercase.

The same rules apply to *include directives* and *include files.*

VCL and LCL

Porting a component from Delphi to Lazarus does not only mean porting from one compiler (`dcc32.exe`) to another (FPC), but also from one GUI platform (usually Windows) to another: the LCL (Lazarus Component Library).
The LCL is by no means a simple re-implementation of Delphi's VCL. It is more accurate to describe the LCL as a complete cross-platform toolkit, independent of the underlying operating system or graphical subsystem. It offers a well-defined API, which is the same on all supported platforms. A component written for the LCL will work on all supported platforms.

7.2.2 Differences in architecture

Porting to the LCL therefore implies changing from the Windows API to the API offered by the LCL. The LCL offers a message system resembling the Windows message system, but there the resemblance ends. Many Windows API calls and messages are not present in the LCL.

A Lazarus application comprises three layers:

- The application code, this is the actual program.
- The LCL classes – a library of classes resembling the VCL.
- The LCL interface. This is an abstraction layer for the underlying GUI.

The application programmer does not have to worry about the bottom layer, the LCL interface. It is sufficient to know the LCL classes. They are constructed to resemble their VCL counterparts as much as possible. However, if you need to port components, then understanding how the LCL interface abstraction layer functions is essential, since any Windows API calls must be translated into the LCL interface equivalents.
Currently, there are implementations of the abstraction layer for GTK, GTK 2, Qt4, Carbon and, of course, 32/64-bit Windows.
The abstraction layer is implemented as a single class, a descendant of *TInterfaceBase* (in the unit interfacebase). The class implementing the interface for GTK 2 is called *Tgtk2WidgetSet*. If the LCL is compiled, a descendant of *TInterfaceBase* must be instantiated, and this instance is used by all classes in the LCL. This instance provides all calls that the LCL needs to handle GUI events, show new windows and so on.
In short, it contains all calls that interact with the graphical system.

The following is part of the interface:

```
Procedure HandleEvents;
procedure WaitMessage;
Procedure AppInit;
procedure AppTerminate;
function IntSendMessage3(LM_Message; Integer; Sender : Tobject; Data:
                   Pointer) : Integer;
function CreateDIBitmap(DC : HDC; Var InfoHeader : TbitmapInfoHeader;
                   dwusage : Dword; InitBits: Pchar; var InitInfo :
                   TbitmapInfo; wusage: UINT) : Hbitmap;
```

These methods are abstract, and must be implemented by a descendant such as *Tgtk2WidgetSet* (obviously, there are more calls than those shown here). The interface object communicates with the classes mainly by means of messages, sometimes by means of direct method calls. The system is very much like the Windows messaging system, although the message numbers will differ. However the message names have been kept similar. For example the Windows WM_SIZE message has been renamed to LM_SIZE to be more platform independent. FPC supports the concept of 'message handling' methods as introduced in Delphi, which means that for a control to respond to the LM_SIZE message, the following method can be implemented:

```
procedure WMSize(var Message: TLMSize); message LM_SIZE;
```

As can be seen, this is very similar to the method as it would be implemented under Delphi. The type name *TWMSize* has been changed to *TLMSize* and the message identifier has been changed to LM_SIZE. The LCL layer will see to it that the message is delivered to the control.
On the other hand, the LCL classes mainly use methods of the *TInterfaceBase* class to talk to the interface. Messages are seldom sent from the LCL classes to the interface layer, so if a component relies heavily on sending messages, the chances are that it will be hard to port to the LCL.
Messages in the LCL are considered mainly to be a means of internal communication, so it is not a good idea to rely on them. In general, for each message there will be a corresponding method in the LCL base classes (*TControl* and *TWinControl*) which will be called by that message handler. Therefore when porting, it is a good idea to use the message methods as little as possible, and instead to override the method that corresponds to the ported message. In the case of LM_SIZE, this means overriding your component's *DoSetBounds* method.
Unfortunately, there is no comprehensive list either of the supported messages nor of the methods that correspond to them. In order to find out what is possible and what not, you will have to study the LCL sources. The `controls` unit in the LCL provides a nice overview of most message handlers, and is the best place to start exploring before you look elsewhere.

Interface units
Because Delphi creators encapsulated much of Windows' functionality in the Windows unit delivered with Delphi, this unit will be encountered in most Delphi programs.
The same is true for several other low-level units such as `Messages.` Needless to say, these units are not very portable. As a result they are not included in the LCL classes, but replaced by other units.
With the exception of these non-portable Windows-centric base units, the LCL attempts to reproduce as much of Delphi's unit and class naming scheme as possible. This means that for an average ported application the uses clause can stay mainly untouched apart from the notable cross-platform case sensitivity issue noted above. Below are some further relevant points.

- The functionality provided by the Delphi `Windows unit` is divided over several Lazarus units: `interfacebase` for most GUI-related calls. Most type and constant definitions have been moved to the `LCLType unit` and are provided mostly for compatibility.
- Messages (names as well as record definitions) will be found in the `LMessages` unit.
- The `IntfGraphics unit` contains most of what is needed for handling images (bitmaps).

However, this list will not solve all 'Identifier not found' compiler errors that may occur when porting a Delphi component to Lazarus. It may well be that the particular message or structure or call does not exist in Lazarus, in which case you will have to use or try something else.

7.3 The porting process

We will demonstrate all the explanations of the previous sections by porting a small Delphi component to Lazarus, by way of example. Porting to Lazarus can be done in Windows. However, there are good reasons for trying a port on Linux: the `Windows unit` is delivered with FPC in the Win32 distribution. Thus, the compiler will happily compile all calls to that unit without complaining. Not so on Linux: the `Windows unit` is not present, and this will force the person porting the component to pay attention to all occurrences of the `Windows unit` in the sources, and remove them (because otherwise the compiler will report an error).

A second reason for attempting a port on Linux is the immediate verification that the component works cross-platform. Last but not least, the Linux file system is case sensitive. This will force correct choice of case for the names of all units involved in the port.

The Delphi example to port is an edit component (*TEditBtn*) which is a regular edit control, with a speedbutton attached to it. The purpose of the speedbutton is to provide a means to pop up a dialog which allows the user to select a value. The component then inserts that value in the edit control. Possible variations on the basic component might include:

- Showing a *file dialog* to select a file.
- Showing a *directory dialog* to select a directory.
- Showing a *calendar* to pick a date.
- Showing a *calculator* to perform a calculation.
- Showing a *form with a grid* containing a dataset and suitable controls designed to search for a particular value in the dataset.
- Anything else you might wish to do that fits the above paradigm.
  In fact, specialized descendants of the general purpose component are being created to perform the first four tasks, and may be on Lazarus' Component Palette by the time you read this.

The original component *TEditBtn* (by Louis Louw) was found on Torry's pages.
The class declaration is quite simple (the published properties have been left out):

```
 TEditBtn = class(TEdit)
 FButton: TSpeedButton;
 FEditorEnabled: Boolean;
 FOnBtnClick : TNotifyEvent;
 procedure SetGlyph(Pic: TBitmap);
 function GetGlyph : TBitmap;
 procedure SetNumGlyphs(ANumber: Integer);
 function GetNumGlyphs:Integer;
 function GetMinHeight: Integer;
 procedure SetEditRect;
 procedure WMSize(var Message: TWMSize); message WM_SIZE;
 procedure CMEnter(var Message: TCMGotFocus); message CM_ENTER;
 procedure CMExit(var Message: TCMExit); message CM_EXIT;
 procedure WMPaste(var Message: TWMPaste); message WM_PASTE;
 procedure WMCut(var Message: TWMCut); message WM_CUT;
protected
 procedure GetChildren(Proc: TGetChildProc; Root: TComponent);
      override;
 function IsValidChar(Key: Char): Boolean; virtual;
 procedure aClick (Sender: TObject); virtual;
 procedure KeyDown(var Key: Word; Shift: TShiftState); override;
 procedure KeyPress(var Key: Char); override;
 procedure CreateParams(var Params: TCreateParams); override;
 procedure CreateWnd; override;
public
 constructor Create(AOwner: TComponent); override;
 destructor Destroy; override;
 property Button: TSpeedButton read FButton;
end;
```

From the listing it is clear what methods we will need to look at as we consider porting – the message methods to start with. The *CreateParams* method and *CreateWnd* calls are also dangerous – in Windows they serve to create the window handle for the component. As the LCL has its own mechanism for creating a window handle, these calls also will need to be adapted.

First we will consider the *uses* clause, which in the original reads as follows:

```
uses
   Windows, Messages, SysUtils, Classes, Graphics, Controls,
   Forms, Dialogs, StdCtrls, Mask, Buttons, ExtCtrls;
```

Keeping in mind the remarks made earlier, this is changed to:

```
uses
   LCLType, LMessages, Messages, SysUtils, Classes, Graphics,
   Controls, Forms, Dialogs, StdCtrls, Buttons, ExtCtrls;
```

The `Mask unit` has been removed, as it isn't needed at all.
We then take the following actions to adapt the message methods:

The *WMSize* call is removed because the necessary actions will be taken in the *DoSetBounds* method which is overridden in the component.

The *CM_ENTER* message is defined but does not work. Instead we will use the *LM_SETFOCUS* message.
The *TCMGotFocus* record has a corresponding Lazarus record called *TLMSetFocus*. Taking this into account, we change the declaration of the *CMEnter* method to the following:

```
procedure WMSetFocus(var Message: TLMSetFocus); message LM_SETFOCUS;
```

The *TCMGotFocus* message record is absent from the LCL, so the general *TLMessage* record is substituted.

Likewise, the message *TCMExit* does not exist in the LCL, which leads to the following adaptation of the *CMExit* method:

```
procedure WMKillFocus(var Message: TLMKillFocus); message LM_KILLFOCUS;
```

The *WMPaste* and *WMCut* methods are removed because they are not yet supported by Lazarus, although the message constants: *LM_PASTEFROMCLIP* and *LM_CUTTOCLIP* are defined.

The *CreateWnd* and *CreateParams* are removed, since the LCL doesn't provide the same functionality these methods require.

The following methods have also been removed, as they are useless and serve no function in the original component.

```
function IsValidChar(Key: Char): Boolean; virtual;
procedure KeyDown(var Key: Word; Shift: TShiftState); override;
procedure KeyPress(var Key: Char); override;
```

The implementation of these methods presents no problems and they compile without needing changes. But the implementation of some methods does need thinking through. Let's consider the constructor first:

```
constructor TEditBtn.Create(AOwner: TComponent);
begin
  inherited Create(AOwner);
  FButton := TSpeedButton.Create (Self);
  FButton.Width := 15;
  FButton.Height := 17;

  If csDesigning in ComponentState
  Then  FButton.Visible := True
  Else FButton.Visible := False;

  FButton.Parent := Self;
  FButton.OnClick := aClick;
  FButton.Cursor:= crArrow;
  ControlStyle := ControlStyle - [csSetCaption];
  FEditorEnabled := True;
end;
```

At first sight, there is nothing wrong with this code. The only code that actually needs changing is the setting of the *Parent* since in Lazarus, not all widgets are able to contain child widgets. Accordingly, we must change the line which sets the *Parent*, so that the form is made *Parent* of the button. This also means that the *Top* and *Left* coordinates of the button will be measured relative to the form, rather than relative to the edit control. Subsequent methods must take account of this. All the rest of the code will compile and work just fine. Our changed constructor body then looks like this:

```
inherited Create(AOwner);
FButton := TSpeedButton.Create(Self);
FButton.Width := Self.Height;
FButton.Height := Self.Height;
FButton.FreeNotification(Self);
CheckButtonVisible;
FButton.OnClick := @DoButtonClick;
FButton.Cursor := crArrow;
ControlStyle := ControlStyle - [csSetCaption];
FDirectInput := True;
```

Some variable names have been changed for clarity. The *CheckButtonVisible* method checks whether the button should be made visible or not.
The *ButtonOnlyWhenFocused* property (omitted in the class declaration above) determines whether the button is visible when the edit control does not have focus. Since the check must be made at various places, the code for it has been moved to a separate procedure. The button width can be set by the user through the *ButtonWidth* property, and initially, the button is made square: the height is the same as the width.
The next method that causes problems is *SetEditRect*:

```
procedure TEditBtn.SetEditRect;
var
 Loc: TRect;
begin
 SendMessage(Handle, EM_GETRECT, 0, LongInt(@Loc));
 Loc.Bottom := ClientHeight + 1; {+1 is workaround for Windows paint bug}
 Loc.Right := ClientWidth - FButton.Width - 2;
 Loc.Top := 0;
 Loc.Left := 0;
 SendMessage(Handle, EM_SETRECTNP, 0, LongInt(@Loc));
 SendMessage(Handle, EM_GETRECT, 0, LongInt(@Loc)); {debug}
end;
```

Under Windows, the *SetEditRect* call serves to limit the editing area of the edit control, and the button is drawn inside the edit control. This code makes sure the cursor will never disappear 'under' the button by telling Windows that only the area not under the button can be used for editing. This call disappears for two related reasons:

1. The button is drawn outside the edit control in the LCL.
2. The call is not supported in Lazarus, where an edit control cannot contain a button, so adding the call would make little sense. Therefore, the call is removed.

The next method implementation that needs checking is the WMSize message handler. Its functionality has been moved to the *DoSetBounds* call:

```
procedure TCustomEditButton.DoSetBounds(ALeft, ATop, AWidth,
  AHeight: Integer);
begin
  inherited DoSetBounds(ALeft, ATop, AWidth, AHeight);
  DoPositionButton;
end;
```

The actual positioning of the button is handled in the *DoPositionButton* call (made virtual, so it can be overridden):

```
procedure TCustomEditButton.DoPositionButton;
begin
 if (FButton<>nil) then
 FButton.SetBounds(Left+Width, Top, FButton.Width, Height);
end;
```

This method does not do anything special. The button width is kept, as it can be set by the user through the *ButtonWidth* property.
The *GetMinHeight* method is removed. It is not really needed since the LCL makes sure the controls are big enough.
The code of the final ported component can be found on the CD-Rom accompanying this book. It will most likely be included as a core Lazarus component, together with some descendent components.

7.3.1 Installing the component in Lazarus

After the code of a Delphi component has been ported to Lazarus successfully, you probably want to have it available on the Component Palette. In Delphi, you would do this using a package – you would create a package, insert the unit in it, recompile the package and install it in the IDE. For single components such as the edit button, the special dclusr package can be employed which contains all Delphi components that are not explicitly part of a package. Unfortunately, Lazarus (or better, FPC) does not yet support loading packages dynamically. But the Lazarus designers have made it really easy to install new components. Since Lazarus is open source, it comes with all the sources. Thus, to install a new component, you simply have to recompile Lazarus with the new component included. The IDE provides two menu options for this under the *Tools* menu:

Build Lazarus This will recompile Lazarus, and will add to the component palette any packages marked for inclusion.

Configure "Build Lazarus"
This allows you to configure the actions taken when *Build Lazarus* is called. In this dialog, use the *Profile to Build* combobox dropdown to select the *Build IDE with Packages* option so that packages with components are included.

So, to include the edit button in the component palette, first set the *Build IDE with Packages* option in the *Configure "Build Lazarus"* dialog. Then the *editbtn* unit must be added to an existing package, or a new package must be created. The *File* →*New* menu pops up a dialog which contains a *Package* entry – double-click on this to create a new package, which opens the Package Editor. In the Package Editor, the *Add* [+] button can be used to add a unit to the package, as can be seen in figure 7.4.

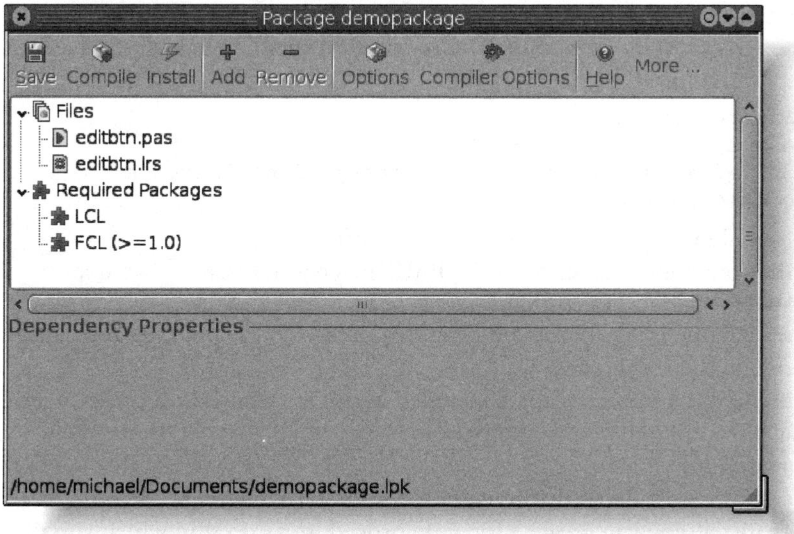

Figure 7.4 The Lazarus Package Editor with source file and resource file added. All components need the LCL as requirement.

When adding a unit to a package you have to tell Lazarus whether the unit has a *Register* procedure to register components. If the flag *Has register procedure* is set, then Lazarus will call the *Register* procedure of the unit. As a result the component will be included on the component palette.
The *Virtual unit* option is meant for cases where the package registers components in units that are not part of the package file list. In that case the units not contained in the package are added to the file list as 'virtual units'. This allows Lazarus to determine package dependencies correctly. For examples of this usage look at the *sqldblaz* or *dbflaz* packages which are included in the default Lazarus distribution, both of which contain virtual units.
Thus, to register the edit button, add the `editbtn unit` to a package (call it *editbutton*), and set the *Has register procedure* flag.
The package can be marked for inclusion in the IDE with the Package Editor's *Install* button. When the IDE is rebuilt, the package will be included. All that remains to do is to install the package, rebuild Lazarus from the *Tools* menu, and after everything has compiled successfully, restart Lazarus. There should be a new component palette page called 'MBS' which contains the edit button.

7.3.2 The component palette

The usual way to add an icon to the component palette in Delphi is to create a resource file with a bitmap that has the name of the component. Lazarus is no different, except that the procedure to add the resource differs. This is because older FPC compilers did not support including of native resources on platforms other than Windows. Therefore, Lazarus created its own resource mechanism.
So, to add an icon to the Lazarus component palette you must do the following:

1. Extract the bitmaps from the original Delphi resources. You can do this using Delphi's Image Editor, or you may prefer to recreate them from scratch.
2. If the *lazres* tool did not come in compiled form with your copy of Lazarus, compile and install it:
   ```
   cd lazarus/tools
   make all
   strip lazres svn2revisioninc updatepofiles lrstolfm
   sudo make install
   ```
   This should install the *lazres* tool in your path.
3. On the command-line, convert the BMP image to a Lazarus resource:
   `lazres editbtn.lrs editbtn.bmp`
4. More than one image name can be added on the command-line, each image will be inserted in the resources.
5. Ensure that the *lresources* unit is included in the *uses* clause of a component unit (usually the unit where the component is registered). The IDE normally does this automatically.
6. Include the `.lrs` file in the initialization section of the unit.
   Alternatively, you can create a separate procedure to do this, which you then call from the initialization section of the unit:

```
begin
  {$I editbtn.lrs}
end;

initialization
 LoadResources;
end.
```

In general, the resources must be loaded before the program will need access to them. You follow the same steps to add almost any resource to a binary file.
The *LazarusResources* instance class manages all resources added in this way. For example, to load an image that has been added as a resource, use the following code:

```
With TPixmap.Create do
   begin
   LoadFromLazarusResource('TEditButton');
   // other code
   end;
end;
```

The resources are searched case-insensitively.
The IDE interface for property and component editors works similarly to Delphi's property and component editor interfaces. Other interfaces are completely different.

The *IDEIntf* package contains all the Lazarus IDE interfaces, and also contains examples of over more than 30 property editors in the `propedits.pp` and `graphpropedits.pas` units, as well as many examples of component editors in the unit `componenteditors.pas`.

Chapter 8
Files and Devices

By Felipe Monteiro de Carvalho and Jörg Braun

All programs have to deal with files in one way or another. Lazarus offers many ways for handling files. Which one we use depends on the result we want to achieve. A simple example is the need most programs have to save configuration data in a file for later use. The *TIniFile* class offers a convenient encapsulation of file routines for doing exactly that. There may also be cases where a user will need to choose the required settings from a list of alternative configurations.

8.1 File Dialogs in Lazarus

Lazarus provides platform-independent ways of opening and saving files, by making use of controls from each platform's widget-set.

Property	Function
DefaultExt	The predefined file name extension, a string.
FileName	The predefined or selected file name after the dialog is closed.
Filter	A list of file type descriptions and their associated extensions.
Filterindex	Determines which description will be show when the dialog is opened. Usually set to 1.
InitialDir	Initial directory on opening the dialog. Normally empty, in which case the current directory will be used.
Options	A set of options indicating whether hidden files and directories should be displayed, whether creating new files is allowed, etc.
Title	Title line shown at the top of the dialog.
Width, Height	Height and width of the dialog. These should normally be left at 0 to get the predefined values.
Tag	The component tag.

Table 8.1: The properties of file and directory dialog components

The Component Palette's Dialogs tab contains the following file selection controls: *TOpenDialog*, *TSaveDialog*, *TSelectDirectoryDialog*, *TOpenPictureDialog* and *TSavePictureDialog*. Each name describes its purpose. *TSelectDirectoryDialog* differs from the other four components, in that it uses a completely different control in Windows compared to Gtk+/Gtk2 and Qt. The properties shared by the file dialogs are listed in Table 8.1. File dialog events are the same in all five dialogs (see Table 8.2).

Event	The event is triggered
OnCanClose	When the user tries to close the dialog. Can be disabled by setting *CanClose* to *False* in the event procedure.
OnClose	When the dialog closes.
OnFolderChange	When the directory changes.
OnHelpClicked	When the *Help* button is pressed.
OnSelectionChange	When the file selection changes.
OnShow	When the dialog opens.
OnTypeChange	When the filter type changes.

Table 8.2: The event handler for file dialogs

Usually there is no need to react to these events. All dialogs save the file name (including the path) into the property *FileName* when the *Execute* method is called. *TSelectDirectoryDialog* loads a target path only. This is only true if the method completes successfully, meaning that the dialog was closed with the OK button and not with Cancel. (The keys [Enter] and [Esc] can be used instead of these buttons). This is a code example of using a *TOpenDialog*:

```
if OpenDialog.Execute then
  Memo1.Lines.LoadFromFile(OpenDialog1.FileName);
```

That is all there is to selecting a file for reading. When we want to save the file it will look as follows:

```
if OpenDialog.Execute then
  Memo1.Lines.SaveToFile(OpenDialog1.FileName);
```

For loading and saving pictures the two *xxxPictureDialogs* should be used. They differ from the normal dialogs in that they provide previews and they have a different default for the filter property. This list comes already filled with the graphical formats supported by Lazarus:

```
Graphic
(*.bmp;*.xpm;*.png;*.pbm;*.pgm;*.ppm;*.ico;*.icns;*.cur;*.jpg;*.jpeg;
                                        *.jpe;*.jfif;*.tif;*.tiff;*.gif)
|*.bmp;*.xpm;*.png;*.pbm;*.pgm;*.ppm;*.ico;*.icns;*.cur;*.jpg;*.jpeg;
                                        *.jpe;*.jfif;*.tif;*.tiff;*.gif|
Bitmaps (*.bmp)|*.bmp|
Pixmap (*.xpm)|*.xpm|
Portable Network Graphic (*.png)|*.png|
Portable PixMap (*.pbm;*.pgm;*.ppm)|*.pbm;*.pgm;*.ppm|
Icon (*.ico)|*.ico|
Mac OS X Icon (*.icns)|*.icns|
Cursor (*.cur)|*.cur|
Joint Picture Expert Group
(*.jpg;*.jpeg;*.jpe;*.jfif)|*.jpg;*.jpeg;*.jpe;*.jfif|
Tagged Image File Format (*.tif;*.tiff)|*.tif;*.tiff|
Graphics Interchange Format (*.gif)|*.gif|
All files (*.*)|*.*|
```

If you only work within the LCL as in our example everything works very intuitively and cleanly. Things get more complicated when the LCL and RTL are used together, because the LCL routines all work with Unicode (UTF8) names. To make the functions and procedures correspond to those in the runtime units, all string parameters need to be normalized. You need to use an encoding conversion function as follows:

```
AssignFile(f, UTF8ToSys(OpenDialog1.FileName);
```

Without the call to *UTF8ToSys* no file or directory with umlauts or other special characters in its name will be found! For *Memo1.LoadFromFile()* and *Image1.Picture.LoadFromFile()* this is not necessary, because these calls are all internal to the LCL (none from the RTL).
The reverse transformation can be done with *SysToUTF8()*.
These four file dialogs encapsulate the operating system file dialogs. In Windows *TSelectDirectoryDialog* is not handled by the normal file routines, but by the shell directory dialog, which is imported as *SHBrowseForFolder* instead. A knowledgeable Windows developer will see the constraints involved in developing platform-independent software here, since the shell API dialog is a lot more powerful than the Lazarus component. To use it fully, you would have to write a proprietary Windows component or handle the import manually within the program.
The Windows API function *SHBrowseForFolder* is exported by the library shell32.dll and is declared as follows (in Pascal syntax here):

```
function SHBrowseForFolderA(var lpbi: TBrowselnfoA): PltemListld;
                                                          StdCall;
function Sh8rowseForFolderW(var lpbi: TBrowseInfoW): PltemIDList;
                                                          StdCall;
```

So there are two variants of this function, one with *AnsiStrings*, the other with *WideStrings*. Also you clearly see some special records being used. *SHBrowseForFolder* is already defined in Lazarus, but instead of the generic *lpbi* shown here, we will have to use a pointer to the structure *Browselnfo*, unless we want to declare the structures again ourselves and compatibly with Delphi (we could do that if we wanted to).

```
BrowseInfoA = record
  hwndOwner : HWND;                  { owner's window handle }
  pidlRoot : PItemIDList;            { ItemList pointer to a structure for the root name }
                                     { NIL for the desktop folder }
  pszDisplayName : PAnsiChar;        { memory area for display name of selected item }
                                     { must be MAX_PATH long }
  lpszTitle : PAnsiChar;             { text to go in the title above the tree }
  ulFlags : UINT;                    { a set of flags that control the return stuff }
  lpfn : TFNBFFCallBack;             { pointer to a callback function }
  lParam : LPARAM;                   { extra info that's passed back in callbacks }
  iImage : LongInt;                  { output var: where to return the Image index }
                                     { of the user-selected folder }
end;

PBrowseInfoA = ^BrowseInfoA;
```

```
BrowseInfoW = record
  hwndOwner : HWND;               { for descriptions see above record structure }
  pidlRoot : PItemIDList;         { the record is identical except for the WideChars }
  pszDisplayName : PWideChar;
  lpszTitle      : PWideChar;
  ulFlags        : UINT;
  lpfn           : TFNBFFCallBack;
  lParam         : LPARAM;
  iImage         : LongInt;
end;

PBrowseInfoW = ^BrowseInfoW;
```

However these records (both the Ansi and Wide versions) leave some unanswered questions. Table 8.3 shows the predefined constants for the flags in the field *ulFlags*:

Constant	Value	Description
BIF_BROWSEFORCOMPUTER	$1000	Only computers will be returned. If the user makes a different selection, the OK button will be disabled.
BIF_BROWSEFORPRINTER	$2000	Only printers will be returned, otherwise the OK button is disabled.
BIF_DONTGOBELOWDOMAIN	$0002	Network folders below the domain will not be shown.
BIF_RETURNANCESTORS	$0008	Only return file system ancestors. If the user selects something else, the OK button will be grayed out.
BIF_RETURNONLYFSDIRS	$0001	Only directories will be returned, otherwise OK is disabled.
BIF_STATUSTEXT	$0004	Include a status area in the dialog box. The callback may enter text into it.

Table 8.3: The contants for ulFlags may be combined

8.1 File Dialogs in Lazarus

```
uses  Windows, ActiveX, ShellAPI;
// This shell function, unlike the other two listed above, is not predefined in Lazarus:
function SHGetMalloc(var ppMalloc: IMalloc): HResult; StdCall;
                           external'shell32.dll';
procedure TForm1.Button1Click(Sender: TObject);
  var ppMalloc      : IMalloc;              // declared in Lazarus!
      pBuffer       : PChar;
      pidlPrograms  : PItemIDList;          // PIDL for 'Program Files' folder
      pidlBrowse    : PItemIDList;          // PIDL for selected program group
      bi            : BrowseInfo;           // already defined!
      sResult       : String;
begin
// obtain pointer to Malloc interface:
  SHGetMalloc(ppMalloc);
  if ppMalloc = NIL then Exit;
// Allocate memory for text display of user's selection
  pBuffer := ppMalloc.Alloc(MAX_PATH);
  if pBuffer = NIL then Exit;
// PIDL to determine Application folder selection: passing the owner handle, an internal identifier of the special folder
// (here CSIDL_PROGRAMS) The return is in a PItemIDList:
  SHGetSpecialFolderLocation(Handle, CSIDL_PROGRAMS, pidlPrograms);
  if pidlPrograms = NIL then
  begin
    ppMalloc.Free(pBuffer);
    Exit;
  end;
// initialize BROWSEINFO
  with bi do begin
    hwndOwner := Handle;
    pidlRoot := pidlPrograms; // the result of SHGetSpecialFolderLocation
    pszDisplayName := pBuffer;
    // Note: UTF8 to AnsiString conversions are not always elegant or easy to understand:
    lpszTitle := PChar(UTF8ToSys('Select a program group'));
    ulFlags := 0;
    lpfn    := NIL;
    lParam := 0;
  end;
// The user can select a program group. With the definition of BrowseInfo in Lazarus you can use the following declaration:
  pidlBrowse := SHBrowseForFolder(@bi);
  if pidlBrowse = NIL then
  begin
    ppMalloc.Free(pidlPrograms);
    ppMalloc.Free(pBuffer);
    Exit;
  end;
// display name and show the path
  sResult := 'Selected program group:' + LineEnding;
  sResult := sResult + 'Display name: ' + SysToUTF8(pBuffer);
// normalise string and output the result;
  if SHGetPathFromIDList(pidlBrowse, pBuffer) then
    sResult := sResult + #13#10 + 'Path: ' + SysToUTF8(pBuffer);
  ShowMessage(sResult);
// Clean up:
  ppMalloc.Free(pidlBrowse);
  ppMalloc.Free(pidlPrograms);
  ppMalloc.Free(pBuffer);
end;
```

The method shown here is just to illustrate how to integrate a system dialog into a program for special purposes.

Constant	Value	Folder	Description
CSIDL_BITBUCKET	000Ah	Recycle bin	Directory in the file system containing the files in the user's recycle bin.
CSIDL_CONTROLS	0003h	Control Panel	Virtual folder containing the control panel symbols.
CSIDL_DESKTOP	0000h	Windows Desktop	Virtual folder at the root of the name space.
CSIDL_DESKTOP DIRECTORY	0010h	Physical desktop	Directory where the file objects visible on the desktop are physically saved (not to be confused with the Desktop folder itself).
CSIDL_DRIVES	0011h	Workspace	Virtual folder containing everything on the PC: Storage media, printers and control panel.
CSIDL_FONTS	0014h	Fonts	Virtual folder containing the fonts.
CSIDL_NETHOOD	0013h	Network	Directory containing the objects in the network neighbourhood.
CSIDL_NETWORK	0012h	Network environment	Virtual folder representing the top layer of the network hierarchy.
CSIDL_PERSONAL	0005h	Personal directory	Directory of the file system as common storage location for documents.
CSIDL_PRINTERS	0004h	Printer folder	Virtual directory holding the installed printer.
CSIDL_PROGRAMS	0002h	Programs	Directory holding the user's program groups.
CSIDL_RECENT	0008h	Recent	Directory with the user's most recently used documents.
CSIDL_SENDTO	0009h	Send to	Directory holding the entries of the "Send to" menu.
CSIDL_STARTMENU	000Bh	Start menu	Directory holding the entries in the Start menu.
CSIDL_STARTUP	0007h	Autostart	Directory in the file system corresponding to the user's program group Startup.
CSIDL_TEMPLATES	0015h	Common files	Directory of the file system used as common storage location for document templates.

Table 8.4: Possible values for the nFolder parameter in the SHGetSpecialFolderLocation function

As can be seen from the declaration, the functions *SHGetSpecialFolderLocation* used to create a basis for *SHBrowseForFolder* and *SHGetPathFromIDList* which gets the path from its result, have both already been declared in the Lazarus libraries. On the other hand *SHGetMalloc* (which is used to reserve memory) is not published in the Lazarus libraries, so it needs to be imported.
The example listing shows how the *SHBrowseForFolder* function can only be used after *SHGetSpecialFolderLocation*. This function has been translated for the LCL and there it is declared as follows:

```
function SHGetSpecialFolderLocation(hwndOwner:HWND; nFolder: Integer;
                                     var ppidl: PItemIDList): HResult;
```

The parameter *nFolder* is very important. It has to be passed one of the constants from Table 8.4. After the call, *PItemIDList* will be filled with the value needed for *SHGetSpecialFolderLocation.*

The call to *SHGetPathFromIDList* in the example above is more straightforward, returning just the absolute path of a special folder in the file system. For a program group that is its absolute path. This information is necessary when installing a program to be able to add links to a program group. This function reuses the structure *ItemIDList* we already know, and returns complete name as a string in the buffer declared as a *PChar*. The record is defined in the LCL in the file `struct.inc`:

```
SHITEMID = record
  cb : USHORT;
  abID : array[0..0] of BYTE;
end;
LPSHITEMID  = ^SHITEMID;
LPCSHITEMID = ^SHITEMID;
_SHITEMID   = SHITEMID;
TSHITEMID   = SHITEMID;
PSHITEMID   = ^SHITEMID;

ITEMIDLIST = record
  mkid : SHITEMID;
end;

LPITEMIDLIST  = ^ITEMIDLIST;
LPCITEMIDLIST = ^ITEMIDLIST;
_ITEMIDLIST   = ITEMIDLIST;
TITEMIDLIST   = ITEMIDLIST;
PITEMIDLIST   = ^ITEMIDLIST;
```

The shell function we have not explained so far is *SHGetMalloc*. This is used to reserve memory for shell objects and to initialize them. Lazarus defines the interface needed in the `shellapi.pp` file:

```
type
{ IMalloc interface }
IMalloc = interface(IUnknown)
  ['{00000002-0000-0000-C000-000000000046}']
  function Alloc(cb: Longint): Pointer;
  function Realloc(pv: Pointer; cb: Longint): Pointer;
  procedure Free(pv: Pointer);
  function GetSize(pv: Pointer): Longint;
  function DidAlloc(pv: Pointer): Longint;
  procedure HeapMinimize;
end;
LPMALLOC = ^IMalloc;
PMALLOC  = ^IMalloc;
```

The simplest way to initialize it is shown in the listing above. The *Free* method is used to release the memory again.

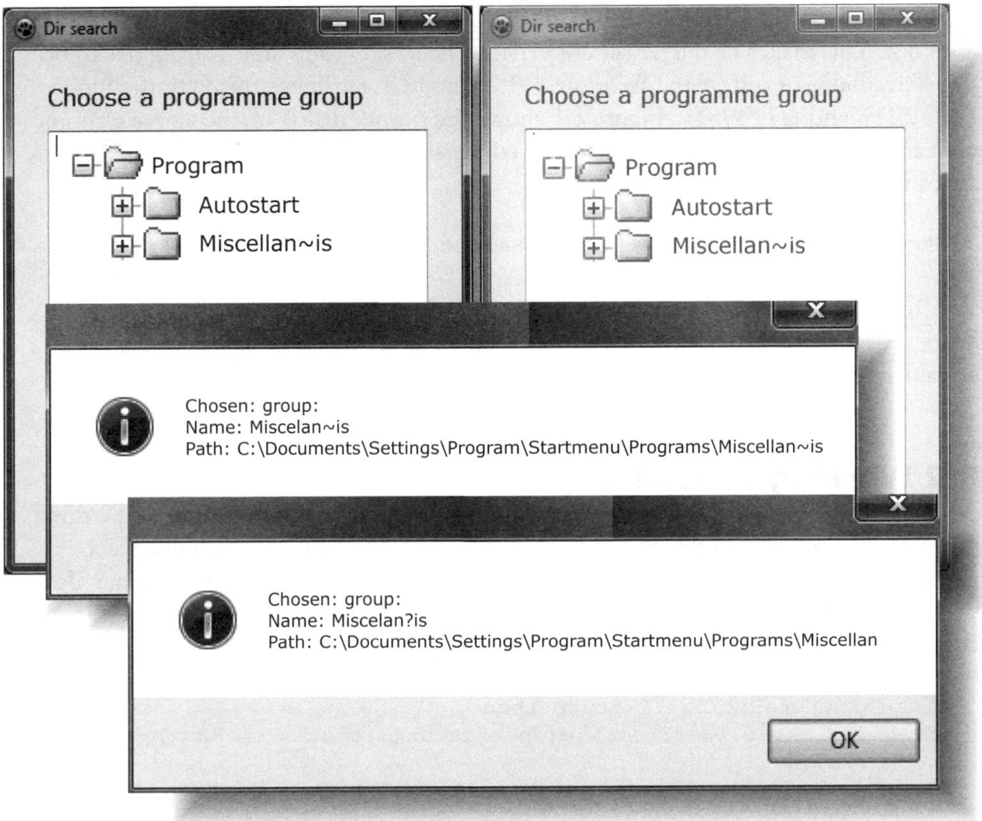

Figure 8.1: When working with API functions in Windows, character set conversions are very important. The textual error in the title (top right) is not as bad as the defective path return value in the result dialog at the bottom right (see the third line of message dialog).

As we can see from our little example, working with the Windows shell API, its folders and dialogs takes quite a lot of work. The definitions in the LCL are often not exactly compatible with those in the VCL, so code conversion from Delphi to Lazarus requires inside Windows knowledge. Of course we also have to keep in mind that a program which uses these routines, cannot be transferred to other platforms later.
Unfortunately when we have to work with files and directories in Windows it is almost impossible to avoid using the shell.

Also remember that Lazarus works with the UTF8 character set internally, and Windows does not. This makes character set conversions necessary each time a string has to be transferred into or out of the Windows API. The LCL facilitates this with the functions *SysToUTF8* and *UTF8ToSys*. Figure 8.1 shows the output dialog of the above example with and without use of the character set conversion routines.
As can be seen from the line:

```
lpszTitle := PChar(UTF8ToSys('Select a program group'));
```

sometimes horrible type conversions are needed to make the text appear correctly in a dialog. Even more important is the correct handling of directory paths containing umlauted characters.

8.2 Working with files

As long as we only use the components supplied with Lazarus for reading and writing data of any type, file-handling works very intuitively. A typical control will have a *LoadFromFile* method for opening and a *SaveToFile* method for saving files. When dealing with a memo field or a complex SynEdit control, we are handling *lines* in a text file. When dealing with *TImage* we are handling its *Picture* property:

```
if OpenPictureDialog1.Execute then
  Image1.Picture.LoadFromFile(OpenPictureDialog1.FileName);
```

It's worth examining these *Load...* and *Save...* methods in more detail. Simple storage classes like *TBitmap* and *TJpegImage* also have *LoadFromFile* and *SaveToFile* methods. They have inherited them from abstract methods of the *TGraphic* class.
This important base class is defined in the unit `Graphics`:

```
TGraphic = class(TPersistent)
  private
   // omitted
  protected
   // omitted
  public
    procedure Assign(ASource: TPersistent); override;
    constructor Create; virtual;
    procedure Clear; virtual;
   {$IF declared(vmtEquals)}
    function Equals(Obj: TObject): Boolean; override; overload;
   {$ENDIF}
    function LazarusResourceTypeValid(const AResourceType: string):
                                               boolean; virtual;
    procedure LoadFromFile(const Filename: string); virtual;
    procedure LoadFromStream(Stream: TStream); virtual; abstract;
    procedure LoadFromMimeStream(AStream: TStream; const AMimeType:
                                                string);virtual;
    procedure LoadFromLazarusResource(const ResName: String);
                                                        virtual;
    procedure LoadFromResourceName(Instance: THandle; const ResName:
                                                String); virtual;
    procedure LoadFromResourceID(Instance: THandle; ResID: PtrInt);
                                                        virtual;
    procedure LoadFromClipboardFormat(FormatID: TClipboardFormat);
                                                        virtual;
    procedure LoadFromClipboardFormatID(ClipboardType:
              TClipboardType; FormatID: TClipboardFormat); virtual;
    procedure SaveToFile(const Filename: string); virtual;
    procedure SaveToStream(Stream: TStream); virtual; abstract;
    procedure SaveToClipboardFormat(FormatID: TClipboardFormat);
                                                        virtual;
    procedure SaveToClipboardFormatID(ClipboardType: TClipboardType;
                            FormatID: TClipboardFormat); virtual;
    procedure GetSupportedSourceMimeTypes(List: TStrings); virtual;
    function GetResourceType: TResourceType; virtual;
    class function GetFileExtensions: string; virtual;
    class function IsStreamFormatSupported(Stream: TStream): Boolean;
                                                        virtual;
  public
    property Empty: Boolean read GetEmpty;
    property Height: Integer read GetHeight write SetHeight;
    property Modified: Boolean read FModified write SetModified;
    property MimeType: string read GetMimeType;
    property OnChange: TNotifyEvent read FOnChange write FOnChange;
    property OnProgress: TProgressEvent read FOnProgress
                                      write FOnProgress;
    property Palette: HPALETTE read GetPalette write SetPalette;
    property PaletteModified: Boolean read FPaletteModified
                                    write FPaletteModified;
    property Transparent: Boolean read GetTransparent
                                write SetTransparent;
    property Width: Integer read GetWidth write SetWidth;
  end;
```

The definitions are defined as virtual, which means the descendants will have to provide an implementation. The definition is shown here without its private and protected parts. We can see there are other possible sources and targets besides normal files.

8.2.1 Reading and writing files

Lazarus's internal functions allow us to do many things already, particularly with text files. But if the data needs any preprocessing before displaying it in an edit field, we will have to resort to the standard Pascal functions of the RTL. This is true for both reading and writing. Free Pascal and Lazarus offer the data types *File* and *Textfile*. Files declared with *File* can optionally have an associated type. This is then specified with the declaration. Before we can work with a file, we need to associate a name with a *file handle*.
You do this with the *AssignFile* procedure (or its older equivalent *Assign*).

Binary file access

Pascal distinguishes between *text* files and *binary* files. Text files are defined as type *Text* or type *Textfile*. In fact *Text* and *Textfile* refer to the same thing, but you should always use *Textfile*. Delphi introduced the name *Textfile* to make a clear distinction between text files and the abundance of components which have *Text* properties. The name is available in Lazarus as well. All other files, i.e. binary files, are of the *File* type.
Each file needs to have a *handle* associated with it. However this is not assigned by the operating system, but by Pascal itself. The simplest example looks like this:

```
var  f: File of Byte;
begin
// convert filename encoding:
  AssignFile(f, UTF8ToSys(OpenDialog1.FileName));
```

Data in files typed as *File of Byte* is read and/or written one byte at a time.
After this call the file is no longer addressed by name, but only through the assigned handle. However, the file is not yet open. It may be necessary to set the access mode first. Pascal opens typed and untyped files by default for both reading and writing, regardless of how they will be used later. The access mode is stored in a system variable named *FileMode*. It has three possible values:

0 All files are opened for reading only.
1 All files are opened for writing only.
2 All files are opened for both reading and writing.

It is important to assign the correct value to the *FileMode* variable before opening the file, because if we try to open a file for write access when we are not allowed to modify it, an error or an exception will result, which has to be trapped (or else the program will crash). The default *FileMode* value is 2, so if it is not changed the operating system will be asked to make the file available for writing, which is not possible if writing is not allowed.
In Pascal, existing files are opened with the command *Reset*. *Rewrite* will create a new file or overwrite an existing one. Use *Append* to add data to the end of an existing file.
Calling *Reset* or *Append* on a nonexistent file will result in an error.

Rewrite will also cause an error if the operating system is not able to create the new file. There are two possible ways to catch the errors that can occur when opening a file. The simplest way is to switch off checking for I/O operations with the compiler directive *{$I-}*:

```
AssignFile(f, ...);
{$I-}                          // turn off I/0 checking
Reset(f);
if IOResult <> 0 then // the file could not be opened!
   ...
{$I+)                          // I/0 checking is turned on again
```

A more modern approach is to create an exception handler for the file routine. To make this work, checking of I/O operations has to be enabled (which is the default setting):

```
AssignFile(f, ...);
try
  Reset(f);
except
  ShowMessage('File cannot be opened!');
  Exit;
end;
```

However, many file access failures can be prevented by correctly setting *FileMode* in advance.
To read all the data sequentially from the file we opened in the *AssignFile* statement above, we have to set up a loop:

```
FileMode := 0;                          // file is read-only
Reset(f);                               // file is opened for reading
while not EoF(f) do begin ... // while the file end has not been reached...
```

EoF (for "End of File") is a file function which returns *True* when we have reached the end of the file with handle *f*. There is a similar function we can use when we want to read a file backwards. This function - *BoF* (for "Beginning of File") - will tell us we have reached the beginning of the file.
The size of a file can be retrieved with the function *FileSize*. This function takes the file name including path as a parameter and returns the size of the file as a 64-bit integer. *FileSize* and numerous other functions for handling files are available in the *FileUtils* and *SysUtils* Free Pascal units. Another interesting function in this area is *FileSize* from the System unit. As this function has the same name and it is included first, we need to qualify it when importing it. This function does not return the size in bytes, but in *records*. For a *File of Byte* that is an identical value, but not for a *File of Word*, because then each record has a size of two bytes instead of one.

This will result in

```
 I := FileSize(UTF8ToSys(Dialog1.FileName));
```

and

```
 I := System.FileSize(f);
```

returning different sizes for the same file f.

Records can be interesting and very complex data types. So *System.FileSize* returns the number of records in a file of records and *FileUtils.FileSize* will return the overall size in bytes of the file of records. Apart from the *typed files* there are also *untyped files*. When reading untyped files their contents are written into a memory buffer without regard to the data type. This buffer may be either in the heap or in the data area. The size of the data to be read or written is specified when reading or writing. The larger it is, the faster the program will operate and the more working memory will be needed.
Here is the classical example of a file copy routine. Source and destination must have been set beforehand in an open dialog and a save dialog.

```
procedure TForm1.Button1Click(Sender: TObject);
  var SourceF, TargetF: File;               // file handles
      Buffer: array[1..2048] of Char;       // (any) buffer
      NumRead, NumWritten: Int64;           // counter for Blockread/write
begin
  AssignFile(SourceF, UTF8ToSys(OpenDialog1.FileName));   // source file
  try
    Reset(SourceF, 1);              // you must specify the record size of untyped files!
  except
    ShowMessage('Error when opening '+ OpenDialog1.FileName + '!');
    Exit;// source file could not be opened
  end;

  AssignFile(TargetF, UTF8ToSys(SaveDialog1.FileName));   // destination file
  try
    Rewrite(TargetF, 1);            // a new file – the record size for reading and writing
                                    // must necessarily be mde equal
  repeat
    BlockRead(SourceF, Buffer, SizeOf(Buffer), NumRead); // read ... and
    BlockWrite(TargetF, Buffer, NumRead, NumWritten);    // write
    until  (NumRead = 0)            // there is nothing left to read
    or (NumWritten <> NumRead);     // last block was shorter -> end of file
  finally                           // and even if it goes wrong:
    CloseFile(SourceF);             // the two files are closed and
    CloseFile(TargetF);             // their handles are released
  end;
  ShowMessage(OpenDialog1.FileName + ' was copied to ' +
                                           SaveDialog1.FileName);
end;
```

8.2.1 Reading and writing files

Function	Description
procedure Append(var F:TextFile | File**);**	*Append* opens an existing file. All data written to F is added at the end of the file. Only text files can be opened in append mode. After calling *Append* the file F is protected for writing until the final *CloseFile*. Concurrent access by other programs is not possible after calling *Append*. *Append* can only be used on existing files. If the file does not exist a run time error occurs.
procedure AssignFile(var F:TextFile | File; const s:string**);**	*Assign* and *AssignFile* assign a name to a file. This works for any file type. However this call does not open the file. It only associates a name with a file variable and will mark the file as closed.
procedure CloseFile(var F:TextFile | File**);**	*Close* or *CloseFile* both close a file.
function EoF(var F: TextFile | File**);** boolean;	Checks whether the End-of-File has been reached.
procedure Erase(var F: TextFile | File**);**	Deletes an unopened file from the file system. The file has to be assigned with *Assign*, and may not have been opened with *Reset* or *Rewrite*.
procedure Flush(var F: TextFile | File**);**	Flush empties the memory buffer of an open file F and writes the contents to the storage medium. It does not close the file.
procedure ReadLn(var F: Text; Args: Arguments**);**	Reads one or more values from file F and saves the result in the specified parameters Args. After that the file pointer is
procedure ReadLn(Args: Arguments**);**	advanced to the next line in the file. The end of a line in text files is marked with the (platform-dependent) end of line character(s). Under Windows this is CRLF, under Unix it is CR and in MacOS it is LF. The end of line mark does not count as part of the line and is ignored. If no file F has been specified, the standard input will be read.
procedure Rename(var F: Textfile | File; const s: string**);**	Rename changes the name of the associated file F.
procedure Reset(var F: TextFile | File**);**	Opens the file for reading.
procedure Rewrite(var T: TextFile | File**);**	Opens the file for writing.
procedure Seek(var F: Textfile | File; Pos: Int64**).**	Sets the file read/write position.
function SeekEOF(var t: TextFile | File**);**	Boolean;Sets the file position to end-of-file.
procedure Truncate(var F:TextFile | File**);**	Truncate cuts off the (open) file F at the current file position.
procedure Write(Args: Arguments**);** **procedure Write(**var F: Textfile | File; Args: Arguments**);**	Write writes the content of the Args parameters into text file F. If the F parameter is omitted, the text will be written to the standard output. Numeric types will be converted, strings and string pointers will be written as they are stored in memory.
procedure WriteLn(Args: Arguments**);** **procedure WriteLn(**var F: Textfile; Args: Arguments**);**	Does the same as Write, but adds the platform-specific End-of-Line character(s) to the end of the string.

Table 8.5: The most important routines for untyped files. Part 1.

Function	Description
Procedure Reset(var F[:File; RecSize : Word]**);**	Opens an untyped file. If no record size is specified, 128 is assumed.
procedure BlockRead(var F: file; var Buf; Count: Integer[; var AmtTransferred: Integer]**);**	Blockwise reading from an untyped file F into buffer Buf. Maximum number of records read is Count. If all reads were successful, AmtTransferred will be equal to Count after the call.
procedure BlockWrite(var f: file; var Buf; Count: Integer[; var AmtTransferred: Integer]**);**	Blockwise writing of data from a storage area to an untyped file. The maximum number of records to write is Count. If all writes were successful, AmtTransferred I wil be equal to Count after the call.

Table 8.5: The most important routines for untyped files. Part 2 (continuation)

For EoF, AssignFile, CloseFile and so on see Table 8.5

Standard input, standard output and standard error

When working with text files, some special restrictions apply. Strictly speaking "text files" are not limited to data read from or written to storage media. Free Pascal offers four standard variables for TextFile: *Input*, *Output*, *ErrOutput* and *StdErr*. *Input* and *Output* refer to the standard input/output device. Normally this is the console. Input is read-only, Output is write-only. *StdErr* is the same as *ErrOutput* and is normally directed to the console as well. It should normally be used to read debug information only. In reality this happens very rarely and debug information is written directly to the Output.
If these channels are available (this depends on the operating system), all these standard TextFile variables will be open and ready to use as soon as your program starts.
This is always true in Unix and DOS for instance. Under Unix the output is sent to the console. If a program is started from the console, that is where its output will be visible. If not, everything sent to Output will vanish.
Under Windows using the standard TextFile variable yields an error, unless the application was compiled in console mode, as only that mode allows access to the console. To set *console mode* in Windows use the directive *{$apptype console}* in your main program file. If the parameter *TextFile* is omitted in calls to *ReadLn* or *WriteLn* the operation will be executed on *Input* for reading and on *Output* for writing.
The following example shows how the procedures *Write*, *WriteLn* and *ReadLn* can be used with the console. The user is asked to type his name in the console and then to press [Enter]. The program will then output this name to the console.

```
program ShowName;
{$apptype console}
  var  Str: String;
begin
  // Writes the specified text without a newline character at the end
  Write('Please write your name and press [Enter]: ');
  ReadLn(Str);         // ReadLn reades text up to the next line break
  WriteLn('Your name is: ' + Str);        // writes a line to the console
end.
```

If the standard channels are to be used, no file assignments should be made. However, if you wish to access files, use the same routines as for access to binary files.

Procedure	Description
AssignFile/Assign	Associates the file name with the handle, just as is done with typed files.
CloseFile/Close	Releases the file handle just as for typed and untyped files.
Reset and Rewrite	Opens/creates a file just as for typed files.
Read	Reads from a file without the following line ending.
ReadLn	Reads a whole line including line ending from the file.
Write	Writes a line without the final line ending.
WriteLn	Writes a whole line including line ending to the file.

Table 8.6: The basic functions for handling text files (files of data type TextFile)

For text files you should always declare the type to be *TextFile* (*Text* is out-dated). The variable *FileMode* does not affect text files. Just as for binary files the file names for opening and closing have to be converted between LCL and system API with *UTF8ToSys* and *SysToUTF8*. These functions can also be used to convert data (for instance from Windows ANSI or FreeBSD ISO strings into UTF8 and back) in an operating-system-independent way. Another small problem when working with text files are the line endings, which are not standardized at all. Windows always uses CRLF, Unix uses LF and MacOS uses CR. To be able to work in a portable way you should always write line endings using the constant *LineEnding* (and not in the DOS/Windows way with #13#10 or ^M ^J; also see chapter 5.1).

8.2.2 Working with streams

A new system for file access was introduced in modern Pascal run-time environments with *TFileStream*. It has some advantages over the standard routines, such as more intuitive method names, exception handling instead of run time errors, and object orientation. On the other hand there are still many useful applications for the standard system, which can access data from the console as well as from files since there is a natural integration with functions for handling the console (many command-line tools do this, for instance). Both file access systems are equivalent, and it is possible to convert between them with the function *AssignStream* from the *StreamIO* unit. The following function illustrates how simple it is to convert from standard routines to streams. This example is a simple file copier, which completely replaces the one we saw earlier when we discussed untyped files:

```
procedure CopyFile(Source, Target: String);
  var  S: TFileStream = NIL; T: TFileStream = NIL;
begin
  S := TFileStream.Create(Source, fmOpenRead);
  try T := TFileStream.Create(Target, fmOpenWrite or fmCreate);
    T.CopyFrom(S, S.Size);
{$ifdef Windows}
    FileSetDate(T.Handle, FileGetDate(S.Handle)); // file date
{$endif}
  finally
    if T <> NIL then T.Free;
    S. Free;
  end;
end;
```

The function works with standard strings again, so it has to be handed strings converted with *UTF8ToSys* if the source and destination are to be determined using the LCL. This function is not just a replacement for Blockread/Blockwrite, but also for the routine with the same name from the kernel DLL in the Windows API. As can be seen in the example, streams can both be the source and the destination of data. All streams are derived from the class *TStream*, which contains abstract methods for operations like reading and writing stream data, which work independently of the nature of the input/output device. If the right descendant of *TStream* is passed, the input/output operation on the device will be handled by the method from the derived class. The Free Pascal RTL offers many *TStream* descendants in the unit `Classes,` which are fully documented in the *Free Pascal 2 Reference Guide*. We will only summarize them here: *TFileStream* saves data in a named file on a storage device, *TMemoryStream* saves data in memory, *TResourceStream* is for internal resources of executable files, *TCustomMemoryStream* is the base class of all streams which keep their data in memory, *TStringStream* saves string data, *THandleStream* is the base class of all streams which are identified by the file system, and *TOwnerStream* handles streams which save data based on another stream. There are many other *TStream* descendants available in the FCL, in particular some for compression and sockets. We will discuss the most important streams again later in this chapter.

Constant	Description
fmOpenRead	Opens a file for reading only.
fmOpenWrite	Opens a file for writing only.
fmOpenReadWrite	Opens a file for reading and writing.
fmShareExclusive	Locks a file for exclusive use.
fmShareDenyWrite	Locks a file so that other processes can only read it.
fmShareDenyRead	Locks a file so that other processes cannot read it.
fmShareDenyNone	Does not lock a file.
fmCreate	Creates a new file

Table 8.7: Modes for opening a file with TFileStream

Object Pascal streams were introduced in 1990 in Turbo Vision 1.0 with Turbo Pascal 6.0. Later streams were updated for the new object oriented Delphi syntax. They are available in the Free Pascal Runtime Library in the unit *Classes* and form a very important part of the Object Pascal programming model. Streams are based on a very simple model and have only two properties: *Size* and *Position*. Their three main methods are *Seek*, *Read* and *Write*. The *Position* is the location in the stream where a read or write operation is executed. When a stream is read or written, the current position is increased by the number of items read or written. The Size is the number of bytes currently in the stream. *Seek* can be used to change the current position. *Read* reads data from the stream and *Write* writes into the stream. The *Size* and *Position* of a stream need to handled with care, as pipe, socket, FIFO, compression and decompression streams do not have these properties.

Tstream

TStream is an abstract class. That means it only specifies an interface for all its derived classes. It is not possible to create stream instances from it. When writing stream-related routines, we normally use a parameter of type *TStream* to accept all derived types of TStream. It is up to the caller to pass the correct derived class. Here is the class definition (without the private and protected parts) as it is found in *classesh.inc*.

```
TStream = class(TObject)
  protected
    // omitted
  public
    function Read(var Buffer; Count: Longint): Longint; virtual;
    // Read reads data from the stream into a buffer and returns the number of bytes read
    function Write(const Buffer; Count: Longint): Longint; virtual;
    // Write writes data from a buffer to the stream and returns the number of bytes read.
    function Seek(Offset: Longint; Origin: Word): Longint; virtual;
                                                   overload;
    function Seek(const Offset: Int64; Origin: TSeekOrigin):
       Int64; virtual; overload;   // Seek sets the current position in the stream
    // The origin can be: soFromBeginning, soFromCurrent or soFromEnd.
    // Offset must be negative if Origin is soFromEnd. It must be positive for, soFromBeginning can accept both
    // directions and thus both positive and negative values for soFromCurrent.
    procedure ReadBuffer(var Buffer; Count: Longint);
    procedure WriteBuffer(const Buffer; Count: Longint);
    function CopyFrom(Source: TStream; Count: Int64): Int64;
    // CopyFrom copies data from one stream to another.
    function ReadComponent(Instance: TComponent): TComponent;
    // ReadComponent reads a component's state from the stream and transmits this state to the specified Instance
    // instance. If Instance is nil the instance is first created based on the data in the stream.
    // ReadComponent returns the data as read from the stream.
    function ReadComponentRes(Instance: TComponent): TComponent;
    procedure WriteComponent(Instance: TComponent);
    // WriteComponent writes the published properties of the instance, so that they
    // can be read later with TStream.ReadComponent
    // This method is intended for use in an IDE, so that the state of a window
    // or a Datamodule can be stored and then reinstated later in the IDE used to create it.
    procedure WriteComponentRes(const ResName: string;
                                 Instance: TComponent);
    procedure WriteDescendent(Instance, Ancestor: TComponent);
    procedure WriteDescendentRes(const ResName: string;
             Instance, Ancestor:TComponent);
    procedure WriteResourceHeader(const ResName: string;
                                 {!!!:out} var FixupInfo: Integer);
    procedure FixupResourceHeader(FixupInfo: Integer);
    procedure ReadResHeader;
    function ReadByte : Byte;              // reads and returns a Byte from a stream
    function ReadWord : Word;              // reads and returns a Word from a stream
    function ReadDWord : Cardinal;         // reads and returns a DWord from a stream
    function ReadQWord : Qword;            // reads and returns a Qword from a stream
    function ReadAnsiString : String;      // reads and returns an AnsiString
    procedure WriteByte(b : Byte);         // writes a Byte to the stream
    procedure WriteWord(w : Word);         // writes a Word to the stream
    procedure WriteDWord(d : Cardinal);// writes a DWord to the stream
    procedure WriteQWord(q : Qword);       // writes a QWord to the stream
    procedure WriteAnsiString (const S : String);// writes an AnsiString
    property Position: Int64 read GetPosition write SetPosition;
    // the current stream position in bytes relative to the starting position
    property Size: Int64 read GetSize write SetSize64;
    // the current size of the stream in bytes
  end;
```

The following diagram demonstrates graphically the state of the stream after each access:

```
procedure WriteMagicNumberToStream(AStream: TStream);
begin
 AStream.WriteByte($AA);

 AStream.WriteWord($BBBB);

end;
```

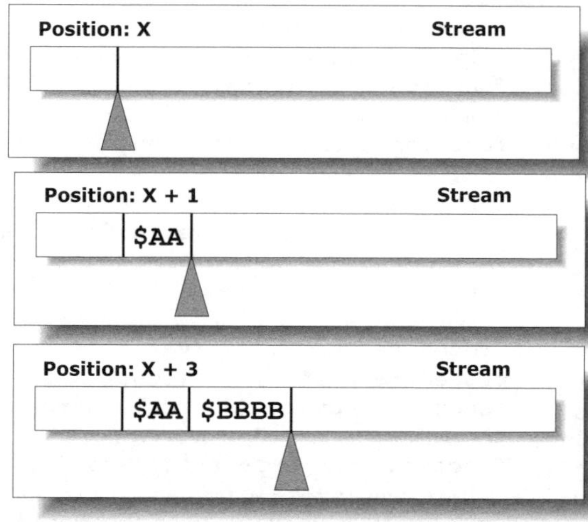

All other streams are based on the *TStream* class.

TMemoryStream

A *TMemoryStream* is a stream located in memory. It has a *LoadFromFile* method which can be used to create a cache filled with data from a file. This can later be read several times. This will improve the execution speed of the operation, as memory access is usually a lot faster than file access. The *SaveToFile* method will store the contents of a memory-based stream to a file.

TStringStream

TStringStream is very useful for converting a stream into a string and vice versa. If a string has to be converted from a stream, it can be read directly from the property *DataString*.
A string is converted into a stream with the *Create* constructor of the class by passing the string as a parameter to the constructor. This class should only be used for communication with strings. It needs the string for saving its data. For each *Write()* operation a *SetLength()* is needed. However this is less efficient than using the method based on memory chunks from *TMemoryString*.
The class is defined in `classesh.inc`:

```
 TStringStream = class(TStream)
// private and protected sections omitted
 public
   Constructor Create(const AString: String);
   function Read(var Buffer; Count: LongInt): LongInt; override;
   function ReadString(Count: LongInt): String;
   function Seek(Offset: LongInt; Origin: Word): LongInt; override;
   function Write(const Buffer; Count: LongInt): LongInt; override;
   procedure WriteString(const AString: String);
   property DataString: String read FDataString;
 end;
```

TCompressor and TDecompressor

The Free Pascal FCL contains many ready-to-use *TStream* descendants.
Amongst them are compression, socket and encryption streams. We will now look at *TCompressionStream* and *TDecompressionStream* from the unit `zstream`.

These classes are ideal for compressing and decompressing data in *Zlib* format (see `http://www.zlib.net/`), which is one of the most efficient compression methods. Far from being merely an interface to the original C source code, these classes are a completely new implementation in Object Pascal, which improves their portability over providing just a simple interface to a library.

```
TCompressionStream = class(TCustomZlibStream)
protected
  raw_written, compressed_written: longint;
public
  Constructor Create(level: TCompressionlevel; dest: TStream;
                     ASkipHeader: Boolean = False);
  destructor Destroy; Override;
  function Write(const buffer; count: Longint): Longint; Override;
  procedure Flush; // since Free Pascal 2.2.2: immediate compression
  function get_compressionrate: Single;
end;

TDecompressionStream = class(TCustomZlibStream)
protected
 // omitted ...
public
  Constructor Create(ASource: TStream; ASkipHeader: Boolean = False);
  destructor Destroy; Override;
  function Read(var buffer; count: Longint): Longint; Override;
  function Seek(offset: Longint; origin: Word): Longint; Override;
  function get_compressionrate: Single;
end;
```

To compress data we need an instance of *TCompressionStream*. Its constructor takes two parameters: the compression level (see Table 8.9) and a target stream where the data has to be stored. Data is sent to the compressor with the *Write* method (or one of *Write's* variants, or with another method that calls it such as *CopyFrom*).

Simply sending the data will only result in it being stored. It is only compressed when *TCompressionStream* is released. As that is not always very convenient, an additional method Flush was introduced with Free Pascal 2.2.2, which can be used to compress the data without first releasing the compressor.
For uncompressing data an instance of *TDecompressionStream* is needed. Its constructor has a parameter which will be the data source. Compression level does not have to be provided, as this will be encoded in the input data. The uncompressed data can be retrieved with the *Read* method or one of its variants. Please note that *TDecompressionStream* does not have a *Size* property. This means it is not possible to read compressed data with the CopyFrom method as is possible with other streams. So we will have to create a loop and call *Read* until no more data is returned, or we will have to use a method like *TStrings.LoadFromStream* from the Free Pascal RTL, which contains a similar implementation. Delphi programmers should be careful, as the Delphi implementation of *TStrings.LoadFromStream* does not have this functionality. It is not meant to be used in this way.

Value	Effect
clNoneNo	compression, the data is simply copied.
clFastest	Use the fastest compression method available.
clDefault	A compromise between speed and output size. This is the preferred value to use.
clMax	The slowest compression method, resulting in the smallest data output size.

Table 8.8: The possible values of TCompressionLevel

The following short example program demonstrates how to pack and unpack string data. After pressing the button, the string in the first text field is compressed and then decompressed again. The byte values of the compressed string are shown in the memo in hexadecimal format. To demonstrate the successful compression and decompression the unpacked string is shown in the edit field.
Decompression is handled by the *TStrings.LoadFromString* method. This saves us the trouble of reading in a loop until we have retrieved the right number of bytes. The implementation follows the directions about using the compression classes given above. The compressed data appears to be rather lengthy compared to the original data! This is due to the fact that its input is very short and will therefore contain very little redundant information. If we feed longer strings, we can observe how the length of the compressed data changes.

```
uses zstream;
procedure TformCompressor.buttonCompressClick(Sender: TObject);
  var  Compressor     : TCompressionStream;
       Decompressor   : TDecompressionStream;
       SourceString   : TStringStream;
       CompressedData: TMemoryStream;
       DestString     : TStringList;
       i: Integer;
begin
  SourceString := TStringStream.Create(editOriginalString.Text);
  CompressedData := TMemorystream.Create;
  Compressor := TCompressionStream.Create(clDefault, CompressedData);
  Decompressor := TDecompressionStream.Create(CompressedData);
  DestString := TStringList.Create;

(* compress the string *)
  Compressor.CopyFrom(SourceString, SourceString.Size);
  Compressor.Free;

(* copy copressed string into memo field *)
  CompressedData.Position := 0;
  memoResults.Lines.Clear;
  for i := 0 to CompressedData.Size - 1 do
    memoResults.Lines[0] := memoResults.Lines[0] +
                        IntToHex(CompressedData.ReadByte, 2) + ' ';

(* uncompress the string *)
  CompressedData.Seek(0, soFromBeginning);
  DestString.LoadFromStream(Decompressor);
  editResults.Text := DestString.Text;

  Decompressor.Free;
  CompressedData.Free;
  SourceString.Free;
  DestString.Free;
end;
```

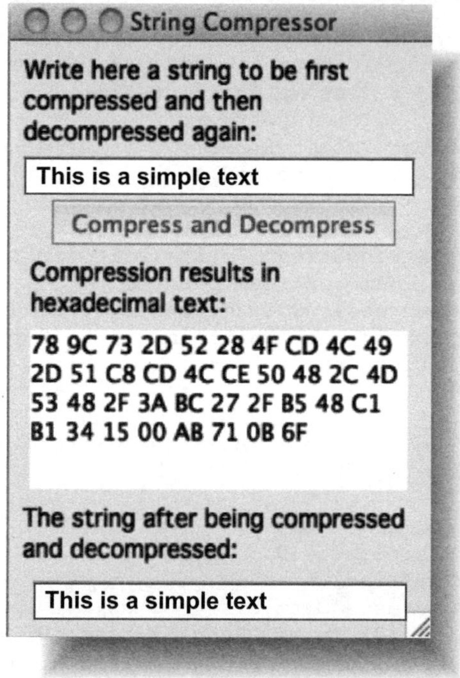

Figure 8.2: The example program demonstrating compression in action

TResourceStream

TResourceStream can be used to read data written into executable files as Windows resources. Lazarus reads resources source code from a file with the extension `.rc` in the same way that other development environments do this. `.RC` files are pure text files. Bitmaps and icons are either stored as dumps or as references to external binary files. These `.rc` files are then processed with a resource compiler. Lazarus uses *WindRes* for this. Resource files created by external programs, like Borland's Resource Workshop or the free XN Resource Editor by Colin Wilson, also create Lazarus-compatible resource files.

The compiled binary `.res` resource files are then linked into the executable Windows file. To do that, a *{$R myresource.rc}* or *{$R myresource.res}* directive is included in the source code of the project or unit file. If an `.RC` file is given, this will automatically be compiled, if its syntax complies with *WindRes*.

When planning a platform-independent application, please keep in mind that these resource files are not portable. Instead of linking this data into the program itself, it may be a better idea to have them read from external files which can be distributed along with the executable.

Sometimes we will have to work with internal resources anyway, for instance when creating Windows installation software, which has to contain the data that needs to be installed. In such cases, *TResourceStream* can be useful. A typical `.rc` resource file has a layout like the following:

```
#include      "resource.h"
// Icons
IDI_ICON1     ICON   "icon1.ico"
IDI_ICON2     ICON   "icon2.ica"
// Bitmaps
IDB_CECAE     BITMAP "cecae.bmp"
// raw data
101 RCDATA
MOVEABLE PURE LOADONCALL DISCARDABLE
BEGIN
  '65 00 02 00 FE FF 74 9C 04 00 10 00 65 9C 00 00'
  'FF FF FE FF 75 9C 04 00 10 00 65 9C 00 00 FF FF'
END
```

We don't always have to use resource streams. For instance, to load a bitmap into a *TBitmap*, we can make use of the *TBitmap.LoadFromResourceID* method, which is easier to use than *TResourceStream*. This class is more suitable for reading raw data, which is referred to as RC_DATA in resource file terminology.
Windows resource files are not limited to Windows only. The resource compiler *WindRes*, which can compile `.rc` files into `.res` files, is also available for 32-bit Linux systems. Besides that there is an additional tool called *fpcresm*, which comes with Free Pascal and can transform `.res` files into `.o` files, which can then be linked into your executable file. But this type of resources does not help to make your application portable.
Under MacOS X such files are completely unknown, so in case of doubt it is best to avoid them.

Persistent objects

Many programs need Pascal classes for saving and changing stored data. If this information is not saved during the program's execution, it will not be available the next time the program is started. The normal way to make sure data in an object will be retained (this is called data persistence), is to pass it to the methods *SaveToStream* and *LoadFromStream*, or to feed it to a *TComponent* descendant. *TStream.ReadComponent* and *TStream.WriteComponent* are then able to write all published properties of these components into a data stream and to read them back again.

The following example shows such a persistent class which handles saving and restoring using the *SaveToStream* and *LoadFromStream* methods. The class has fields *numberData* and *stringData* which can be written to and read from the data stream.

```
type
TMyPersistent = class
  public
    numberData: DWord;
    StringData: String;
    procedure SaveToStream(AStream: TStream); Virtual;
    procedure LoadFromStream(AStream: TStream); Virtual;
end;

//...

TMyPersistent.SaveToStream(AStream: TStream);
begin
  AStream.WriteDWord(NumberData);
  AStream.WriteString(StringData);
end;

TMyPersistent.LoadFromStream(AStream: TStream);
begin
  numberData := AStream.ReadDWord();
  StringData := AStream.ReadString();
end;
```

The following class definition shows a class derived from *TComponent* which does the same thing, but utilising built-in functionality. It is able to persist its properties (as can all classes derived from *TComponent*). *TStream.LoadComponent* and *TStream.WriteComponent* are used to load this class from a stream and to write the class to a stream:

```
type
TMyComponent = class(TComponent)
  private
    FNumberData: DWord;
    FStringData: String;
  published
    property numberData: DWord read FnumberData write FnumberData;
    property StringData: String read FStringData write FStringData;
end;
```

8.3 Searching in Directories

The standard Lazarus file dialogs are ideal for letting a user choose one or more files to work on. But when a user needs to select from a large number of files, or a directory tree needs to be searched for subdirectories and files, such a dialog is too simple. We need firstly to select a working directory (for instance with *TSelectDirectoryDialog*). Thereafter an automatic search for the desired files and directories should be started from that selected directory, and any matching entries discovered should be stored in a temporary location, such as in a stringlist or a custom record. Pascal offers the functions and procedures *FindFirst/FindNext/FindClose* to handle such file search operations. A search action starts with a call to *FindFirst* and (if more than one file or directory needs to be found) continues with repeated calls to *FindNext*. Each search operation must be ended with *FindClose*. These functions are used in exactly the same way as in Delphi. It is important to give the right constant for the path separator. Recursive directory searches can be nested in all operating systems (except in OS/2). As there is no Lazarus for OS/2 anyway, this is not a problem that need concern us. The routines mentioned can be found in the file `fileutilh.inc` and are defined as follows:

```
function FindFirst(const Path: String; Attr: LongInt;
                   out Rslt: TSearchRec): Longint;
function FindNext(var Rslt: TSearchRec): Longint;
procedure FindClose(var F: TSearchRec);
```

The record *TSearchRec* is defined in the same file, but the declaration depends on the operating system:

```
type
  TSearchRec = record
    Time: Longint;
    Size: Int64;
    Attr: Longint;
    Name: TFileName;
    ExcludeAttr: Longint;
{$ifdef unix}
    FindHandle: Pointer; Mode: TMode;
    PathOnly: AnsiString {$ifndef VER2_2} Deprecated {$endif};
{$else unix}
    FindHandle: THandle;
{$endif unix}
{$if defined(Win32) or defined(WinCE) or defined(Win64)}
    FindData: TWin32FindData;
{$endif}
{$ifdef netware_clib}
    FindData: TNetwareFindData;
{$endif)
{$ifdef netware_libc}
    FindData: TNetwareLibcFindData;
{$endif}
{$ifdef MacOS}
    FindData: TMacOSFindData;
{$endif}
  end;
```

In *FindFirst* we need to specify the file attributes of the items we want to find in *Attr*. Constants for this are also defined in the same file. These have to be used in the search operations:

```
const
{ File attributes }
   faReadOnly  = $00000001;
   faHidden    = $00000002;
   faSysFile   = $00000004;
   faVolumeId  = $00000008;
   faDirectory = $00000010;
   faArchive   = $00000020;
   faSymLink   = $00000040;
   faAnyFile   = $0000003f;
```

Depending on what we want to do with the search results, we will have to specify whether we want them just in a *TStringList*, a memo window, or a specially constructed record with fields for size, attributes, date of last access etc.
The following example program demonstrates how to search a directory. It displays all the directory entries in a memo:

```
procedure TForm1.Button1Click(Sender: TObject);
  var  sr: TSearchRec;
        s: String;
begin
  if SelectDirectoryDialog1.Execute then          // set source directory
  begin
    s := UTF8ToSys(SelectDirectoryDialog1.FileName); // normalise file name
    Memo1.Lines.Add('Contents of ' +
                        SelectDirectoryDialog1.FileName + ':');
    if FindFirst(s + '*,*', faAnyFile, sr) = 0 then   // what is there?
    begin
      Memo1.Lines.Add(sr.Name);         // ... add more
      while FindNext(sr) = 0 do Memo1.Lines.Add(sr.Name);
    end;
    FindClose(sr);
  end;
end;
```

We kept this example very simple. The program does not distinguish between files and directories, and it does not drill down into subdirectories. To search a complete directory structure, we would have to create an outer loop for finding the directories and an inner loop to find the files contained in them. In that case we would use two blocks of *FindFirst*/*FindNext*, each of which would have to be closed with its own call to *FileClose*.

The next example shows a recursive directory search which is a bit more complicated:

```
unit UnitMain;
{$apptype gui}
{$mode objfpc}{$H+}

interface

uses Classes, SysUtils, FileUtil, LResources, Forms, Controls,
     Graphics, Dialogs,StdCtrls;
type { TForm1 }
  TForm1 = class(TForm)
    Button1: TButton;                   // start button
    Memo1 : TMemo;                      // display results in a memo
    SelectDirectoryDialog1 : TSelectDirectoryDialog; // to obtain starting folder
    procedure Button1Click(Sender: TObject);// event that initiates the search
  private
    DirectoryList: TStringList;         // holds the search results
    DosError: Integer;                  // helper variable without which the result
                                        // is harder to read
    procedure Scan(const dir, mask: String); // procedure to do the work of searching
  end;

var  Form1: Tform1;

implementation
{$R *.lfm}

procedure TForm1.Scan(const dir, mask: String);
(* The actual search routine, with only a single string list for folders and files. This can be changed in the procedure's
   first block by adding a different folder list variable (to be defined).                                    *)

  var  sr: TSearchRec; // a record needed both by FindFirst and FindNext
       s : String;     // helper variable
begin
// To construct the stringlist properly we must ensure that the directory always has a DirectorySeparator at the end
  s := Dir;                                                          //  (whichever: / or \)
  if s[Length(s)] <> DirectorySeparator then
    s := s + DirectorySeparator;               // only if no Windows drive letter
  if sr.Name <> '' then                        // if the first sr.Name is not empty
    if sr.Name[Length(sr.Name)] = DirectorySeparator then
      s := s + sr.Name                         // proper string construction
    else
      s := s + DirectorySeparator + sr.Name;
  Directorylist.Add(s);                        // copy from the helper variable into the list

// After the initial directory is entered in the string list, then all the files in the directory follow. The VolumeID
//  (drive letters of DOS / Windows and its subdirectories) are ignored here Only file entries are read:

  DosError := FindFirst(Dir + DirectorySeparator + mask,
              faAnyfile mod faDirectory mod faVolumeID, sr);
                   // mod with the two specified attributes masked
```

```
  while DOSError = 0 do
  begin
    if Dir[Length(Dir)] = DirectorySeparator then
      Directorylist.Add(Dir + sr.Name)
    else
      Directorylist.Add(Dir + DirectorySeparator + sr.Name);
    DosError := FindNext(sr); // iterate through the entire list
  end; { while }

  try
    SysUtils.FindClose(sr);       // at the end of the search close everything
  Except                          // each FindFirst requires a FindClose
  end; { try }

// If the files are processed in a directory, in the next Subdirectory level the directories "." (current directory) and
// ".." (parent directory) must be ignored.

  DosError := FindFirst(Dir+DirectorySeparator+'*.*',faDirectory,sr);

  while DosError = 0 do
  begin
    if (sr.Attr and faDirectory = faDirectory) then    // directory found!
    begin
      if (sr.Name <> '.') and (sr.Name <> '..') then   // ignore pseudo-entries
      begin
        if Dir[Length(Dir)] = DirectorySeparator then
          // The current routine is called recursively. First, for direct drive specification, for example C:\)
          Scan(Dir + sr.Name, Mask) // recursive search in the directory
        else
          // search all subdirectory paths
          Scan(Dir + DirectorySeparator + sr.Name, Mask); // recursive search
      end; { if }
    end; { if }
    DosError := FindNext(sr);
  end; { while }

  try
    SysUtils.FindClose(sr);
  Except
  end; { try }
end;
```

```
procedure TForm1.Button1Click(Sender: TObject);
// Initiate the processing in the OnClick event of the button
  Var  i: Integer;
begin
  if SelectDirectoryDialog1.Execute then
  begin
// The string list is created outside of the working procedure and needs to be released again at the end. The working procedure
// always refers to the global DirectoryList in the window class created and referenced here:

    DirectoryList := TStringList.Create;            // create list

// The actual work procedure. TSelectDirectoryDialog provides a path with an appended path separator so the
// search string is attached directly here. In the example we search for *.*, although any kind of mask can be specified.
//  Searching only for files and not for the names of subdirectories:

    Scan(UTF8ToSys(SelectDirectoryDialog1.FileName), '*.*');// working...

// The file names are collected by the end of this routine. The disadvantage is that during the processing nothing is displayed,
// the search is dramatically faster than if a window is constantly refreshed. A message "Searching ..." would reduce the
// user's anxiety

    for i := 1 to DirectoryList.Count do
      Memo1.Lines.Add(SysToUTF8(DirectoryList[i-1]));

// ... any other processing is also possible here. It is important that the file names displayed in the memo are
// normalized so that special characters are displayed properly.

    DirectoryList.Free;      // the list is released at the end
    end;
end;

initialization
{$I UnitMain.lrs}
end.
```

This program is not too complex and if you leave out the comments it isn't even very long, but it forms a good basis for a search function in a program, and it can easily be extended. The search results could be displayed in a grid or in a treeview as well. The memo used here for display is just a simple example. A disadvantage of such an encapsulated procedure as *Scan()* is that there is no progress indication while it is working on a large directory structure. We could provide some feedback to the user at the start of the scanning procedure:

```
StatusBar1.SimpleText := 'Searching ' + s;
Update;.        // force window to update
```

This would help the user to see that the program is still alive. It is not a good idea to write strings into the memo field while the search is still in progress, as this slows the program down too much. It is better to notify the user about the search activity in the status bar and clean it up again with:

```
StatusBar1.SimpleText := '';
```

from the routine that started the search action.
Free Pascal (and hence Lazarus too) contains many more functions for handling files. We list some of the most useful ones here. The functions they perform should be clear from their names, and they are listed because it is useful to know that they exist.
They are all found in the *SysUtils* unit:

```
function ChangeFileExt(const FileName: String; const Extension:
                                                       String): String;
function CreateDir(const NewDir: String): Boolean;
function DeleteFile(const FileName: String): Boolean;
function DirectoryExists(const Directory: String): Boolean;
function ExeSearch(const Name, DirList: String) : String;
function ExtractFileDir(const FileName: String): String;
function ExtractFileDrive(const FileName: String): String;
function ExtractFileExt(const FileName: String): String;
function ExtractFileName(const FileName: String): String;
function FileExists(const FileName: String): Boolean;
function FileSearch(const Name, DirList: String;
                          ImplicitCurrentDir: Boolean = True): String;
function FileIsReadOnly(const FileName: String): Boolean;
function RenameFile(const OldName, NewName: String): Boolean;
```

The following two routines can be used to retrieve or set the attributes of a file. The attributes are an ORed combination from a collection of file attribute constants. Possible constants are *faReadOnly* (file can only be read), *faHidden* (file is hidden; in Unix the name of such a file starts with a dot), *faSysFile* (the file is a system file; in Unix it can be a text, block or FIFO file), *faVolumeId* (volume label, this is a Windows-specific constant), *faDirectory* (the file is a directory) *faArchive* (the file is an archive, this is Windows-specific).

```
function FileGetAttr(const FileName: String): Longint;
function FileSetAttr(const Filename: String; Attr: Longint): Longint;
```

The following routines read and write a file's date:

```
function FileGetDate(Handle: THandle): Longint; // you must assign a file handle
function FileSetDate(Handle: THandle; Age: Longint): Longint;
function FileSetDate(const FileName: String; Age: Longint): Longint;
                                                     // no file handle here
```

And this function reads a file's last access date:

```
function FileAge(const FileName: String): Longint;
```

The file date is retrieved in a special format. However there are routines to convert that into the standard Pascal *TDateTime* format:

```
function FileDateToDateTime(Filedate: Longint): TDateTime;
function DateTimeToFileDate(DateTime: TDateTime): Longint;
```

8.4 Communication with Devices

ISA and PCI boards and the parallel port communicate with the computer through a parallel protocol. The serial port and USB devices use a serial protocol. Parallel protocols send data in blocks, which may be 8, 16, 32 or even 64 bits wide, requiring an equal number of parallel wires in the hardware. Serial protocols on the other hand use only one or two data lines (two in a full duplex connection, where both sides can send data simultaneously). One data line is used for each direction, over which only one state (1 bit) is transmitted at a time. Libraries and software that use a serial interface for sending data in chunks or blocks make it easier to process the data later.

There are three different ways to send and receive data to/from parallel hardware: through a hardware *port*, through *interrupts* and through **DMA** (Direct Memory Access). The first method, using a hardware interface *port*, involves sending the address of an I/O port to the software through the BIOS and the operating system. When the software sends data to this address, it become available to the device. And when the software reads data from the device, it is also immediately available, there is no time delay in processing the input. While the application is waiting for the hardware to provide data, the software runs in a loop, polling the hardware from time to time to check whether data is available. This is the simplest of the three communication models.
If *interrupts* are used, the hardware sends a signal to the software when data is available. This makes waiting in a polling loop unnecessary, and makes it possible to respond to new data more quickly.
The fastest method to use is *DMA*. When this is used, the hardware is able to access the computer memory directly and to fetch or deposit the data itself. This takes no processor time. This method is used most often for devices like hard disks, CDROM drives and other mass storage devices, which have to deal with large amounts of data. Modern operating systems require a device driver for interrupt service routines and for the implementation of *DMA*. These are usually quite complex.
The simplest approach is to use a parallel port and this is what we will discuss in this chapter. The serial protocols require much more complicated hardware than the parallel ones, so most serial interfaces work with special logic circuits or built-in microcontrollers. Lazarus offers the platform- independent serial communications library *Synaser*.

Technology	Data transfer speed	Hardware complexity
Serial port	Very slow (< 105 Bit/s)	Average
Parallel port	Slow (~ 106 Bit/s)	Easy
ISA card	Average (~ 107 Bit/s)	Average
USB	Average (~ 107 Bit/s)	Complicated
PCI card	Very fast (> 109 Bit/s)	Very complex

Table 8.9: Hardware access protocol overview

8.4.1 The parallel port

Most desktop computers, even modern ones, still have a standard parallel port.
If there is no parallel interface on the motherboard, it can still be installed by adding a PCI card or USB adapter with a parallel port. Many printers (unless they use a network or USB interface) are connected to the PC through the parallel port. This goes for all older printers, but also for modern printers in the higher price bracket. The parallel port can also be used for purposes other than printing. We will concentrate on direct communication by sending/receiving data through a hardware interface on the PC. (Communication with other parallel devices like ISA and PCI cards is also possible by exchanging the hardware port, which is often used for development of custom hardware.) The standard parallel port has eight data pins for I/O, five status pins to read the state of the device, and four control pins to send commands. This makes interfacing a lot easier compared to other protocols that do not provide special status pins. If there are no extra pins available some data pins have to be used for communicating status and control information. The parallel port is usually addressed through the ports 3BCh to 3BFh, 378h to 37Fh, and 278h to 27Fh. The operating system will provide the addresses of the parallel ports. Under Windows the address can be found in the properties of the LPT port in the *Device Manager* in *Control Panel*. The hardware address will be listed there.

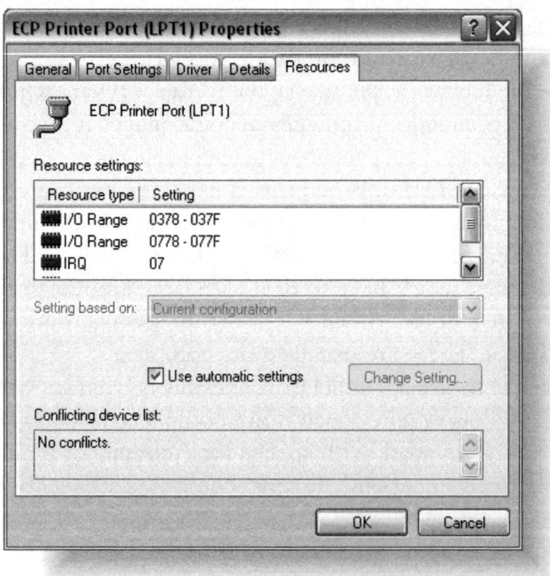

Figure 8.3: Information about the parallel port in control panel in Windows XP

8.4.1 The parallel port

The outputs from the parallel port are usually normal TTL levels, with +5 V for a 1 and 0 V for a 0. The current available from the pins depends on the port and is usually somewhere between 4 mA and 20 mA per pin (for source and sink). For connecting very simple hardware like a few LEDs or for direct reading of the pins it may be possible to get the current directly from the port pins. For connecting more complex hardware, it is advisable to add a buffer with an external power source, to minimize the load on the parallel port.
For communication through the parallel interface in x86 computers two special assembler opcodes are needed: IN and OUT. However, only the Windows 9x line (95, 98 and ME) allows direct access to these calls. The Windows NT series only allows its use in device drivers. There is a solution in the form of the library `inpout32.dll` (a version for 64-bit Windows also exists). It can be downloaded from `http://iogix4u.net/` and it is free and open source software. When it finds a Windows NT on the system, it will unpack the kernel device driver `HWlnterface.sys` and install it. If a Windows 9x is found, the assembler opcodes will be used to address the hardware directly.

Pin No (DB25)	Signal name	Direction	Register bit	Hardware inverted?
1	nStrobe	Out	Control-0	Yes
2	Data0	In/Out	Data-0	No
3	Data1	In/Out	Data-1	No
4	Data2	In/Out	Data-2	No
5	Data3	In/Out	Data-3	No
6	Data4	In/Out	Data-4	No
7	Data5	In/Out	Data-5	No
8	Data6	In/Out	Data-6	No
9	Data7	In/Out	Data-7	No
10	nAck	In	Status-6	No
11	Busy	In	Status-7	Yes
12	Paper-Out	In	Status-5	No
13	Select	In	Status-4	No
14	Linefeed	Out	Control-1	Yes
15	nError	In	Status-3	No
16	nInitialize	Out	Control-2	No
17	nSelect-Printer	Out	Control-3	Yes
18-25	Ground			

Table 8.10: The pinout of the 25-way parallel connector

Signal names starting with an n indicate active low. Pins are counted as seen from the computer side. Some pins are inverted in the parallel port hardware. This means that applying a high level (+5 V) will result in a 0 being read by the software.

The library is very simple and intuitive to use. It has only the functions *Inp32* and *Out32*. *Inp32* reads a byte from the parallel device at the given port, and *Out32* sends a byte. We will show how to use this library in an example.
In Linux and other Unix-like systems the solution for parallel communication looks different, so in platform-independent applications for parallel communication, we will always have to use *{$ifdef}* directives.

8.4.1 The parallel port

On Unix we have to start by establishing permissions to address the port (address range) by calling *ioperm*. This routine is part of *LibC*. To use it, the `clib unit` has to be included in the uses clause of your program. Once the access permissions are established, the data can be read and written with the unit ports. Under Windows this will make use of the assembler instructions IN and OUT.

The following example program for parallel communication has a text field for the information about the value to send and the port address of the device. It also has buttons to initiate the sending and receiving of the data. This program is useful to illustrate the way to work with parallel devices, but it can also be used to test new hardware or simple devices.

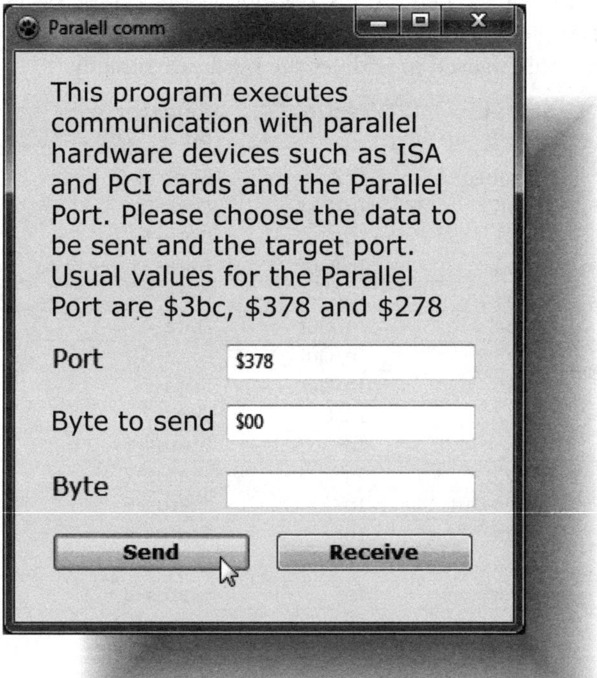

Figure 8.4: The application for parallel communication in action

```
unit parallel_form;
{$mode objfpc}{$H+}
interface

uses  Classes, SysUtils, FileUtil, LResources, Forms,
      Controls, Graphics, Dialogs, StdCtrls, ExtCtrls
  {$IFDEF WIN32}
    , Windows
  {$ENDIF}
  {$IFDEF Unix}
    , clib, ports    // for the library and port operations
  {$ENDIF}
  ;
type    { TformParallel }
  (* Address represents the address of  the port you want to access Out32 sends data to the port
    specified by Address Inp32 returns a byte from the port specified by Address *)

   TInp32 = function(Address: SmallInt): SmallInt; StdCall;
   TOut32 = procedure(Address: SmallInt; Data: SmallInt); StdCall;
   TformParallel = class(TForm)
     buttonSend: TButton;
     buttonReceive: TButton;
     editPort: TEdit;
     editSend: TEdit;
     editReceived: TEdit;
     Label1: TLabel;
     Label2: TLabel;
     Label3: TLabel;
     Label4: TLabel;
     procedure buttonReceiveClick(Sender: TObject);
     procedure buttonSendClick(Sender: TObject);
     procedure FormCreate(Sender: TObject);
     procedure FormDestroy(Sender: TObject);
   private
     Inpout32: THandle;
     Inp32: TInp32;
     Out32: TOut32;
   end;

var formParallel: TformParallel;

{$Ifdef Unix}
function ioperm(from: Cardinal; num: Cardinal; turn_on: Integer):
 Integer; CDecl; external clib;
{$endif}

implementation

{ TformParallel }
```

```
procedure TformParallel.FormCreate(Sender: TObject);
// Under Windows the helper library is loaded dynamically
begin
  {$ifdef Win32}
  {$ifdef CPUX86}
  Inpout32 := LoadLibrary('inpout32.dll');    // this only for 32-bit Windows
  {$else}
  Inpout32 := LoadLibrary('inpoutx64.dll'); // In 64-bits Windows use:
  {$endif}                                    // inpoutx64.dll
  if Inpout32 <> 0 then begin
    Inp32 := TInp32(GetProcAddress(Inpout32, 'Inp32'));
    if @Inp32 = NIL then Caption := 'Error';
    Out32 := TOut32(GetProcAddress(Inpout32, 'Out32'));
    if @Out32 = NIL then Caption := 'Error';
  end else
    Caption := 'Error';
  {$endif}
end;

procedure TformParallel.buttonSendClick(Sender: TObject);
  var  PortAddress: Integer; Data: Byte;
begin
  PortAddress := StrToInt(editPort.Text);
  Data := StrToInt(editSend.Text);
  {$ifdef Win32}
  Out32(PortAddress, Data);
  {$endif}
  {$ifdef Unix}
  ioperm(PortAddress, 8, 1);
  port[PortAddress] := Data;
  {$endif}
end;

procedure TformParallel.buttonReceiveClick(Sender: TObject);
  var  PortAddress: Integer;
begin
  PortAddress := StrToInt(editPort.Text);
  {$ifdef Win32}
  editReceived.Text := IntToHex(Inp32(PortAddress), 2);
  {$endif}
  {$ifdef Unix}
  editReceived.Text := IntToHex(Port[PortAddress], 2);
  {$endif}
end;

procedure TformParallel.FormDestroy(Sender: TObject);
begin
  {$ifdef Win32}
  FreeLibrary(Inpout32);
  {$endif}
end;

initialization
  {$I parallel_form.lrs}
end.
```

This program is in no way perfect. If a 64-bit application is needed, another driver should be used and tested.

8.4.2 Serial communication

Communication through the serial port is used frequently, for instance in the Internet protocol TCP/IP and other network protocols, on normal COM ports and even on USB devices. This section will deal with the COM port and with USB devices which have been configured to behave like COM ports.
The COM port or serial port is best known from the RS-232 connector, but the format of the connector and its pinout can take many different forms, depending on the hardware.

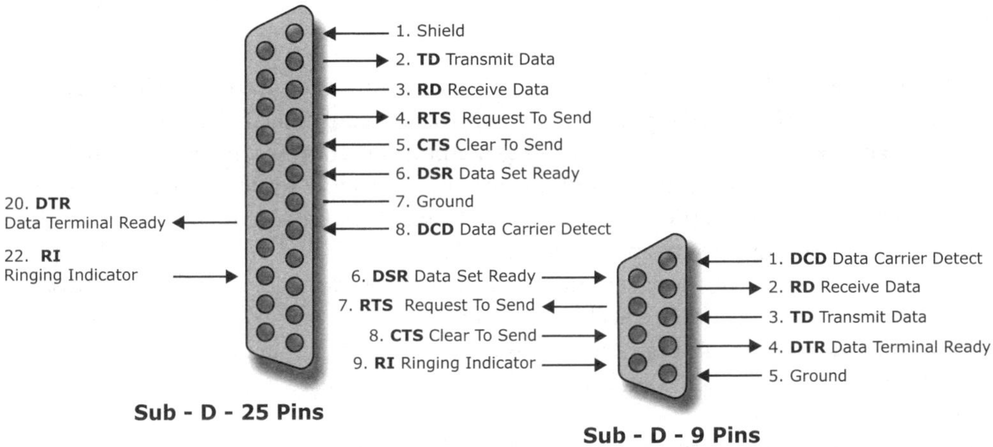

Figure 8.5: The pinout of the serial connector

A computer may have many COM ports, which are numbered COM1, COM2, COM3 etc. Under Linux they are available as `/dev/ttyS0, /dev/ttyS1, /dev/ttyS2` etc., under FreeBSD the ports are called `/dev/ttyu0` etc. To be able to communicate with a serial device, you have to know which port it is connected to and what the parameters of its serial protocol are. The properties are speed (in bits per second), number of data bits, parity bit, stop bit and *handshake* protocol, if any. If we know these key properties, we can connect to any serial device.
USB devices can also be treated as if they were normal COM ports, but this requires an installed driver to implement this behaviour. The manufacturer of the USB chip to use should provide information about whether he is offering virtual COM port drivers. A chip which can be recommended for this is the FT245RL from FTDI, which offers licence-free, virtual COM port drivers for several operating systems like Windows, Linux, MacOS X and Windows CE (see `http://www.ftdichip.com/FTProducts.htm`).
A good platform-independent library for serial communication is *Synaser* from the Synapse project. It does not come standard with Free Pascal, but it can be easily acquired from `http://synapse.ararat.cz/doku.php/download`

The library is offered under a modified BSD licence, which allows its use in commercial and proprietary projects. There is comprehensive documentation available about the classes, methods, data types and constants of the `Synaser unit`, which you can find at `http://synapse.ararat.cz/doc/help/synaser.html`
The following example is based on *Synaser* release 16 and shows everything we need to work with this unit.
The serial connection test program shows how to work with the *Synaser* unit.
An instance of the *TBlockSerial* class is created in the window's *OnCreate* event.
This is the main serial communication class in *Synaser*. But creating the class in not enough to connect to the device which requires calling a dedicated function. It is also important to release the instance again with *Free* (in the *OnDestroy* method or at another strategic location in the program) otherwise the connection will stay open after the program has ended.

If the user presses the Connect button in the window, the method *Connect* will be used to create a connection to a serial port. An edit control is used to specify which port to use (in the example it is COM1). Then the *Config* method is used to set the data rate, the number of data bits, the parity, the stop bit and the handshake protocol of the serial port. Then everything has been prepared for using *RecvByte*, *SendByte* and the related methods to send and receive data to/from the serial interface. The *Recv** methods have a *Timeout* parameter. They will wait for data until the number of milliseconds specified in *Timeout* has passed. If data is received, it will be returned.
The Connect button will not only activate the communication, but also a timer which will repeatedly test whether data is available at the serial interface. If it is, it will be written into the *memo* window.
Here is the declaration of the methods in class *TBlockSerial:*

```
procedure Connect(comport: String);
procedure Config(baud, bits: integer;
                 parity: char; stop: Integer;
                 softflow, hardflow: Boolean);
function sSendBuffer(buffer: Pointer; length: Integer): Integer;
procedure SendByte(data: Byte);
procedure SendString(data: String);
procedure SendInteger(Data: Integer);
procedure SendStream(const Stream: TStream);
function RecvBufferEx(buffer: Pointer; length: Integer;
                      timeout: Integer): Integer;
function RecvByte(timeout: Integer): byte;
function RecvString(timeout: Integer): String;
function RecvInteger(Timeout: Integer): Integer;
procedure RecvStream(const Stream: IStream; Timeout: Integer);
```

This class not only offers these important methods, but some important properties as well. The device name is saved in *Device*. Synaser also fills in the properties *LastError* and *LastErrorDesc* after each operation. The result of the last operation is saved in *LastError*: *Null* for success or an error code in case of a failure. A human-readable description of the error will be written to *LastErrorDesc*. If an error occurs, *Synaser* will check the property *RaiseExcept*. If this is *True* an exception with the error information will be raised. If it is *False* (default), it will just fill *LastError* and *LastErrorDesc* and no exception will be raised. So then, we have to check *LastError* to find out whether the operation was successful.

```
property Device: String Read FDevice;
property LastError: Integer Read FLastError;
property LastErrorDesc: String Read FLastErrorDesc;
property RaiseExcept: Boolean Read FRaiseExcept
                              Write FRaiseExcept Default False;
```

The test program was tested with a serial mouse and it was able to accept data from it. Serial port COM1 was configured for 1200 bits per second, 7 data bits, no parity, 1 stop bit and no *handshake*.
The same program can also communicate with USB devices, if a serial-USB converter is connected or if a virtual COM port driver like the one from FTDI is used for the USB port.

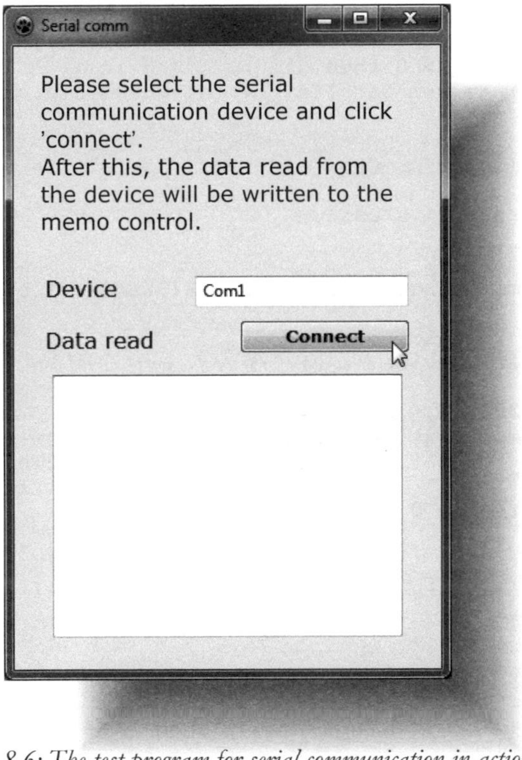

Figure 8.6: The test program for serial communication in action

```
unit comm_form;
{$mode objfpc}{$H+}
interface
uses Classes, SysUtils, FileUtil, LResources, Forms, Controls,
     Graphics, Dialogs, StdCtrls, ExtCtrls, ComCtrls, Synaser;
type { TformComm }
  TformComm = class(TForm)
    buttonConnect: TButton;
    editDevice: TEdit;
    Label1: TLabel;
    Label2: TLabel;
    Label3: TLabel;
    memoData: TMemo;
    statusBar: TStatusBar;
    timerRead: TTimer;
    procedure buttonConnectClick(Sender: TObject);
    procedure FormCreate(Sender: TObject);
    procedure FormDestroy(Sender: TObject);
    procedure timerReadTimer(Sender: TObject);
  private
    connected: Boolean;
    ser: TBlockSerial;
  end;

var formComm: TformComm;
implementation  { TformComm }
procedure TformComm.timerReadTimer(Sender: TObject);
  var Data: Byte;
begin
  if not connected then Exit;
  Data := ser.RecvByte(timerRead.Interval div 2);
  if ser.LastError <> 0 then Exit;
  memoData.Text := memoData.Text + IntToHex(Data, 2) + ' ';
end;

procedure TformComm.FormCreate(Sender: TObject);
begin
  ser := TBlockSerial.Create;
end;

procedure TformComm.buttonConnectClick(Sender: TObject);
begin
  if connected then Exit;
  ser.Connect(editDevice.Text); // specification of COM port
  Sleep(1000);
  ser.Config(1200, 7, 'N', SB1, False, False);
  StatusBar.SimpleText := 'Device: ' + ser.Device + ' Status: ' +
                  ser.LastErrorDesc + ' ' + IntToStr(ser.LastError);
  Sleep(1000);
  if ser.LastError = 0 then connected := True;
end;

procedure TformComm.FormDestroy(Sender: TObject);
begin
  ser.free;
end;

initialization
  {$I comm_form.lrs}
end.
```

Under Windows there is another very comprehensive solution for communication with the serial interface in *TSerial*. The current version 4.4 was published in issue 3-4/2009 of the magazine *Toolbox*. It is not free open source, but readers of the magazine are allowed to use it in any project. *TSerial* is a set of components for Delphi, but it can also be installed in the Windows version of Lazarus. Programs written with it cannot be transferred to other platforms however.

8.4.3 The printer

Lazarus offers a well-designed platform-independent interface for printer access.
The printing functionality is implemented in two packages:
Printers4lazide adds an entry *Print* to the *File* menu in the IDE to print the current file. Lazarus Version 0.9.26 and beyond also offer printing of just the current selection only.
Printer4lazarus is the base package for printer support in the LCL.
It contains the system-specific parts of the printing system.
This package has to be added to your printing-enabled project. To do that, go to the menu *Project* → *Project Inspector*, select the [+] button (Add) to add a new entry in the project dialog, then select *Printers4Lazarus* and finally click *OK*. The reason why the printing system is in a separate package is that printing is normally not part of the standard operating system in Unix and – by contrast with Windows – graphical user interfaces without printer support are allowed and even quite common.

The basis for printing is the *TPrinter* class in the `unit Printers`, which is part of the LCL and provides an interface to the user's currently selected printer. The unit contains a variable *Printer*, which is instantiated by the `OSPrinters unit` in the package *Printer4Lazarus*. *TPrinter* has many properties and methods. Its main property is an instance of *TCanvas*, which represents the page to print on.
This object's methods allow us to start printing text or graphics, set page margins and eject sheets of paper. Before printing, you should always present the user with a *TPrinterDialog*, which allows you to select a printer, set the margins and paper size and change other configurable items. (To select a printer, an instance of *TPrinterDialog* is called from the *PrinterDlgs* unit.) When the dialog is closed, the *Printer's* settings are automatically updated, applying the settings to the selected printer.

When printing the *Canvas* plays a central role. It is the main property of the *Printer* object. *Printer.Canvas* is responsible for drawing pictures and text on the page. *TCanvas* is discussed in Chapter 9 when we deal with graphic controls, but it is the same as the *TCanvas* used in printing; this compatibility makes it easy to exchange drawing code between drawing to the screen and drawing to the printer. The origin of the *Canvas* is position (0, 0) in the top left corner of the paper. It is important to keep in mind that printers don't usually print the full page, i.e. there is an unprintable border, which is determined by a *TRect* property: *Printer.PaperSize.PaperRect.WorkRect*.

Method	Effect
procedure Abort;	Terminates the current print job. If the printing has already started, it will be interrupted.
procedure BeginDoc;	This should be the first method to be called when sending data to the printer, used after any printing dialogs have been shown to the user. After this method is called then images and text can be drawn using the *Canvas* property. The printer won't actually start printing until *EndDoc* is called.
procedure EndDoc;	By this call you indicate that the print data has been fully prepared and tell *TPrinter* to send it to the printer to do the actual printing.
procedure NewPage;	Starts a new printing page with a clean *Canvas*. Increments the property *PageNumber* by 1.
procedure TPrinter.Set-Printer(aName: String);	Changes the current printer. Check the property *Printers* to see a list of all available printers.

Table 8.11: The most important methods of TPrinter

Property	Effect
property PaperSize. PaperRect.WorkRect: TRect; [read-only]	The print-accessible surface of the currently selected paper. It changes according to the paper selected in *Papername*, which is usually either A4 or letter.
property Orientation: TPrinterOrientation; [read-write]	Orientation of the document. The most common values are *poPortrait*, for portrait, and *poLandscape*, for landscape orientation. Some printers also allow the value *poReverseLandscape* and *poReversePortrait* for a reversed version of the first two options.
property PrinterState: TPrinterState; [read-only]	The state of the printer, which may be: *psNoDefine* – for undefined; *psReady* – Ready to print; *psPrinting* – Currently printing; *psStopped* – the current print was stopped.
property Copies: Integer; [read-write]	Number of Copies of the current document.
property Printers: Tstrings;[read-only]	List of available printers.
property Fonts: Tstrings; [read-only]	List of available fonts.
property Canvas: Tcanvas;	The main property of the printer. Defines the surface where the images and text to be printed should be drawn.
property PageHeight: Integer;[read-only]	The height of the canvas in pixels.
property PageWidth: Integer;[read-only]	The width of the canvas in pixels.
property PageNumber: Integer;[read-only]	The number of the page being printed currently.
property Aborted: Boolean; [read-only]	*True* if printing of the document has been prematurely terminated by operator command.
property Printing: Boolean;[read-only]	Indicates if the document is currently in process of being printed.
property Title: String; [read-write]	Name of the current printer.
property PrinterType: TPrinterType; [read-only]	Has value *ptLocal* for a local printer or *ptNetwork* for network printers.
property CanPrint: Boolean;[read-only]	*True* if the current printer is enabled, *False* if disabled.
property XDPI: Integer; [read-only]	Horizontal resolution of the current printer in dots per inch.
property YDPI: Integer; [read-only]	Vertical resolution of the current printer in dots per inch.

Table 8.12: The most important properties of TPrinter

8.4.3 The printer

When we present the user with a *TPrintDialog* for selecting printing parameters, we must keep in mind that some of these capabilities are implemented automatically by the operating system, while others have to be read first from *TPrintDialog*, before we can meet the user's wishes. The most common non-automatic setting is the page range to be printed. We have to set *TPrintDialog.MinPage* and *TPrintDialog.MaxPage* before calling *TPrintDialog.Execute* to make it possible to show the minimum and maximum available page number the user can select. *MinPage* is usually 1, *MaxPage* is usually the number of pages in the current document. After executing the dialog, *TPrintDialog.PrintRange* will use *TPrintDialog.FromPage* and *TPrintDialog.ToPage* to read the page range the user has selected. Some capabilities are implemented automatically by the operating system, such as the number of copies to print (the operating system just takes the document to print and reproduces the number of desired copies), and the page sort order. In MacOS X the number of pages to print on each sheet can also be selected on the Layout tab. This all happens transparently for the user.

Constant	Effect
Collate: Boolean default False	Affects the printing of multiple copies. When False, first all copies of the first page will be printed, then all copies of the second page will be printed, etc. When True each successive page is printed once and then this process is repeated again for each document page. This property is handled automatically by the operating system.
Copies: Integer default 1	The number of copies to be printed. This property is handled automatically by the operating system.
FromPage: Integer default 0	A 1-based index to the starting page of the user's range selection.
MinPage: Integer default 0	Indicates to the dialog user what the minimum allowed age number is for this print. Zero indicates that there will be no restriction.
MaxPage: Integer default 0	Indicates to the dialog user what the maximum allowed page number is for this print. Zero indicates that there will be no restriction.
Options: TPrintDialog-Options default []	Contains a set of possible options for customizing the dialog's appearance and behaviour. Possible values are listed in Table 8.15.
PrintToFile: Boolean default False	Defines if the printing will be done to a file instead. This is a Windows-only property and is handled automatically by Windows.
PrintRange: TPrintRange default prAllPages	The possible values are explained in Table 8.16.
ToPage: Integer default 0	End page of the user's range selection.

Table 8.13: The most important properties of TPrinter

Method	Description
poPrintToFile	Activates by default the option "Print to file" present only in Windows dialogs. This option generates a printing .prn file, which can be used to print the file later, instead of printing now. Don't confuse with the option to print to a PDF, which is available in Mac OS X and Linux dialogs.
poPageNums	Allows the user to specify the number of pages to be printed in the dialog.
poSelection	Allows the user to specify a selection of pages to be printed in the dialog.
poWarning	A Windows option to show a warning message if the user tries to print to an uninstalled printer.
poHelp	Shows a button offering the standard operating system help for printing.
poDisable-PrintToFile	Prevents the user selecting the option "Print to file" which is only available in Windows dialogs. See *poPrintToFile* above for more details.

Table 8.14: The most important properties of TPrintDialog

Value	Description
prAllPages	All pages should be printed.
prSelection	Only some pages should be printed. The page range selected is specified in the properties *FromPage* and *ToPage*.
prPageNums	Which pages should be printed.
prCurrentPage	Only the current page should be printed.

Table 8.15: The possible values of PrintRange

The following example takes the text from a memo control and prints it in the top left corner of the page, taking the printer margins into account:

```
uses Printers, PrintersDlgs;

procedure TformPrint.buttonPrintClick(Sender: TObject);
  var PaperWorkRect: TRect;
      PrintDlg     : TPrintDialog;
begin
  Application.Initialize;
  PrintDlg := TPrintDialog.Create(NIL);
  try
    PrintDlg.MinPage := 1; PrintDlg.MaxPage := 1;
    if PrintDlg.Execute then
    begin
      PaperWorkRect := Printer.PaperSize.PaperRect.WorkRect;
      Printer.BeginDoc;
      Printer.Canvas.TextOut(PaperWorkRect.Left, PaperWorkRect.Top,
                             memoPrint.Lines.Text);
      Printer.EndDoc;
    end;
  finally
    PrintDlg.Free;
  end;
end;
```

Chapter 9
Graphics Programming

By Felipe Monteiro de Carvalho

When we speak about "graphics", we could be referring to two separate topics. On the one hand we may be talking about the manipulation of pictures or images – how to handle existing graphic data. On the other hand, we may be thinking about how to draw on a canvas and display a picture. These are related and overlapping topics.
Lazarus offers very powerful tools for both these activities. The *TImage* control can load graphics in several formats from files and resources; and various visual controls together with the TCanvas class provide a drawing surface, which can be manipulated and drawn upon.

9.1 The Canvas

The *canvas* is the basis for all drawing operations. The *canvas* is a property of visual components and it is derived from graphics classes such as *TBitmap*. Being a class property *Canvas* has no memory of its own. That is why an error occurs if you try to use a canvas before you have instantiated a visual control for it. The **LCL** takes care of the necessary preparations for drawing visual components on a form, and for displaying visual components onscreen.
Drawing on a canvas is always done using X,Y co-ordinates. The co-ordinate system's origin is always at the top left corner of the working area. The window's title bar is outside this area, so it is not affected. Drawing is done either using separate X and Y integer co-ordinates, or using co-ordinates which are grouped together as records, either as a *TPoint* (a record linking an X and a Y co-ordinate) or a *TRect*. Some graphic methods do not work with absolute co-ordinates, but with a *TSize* record instead. Such a record only defines the width and height, but not the target position.

```
TPoint = record
  X: LongInt;
  Y: LongInt;
end;
PPoint = ^TPoint;

TRect = record
  case Integer of
    0: (Left, Top, Right, Bottom: LongInt);
    1: (TopLeft, BottomRight    : TPoint);
  end;
PRect = ^TRect;

TSize = record
  cx : LongInt;
  cy : Longint;
end;
PSize = ^TSize;
```

The real declaration is more complex. It ensures that the type declarations are identical in the units *Classes*, *Types* and *Windows*. However, the result shown above is how developers see it (and should see it). A little example will show how simple the philosophy behind Lazarus drawing operations is. We create a new Lazarus application and extend the *FormMouseDown* event of the window with just two lines:

```
procedure TForm1.FormMouseDown(Sender: TObject; Button: TMouseButton;
                               Shift: TShiftState; X, Y: integer);
begin
  Canvas.MoveTo(x, y);
  Canvas.LineTo(100, 100);
end;
```

After a mouse press on the form X and Y will contain the actual X and Y co-ordinates. The drawing tool is moved to that location and then a line is drawn to the pre-programmed location (100, 100) in the window. This drawing operation is done on the window canvas. This will always happen, unless a different control's canvas is specified. This work is volatile. If the window is updated (for instance when its size changes) the lines drawn earlier will disappear.
The canvas is capable of many more operations than this simple one.
The most important methods and properties in the following definition are briefly explained in Table 9.1. We will see more in the examples that follow later.

As the work done on the form's canvas is not retained, the graphic data will have to be painted again after every update of the control. For the graphic to persist, therefore, we will have to keep a list ourselves of the completed drawing operations in a buffer.

Invisible buffer objects will have to be created before drawing can begin. We see next a simple example in the use of a *bitmap* as a buffer for drawing:

```
procedure TMyForm.FormPaint(Sender: TObject);
  var  MyBitmap: TBitmap;
begin
  MyBitmap := TBitmap.Create; (* Create the working buffer *)
  try
    MyBitmap.Height := 100;     (* set the image size *)
    MyBitmap.Width  := 100;
   (* After the bitmap's memory is allocated, we can start drawing: *)
    MyBitmap.Canvas.Rectangle(0, 0, 100, 100);
   (* Draw the bitmap on the window's canvas *)
    Canvas.Draw(0, 0, MyBitmap);
  finally
    MyBitmap.Free;                 (* free the memory buffer *)
  end;
end;
```

To draw on the canvas we only need to supply the co-ordinates where objects are to be drawn. The basic properties of these objects are already established in the canvas drawing tools, listed below.

Method / Property	Description
procedure Arc	Draws an Arc using the Pen.
procedure CopyRect	Copies a part of another canvas.
procedure Draw	Draws an image class (such as *TBitmap*) to the Canvas.
procedure StretchDraw	Draws a scaled version of an image.
procedure Ellipse	Draws an Ellipse outline using the Pen.
procedure FloodFill	Fills surface of connected pixels with one colour.
procedure Line	Draws a single line using the Pen.
procedure Polygon	Draws a Polygon outline using the Pen.
procedure Polyline	Draws a sequence of connected lines using the Pen.
procedure Rectangle	Draws a rectangular frame using the Pen and fills its contents using the Brush.
procedure TextOut	Draws text using the Font tool.
procedure TextRect	Draws text within a specified rectangle.
function TextExtent	Returns the width, height (or both in the case of TextExtent)
function TextHeight	which the text would have when drawn using the
function TextWidth	current Font tool.
property Pixels: Tcolor; [read/write]	Each individual image pixel can be set with this property. It draws a dot (the equivalent of drawing a *TPoint*).

Table 9.1: The most important drawing methods of TCanvas.

The most important basic properties of the canvas are the *Style* and *Color* of the drawing brush (which fills the surfaces when drawing a circle or rectangle); the *Pen* which is used to draw an object's contours and any lines or curves, and the *Font* used to output text.
The *TCanvas* class handles an application's basic drawing operations.
If further operations are needed, you can implement those yourself.
The classes *TPen*, *TBrush* and *TFont* extend the *TCanvas* class.

9.1.1 Colours

Colours of type *TColor* are used to draw on the canvas. *TColor* is imported by the classes *TPen*, *TBrush* and *TFont*. The colour names are valid system-wide and they are defined to be the same for all platforms. It is therefore no use to try to cast the loop counter in a loop to a *TColor*. The same is true of patterns.
For example:

```
   var i: integer;
 Pen.Color := TColor(i);
```

is syntactically correct – but useless! We always need to use the constants defined in the Graphics unit. Only the most important ones are listed here:

```
clBlack    TColor($000000);          // Black
clMaroon   TColor($000080);          // Maroon
clGreen    TColor($008000);          // Green
clOlive    TColor($008080);          // Olive
clNavy     TColor($800000);          // Navy
clPurple   TColor($800080);          // Purple
clTeal     TColor($808000);          // Teal
clGray     TColor($808080);          // Gray
clSilver   TColor($C0C0C0);          // Silver
clRed      TColor($0000FF);          // Red
clLime     TColor($00FF00);          // Lime
clYellow   TColor($00FFFF);          // Yellow
clBlue     TColor($FF0000);          // Blue
clFuchsia  TColor($FF00FF);          // Fuchsia
clAqua     TColor($FFFF00);          // Aqua
clLtGray   TColor($C0C0C0);          // = clSilver alias Light Gray
clDkGray   TColor($808080);          // = clGray alias Dark Gray
clWhite    TColor($FFFFFF);          // White
StandardColorsCount = 16;

// Extended colors
clMoneyGreen = TColor($C0DCC0);  // a brilliant keynote
clSkyBlue    = TColor($F0CAA6);  // sky blue
clCream      = TColor($F0FBFF);  // very light gray
clMedGray    = TColor($A4A0A0);  // another medium gray
ExtendedColorCount = 4;
```

In addition to this list, there are a large number of system colours. Lazarus also includes the colours defined by Borland in the CLX for Kylix, but these are outdated and should not be used. And of course we can define our own colours too. To do that, you need to know how colours are defined. Colours are coded as 24-bit numbers in *BBGGRR* format. A channel is blacked out, if the corresponding number is set to zero. It will light up at full strength when it gets the number $FF. All intermediate values are possible.
The standard colours are simple examples of how this is used: "Maroon", a reddish colour, is attained by applying $80 in the red channel. Bright red is produced with $FF. The other channels remain off for this. To produce gray colors all three channels get the same value; the higher the value, the lighter the colour. This goes up to $FFFFFF for white. The following routine shows an example of this:

```
procedure Tform1.FormMouseDown(Sender: TObject; Button: TMouseButton;
                               Shift: TShiftState; X, Y: Integer   );
begin
  with Canvas do
  begin   // red component  green component    blue component
    Pen.Color := Random($FF)   + Random($FF)  * $100 +
                                 Random($FF)  * $10000;
    MoveTo(100, 100);
    LineTo(X, Y);
  end;
end;
```

There are some special colours that deserve special attention. Their 32-bit values are as follows:

```
// Special colours
clNone     = TColor($1FFFFFFF);
clDefault  = TColor($20000000);
```

There are tools to help us define colours. Lazarus has two components for choosing colours in a professional way from the available palette. The basis of assigning colours is *TColorButton* on the *Misc* tab of the Component Palette. The button in this component calls a *TColorDialog* from the Dialogs tab of the Component Palette. The *TColorDialog* does not have an *Execute* routine, as can be seen in its definition:

```
TColorDialog = class(TComnonDialog)
  private
    // ... omitted
  protected
    // ... omitted
  public
    constructor Create(TheOwner: TComponent); override;
    destructor Destroy; override;
  published
    property Title;
    property Color: TColor read FColor write FColor;
   // Entry looks like ColorA = FFFFOO ... ColorX = COCOCO
    property CustomColors: TStrings read FCustomColors
                                    write SetCustomColors;
end;
```

The properties available are not needed to work with the colours in the dialog. This is all handled by the colour button control *TColorButton*. The most important method of this speed button descendant is *Click*, and its most important properties are *ColorDialog* and *ButtonColor*. Its most important event is *OnColorChange*. (*ColorDialog* can be used to. assign a colour dialog, but this is only needed if we don't want to use the prepared standard dialog. If we leave the property empty, a dialog will be included anyway. This happens automatically when the button is clicked). The dialog always saves the currently selected colour in *ButtonColor* (not in *Color*!). The selected colour will not be transferred in the *OnClick* event. This holds the current colour (just in case you wanted to know!). The new colour will be available in *OnColorChanged* event. This can then simply be assigned to a *Color* property in the program, for instance (anticipating the next section) like this:

```
Canvas.Pen.Color := ColorButton1.ButtonColor;
```

To assign the original *Color* at your program's start, transfer this value in your main form's *OnCreate*. If your program does not contain a toolbar, you will have to use the *TColorButton* from the Component Palette's *Misc* tab, with its *Visible* property set to False. Its *OnClick* routine can then be activated from a menu selection, for instance.

9.1.2 TPen

The *TPen* (a stylus or pen class) determines the properties of dots, lines and curves when they are drawn, and it has the properties *Color*, *Width*, *Style*, *Mode*, *JoinStyle*, *EndCap* and *Cosmetic*:

```
TPen = class(TFPCustomPen)
  private
    // omitted
  protected
    // omitted
  public
    constructor Create; override;
    destructor Destroy; override;
    procedure Assign(Source: TPersistent); override;
    property Handle: HPEN read GetHandle write SetHandle; Deprecated;
    property Reference: TWSPenReference read GetReference;
    function GetPattern: TPenPattern;
    procedure SetPattern(APattern: TPenPattern); Reintroduce;
  published
    property Color: Tcolor read Fcolor
                           write SetColor default clBlack;
    property Cosmetic: Boolean read Fcosmetic
                               write SetCosmetic default True;
    property EndCap: TPenEndCap read FEndCap
                               write SetEndCap default pecRound;
    property JoinStyle: TPenJoinStyle read FJoinStyle
                               write SetJoinStyle default pjsRound;
    property Mode default pmCopy;
    property Style default psSolid;
    property Width default 1;
end;
```

The predefined colour for all activities is black, but *Color* can be set to any *TColor* value you like. *Width* has a predefined value of 1 and determines the width of the line to be drawn. *Mode* determines how the drawn line will interact with the background. Its predefined and most commonly used value is *pmCopy*, which means the line will have the colour set in the *Color property*. The other possible values are listed in Table 9.2.

Constant	Description
pmCopy	Draws in the colour set in *Color*.
pmBlack	Draws in black.
pmWhite	Draws in white.
pmNop	Does not draw at all.
pmNot	Inverts the background colour.
pmNotCopy	Draws in the inverse of the colour set in *Color*.
pmMergePenNot	Combines the colour in *Color* with the inverse background colour.
pmMaskPenNot	Paints with colours common to *Color* with the inverse of the background colour.
pmMaskNotPen	Combines the inverse of the colour in *Color* with the background colour.
pmMerge	Combines the colour in *Color* with the background colour.
pmNotMerge	Draws in the inverse colour of *pmMerge.*
pmMask	Combination of colors common to both Pen and canvas background.
pmNotMask	Draw in the inverse colour of *pmMask*.
pmXor	Combines *Pen* colour with background colour with the XOR operation.
pmNotXor	Draw in the inverse colour of *pmXor.*

Table 9.2: The possible values for Mode and the interaction with the canvas background

Since Lazarus 0.9.28 new properties are available which make the pen more versatile. These extend its possibilities beyond those offered in Delphi and they are named *JoinStyle*, *EndCap* and *Cosmetic*. *JoinStyle* controls the way two connected lines are drawn and it can take the values listed in Table 9.3.

Constant	Description
pjsRound	Draws a rounded connection. This is the default value.
pjsBevel	Draws connections with a diagonal cut.
pjsMiter	Draws a sharp straight connection.

Table 9.3: JoinStyle's options for drawing connected lines

The *JoinStyle* only works for lines that are connected. It has no effect if lines are drawn in sequence with the routines *Line, MoveTo* or *LineTo*. These are always considered non-connected, even when they are drawn immediately after each other. *JoinStyle* works on *Polyline* (which draws several connected lines in one operation) and on polygons.

```
procedure TfrmPen.FormPaint(Sender: TOhject);
  var  MyBitmap : TBitmap;
       MyLine   : array[0..2] of TPoint;
begin
 // ... omitted
 // join style
  MyBitmap.Canvas.TextOut(200, 225, 'Join Style:');
  MyBitmap.Canvas.Pen.Width := 10;
  MyBitmap.Canvas.Pen.EndCap := pecRound;

  MyBitnap.Canvas.TextOut(200, 250, 'pjsRound');
  MyBitnap.Canvas.Pen.JoinStyle := pjsRound;
  MyLine[0] := Point(200, 275);
  MyLine[1] := Point(250, 275);
  MyLine[2] := Point(250, 325);
  MyBitmap.Canvas.Polyline(MyLine);
 // ... omitted
end;
```

EndCap determines the way the endings of simple lines drawn with *Line*, *MoveTo* and *LineTo* will be drawn. This property also determines the appearance of the end points of line sets drawn with *Polyline*. It can take one of the following values: *pecRound* (default value, round ending), *pecSquare* (sharp, right-angled ending) and *pecFlat* (tiny point). The latter looks the same as *pecSquare* for simple lines, but the line will be a bit shorter, as the pointed edge takes up some space.

The behaviour of the line endings can be seen in the following example.

```
procedure TForm1.FormCreate(Sender: TObject);
begin
  i := 0; // initialize the loop variable
end;

procedure TForm1.FormMouseDown(Sender: TObject; Button: TMouseButton;
                               Shift: TShiftState; X, Y: Integer);
Begin
  Inc(i);
  with Canvas do begin
    Pen.Width := 10;                                // Line thickness
    Pen.EndCap := pecFlat;                                // Starting value, small!
    if i mod 2 = 0 then Pen.EndCap := pecRound;
    if i mod 3 = 0 then Pen.EndCap := pecSquare;
    if i = 3 then i := 0;
    Pen.Color := Random($FF) + Random($FF) * $100 +
                                                  Random($FF) * $10000;
    MoveTo(100, 100);
    LineTo(X, Y);
  end;
end;
```

The loop counter used here is defined as an integer class variable in the Form1 declaration.

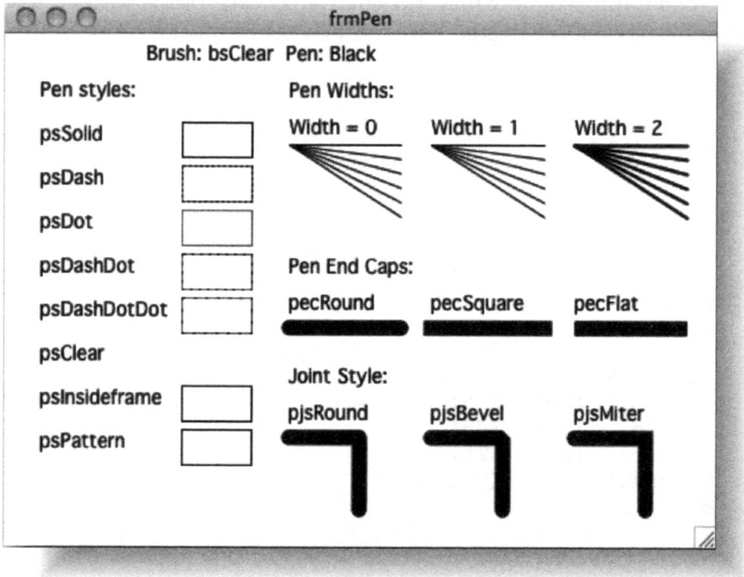

Figure 9.1: The effect of different TPen properties

The *Cosmetic* property indicates that the pen will always be 1 pixel wide. Some libraries need this information to simplify their drawing routines. This will make these operations execute faster. If the width is greater than 1, this property will be ignored, so it can simply be left at its default value; its only purpose is to ensure that the faster drawing methods for single-pixel-wide pens will be used, if possible.

9.1.3 TBrush

The *TBrush* (a brush) is the tool used to fill in areas in the drawing.
It has a simple structure and just three main properties: *Color*, *Style* and *Bitmap:*

```
TBrush = class(TFPCustomBrush)
  private    // ... omitted
  Protected // ... omitted
  public
    procedure       Assign(Source: TPersistent); Override;
    constructor Create; Override;
    destructor Destroy; Override;
    property Bitmap: TCustomBitmap Read FBitmap Write SetBitmap;
    property Handle: HBRUSH Read GetHandle Write SetHandle;
                                                        Deprecated;
    property Reference: TWSBrushReference Read GetReference;
  published
    property Color: TColor Read FColor Write SetColor Default
                                                          clWhite;
    property Style Default bsSolid;
end;
```

Style indicates which areas should be filled with the brush *Color* and which should not (i.e. those areas will remain in their current *Color*); the patterns *bsSolid*, *bsClear*, *bsHorizontal*, *bsVertical*, *bsFDiagonal*, *bsBDiagonal*, *bsCross* and *bsDiagCross* are available. The following example routine demonstrates what these look like:

```
procedure TForm1.Button1Click(Sender: TObject);
  var  i: Integer;
begin
  with Canvas do for i := 0 to 7 do
  begin
    case i of
      0: begin Brush.Style := bsSolid;     Brush.Color := clBlack;end;
      1: begin Brush.Style := bsClear;     Brush.Color := clWhite;end;
      2: begin Brush.Style := bsHorizontal;Brush.Color:= clGreen;end;
      3: begin Brush.Style := bsVertical; Brush.Color := clOlive;end;
      4: begin Brush.Style := bsFDiagonal;Brush.Color := clNavy; end;
      5: begin Brush.Style := bsBDiagonal;Brush.Color :=clPurple;end;
      6: begin Brush.Style := bsCross;     Brush.Color := clTeal; end;
      7: begin Brush.Style := bsDiagCross;Brush.Color := clRed;  end;
    end;
    FillRect(i * 100, 0, i * 100 + 100 + i, 100);
  end;
end;
```

The brush definitions do not affect the way lines are drawn. In the following example the squares drawn around the patterns will all be yellow:

```
procedure TForm1.Button1Click(Sender: TObject);
  var  i: Integer;
begin
  with Canvas do begin
    Pen.Color := clYellow;                    // draw lines in yellow
    for i := 0 to 7 do
    begin
    case i of
      0: begin Brush.Style := bsSolid;  Brush.Color := clBlue;   end;
      1: begin Brush.Style := bsClear;  Brush.Color := clWhite;  end;
      2: begin Brush.Style := bsHorizontal;Brush.Color:= clGreen;end;
      3: begin Brush.Style := bsVertical;Brush.Color := clOlive; end;
      4: begin Brush.Style := bsFDiagonal;Brush.Color := clNavy; end;
      5: begin Brush.Style := bsBDiagonal;Brush.Color:= clPurple;end;
      6: begin Brush.Style := bsCross;  Brush.Color := clTeal;   end;
      7: begin Brush.Style := bsDiagCross; Brush.Color := clRed; end;
    end;
    FillRect( i*100, 0, i*100+100+i, 100);   // here the brush is drawing
    Rectangle(i*100, 0, i*100+100+i, 100);   // here the pen (not brush) is drawing
    end;
  end;
end;
```

In addition to the predefined brushes, it also possible to define your own. Normally TBrush.Bitmap is set to NIL. To set your own brush, change the Style to *TBitmap*. The defined area will then be filled with the data from this bitmap, using the colours of the bitmap image. The properties Color and Style are not used in this case.

The routine

```
procedure TfrmBrush.FormPaint(Sender: TObject);
  var MyBitmap: TBitmap;
begin   // ... omitted
        // image brushes
  MyBitmap.Canvas.TextOut(25, 250,'Canvas-aligned bitmapped Brush:');
  MyBitmap.Canvas.Brush.Bitmap := TBitmap.Create;
  MyBitmap.Canvas.Brush.Bitmap.Height := 20;
  MyBitmap.Canvas.Brush.Bitmap.Width := 20;
  MyBitmap.Canvas.Brush.Bitmap.Canvas.Brush.Color := clWhite;
  MyBitmap.Canvas.Brush.Bitmap.Canvas.FillRect(0, 0, 20, 20);
  MyBitmap.Canvas.Brush.Bitmap.Canvas.Brush.Color := clRed;
  MyBitmap.Canvas.Brush.Bitmap.Canvas.Ellipse(0, 0, 20, 20);
  MyBitmap.Canvas.Rectangle(Bounds( 25, 275, 50, 50));
  MyBitmap.Canvas.Rectangle(Bounds(100, 275, 50, 50));
  MyBitmap.Canvas.Brush.Bitmap.Free;
  MyBitmap.Canvas.Brush.Bitmap := NIL;
        // ... omitted
end;
```

will draw the two brush patterns shown at the bottom in figure 9.2.

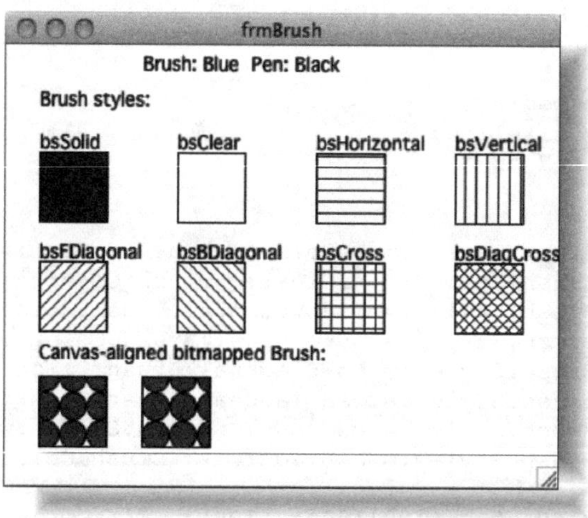

Figure 9.2: The effect of the Brush property

The bitmap masks depend on more than one factor. On the one hand they are of course affected by the image used, but on the other hand the way the image is blended has an effect too. The two different results in the picture arise from the fact that they have a different origin in the same bitmap (see figure 9.3).
The procedure is therefore called "canvas aligned, bitmapped brush", because the pattern drawn depends on the location of the area on the canvas.

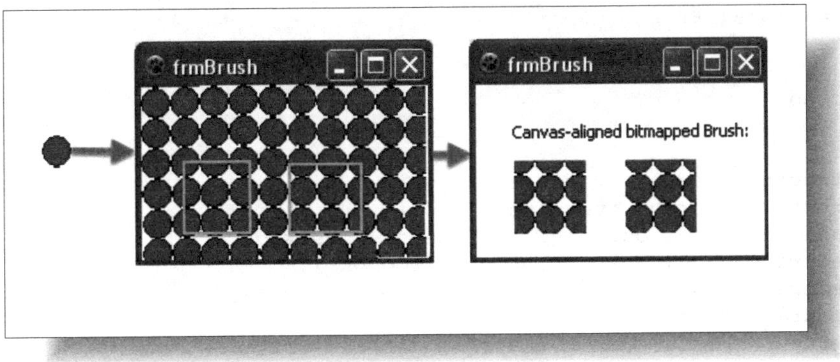

Figure 9.3: Generating different brushes from the same bitmap

When we want to fill the shapes with fixed colors and styles again, we just need to set the property *Bitmap* back to NIL. It is important to manually free the bitmap again. This is not done automatically when *TBrush* is freed.
Normally the brush is only used for filling shapes. An exception to this is *TCanvas.FrameRect*, which uses the brush properties for drawing the lines as well.

9.1.4 Fonts

Most computer users are familiar with the concept of fonts, especially if they are used to working with text editors. A font describes how characters are represented on the output device, making several styles and typefaces possible. Lazarus works with Unicode, allowing a great number of possible characters. But not every font will contain every possible character. When we select a font, we must keep in mind that foreign-language applications should be able to work as expected.
Fonts in Lazarus have the basic properties *CharSet*, *Color*, *Height*, *Name*, *Pitch*, *Size* and *Style* (see Table 9.4). The font information is defined in the *Graphics* unit as follows:

```
type
  TFontPitch      = (fpDefault, fpVariable, fpFixed);
  TFontName       = String;
  TFontDataName   = String[LF_FACESIZE -1];
  TFontStyle      = (fsBold, fsItalic, fsStrikeOut, fsUnderline);
  TFontStyles     = set of TFontStyle;
  TFontStylesbase = set of TFontStyle;
  TFontCharSet    = 0..255;
  TFontQuality    = (fqDefault, fqDraft, fqProof, fqNonAntialiased,
                    fqAntialiased, fqCleartype, fqCleartypeNatural);

TFontData = record
  Handle : HFont;
  Height : Integer;
  Pitch  : TFontPitch;
  Style  : TFontStylesBase;
  CharSet: TFontCharSet;
  Quality: TFontQuality;
  Name   : TFontDataName;
  Orientation: Integer;
end;
```

```
TFont = class(TFPCustomFont)
private
    // .. omitted
protected
    // .. omitted
public
 constructor Create; override;
 destructor Destroy; override;
 procedure Assign(Source: TPersistent); override;
 procedure Assign(const ALogFont: TLogFont);
 procedure BeginUpdate;
 procedure EndUpdate;
 property FontData: TFontData read GetData write SetData;
 function HandleAllocated: boolean;
 property Handle: HFONT read GetHandle write SetHandle; deprecated;
 function IsDefault: boolean;
 function IsEqual(AFont: TFont): boolean; virtual;
 property IsMonoSpace: boolean read GetIsMonoSpace;
 procedure SetDefault;
 property CanUTF8: boolean read GetCanUTF8;
 property PixelsPerInch: Integer read FPixelsPerInch
                                 write FPixelsPerInch;
 property Reference: TWSFontReference read GetReference;

published
 property CharSet: TFontCharSet read GetCharSet write SetCharSet
                                default DEFAULT_CHARSET;
 property Color: TColor read FColor write SetColor
                                default clWindowText;
 property Height: Integer read GetHeight write SetHeight
                                stored IsHeightStored;
 property Name: string read GetName write SetName
                                stored IsNameStored;
 property Orientation: Integer read GetOrientation
                                write SetOrientation
                                default 0;
 property Pitch: TFontPitch read GetPitch write SetPitch
                                default fpDefault;
 property Quality: TFontQuality read FQuality write SetQuality
                                default fqDefault;
 property Size: Integer read GetSize write SetSize stored false;
 property Style: TFontStyles read GetStyle write SetStyle default [];

end;
```

Apart from the basic properties there are also methods provided for getting and setting data and for assigning fonts. Text output is handled by the *Textout* method of the canvas. In your code this might look something like this:

```
with Canvas do begin
  Font.Name  := 'Courier';                  // the font name (a string)
  Font.Color := clRed;                      // colour (a TColor)
  Font.Size  := 24;                         // size in points
  Font.Style := [fsBold, fsItalic]; // a set combining various style values
  TextOut(20, 20, 'Lazarus');
end;
```

TextOut writes the specified text at the specified X and Y co-ordinates. However a

```
TextOut(20, 20, 'Lazarus'^J'is'^J'Great!');
```

will not have the result you might expect. To produce text with multiple lines you have to use more complicated code:

```
TextOut(20, 20, 'Lazarus');
TextOut(20, 20+36, 'is');
TextOut(20, 20+36+36, 'Great!');
```

The value 36 will result in a proper 12-point line separation for the 24-point font we are using.
Height is the font size in pixels, which can also be set in the *Size* property, measured in points (1/72 of an inch). Positive sizes exclude the line spacing, so you can also use negative sizes which include the line spacing. These two alternative properties for specifying the height of a font (*Height* and *Size)* are based on the two common text output destinations either to the screen or printed onto paper. Note that a 'pixel' can have different sizes, depending on the circumstances. The *Size* and the *Height* of a font are related by the following formula:

```
Font.Size = -(Font.Height * 72) / Font.PixelsPerInch
```

Pitch is the distance between the characters. This can be *fpDefault*, *fpFixed* or *fpVariable* and indicates to the library which font should be used, based on this parameter. For *fpFixed* a monospaced font (such as Courier) will be used; for *fpVariable* a proportional one. *fpDefault* indicates that this parameter should be ignored in the selection of a font. Should the pitch parameter be impossible for the selected font, the library will ignore the given font name and substitute another instead. *TFont.IsMonospace* does not give the actual font, but rather a specification indicating whether a particular font is proportional or not.

Since Lazarus 0.9.28 we can also set the *Orientation* of the text to be drawn. This property should be set to the angle between the base line of the text with the X axis of the canvas (in tenths of a degree). An important function used for text output is:

```
function TextExtent(const Text: string): TSize; virtual;
```

Property	Description
CharSet	The character set or codepage. This property exists only for compatibility with Delphi. Lazarus uses UTF-8 to encode text strings (which shows all existing characters without the need to choose a codepage), so this property is ignored.
Color	The text colour.
Height	The font size in pixels.
Name	The name of the font.
Pitch	The distance between characters. Can be *fpDefault*, *fpFixed* or *fpVariable*.
Size	The size of the font in 1/72 of an inch (also known as points). Negative numbers indicate that the space between lines is included in the size; positive values exclude line spacing.
Style	A set combining any or none of the following styles: *fsBold*, *fsItalic*, *fsStrikeOut*, *fsUnderline*.

Table 9.4: The basic properties of TFont.

9.1.5 The most important graphics routines

Now that we know about *TColor*, *TPen*, *TBrush* and *TFont*, we can finally start working with the methods of the canvas we mentioned earlier.

Pixels

It is possible to set each pixel of an image individually. However we must realize that this is a very slow process and for moving images it is totally impractical.

```
property Pixels[X, Y: Integer]: TColor read GetPixel write SetPixel;
```

Because the Pixels property reads or writes one specific image pixel, additional functions or properties like brush or pen are not needed for this. Pixels can be set by directly assigning a colour constant or an RGB value to them:

```
Canvas.Pixels[10, 20] := clBlack;

Reading is just as simple:
  var  MyColor: TColor;
begin
  MyColor := Canvas.Pixels[10, 20];
```

Lines

Lines are drawn simply by setting the start point and then drawing towards the end point by means of a call to *MoveTo* followed by a call to *LineTo*. Each *LineTo* moves the drawing cursor to a new starting position for further *LineTo* commands.

```
procedure MoveTo(x, y: Integer);
procedure MoveTo(p: TPoint);
procedure LineTo(x, y: Integer);
procedure LineTo(p: TPoint);
```

The next line's starting position is stored in the PenPos property, which can both be read and written:

```
property PenPos: TPoint read FPenPos write SetPenPos;
```

A direct assignment to PenPos has the same effect as a call to MoveTo. A combination of a MoveTo followed by a number of LineTo calls will draw any polygon. In the following routines, MoveTo is no longer needed to set the starting position. With Line both the starting and ending position are passed as parameters. This can be done either directly, in co-ordinate pairs, or in the form of a TRect structure.

```
procedure Line(x1, y1, x2, y2: Integer);
procedure Line(const p1, p2: TPoint);
procedure Line(const Points: TRect);
```

Polygons

Polyline replaces the turtle in drawing polygons. Co-ordinates can be passed in several ways, either in a typical Pascal format as an array of TPoint, by giving the points to use in an array, or in a more C-like style by passing a pointer to a TPoint array. All three versions result in lines connecting all the points listed in the array.

```
procedure Polyline(const Points: array of TPoint);
procedure Polyline(const Points: array of TPoint; Startindex:
                                       Integer; NumPts: Integer = -1);
procedure Polyline(Points: PPoint; NumPts: Integer);
```

The method to draw filled polygons is called Polygon. The outside frame is drawn with the pen; the filling of the area is done with the brush. Just like Polyline, Polygon needs an array of TPoints to list the points to be connected:

```
procedure Polygon(const Points: array of TPoint; Winding: Boolean;
                      Startindex: Integer = 0; NumPts: Integer = -1);
procedure Polygon(Points: PPoint; NumPts: Integer;
                                  Winding: boolean = False); virtual;
procedure Polygon(const Points: array of TPoint);
```

Rectangles

The canvas has several functions for drawing rectangles. This is because rectangles are the most frequently used elements in graphics work. The simplest routine for drawing rectangles is *Rectangle*, which draws the frame of the rectangle with settings from the canvas *Pen* property, and fills its area with settings from the canvas *Brush* property. *Frame* only draws the frame, but does not fill it. *FrameRect* only draws the frame, just like Frame does, but it uses the properties of *Brush* instead of *Pen*. As *Brush* does not define a line width, as fixed width of 1 is used. *FillRect* works like *Rectangle*, but draws the frame in width 1 with the *Brush* properties, just like *FrameRect*.

We can summarize this as follows:

Method	Frame	Fill
Rectangle	Pen	Brush
Frame	Pen	None
FillRect	Brush	Brush
FrameRect	Brush	None

Table 9.5: The different rectangle drawing methods

These four routines all cover the same total area when called with the same rectangle coordinates.

```
procedure Rectangle(X1, Y1, X2, Y2: Integer);
procedure Rectangle(const ARect: TRect);
procedure Frame(const ARect: TRect);
procedure Frame(X1,Y1,X2,Y2: Integer);
procedure FrameRect(const ARect: TRect);
procedure FrameRect(X1, Y1, X2, Y2: Integer);
procedure FillRect(const ARect: TRect); virtual;
procedure FillRect(X1, Y1, X2, Y2: Integer);
```

Apart from these basic functions there are extended functions for drawing visual control elements. *DrawFocusRect*, for instance, indicates that an object has the input focus.
The result of this is platform-dependent. Under Windows the result is the frame of the rectangle is drawn in dotted lines, with the dots alternating between the original background colour and its complementary colour. In MacOS X it will result in a fat blue frame being drawn.

```
procedure DrawFocusRect(const ARect: TRect);
```

Another special rectangle routine is *RoundRect*, which draws the frame in the *Pen* colour with rounded corners and fills the resulting area with the *Brush*. This method covers the same area as the other rectangle routines – with the exception of the rounded corners.

The radius of the rounded corners is determined by an ellipse with radiuses RX and RY:

```
procedure RoundRect(X1, Y1, X2, Y2: Integer; RX, RY: Integer);
procedure RoundRect(const Rect: TRect; RX, RY: Integer);
```

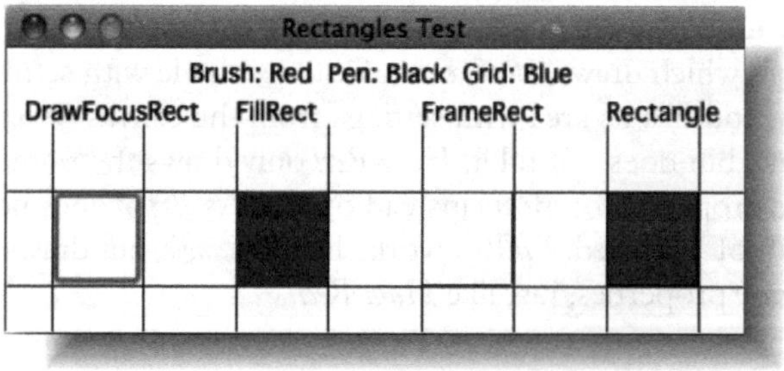

Figure 9.4: The geometry of the TCanvas rectangle methods

Circles and ellipses

The *Ellipse* method draws a circle or an ellipse within a rectangular area. The circumference is drawn with the *Pen* settings; the area is filled with the current *Brush*. This procedure has two variants: one takes the points of the enclosing rectangle in the form of a *TRect*, the other takes the co-ordinates of the top left and bottom right corner directly as X and Y values. Since a circle is just a special ellipse there is no separate routine for it. You draw circles by defining a square as the surrounding rectangle of an ellipse.
If you work under older Windows versions, you have to take into account a problem in the Windows 9x and ME API, namely that the sum of x1 + x2 + y1 + y2 may not exceed 32768. That is admittedly quite a large number, but it is nevertheless something you should be aware of.

```
procedure Ellipse(const ARect: TRect);
procedure Ellipse(x1, y1, x2, y2: Integer);
```

It is also possible to draw only a section of an ellipse. *Arc* draws part of the edge of an ellipse. Drawing starts at *Angle16Deg* and goes in a clockwise direction up to *Angle16DegLength*. Both parameters (and this explains their odd names) are measured in units of 1/16 of a degree. So a value of 16 corresponds to an angle of 1°. The Arc procedure draws the part-edge of the ellipse using only the pen settings – it does not fill the area.

Chord is an extension of *Arc*. This method completes the part-ellipse with a straight line between the two end points. This results in an enclosed area, which is then filled with the *Brush*.
Pie is also derived from *Arc*. Pie sections drawn with *Pie* are started by drawing an arc after which straight lines are drawn from each of the end points to the centre of the ellipse. Again the border lines are drawn with the Pen and the resulting enclosed area is filled with the *Brush*. The area drawn is bordered by two lines from the ellipse's centre to the points (`StartX, StartY`) and (`EndX, EndY`).

```
procedure Arc(ALeft, ATop, ARight, ABottom, Angle16Deg,
                                        Angle16DegLength:  Integer);
procedure Arc(ALeft, ATop, ARight, ABottom, SX, SY, EX, EY: Integer);
procedure Chord(x1,y1, x2,y2, Angle16Deg, Angle16DegLength: Integer);
procedure Chord(x1, y1, x2, y2, SX, SY, EX, EY: Integer);
procedure RadialPie(x1, y1, x2, y2, StartAngle16Deg,
                                         Angle16DegLength: Integer);
procedure Pie(EllipseX1, EllipseY1, EllipseX2, EllipseY2,
                              StartX, StartY, EndX, EndY: Integer);
```

These routines are shown in the following example:

```
procedure TfrmEllipse.FormPaint(Sender: TObject);
begin
  with Canvas do
  begin
    Brush.Color := clBlue;
    TextOut(50, 30, 'Ellipse');
    Ellipse(50, 50, 100, 100);
    TextOut(150, 30, 'Arc');
    Arc(150, 50, 200, 100, 0, 90 * 16);
    TextOut(50, 130, 'Chord');
    Chord(50, 150, 100, 200, 0, 90 * 16);
    TextOut(150,130, 'Pie');
    Pie(150, 150, 200, 200, 200, 175, 175, 150);
  end;
end;
```

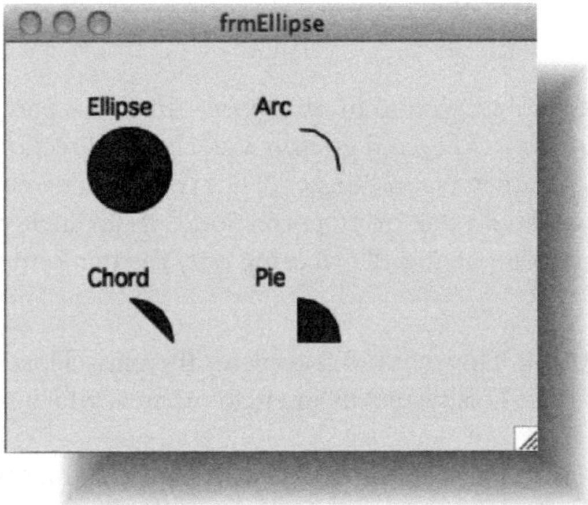

Figure 9.5: The geometry of the TCanvas ellipse

Text methods

Text can be output with two different methods. *TextOut* draws the text starting from the top left corner (X, Y) to the right. It also does this if the writing direction of the selected language is from right to left or from top to bottom. *TextRec* works exactly the same as *TextOut,* but in addition it cuts off any text that would have been drawn outside the rectangle specified in *ARect*:

```
procedure TextOut(X, Y: Integer; Const Text: String);
procedure TextRect(const ARect: TRect; X, Y: integer;
                                             const Text: String);
```

Both methods draw the *Text* on the canvas at the size defined by the *Font.* The following three methods can be used to calculate the size of the *Text. TextHeight* returns the height of a string and *TextWidth* returns its width. *TextExtent* gives both the height and the width:

```
function TextExtent(const Text: String): TSize;
function TextHeight(const Text: String): Integer;
function TextWidth (const Text: String): Integer;
```

9.2 Graphics components

Lazarus's graphic controls allow us to load, save and manipulate images. The basic visual controls for such operations are TImage from the Additional tab and *TImageList* from *Common Controls*. If it is necessary to scroll larger images, we can drop the image component in a scrollbox (a scrolling container for other controls, found on the *Additional* tab).
On the same tab there is also the *TPaintBox* component, which also has a canvas.
The main difference from *TImage* is that the *TPaintBox* does not offer permanent storage for the image. This means the contents of a paintbox have to be recreated every time the window needs to be refreshed. It is perfectly possible to draw outside the paint event with some Lazarus interfaces, but everything will be wiped out at the next refresh.
In Carbon and Qt this is not even possible, so it is advisable to refrain from doing this at all.
Images can be loaded and saved with the normal open and save dialogs, but it is better to use the predefined *TOpenPictureDialog* and *TSavePictureDialog* as these feature a convenient preview of the image.
A simple image viewer can be created with just a few lines of source code.
All that is needed is a *TImage* and a *TOpenPictureDialog*.

The image will be put into a window and its magnification (*Align*) can be set to *alClient*:

```
procedure TForm1.Image1DblClick(Sender: TObject);
begin
  if OpenPictureDialog1.Execute then
    Image1.Picture.LoadFromFile(OpenPictureDialog1.FileName);
end;
```

As the dialog is pre-configured to show all Lazarus-supported image formats, this minimal program can already be used as a real image viewer. However it does not offer the ability to scroll larger images. For that a scrollbox would be needed.
The order of placing controls in the Designer would then be as follows:
Form1 → *ScrollBox1* → *Image1*. The scrollbox *Align* is given the value *alClient*, the *TImage* component in the scrollbox gets starting co-ordinates *Left 0* and *Top 0*, and a size smaller than the size of the scrollbox in the design mode. Image1 gets an Align value of *alNone* (important!) and the *AutoSize* property is set to *True*.

Now if you load a picture that is larger than the current window, the scrollbox will react and display scrollbars that can be used to scroll the invisible parts of the picture into view. This looks as follows in form's resource data (`.lfm`):

```
object ScrollBox1: TScrollBox
  Left = 0
  Height = 229
  Top = 0
  Width = 368
  Align = alClient
  AutoSize = True
  ClientHeight = 225
  ClientWidth = 364
  TabOrder = 0
  object Image1: TImage
    Left = 0
    Height = 128
    Top = 0
    Width = 256
    AutoSize = True
    OnDblClick = Image1DblClick
  end
end
```

This completes our rudimentary picture viewer. We will use this code as the basis for the following extensions.
As can be seen when we open the initial *TPictureDialog*, Lazarus is already capable of handling a great number of graphical formats. *TImage's* method *LoadFromFile* supports all these formats when loading an image into its *Picture property* (of type *TPicture*). *TImage* is derived from *TCustomImage*. Its full list of available methods and properties is as follows:

```
TCustomImage = class(TGraphicControl)
  private     // ... omitted
  protected   // ... omitted
  public
    constructor Create(AOwner: TComponent); Override;
    destructor Destroy; Override;
    property Canvas: TCanvas read GetCanvas;
  public
    property Align;
    property AutoSize;
    property Center: Boolean read FCenter write SetCenter default False;
    property Constraints;
    property Picture: TPicture read FPicture write SetPicture;
    property Visible;
    property OnClick;
    property OnMouseDown;
    property OnMouseMove;
    property OnMouseUp;
    property Stretch: Boolean read FStretch write SetStretch
           default False;
    property Transparent: Boolean read FTransparent
           write SetTransparent default False;
    property Proportional: Boolean read FProportional
           write SetProportional default False;
    property OnPictureChanged: TNotifyEvent read FOnPictureChanged
          write FOnPictureChanged;
  end;

  TImage = class(TCustomImage)
  published
    property Align;
    property Anchors;
    property AutoSize;
    property BorderSpacing;
    property Center;
    property Constraints;
    property DragCursor;
    property DragMode;
    property Enabled;
    property OnChangeBounds;
    property OnClick;
    property OnDblClick;
    property OnDragDrop;
    property OnDragOver;
    property OnEndDrag;
    property OnMouseDown;
    property OnMouseEnter;
    property OnMouseLeave;
    property OnMouseMove;
    property OnMouseUp;
    property OnMouseWheel;
    property OnMouseWheelDown;
    property OnMouseWheelUp;
    property OnPaint;
    property OnPictureChanged;
    property OnResize;
    property OnStartDrag;
    property ParentShowHint;
    property Picture;
    property PopupMenu;
    property Proportional;
    property ShowHint;
    property Stretch;
    property Transparent;
    property Visible;
  end;
```

The purposes of the different properties of both classes in the *ExtCtrls* unit should be clear from their names. But – as you have probably noticed – the definition does not contain any methods. These are all located inside the *Picture* property which is imported in the *Graphics* unit and which is a lot more complex than the *TImage* control itself:

```
TPicture = class(TPersistent)
  private
      // ... omitted
  protected
      // ... omitted
  public
    constructor Create;
    destructor Destroy; Override;
    procedure LoadFromFile(const Filename: String);
    procedure SaveToFile(const Filename: String;
              const FileExt: String = '');
    procedure SaveToStreamWithFileExt(Stream: Tstream;
                                      const FileExt: String);
    procedure LoadFromStreamWithFileExt(Stream: Tstream;
                                      const FileExt: String);
    procedure LoadFromLazarusResource(const AName: String);
    procedure LoadFromClipboardFormat(FormatID: TClipboardFormat);
    procedure LoadFromClipboardFormatID(ClipboardType:
                        TClipboardType; FormatID: TClipboardFormat);
    procedure SaveToClipboardFormat(FormatID: TClipboardFormat);
    class function SupportsClipboardFormat(FormatID:
                                     TClipboardFormat): Boolean;
    procedure Assign(Source: TPersistent); Override;
    class procedure RegisterFileFormat(const AnExtension,
                    ADescription: String; AGraphicClass:TGraphicClass);
    class procedure RegisterClipboardFormat(FormatID: TClipboardFormat;
                                    AGraphicClass: TGraphicClass);
    class procedure UnregisterGraphicClass(AClass: TGraphicClass);
    procedure Clear; virtual;
    function FindGraphicClassWithFileExt(const Ext: String;
                 ExceptionOnNotFound: boolean = true): TGraphicClass;
```

The class does not contain a published clause, as that is already part of *TImage*. Very important in this class are the properties under the second public definition:

```
  public
    property Bitmap: Tbitmap   read GetBitmap write SetBitmap;
    property Icon: TIcon       read GetIcon   write SetIcon;
    property Jpeg: TJpegImage  read GetJpeg   write SetJpeg;
    property Pixmap: TPixmap   read GetPixmap write SetPixmap;
    property PNG: TPortableNetworkGraphic read GetPNG write SetPNG;
    property PNM: TPortableAnyMapGraphic  read GetPNM write SetPNM;
    property Graphic: TGraphic read FGraphic  write SetGraphic;
    property Height: Integer   read GetHeight;
    property Width: Integer    read GetWidth;
    property OnChange: TNotifyEvent read FOnChange write FOnChange;
    property OnProgress: TProgressEvent read FOnProgress
                               write FOnProgress;
 end;
```

To summarize: *TImage* is a very simple component which shows a static image, and which can be accessed as the *TImage.Picture* property (of type *TPicture*). *TImage* can be used to display simple images loaded from file, or images that only rarely change, or images that are only drawn incrementally.
An important consideration when using *TImage* is that its size is totally unrelated to the size of the image being handled; both sizes have to be controlled individually.
Each *TImage* consists of two parts: a *TGraphic* (a PNG picture, a bitmap, a JPEG image etc.) which contains the persistent image, and the visible region which is repainted after every *OnPaint* event. The image itself can be accessed through *TImage.Picture.Graphic* (or through *TImage.Picture.Bitmap*, which is basically the same).
The canvas is accessed via TImage.Picture.Graphic.Canvas (or *TImage.Picture.Bitmap.Canvas*). We must keep in mind that *TImage.Canvas* points to the volatile visible area during the control's *OnPaint* event, not to *TImage.Picture.Graphic.Canvas*. It is best to avoid accessing this visible canvas. Drawing should be done on the *Graphic* in *TImage* as you can see in the following example. Here we draw a rectangle filling the whole image. Drawing in a *TImage* can be done at any time, for instance in the *OnClick* event of a button. The results will be retained in the image:

```
procedure TForm1.Button1Click(Sender: TObject);
begin
  Image1.Canvas.Brush.Style := bsSolid;
  Image1.Canvas.Brush.Color := clBlue;
  Image1.Canvas.Rectangle(0, 0, Image1.Width, Image1.Height);
end;
```

The *public* section of *TPicture* contains the definitions of the graphical formats.
Not all formats that the FCL handles can also be processed by Lazarus.
The FCL contains the low-level classes for reading images from files and writing them back and in Lazarus the images are handled through a more or less platform-independent interface.
The *Graphics* unit contains Lazarus's image classes which are all derived from *TRasterImage*. This ancestor class provides as a minimum a *TCanvas* for drawing the image and basic properties like *Width*, *Height*, *PixelFormat*, *TransparentColor* and *TransparentMode*. These properties are available even when the descendent class represents a format that allows multiple images, such as *TIcon*, *TCursorImage* and *TIcnsIcon*. In that case the properties represent the state of currently selected image.

9.3 Graphics Formats

The graphics formats supported by Lazarus are arranged in a hierarchy.

9.3.1 TGraphic

Tgraphic is the base class for all pixel image formats. The next level, *TRasterImage*, builds directly on top of this. *TGraphic* introduces all the basic image properties. *TGraphic's* main public properties are:

- *Empty*: This indicates whether the image is empty.
  Normally its height and width will be zero if that is the case.
- *Height* and *Width*: The size of the image.
- *Modified*: This is an auxiliary property which can be set to *False*. It can be used to check whether the image has been changed since the property was set.
- *Transparent*: A flag indicating whether the image contains transparency.
  This may be either colour transparency or an alpha channel.

The *OnChange* and *OnProgress* events are triggered when the image is changed or when saving or loading is in progress. You can use this for progress indicators.
Tgraphic also defines the main methods for all graphical formats. These are:

- *Assign* (to copy contents from another image.
  You can use this for format conversion).
- *Clear* (which sets the image size to (0, 0) thereby clearing all data).

Loading and saving is done with *LoadFromFile*, *LoadFromStream*, *LoadFromLazarusResource*, *SaveToFile and SaveToStream*, depending on the situation.

9.3.2 TRasterImage

TRasterImage is the base class for all LCL image classes. It descends from *TGraphic* and offers an API for working with image data. The key elements in this are the properties *Canvas*, *BitmapHandle* (for *LCLIntf API* calls), *PixelFormat* as the format for saving pixel images, and *TransparentColor* and *TransparentMode*, which indicate whether a colour is transparent (which is an alternative to using an alpha channel for transparency). The colour defined to be transparent is then converted to a mask, which is used in drawing the image. The main routine in *TRasterImage* is *LoadFromDevice*, which is used to load the image from the canvas handle. If Null is passed in the parameter to *LoadFromDevice*, a screenshot is created and loaded into the image. This method does not work with the (out-dated) Gtk 1, but it does work with all the other interfaces: Win32/64 (pre-Windows 7), WinCE, Gtk 2, Qt and Carbon.

```
procedure TfrmScreenshot.btnScreenshotClick(Sender: TObject);
  var  bmp: TBitmap;
begin
  bmp := TBitmap.Create;
  bmp.LoadFromDevice(0);
  imgScreenshot.Picture.Bitmap.Assign(bmp);
  FreeAndNil(bmp);
end;
```

```
procedure TfrmScreenshot.btnScreenshotClick(Sender: TObject);
  var  bmp: TBitmap;
begin
  bmp := TBitmap.Create;
  bmp.LoadFromDevice(0);
  imgScreenshot.Picture.Bitmap.Assign(bmp);
  FreeAndNil(bmp);
end;
```

Like *TGraphic*, *TRasterimage* does not have any properties defined as published. Raster images consist of a two-dimensional area with a height and width defined in pixels. A 'pixel' is the smallest square area that can be represented on the display surface.

The exact size of a 'pixel' depends on the resolution of the monitor (usually between 72 and 135 dpi) and printer (depending on the quality of the printer this is typically between 150 and 1200 dpi).The current resolution can be obtained from the globally available properties *Screen.PixelsPerInch* and *Printer.PixelsPerInch.*
Raster images can be changed in size by rotating and scaling (or both simultaneously). For instance with the following routine, which uses *TCanvas.CopyRect* to transfer the image to a new canvas:

```
  var  MyBitmap: TBitmap;
begin
 // create a bitmap of size 100 x 100 pixels
  MyBitmap := TBitmap.Create;
  MyBitmap.Width := 100;
  MyBitmap.Height := 100;
 // draw in this newly defined bitmap
  MyBitmap.Canvas.Brush.Color := clBlue;
  MyBitmap.Canvas.Pen.Color .= clBlue;
  MyBitmap.Canvas.Rectangle(20, 20, 80, 80);
 // now resize to 200 x 100 pixels
  MyBitmap.Width :=200;
  MyBitmap.Canvas.CopyRect(Bounds(0, 0, 200, 100), MyBitmap.Canvas,
                           Bounds(0, 0, 100, 100));
  MyImage.Canvas.Draw(0, 0, MyBitmap); // draw on the canvas
  MyBitmap.Free;                       // free the bitmap instance
end;
```

All pixels are transferred to a location on the new canvas and if there are 'holes' between them, they are filled with the nearest values. These can be available values from adjacent pixels, or calculated intermediate values. This calculation of intermediate values is called anti-aliasing. The property *TCanvas.AntiAliasingMode* determines whether anti-aliasing will be applied. An anti-aliased image that is stretched in one direction while applying anti-aliasing may look properly rounded or it may look blurred. If anti-aliasing is off, the edges are always sharp, but they may be jagged. We also need to keep in mind that the setting *amDontCare* may lead to different results on different platforms. Therefore it is often better to switch off anti-aliasing for all platforms with *amOff*. In Carbon the default setting is amOn. In all other interfaces, the default setting is *amOff*.

The Windows inter-face does not handle anti-aliasing at all, so switching it off may generally be a good idea.

```
type
  TAntialiasingMode = (amDontCare, // default
                       amOn,        // turn anti-aliasing on
                       amOff);      // turn anti-aliasing off

  property AntialiasingMode: TAntialiasingMode read FAntialiasingMode
                             write SetAntialiasingMode default amDontCare;
```

This is a good point to mention the image copying routines of *Tcanvas*:

- CopyRect copies a rectangular area in Source from the source canvas to the rectangular area in Dest.
  If Source and Dest are not the same size, the image will be scaled accordingly.
- Draw draws an image without distorting it. The top left co-ordinate of the destination location is given in the co-ordinates X and Y.
- StretchDraw does the same as Draw, but adjusts the size of the image to the target area.

```
procedure CopyRect(const Dest: TRect; SrcCanvas: Tcanvas;
                   const Source: TRect);
procedure Draw(X, Y: Integer; SrcGraphic: TGraphic);
procedure StretchDraw(const DestRect: TRect; SrcGraphic: TGraphic);
```

Instead of these basic routines, you can also use the *StretchBlt* routine from the `LCLIntf unit`. The parameters of this very versatile function are (in this order):
the target canvas,
the target area within it,
the source canvas,
the source area within it,
the copy mode "Rop"
This defines the way the image is transferred: for instance, whether the colors of the source image should be inverted, and whether multiple images should be combined. The copy modes (see also Table 9.6) are defined in the `LCLType unit`, but unfortunately the extent of their implementation in different widget-sets varies widely. One thing that always works is the normal copy mode, for which the constant *SRCCOPY* should be specified. The rest will have to be tested on your individual platform.

```
function StretchBlt(DestDC: HOC; X, Y, Width, Height: Integer;
   SrcDC: HOC; XSrc, YSrc, SrcWidth, SrcHeight: Integer;
                                        Rop: Cardinal): Boolean;
```

In the last example, StretchBlt should be called as follows to replace the call to *CopyRect* shown:

```
LCLIntf.StretchBlt(MyBitmap.Canvas.Handle, 0, 0, 200, 100,
                   MyBitmap.Canvas.Handle, 0, 0, 100, 100, SRCCOPY);
```

Constant	Value	Formula
SRCCOPY	00CC0020h	Target = Source
SRCPAINT	00EE0086h	Target = Source OR Target
SRCAND	008800C6h	Target = Source AND Target
SRCINVERT	00660046h	Target = Source XOR Target
SRCERASE	00440328h	Target = Source AND (NOT Target)
NOTSRCCOPY	00330008h	Target = (NOT Source)
NOTSRCERASE	001100A6h	Target = (NOT Source) AND (NOT Target)
MERGECOPY	00C000CAh	Target = (Source AND Target Brush)
MERGEPAINT	00BB0226h	Target = (NOT Source) OR Target
PATCOPY	00F00021h	Target = Target Brush
PATPAINT	00FB0A09h	Target = (Target Brush OR NOT Source) OR Target
PATINVERT	005A0049h	Target = Target Brush XOR Target
DSTINVERT	00550009h	Target = (NOT Target)
BLACKNESS	00000042h	Target = BLACK
WHITENESS	00FF0062h	Target = WHITE

Table 9.6: Raster operations (many are not implemented on all platforms!) for StretchBlt

9.3.3 Bitmaps

The Windows bitmap format, which is also available on the other Lazarus-supported platforms, has been extended with the OS/2 bitmap format since version 0.9.28.
This is the simplest graphical format. Color depths between 1 bit per pixel and 32 bits per pixel are possible. The 32 bit format defines an *alpha channel* in addition to the three 8-bit colour channels Red Green and Blue of the 24-bit format. In theory the data can be compressed, but Lazarus does not support this.

All *TBitmap's* properties and methods are derived from its ancestor classes, most of them from *TRasterImage*, but a few of them from *TFPImageBitmap* and *TCustomBitmap*.
The only thing implemented in *TBitmap* itself, is the method for reading and writing the file format. Besides that the list of accepted filename extensions is defined.

TFPImageBitmap is the direct ancestor of *TBitmap*. The only new routine made available by this class is *IsFileExtensionSupported*, which checks whether the class knows the extension. *TFPImageBitmap* is derived from *TCustomBitmap*. This intermediate class has two new properties. These are a bitmap Handle for the *LCLIntf API* (based on the Windows API) and *Monochrome*.

The latter is a boolean property indicating whether the *TRasterImage.PixelFormat* of the bitmap is *pf1bit* (meaning it has a single bit size). *TCustomBitmap* is derived from *TRasterImage:*

```
TCustomBitmap = class(TRasterImage)
  private   // ... omitted
  public    // ... shortened
    property Handle: HBITMAP read GetBitmapHandle
                             write SetBitmapHandle;
                            // for custombitmap handle = bitmaphandle
    property HandleType: TBitmapHandleType read GetHandleType
                                           write SetHandleType;
    property Monochrome: Boolean read GetMonochrome
                                 write SetMonochrome;
  end;

TFPImageBitmap = class(TCustomBitmap)
  protected  // ... omitted
  public     // ... shortened
    class function IsFileExtensionSupported(const FileExtension:
                                                  string): boolean;
  end;

TBitmap = class(TFPImageBitmap)
  protected  // ... omitted
  public
    class function GetFileExtensions: string; override;
    procedure LoadFromStream(AStream: TStream; ASize: Cardinal);
                                                          override;
  end;
```

The other graphical formats *TPixmap*, *TPortableNetworkGraphic* and *TPortableAnyMapGraphic* have no extra properties or functions compared to *TBitmap* and they are used in exactly the same way. For PNG graphics it is not even possible to select the compression. The three other classes are descendants of *TFPImageBitmap* like *TBitmap.*

9.3.4 TJpegImage

JPEG is a standardized graphical format. The actual format named JFIF is useable not only for static images, but is used in video formats too. As in Delphi and other development environments, the JPG support in Free Pascal and Lazarus is based on the routines from the Independent JPEG Group.
The class itself is derived from *TFPImageBitmap*, so everything we discussed about class that applies here too. Apart from the *TBitmap* functions you can also control the compression when loading or saving to a file or a stream.

```
TFPJPEGCompressionQuality = 1..100; // 100=best quality, 25=moderate quality
TJPEGReadPerformance = (jpBestQuality, jpBestSpeed);

TJPEGQualityRange = TFPJPEGCompressionQuality;
TJPEGPerformance  = TJPEGReadPerformance;

TJPEGImage = class(TFPImageBitmap)
private
  // ... omitted
protected
  // ... omitted
public
  constructor Create; override;
  class function GetFileExtensions: String; Override;
                                                   // see TFPImageBitmap
public
  property CompressionQuality: TJPEGQualityRange read FQuality
                                                 write FQuality;
  property GrayScale: Boolean read FGrayScale;
  property ProgressiveEncoding: boolean read FProgressiveEncoding;
  property Performance: TJPEGPerformance read FPerformance
                                         write FPerformance;
end;
```

The properties *CompressionQuality* and *ProgressiveEncoding* only apply for writing, and Performance applies when reading. *CompressionQuality* accepts values of 0 to 100 (percent). The higher its value, the better the image quality. *ProgressiveEncoding* performs a compression in multiple stages.

This results in displaying a low quality overview first, with improving quality as loading progresses. This is often used in websites, which is the intended use of this feature. *Performance* is a measure of the speed in loading and displaying the file. The best quality is attained with *jpBestQuality*. This will continue reading until the best quality is reached. *jpBestSpeed* will decompress the data faster, at the price of possible loss in quality.
The next example shows how a JPEG image is written.

It first creates a JPEG image, then paints a blue triangle on a black background and then writes the data into the selected file. The image quality is set with a *TTrackBar*:

```
procedure TfrmDraw.btnDrawJPEGClick(Sender: TObject);
  var jpeg       : TJPEGImage;
      Points     : array[0..2] of TPoint;
      SaveDialog: TSaveDialog;
begin
  jpeg        := TJPEGImage.Create;
  SaveDialog := TSaveDialog.Create(NIL);
  try
   // Draws a blue triangle on a black background:
    jpeg.Width  := 100;
    jpeg.Height := 100;
    jpeg.Canvas.Brush.Color := clBlue;
    Points[0]   := Point(50, 25);
    Points[1]   := Point(25, 75);
    Points[2]   := Point(75, 75);
    jpeg.Canvas.Polygon(Points);

   // prepares the SaveDialog and the compression configuration
    SaveDialog.DefaultExt := 'jpg';
    jpeg.CompressionQuality := trackJPEG.Position;

   // Write the file:
    if SaveDialog.Execute then
      jpeg.SaveToFile(SaveDialog.FileName);
  finally
    jpeg.Free;             // Free ...
    SaveDialog.Free;       // ... the objects
  end;
end;
```

9.3.5 Icons

While most classes in Lazarus are similar to their Delphi counterparts, this is not true for *TIcon*. While Delphi's *TIcon* can only contain one image, the Lazarus version of *TIcon* includes all the image variants available in the icon file. Each platform has its own icon format. In Windows they are files with extension `.ico`, in MacOS X they are called *.icns*. A *TIcnsIcon* class is available for this in Lazarus. The typical Unix icons in pixmap format are handled by the class *TPixmap*.

The programmer normally does not have to work with these base classes, because the LCL uses *TIcon* everywhere where an icon is required, automatically converting the image to the right format.

The structure of *TIcon* is derived from *TRasterImage*, just like *TBitmap* and the other LCL image classes. This means the image has a canvas, a pixel format and a size.

Although *TIcon* is actually a container with more than one image, these properties refer to the currently selected image.

When loading, the largest or most colourful image is selected as the current one, the others can be accessed by changing the value of property *Current. Current* is a zero-based index to the selected image. The property *Count* gives the number of images in the icon file and the methods *Add* and *Delete* can be used to add or delete icons. Other important *TIcon* methods are *Clear* to *delete* all images,
and *GetDescription* for a quick check of the basic properties of a selected image.
This latter method takes the index of the image as a parameter and returns its height, width and pixel format.
A suitable image for a given image size can be found with *GetBestindexForSize*.
The desired size is given in a parameter of type TSize.

```
property Current: Integer read FCurrent write SetCurrent;
property Count: Integer read GetCount;
procedure Add(AFormat: TPixelFormat; AHeight, AWidth: Word);
procedure Delete(Aindex: Integer);
procedure Clear; Override;
procedure GetDescription(Aindex: Integer; out AFormat: TPixelFormat;
                         out AHeight, AWidth: Word);
function GetBestIndexForSize(ASize: TSize): Integer;
```

The following listing shows a routine that displays all of an icon's images in a window:

```
procedure TForm1.Button1Click(Sender: TObject);
  var Ico: TIcon;                    // a named variable
      i, j, k, x, y: Integer;        // various counting variables
begin
  with OpenPictureDialog1 do
  begin
    Filter := 'Icon (*.ico)|*.ico';      // restrict file selection to icons
    Options := [ofEnableSizing, ofViewDetail, ofReadOnly];
    // ensure read-only option is set
  end;

  if OpenPictureDialog1.Execute then
  begin
    Caption := 'Icon Viewer: '
       + ExtractFileName(OpenPictureDialog1.FileName);
    // The icon images are shown as TImage controls inside a panel
    // Ensure we remove any images from a previous icon

    while Panel2.ComponentCount > 0 do
      Panel2.Components[0].Free;
    Ico := TIcon.Create;
```

```
try
  Ico.Width  := 256;                                    // use preset size for the base icon
  Ico.Height := 256;
  Ico.LoadFromFile(OpenPictureDialog1.FileName);
  x := 10;                                              // left coordinate of each image
  y := 0;                                               // default window height

  if Ico.Count > -1 then                                // Check if there are images in the icon
    for i := 0 to Ico.Count - 1 do                      // All Icons in the file
      with TImage.Create(Panel2) do                     // the unnamed TImage is dynamic,
      begin                                             // so access using With
        Parent   := Panel2;                             // image shown on the panel
        Enabled  := True;                               // and enabled
        AutoSize := False;                              // size to fit
        Top      := 25;                                 // Leave space above for the text
        Left     := x;                                  // X is used to calculate the left pos
        Ico.Current := i;                               // current icon in the file
        Picture.Bitmap.Height := Ico.Height; // image and component
        Picture.Bitmap.Width  := Ico.Width;  //...
        Height   := Ico.Height;                         // share the same size!
        Width    := Ico.Width;

        if Height > y then
          y := Height;                                  // adjust window height
        for j := 0 to Ico.Width do                      // all pixels of current
          for k := 0 to Ico.Height do                   // image are sent
            Picture.Bitmap.Canvas.Pixels[j, k]:= Ico.Canvas.Pixels[j, k];
        Show;     // Show the image

        if CheckBox1.Checked then

        // view the image size in a label over the image:
          with TLabel.Create(Panel2) do
          begin // unnamed dynamic label
            Caption    := Format('%dx%d', [Ico.Width,Ico.Height]);
            Autosize   := True;
            Parent     := Panel2;
            Left       := x;
            Top        := 5;
            Show;
          end;

        x := x + Ico.Width + 10;    // Increase the left position

      end; {with TImage....}

    Ico.Free;                                           // Make sure that the icon is freed

    if Width < x + 10 then
      Width := x + 10;                                  // Adjusts the width of the form

    if Height < y + 50 + Panel1.Height then
      Height := y + 50 + Panel1.Height;                 // Corrects the form height

  end; { if OpenPictureDialog1..}
end;
```

After loading an icon file, this program will dynamically create a *TIcon*, containing all the image data. As we don't know in advance how many images have to be displayed, the icon is not in a *TImage*. If there is at least one icon in the file, the program will iterate over all images. For each of the contained images, a *TImage* is created. Please keep in mind that:

- The image is created dynamically and it does not have a name. Therefore it can only be accessed in a loop, using the with operator.
- The size of the contained bitmap and the image control need to be set. To do this the current icon's data is read from the file.
- The icon data in the image bitmap is processed pixel by pixel in a loop. The canvases of both components are used for that.

The rest of the program is mainly cosmetic, like erasing previously displayed symbols and text when the *OpenPictureDialog* is called again. This does lead to a complication in Lazarus. If we try to erase the labels in a for loop:

```
for i = 0 to Panel2.ComponentCount-1 do begin
  if (Panel2.Components[i] is TLabel) or
     (Panel2.Components[i] is TImage) then Panel2.Components[i].Free;
```

Everything seems to look correct at first. But this would lead to a list error. The reason is, the internal component index will change after erasing the first element. The loop would start deleting element 0, and as a result of this all elements immediately (!) shift one position down. Our loop does not know about that, so it would continue deleting element 1 (which used to be #2) etcetera. When it is halfway through the operation it will have reached the end of the list and the next attempt will result in an error.

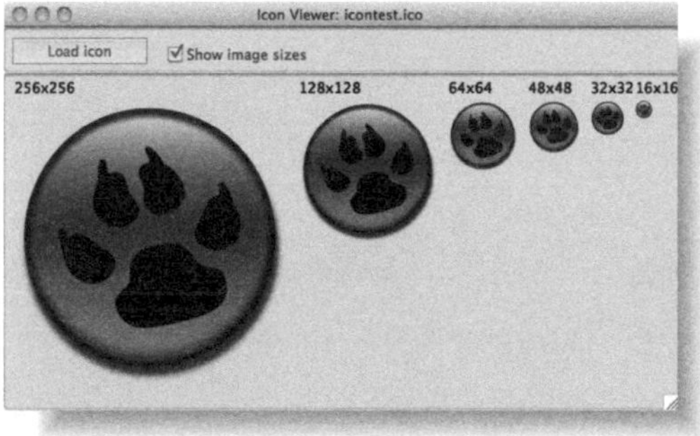

Figure 9.6: The different icons present in one of the icon files that come with Lazarus

In this case we can solve the problem by using a while loop

```
while Panel2.ComponentCount > 0 do Panel2.Components[0].Free;
```

However, this will only work if we want to remove all the control elements of a parent. Accessing the elements in a for loop is only possible if the number of elements is not changing while we are in the loop!

Chapter 10
Processes and threads

By Felipe Monteiro de Carvalho

In all modern operating systems it is possible to run multiple programs at the same time. On multiprocessor systems and multicore-PCs programs can actually run concurrently. On single processor systems they only appear to do so, by means of the scheduler modern operating systems incorporate to handle the division of CPU time between running processes.

Windows, MacOS X and the modern Unix derivatives all allow pre-emptive multitasking. In a 32-bit operating system the maximum amount of memory that can be assigned to a single process is 4 Gbytes. This limitation is imposed by the 32-bit address bus, which can address exactly 232 bytes = 4,294,967,296 bytes = 4,194,304 kbytes = 4,096 Mbytes = 4 Gbytes. This memory has to be requested as needed – it is not immediately available to the process. This address space has to store not only the program itself, but also its data, its resources and any loaded libraries.

The process itself does not know about a forced context change. Each process thinks it is the only one running in the CPU. This means that each context change is quite costly since all the current process information has to be saved, and all the other process's information has to be restored, before that process can continue to run.

It seems like a good idea to create more than one process for a complex program, because while a process is waiting for user response another process can meanwhile be doing some other needed task such as saving data in the background. For this reason a process is often split into small independent parts, called *threads*. Each process has at least one thread. All the threads of one process share a common address space (in contrast to the different processes running in the operating system in different address spaces). All threads together can use this common storage area. Of course we have to be very careful when we access this common memory, because synchronization problems may arise. It is assumed that threads have a cooperative character and can access their common memory without restrictions.
Each process can tell the operating system how it should respond to errors. Possible errors are critical errors, protected memory access violations, and failure to open a requested file.
One process is not allowed to access the address space of another process. The operating system monitors this. But sometimes processes need to exchange data. How then can they do that? For this purpose the operating system offers so-called *kernel objects*.
The kernel is the lowest level of the operating system, responsible for task-scheduling and other system operations. Because the operating system has control over all processes, it is in a position to organise synchronization and communication between processes.

Each process or thread is represented by a kernel object. Because each process has at least one thread, communication always takes place between the threads of the processes involved. To make communication possible, the kernel makes use of special objects, the so-called synchronization objects. The main multitasking objects are:

- Process objects
- Thread objects
- Mutex objects
- Semaphore objects
- Event objects

10.1 Processes

A process can create other processes. Because a process is considered an independent program under Windows, MacOS X and Unix/Linux, this means a program has to call another program to create a new process instance. To do this, the operating system initializes the necessary kernel objects and makes available an individual address space. Particularly under Windows there are several convenient methods to start new processes. The most complex one of these is offered by the *CreateProcess API*. Its encapsulation in Pascal looks like this:

```
function CreateProcess(
           lpApplicationName    : PChar;
           lpCommandLine        : PChar;
           lpProcessAttributes,
           lpThreadAttributes   : PSecurityAttributes;
           bInheritHandles      : Bool;
           dwCreationFlags      : DWord;
           lpEnvironment        : Pointer;
           lpCurrentDirectory   : PChar;
           const lpStartupInfo : TStartupInfo;
           var lpProcessInformation : TProcessInformation) : Bool;
                                                            StdCall;
```

Lazarus offers a wrapper called *TProcess* for this Win32 API function. This directly controls calling new programs. As can be seen from the definition with its many options, we can influence the start of a new program in many ways, but thanks to the LCL wrapping, most of that need not concern us.
The *TProcess* component has many properties, most of which correspond to the arguments of the *CreateProcess* Windows API function.

A short description of these properties follows:

- *Active:* If this boolean property is *True*, the program will be executed with the specified options. This corresponds to calling the *Execute* method.
  If the property is *False*, a running application is ended.

- *ApplicationName*: This string property contains the exact name of the program to be executed in the syntax required by Windows. Windows does not search for the program to be executed in the path. If a complete path is not given it only searches the current directory. It is not necessary to specify an extension – Windows assumes this will be .exe by default. This property can also be left empty.
An example is `C:\Windows\notepad.exe`.

- *CommandLine*: This property contains the command-line as it will be seen by the application. It consists of the program name, followed by any options to be transferred to the program. Windows searches for the program to be executed in the path. If it is empty the *ApplicationName* property is used instead.
An example is `notepad process.pas`.

- *ConsoleTitle*: If the application is a console program this string will be used as the title of its console window. If this is empty the name of the executable program will be used as the window title.

- *CurrentDirectory*: This string property specifies the starting directory for the process. If set, the starting directory of the program will be set to this value.
If it is not set, the current directory of the calling process will be used.

- *DeskTop*: In Windows NT (and possibly also in Windows 2000) this is the name of the desktop where the application's initial window will be shown.

- *Environment*: A list of *Name=Value* pairs, which will be used as environment variables for the new process. If the list is empty, the environment of the current process will be used.

- *FillAttribute*: The initial foreground and background colours of the application's console. This option can only be used if the value *suoUseFillAttributes* has been entered in *StartupOption*. More information about this option can be found in the help for the *STARTUPINFO* record in the Win32 API Reference.

- *InheritHandles*: If *True*, the new application will inherit all (file) handles of the current application. If *False* a new set of handles will be created.

- *Options*: A set of options each of which can be either on or off.
Details about these will be explained later.

- *Priority*: The scheduling priority for the process to be created.
The standard value is *ppNormal*, other values are *ppHigh*, *ppIdle* and *ppRealTime*.

- *StartUpOptions*: This controls which window properties will be in effect when the application is launched. If an option is included the corresponding property will be in effect.

- *ShowWindow*: Determines how the window of the created process will be displayed. The values are self-explanatory. This property will be ignored if *StartupOptions* does not contain the value *suoUseWindow*.

- *WindowColumns* and *WindowRows*: For a console application these values determine the number of lines and columns in the console buffer. This property is ignored unless *StartupOptions* contains the value *WindowHeight* and *WindowWidth*.

- *WindowHeight* and *WindowWidth*: Determines the initial window's height and width (in pixels). *StartupOptions* has to include the value *suoUseSize* for this to be effective.

- *WindowLeft*, *WindowTop*: Sets the initial window's top left position (in pixels). It is ignored if *StartupOptions* does not contain the value *suoUsePosition*.

When all properties have been set, the external program can be called with the component's *Execute* method.

Option	Affects the Properties
suoUseShowWindow	ShowWindow
suoUseSize	WindowHeight, WindowWidth
suoUsePosition	WindowTop, WindowLeft
suoUseCountChars	WindowColumns, WindowRows
suoUseFillAttributeFill	Attribute

Table 10.1: Effect of the StartupOptions Flags

The property *Options* controls what happens when the process is started. This property is a set containing one or more of the following elements:

- *poRunSuspended*: When a process is created, it will be in a suspended state; this means the program is not running until it receives a *Resume* command. This command is sent to the process by the method *TProcess.Resume*. This option cannot be combined with the option *poWaitOnExit*.

- *poWaitOnExit*: If the *Execute* method is called after the process has been created, it will wait until the process ends by calling the method *WaitOnExit*. This method cannot be used together with the option *poRunSuspended*.

- *poUsePipes*: The standard input/output file descriptors of the newly created program will be redirected to pipes.

- *poStderrToOutPut*: When pipes are created, the same pipe will be used for the standard error and the standard output file descriptor. This will make it possible to read both standard output and standard error from the same stream.

- *poNoConsole*: For console applications: the created process will not be allowed access to the console of the calling application. This option should be used with pipes. It cannot be used together with the option *poNewConsole*.

- *poNewConsole*: Create a new console for the process to be created. This option cannot be used together with the option *poNoConsole*.

- *poDefaultErrorMode*: Not the error mode of the calling process, but the creation of a new error mode. For more information about this option see the reference to the *CreateProcess* function.

- *poNewProcessGroup*: Create a new process group. For more information about this option see the reference to the *CreateProcess* function.
- *poDebugProcess*: If the current process is a debugger, this option allows receiving debug events from the process to be created.

- *poDebugOnlyThisProcess*: If the current process is being debugged, the default behaviour is to debug a process created by *CreateProcess* as well. This option prevents this from happening, so the new process will not be debugged.

In addition, the following published properties can be examined while the process is running, or after it has ended.

- *IsRunning*: indicates whether the process is still running or has ended.
- *ProcessInformation*: the process information as returned by Windows.
- *Handle*: the handle of the newly created process. (This is a process information record).
- *ExitStatus*: gives the return status of the process after it has ended.
- *ThreadHandle*: returns the handle of the main thread of the process. This handle is available for suspending, resuming or ending the process. (This is a process information record).

If the option *poUsePipes* was included in the property *TProcess.Options* new streams will be created for the standard input, output and standard error of the new process:

- *Input*: A stream descendant for writing to the input file of the newly created process. It is important to release the stream after sending information, otherwise the process will not be able to detect an end of file condition.

- *Output*: A stream descendant for reading the data the newly created process writes to its standard output file.

- *StdErr*: A stream descendant for reading the data the newly created process writes to its standard error file.

If the constant *poStdErrToOutput* is included in *Options*, *Output* and *StdErr* will be sent to the same stream.

Please note the newly created process will have to use the standard handles for accessing its standard input, output and error files. If the process does not use these file descriptors, reading or writing the pipe streams will be blocked for the calling process. Delphi-generated programs do not use these standard file descriptors for their input and output files, whereas Free Pascal-generated console applications do.
These standard file descriptors can be acquired with the following calls:

```
  var StdInputHandle, StdOutputHandle, StdErrorHandle: INTEGER;
begin
  StdInputHandle  := GetStdHandle(STD_INPUT_HANDLE);
  StdOutputHandle := GetStdHandle(STD_OUTPUT_HANDLE);
  StdErrorHandle  := GetStdHandle(STD_ERROR_HANDLE);
end;
```

With these handles you can create a *THandleStream*, or you can call the file handling routines from the *SysUtils* unit.

Method	Description
Execute	Creates and then runs the process with the parameters described in the respective properties. If the call to *CreateProcess* fails, an exception will be raised. If the option *poWaitOnExit* is activated, the caller application will remain stopped in the call to *Execute* until the created process finishes.
Suspend	Increases the suspend counter of the running process. The function returns this number as a result and if it is different from zero, the created process will be stopped.
Resume	Decreases the suspend counter of the running process. The function returns this number as a result and if it is zero, the created process will be resumed.
Terminate(AExitCode: Integer)	This function terminates the execution of the Process. It closes with the exit *code AExitCode*. The function returns True if successful, *False* otherwise.
WaitOnExit	This call will wait and only return when the created process ends. This function will return a boolean value indicating whether it was successful or not. A failure in this function under Windows will most likely be caused by a problem in the call to *WaitForSingleObject*, while on UNIXes it will most likely be caused by a problem in the call to *fpWaitPid*.

Table 10.2: The methods of TProcess

The public methods and functions of the *TProcess* component are summarized in Table 10.2. This is a very versatile component, but also a very complex one, so we will summarize all relevant definitions once again:

```
type
  TProcessOption = (poRunSuspended,      poWaitOnExit,
                    poUsePipes,          poStderrToOutPut,
                    poNoConsole,         poNewConsole,
                    poDefaultErrorMode, poNewProcessGroup,
                    poDebugProcess,      poDebugOnlyThisProcess);

  TShowWindowOptions = (swoNone, swoHIDE, swoMaximize, swoMinimize,
            swoRestore, swoShow, swoShowDefault, swoShowMaximized,
                  swoShowMinimized, swoshowMinNOActive, swoShowNA,
                               swoShowNoActivate, swoShowNormal);

  TStartupOption = (suoUseShowWindow, suoUseSize, suoUsePosition,
                          suoUseCountChars, suoUseFillAttribute);

  TProcessPriority = (ppHigh, ppIdle, ppNormal, ppRealTime);

  TProcessOptions = set of TProcessOption;
  TStartupOptions = set of TStartupOption;


type
  TProcess = Class(TComponent)
  private // omitted
  protected // omitted
  public
    constructor Create (AOwner : TComponent); Override;
    destructor Destroy; Override;
    procedure Execute; Virtual;
    procedure CloseInput; Virtual;
    procedure CloseOutput; Virtual;
    procedure CloseStderr; Virtual;
    function Resume: Integer; Virtual;
    function Suspend: Integer; Virtual;
    function Terminate(AExitCode: Integer): Boolean; Virtual;
    function WaitOnExit: Boolean;
    property WindowRect: TRect Read GetWindowRect
                               Write SetWindowRect;
    property Handle: THandle Read FProcessHandle;
    property ProcessHandle: THandle Read FProcessHandle;
    property ThreadHandle: THandle Read FThreadHandle;
    property ProcessID: Integer Read FProcessID;
    property ThreadID: Integer Read FThreadID;
    property Input: TOutputPipeStream Read FInputStream;
    property Output: TInputPipeStream Read FOutputStream;
    property Stderr: TinputPipeStream Read FStderrStream;
    property ExitStatus: Integer Read GetExitStatus;
    property InheritHandles: Boolean Read FInheritHandles
                                     Write FInheritHandles;
```

```
  published
    property Active: Boolean Read GetRunning Write SetActive;
    property ApplicationName: String Read FApplicationName
                              Write SetApplicationName;
    property CommandLine: String Read FCommandLine Write FCommandLine;
    property ConsoleTitle: String Read FConsoleTitle
                              Write FConsoleTitle;
    property CurrentDirectory: String Read FCurrentDirectory
                              Write FCurrentDirectory;
    property Desktop: String Read FDesktop Write FDesktop;
    property Environment: TStrings Read Fenvironment
                              Write SetEnvironment;
    property Options: TProcessOptions Read FProcessOptions
                               Write SetProcessOptions;
    property Priority: TProcessPriority Read FProcessPriority
                              Write FProcessPriority;
    property StartupOptions: TStartupOptions Read FStartupOptions
                              Write FStartupOptions;
    property Running: Boolean Read GetRunning;
    property ShowWindow: TShowWindowOptions Read FShowWindow
                              Write SetShowWindow;
    property WindowColumns: Cardinal Read dwXCountChars
                              Write SetWindowColumns;
    property WindowHeight: Cardinal Read dwYSize
                              Write SetWindowHeight;
    property WindowLeft: Cardinal Read dwX Write SetWindowLeft;
    property WindowRows: Cardinal Read dwYCountChars
                              Write SetWindowRows;
    property WindowTop: Cardinal Read dwY Write SetWindowTop;
    property WindowWidth: Cardinal Read dwXSize Write SetWindowWidth;
    property FillAttribute: Cardinal Read FFillAttribute
                              Write FFillAttribute;
end;
```

Although we have mentioned only Windows so far, this component can – as usual with Free Pascal – be used on all supported platforms. *TProcess* can also be used to manage the called program, which is not a trivial thing to do – after all, processes are supposed to be mutually independent. The method *WaitOnExit* is responsible for this. We are talking about synchronous calls here. Normal calls to external programs are much simpler, but those are always asynchronous. The calling program has no control over the child process.

Under Windows there are two families of API functions that can be used to start other programs. The routines from the shell API are the simplest to use. The basic function is called *ShellExecuteA* or *ShellExecuteW*:

```
function ShellExecuteA/W(hWnd: HWND;
                         Operation, FileName, Parameters,
                         Directory: Pchar; ShowCmd: Integer): HINST
```

An exciting feature of *ShellExecute* is its ability to do more than just run a program.

If we call this routine with the name of any data file as its parameter, the API will check which program file in the registry is linked to that extension, and will then load the program with the file as parameter. If no suitable program can be found for this filename extension the Windows shell asks the user to specify one - either just for now, or in future too. Nor are *ShellExecute's* capabilities limited to executing programs. It can also be used to open a directory in Windows Explorer, or send a file to the printer (see Table 10.3).

String	Description
open	The file in the *lpFile* parameter will be opened. This file can either be an executable or a document. It may also be a directory, in which case it will be displayed using Windows Explorer.
print	The file in the *lpFile* parameter will be printed. This file should be a document. If an executable is passed, it will be opened, just as if the open option had been selected.
explore	The contents of the folder specified by *lpFile* will be shown using the Windows Explorer.

Table 10.3: Strings for the parameter lpOperation of the ShellExecute function

The parameter *hWnd* is used to pass the parent window's handle. This parent window's handle is needed if an error message window (or any other window) has to be created by the application. *lpOperation* is a pointer to the null-terminated string indicating the operation to be executed. *lpFile* is a pointer to a null-terminated string referring to the file to be opened or printed or to the folder to be opened.

API Constant	Value	Description
	0	The Operating System has no more memory or resources available.
ERROR_FILE_NOT_FOUND	2	The given file was not found.
ERROR_PATH_NOT_FOUND	3	The given path was not found.
ERROR_BAD_FORMAT	11	The executable file (.exe) given is invalid (either it is not a Win32-exe, or it is corrupted).
SE_ERR_ACCESSDENIED	5	The operating system doesn't allow access to the given file. This error usually happens because the user does not have permission to access the file.
SE_ERR_ASSOCINCOMPLETE	27	The extension of the file name is incomplete or invalid.
SE_ERR_DDEBUSY	30	The DDE transaction could not be completed, because other DDE transactions were in progress.
SE_ERR_DDEFAIL	29	The DDE transaction failed.
SE_ERR_DDETIMEOUT	28	The DDE transaction could not be completed; a timeout occurred.
SE_ERR_DLLNOTFOUND	32	The selected DLL was not found.
SE_ERR_FNF	2	The selected file was not found.
SE_ERR_NOASSOC	31	No application associated with the specified file name extension was found.
SE_ERR_OOM	8	Insufficient memory was available to complete the operation.
SE_ERR_PNF	3T	he selected path was not found.
SE_ERR_SHARE	26	An access conflict was detected.

Table 10.4: Possible return values of the ShellExecute function (Windows only)

lpParameters is used to pass a pointer to a null-terminated string containing the parameter for an executable file. For documents a NIL should be passed. *lpDirectory* is a pointer to a string representing the standard directory for the calling application. If *lpFile* refers to an executable file, *nShowCmd* controls how this program will be displayed. For documents a 0 should be passed.
The following short program demonstrates how easy it is to use this function. It implements a classic `shellexec.exe` for Windows Cds:

```
program shellexec; { shellexec.lpr }
{$APPTYPE GUI}    (* Very important in this Program *)
{$mode Delphi}

(* direct import of API function saves space *)
function ShellExecute(HWND: LongInt;
                      lpOperation, lpFile, lpParameters, lpDirectory:
                      PChar; nShowCmd: Integer): LongInt; StdCall;
  External 'Shell32.dll' Name 'ShellExecuteA';

  var  s: String;
begin
  if ParamCount > 0 then
  begin
    s := ParamStr(1);
    (* only use ParamStr(1) – no parent handle or other information *)
    ShellExecute(0, 'open', PChar(s), nil, '', 0);
    Halt(0);          // No error analysis done – just quit the program
  end
  else
    Halt(1);          // No parameter given, so quit with error indication
end.
```

If we pass this program a file name on the command-line, or drop a data file on the executable program file, the associated program will be launched and – if the application allows it – immediately load the selected file.

API Constant	Value	Description
SW_HIDE	0	The window will be hidden and another one will be activated.
SW_MAXIMIZE	3	The window will be activated and maximized to occupy the screen.
SW_MINIMIZE	6	The window will be shown as an icon in the taskbar and the next window in the program z-order will be activated.
SW_RESTORE	9	The window will be activated and shown. If it was previously maximized, it will be maximized again, if not, then it will be shown with its previous size and position. This option should be used to restore minimized windows.
SW_SHOW	5	The window will be shown at its current position and size.
SW_SHOWDEFAULT	10	The window will be shown with the options specified in the *STARTUPINFO* record of the *CreateProcess* call which started the program, based on the SW_ flag. An application should set this flag when calling *ShowWindow*, to set the original show state.
SW_SHOWMAXIMIZED	3	The window will be activated and maximized to occupy the entire screen.
SW_SHOWMINIMIZED	2	The window will be activated and shown as an icon in the taskbar.
SW_SHOWMINNOACTIVE	7	The window will be shown as an icon in the taskbar. The currently active window remains active.
SW_SHOWNA	8	The window will be shown at its current position and size. The currently active window remains active.
SW_SHOWNOACTIVATE	4	The same as **SW_SHOWNA**
SW_SHOWNORMAL	1	The window will be activated and shown. If it is currently maximized or minimized, Windows restores its previous size and position before being maximized / minimized. An application should set this flag to show a window for the first time.

Table 10.5: Values for the nShowCmd parameter for the ShellExecute function (Windows only)

In addition to the *ShellExecute* function the shell API offers a function *ShellExecuteEx*, which takes fewer parameters. All data is transferred to it in a single structure, but it offers the same functionality.

Calling the associated program when a data file is clicked is a Windows-specific feature which cannot be ported to other platforms. To offer something like this on other platforms, you would have to create an initialization dialog similar to the one Windows offers for extensions that do not have a pre-defined file association.

Because *ShellExecute* is available only in Windows, programs that are intended to be platform-independent should not use it (or restrict its use by conditional compilation). However we don't have to work with *CreateProcess's* complex parameters

The *SysUtils* unit offers a simpler way to call other programs:

```
function ExecuteProcess(const Path: AnsiString;
                         const ComLine: AnsiString): Integer;
function ExecuteProcess(const Path: AnsiString;
                         const ComLine: array of AnsiString): Integer;
```

This is the preferred function to use, even in Windows, where it replaces the outdated *WinExec*, (which is no longer available in Vista or Win7). It starts the program specified in *Path* and transfers the parameters in *ComLine* to it. The function waits until the program has ended and then returns its Exitcode as return value. If just one string is passed in *ComLine* (the first variant shown above), the function will parse it for parameters with the usual separating and masking characters. If the program to be executed cannot be found, the function will throw an exception of type *EOSError*. This is declared in the `sysutilsh.inc` file as follows:

```
type  EOSError = class(Exception)
public
  ErrorCode: LongInt; // operating system error code.
end;
```

As you may have guessed from *ExecuteProcess's* parameter's name: *Path*, the program to start should be specified by its full path name, not just the name of the executable. In Linux and FreeBSD this is easy, as most programs reside in `/usr/bin` (Linux) or `/usr/local/bin` (FreeBSD) (we might even search these directories for the program name). In PC BSD it may be a bit more difficult, and in Windows it can be quite complex and unfeasible for generic applications. Specifying the complete path to the child application is a design requirement, since it reduces the chance of executing a Trojan. It is no use parsing the system variable *PATH* since in recent versions of Windows most programs will not be found by doing that.

10.2 Threads

Threads are the locations where a program is executed. If a program has more than one thread, it is able to execute several actions simultaneously. In a single processor system, each thread is allowed to execute during short time slots, giving the impression several actions are taking place at the same time. This strategy is called *timesharing*.
In multiprocessor systems it is possible for more than one thread to be actually running at the same time, but never more than there are CPUs in the system, of course.

There are several reasons for going to the trouble of creating multithreaded applications. One reason is to allow the user to continue working while a time-consuming task is being executed. Another reason can be the necessity to execute several processor-intensive activities at the same time in a way that makes use of all the resources of a multiprocessor system. One thread is always executed by one processor, so a single-threaded program is not able to make use of multiprocessor capabilities.

Using threads also has disadvantages, so we should always consider whether it brings sufficient advantages for the problem we wish multithreading to solve. Multithreaded applications are more difficult to debug, because the time it takes to perform a threaded activity will vary.

Every process has at least one thread, which will first execute the initialization of all units and then go to the beginning of the main program. This thread is called the *main thread.* The application ends when the main thread ends. It is the only thread able to call libraries that are not thread-safe.
All threads of the process share the same storage space, so they are all able to read and write the global variables. Each thread has its own stack and its own register image, so they also have their own local variables. This means that passing local variables to other threads can be problematic: they are no longer valid when the thread leaves the procedure where they were declared.

This is not a problem for reference-counted objects such as strings.

Unix systems have a very modular structure (in contrast to Windows which is monolithic) and many functions are not part of the initial installation, but are only added in later installations. This means we cannot be certain that a Unix system has all required resources installed. This is also true for the POSIX thread library, since it is not a basic requirement for running the operating system. Such extended functionality is installed by adding libraries to a Unix system as the need arises. So we must take care to have a suitable resource manager installed. In this case we need a thread manager. This is handled by linking the *cthreads* unit into your program. This will load the *pthreads* library in your program initialization.

To make this work, the *cthreads* unit has to be included before all the other units that make use of it. Here is an example uses clause:

```
program myproject;
  uses
    {$IFDEF UNIX}
  cthreads,
    {$ENDIF}
    //... other units are declared after cthreads
```

10.2.1 The TThread class

The Free Pascal *TThread* class represents an operating system thread. Before we can use it, we first have to make a derived class implementing the abstract *Execute* method.

Property	Description
procedure Resume;	Resumes the thread's execution.
procedure Suspend;	Suspends the thread.
procedure Terminate;	Signals to the thread that it should terminate.
procedure Synchronize(AMethod: TThreadMethod);	Executes *AMethod* in the main thread. *AMethod* should be of type procedure of object.
function WaitFor:	Integer;Waits for the thread to terminate and returns the exit status.
property FreeOnTerminate: Boolean; [rw]	Indicates whether the thread should free itself when it stops executing. The default value is *False*.
property Handle: TThreadID; [r]	Returns the thread handle.
property Priority: TThreadPriority; [rw]	Returns the thread priority.
property Suspended: Boolean; [rw]	Indicates whether the thread is suspended.
property OnTerminate: TNotifyEvent; [rw]	The event called when the thread terminates.

Table 10.6: The most important methods and properties of TThread

The code in the *Execute* method is executed when the thread is running. To create local storage for the thread, we can add fields to the derived class. When deriving a class from *TThread* we create a new thread, when releasing it we are releasing the thread. Some methods in *TThread* make it possible to wait for its termination. We can also indicate whether it should start immediately or only later. The property *Terminated* indicates it should be ended. This property is really only a flag and does not take any action. It is up to the code in the *Execute* method to check it from time to time. If *Terminated* is set, the thread should end.

Suspend and Resume

Although *TThread* offers the method *Suspend*, it should never be used! *Resume* on the other hand can be used to resume a thread that has been stopped (safely). But because *Suspend* should not be used, *Resume* is useless as well.

It is easy to explain why *Suspend* and *Resume* should not be used: *Suspend* is dangerous, because it can lead to race conditions because it does not let you control at what point the thread is stopped. It might very well be in a critical section, blocking other threads from using that section when they need it.

Therefore the POSIX standard does not offer ways to suspend a thread in a non-cooperative way. The result is that *Suspend* is not available in any Unix system. Windows does support *Suspend* completely, but we should not use it to prevent problems when we want to convert the program to a Unix platform.

Usually it is possible to use a variable to inform a thread it should halt instead of using *Suspend*. The target thread should check this variable from time to time and suspend itself when needed, until the variable tells it to resume again.

Priority

Threads can have different priorities. Threads with a high priority are more likely to get a chance to run and/or will get larger time slices than low-priority tasks. A typical example is to give I/O operations a higher priority than CPU-bound threads that merely perform calculations. Most of the time an I/O-bound thread is just waiting for an input or output operation to complete, hardly making use of any CPU capacity. For this reason it can be allowed a higher priority. This enables it to respond quickly and prepare for the next I/O operation. A purely CPU-bound thread with a high priority would consume most of the CPU capacity, blocking other tasks with a lower priority.
In general the use of multiple threads should be very well thought through to ensure you actually attain the benefit of the intended higher execution speed. Wrong decisions can have very negative effects on the performance. It may even be so difficult to test and fine-tune the priorities that the possible improvement is not worth all the effort it takes.

Constant	Description
tpIdle	Thread only runs when other processes are idle.
tpLowest	Thread runs at the lowest priority.
tpLower	Thread runs at a low priority.
tpNormal	Thread runs at normal priority.
tpHigher	Thread runs at high priority.
tpHighest	Thread runs at highest possible priority.
tpTimeCritical	Thread runs at real-time priority.

Table 10.7: Possible values for TThread.Priority

Synchronization and Critical Sections

The synchronization mechanism was introduced to allow the main thread to call different threads that may use libraries which are not thread-safe. To make this possible, the execution of the threads is suspended until the main thread has executed this code.
The LCL – like most GUI-libraries – is not thread-safe. Therefore all LCL-based code should be in the main thread or in synchronization blocks.

Considering a Critical Section – also known as a Mutex (Mutual exclusion) – is a good way of explaining the synchronization mechanism. When a thread wants to enter a Critical Section, it is suspended if there is already another thread within that section. This ensures the operation is completed and the result is available before another thread can enter the same critical section. The class *TCriticalSection*, which is located in the *SyncObjs* unit, offers two simple methods: *Enter* and *Leave*. The first one indicates the thread is entering a critical section, and prevents other tasks from entering until *Leave* has been called. The threads waiting to enter the critical section are sleeping and will automatically be woken by the operating system when it is their turn.

A thread can be stopped between any two machine code instructions when the operating system executes a task switch. This may even be in the middle of an Object Pascal instruction, as most instructions consist of more than one machine instruction.

MyVar might start with the value 0.

Now the first thread starts to run. It reads *MyVar* and adds 4 to that.
Now the operating system does a task switch. The second thread executes all the code.
It still reads *MyVar* as 0 and it adds 4 too.

So now *MyVar* equals 4, and the operating system switches back to the first thread, which also stores 4 in MyVar. The problem is that *MyVar* might also have become 8, if the first thread had not been stopped exactly at that point.
If more than two threads are running the problem can get even worse and like all timing problems it is very difficult to find out what is going on.
We can code this section differently to prevent this problem using a *TCriticalSection*.
The class is short and easy to understand:

```
type
  TWaitResult = (wrSignaled, wrTimeout, wrAbandoned, wrError);

  TSynchroObject = class(TObject)
    procedure Acquire; Virtual;
    procedure Release; Virtual;
  end;

TCriticalSection = class(TSynchroObject)
  private
    CriticalSection: TRTLCriticalSection;
  public
    procedure   Acquire; Override;
    procedure   Release; Override;
    procedure   Enter;
    procedure   Leave;
    constructor Create;
    destructor  Destroy; Override;
  end;
```

Critical sections are related to the typical problem of race conditions.
A *race condition* is a section of code which may produce different results, depending on the order in which it is executed by multiple threads.
This scenario is error-prone and often very difficult to debug.
Let's assume two threads execute the following code:

```
Local := MyVar;
Local := Local + 4;
MyVar := Local;
```

Time	Thread 1	Local	Thread 2	Local	MyVar
1	Local := MyVar;	0			0
2	Local := Local + 4;	4			0
3		4	Local := MyVar;	0	0
4		4	Local := Local + 4;	4	0
5		4	MyVar := Local;	4	4
6	MyVar := Local;	4			4

Table 10.8: A race condition between two tasks leads to an error

The critical section has to be global and is specific for the global variable accessed, which is why we call it *MyVarCS* here. Before the code can be executed, the variable has to be initialized by creating an instance of the *TCriticalSection* class:

```
MyVarCS.Enter;
try
  Local := MyVar;
  Local := Local + 4;
  MyVar := Local;
finally
  MyVarCS.Leave;
end;
```

This new code ensures there is never more than one thread in this code block. The `try...finally` construct is a safety measure, making sure the critical section will be released for other threads in case an exception occurs.

Time	Thread 1	Local (Thread1)	Thread 2	Local (Thread2)	MyVar
1	MyVarCS.Enter;	?			0
2	Local := MyVar;	0			0
3	Local := Local + 4;	4			0
4		4	MyVarCS.Enter;	?	0
5	MyVar := Local;	4		?	4
6	MyVarCS.Leave;	4	?		4
7			Local := MyVar;	4	4
8			Local := Local + 4;	8	4
9			MyVar := Local;	8	8
10			MyVarCS.Leave;	8	4

Table 10.9: The same calculation, stabilized with critical sections

Here is the complete, translatable version of the application with proper multi-threading. This code does the same as the above example and prints the value of *MyValue*, which is always 8, on the console. The result does not depend on the order in which the operating system executes the threads.

```
program criticalsection;
{$apptype console}
{$mode objfpc}{$H+}
uses {$IFDEF UNIX}
       cthreads,
     {$ENDIF}
       Classes, SyncObjs;

type TMyThread = class(TThread)
     public
       procedure Execute; override;
     end;

var  MyVar  : Cardinal;
     MyVarCS: TCriticalSection;
     Thread1, Thread2: TMyThread;

  procedure TMyThread.Execute;  (* The procedure being executed with a Critical Section *)
    var Local: Cardinal;
  begin
    MyVarCS.Enter;
    try
      Local := MyVar;
      Local := Local + 4;
      MyVar := Local;
    finally
      MyVarCS.Leave;
    end;
  end;

{ program criticalsection }
begin
  MyVar    := 0;                          (* Initializes MyVar          *)
  MyVarCS  := TCriticalSection.Create;    (* Creates the Critical Section *)
  Thread1  := TMyThread.Create(False);    (* Creates and       *)
  Thread2  := TMyThread.Create(False);    (* starts the threads *)
  Thread1.WaitFor;                        (* Waits until the threads *)
  Thread2.WaitFor;                        (* finish executing      *)
  Thread1.Free;                           (* Release the threads ... *)
  Thread2.Free;
  MyVarCS.Free;                           (* ... and the critical section *)
  WriteLn('MyVar = ', MyVar);             (* Show the result on screen *)
end.
```

Chapter 11
Network Programming

by Inoussa Ouedraogo

TCP/IP is a network protocol that allows two computer programs (whether running on the same computer or on different computers) to communicate with each other. Usually the protocol is used in a client-server communication scheme. This allows a server process to listen and respond to clients requests, the client processes usually being located on different computers.

The listings in this chapter are too long to be printed. They will be included in the downloadable code that belongs to this book.

The code will be provided by our website at
`www.blaisepascal.eu`

11.1 TCP/IP programming

This chapter presents a simple guide to TCP client and server programming. The code has been simplified to highlight just the essential points. So no full error checking is done as it needs to be in actual production-quality professional software.

The **Synapse** sockets library will be used as the base TCP library. This library can be downloaded for free from this address:
`http://www.ararat.cz/synapse/`

The complete source code of the chapter is provided in the `tcp` sub-folder of the `sources` folder of the disk accompanying this book.

In a TCP/IP network, every computer is uniquely identified by its IP address. A server process running on a computer listens for clients' requests on a specified port. A TCP port is identified by a positive integer. Only one server process can listen on a given port at a time. A client process is then able to open a connection to a server process given the server computer's IP address and the port number the server process is listening on.
In this chapter we will build a simple server process that listens on port 1234 in order to provide simple integer calculation functionality (Add, Subtract, Multiply and Divide) to its clients. So a client request will have to specify both what the desired numerical operation is, and provide appropriate numerical arguments to be operated on. We start by defining a data structure to represent this client request:

```
<Code ID = 1>
 TIntType   = ShortInt;
 TChar = ansichar;

 TCalcRequest = packed record
   Operation: TChar;
   ArgumentA: TIntType;
   ArgumentB: TIntType;
 end;
</Code>
```

and another data structure to represent the server's response:

```
<Code ID = 2>
 TCalcResponse = packed record
   Operation: TChar;
   ArgumentA: TIntType;
   ArgumentB: TIntType;
   ResultArg: TIntType;
 end;
</Code>
```

The response data structure includes the query's items and the *ResultArg* that holds the result of the computation. Interaction between the server and the client occurs as follows:

1. The server listens for client connections
2. A client connects to the server
3. The client sends a buffer stream representing its request *TCalcRequest* to the server
4. The server reads the buffer stream into a request variable *TCalcRequest*
5. The server performs the computation and stores the request's data and the result of the computation to the result variable *TCalcResponse*
6. The server returns the result variable to the client
7. The client reads and displays the result
8. The client disconnects from the server

The sequence of actions from (3) to (7) can be repeated as needed by the client. The required data structures are defined in the file `service_intf.pas`.

```
unit service_intf;

{$mode objfpc}{$H+}

interface

type

   TIntType = ShortInt;
   TChar = ansichar;

   TCalcRequest = packed record
      Operation: Char;
      ArgumentA: TIntType;
      ArgumentB: TIntType;
   end;

   TCalcResponse = packed record
      Operation: Char;
      ArgumentA: TIntType;
      ArgumentB: TIntType;
      ResultArg: TIntType;
   end;

implementation

end.
```

11.1.1 The Client program

The client program is a simple one that takes two operands and an operator to do the calculation and print the result. An execution session and the program's code are shown below.

```
<Session ID = 1>
      E:\book\tcp\client>client.exe
      Client demo program.
        Enter first operand ( -120 < x < 120 ) : 12
        Enter second operand ( -120 < x < 120 ) : 10
        Enter operator ( +, -, *, / ) : +
          12 + 10 = 22

        Continue (y/n) ? : y
        Enter first operand ( -120 < x < 120 ) : 12
        Enter second operand ( -120 < x < 120 ) : 10
        Enter operator ( +, -, *, / ) : -
          12 - 10 = 2

        Continue (y/n) ? : n
</Session>
```

11.1.1 The Client program

```
<Code ID = 3>
 1  program client;
 2  {$mode objfpc}{$H+}
 3  uses
 4     Classes, SysUtils,
 5     service_intf, client_imp;
 6  var
 7     a, b, c: TIntType;
 8     op: Char;
 9     s: string;
10  begin
11     InitConnection();
12     try
13     WriteLn('Client demo program.');
14     while True do begin
15        Write('Enter first operand ( -120 < x < 120 ) : ');
16        ReadLn(a);
17        Write('Enter second operand (  -120 < x < 120 ) : ');
18        ReadLn(b);
19        Write('Enter operator ( +, -, *, / ) : ');
20        ReadLn(op);
21        if ( op in ['+', '-', '*', '/'] ) and
22          not ( ( op = '/' ) and ( b = 0 ) )
23          then begin
24          c := Compute(a,b,op);
25          WriteLn();
26          WriteLn( '    ', a, ' ', op, ' ', b, ' = ', c);
27        end else begin
28          WriteLn('Wrong arguments and/or operation.');
29        end;
30        WriteLn('');
31        Write('Continue (y/n) ? : '); ReadLn(s);
32        if ( UpperCase(s) <> 'Y' ) then
33          Break;
34        WriteLn();
35     end;
36     finally
37     CloseConnection();
38     end;
39  end.
</Code>
```

The code starts by preparing and opening the connection to the server (line 11) and finishes by closing the connection (line 37). The connection is a global variable *SocketCnx* declared in `client_imp.pas`. The routines that open and close the connection, namely *InitConnection* and *CloseConnection*, can also be found in the `client_imp.pas` file. *InitConnection* simply checks if the connection has been established, and if not it creates the connection and initializes it.

```
<Code ID = 4>
var
  SocketCnx: TTCPBlockSocket = nil;

procedure InitConnection();
var
  cnx: TTCPBlockSocket;
begin
  if ( SocketCnx = nil ) then begin
    cnx := TTCPBlockSocket.Create();
    try
      cnx.RaiseExcept := True;
      cnx.Connect(SERVER_ADDRESS, IntToStr(SERVER_PORT));
      SocketCnx := cnx;
    except
      on e : Exception do begin
        cnx.Free();
        raise;
      end;
    end;
  end;
end;
</Code>
```

The connection details of serialization, communication with the server, and deserialization are handled at "line 24 code ID 3" by the Compute routine which is defined in the file `client_imp.pas`.

```
<Code ID = 5>
function Compute(
         const A,B: TIntType;
         const AOp: Char
         ): TIntType;
var
  RequestBuffer: TCalcRequest;
  ResponseBuffer: TCalcResponse;
  cnx: TTCPBlockSocket;
  bufferLen: Integer;
begin
  RequestBuffer.ArgumentA := A;
  RequestBuffer.ArgumentB := B;
  RequestBuffer.Operation := AOp;
  cnx := SocketCnx;
  cnx.SendBuffer(@RequestBuffer,SizeOf(RequestBuffer));
  cnx.ExceptCheck();
  bufferLen := cnx.RecvBufferEx(
       @ResponseBuffer,SizeOf(ResponseBuffer),100 );
  cnx.ExceptCheck();
  if ( bufferLen <> SizeOf(ResponseBuffer) ) then
    raise Exception.Create('Invalid server response.');
  Result := ResponseBuffer.ResultArg;
end;
</Code>
```

The Compute routine executes instructions in the following order:
1. the request buffer is filled (lines 11-13)
2. the request buffer is sent to the server (line 15) and checked for error(s) (line 16)
3. the response buffer sent by the server is read (lines 17-18) and checked for error(s) (line 19)
4. the received buffer length is compared to the size of the response size and if it does not match an exception is raised (line 21)
5. finally the function's result is filled with the server's response *ResultArg* (line 22)

Compiling the client code

The chapter's source code is organized in three folders:
- `client`: this folder contains the client-specific code;
- `shared`: the shared folder contains the code shared between the client and the server, mainly the interface unit, `service_intf.pas`, that defines the data structures passed between the client and the server;
- `server`: this folder contains the server-specific code.

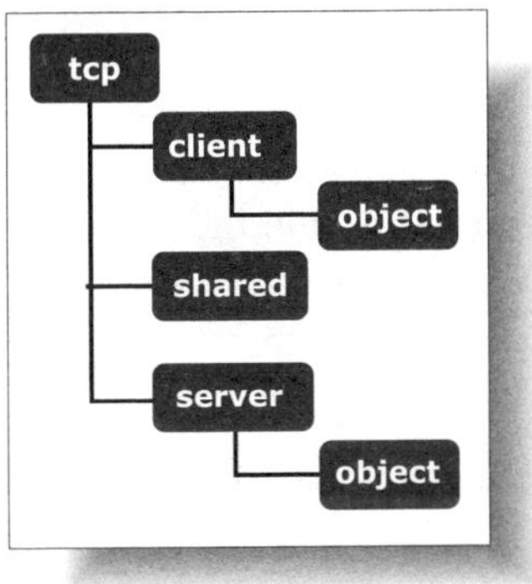

Figure 11.1 Overview of the structure

The `client` folder contains a single Lazarus project file `client.lpi`. You need to download and install the **Synapse** library (by unpacking the `synapse.zip` file to a specified folder) before you can compile the project. The Synapse library is available freely from `http://www.ararat.cz/synapse/`. You also need to update your project's unit search folder to include the ...`\synapseXYZ\source\lib\` folder, where the `XYZ` of `\synapseXYZ\` needs to be changed to the appropriate version number of the Synapse release you have downloaded.

11.1.2 The server program

The server program listens on a defined port for clients' connections and requests. The socket library we are using – Synapse – uses a blocking algorithm, so every client needs to be handled in its own dedicated thread. The server process has a listening thread that is waiting for a client connection request. Once a client requests a connection, the server listening thread creates a thread that will handle that client exclusively. The server program's code is presented below:

11.1.2 The server program

<Code ID = 6>

```
program tcp_server;
{$mode objfpc}{$H+}
uses
   Classes, SysUtils,
   service_intf, server_imp;
var
   serverThread: TServerListnerThread;
begin
   WriteLn('Starting the server listening thread ...');
   serverThread :=
      TServerListnerThread.Create('vmwinxp',1234);
   WriteLn('Listening on port # 1234');
   WriteLn('Hit <enter> to stop.');
   ReadLn;
   WriteLn('Terminating ...');
   serverThread.Terminate();
   Sleep(500);
   serverThread.Free();
   WriteLn('Finished.');
end.
```

</Code>

The program starts by creating the listening thread, specifying the port on which it will be listening. There is only one listening thread in the server process. The listener thread once created starts automatically. The following code shows the listener thread Execute method:

<Code ID = 7>

```
procedure TServerListenerThread.Execute();
var
   ClientSock: TSocket;
begin
   FSocketObject.RaiseExcept := True;
   FSocketObject.CreateSocket();
   FSocketObject.SetLinger(True,10);
   FSocketObject.Bind(FIP,IntToStr(FPort));
   FSocketObject.Listen();
   while not Terminated do begin
      if FSocketObject.CanRead(DefaultTimeOut) then begin
         ClientSock := FSocketObject.Accept();
         TClientHandlerThread.Create(ClientSock);
      end;
   end;
end;
```

</Code>

11.1.2 The server program

The server socket is prepared (lines 5-8) and then starts listening (line 9). A thread loop then begins (line 10), waiting for a client connection request. When a client makes a connection request, a thread is created to handle its communication with the server (lines 11-13). The client handling thread, once created, starts automatically. The code below presents the client handling thread main execution method:

```
<Code ID = 8>
  1    procedure TClientHandlerThread.Execute();
  2    begin
  3       FSocketObject := TTCPBlockSocket.Create();
  4       try
  5          FSocketObject.Socket := FSocketHandle;
  6          FSocketObject.GetSins();
  7          while not Terminated do begin
  8             ClearBuffers();
  9             if ReadInputBuffer() then begin
 10                Compute();
 11                SendOutputBuffer();
 12                ClearBuffers();
 13             end;
 14          end;
 15       finally
 16          FreeAndNil(FSocketObject);
 17       end;
 18    end;
</Code>
```

The client handling thread prepares the socket object and then enters its execution loop. At line 9, the thread tries to read from the socket, which may or may not have been filled depending on whether the remote client has made a calculation request or not. If the read operation succeeds the following sequence occurs:

- the input buffer is filled;
- the calculation is completed and the output buffer is filled;
- the output buffer is sent back to the remote client;
- the input and output buffers are cleared.

Compiling the server code

As for the client program, you must have installed a copy of the **Synapse** library into its own folder. The `server` folder contains a single Lazarus project `file tcp_server.lpi`. Before compiling the project, make sure you update the project's `search` folder to include the `Synapse library` folder.

A cross-platform issue to note if using multi-byte types

The request and response data structures defined in the shared interface file, `service_intf.pas`, are packed records, and their members are single-byte types (ShortInt or ShortInt aliases). If we had used multi-byte types such as Word, LongInt or Double, we would have had to take care of those data members' byte order in order for the programs not to depend on the underlying processor's endianness.

Raw *TCP/IP* programming does have some technical issues that get harder to manage with the developers' need to use some features that appear, by compiler magic, natural to Object Pascal developers such as :

- multi-byte types (*Word, LongInt, Cardinal, Int64, Single, Double, ...*),
- long strings (*AnsiString, WideString*),
- dynamic array,
- classes instances,
- enumerations.

The developer would have to handle:

- the endianness of the processors, in the case of a cross-platform application, to handle multi-byte types: the byte order of "on the wire" buffer; the two most used are Big-Endian (most significant byte at lower memory address) found on ARM, PowerPC, SPARC processors and Little-Endian (least significant byte at lower memory address) found on x86, x86-64;
- serialize Object Pascal's managed types (String, Array) into a suitable format,
- pointer based type or type making use of pointer, make sure the serialized format can be set up from the serialized data. This includes classes' instances, record with pointer members.

The "**Web Service Toolkit**", **WST** for short, presented in the next section, solves all these problems by handling the serialization of the parameters in a cross platform way making use of the de-facto industry standards *(XML* with *SOAP* and *XmlRPC, JSON)* or a WST custom cross-platform binary format. WST goes further to allow the use of the HTTP protocol and a custom dynamic linking (Windows DLL/(x)nix SO) based protocol(services hosted on libraries modules).

11.2 Webservices

A webservice is nothing but an **RPC** (Remote Procedure Call) – older readers will most likely know this. But webservices distinguish themselves from simple RPC functions in several ways. Through webservices technology two software components can communicate with each other remotely. The two components are a provider (service-provider or server) and a consumer (service-consumer or client). They are able to do this without regard to either component's location, hardware, operating system, or the language used in their development.

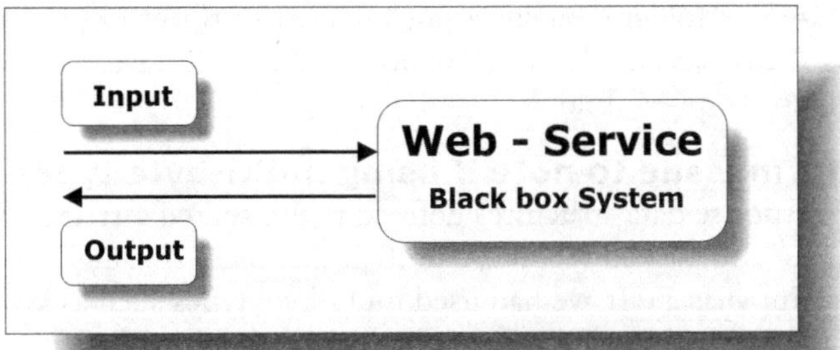

Figure 11.2 The Black box principle

Simply put, a webservice is a program function which is called at a fixed address on the internet. The communication between programs happens with the exchange of standardised messages in XML format. The webservice can be integrated into a program and called subsequently as if it were part of the program. The developer does not need to know how the function was implemented, he just needs the URL of the service.

The W3C has published specifications designed to set standards to accomplish this goal:

- **SOAP** (Simple Object Access Protocol, `http://www.w3.org/TR/soap`): The format of messages exchanged between the consumer and the provider.
- **WSDL** (Web Services Description Language, `http://www.w3.org/TR/wsdl)`: The formal definition of the interfaces for the services: what each service provides and how and where to invoke the service.

Other specifications have been defined by groups independent of W3C such as:

- **XmlRPC** (`http://www.xmlrpc.com`): A Remote Procedure Call model where exchanged messages are XML-based and transport is over HTTP. XmlRPC is far simpler than SOAP.
- **JsonRPC** over HTTP (`http://json-rpc.org`): Similar to XmlRPC, but the messages are JSON formatted.

And lastly there are the less formal **REST** style web services (REpresentational State Transfer). See: `http://www.ics.uci.edu/~fielding/pubs/dissertation/top.htm`
The FPC/Lazarus developer should use the Web Service Toolkit (WST) when working with webservices. This software package makes it much easier to consume webservices (consumer side) and to create them (provider side). It frees developers from needing to tangle with all the details involved in coding the format of exchanged messages (SOAP, XMLRPC or JSON) and the transport protocol (HTTP, TCP and – as will be seen shortly – a protocol specific to WST).

In WST, the format of the messages exchanged between the service consumer (client) and the service provider (server) does not depend on the transport protocol, and vice versa. Quite the contrary: programs created with WST - both client and server - are very flexible about combining different message formats and transport protocols. WST supports the following message formats: SOAP 1.1, XmlRPC, JSON and a custom binary format optimized for speed and memory performance.

On the server side, out of the box, WST allows the creation of services hosted in:

- a single executable file as an Indy-based HTTP server
- a single executable file as an Indy-based TCP server
- a single executable file as a Synapse-based TCP server
- an Apache HTTP server module
- a dynamic library (specific to WST)

WST's server side can easily be hosted on a custom application server by writing minimal code.

On the client side, WST provides several transport implementations:

- Indy-based HTTP transport
- Indy-based TCP transport
- Synapse-based HTTP transport
- Synapse-based TCP transport
- ICS-based HTTP transport
- ICS-based TCP transport
- A dynamic library transport protocol specific to WST
- An in-process transport protocol where the server and client are in the same executable module

For the remote functionality through network access, one of the frameworks Indy, ICS or Synapse must be installed. The Indy components available from `http://www.indyproject.org/Sockets/fpc/` can be used with FPC, and the Indy packages can be installed in Lazarus. The internet component suite ICS is hosted on `http://www.overbyte.be/`. Synapse can be downloaded from `http://www.ararat.cz/synapse/`. These 3 suites offer well-tested TCP/IP components and WST is able to use all three as transport layers over HTTP. Server services can be developed with the HTTP server from Indy or with the TCP-server from ICS.
WST itself is available for free from the location `http://inoussa12.googlepages.com/webservicetoolkitforfpc%26lazarus` or from `http://wiki.freepascal.org/Web_Service_Toolkit`

In this chapter we will see how easy and straightforward it is to define and use a web service with Lazarus and WST.

11.2.1 Programming the server

A web service is made of three basic modules

- the **interface** that defines *what* the service provides
- the **binding** that specifies *how* the service is provided
- the **endpoint** that specifies *where* the service is provided

The **interface** defines what the service offers in terms of the operations consumers can request as they use that service's functionalities. It defines the operations as well as the messages and data structures which are exchanged between the consumers and providers of the service.

The **binding** specifies the inner details of these messages and the transport protocol, and specifically the operation's style and requirements (such as the SOAP headers and binding style), the message format protocol (such as SOAP serialization or JSON or XmlRPC serialization) and the transport protocol (such as HTTP or TCP).

The **endpoint** specifies where the service is located and which bindings are available at this address. For example an endpoint can expose a SOAP interface to a web service located at the address:

```
http://wst-services/services/CalcService?format=soap
```

Webservice authoring using WST is usually accomplished in four basic steps: describing the service; generating the Object Pascal support files for the service; completing the service's implementation class; and hosting the service on an application server.

Step 1: Describe the service
WST describes the service using the standard Web Services Description Language (**WSDL)**. For this, it provides a Type Library Editor that produces WSDL files as its native storage format. It has a graphical user interface, so there is no need to code WSDL files by hand.

The Type Library Editor is provided in two formats: A standalone Lazarus application `typ_lib_edtr.exe` that operates outside any IDE. The application source is provided with WST and is located in the `type_lib_edtr` folder. Secondly as a Lazarus extension package that adds several menus entries to the Lazarus IDE. When installed, it adds an entry Type Library Editor to the Project menu that invokes the type library editor within the Lazarus IDE. The package source code is provided with WST and is located in the `ide\lazarus` folder.

Step 2: Generate the Object Pascal support files for the service
Step 1 produced a WSDL file which has to be translated to Object Pascal to be usable by the Free Pascal compiler. WST provide two tools to facilitate this process:

- GUI Type Library Editor seen in the previous step provides an export dialog that can be invoked through its *'File'→'Save generated files...'* menu item, or via the pop-up menu item *'Save generated files ...'* if you right-click on a source file viewed in the editor pages. In this dialog the user can select the type of files that must be exported and set various options before the translation to Pascal starts.
- A command-line program `ws_helper.exe`. This utility provides several options for translating WSDL files and **XSD** (*XML Schema Definition*) files to Object Pascal language files. To get an overview of its capabilities, just run it without any parameters then it will output its usage details to the console.

The following files are needed for a service provider implementation:

- An interface file appropriate to the service interface. This file contains the data structures (enumerations, compound structures, ...) and a representation of the operations in the WSDL file as a regular Object Pascal interface. Service developers should not modify this file.
- A binder file that contains the service binder class. This class is responsible for the messages' serialization and deserialization, for setting up the call stack, and making the call to the service implementation class. Service developers should not modify this file either.

- The implementation file contains the actual service implementation class. This file will contain a skeleton for a class implementing the service interface defined in the interface file.

These files are generated either by the *Type Library Editor* or `ws_helper.exe`.

Step 3: Complete the service's implementation class
A web service is represented in Object Pascal by a regular interface which inherits from *IInvocable.* The service implementation class - the class that actually provides the service functionalities - is an Object Pascal class that inherits from *TBaseServiceImplementation* or *TactivableServiceImplementation.* This class implements the service interface. The implementation file generated by the WST tools contains a skeleton implementation class that has to be completed by the service developer.

Step 4: Host the service into an application server
Once the three previous steps have been completed, the service is ready to be embedded in an application server called the host. The hosting environment provides the transport infrastructure for the service. The WST architecture is flexible enough to allow WST-based services to be hosted on a variety of servers. Out of the box, WST provides support for INDY-based HTTP and TCP servers, Synapse-based TCP servers, dynamic linked/shared library (dll/dso) based servers, and Apache HTTPD server based modules.

Definition of the service interface

The first example in this chapter deals with a simple integer calculation service. This service provides two integer operations: Add and Subtract. To define the service interface we will use the WST Type Library Editor. An interface is created defining two operations for that interface. We use the interface creation dialog to create the interface, which is available through the menu item '*Edit→Create Interface*' as shown in the following screenshot. Note that the interface creation dialog is also available through the pop-up menu item '*Create Interface*' obtained by right-clicking on any of the editor's source view pages.

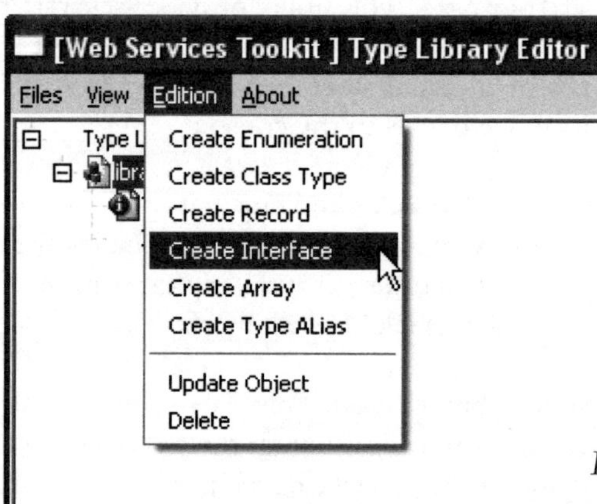

Figure 11.3: The 'Create Interface' menu item

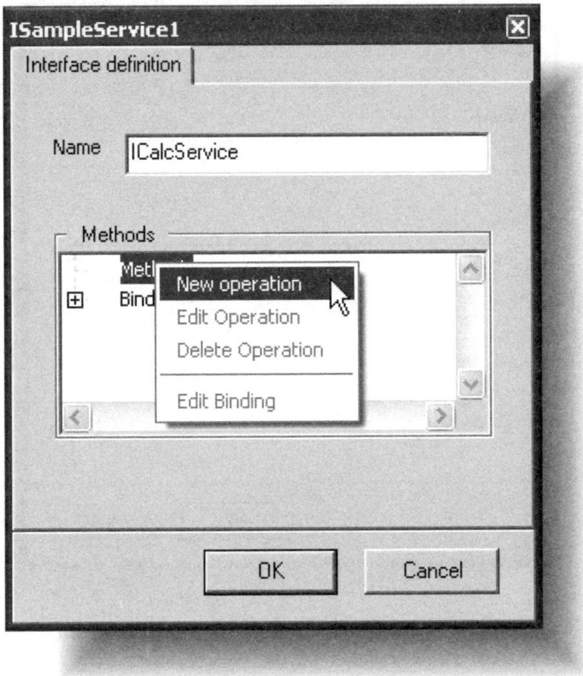

Figure 11.4: The service properties dialog

Figure 11.4 shows the interface properties and Figure 11.5 the dialog which creates the operation of the interface.

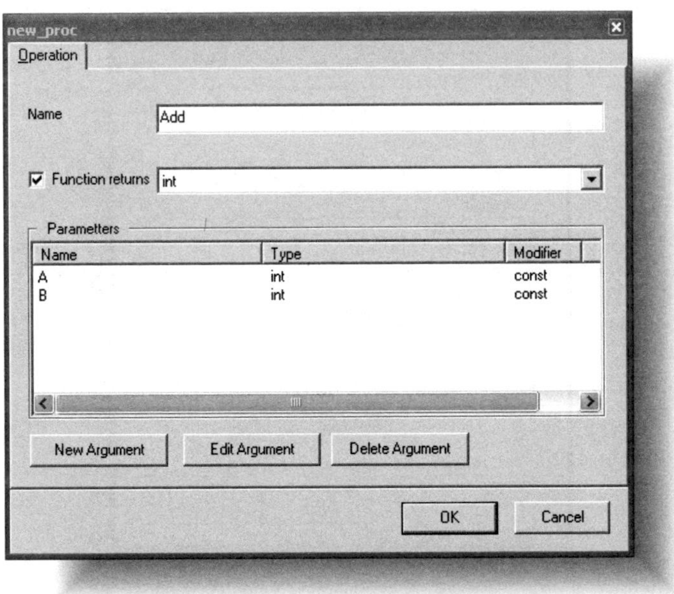

Figure 11.5: Dialog to create the operations

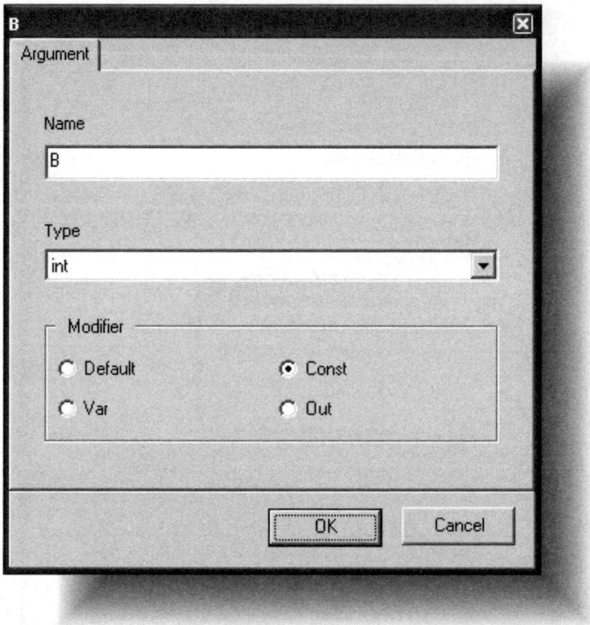

Figure 11.6: Dialog showing argument properties

The *Operation properties* dialog provides buttons to add, edit and delete operation arguments. The *Argument* dialog (shown above) has then been used to add the arguments needed for the operation named *Add*. Once all operations have been added to the interface, the binding editor dialog is called through the *'Edit binding'* pop-up menu item as shown in Figure 11.7.

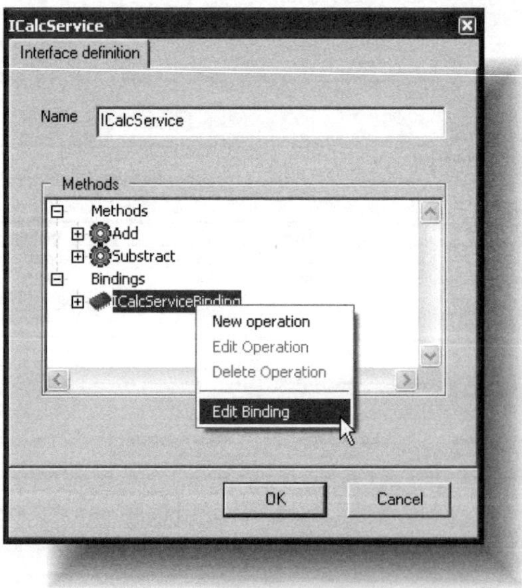

Figure 11.7: The Edit binding menu item

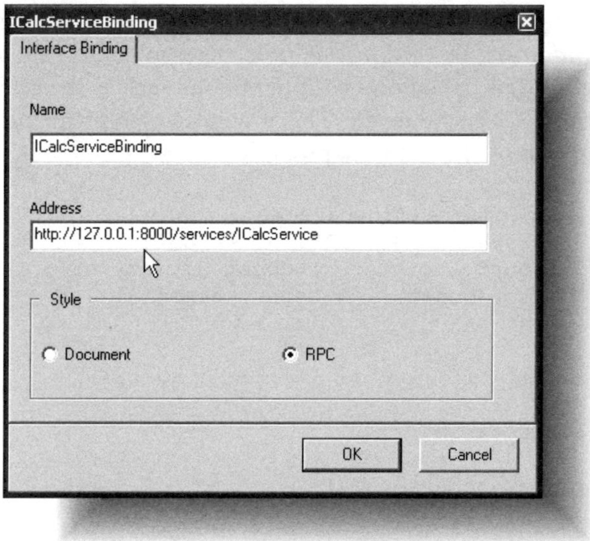

Figure 11.8: Properties of a binding

Once the WSDL is complete, the Object Pascal files needed for the service must be generated. To do this, the '*Export file options…*' dialog must be used, through the '*Files→ Save generated files ...*' menu item. It is shown in Figure 11.9.

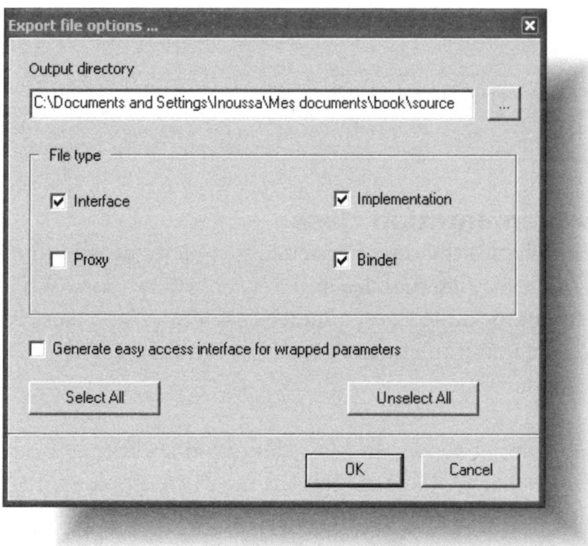

Figure 11.9: Generate files dialog

Hint: The '**Generate easy access interface for wrapped parameters**' checkbox instructs the generator to create a simpler interface for wrapped literal document web services. This is mostly used by implementations of Microsoft .Net web services.

An extract of the interface file follows giving the generated Object Pascal interface type. Note the *Register_calcservice_ServiceMetadata()* procedure (in `calcservice.pas`) that records the service and its operation's custom options such as the service default address, style (document or RPC), encoding etc. This routine is used by the proxy and binder to handle the serialization of the call stack properly.

```
ICalcService = interface(IInvokable)
  ['{090EADB7-6B25-4F35-9419-2AF113D44BF8}']
  function Add(const A: integer; const B: integer): integer;
  function Subtract(const A: integer; const B: integer): integer;
end;

procedure Register_calcservice_ServiceMetadata();
var
  mm : IModuleMetadataMngr;
begin
  mm := GetModuleMetadataMngr();
  mm.SetRepositoryNameSpace(sUNIT_NAME, sNAME_SPACE);
  mm.SetServiceCustomData(sUNIT_NAME, 'ICalcService',
     'TRANSPORT_Address',
     'http://127.0.0.1:8000/services/ICalcService');
  mm.SetServiceCustomData(sUNIT_NAME, 'ICalcService',
     'FORMAT_Style','rpc');
  mm.SetOperationCustomData(sUNIT_NAME, 'ICalcService',
     'Add','_E_N_','Add');
  mm.SetOperationCustomData(sUNIT_NAME,'ICalcService','Add',
     'FORMAT_Input_EncodingStyle','literal');
  mm.SetOperationCustomData(sUNIT_NAME,'ICalcService','Add',
     FORMAT_OutputEncodingStyle','literal');
............{same for subtract}
end;
```

The service implementation class

The implementation class is the one that actually implements the functionalities provided by the service (In our example, the *Add* and *Subtract* operations). WST generates, through *ws_helper*, an implementation file that contains a skeleton class, namely *TCalcService_ServiceImp*, that implements the service interface. All that remains to be done is to complete this class.

The following code snippet shows the class definition and the *Add()* method implementation. Note that we have completed the *Add()* implementation manually, so it is no longer a skeleton. Once the service implementation is provided, the service has to be registered in the services implementation registry so that the WST runtime will know about it. The generated implementation unit contains a procedure *RegisterCalcServiceImplementationFactory* that does this.

```
TcalcService_ServiceImp=
     class(TBaseServiceImplementation, ICalcService)
Protected
   function Add(const A: integer; const B: integer): integer;
   function Subtract(const A: integer; const B: integer): integer;
end;
...
function TCalcService_ServiceImp.Add(
   const A: integer; const B: integer): integer;
begin
   Result := A + B;
end;
```

The Application Server

Once the service is defined and implemented, it has to be hosted by an *application server*. The application server provides the transport infrastructure for the service. For the HTTP application server we are going to build, this means that it:

- will be an HTTP server listening for client connections
- carries the client request payload to the WST runtime
- returns the resulting response stream to the client

The WST runtime is designed as a *server listener object model* which implements the actual transport layer. That means it offers objects which listen for client requests, accept client connections and handle the connection and communication details during the lifetime of the connection. For each supported protocol, a specialized listener object is implemented. In the example an **INDY**-based HTTP server listener is used. The complete source code of the program's main unit is shown below. The complete source code of the server is in the `sources\web-services\server` folder.

The program registers the SOAP serialization format in *Server_service_RegisterSoapFormat()*, in order for the WST runtime to accept this format. This routine is located in the `server_service_soap.pas` unit. Then it registers the implementation and binder for *CalcService* in the WST runtime registry. The implementation and the binder are defined in the `calcservice_imp` and `calcservice_binder` units.

It then creates the INDY-based object which will listen for HTTP requests (the HTTP listener). The object instance is stored in the variable *AppObject* which is declared as an instance of *TwstListener*. This is the base class from which every listener inherits. *TwstListener* is an abstract class that defines the WST listener model. This class is defined in the `server_listener` unit. *TwstIndyHttpListener* is a class that inherits from the base listener class and implements an HTTP server transport infrastructure using the INDY HTTP library for the application server. The INDY HTTP listener is defined in the `indy_http_server` unit. The program then invokes the listener and waits for incoming requests.

The remaining unit `metadata_service` has not been introduced. It provides a metadata service implementation exposing the services registered in the WST runtime registries. A simple test of the HTTP listener can be done by opening a browser and pointing it to the address `http://127.0.0.1:8000/`. An HTTP page presenting a list of the registered services should be displayed. It will contain links to the description of its service in the WSDL format. Note that these descriptions are generated at runtime.

```
program srv_calc;
   $mode objfpc}{$H+}
uses
   {$IFDEF UNIX}cthreads,{$ENDIF}
   Classes, SysUtils,
   server_listener, indy_http_server,
   server_service_intf, server_service_soap, metadata_service,
   calcservice, calcservice_binder, calcservice_imp;
var
   AppObject: TwstListener;
begin
   Server_service_RegisterSoapFormat();
   RegisterCalcServiceImplementationFactory();
   Server_service_RegisterCalcServiceService();
   AppObject := TwstIndyHttpListener.Create('127.0.0.1',8000);
   try
      WriteLn('"Web Service Toolkit" HTTP Server listening at:');
      WriteLn('');
      WriteLn('http://127.0.0.1:8000/');
      WriteLn('');
      WriteLn('Press enter to quit.');
      AppObject.Start();
      ReadLn();
   finally
      FreeAndNil(AppObject);
   end;
end.
```

A library- based Application Server

WST web services can be hosted using a dynamic library (a Windows Dynamic Linked Library DLL, or Unix Shared Objects SO). At runtime the library is loaded into the client process so that the client and server code then run in the same process. Library-based application servers can be used for a high performance scenario as the server and the client share the same address space and no remote protocol stack is used. The library transport protocol uses the local process address space to share client requests and server responses buffers. Every library-based application server exports a function *wstHandleRequest* located in the `library_server_intf` unit, which is used by the client library protocol implementation to invoke the server code. The following code shows the function signature. The *ARequestBuffer* parameter is the one used to share request and response buffers.

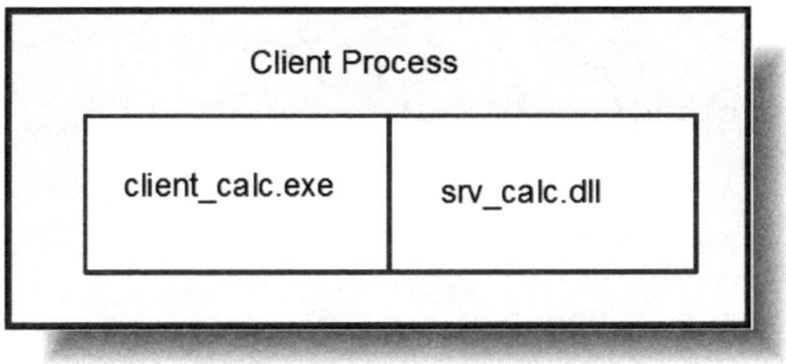

Figure 11.10 Client and server modules in the client process

Library-based application servers are well suited for plug-in development as the plug-in interface is defined in a high level language and the developer does not have to worry about low level library code. The complete source code of a sample server is located in the `sources\web-services\protocols\library_server` folder. This server can be used with the client located in the `sources\web-services\protocols\client` folder, choosing the library protocol when executed.

```
unit = library_server_intf.pas>
function wstHandleRequest(
  ARequestBuffer: IwstStream;
  AErrorBuffer: Pointer;
  var AErrorBufferLen: LongInt
  ):LongInt;
```

SOAP headers

A SOAP header is an optional part of a SOAP message. It contains meta-information about the message. It can be used for example for encryption information or to give routing instructions. WST supports SOAP headers both on the server side and on the client side. In WST, *THeaderBlock* descendants (shown below) are used to represent header entries. This class has three important properties, firstly: *Direction* which specifies whether the header is an incoming our an outgoing header. Secondly: *mustUnderstand* maps to the SOAP header property of the same name that instructs the server that the understanding of this header is mandatory. Thirdly: *Understood* is used by the service developer to indicate whether the header has been understood or not. If the header is mandatory (*mustUnderstand* = 1), the WST runtime checks for this property to be True or else it returns an exception to the caller. So at the server side, all understood headers must be marked as such.

The *ICallContext* interface (see below) provides methods to access, add and delete headers in the context of preparing to make or execute calls. The source code of a complete example server side project and client side project can be found in the `sources\web-services\headers` folder.

```
type
  THeaderDirection = ( hdOut, hdIn );
  THeaderBlock = class(TBaseComplexRemotable)
...
public
  property Direction: THeaderDirection read FDirection write
     FDirection;
  property Understood: Boolean read FUnderstood write FUnderstood;
published
  property mustUnderstand: Integer read FmustUnderstand
  write SetmustUnderstand stored HasmustUnderstand;
end;

ICallContext = Interface
  ['{855EB8E2-0700-45B1-B852-2101023200E0}']
  procedure AddObjectToFree(const AObject: TObject);
  procedure Clear();
  function AddHeader(
     const AHeader: THeaderBlock;
     const AKeepOwnership: Boolean
  ):Integer;
  function GetHeaderCount(const Adirections:
     THeaderDirections):Integer;
  function GetHeader(const AIndex: Integer: THeaderBlock;
  procedure ClearHeaders(const ADirection: THeaderDirection);
end;
```

Server side SOAP headers

Using the WST *Type Library Editor* to define a header entry class is as simple as creating the class and making sure the class inherits directly (or through a parent class) from *THeaderBlock*. Figure 11.11 shows the dialog used to define the *TLoginHeader* used in this chapter's example.

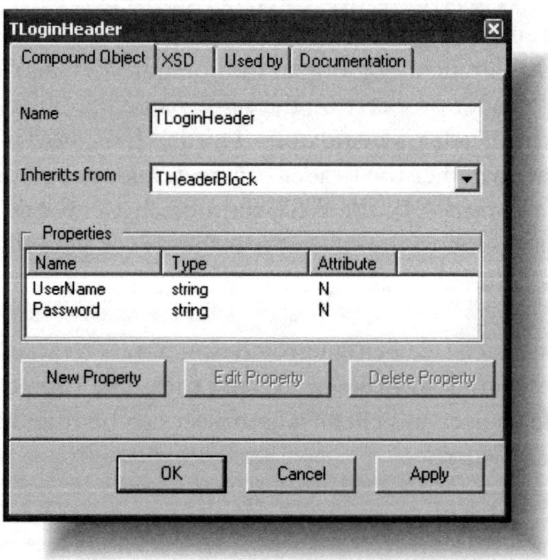

Figure 11.11: SOAP-header class definition

You can obtain the context of a call executing at the server side in the implementation class, through the *GetCallContext* method of *TBaseServiceImplementation* from which every service implementation class descends. In a service extension the context is a parameter of the *ProcessMessage* method. Note that for an added header to be sent to the server its direction must be set to *hdOut*.

Client side SOAP headers
For handling client side headers, you have to make sure that the header class inherits directly or through a parent class from *THeaderBlock*. For a WST web service, the WST Type Library Editor generated WSDL file contains such indications. The context of the call is obtained by casting the service proxy using the as operator, as shown in the following code excerpt. Note that for an added header to be sent to the server its direction must be set to *hdOut*.

```
callContext := theProxy as ICallContext;
```

Server side multi serialization format support
An application server hosting WST web services can be developed to accept clients which use various different serialization formats. The WST server side provides support for the following serialization formats:

- **SOAP**: The supported version is SOAP 1.1, which is the widely used version. The implementation is provided by the `server_service_soap` unit.
- **XmlRPC**: The implementation is provided by the `server_service_xmlrpc` unit.
- **JSON**: The WST implementation of the JsonRPC is done in a client-server oriented manner, not the peer-to-peer way expressed in JsonRPC 1.0. The WST implementation supports both the JsonRPC 1.0 format and the JsonRPC 1.1 format. The implementation can be found in the `server_service_json` unit.
- **Binary**: This is a WST custom binary format. The implementation can be found in the `server_binary_formatter` unit.

Note that to use a serialization protocol, its implementation has to be registered with the WST runtime. Every serialization format implementation unit provides a registration procedure that must be called by the hosting application server before starting the listener object(s). The registration procedures names are self-explanatory as illustrated in the following source code excerpt. (The complete source code of the sample is located in the `sources\web-services\protocols` folder). The server project uses the logging extension to log the exchanged messages to file. The client project allows the user to select the serialization format.

```
Server_service_RegisterSoapFormat();
Server_service_RegisterXmlRpcFormat();
Server_service_RegisterJsonFormat();
Server_service_RegisterBinaryFormat();
```

Server side multi transport protocol support
The WST listener model simplifies the handling of multiple transport protocols. To handle several protocols an application server just has to create the needed listeners and start them. The WST server side provides support for the following transport protocols:

- **HTTP**: The implementation (based on the INDY socket library) is provided by the `indy_http_server` unit.
- **TCP**: WST provides two transport implementations using different socket libraries : The INDY socket library (implemented in the `indy_tcp_server` unit) and the SYNAPSE socket library implemented in the `synapse_tcp_server` unit.

Note that each active listener must have a unique port. The following source code excerpt shows the creation and running of both HTTP and TCP listeners. The complete sample source code is located in the `sources\web-services\protocols\server` folder.

```
...
 listener := TwstIndyHttpListener.Create('127.0.0.1',8000);
 listenerList.Add(listener);
 listener.Start();
 listener := TwstIndyTcpListener.Create('127.0.0.1',1234);
 listenerList.Add(listener);
 listener.Start();
...
```

11.2.2 Programming the client

Overview

The Web Services Toolkit (*WST*) enables Object Pascal developers to develop software that consumes web services regardless of the hardware and operating system on which the service provider is running, and regardless of the development language used to program the service provider. To be able to do this, WST parses the WSDL description file and then creates an Object Pascal language file that represents the service described in it. The latter contains a regular Object Pascal interface definition whose procedures and functions match the service operations' descriptions and which includes all the needed type definitions. The file also contains the options for the serialization and transport protocols needed to compose the messages exchanged between the service provider and the consumer.

Based on the result of the previous step, WST then creates a proxy class. This is an Object Pascal class that implements the interface created above representing the service. The proxy class marshals the call between the local client and the remote service provider and it is located in a separate Object Pascal unit file.

Through the proxy class, the service appears as a regular Pascal interface to the Object Pascal developer. The developer can use it to create an instance that represents the service implementation and consume the functionalities provided by the service.

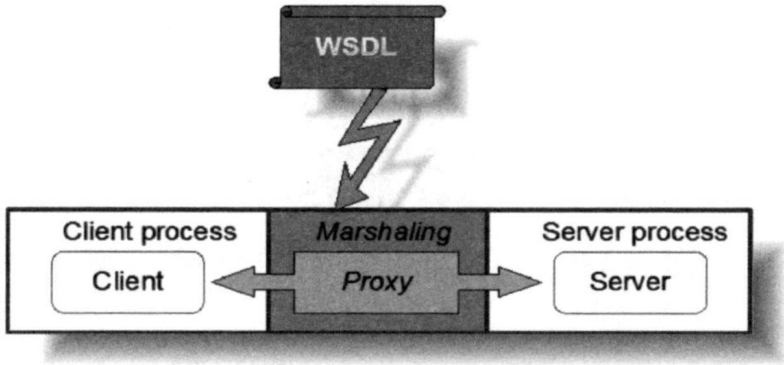

Figure 11.12: The WST client process

WST provides two ways of parsing WSDL files: A console program, `ws_helper.exe`, which parses Web Services Description Language *(WSDL)* files and XML Schema Definitions *(XSD)* files, and a WSDL importer wizard integrated into Lazarus as a package, `wst_design.lpk`. This file is part of the package `wsdl-<versionnumber>.zip` which can be downloaded from the author's Googlepages at:
`http://inoussa12.googlepages.com/webservicetoolkitforfpc%26lazarus`

After the download, the archive can be unpacked in the Lazarus installation's components directory, and the version should be removed from the directory name. In Lazarus, the *Package→Open* package file menu must be used to select the file `wst_design.lpk` from the directory `wst\ide\lazarus` (see Figure 11.13).

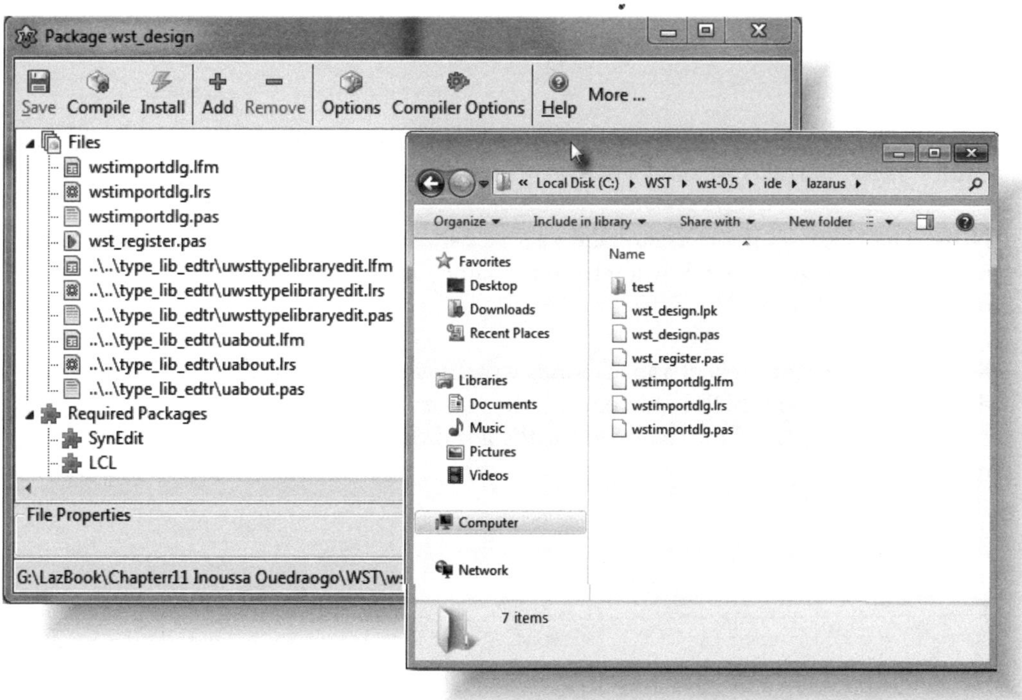

Figure 11.13: Using the Package→Open package file menu item the .lpk file is chosen, compiled in the Package dialog and subsequently installed

In the package dialog that follows, `wst_design` must first be compiled and then installed. This will cause Lazarus to be recompiled (see Figure 11.14).

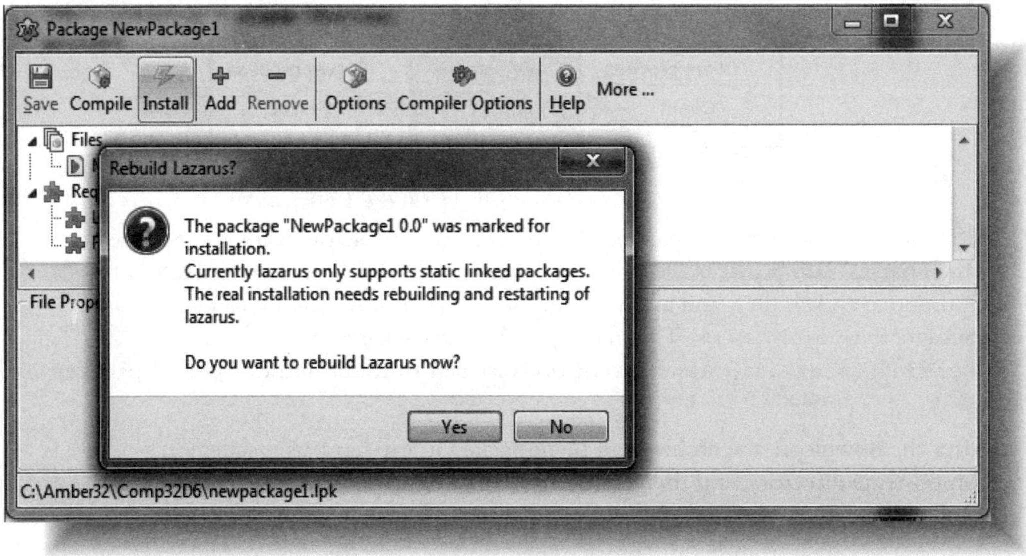

Figure 11.14: Lazarus must be recompiled to install a package

After all this, the IDE Project menu contains a new submenu *Web services Toolkit* with two entries: *Import WSDL File...* and *Type library editor...* .

Note: The Lazarus import wizard and `ws_helper.exe` are two front ends for the same parser and code generator. Starting from the same file, both tools will produce the same output.

Subsequently, a simple client application is written which will consume the CalcService defined earlier. The WSDL is parsed with the two front ends, starting with `ws_helper`. The implementation of the transport protocol is provided by the Synapse HTTP transport.

Translating WSDL files to Object Pascal

To parse the file, invoke `ws_helper` on from the command-line:

```
ws_helper\ws_helper -p -uA .\samples\book\ws\calcservice.wsdl
-a.\samples\book\ws\client\
```

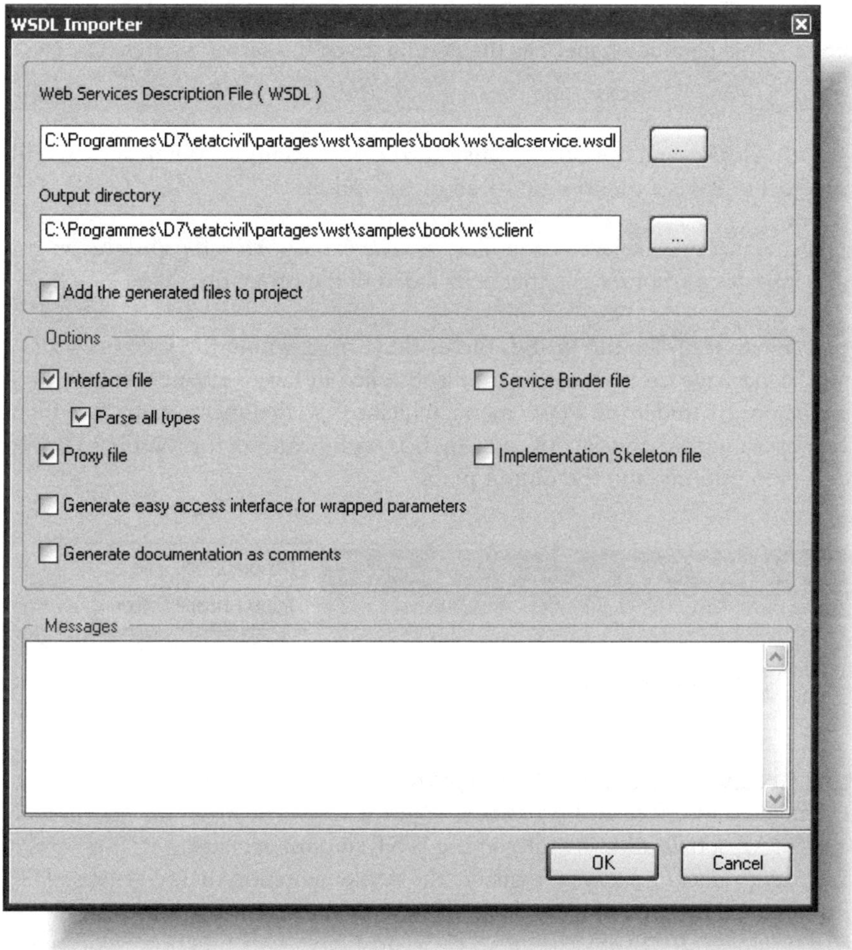

Figure 11.15: The WSDL importer dialog

```
ws_helper, Web Service Toolkit 0.6 Copyright (c) 2006, 2007, 2008 by
   Inoussa OUEDRAOGO
Parsing the file: .\samples\book\ws\calcservice.wsdl
Interface file generation...
Proxy file generation...
Metadata file generation...
File ".\samples\book\ws\calcservice.wsdl" parsed successfully.
```

The parameters have the following meaning:

Parameter	Description
-p	Generate a proxy file
-uA	Parse and generate descriptions for all the type descriptions in the input file. This option is useful when there are some types not used directly by the service operations
-a<path>	This parameter specifies the port on which the server is listening

Table 11.1: Three useful command-line options for ws_helper

`ws_helper` provides several options for customizing its execution. When started without any parameters it outputs a description of all of its options.

`ws_helper` generates two Object Pascal files, the *interface description* file and the *proxy* file. Additionally, it writes a resource file that is included in the proxy file.

It is also possible to translate the WSDL file working from within the Lazarus IDE. When the WST package (`wst_design.lpk`) is installed in Lazarus, a new submenu *Web Services Toolkit* appears under the *Project* menu, which offers two menu items (see Figure 11.16). The import wizard consists of a dialog box with prompts for the file to import, the customization options, and the output path.

Figure 11.16: The menu items after installation of the WST package

Using the proxy in the client program

Using the generated interface and proxy is straightforward. The `soap_formatter` unit registers the SOAP serialization handler in the WST runtime registry. *SYNAPSE_RegisterHTTP_Transport* registers the implementation of the synapse HTTP transport protocol. This procedure is declared in the `synapse_http_protocol.pas` unit. *wst_CreateInstance_ICalcService* creates a proxy instance. This function is located in the generated proxy unit, `calcservice_proxy.pas`. The rest of the code simply asks the user to enter the operands and operator required for the calculation.

```
program client_calc;
   {$mode objfpc}{$H+}
uses
   Classes, SysUtils,
   soap_formatter, synapse_http_protocol, calcservice,
   calcservice_proxy;
var
   theProxy: ICalcService;
   a, b: Integer;
   op, c: Char;
begin
   SYNAPSE_RegisterHTTP_Transport();
   theProxy := wst_CreateInstance_ICalcService();
   WriteLn('Calculator Client demo');
   repeat
      Write('Enter first operand : '); ReadLn(a);
      Write('Enter second operand : '); ReadLn(b);
      Write('Enter operator ( + or - ) : '); ReadLn(op);
      case op of
         '+' : WriteLn(a,' + ',b,' = ',theProxy.Add(a,b));
         '-' : WriteLn(a,' - ',b,' = ',theProxy.Subtract(a,b));
         else WriteLn('Unknown operator : ',op);
      end;
      WriteLn(''); Write(' Continue (y/n) ? : '); ReadLn(c);
      WriteLn('')
   until ( c <> 'y' );
end.
```

Client connection parameters

The *TBaseProxy* class, which is defined in `service_intf.pas` and from which every service proxy class must descend, provides a virtual constructor that can be used to customize the serialization and connection properties.

```
TBaseProxy = Class(TInterfacedObject,IInterface,ICallContext)
...
public
  constructor Create(
  Const ATarget : String;
  Const AProtocolData : string;
  Const ATransportData : string
  );overload; virtual;
...
End;
```

The above code excerpt shows the constructor and its parameters. *ATarget* is the target web service name, *AProtocolData* specifies the serialization protocol (SOAP, XmlRPC, JSON or binary) and its parameters (such as SOAP rpc/Document style, or SOAP Encoded/Literal encoding style). The *ATransportData* parameter specifies the transport protocol (HTTP, TCP, WST) and its parameters (such as address and port for TCP transport, and address and proxy parameters for HTTP transport).

The general format of the serialization and the transport connection string is:
```
protocol:paramName=paramValue(;paramName=paramValue)*
```

If no parameter is specified the string becomes:
```
protocol:
```

Where *protocol* stands for the name of the transport protocol, for example *http*. The following is an example of two parameters
http:address = `http://ws.sample/service;ProxyServer=192.168.10.1`

Three parameters:
http:address = `http://ws.sample/service;ProxyServer=192.168.10.1;`
ProxyPort=4567

The parameters are separated by semicolons.

Currently, WST supports the serialization protocols listed in Table 11.2.

Protocol	Description	
SOAP	the supported version is SOAP 1.1, which is the widely used version. The implementation is provided by the `soap_formatter` unit. The available parameters are:	
	Style	this parameter specifies the SOAP document style. The possible values are *rpc* or *Document*.
	EncodingStyle	this parameter specifies the SOAP encoding style. The possible values are *Literal* or *Encoded*.
XmlRPC	The implementation is provided by the `xmlrpc_formatter` unit. This protocol has no parameters.	
JSON	The WST implementation of the JsonRPC is done in a client-server oriented manner, not the peer-to-peer way found in JsonRPC 1.0.	
	The implementation supports the formats of both JsonRPC 1.0 and JsonRPC 1.1. The implementation is provided by the `json_formatter` unit. The available parameters are:	
	Version	This parameter specifies the version of the protocol. The possible values are 1.0 or 1.1. The `base_json_formatter` unit contains the symbolic constants *s_json_rpc_version_10* and *s_json_rpc_version_11* that map to 1.0 and 1.1, which can also be used.
Binary	This is a WST custom binary format. The implementation is provided by the `binary_formatter` unit. This format has no parameters.	

Table 11.2: Serialization protocols supported by WST

11.2.2 Programming the client

To be able to use a serialization protocol, its implementation has to be registered with the WST runtime. You have to add the unit implementing the specific protocol to the *uses* clause of the project file in at least one of your project's units. The client side serialization protocol implementation units are automatically registered in their initialization section. Examples of strings to select a serialization:

```
'SOAP:'
'SOAP:Style=rpc;EncodingStyle=Literal'
'XMLRPC:'
'JSON:Version=1.0'
```

WST offers the following HTTP transport implementations:

- The INDY socket library is located in the `indy_http_protocol` unit.
- The SYNAPSE socket library is located in the `synapse_http_protocol` unit.
- The ICS socket library is located in the `ics_hyyp_protocol` unit.

The available parameters are :

Parameter	Description
Address:	This parameter specifies the web service HTTP address.
ProxyServer:	This parameter is used when the connection is done through a proxy. It specifies the address of the proxy server.
ProxyPort:	This parameter is used when the connection is done through a proxy. It specifies the port of the proxy server.
ProxyUsername:	This parameter is used when the connection is done through a proxy. It specifies the user name for proxy server authentication.
ProxyPassword:	This parameter is used when the connection is done through a proxy. It specifies the user password for proxy server authentication.

Table 11.3: HTTP transport parameters

WST offers the following TCP transport implementations:

- The INDY socket library is located in the `indy_tcp_protocol` unit.
- The SYNAPSE socket library is located in the `synapse_tcp_protocol` unit.
- The ICS socket library is located in the `ics_tcp_protocol` unit.

The available parameters are :

Parameter	Description
Target:	This parameter specifies the web service name as registered by the server.
Address:	This parameter specifies the server IP address.
Port:	This parameter specifies the port on which the server is listening.

Table 11.4: TCP transport parameters

Table 11.5 lists the parameters for the WST-specific *LIB transport* protocol to use services hosted using a Windows DLL (dynamic linked library) or Unix dynamic shared objects (DLL/DSO). The implementation is located in the `library_protocol` unit.

The available parameters are:

Parameter	Description
Target:	This parameter specifies the web service name as registered by the server.
FileName:	This parameter specifies the server dynamic library file name.

Table 11.5: LIB transport parameters

11.2.3 Logging server exchanged messages

While programming web services it is useful to consult the messages received from and sent to clients by the server. To facilitate that, WST provides a service extension you can use to log all client-server message exchanges to a file. To use this, the `file_logger_extension` unit must be included in the project, and the logging file location must be specified by setting the value of the *LogFileCompleteName* variable (this variable is defined in the above unit); and lastly the extension must be registered with the service implementation that will be the target of the logging.

It is important to make sure that the target service implementation is already registered in the implementation registry. The following code excerpt shows how to register the file logger extension with the implementation of the *ICalcService*. The complete source of this example is located in the `sources\web-services\logging` folder. Before it can be tested, both the server and client projects must be compiled. Then you need to open a shell terminal and navigate to the server folder. First the server process must be started, after which the client can be started. At least one calculation should be done which will invoke the server. Note that the client should be started in a separate shell terminal. After stopping the server, the logging file should contain some messages marked with a time stamp.

```
...
LogFileCompleteName := Format('.%slog.txt',[PathDelim]);
theFactory :=
  GetServiceImplementationRegistry().FindFactory('ICalcService');
if ( theFactory <> nil ) then
  theFactory.RegisterExtension(['TFileLoggerServiceExtension'])
else
  WriteLn('Unable to find the service implementation factory.');
...
```

11.2.4 Implementing Web Services object pooling

Object pooling is a factory pattern used to accelerate object creation. This technique creates a pool of objects well before they are requested, and the objects are recycled for later requests instead of destroying them. Object pooling can greatly enhance the performance of an application, if the application repeatedly needs to create objects with a lot of parameters. The performance gain becomes clear when you realise the high cost of creating many objects. For example, it is usually expensive to create objects that establish a connection to a remote database engine. In such situations, recycling these objects for future reuse can improve performance greatly. The object pool can be a factor in improving software scaling through adjustment of the pool capacity according to the hardware on which the software has to run.

WST provides all the tools needed to implement object pooling. The default object factory for web services implementation objects provided by WST, *TImplementationFactory* (defined in `server_service_intf.pas`) has pooling functionalities that simply need to be activated for implementation objects that support pooling. The implementation objects must implement the *IObjectControl* interface defined in `server_service_intf.pas`.

Pools as implemented in WST have three main properties. *PoolMax* specifies the pool capacity. The pool cannot contain more objects than this value. *PoolMin* specifies the minimum number of objects created when the pool itself is created. Usually a pool is created with its minimum number of created objects, and as the number of simultaneous requests grows, the pool is filled, as needed, up to capacity. The valid values of this property are between zero and the capacity of the pool. *TimeOut* specifies the maximum amount of time an object requester can wait for the pool to obtain an available object. Past this time the pool raises an exception to mark the failure. The timeout value is given in milliseconds. At the time of writing, the timeout functionality is available only on the Windows platform.

Developing Poolable objects

Poolable objects can be developed in 2 basic steps: The *IObjectControl* interface must be implemented, and the object must be registered as a poolable object by specifying the pool properties.

Step 1: Implementing the IObjectControl interface

Using the *IObjectControl interface* – defined in `server_service_intf.pas` – the WST runtime manages the object's lifetime. It is used to activate an object before its use and to test whether or not the object can return to the pool once the object is released.

```
IObjectControl = interface
['{C422C7CA-4C95-48A4-9A82-2616E619F851}']
  procedure Activate();
  procedure Deactivate();
  function CanBePooled(): Boolean;
end.
```

These methods have the following meanings:

Activate is called by the runtime when an object is retrieved from the pool and is about to be used. This is the appropriate moment for the object to prepare itself to handle a request. *Deactivate* is called by the runtime when the object has been used and is no longer needed. This is the appropriate moment for the object to prepare itself to be pooled again or to be discarded. *Deactivate* is called before the object is queried for its capability to be pooled through the *CanBePooled* method. *CanBePooled* is called by the pool to determine if an object can be pooled for later reuse. If it returns True, the object is added to the pool's inactive objects list. If not, the object is freed.

In the `server_service_intf.pas` unit, WST defines *TactivableServiceImplementation*, a class that implements *IObjectControl* and which can be used as the base class for poolable objects. The implementation of *IObjectControl* provides empty methods for *Activate* and *Deactivate* while *CanBePooled* returns False. These methods are virtual, and descendent classes must override them. A poolable object should assess its ability to be pooled when the *Deactivate* method returns. An incoherent internal state may cause a poolable object to discard itself by returning False in *CanBePooled*.

Step 2: Registering the poolable object
Objects implementing webservices, whether poolable or not, have to be registered with the WST runtime. Actually it is an implementation factory that gets registered so that the WST runtime can create an implementation object by invoking the *CreateInstance* method of that factory. *CreateInstance* is a method of *IItemFactory* and is declared in `base_service_intf.pas`. The skeleton implementation file generated either by the WST Type Library Editor or `ws_helper.exe` contains a procedure that registers the implementation object with the implementation registry:

```
procedure RegisterCalcServiceImplementationFactory();
begin
  GetServiceImplementationRegistry().Register(
    'ICalcService',
    TImplementationFactory.Create(
    TCalcService_ServiceImp,wst_GetServiceConfigText('ICalcService')
    ) as IServiceImplementationFactory
  );
end;
```

The *factory Create* method uses an overloaded constructor which expects two parameters: the implementation class, and a string describing its properties. In the code above a default properties string is retrieved by the *wst_GetServiceConfigText* function defined in the `config_objects.pas` file. The properties string is the most direct way to configure the implementation factory. Its general format is a list of name/value pairs separated by semicolons in the following format:

```
name=value(;name=value)*
```

If the parameter *Pooled* appears in the string, it must be in the last position. The string can also be empty. The name specifies the pool parameter the developer wants set to a value. To set up a pool with a capacity of ten with a minimum of three created instances, the following properties string would be used:

```
'PoolMax=10;PoolMin=3;Pooled=True'
```

It is also possible to configure the pool through a configuration file. This is an **XML** file that can be used by the developer to specify service configuration properties. You can obtain the file location by calling the *wst_GetConfigFileName* function located in the `config_objects` unit. Note that the WST runtime does not automatically create this file. The unit contains a function *wst_CreateDefaultFile* that can be use to create a default configuration file which contains all the services registered in the WST runtime with default values.

The following sample content duplicates the configuration produced by the properties string given earlier.

```
<?xml version="1.0"?>
<Application xmlns:ns1="urn:wst_base">
  <WST_Configuration>
  <Services>
     <service Name="IWSTMetadataService">
        <PoolMax>0</PoolMax>
        <PoolMin>0</PoolMin>
        <Pooled>false</Pooled>
        <TimeOut>0</TimeOut>
     </service>
     <service Name="ICalcService">
        <PoolMax>10</PoolMax>
        <PoolMin>3</PoolMin>
        <Pooled>true</Pooled>
        <TimeOut>0</TimeOut>
     </service>
     </Services>
  </WST_Configuration>
</Application>
```

The `sources\web-services\protocols` folder contains a complete source code example. The registration procedure of the implementation object registers the object as a singleton. The object displays its pointer address in the terminal at its construction, its moment of execution, and at its destruction. As the object is a singleton, multiple calls to the server will display the same object pointer address. A specific instance can handle up to five (5) requests and then returns False in *CanBePooled.* So the object pointer address will be shown five times before a new object is created with a new address, while the old one is destroyed.

11.2.5 Service extensions

Service extensions allow the service developer to plug into the request processing stages. Client request handling can be subdivided into four stages as shown in Figure 11.17.

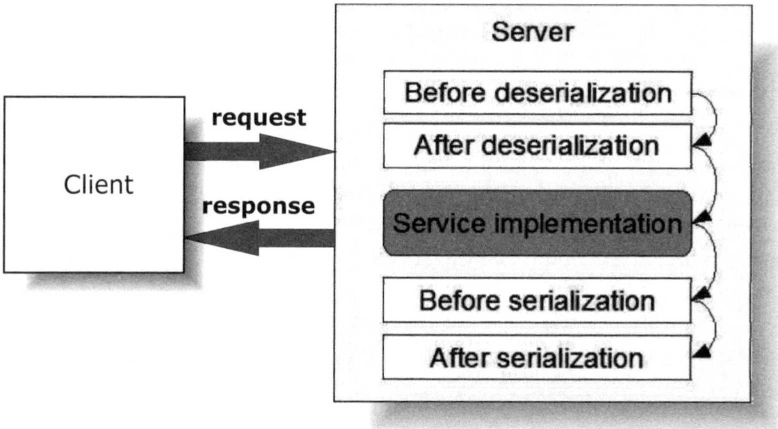

Figure 11.17: Stages during client request processing

The service extensions mechanism provided by the WST runtime offers access to these four stages through the *IServiceExtension* interface:

Property	Effect
msBeforeDeserialize:	The runtime has just received the request buffer. At that stage the *AMsgData* is an *IRequestBuffer* reference.
msAfterDeserialize:	The request buffer has been deserialized into an *IFormatterResponse* that corresponds to the *AMsgData*.
msBeforeSerialize:	The service implementation object has already handled the call. The call stack is about to be serialized to the response buffer. The *AMsgData* still contains a reference to an *IFormatterResponse*.
msAfterSerialize:	The call stack has been serialized and the response buffer is ready to be sent to the client. The *AMsgData* contains a reference to an *IRequestBuffer*.

Table 11.6: Possible TMessageStage values

A service extension has to implement this interface and be registered with the service extensions registry, which is available through the *GetServiceExtensionRegistry* function declared in `server_service_intf.pas`. For a service extension to be invoked on a service implementation's processing stages, the implementation has to register the service extension. The *IServiceImplementationFactory* provides a *RegisterExtension* method to do that.

```
TMessageStage = (
  msAfterDeserialize, msAfterSerialize, msBeforeDeserialize,
  msBeforeSerialize
  );
IServiceExtension = interface
['{E192E6B3-7932-4D44-A8AC-135D7A0B8C93}']
procedure ProcessMessage(
  const
     AMessageStage: TMessageStage;
     ACallContext: ICallContext;
     AMsgData: IInterface
     );
end;
```

A service extension is developed in the following steps:

- A class must be created that implements the *IServiceExtension* interface. Using *TSimpleFactoryItem* as a base class will free the developer from needing to create a factory implementation as the *TSimpleFactory* can be used.
- The service extension must be registered with the service extensions registry. Ideally this is done in the *initialization* section of the containing unit. The service extensions registry is available through the *GetServiceExtensionRegistry* function.
- All implementation classes of services that need the extension can register it through their factory with the method *RegisterExtension*. Given the service name, the implementation factory is found through the *FindFactory* method of the services implementation registry.

References

Specifications :

- **SOAP** `http://www.w3.org/TR/soap`
- **WSDL** `http://www.w3.org/TR/wsdl`
- **JSON** `http://www.json.org/`
- **JsonRPC** `http://json-rpc.org/`
- **XmlRPC** `http://www.xmlrpc.com`
- **Synapse** socket library `http://synapse.ararat.cz/`
- **Indy socket library for Lazarus**
  `http://www.indyproject.org/Sockets/fpc/index.EN.aspx`
- **ICS socket library**
  `http://www.overbyte.be/eng/products/ics.html`

WST sites :

- **Home page :**
  `http://inoussa12.googlepages.com/webservicetoolkitforfpc%26lazarus`
- **Google group**
  `http://groups.google.com/group/wst-list`
- **Wiki page at the Lazarus wiki site**
  `http://wiki.freepascal.org/Web_Service_Toolkit`
- **development sources (svn)**
  `https://lazarus-ccr.svn.sourceforge.net/svnroot/lazarus- ccr/wst/trunk`

Chapter 12
Database Access

by Michael Van Canneyt

Database access

Many applications (by no means only business applications) display and manipulate data coming from various sources. The data may come from a database server or from regular files, and is commonly stored on the local hard disk.

12.1 Architecture

The Lazarus IDE and LCL do not provide their own database engine, nor do they offer a complete database management system. All database systems have their peculiarities, and most come with their own specialised tools to create and maintain their databases. General-purpose tools cannot hope to match that specialised functionality. Therefore when you develop database applications in Lazarus, you will also need whatever native database tools are available (for instance mysqladmin when working with MySQL, or FlameRobin when working with Firebird).
Instead of attempting to duplicate what the database engines and tools do best, Lazarus and its LCL offer two kinds of support for creating database applications, which focus on connecting to as many database systems as possible.

12.1.1 Database access

Access to different data sources in Lazarus is achieved through a unified database interface, provided in the form of components. Most standard controls available for writing a user interface have a corresponding data-aware version. The data-aware control knows how to get data from the data interface, and how to communicate any data changes back to the database.
Thanks to this unified architecture, you don't have to change your user interface to develop it as a database application which can edit an underlying database. The database layer is not dependent on the visual controls, and therefore it can also be used in service or web applications.
The database interface is written in pure Object Pascal – and is therefore fully accessible – and Lazarus contains ready-made components for access to many different database types and file formats, regardless of whether they are open source or not: CSV data (comma-separated values), DBF files, Firebird and Interbase databases, MySQL databases (version 4.0, 4.1 or 5), Oracle databases, PostGreSQL databases, embedded SQLite databases and any other database for which an ODBC driver is available. Additionally, Lazarus offers components to keep data in memory.
The advantage of this Object Pascal approach is that data can be shown in the IDE, where it can be inspected at design time. You don't have to run your application just to view the data.

Alternatively, there are database access interfaces from third parties. For instance, the Advantage Database Server, the ZeosLib components for access to different databases, and several Firebird/Interbase components from UIB (whose main components are not based on the Lazarus *TDataset* class). FBLib also offers access to Firebird/Interbase databases. In theory, anyone can develop components for database access.

Components designed for database connectivity in the LCL (or FCL) fit into one of two distinct categories: the data access layer (*TDataset* descendants) and the presentation layer (various visual components, such as *TDBGrid*). The two categories are connected through a *TDatasource* instance. This component connects the presentation components to the database access layer. The Component Palette's *Data Access* page contains a series of components for connecting to a database in order to send data to (or receive data from) that database. The visual components that are the source of the data are the subject of this chapter.

To develop a GUI database application you will use both data-access and data-presentation components. This usually involves three (or four) steps:

1. Dropping a database connection component on a form. (You can skip this step for most flat-file databases).
2. Dropping one or more *TDataset* descendants on a form and connecting them to the database connection component created in step 1.
3. Dropping a *TDatasource* component on the form for each *TDataset* descendant created in step 2, and connecting it to the corresponding *TDataset* descendant.
4. Finally, to see the data, you place as many data-aware controls on the form as are needed. Each of them must be connected to a *TDatasource* instance created in step 3.

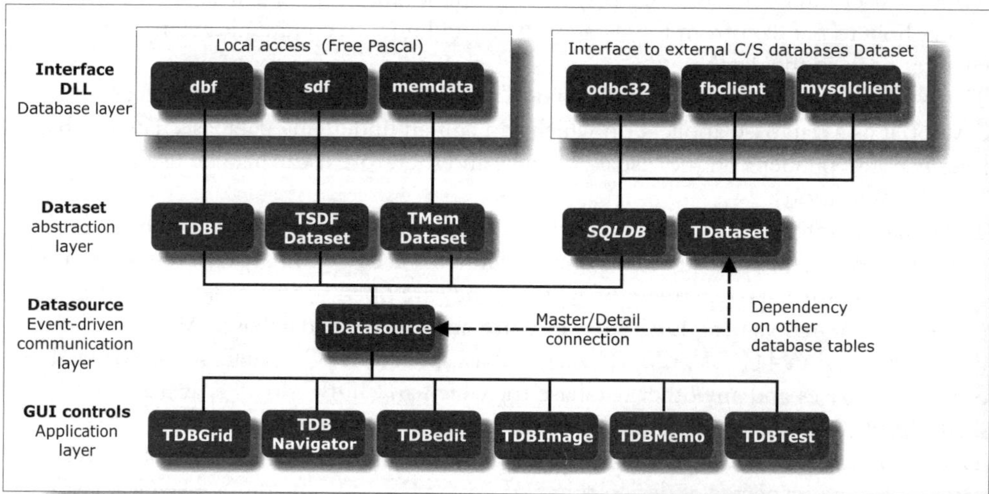

Figure 12.1: The database access layers in Lazarus

The first step is dropping a database connection on a form. This begs the question: which database should you use? This is the theme of the next section.

12.1.2 The case for database engines

Whenever an application has to store data (of whatever kind) the programmer must decide what format to store it in. You always have a choice between using custom-format data files or using an existing database engine to read and write the data. Object Pascal has very flexible file reading and writing routines, which makes it easy to read and write data stored in files, whatever their format. It is tempting therefore to write data to regular files using custom routines. Indeed, in many cases this is a valid choice.
However, for large amounts of data or when sharing data with other applications, this may not be the best choice because it forces the other applications to duplicate your file reading-and-writing code. There may also be concurrency issues when two applications try to access the same data simultaneously. In such cases, it is better to opt for some kind of database engine to manage the data.
There are many different kinds of database engines. How they store the data which they manage constitutes one important difference between them. Some store their data in simple flat-files while others store their data in large database files or even entire disks. In general, the data is written in a format private to the database engine.
The database engines can store various kinds of information. Some databases allow a very free format, where the various items of data can have widely differing structures. Examples of databases which allow variously structured data are `XML`-like files, `.INI` files, or something like the Windows Registry. These are often used to store configuration data (which usually contains many differently structured kinds of data).
A distinctly different type of engine will store only strictly tabular data. Each *table* contains only identically structured items. Each item is called a *record*, and the various entries in each record are called *fields*. In such systems, to store differently structured records requires the creation of different tables. Storage of measurement data, addresses, lists of users and more complex data are typical uses for such systems. A collection of such tables is then called a *database*. The various tables in the database can be related. For example a table containing invoices can be linked to a table containing customer data, making it easy to retrieve a list of invoices per customer, or to get a warning when deleting a customer in the customer table, if that customer still has outstanding invoices. All this is described in **RDBMS** (Relational Database Management System) theory – which is in fact a mathematically described model.

There are many commercial RDBMS engines such as Oracle, MS-SQL server, DB2 as well as Open Source alternatives such as Firebird, PostGreSQL and MySQL.
RDBMS engines have features that extend beyond merely storing tabular data. They provide mechanisms to collect various pieces of information from several tables at once. It is unnecessary to access the tables individually – cross-table queries are an integral part of an RDBMS.

12.1.2 The case for database engines

To be able to quickly locate specific data, an RDBMS will create *indexes* on its tables. An index is a lookup table. It contains a series of *keys*, and a pointer to the corresponding row in the table – for instance, the invoice number in an Invoices table is a good candidate for an index.

The RDBMS can create an index on the invoice number field, which means that it will keep an ordered list of invoice numbers, together with the location of the corresponding invoice record in the Invoices table. When looking for the record of a particular invoice, the RDBMS will look in the index for that invoice number – a fast operation since the numbers are ordered – and when it finds the number, it will then use the location information to quickly look up the invoice record in the Invoices table. If there were no index, it would have to scan every record in the Invoices table, and check its invoice number field, until it found the right record (possibly very slow for a large Invoices file).

Some flat-file systems also have support for indexes and can have index files associated with them (dBase files are one example). Such index files let you quickly show the records in a particular order.

Besides storing data and allowing you to retrieve and modify this data, most RDBMSs also allow you to write procedures which are stored in the database, and which are executed by the database engine. Often this offers significant speedups because transferring data from the database to the application, modifying it, and sending the modifications back to the database are all time-consuming operations. Stored procedures are designed to avoid the need for such time-consuming data transfers.

Additionally, an RDBMS will offer sophisticated management routines. Applications change, and sometimes need to store additional data – for instance, a shipping address. In the case of data in flat-files, this would mean writing some kind of conversion routine to add additional storage space for the shipping address to the flat files. RDBMSs have a built-in capability for doing this.

All RDBMSs offer a common interface to enable you to manipulate the data and the structure of the data. They use a language called SQL (Structured Query Language). Using this language means that – in theory – the data can be transferred from one engine to another and very little of the application must be changed as long as you use SQL to retrieve and manipulate the data. This makes RDBMSs more attractive to programmers when compared to XML-like or registry-like mechanisms.

In reality, SQL compatibility across RDBMSs is not so reliable. The programming models and communication interfaces of these engines differ widely. Each of them offers an API (Application Programming Interface) to access the data in the database.

This is usually a library (DLL) which contains the routines needed to execute SQL statements and retrieve the results (if any).

These routines differ from engine to engine.

For some database mechanisms the shared library is all there is to the engine – the whole database engine is contained in the shared library and so becomes part of the application. The engine is *embedded* in the application.

With other database mechanisms, the shared library just contains a communication entry point to the external database engine which is a separately running process, managing the actual databases.

Examples of the embedded approach are MS Access, Advantage Database System, SQLite or even Berkeley DB. Other RDBMSs use the latter approach in which a separate process runs (perhaps on another computer) and manages the database, and a DLL (client library) is needed to communicate with this process.
Some systems, such as Firebird, offer a hybrid approach, with both an embedded form and a client/server option.
It hardly needs to be said that having a separate process to manage the databases requires more processing power on the PC where the application is supposed to run.
The required server also needs to be set up (a task which may be beyond the average user), and it also needs more ongoing maintenance than when the database layer is embedded in the application.
To solve the problem of the differing interfaces to the various database engines, the **ODBC** (Open Database Connectivity) system was devised. This system offers a single, well-defined API, which allows an application to connect to any database, from any programming language. The ODBC system handles the details of the connection to the various databases through driver libraries.
This works well when speed is not an issue, and when a driver is available for the particular database that needs to be accessed. ODBC exists for most available platforms and would therefore seem like an ideal candidate for use as a database access layer in Free Pascal or Lazarus.

Rather than relying on ODBC for access to data, Free Pascal has implemented its own abstraction layer (as found in Delphi) in which all tabular data is represented by a *TDataset* class. The use of the *TDataset* class assumes that the data to be managed has a uniform structure. You must be able to structure your data as a series of records, all of which have the same form, i.e. each record has the same set of fields.
That is to say, the data is in tabular form, consisting of rows (records) and columns (fields). The *TDataset* class offers a set of routines to navigate the data, to retrieve the values in the various columns (fields) and to change those values.
The origin of the data managed by the *TDataset* component is irrelevant – it is only known to the actual *TDataset* descendants. It could be the content of a structured flat-file, the result of an SQL query or even simple, in-memory data.
Tdataset is an abstract class, from which descendants must be created.
In practice, Lazarus/FCL already provides descendant classes for each kind of database engine.
For instance *TDBF* is a *TDataset* descendant that can handle data from dBase files. *TSQLiteDataset* is a *TDataset* descendant that lets you work with data from a SQLite database. Both these engines are descendants of *TDataset*, which means that the same set of methods can be used to navigate through the data or to modify the data.
Many such descendants have been implemented by the Free Pascal team and are included in each release.
The DB unit, in which the *TDataset* component is defined, also contains classes to describe index definitions (*TIndexDef*) and parameters for queries (*TParameter*).
These classes have no other function than to describe the indexes of a table or the parameters of a query. They introduce no further functionality.

12.1.3 The Database Desktop application

In addition to the components needed to access databases, Lazarus comes with an application called the *Lazarus Database Desktop*. It can be used to:

- Access all the databases which Lazarus supports.
- Execute SQL queries on SQL-based databases, and view the results.
- Create databases.
- Create common SQL statements for tables.
- Create and maintain data dictionaries, which can be applied to datasets in an application.
- Export data in different formats.
- Generate code for object oriented coding based on the database structure.

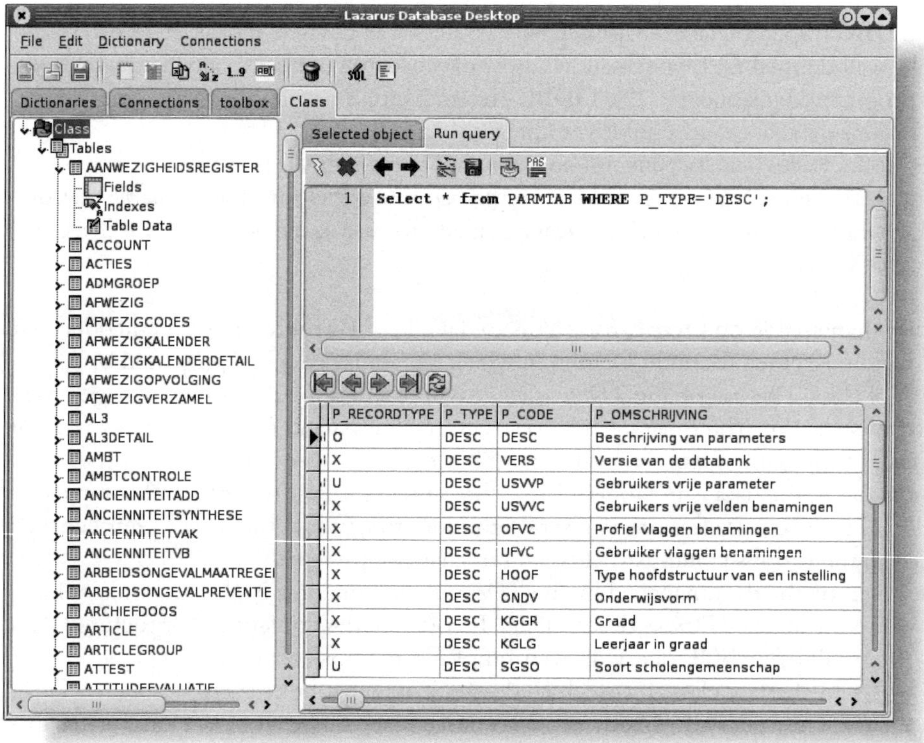

Figure 12.2: The Lazarus Database Desktop

The Database Desktop is not a database management system, although it can perform general tasks, but rather it is an aid for database development. It understands both databases and the LCL mechanisms for accessing databases, and can therefore be used to create code in the Lazarus IDE. It is described in more detail in section 12.4.

12.2 The Database Access classes

12.2.1 TDataset

TDataset is the base component from which all database components descend which manipulate tabular data. It provides the foundation for all database operations.
No *TDataset* descendant adds much functionality to *TDataset*, since the methods and properties which are relevant to data-aware applications are already defined in *TDataset*. In order to work with these descendants, you only need to know *TDataset*. In fact, all the visual database components know only *TDataset* and are thereby able to work with any of its descendants.

The core of *TDataset* is a memory buffer that contains the data. The source of this data has to be specified in its descendants. The data is organized in rows (records) – comparable to rows in a grid. To complete the two-dimensional database structure, vertical columns are also provided. You can access these columns in the horizontal direction via their names: the fields. There can be one or more fields or columns.
The *TDataset* class introduces methods to navigate and manipulate the data. It also introduces a cursor in the data. Only the data at the current location of the cursor (the current record) can be shown and manipulated. In order to change data in another row, the cursor must be moved to that other row. *TDataset* provides the necessary methods and properties to navigate through the data.

TDataset does not itself provide access to data. The actual data is fetched by a descendent class, which must override a number of abstract, protected methods of *TDataset*, by which the data is copied to the memory buffers managed by *TDataset*. Changes to the database or file are applied automatically whenever the data in memory has changed. All this is hidden from the user, who needs to know only four data manipulation methods.
TDataset is an abstract class, which should never be instantiated in memory. There are lots of descendants, and you choose the one to use depending on the data to be accessed.
There are several companion components to *TDataset*, which you need to understand in order to work with a *TDataset* descendant:

- **TField:** The *TField* class represents a single field in the current record, and it offers methods to retrieve the value of the field, or to set the value of the field. The value can be retrieved or set as any of the basic types supported by Object Pascal, such as string, integer, floating point, currency or *TDateTime* types. In the case of BLOB fields the value can be retrieved as text or in a memory buffer, or it can be saved to file. Various properties are provided which you can use to specify how the value should be displayed in a GUI.

- **The TDataset** component contains an array property named *Fields*, which gives access to the various fields in the current record – the elements in this array are descendants of *TField*. There is a different descendant for each data type present in the record.

- **TDatasource** is a companion component to *TDataset* which communicates changes in the dataset to any third component (usually a GUI control). GUI controls never communicate directly with a *TDataset* instance, but always use a *TDatasource* as a mediator. A single *TDataset* can be connected to many *TDatasource* instances.
  This enables you to selectively distribute data-update events to other components, for example to GUI controls.

- **TDatamodule:** Although it is possible to place a *TDataset* or a *TDatasource* on a form, it is bad design practice to do so. To clearly separate GUI logic from data logic, it is better to create a *TDatamodule* descendant. The *TDatamodule* component itself introduces no functionality. It exists solely for the benefit of easy separation of data and GUI logic while nevertheless allowing all the easy manipulations offered by a RAD environment. Datamodules act as containers for all dataset components, and have a visual representation in the Lazarus IDE, so they can be manipulated as you would manipulate a form. Datamodules are not visible in your running application (they exist only in the application's memory).
  To connect the GUI elements of a form to the datasets or datasources on a datamodule, the unit in which it resides must be added to the form unit's *uses* clause. The controls on the form can then be connected to the right *TDatasource* instance by simply selecting it from the control's *DataSource* property's dropdown list.

The four classes above are part of the way Lazarus implements its data-access mechanism. The actual connection is implemented by descendants of *TDataset*. Often these descendants refer to another component, which represents the connection to a database. It may be that your dataset (e.g. representing different tables, or the result of a query) is connected to a single database component. They are not the only possibility to connect to database tables. There are also many data components that do not need a database connection. Single-file datasets such as the *TDBF* component have no concept of a database, they handle only individual files on disk using a flat-file model. Therefore the basic Lazarus data architecture provides no abstraction for the database concept.

Navigating through data

The dataset concept makes use of a cursor which represents the position of the current record in the dataset's record set. Only the current record's data can be read or manipulated. Navigating the dataset means moving the cursor over the records in the dataset. To change a table record, you have to navigate to that specific record before you can edit that record's contents. *TDataset* introduces methods to navigate to and examine the records in the dataset, and also offers the properties listed in Table 12.1.

Properties	Description
Active	A boolean property. If it is True, the dataset is open, and the data is available for browsing and editing. If it is False, the dataset is closed, and the data is unavailable. The property can be set to True or False to open or close the dataset, which can be done either in the IDE, or at runtime in code. Opening the database will access the real data, which means that a file on disk is opened, or a query is run on the database. Note that this can cause an exception to be raised (for instance if the SQL statement contains an error or if the file from which data should be read is not available).
RecNo	This is the current position of the cursor in the rows of the dataset. This cannot always be relied upon. Some datasets are unidirectional (only forward navigation is allowed), because the underlying data access mechanism does not allow navigation back and forth between the rows.
RecordCount	This indicates the number of records in the dataset. This number is not always available or even reliable. Some datasets fetch additional records as the cursor is moved through the data, and update the record count as they fetch more records.
BOF	The cursor is at the beginning of the set. Moving to the prior record will have no effect.
EOF	The cursor is at the end of the set. Moving to the next record will have no effect.
Fields	This is an indexed array of *TField* instances. Each instance represents a field in the current record. The fields can be accessed by index, or by name (see below).
Modified	Indicates whether the data in the buffer has been modified.
State	The state property indicates the current state of the dataset and is a read-only property. The commonest states are: *dsInactive* when the dataset is closed; *dsBrowse* when data is being browsed; *dsEdit* when editing the current record; *dsInsert* when a new record is being added.

Table 12.1: The properties of Tdataset (part 1)

Properties	Description
FieldDefs	This is a collection of *TFieldDef* items. Each item contains the definition of a field in a row, and for each of the elements in this collection, there is a corresponding *TField* instance in the Fields array. This collection is automatically filled by *TDataset* descendants so it accurately represents the data you are trying to access. When a dataset is opened, the *TDataset* descendant will use the FieldDefs collection to create each required *TField* instance. Because this happens behind the scenes it is not usually necessary to access the FieldDefs collection directly. In-memory datasets are a notable exception, where to be able to create the actual data you must fill the FieldDefs collection with appropriate definitions.
Filter	A filter expression to filter the records in the dataset. Whether this is implemented or not depends on the particular *TDataset* engine in use because *TDataset* itself does not contain an implementation of filters. This means that the syntax of the filters depends on the actual *TDataset* descendant in use, although most implementations stick to an SQL-compliant syntax for the filters.
Filtered	A boolean property which indicates whether the filter expression in the Filter property should be applied or not.

Table 12.1: The properties of TDataset (Continuation)

If a dataset is open, and both EOF and BOF are *True*, it means that the dataset is empty (containing no records). It is not advisable to check for RecordCount=0, because this may not be implemented for the *TDataset* descendant in use. The following is the only correct check:

```
  Var D : TDataset;
begin
  D.Active:=True;
  try
    if (D.EOF and D.BOF) then
      raise Exception.Create('No data available!');
    // Do something with D if there is data.
  finally
    D.Close;
  end;
end;
```

Methods

The methods available to navigate the data are listed in Table 12.2.

Methods	Description
Open	Opens the dataset. This is equivalent to setting the Active property to True. Opening a dataset twice has no effect - the second call will simply return without doing anything.
Close	Closes the dataset. This is equivalent to setting the Active property to False. Again, closing a dataset twice has no effect - the second call will simply return without doing anything.
Next	Moves the cursor to the next record in the dataset. If EOF is True, this has no effect.
Prior	Moves the cursor to the previous record in the dataset. If BOF is True, this has no effect. Not all *TDataset* descendants support this operation. Some datasets are unidirectional and only allow forward navigation.
First	Moves the cursor to the first record in the dataset. After a call to First, BOF is True. Again, not all *TDataset* descendants support this operation.
Last	Moves the cursor to the last record in the dataset. After a call to Last, EOF is True. All datasets support this method.
MoveTo	This method accepts a 1-based record number (RecNo) as a parameter. It will jump to the numbered record. Again, not all *TDataset* descendants support this operation.
Refresh	Refreshes the data in the dataset from its actual source, but does not change the current record position (if possible). For a file-based dataset, this means that the file is re-read from disk.

Table 12.2: Methods of navigation

With these methods and properties, most read-only operations can be performed on a dataset. The following code example will allow you to traverse all records in a dataset, and perform some operation on each record:

```
  Var D : TDataset;
begin
  D.Open;
  Try
    While Not D.EOF do begin
      DoSomeOperation(D);
      D.Next;
    end;
  Finally
    D.Close;
  end;
end;
```

Note the *Try...Finally block*:
If an exception occurs during manipulation of the data, the dataset will be closed anyway at the end of the routine. For short operations, it is good practice to do this.

Accessing field data

The field values in the current record can be accessed through the Fields property. This is a property of the *TFields* class, which has as a default property an indexed array of *TField* descendants. The array is zero based and valid indexes range from 0 to Count-1 (Count is a property of Fields) Thus, the following code accesses the field with index 0:

```
  Var F : TField;
begin
  F:= Dataset.Fields.Fields[0];
end;
```

Each of the elements is always a descendant of class TField. Table 12.3 lists the most important properties of the *TField* class, properties which give information about the field content.

Properties	Description
FieldName	The name of the field as it is known in the underlying database.
DataType	The database native type of the data in this field.
FieldKind	Indicates whether this is a data field, a lookup field or a calculated field.
Size	For strings and BCD (Binary Coded Decimal) fields, this indicates the largest possible size of the string or BCD value.
Precision	for BCD values this indicates the number of decimal places.
Required	This property will be True if the field requires a value, and a value must be set before posting any data to the record. When posting data, *TDataset* will check if all fields that have Required set to True are not empty, raising an exception if this is not the case. By default it will be set to the value supplied by the underlying database, but this can be modified, for instance when a particular situation requires a certain field to be set, even when it is not required by the database.
ReadOnly	Indicates whether the field is read-only. For instance, this might be the case for a computed field in a SQL database.

Table 12.3: Properties of TField

The properties listed in Table 12.3 determine what kind of (and how much) data a field can contain. Normally, a field contains only one kind of data, i.e. it is not possible to store a string in an integer field. To access the data in the field, the following read/write properties are provided:

To access the data in the field, the following read/write properties are provided:

Properties	Description
AsInteger	The value of the data as an integer.
AsString	The value of the data as a string.
AsDateTime	The value of the data as a *TDateTime* value.
AsCurrency	The value of the data as a Currency value.
AsFloat	The value of the data as a Double value.
AsBoolean	The value of the data as a Boolean value.
Value	The value of the data as a variant.

Table 12.4: Properties used to access TField data

Each *AsXYZ* property will attempt to convert the actual data to the requested type. If, for example, the database field is a string field, then reading the value by means of the *AsInteger* property will attempt to convert the string value to an Integer. If the string value in the database is not a valid representation of an integer, then an *EConvertError* will be raised. Conversely, setting the property will convert the value to the type expected by the database.

Assuming that the first field in a dataset is an integer field, and that the field in the current record has the value 123, then the following assignment can be made:

```
  Var S : String;

begin
  S := Dataset.Fields[0].AsString;
end;
```

As a result, the string S will contain '123' – the data has been converted to the correct type. The following routine dumps all data in the current record of dataset D to the console:

```
Procedure DoSomeOperation(D : TDataset);
  Var I : Integer;
      F : TField;
begin
  For I := 0 to D.Fields.Count - 1 do
    begin
      F := D.Fields[I];
      Write(F.FieldName:32,':');
      If (F.DataType = ftBlob) then
        Writeln('<BLOB>')
      else
        Writeln(F.AsString);
    end;
end;
```

Combined with the navigation example above, this would dump all data in a dataset to screen.
If the names of the fields are known, they can be accessed with *TDataset's FieldByName* method. Continuing the example above, if the dataset D contains the result of an SQL Query like the following:

```
SELECT FirstName, LastName, BirthDay From Persons;
```

then the DoSomeOperation could be coded like this:

```
Procedure DoSomeOperation(D : TDataset);
  Var BD : TDateTime;
begin
  Writeln('FirstName : ',D.FieldByname('FirstName').AsString);
  Writeln('LastName : ',D.FieldByname('LastName').AsString);
  BD := D.Fields.FieldByName('BirthDay').AsDateTime;
  Writeln('BirthDay : ',DateToStr(BD));
end;
```

Note that the variable BD is retrieved from the Fields property. The method FieldByName will raise an exception if the dataset does not contain a field with the requested fieldname. If this behaviour is not desirable, the alternative method FindField will simply return Nil if the requested field is not present. This can be used to check for the existence of a field, like this:

```
Function HasField(D : TDataset; FieldName : String) : Boolean;

begin
  Result := D.FindField(FieldName) <> Nil;
end;
```

There is an alternative way to retrieve (or set) the values of the fields, using a variant array. The *TDataset* class has a FieldValues array property of type Variant, declared as:

```
property FieldValues[FieldName : String] : Variant; default;
```

The index in the array is a string with the fieldname, and this array is the default property of the *TDataset* class, so it can be used as follows:

```
Procedure DoSomeOperation(D : TDataset);
  Var BD : TDateTime;
      S : String;
begin
  S := D['FirstName'];
  Writeln('FirstName : ',S);
  S := D['LastName'];
  Writeln('LastName : ',S);
  BD := D['BirthDay'];
  Writeln('BirthDay : ',DateToStr(BD));
end;
```

While this notation resembles the notation used in Visual Basic, Its use is not recommended, since variants are inherently inefficient and their type conversion rules may lead to nasty surprises.
Note that the items in the Fields property are not all of type *TField:* rather they are descendants of *TField* (a descendant is provided for each native database type).
When fetching data from the database, each *TDataset* will map the native database type for each field in the recordset to a *TField descendant*, and will set the DataType property to a value that best describes the type of the data in the database.

Several standard **TField descendants** are available:

Descendants	Description
TIntegerField	for up to 32-bit signed integer values. DataType will be *ftInteger.*
TSmallIntField	for up to 16-bit signed integer values. DataType will be *ftSmallInt*.
TWordField	for up to 16-bit unsigned integer values. DataType will be *ftWord*.
TLargIntField	for 64-bit integer values. DataType will be *ftLargeInt*.
TFloatField	for floating point values. DataType will be *ftDouble*.
TStringField	for string values. DataType will be *ftString*.
TBCDField	for BCD values. DataType will be *ftBCD*.
TDateField	for date values. DataType will be *ftDate*.
TTimeField	for time values. DataType will be *ftTime*.
TDateTimeField	for *TDateTime* values. DataType will be *ftDateTime*.
TBLOBField	for BLOB data (binary data without form). DataType will be *ftBLOB*.
TMemoField	for BLOB data containing only text. DataType will be *ftMemo*.

Table 12.5: Standard descendents of TField

Which field is used depends on the *TDataset* descendant. More specialised *TField* descendants exist, and although they are rarely used, some *TDataset* descendants use specialised *TField* descendants to encapsulate database-specific behaviour for their field types.
Not all fields in a record need to contain data - they could be empty. It is possible to test whether a field is empty using the boolean IsNull property. If it is True, the field has no value. It corresponds to the SQL value NULL.

The following will test whether all fields in the current record have a value:

```
With MyDataset do
 For i:=0 to Fields.Count-1 do
   if Fields[i].IsNull then
     Writeln('Field ',Fields[i].FieldName,' is empty');
```

Locating records

Sometimes it is necessary to jump to a record which has a specific value in a certain field. This can be done using the Locate method, which is defined as follows:

```
Type TLocateOption = (loCaseInsensitive, loPartialKey);
     TLocateOptions = set of TLocateOption;

function Locate( const keyfields: string;
                 const keyvalues: Variant;
                 Options: TLocateOptions  ) : boolean;
```

The parameters are a semicolon-separated list of field names; a single value or a variant array of values; and then the locate options:

- Should the search be case insensitive?
- Should a partial key match be considered, that is, should a string match partially or not?

The function returns True if a record is found that matches the search criteria. The dataset will then be positioned on the first matching record. The search is always from the first record in the dataset. This means that the following call will search for the record which has AName in the 'FirstName' field:

```
Function FindFirstName(D : TDataset; AName : String) : boolean;

begin
  Result := D.Locate('FirstName',AName,[]);
end;
```

To construct the variant array, the VarArrayOf function from the `variants` unit can be used, as in the following routine:

```
Function FindPerson(D : TDataset;
  Const AFirstName,ALastName : String) : boolean;

begin
  Result := D.Locate('FirstName;LastName',
    VarArrayOf([AFirstName,ALastName]),[loCaseInsensitive]);
end;
```

In this case, the search will be performed case-insensitively.

Using bookmarks

Sometimes you want to return to a particular record in the dataset after navigating through the other records. This can be done by retrieving a bookmark, and later returning to this same bookmark. The Bookmark property of *TDataset* can be used for this. It is declared as follows:

```
property Bookmark: TBookmarkStr read GetBookmarkStr
                                write SetBookmarkStr;
```

A bookmark on a certain record can be retrieved by reading the Bookmark property. Setting the bookmark will jump to the position in the dataset that the bookmark referred to. This can be used to implement a search routine, for instance:

```
Function HasFirstName(D : TDataset; AName : String) : boolean;
  Var B : TBookMarkStr;
begin
  B := D.BookMark;
  Try
    Result := D.Locate('FirstName',AName,[loCaseInsensitive]);
  Finally
    D.BookMark := B;
  end;
end;
```

This routine will return True if the dataset contains a first name AName, but will not move the cursor from the current location. More than one bookmark can be retrieved. For example, you could use this to maintain a selection of records in the dataset.

Manipulating data

TDataset also has methods for editing, adding and deleting data. They are listed in Table 12.6. While the dataset is in editing mode, any navigation command will attempt to post the modified data prior to executing the navigation method itself.
If the data is incomplete or otherwise invalid, an exception will be raised, and the dataset will remain in the editing state.
The State property of the dataset can be checked to see whether the dataset is currently in one of the edit modes. In fact, the special *dsEditModes* constant is a set that contains all edit modes. The following function will return True if the dataset is currently in one of the editing modes:

Methods	Description
Edit	Puts the dataset in edit mode. After this command, the contents of the current record can be modified. (The State property will equal *dsEdit*).
Insert	Puts the dataset in insert mode at the current location: a new record is added. After this command, the contents of the new record can be modified. (The State property will equal dsInsert).
Append	Is equal in functionality to Insert, except that the new record is added at the end of the recordset. The State property will likewise equal *dsInsert*.
Post	If the dataset is in edit or append mode, then the Post command will commit the changes to the record buffer, and will put the dataset back into browse mode, and at the same time the changes will also be committed at once to the underlying database.
Cancel	If the dataset is in edit or append mode, then the Cancel command will revert any changes and return the dataset to the state it was in prior to the Edit, Insert or Append command.
Delete	This command deletes the current record from the record buffer and - depending on the particular *TDataset* descendant being used - from the underlying database. No Post is needed to commit this action to the database. It follows that this action is irreversible, and cannot be undone with Cancel.

Table 12.6: Methods for editing, adding and deleting data

```
Function CheckEditing(D : TDataset) : Boolean;
begin
  Result := D.State in dsEditModes;
end;
```

Modifying existing data

In general, modifying existing data happens by navigating to the correct record in the dataset, and putting the dataset into the edit state, so the State property equals *dsEdit*. Then the data can be modified by setting the field values through one of the *AsXYZ* properties described in Table 12.4. Clearing the value of a field can be done by calling the field's Clear method.

When all editing is done, the Post method can be used to apply the edits to the underlying database. Prior to the Post method, all edits are only in memory: no actual data has been modified so far. After the Post method, the dataset is again in browse mode.

The following code is an example of a DoSomeOperation implementation that modifies the data in a dataset:

```
Procedure DoSomeOperation(D : TDataset);
  Var I : Integer;
      F : TField;
begin
  If D.FieldByName('NeedsCheck').AsBoolean then
    begin
      Edit;
      I := FieldByName('CheckField').AsInteger;
      FieldByName('CheckField').AsInteger := I+1;
      FieldByName('NeedsCheck').AsBoolean := False;
      Post;
    end;
end;
```

The above code will check the boolean field NeedsCheck. If it is True, it will augment the value of the CheckField field with 1, and set the NeedsCheck field to False. If this method is called for all records in a table called CheckTable, that operation would be equivalent to the following SQL statement:

```
UPDATE CheckTable SET
  CheckField = CheckField + 1,
  NeedsCheck = False
WHERE
  NeedsCheck = True;
```

Likewise, it is possible to clear a particular field (column) in the entire dataset by writing a loop as follows:

```
Procedure ClearIfNeedsCheck(D : TDataset);
  Var F : TField;
begin
  With D do
    While not EOF do
    begin
      If FieldByName('NeedsCheck').AsBoolean then
      begin
        Edit;
        FieldByName('CheckField').Clear;
        Post;
      end;
      Next;
    end;
end;
```

Obviously, this will only work if the 'Checkfield' field is not a required field. The above code could be done in SQL using the following statement:

```
UPDATE
  CheckTable
SET
  CheckField = Null
WHERE
  NeedsCheck = True;
```

Inserting new data

Append or Insert can be used to insert a new record in a dataset. Both methods create a new record. The former appends the record to the end of the dataset, the latter tries to insert the record at the current position, or falls back to appending if inserting at a specific position is not supported (not all databases have a notion of record position in a table). File-based datasets such as TDBF for dBase files do support inserting a record at the current position.

As with the editing of existing data, the new record exists in memory only, and is not actually inserted in the database until the Post method of the dataset is called.

The following will insert a new record in the dataset of the previous example:

```
Procedure CreateNewRecord(D : TDataset);
begin
  With D do
  begin
    Append;
    FieldByName('CheckField').AsInteger := 0;
    FieldByName('NeedsCheck').AsBoolean := True;
    Post;
  end;
end;
```

in SQL this insert operation is written as

```
INSERT INTO CheckTable
  (CheckField,NeedsCheck)
VALUES
  (0,True);
```

In fact, some *TDataset* descendants would, during the Post operation, generate such a statement, and execute it on the underlying database.

Deleting data

To delete a record, the correct procedure is to position the cursor on the record that should be deleted and then call the *Delete* method. The current record will then be deleted, and the cursor will be positioned on the next record in the dataset.
Note that no call to the 'Post' method is necessary: the delete statement is effective immediately.
So, the following code will delete all records in the dataset:

```
Procedure DeleteAllRecords(D : TDataset);
begin
  D.First;
  While not D.EOF do
  D.Delete;
end;
```

Note that no explicit navigation is done, other than placing the dataset on the first record. The above would be done in SQL as

```
DELETE FROM CheckTable;
```

The following would delete every odd-numbered record in the dataset:

```
Procedure DeleteEverySecondRecord(D : TDataset);
begin
  D.First;
  While not D.EOF do
  begin
    D.Delete;
    D.Next;
  end;
end;
```

Cancelling edits

When fields are modified either by insertion of a new record or editing an existing record, it may happen that the operation must be undone. For instance, the user starts editing the address of a customer, and then notices that the wrong customer has been selected. To undo the edits, the Cancel method can be called. This will restore the record to the state it was in prior to the Edit call.
Another scenario is when a Post operation fails: an exception will be raised in such case, and the dataset will remain in edit or insert mode. To restore the dataset to browse mode, the edit mode must be cancelled.

If the 'NeedsCheck' field of the previous examples is a required field, then the following code will raise an exception on the Post operation:

```
Procedure TryInsert(D : TDataset; AValue : Integer);
begin
  Try
    D.Append;
    D.FieldByName('CheckField').AsInteger := AValue;
    D.Post;
  except
    On E : Exception do
    begin
      D.Cancel;
      Raise;
    end;
  end;
end;
```

The exception handler will catch the exception, and will cancel the edit (returning the dataset to browse mode), and re-raise the exception.

Errors when manipulating data

Note that various things can go wrong when editing data in a dataset.
Errors are reported through exceptions since the *TDataset class* and its helper classes do a lot of checking and report any errors they find.
The usual class used when reporting errors is *EDatabaseError*.
First consider the type of error you will produce by attempting to edit data when the dataset is not in edit mode. The following code will result in an *EDatabaseError* exception:

```
With MyDataset do
begin
  Open;
  FieldByName('MyField').AsString := 'Some string';
  Post;
end;
```

The Post operation will never be reached, because writing to fields when the dataset is not in edit mode is not allowed.
Then another common type of error is attempting to write the wrong kind of data to a field. Suppose you have a CUSTNO field of SQL type INT (this will normally correspond to a *TIntegerField class*, whose DataType value is *ftInteger*).
The following code will raise an *EConvertError*.

```
With MyDataset do
begin
  Open;
  Append;
  FieldByName( 'CUSTNO' ).AsString := 'Some string';
  Post;
end;
```

The error is raised because the dataset expects an integer value for the 'CUSTNO' field, and 'Some String' is not a valid integer.
Yet another kind of error is failure to supply all required fields for a record. Consider a dataset which has two string fields, MyField and MyRequiredField. The following code will raise an exception when the Post command is executed:

```
With MyDataset do
begin
  Open;
  Append;
  FieldByName( 'MyField' ).AsString := 'Some string';
  Post;
end;
```

This will cause an *EDatabaseError* error saying that MyRequiredField needs a value, since no value was supplied. **Note** that supplying an empty string would solve this, because an empty string is a valid value. The following code would not give an error:

```
With MyDataset do
begin
  Open;
  Append;
  FieldByName('MyField').AsString := 'Some string';
  FieldByName('MyRequiredField').AsString := '';
  Post;
end;
```

The same error can also occur when editing data, when a field is cleared:

```
With MyDataset do
begin
  Open;
  Edit;
  FieldByName('MyField').AsString := 'Some string';
  FieldByName('MyRequiredField').Clear;
  Post;
end;
```

The **Clear** method of *TField* clears the contents of the field. Since the field is required, this is not allowed by the Post operation. It is important to be aware of the errors that can occur, because the dataset will be left in an inconsistent state after the error occurred, and action to correct the situation will be required. If an error occurs in the Post operation (e.g. when no value for a required field is given), then the dataset will be left in the edit state. The following code for instance will result in an exception:

```
With MyDataset do
  While Not EOF do
  begin
    Try
      Edit;
      FieldByName('MyRequiredField').Clear;
      Post;
    Except // Silently ignore any errors.
    end;
    Next;
  end;
```

Even though it looks like the code takes care of errors, it does not: if an exception is raised, then the exception is caught by the *Try...Except* block, but the dataset is left in edit mode. The *Next* statement that follows will try to post the pending changes anyway, and an exception will be raised again - but this time not caught by the *Try...Except* block. The correct way of handling this error is by cancelling the pending changes, as outlined in the previous section:

```
With MyDataset do
  While Not EOF do
  begin
    Try
      Edit;
      FieldByName('MyRequiredField').Clear;
      Post;
    Except
     // Silently ignore any errors.
      Cancel;
    end;
    Next;
  end;
```

If an error arises, the Cancel will cancel the changes, and put the dataset back into the browse state. The *Next* statement will then simply move to the next record. Whether or not a particular error can be ignored or the exception should be re-raised depends on the situation. What matters is that the dataset should be put back into a consistent state, hence the need for a *Cancel*.

Dataset events

The error handling illustrated in the previous section should have made it clear that you have to do some error checking. This is easy when doing everything in linear code as in the examples, but if the data is edited in a GUI and the actions are driven by user-generated events (e.g. by clicking the buttons of the *TDBNavigator* control), then error checking is not so easy.

Luckily, *TDataset* offers a lot of events to cater for this. For almost all methods discussed in the previous sections, there are 2 events. The events are consistently named with a prefix 'Before' and 'After' or 'On'.
These events are of type *TDataSetNotifyEvent*, which is declared as:

```
TDataSetNotifyEvent = procedure(DataSet: TDataSet) of object;
```

Note that the argument is of type *TDataset* instead of *TObject* as in a normal *TNotifyEvent event handler*.
If an exception happens in a 'Before' event handler, then the action will not be executed: it will be as if the call had not been done. This can be used to check if all necessary conditions to successfully execute the method have been fulfilled.

Table 12.7 lists the available Before events.

Events	Description
BeforeOpen	is executed by the 'Open' method, before the dataset is actually opened. This is usually the very first event to be executed in the lifetime of a dataset. The dataset is still in *dsInactive* state.
BeforeScroll	is executed before the cursor is moved to another record, no matter in which direction or to which position, or by what cursor repositioning method (such as when the cursor is positioned on a new record). This event will be triggered often, so time-consuming tasks should be avoided in this event handler.
BeforeEdit	is executed by the *'Edit'* method. The dataset is not yet in *dsEdit* state.
BeforeInsert	is executed by the 'Insert' or 'Append' methods. The dataset is not yet in *dsInsert* state.
BeforePost	is executed by the 'Post' method. The dataset's check on whether all required fields have a value has already been performed before this event is triggered, and it may have given an exception, in which case the event is not triggered. The dataset is still in one of the *dsEdit* or *dsPost* states.
BeforeDelete	is executed by the Delete method.
BeforeCancel	is executed before the Cancel method.
BeforeRefresh	is executed before the Refresh method.
BeforeClose	is executed by the Close method. The dataset is still in *dsActive* state.

Table 12.7: Before events

For all these events, there is also a corresponding 'After' event which is executed after the method has executed successfully. If an exception occurs during the method's execution the 'After' event handler will not be triggered.

There are some special events, which have no 'Before' or 'After' variations:

Events	Description
OnNewRecord	happens whenever a new record must be allocated. It can be used to initialize certain fields. It is triggered after the BeforeInsert but before the AfterInsert
OnPostError	happens when an error is detected during the Post method. An instance of the exception object is passed to this event handler, plus a variable that can be set so the post operation will be attempted again. This can be used to correct errors.

Table 12.8: Events without Before or After variations

Using persistent fields

Fields in a dataset have additional properties that can be set to control the display of their contents, and to control the way any connected data-aware controls behave when they display or edit the field data. Under normal circumstances the fields do not exist unless the dataset is active, so their properties cannot be set. If the dataset contains different fields each time it is opened, this is normal and expected behaviour.

Fields are created for the actual data returned by the dataset. For instance, if you create a form that allows you to enter an SQL statement, and its resulting dataset in a DBGrid, the number and type of fields that are created when the query is opened depends on the SQL statement that you entered.
For example, if the Customer table in a database has a field 'FirstName', and all records of the Customer table are shown in a grid,, then every time the dataset for this table is opened, an instance of *TField* is created which contains – among other things – the field name. The grid that shows this data will create a column for each of the fields thus created. The title of the columns will be set to the DisplayLabel property of the *TField* instance. The title of the customer name field will always be 'FirstName', because the field name is all that is available, and this will be returned by default by the DisplayLabel property. All the other *TField* properties that control the display of that field's contents are also filled with default values. This will confuse the user of the application.

If the developer knows that each time the table Customers is accessed, a 'FirstName' field will be returned, a persistent field can defined, which is a place holder for the relevant information for the 'FirstName' field (and any other fields the developer cares to define). In this place holder, for instance, the DisplayLabel property can be set to 'Customer first name'. The grid will then use this value as the title for the column for this field. When the dataset is opened and it encounters a field 'FirstName', it will first look for a persistent field with the same field name. If it finds such a persistent field, it will use it. If no persistent fields are present, a *TField* instance is created to represent the field, and filled with default values.
Creating persistent fields means that all fields in the dataset will be defined as fields in the form declaration, just as any other control on the form is declared as a field. Indeed, a *TField* is a *TComponent* descendant.
Creating persistent fields allows you to set display properties for the fields ahead of time, and these display properties will be streamed together with the rest of the form and will be available subsequently in the form at runtime.
Additionally, persistent fields provide easy access to your fields. Suppose a field ItemCount exists in a dataset, then creating persistent fields, and renaming the field component to ItemCount (the default name will be 'DatasetNameItemCount'), allows you to alter its content like this:

```
Procedure TMyForm.MyMethod;
begin
  ItemCount.AsInteger := 0;
end;
```

The data field of the dataset is available as a form 'field' of the form class (where 'field' is used in the Object Pascal sense).

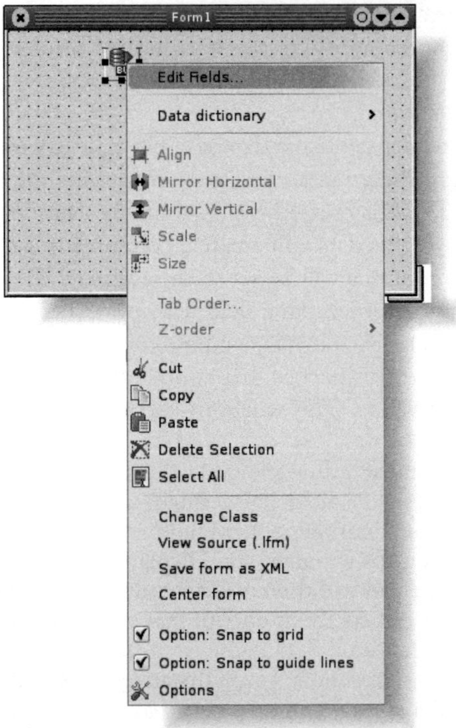

Figure 12.3: The context menu for datasets

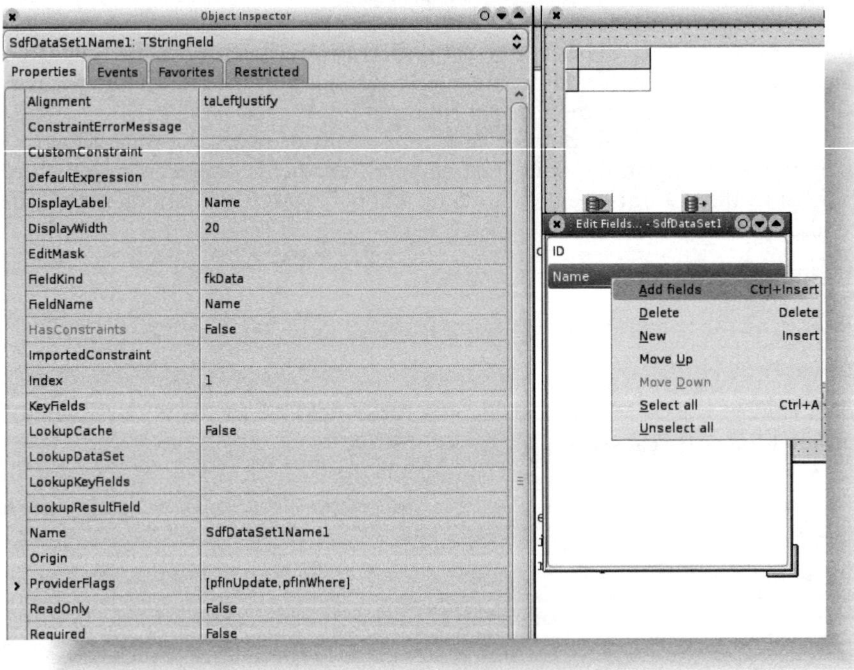

Figure 12.4: The field editor and its context menu

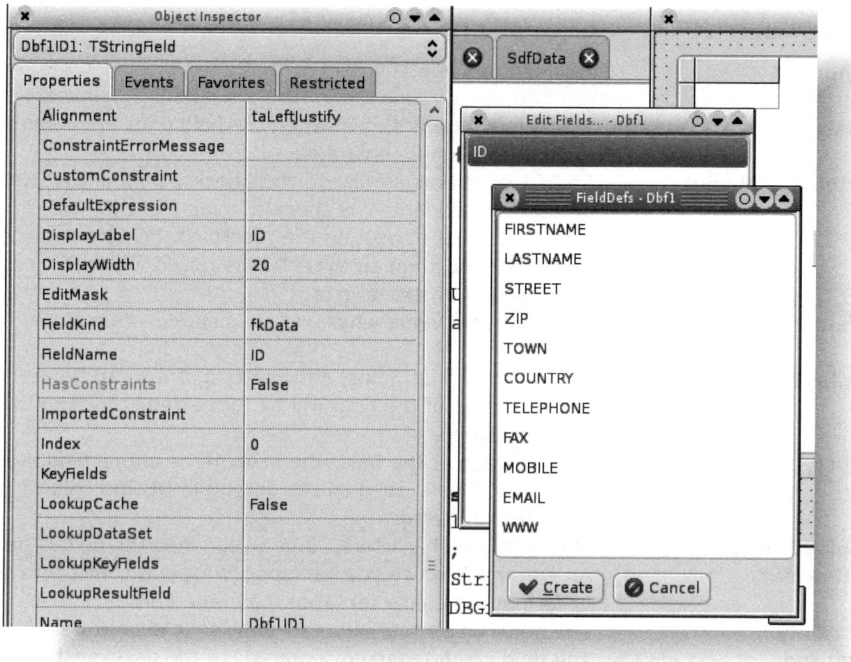

Figure 12.5: The fielddefs window

Persistent fields can be created by right-clicking the dataset to display the context menu (see Figure 12.3) and selecting the *Edit Fields...* menu item. The Fields Editor will pop up (as in Figure 12.4), and the Add fields menu item can be chosen from its context menu via a right-click. This will pop up a list of fields that can be added (see Figure 12.5). Clicking the [Create] button will create the field and add it to the form. It will also be selected in the Object Inspector, where the properties listed in Table 12.9 will be displayed and can be set.

Fields properties	Description
Alignment	This controls how the field contents are displayed e.g. in a grid column.
ConstraintErrorMessage	Which message is shown when the field does not conform to the CustomConstraint constraint.
CustomConstraint	An SQL condition, similar to the Check Constraint in SQL. Some dataset descendants will check the value of the field with this constraint prior to posting the record. If the field does not satisfy the constraint, then an exception is raised with the message specified in ConstraintError.
DefaultExpression	A default field value which will be inserted when a new record is created.
DisplayFormat	For BCD and float fields, a formatting string can be specified, and the value of the field will be formatted according to the mask specified.
DisplayLabel	A description of the field when the name of this field must be displayed. This is used as the default in DBGrid column headers or in error messages.
DisplayWidth	The width, in characters, to be used when the field is displayed.
EditFormat	An edit mask which you can specify for edit controls to constrain or format the characters that may be entered.
ReadOnly	The field can be marked read-only, so it will not be editable.
Required	The field can be marked required, so the user must enter a value before the data can be posted. Conversely, database required fields can be marked as not required if the insert query will supply a default value.
Visible	Can be set to False so a field won't be shown in the DBGrid.

Table 12.9: Fields Editor properties

Most of these properties control how a field's value is shown to the user. This can also be done at the GUI control level, but by setting it at the field level, the field will be displayed consistently in all locations where it is shown (e.g. in both DBGrid and DBEdit controls). Setting the field format in a single place affects all connected data-aware controls identically.

In addition to the properties, the events listed in Table 12.10 are also available.

Events	Description
OnChange	Is executed after the value of the field has been changed. This event is fired regardless of the way the field value was set (*whether by the user or through code).*
OnGetText	This event can be used to specify an alternative display or edit text for the field.
OnSetText	This event can be used to specify an alternative value for the field when it is set.

Table 12.10: Fields events

An important thing to remember is that when persistent fields have been created, those are the only fields that will be available as components to the data-ware controls. If, at a later point, the dataset retrieves more fields (because they were added to the SQL statement for instance, or the DBF file was restructured to contain more fields), then these new fields will not be available to the data-aware controls until these new fields have also been created as persistent fields.
Consider the following example: a dataset returning the data of the following query:

```
SELECT FIRSTNAME,LASTNAME FROM PERSON;
```

Two persistent fields (FirstName and LastName) are created and displayed in a grid. Later, the query is changed so it also retrieves the BirthDay field:

```
SELECT FIRSTNAME,LASTNAME, BIRTHDAY FROM PERSON;
```

Unless the BirthDay field is also created as a persistent field, it will not be visible in the grid.

12.2.2 The Data module

Instances of *TDataset* and *TDatasource* can be dropped directly on forms. This is easy, quick and in a few moments, a form with some events is ready. It also means that the GUI and data event handlers are mixed in the same unit. Lazarus offers a way to separate GUI from database logic: the datamodule. This can be thought of as an invisible window, which is never shown in the application, but which is kept in memory at runtime. In the IDE, components can be dropped on it, just as if they were dropped on a normal form. Since in this case event handlers are defined in the datamodule and not in a form, all data logic will be written in the datamodule, and not in the form, resulting in a clear separation between data and GUI logic. Service applications – which have no windows – are restricted to datamodules to contain program database logic. Once a datamodule has been created, the visual controls on the form can be connected to any datasource on the datamodule, provided the datamodule unit is added to the uses clause of the application:

- Create a new datamodule with the *File* → *New* menu item.
- On the newly created datamodule, create a database connection, setting all parameters.
- Drop some *TDataset* descendants on the datamodule, and connect them to the database instance. Usually the property connecting the dataset to the database is simply called Database. Finally, the various properties of the dataset must be set to select the appropriate data: the table name or an SQL statement.
- If a form must be connected to a dataset, then a *TDatasource* instance must also be placed on the datamodule, and must be pointed to the right *TDataset* instance by way of its Dataset property.

After these steps, the application can be connected to the database.
If a Database component is present, this can be done by setting the Connected property to 'True'. This means that the IDE will actually attempt to create a connection with the database. If an error occurs, it means the properties of the database component have not been set correctly (wrong database name or username/password pair are strong candidates). It may also be that the underlying database interface library is not present. The database code will attempt to load this library only when a connection is made.
If the connection to the database is established, then the properties of the dataset can also be tested by setting the Active property to True. This will attempt to fetch the data from the database - which data this is depends on the actual dataset and its properties. If the properties of the dataset are not correct, or the database is not available, an error message will be shown, indicating what went wrong. After the test, the Active and Connected properties can remain set on their True values. When the application is run and the datamodule is created, the connection to the database will be re-established, and the data for all active datasets will be fetched from the database.
More likely, some kind of run-time configuration must be done since the database location will change from installation to installation. In these cases, the Active and Connected properties must be set to False before saving the datamodule definition. They can be set to True after the necessary configuration steps have been performed at runtime in the appropriate event handlers.
Figure 12.6 shows a datamodule with a couple of data components in the IDE.

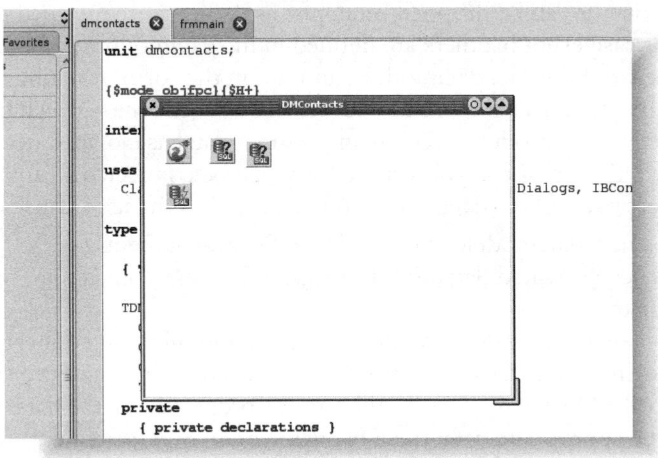

Figure 12.6: A datamodule in designmode

After the datamodule has been created, one or more forms can be created, for example using a *TDBGrid*. Its DataSource property can be set to the datasource instance on the datamodule (more about this in Section 12.2.3). For very simple applications, using only a single dataset and no database component, all this can be done simply on the main form: using a *TDatamodule* in this case complicates things unnecessarily.

12.2.3 Data-aware visual controls

In order to display data in a GUI, Lazarus has implemented a set of data-aware controls which are descendants of standard GUI controls, communicating via a *TDatasource* instance. The *TDatasource* component can be found on the Component Palette's Data Access page. The data-aware controls can be found on the Component Palette's Data Controls page, as shown in Figure 12.7.

Figure 12.7: Standard data-aware controls

Data-aware controls usually have two properties:

Properties	Description
DataSource	The *TDatasource* instance from which data and event notifications should be accepted.
DataField	The name of the field in which the control is interested. The control will display and manipulate the value of this field only, for the current record. Some controls - notably, the DBGrid and DBNavigator control - do not have a DataField property, because they do not act on a single field but on the dataset as a whole.

Table 12.11: Data-aware controls properties:

To display and/or manipulate data from datasets you need to take the following steps in order:

- Drop one or more *TDatasource* components on the form, and connect them to a *TDataset* descendant.
- Drop as many data-aware controls on the form as needed to edit the data fields, connecting them to the *TDatasource* components, and setting each DataField property accordingly.

If everything is set up correctly, then setting the Active property of the *TDataset* instance to True will actually display the data in the form while it is being designed in the Lazarus IDE. Most of this can be accomplished without writing a single line of code.

By default, the following data-aware controls are available in the Lazarus IDE:

Controls	Description
TDBLabel	A simple label control that shows the text of any field.
TDBEdit	A simple edit control to edit the contents of a single field.
TDBMemo	A simple memo control to edit the contents of a single field as multi-line text. It knows about BLOB fields, and can display them.
TDBImage	An image-display control. It shows whatever image it loads from a BLOB field.
TDBListBox	A selection control which allows you to choose the value of a field from a list of items in a listbox.
TDBComboBox	A selection control which allows to choose the value of a field from an item in a combobox list.
TDBCheckBox	A checkbox control allowing you to show and set a boolean field. The values for the checked and unchecked state can be specified.
TDBRadioGroup	A radiogroup control allows you to show the contents of an integer field as a mapping. An underlying integral value is represented in the radiogroup by checking the named (mapped) item whose itemindex corresponds to the value of the field.
TDBCalendar	A calendar control designed to show the value of a *TDateTime* field.
TDBNavigator	is a specialized control containing a series of buttons. Each button corresponds to a *TDataset* navigation method, or to one of its data manipulation methods. Clicking the appropriate button will execute the corresponding action on the dataset. The control keeps track of the state of the dataset, disabling the buttons that cannot be used in the current state of the dataset.
TDBGrid	shows the contents of the dataset in a grid. All records that will fit into the grid are shown, not just the current record. Grid data is editable - clicking any cell will allow you to edit the data in that cell.

Table 12.12 Available data-aware controls in the Lazarus IDE

When compared to their non-data-aware ancestors, most of these controls do not have additional properties beyond their Datasource and DataField properties.

12.3 Available TDataset descendants

As indicated earlier, *TDataset* is an abstract class. After the theoretical considerations of the previous sections, we will now review the various actual implementations. The Lazarus distribution contains several *TDataset* descendants, each of which provides access to a certain type of database. Table 12.13 documents the available datasets, and the Lazarus package in which they are implemented.

Datasets	Description
TDBF	is a dataset that can be used to access dBase files. It is implemented in the DBFlaz package.
TMemDataset	is an in-memory dataset that contains in-memory data. As soon as the dataset is closed, the data is lost, unless manually saved to file. It is in the memdslaz package.
TParadox	is a read-only dataset that can be used to read Paradox files. It relies on an external Paradox reading library. It is in the lazparadox package.
TFixedDataset	in the sdflaz package, allows you to read and write ASCII files with fixed-length values.
TSDFDataset	in the sdflaz package, allows you to read ASCII files with comma-separated value fields (*also known as CSV files*).
TSQLQuery	is part of the SQLDB implementation of Free Pascal. It is located in the SQLDBLaz package. It can be used to connect to a number of databases, such as Firebird, MySQL, Oracle, PostGreSQL and SQLite. For these databases, native access to the database is used, using the client libraries provided by the database. SQLDB can also be used to connect to any other database that has an ODBC driver.

Table 12.13: TDataset descendants available in a default installation

The contents of the Component Palette's Data Access page (which contains some of the standard datasets and the *TDataSource* component) is shown in Figure 12.8. The *TSQLQuery* and various connections are on the Component Palette's SQLDB page.

Figure 12.8: Standard Datasets

In addition to the packages delivered by default with Lazarus, there are externally available packages which must be installed separately in Lazarus before they become available.

Packages	Description
Zeos	A free, mature, database library similar in design to SQLDB, which can be used to access many of the same databases as SQLDB.
AnyDAC	A commercial data access layer, designed to access a wide variety of databases, currently distributed by RemObjects software.
UIB	Unified Interbase is a firebird/Interbase database access layer, which offers a low-level data access mechanism, but also offers a *TDataset* descendant.
FBLib	is a Firebird/Interbase database access layer.
ADS	The Advantage Database Server can also be used with Free Pascal. It should compile with minimal changes.
NexusDB	The commercial Nexus DB is reported to work with Free Pascal and Lazarus.

Table 12.14: (external) packages that work with Lazarus

In the following sections, only the dataset components that are distributed with Lazarus will be discussed. Typical use of these components is shown in Figure 12.9.

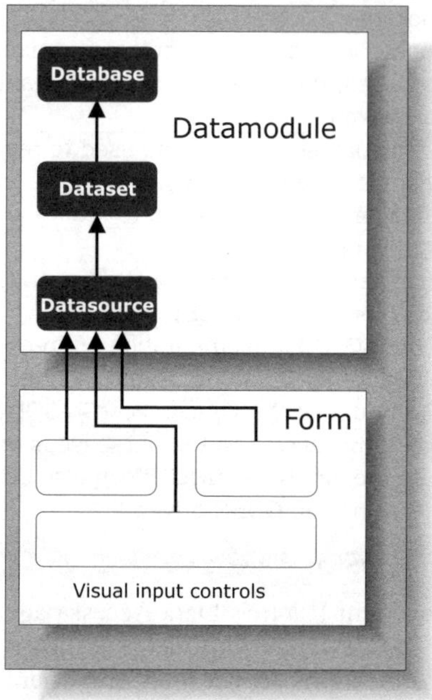

Figure 12.9: The structure of the Database binding in Lazaus

In-memory data

The memdslaz package registers the *TMemDataset* dataset in the Lazarus IDE. This is a Memory Dataset which keeps any data that is written to it in memory. It has methods to load and save the data to disk, and a method to define a new dataset. It is not recommended to use *TMemDataset* for anything other than lookup lists, but it can nevertheless be used as a persistent data store.

TMemDataset does not need an external database engine. It keeps the data as a list of records in memory. The component implements the adding, editing and deleting of records as well as record navigation.

When the dataset is closed, the memory is released and the data is no longer available. If the data must be kept available over multiple runs of the application, then it is possible to save the data to file and load the data from file, for which methods are provided. The stored data is simply a copy of the memory block, and there are no methods to index or search the data. *TMemDataset* inherits all *TDataset*'s properties and methods, and implements some additional ones shown in Tables 12.15 and 12.16.

Property	Description
Filename	The name of the file from which data should be loaded or to which it should be saved.
FileModified	Was the data modified since the file was loaded ?

Table 12.15: The extra properties of TMemDataset.

Method	Description
Clear	Clear data and optionally the list of field definitions.
SaveToFile	Save data and field definitions to file.
LoadFromFile	Load data and field definitions from file.
SaveToStream	Save data and field definitions to a stream.
LoadFromStream	Load data and field definitions from a stream.
CreateTable	Create and open the dataset based on the contents of the fielddefs property.
CopyFromDataset	Copy the structure and optionally the data from another dataset instance.

Table 12.16 The methods of TMemDataset

You must take the following steps to use *TMemDataset:*

1. The table structure (memory layout) must be defined. This is done by adding items to the FieldDefs collection: each item represents a field in the table. This can be done in code or in the IDE, since the FieldDefs property is a normal collection which can be edited using the IDE's collection editor. At least the properties DataType, Size and Name must be set to appropriate values for each field.
2. CreateTable must be called. This will create the necessary memory structures to manage data as defined in the FieldDefs collection, and will open the dataset. CreateTable can be called from the component menu in the IDE (right click on the component and choose Create dataset), or can be called at runtime, for instance in the OnCreate event handler of the form on which the dataset was dropped.
   After editing the data, the table structure and the data can be saved to file with the SaveToFile command. The contents of the FieldDefs collection and the actual data are then written to disk.

The data can be loaded at any time using the LoadFromFile method. This will read the FieldDefs collection from disk, CreateTable is called, and all data in the file will be read into memory. If an opened dataset or a dataset with persistent fields is available, then the method CopyFromDataset can be used to copy its structure into the FieldDefs property of the *TMemDataset* instance. Optionally, the data in the open dataset can also be copied to the memory buffers of the *TMemDataset* instance.

CSV data

CSV format (Comma Separated Values) is a common format for data transfer.
All CSV-structured data looks similar to the following:

```
FieldOne,"Field two, which also has commas.",12345,"Field4"
"Field1","Field 2 in the second record.",,"SingleWordFieldFour"
```

All fields are separated by commas. Text fields with a single word may be enclosed in double quotation marks, although this is not required. It is recommended however, since the CSV parser can then distinguish text from non-text fields.
This is important when importing particularly into Microsoft Excel.
Numerical fields are normally not quoted. If a field contains commas within the text value, then it must also be enclosed in quote characters. Empty (NULL) fields remain empty. Each line in the file is a record in the dataset. The format is not strictly defined, so instead of a comma, the field separator can also be a semicolon or a tab character. The character used depends primarily on which application has generated the file.
Some applications write the field names as the first line of the file.
This is by no means guaranteed, but does make it easier to interpret the data, and is therefore recommended practice.
Lazarus offers a *TSDFDataset* descendant of *TDataset* to deal with this.
It is contained in the *SDFLaz* package. This *TDataset* descendant differs little from *TMemDataset* in its use.
TSDFDataset does not introduce any new methods over *TDataset,* however it does offer some additional properties to describe the CSV file:
There are 2 cases to be considered when working with the TSDFDataset component:
If an existing file with CSV data is available, then it is simply a matter of setting the filename, and possibly the FirstLineAsSchema property. Setting the Active property to True, will read the data from the file. If the first line was not a schema (i.e. the names of the fields) then a set of names will be generated by the component. If the first line was a schema, then the field names given in that schema will be used. Note that all fields will be of type string.

The other situation is when no CSV file exists. In that case, the Schema property must filled with fieldnames: one fieldname per line in the stringlist. The FileMustExist property should be set to False. If the file does not yet exist, then string fields will be created with the names in the Schema property.
As soon as the dataset is closed, it will write to file any changes made to the data, using the FileName property.

Property	Type	Description
Delimiter	String	The character used to delimit fields in each line. The default value is the comma (,).
FirstLineAsSchema	Boolean	This tells *TSDFDataset* to treat the first line as a line containing the fieldnames.
FileMustExist	Boolean	The file must exist on disk, you must not create a new file using a schema.
FileName	String	The name of the file to read when 'Open' is called.
Schema	Tstrings	A list of fieldnames to use when creating a new file.

Table 12.17: TSDFDataset properties

To know how to load a CSV file, the value of the field-separator character must be known, as well as whether or not the first line contains field names.
Where a programmer has created CSV files using the *TSDFDataset* component, he of course knows which character was used as the field-separator. However, where a file from a third party must be opened, the value of the separator character is not usually known. The following routine attempts to detect both the separator character and the presence of fieldnames from the first line in the file:

```
function DetermineSeparator(AFileName: String;
                            var HasFieldNames: Boolean): Char;
  const Seps: array[1..5] of Char = (',', ';', #9, '@', '#');
  var F : TextFile;
      S, S2, T: String;
      I : Integer;
begin
  AssignFile(F, AFileName); // Open file and read first line
  Reset(F);
  try
    ReadLn(F, S);
  finally
    CloseFile(F);
  end;
  Result := #0;

  // Scan the line for the separator character:
  I := 0;
  while (Result = #0) and (I < 5) do
  begin
    Inc(I);
    if Pos(Seps[i], S) <> 0 then Result := Seps[i]
  end;

  // Try and detect the presence of fieldnames:
  // no spaces or double separator:
  if Result <> #0 then
    HasFieldNames := (Pos('', S) = 0) and
                     (Pos(Result + Result, S) = 0);
end;
```

It can be used when opening a file (here named AFileName) :

```
  var B: Boolean;
      C: Char;
begin
  C := DetermineSeparator(AFileName, B);
  if C = #0 then Exit;
  with CSV do
  begin
    Delimiter := C;
    FirstLineAsSchema := B;
    CBFirstLineAsSchema.Checked := B;
    FileName := AFileName;
    Open;
  end;
end;
```

Once the data has been viewed and possibly modified, it can be written to disk again with the 'SaveFileAs' method:

```
CSV.SaveFileAs(CSV.FileName);
```

Once the dataset has been opened, the property FirstLineAsSchema cannot be changed: the dataset must be closed and opened again for it to take effect.
Note that the dataset is closed prior to setting the FirstLineAsSchema property. Setting this property while the dataset is open will result in an exception. If the dataset was open to start with, it is reopened again after setting the property.
The *TSDFDataset* component can be used to create a new CSV file. This is usually achieved in the OnClick event handler of a New menu item:

```
Procedure TMainForm.MINewClick(Sender : TObject);
begin
 With SDCSV do
 if Execute then
 NewCSV(FileName);
end;
```

To create a new CSV file four properties must be known: the filename (in the *FileName* property), the names of the fields (in the *Schema* property), whether the fieldnames must be written as the first line (in the *FirstLineHasSchema* property) and lastly the field separator character (in the *Delimiter* property). When these properties are set, the file can be created. The *FileMustExist* property should be set to *False* which will prevent the component from trying to read an existing file:

```
CSV.Close;
CSV.Schema.Assign(Schema);
CSV.Delimiter := ',';
CSV.FirstlineAsSchema := True;
CSV.FileName := AFileName;
CSV.FileMustExist := False;
CSV.Open;
```

The 'Open' method will do all the work of creating the dataset.

Accessing dBase files

dBase files are an old data format with fixed-length records. The data is stored in binary format in a main (`.dbf`) file, and the indexes are stored in a separate file. They were introduced in the legendary dBase program, and later adopted by FoxPro and Visual FoxPro. The internal structure is handled completely by the dBase engine, so the developer needs to know just the names, types and sizes of the fields he needs, and the engine takes care of the rest.

Although this data format is now quite old, it still is perfectly suitable for small desktop applications that do not need access to a full-blown SQL engine. Even in situations where master-detail relationships between two or three linked tables need to be handled, dBase files are worth considering, particularly since no external code or library is required to handle them.

Property	Description
DateTimeHandling	This is a Delphi compatibility property, and should be set to *dtDatetime* in Lazarus.
Exclusive	This boolean property tells the *TDBF* component whether it should attempt to get exclusive access to the file. This is necessary when creating a new TDBF file, or when manipulating indexes.
FilePath	The directory (relative to the current working directory) in which the table is located.
FilePathFull	The absolute path in which the table is located. This can be set for instance when the application's location is changed.
Filter	Here you can enter a filter expression.
Filtered	Set to True if the Filter expression should be applied to the data (False otherwise).
IndexDefs	contains the Indexes that are defined for this dBase file.
Indexes	is an alias for IndexDefs.
IndexFieldNames	are the fieldnames of the current index. This property can be used to construct simple, temporary, indexes which will order the dataset by the specified fields.
IndexName	The name of the currently active index. This should be one of the indexes in the indexDefs property.
MasterFields	Names of fields in the dataset which MasterSource points to. The names and values of these fields will be used to construct a filter on the `.DBF` dataset.
MasterSource	Datasource which will be used to construct a master-detail relation.
OpenMode	determines how the file is used. Either it is treated as a normal file (omNormal), or it is auto-created (omAutoCreate), i.e. the file will be created if it does not exist. The FieldDefs property is then used to determine the structure of the file.
ShowDeleted	If set to True, records marked as deleted in the dBase file are shown anyway.
Storage	is by default set to stoFile which means that data is kept in files. It can also be set to stoMemory which means that the data is kept in memory.
TableLevel	Can be one of 3, 4, 7 or 25. Levels 3, 4, and 7 correspond to dBase III, IV or VII file formats. Level 25 is used for Foxpro files.
TableName	is the name of the dBase file. When set, the path part of the filename will be cut off and moved to the FilePathFull property. Most of these properties are not required for normal use of this component. Setting the *TableName* property is usually sufficient to open and view a dBase file.

Table 12.18 TDBF component properties (Continuation)

The *TDBF* component was originally written for Delphi, but was ported to Free Pascal as one of its first database components. It can be used to browse `.DBF` files, and supports index files which can be used to determine the record order in the database.
It is possible to create indexes based on an expression. *TDBF* has good support for filtering, and supports constructing master-detail relations between datasets.
You can also create new dBase files using this component.
The support for the *TDBF* component is located in the DBFlaz package.
The component itself is included in the Free Pascal distribution. Compiling and installing this package will register the *TDBF* component on the Component Palette's Data Access page.

Opening existing dBase files

For all its rich feature list, the *TDBF* component is very easy to use. Drop it on a form (or datamodule) and set the TableName property to the name of the `.DBF` file, when a file-selection dialog will pop up. After this, setting the Active property will open the file and display the records.
The properties listed in Table 12.18 influence how the file is opened, and how its contents are treated. Most of these properties are not required for normal use of this component. Setting the TableName property is usually sufficient to open and view a dBase file.
Here is a stepwise guide to accessing dBase files:

1. Drop a *TDBF* from the Data Access tab on a form.
2. Drop a *TDatasource* on the form (Datasource1) and set its Dataset property to DBF1.
3. Drop a *TDBGrid* and a *TDBNavigator* component from the Data Controls tab on the form.
4. Set the Datasource property of the DBGrid1 and DBNavigator1 to Datasource1.
5. In the Object Inspector, set the TableName property to a dBase file (the FilePath and FilePathFull are set automatically).
6. Set the Active property of the *DBF1* component to True.
   This will load the table data and show it in the grid – in the IDE.

No dBase file is encoded in UTF-8 format. Lazarus works internally only with Unicode. As of dBase 7, Borland used Windows ANSI strings in the Borland Database Engine (BDE), which under Windows is available in the control panel's BDE Administrator entry. It proposes by default a Windows ANSI character set, and dBase version 7. This setting is valid for all programs using the database driver. Older versions and specifically dBase III/II+ and IV, were DOS programs and used the DOS character set.

This is specifically true for the data format of these dBase versions. DBase III and dBase IV files should always be treated as DOS files with the US ASCII code page (US ASCII CP 437). In the header of this dBase format there is no entry to designate the character set. If the character set is interpreted wrongly, special characters (such as the German umlaut) are lost, making the data files unusable in the process. This is also a problem when working with Delphi.

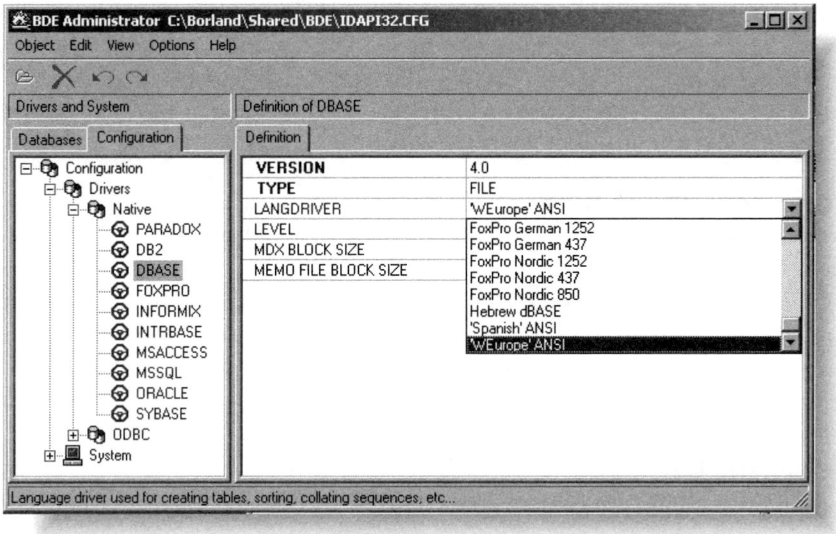

Figure 12.10: The character set definition for dBase files in the Borland Database engine must be observed when using dBase files in Lazarus]

To show and manipulate DOS-encoded tables correctly, after calling Open you must make two character translations.

1. Set the Transliterate property of all fields to True.
2. Implement the OnTranslate event handler of the *TDBF* component.

The following method does the first step:

```
procedure TMainForm.SetTransliterate;
  var I: Integer;
begin
  for I := 0 to DBFFile.Fields.Count-1 do
  if DBFFile.Fields[I] is TStringField then
    TStringField(DBFFile.Fields[I]).Transliterate := True;
end;
```

The *TDataset* implementation does not perform any transliteration by itself. It must be implemented in the standard OnTranslate event of the *TDBF* components. It looks like this:

```
function TMainForm.DBFFileTranslate(Dbf: TDbf; Src, Dest: PChar;
 ToOem: Boolean): Integer;
var
 S: String; L: Integer;
begin
 S := StrPas(Src);
 L := Length(S);
 if L > 0 then begin
 S := ConvertEncoding(S, 'CP437', EncodingUTF8);
 if Length(S)>L then SetLength(S, L);
 Move(S[1], Dest^, L + 1);
 end;
 Result := L;
end;
```

This routine takes the string in the null-terminated *Src* parameter and converts it to the *Dest* string. The *ConvertEncoding* call is part of the LCL (in the `lconvencoding` unit) and will do a conversion from codepage 437 to the standard UTF-8 encoding used by Lazarus. Note that the length together with one additional byte is moved to the result buffer because the terminating NULL character must also be moved.

Creating new dBase files

There are two ways to create a new dBase file. The first and simplest can be done almost completely in the IDE:

- Fill the *FieldDefs* property of the *TDBF* component with an item for each field. Note that *TDBF* does not support all existing field types of *TDataset.*
- Optionally, fill the *IndexDefs* property of the *TDBF* component with index definitions.
- Set the *Exclusive* property to *True.*
- Set the *TableName* property to the required filename.

Then at runtime, calling the *CreateTable* method is all you need to create a new DBF file.

An alternative method is to fill a *TdbfFieldDefs* collection with *TdbfFieldDefItems.* This is the DBF equivalent of the *FieldDefs* property, but the *TDbfFieldDef* class contains additional properties which give finer control over the structure of the DBF file. The *TdbfFieldDefs* collection can then be passed to the *CreateTableEx* method, which will create the DBF file according to the definitions in the collection. In fact, internally, the *CreateTable* method calls the *CreateTableEx* method, which constructs the *TdbfFieldDefs* collection from the items found in the *FieldDefs* method.

SQL databases

SQLDB is the name of the set of components in Free Pascal that can be used to communicate with SQL-enabled databases. SQLDB works simply by using the native client libraries to access each available database. This makes it quite fast and memory efficient. Additionally, it can connect to any database that supports ODBC. The ODBC layer is available by default on Windows and can easily be installed for the Linux or Mac operating systems.
SQLDB support is installed in Lazarus using the SQLDBLaz package. It registers the available components and some property editors in the IDE (the actual code is in Free Pascal). All components are installed in the Component Palette's SQLDB page.
All the connection components load their support libraries dynamically, so the components can be installed and dropped on a datamodule even if a particular database engine is not installed.

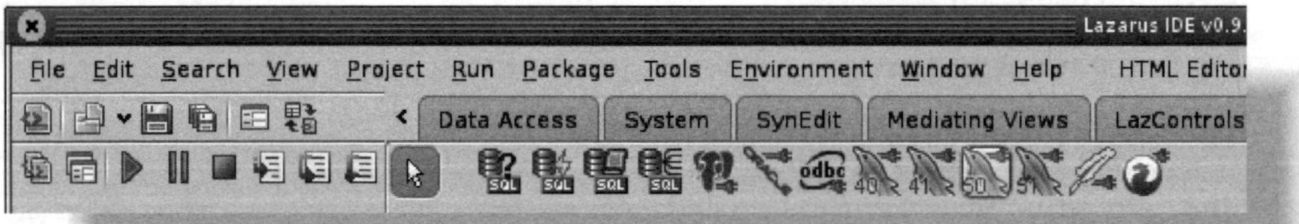

Figure 12.11: Installed SQLDB components

When a connection is activated, SQLDB will load the appropriate client library on-demand. If the client libraries are not installed, this will lead to an error, of course. Currently, SQLDB provides direct access to Firebird, Interbase, MySQL versions 4.0, 4.1 and 5.0, Oracle, PostgreSQL and SQLLite. Other databases can be accessed with the ODBC connection. To connect to a database with SQLDB, at least three components are needed which are listed in Table 12.19

Component	Description
TSQLConnection	or actually, a descendant of *TSQLConnection*. This represents the actual connection to the database, and all data required for connection must be entered here. Usually this is the name of the desired database connection, togther with a username and password.
TSQLTransaction	This component is used to control transactions. An application can have many independent transactions active at the same time. If the native engine does not support this, it is emulated by opening multiple connections to the same database - a fact you should be aware of in case the database uses a per-connection license scheme.
TSQLQuery	This is the *TDataset* descendant, which can be used to run *SELECT* or other queries. This is the central component of a SQLDB based application. It can execute one SQL statement at a time.

Table 12.19: Needed components when using SQLDB

TSQLConnection has several descendants, one for each supported database:

- **TIBConnection** To connect to Firebird or Interbase databases.
- **TMySQL40Connection, TMySQL41Connection, TMySQL50Connection** to connect to MySQL databases using a MySQL client library version 4.0, 4.1 or 5.0 respectively.
- **TOracleConnection** to connect to Oracle databases.
- **TODBCConnection** to connect to a database using the ODBC library.
- **TPQConnection** to connect to a PostGreSQL database.
- **TSQLite3Connection** to connect to a SQLite 3 database.

Note that for MySQL databases, the connection component depends on the installed client library, not on the server version. Normally, a 4.0 client library can connect to a 5.0 server.
If you want to migrate from one type of database to another, then all that is needed is to change the connection component. This is only possible if the structure of the database remains the same, and no database-specific features are used.
Even this can be avoided by using the *TSQLConnector* component. This component is a *TSQLConnection* descendant which acts as a proxy for the actual connection component: It does not perform anything by itself, but creates one of the *TSQLConnection* descendants mentioned above, and simply passes on all properties and method calls to this *TSQLConnection* instance. All that needs to be done is to set the *TSQLConnector*'s *ConnectorType* property to the appropriate connection type.

The three base components presented above (or their descendants) have a tight interrelationship: the *TSQLConnection* descendant refers to a default transaction component, which it uses to collect metadata about the data and the queries that are being run. The *Transaction* property refers to the default transaction. The *TSQLTransaction* refers to a *TSQLConnection* component for which it manages a transaction. The *Database* property contains this reference. The *TSQLQuery* component refers to a *TSQLConnection* component (through its *Database* property) to manage the connection to the database. Additionally, it refers to a *TSQLTransaction* component (through its *Transaction* property) to manage the transaction it operates in. That makes four properties that should be set. Luckily, the components set some of the properties automatically: *TSQLConnection* uses the first *TSQLTransaction* that is connected to it as its default transaction. Similarly, setting the *Transaction* property of a *TSQLQuery* component will set the *Database* property if it was not yet set, and vice versa.

Connecting to a SQL Database

Connecting to a Firebird database using SQLDB is done in the following steps:

- The *File→New* dialog is used to create a new datamodule.
- Drop a *TIBConnection* on the datamodule from the SQLDB tab on the Component Palette. It will be named *IBConnection1* and lets you establish a connection to a Firebird or Interbase database.
- Drop a *TSQLTransaction* component on the datamodule. Its *Database* property should be set to *IBConnection1*. The *Transaction* property of the *IBConnection1* component will automatically be set to *SQLTransaction1*.
- Drop a *TSQLQuery* component on the datamodule. It will be named *SQLQuery1*. Its *Database* property should also be set to *IBConnection1*. Again, the *Transaction* property of the *SQLQuery1* component will automatically be set to *SQLTransaction1*.

Once the components have been dropped on a datamodule (or on a form) and have been properly connected, it is time to set up their properties. For *TSQLConnection* descendants, you must set as a minimum the properties listed in Table 12.20.

Property	Description
Hostname	The hostname on which the database resides. This can be empty if the database is on the current machine.
DatabaseName	The name by which the database can be identified. This can be a path (as in SQLite or Firebird) or a symbolic name (as in MySQL or Oracle). This depends on the actual connection.
UserName	The username with which to connect.
Password	The password of the user.

Table 12.20: Properties of TSQLConnection descendants

Each *TSQLConnection* descendant has descendant-specific properties, which can be set in addition to control the connection. For instance the *TIBConnection* allows you to set the SQLDialect and Charset properties.

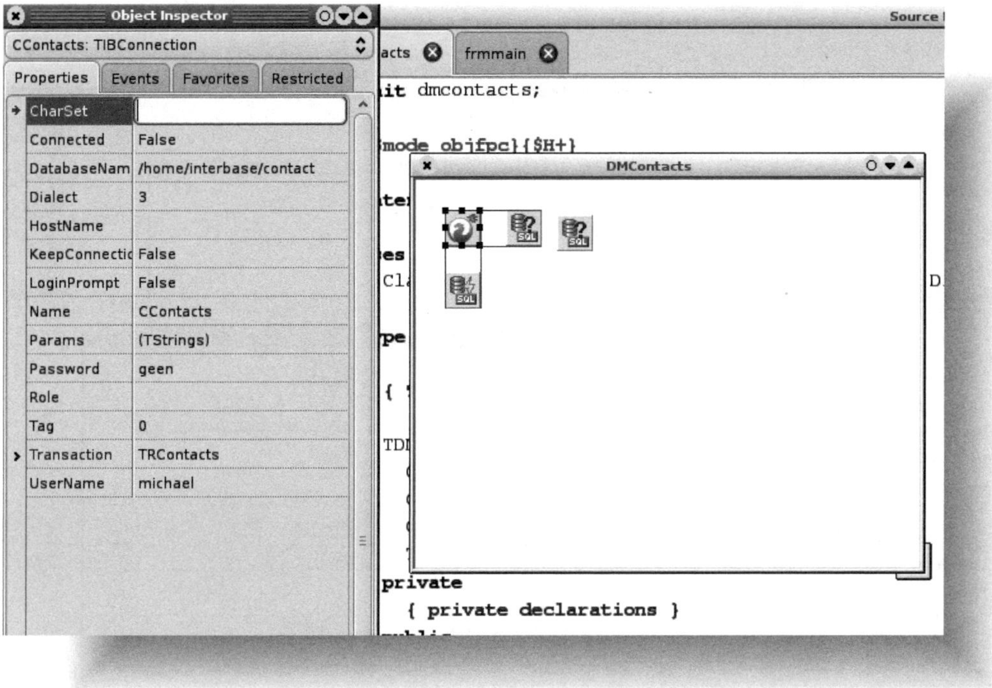

Figure 12.12: : *A typical set-up with SQLDB*

When all these properties have been set correctly, the *Connected* property can be set to *True* to connect to the database. If something goes wrong, a dialog with an exception message may appear as shown in Figure 12.13.

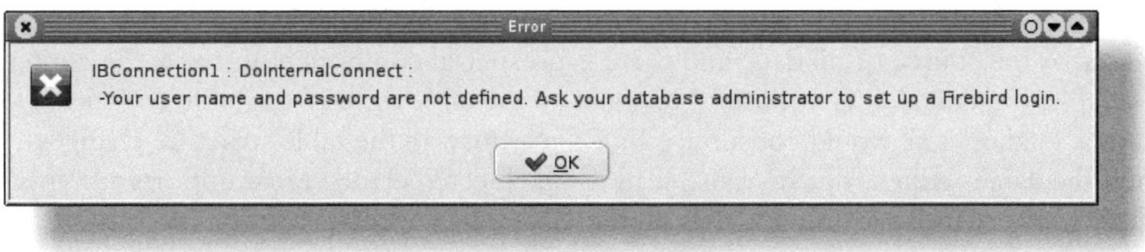

Figure 12.13: Exception message dialog

At runtime, the *Open* and *Close* methods may be used to open or close the connection to the database. When the connection has been made successfully, the *TSQLQuery* component can be configured. The main property is the *SQL* property which is a property of *TStrings* type in which a SQL statement can be entered. Once an appropriate select query has been entered, the *Active* property of the *TSQLQuery* component can be set to *True* to execute the query and fetch the result. The result can be shown in the IDE, by adding a *TDatasource* component to the datamodule, and dropping a *TDBGrid* on a form and setting its *DataSource* property so it points to the datasource on the datamodule. The result will look like Figure 12.14

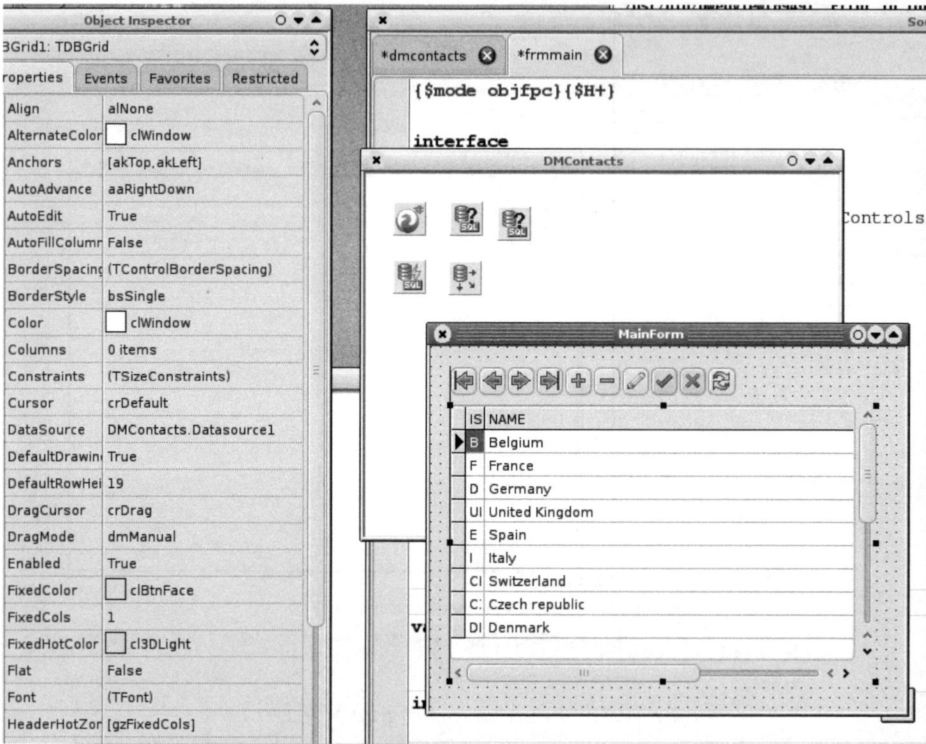

Figure 12.14: Viewing the query result in the IDE

SQL Select queries

SQLDB is oriented towards SQL databases, which means that only SQL statements can be used as the source of all data, and there is no special component to show the contents of a table. In general, it is not useful to show all the table data. If the table contains a lot of data, loading it all would consume a lot of memory. If the table structure changes when the data is edited, this may also lead to unexpected errors. Most importantly, it is simply not very user-friendly to show all the table data – a filtered set of records is usually much better.

Despite all this, it is sometimes necessary to show all the records in a table. Doing so is not fundamentally different from showing the result of a SQL select statement:

1. Configure a *TSQLConnection* descendant for the database in which the table resides.
2. Connect a *TSQLTransaction* component to the connection component.
3. In a *TSQLQuery* component connected to these 2 components, the following SQL statement can be used to select all data in the table:

```
SELECT * FROM MyTable;
```

Where MyTable should of course be replaced with the actual table name. After this, *TSQLQuery* will act much as a *TDBF* component: the data can be edited, sorted or deleted. The sole difference is that *ApplyUpdates* must be called in order to write changes to the database.

Updating data

The data in a *TSQLQuery* dataset is editable, meaning that data can be deleted, inserted or updated. In simple cases (for example when selecting fields from a single table), *TSQLQuery* knows how to update the data in the table, and it will construct and execute the necessary statements by itself. This can either be done immediately when the *Post* call is executed, or the *Update* statements can be buffered, and then executed all at once.
The choice between these two possibilities is up to the programmer. The SQL statements are buffered, and they are only executed when the *ApplyUpdates* method is called. To have the updates always applied immediately after the *Post* operation, the following code can be inserted in the *AfterPost* handler of a *TSQLQuery* component:

```
procedure TDMParams.SQLQuery1AfterPost(DataSet: TDataSet);
begin
 SQLQuery1.ApplyUpdates;
end;
```

To create an INSERT statement, the *TSQLQuery* component doesn't really need help from the programmer since it is quite clear what should be done.
However, for DELETE and UPDATE statements, a WHERE clause must be constructed to uniquely identify the record that must be changed. And here *TSQLQuery* sometimes needs help. The WHERE clause of the SQL statement that will be executed can be controlled using the *UsePrimaryKeyAsKey* property and the *UpdateMode* property. *UpdateMode* can take one of three values, listed in Table 12.22.

Values	Description
upWhereAll	The *WHERE* statement will simply contain all old field values for fields that have *pfInWhere* set in their ProviderFlags property. This means that if another user has simultaneously changed the record, the update statement will fail.
upWhereChanged	The *WHERE* statement will simply contain only the old values of all changed fields that have *pfInWhere* set in their ProviderFlags property. This is slightly less strict than the *upWhereAll* option.
upWhereKeyOnly	This is the least restrictive option. The *WHERE* clause will simply contain conditions for the key fields in the dataset. The key fields are the ones which have *pfInkey* in their ProviderFlags property.

Table 12.21: Possible values for TSQLQuery's UpdateMode property

By default, all fields have *pfInWhere* set in their *ProviderFlags*. By removing the flag for some fields, the statement can be tuned. The default value for *UpdateMode* is *upWhereAll*, but it is recommended that you change this. The *pfInkey* flag can be set manually for the fields that should form the primary key for update statements. However, the *TSQLQuery* component can try to detect which fields should have the *pfInKey* flag set by examining the primary index of the table from which data is fetched. Setting the *UsePrimaryKeyAsKey* property to *True* (the default) will enable this mechanism. If it is set to *False*, the *pfInkey* flag must be set manually on all fields that need it. Obviously, you need persistent fields to be able to do this in the IDE.

In some cases, these properties are still not sufficient for *TSQLQuery* to be able to construct correct update queries. In such cases the required SQL statements can be specified manually using the properties in Table 12.22.

Property	Description
DeleteSQL	The SQL statement needed to delete the current record from the database.
InsertSQL	The SQL statement needed to insert the current record in the database.
UpdateSQL	The SQL statement needed to update the current record with the new values.

Table 12.22: Properties to specify SQL update statements

All three SQL statements must use parameters. The parameters will be scanned and filled with the new values of the fields with the same name in the dataset. To use the old value of a field in the SQL statement, the name of the parameter can be prefixed with OLD_: the value of such a parameter will be replaced with the old value of the field.

Master/detail relationships

Parameters are an important concept in SQLDB: they can be used to parameterise oft-repeated queries, and they must be used when creating SQL UPDATE statements. They are also instrumental when constructing master-detail relationships using SQLDB.
To construct a master-detail relationship is quite easy. The detail query should contain some parameters. The value of these parameters will be fetched in the master dataset. The master dataset can be set in the *Datasource* property. Once this property is set, parameter values which have not been explicitly set will be fetched from the dataset connected to this datasource. A field with the same name as the parameter will be searched, and its current value will be used as the value of the parameter. This is true both when opening a SELECT query and when executing other SQL statements using *ExecSQL*.
What is more, as soon as the current record in the master dataset changes, the detail dataset will be closed, and reopened with the new values for the parameters filled in. All this is possible without a single line of code.

12.4 The Lazarus Data Desktop

The foregoing sections described how to program end-user Lazarus applications which need to handle data. In order to develop such applications, you have to create, design and populate a database. Creating database applications involves repetitive tasks. If you create many forms that often access the same data in different ways, you end up repeating the same tasks: setting display names; setting field sizes; providing hints for controls and so on. The values of these properties for all tables and fields in a database can be put in a single structure, known as a *data dictionary*. It can hold all this visual design information and apply it in the IDE, or at runtime. The data dictionary can even - if so desired - be used to recreate or remodel the database.

The Lazarus Data Desktop has been designed to perform the double tasks of being a database access tool as well as a data dictionary manager. Bonuses are its ability to create Object Pascal code to manage and access your databases, and its integration with the Lazarus IDE - a data dictionary created in the Data Desktop is accessible within the IDE and can be applied to any *TDataset* descendant.

The Lazarus Data Desktop (sometimes called Database Desktop) sports the following features:

- Access to many databases supported by FPC: DBF files, MySQL, Firebird, Oracle, PostGreSQL, SQLite and any ODBC-supported database.
- Creation of a data dictionary for a database, where all *TField* properties can be stored.
- Data dictionary storage either in `.ini` files, or in a database.
- Creation of DDL and DML SQL statements from the data dictionary.
- Examination of table data.
- Execution of any query, and the ability to examine the result.
- Data export to many formats, e.g. XML, JSON, RTF, plain text (CSV), DBF, SQL.
- The creation of code from datasets. You can create an object corresponding to the data resulting from a query, and code to load that object's properties from the query. A special bonus for people using an OPF (Object Persistence Framework) is the ability to create tiOPF code.

All this functionality is present already in the Free Pascal code base, and most of it is available in the Lazarus IDE itself, on the Component Palette. The Data Desktop just exposes this functionality in a tool that is designed to handle everyday database programming tasks.

The API managing all these tasks is designed to be extensible, so it can be extended to suit the needs of your particular project. Depending on what needs to be done, a new class can be written and registered, or an existing class can be enhanced. Since the source code of the Data Desktop ships with Lazarus, it can be recompiled with whatever enhanced functionality you may wish to add.

The Lazarus Data Desktop is under continuous development, as are the APIs that it uses. The best way to take advantage of recent enhancements is to take a recent version from SVN and recompile it. It is located in the `tools/lazdatadesktop` directory. To be able to compile it, several Lazarus packages are needed:

Packages	Description
lazDBF	for DBF support.
lazSQLDB	for SQLDB support, as explained in the earlier sections.
lazDataDict	for data dictionary integration into the IDE.
lazDBExport	for the export components. These components are exposed on the Data Export tab of the component palette.
RuntimeTypeInfoControls	for RTTI controls. The APIs and the Data Dictionary editor make extensive use of this package.

Table 12.23: Lazarus packages

These packages do not need to be installed in the IDE, but doing so makes sure that the necessary unit paths are added to the compiler path when compiling. Opening the *lazdatadesktop* project and compiling it should result in a working binary.
When the Lazarus Data Desktop is started, a form as in Figure 12.15 should appear.

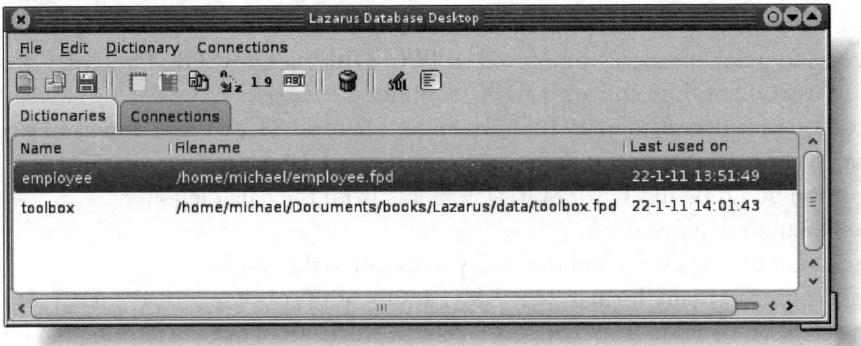

Figure 12.15: The Lazarus Data Desktop on startup

On start-up, a list of recently used data dictionaries (on the first tab) or database connections (the second tab) is shown. Double-clicking an entry will open it in a new tab. Connections can be used to connect to databases when the structure and data of the tables in the database can be viewed. If the database is SQL-based, then query statements can be executed on the database. The results of the queries can be viewed, and exported in one of the supported export formats.

12.4.1 Data dictionaries

Data dictionaries are repositories with meta-information about databases, a kind of meta-database on the database, and describe completely the basic structure of a database (the database schema). Specifically, the following information can be held: a list of all tables and the fields in each table, and all indexes on the tables. The data dictionary also contains extended field attributes which determine how the contents of the fields should be shown: the number of decimals, the currency format, the hint to be shown over the control that shows the field and so on. The data dictionary is still under development, and will be extended in future to manage other kinds of information as well, such as domains, views, triggers, sequences and stored procedures.

Having this metadata available in structured form serves several purposes:

- A data dictionary can be accessed from within a Lazarus program to set field and form properties at run-time (for instance for ad-hoc queries), but it can also be applied in the Lazarus IDE at design time.
- It can be used to create a database: the data dictionary can create SQL statements that will recreate the database whose structure it describes.
- Two data dictionaries can be compared, and the differences can be used to create an update script.

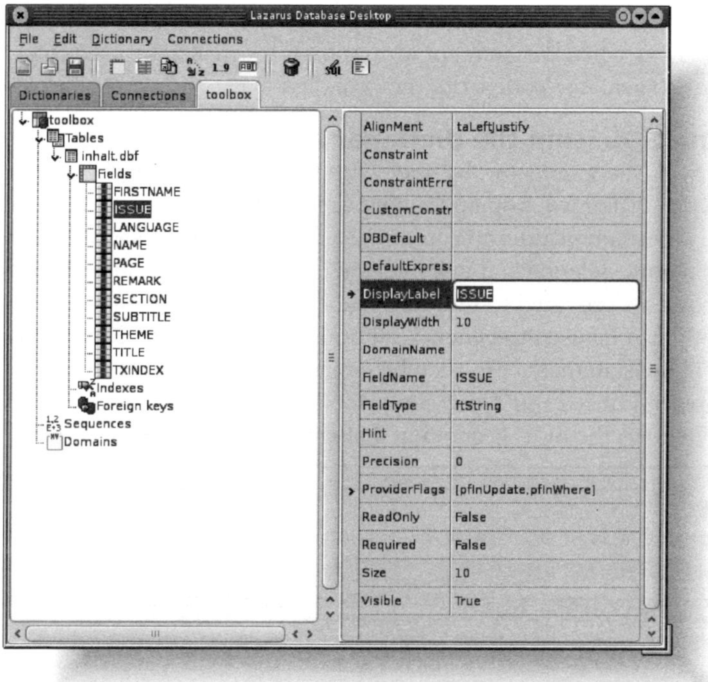

Figure 12.16: The Lazarus Data Dictionary editor

A data dictionary can be created from scratch, but can also be reverse-engineered from an existing database. To create a new data dictionary, use the *File→New* menu. Alternatively, the *Dictionary→ Import* menu can be used to reverse engineer a database and create a new data dictionary or update an existing one. If a dBase file `'contents.dbf'` is imported, then this should result in a new data dictionary, which can be saved e.g. as `'dictionary'`. After expanding the tree with the data structures, a list of field definitions is visible.

Using the data dictionary is quite straightforward. In the left half of the window, the data dictionary shows all available objects in a treeview. Selecting an item will display the properties of the selected item in the Object Inspector grid located in the right half of the window. The tree and Object Inspector can be resized with the help of the splitter control in the middle.

The buttons in the toolbar can be used to add a new object or delete an object. Currently, a table field or index can be created (or deleted) in this way. For a table, the table name and primary key constraint name can be edited. For the fields, all field properties can be set, likewise for an index. Selecting a field in a table definition will display the field's properties in the right half of the screen. You can edit these, and the main form should look more or less as in Figure 12.16. Entering the information for all the fields is a lot of work. The advantage of the data dictionary is that this work needs to be done only once, and that the information can then be used in many places over and over again.

Once the information in the data dictionary is complete, it can be used in a Lazarus application (either when designing or at runtime). It can also be used to generate SQL statements or to generate code from the data dictionary, such as for the result of a query.

Generating SQL from the dictionary

Generating SQL statements can be done with the *[Generate SQL]* button or menu item. When clicked, a dialog will pop up looking like a much-extended version of Delphi's UpdateSQL Component Editor. You can use this dialog to create SQL statements for selecting, updating, deleting and inserting data from any table in the data dictionary. Several options are provided to fine-tune the form of the SQL statements generated. Additionally, it can be used to generate an SQL statement to recreate the table (or part of it) in SQL. These statements can then be copied to your application, for instance to the various properties of a *TSQLQuery* component.

Figure 12.17 shows the SQL generation dialog with various fields selected.

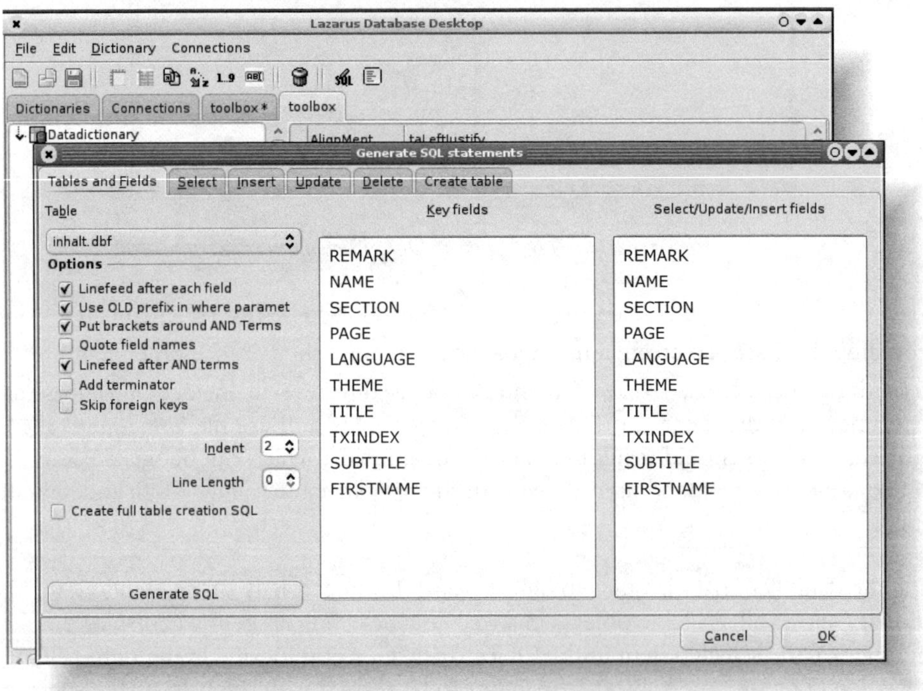

Figure 12.17: Generating SQL from the Data Dictionary

Generating the contents table from Toolbox in a SQL-based database could be done with the following SQL statement:

```
CREATE TABLE CONTENTS (
   EDITION VARCHAR(10),
   REMARK VARCHAR(74),
   NAME VARCHAR(30),
   SECTION VARCHAR(30),
   PAGE VARCHAR(3),
   LANGUAGE VARCHAR(30),
   THEME VARCHAR(30),
   TITLE VARCHAR(74),
   TXINDEX VARCHAR(14),
   SUBTITLE VARCHAR(74),
   FIRSTNAME VARCHAR(30),
   CONSTRAINT CONTENTS_PK PRIMARY KEY (EDITION))
```

The following code shows how to use the data dictionary at runtime in a Lazarus application

```
uses fpdatadict,dbf,db;

  var DD  : TFPDataDictionary; DBF : TDBF;
begin
  DD := TFPDataDictionary.Create;
  DD.LoadFromFile('toolbox.fpd');
  DBF := TDBF.Create(Nil);
  DBF.TableName := 'inhalt.dbf';
  DBF.Open;
  DD.Tables.TableByName('inhalt.dbf').ApplyToDataset(DBF);
  // Alternatively
  // DD.ApplyToDataset(DBF);
end.
```

This code will create a data dictionary instance, and load it from file. Then, it will load the DBF file, and apply the data dictionary to it. As a result, properties such as *DisplayName* and *DisplaySize* will be filled in. If the data is displayed in a grid, the proper column sizes and titles will be shown automatically. Instead of applying the data dictionary at run-time, it can also be applied while designing in the Lazarus IDE. If the *lazDataDict* package is installed, then the IDE will be extended in three ways:

1. A *Data Dictionary* menu item is registered under the *Project* menu which lets you select and configure the data dictionary for a project. The name of the data dictionary will be saved with the project options, and the data dictionary will be reloaded when the project is loaded the next time.
2. A menu item *Database Desktop* is created under the *Tools* menu which starts the Lazarus Data Desktop. When used for the first time, it may ask where the Lazarus Data Desktop application is located.
3. In the Form Designer, a *Data dictionary* menu item is registered in the context pop-up menu which can be used to apply the data dictionary to any *TDataset* descendant. Obviously, this will only work if the following conditions have been satisfied: persistent fields have been created for the dataset (use the Fields Editor to do this), and a data dictionary was selected for the current project.

Connecting to databases

The Data Desktop offers the further functionality of letting you simply connect to existing databases and examine the data in their tables (or run queries on them in the case of an SQL-enabled database). You can connect to all databases supported by FPC. All that is needed is a small class that registers the database support in the data dictionary engine, and the Data desktop will pick it up and offer a connection type. Connecting to a database is done through the *Connection→ New* menu item. Below this item, a list of supported connection types is shown. When you have chosen a type, the connection parameters have to be given, and following the successful establishment of a connection, a new tab will be shown with the contents of the database. Currently, only tables and their indexes will be shown. To connect to a database with DBF files, the directory with the DBF files must be entered. So, to connect to the Toolbox database, a new *'DBF Files'* connection is started, the path to the DBF file is chosen, and the connection is saved with the name *Toolbox*, i. e. the data dictionary's name. As a result, the screen should look like Figure 12.18.

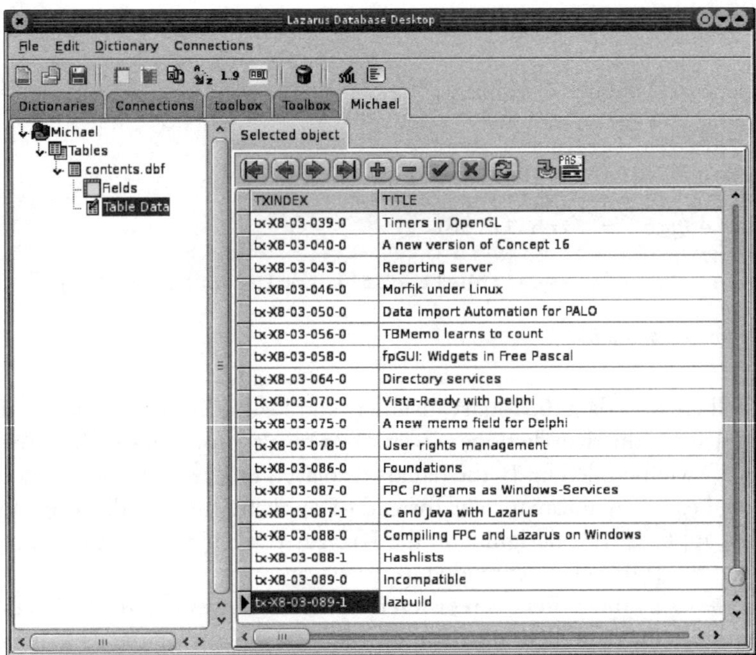

Figure 12.18: The toolbox contents

At the right of the window is a work area which shows the definition of the object chosen at the left, or (in the case of a table) it can show the contents of the table. The table data can be edited, if you wish, since creating test data for an application is one possible use of the Data Desktop. However it has more extensive capabilities. The *Data* view has - besides the navigation buttons - two extra buttons. One lets you export data in a variety of storage formats. Currently, eight formats are available (see below). The other button lets you generate various kinds of Object Pascal code, based on the data shown. Currently, four types of code can be generated.

12.4.2 Exporting data

Exporting the displayed data can be done to the following formats: CSV (Comma Separated Values) text files; fixed-length text files; simple XML files; simple JSON files; SQL statements to fill a table with the data shown; LaTeX tables; RTF tables, and DBF files. More formats are planned. This functionality is suitable for transforming data from one data format to another. The list of export mechanisms can easily be extended with exporters you write yourself. The API for this is in the Free Pascal source code. The relevant unit is called *fpdbexport*, and the many available examples can be studied if you wish to write your own custom export mechanism.
The export mechanism can be applied to the sample data: choosing the XML export format will result in an export configuration dialog shown in Figure 12.19. To the left is the list of fields that can be exported. Any field can be disabled, so it will not be included in the export. To the right, a small grid with export options for this field is shown. In the case of XML the exported name is the name of the XML tag used to represent that field.

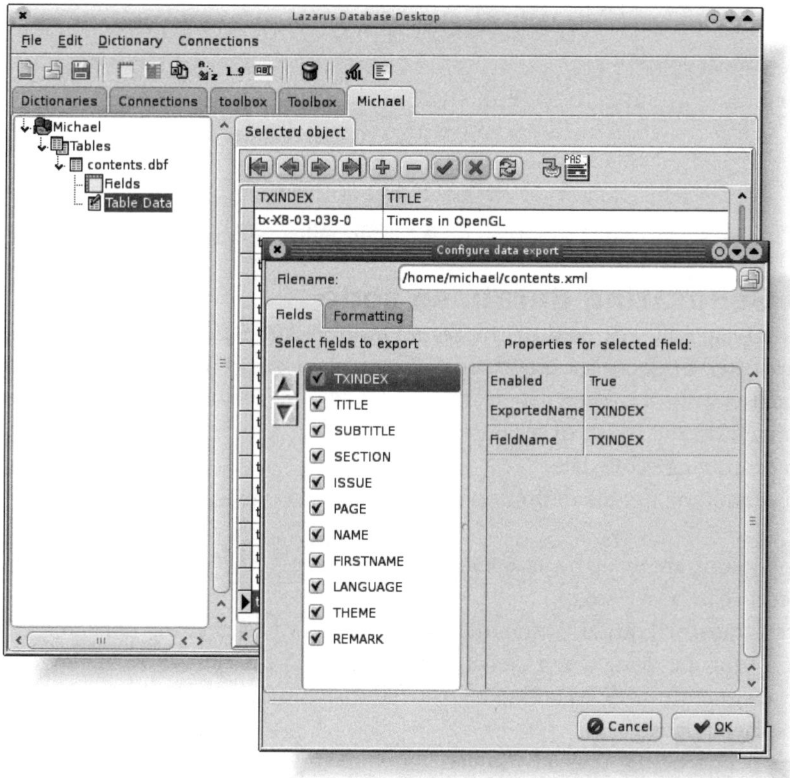

Figure 12.19 Exporting the toolbox contents

The second tab shows some general export options. These mostly control the format of the output. Obviously, the options are different for each of the export formats. Finally, the filename can be filled in at the top of the dialog, and then the data will be exported to the filename given there. The export mechanism can also be used in Lazarus applications: installing the *lazDBExport* package will add a lot of components to the *Data Export* page of the Component Palette. There will be an export component for each data format, plus the *TFPDataExporter* component which shows a selection and configuration dialog for each of the export formats compiled into the application.
To register the standard export formats in the application, a *TStandardExportFormats* component is provided. You can drop this on a form, and the desired formats can be made available to the end-user by setting a simple property. Other custom-made formats would need to be registered in code.
The Toolbox application can be used to demonstrate this: dropping a *TStandardExportFormats* component and a *TFPDataExporter* component (name it DEToolbox) is all that is required. Then the *Dataset* property of the *DEToolbox* component must be set to the DBF file. Lastly, a button *BExport* is added with the following *OnClick* handler:

```
procedure TToolBoxForm.BExportClick(Sender: TObject);
begin
  DEToolbox.Execute;
end;
```

That is all the code you need to add export functionality to any data-aware application!

12.4.3 Generating database code

An important capability offered by the Data Desktop is the creation of very simple to quite complicated Object Pascal code for various purposes. The code can be generated in various places:

- When viewing the result of a query.
- When examining table data.
- When examining a table definition in the data dictionary.

Not all operations are available in every one of these places. Currently, the following kinds of code can be created:

1. You can transform an SQL statement to an Object Pascal string constant. This can only be done when viewing the result of a query.
2. You can generate code to create a DBF file that can be used to store the displayed data.
3. Based on a particular dataset you can generate an Object Pascal class with properties corresponding to the fields in the data. Additionally, you can generate code to load the properties from a dataset.
4. You can generate a tiOPF class declaration with properties corresponding to the fields in the data, and also the necessary visitor classes to persist the class to or from the database.

These code generators are delivered by default with Free Pascal. As with the export formats, it is possible to write additional custom code generators that can be registered in the system. When selecting the *Generate code* functionality, a choice of available code generators is presented, and when a generator is chosen, you see a configuration dialog similar to the export configuration.

As with the export functionality, all code generators can be used in Lazarus programs as well. While not directly useful for end-user applications, this capability can ease the task of writing support tools.

Executing queries

On databases that are SQL-based, the '*Connection*' tab displays a Query Editor which can be used to create and execute queries. If the query is a SELECT query, the result of the query will be shown, and the same export and code generating mechanisms are available as when viewing table data.
The Query Editor currently offers a history list, and the saving and loading of queries from disk. It looks like Figure 12.20

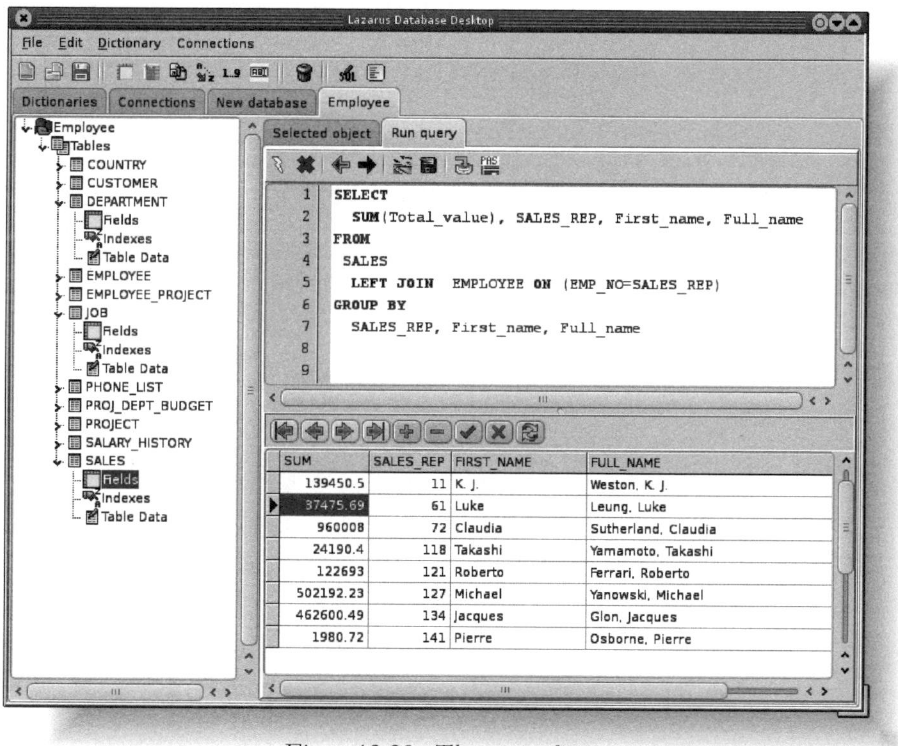

Figure 12.20: The query editor

12.4.3 Generating database code

An extra code generator available in the query editor is the generation of an SQL statement constant. If the following query is typed in the query editor:

```
SELECT
  SUM(TOTAL_VALUE), SALES_REP, FIRST_NAME, LAST_NAME
FROM  SALES  LEFT JOIN EMPLOYEE ON (EMP_NO=SALES_REP)
GROUP BY  SALES_REP, FIRST_NAME, LAST_NAME
```

This results in the following SQL constant declaration

```
Const
 SQL = 'SELECT'+ sLineBreak
   +'  SUM(TOTAL_VALUE), SALES_REP, FIRST_NAME, LAST_NAME'+ sLineBreak
   +'FROM'+ sLineBreak
   +'  SALES'+sLineBreak
   +'  LEFT JOIN EMPLOYEE ON (EMP_NO=SALES_REP)'+ sLineBreak
   +'GROUP BY'+ sLineBreak
   +'  SALES_REP, FIRST_NAME, LAST_NAME';
```

which you can directly copy and paste in the Lazarus IDE.

12.5 A crash course in SQL

SQL is a standardised language used to manipulate relational databases. Most relational database engines support SQL. There are various standards (SQL 92, SQL 99 or 2003) which differ in that they describe progressively more language features. In general, restricting yourself to the SQL 92 standard ensures that the SQL statement will work on any database.

SQL has two kinds of statements:

1. DDL statements (Data Definition Language). These statements can be used to create tables, indexes and other structures in a database.
2. DML statements (Data Manipulation Language). These statements are used to read, write or update data.

12.5.1 Creating a table in SQL

Creating a table in SQL is done using a CREATE TABLE statement.
In general, it looks like this:

```
CREATE TABLE TableName (
  FieldDef1,
  ...
  FieldDefN
);
```

Where FieldDef1.. FieldDefN are the definitions of the fields that must exist in the table. A field definition looks like this:

```
FieldName FieldType [default value] [Not Null]
```

FieldName should be a valid identifier (more or less the same rules apply to SQL identifiers as to Pascal identifiers). Possible field types are listed in Table 12.24.

Name	Type
VARCHAR(N)	A string, maximum N characters long
CHAR(N)	A string which is always N characters long
INT	A 32-bit integer
DATE	A date value
TIME	A time value
DATETIME	A date/time value
BOOLEAN	A boolean value
FLOAT	A floating-point value
SMALLINT	A 16-bit integer value
BLOB	Arbitrary sized data, untyped

Table 12.24: FieldType identifiers

The *Not Null* clause in a field definition means that this field requires a value. The *Default* clause can be used to specify a default value for the field if none is specified when creating a new record. Obviously the specified value must have the correct data type. The following will create a simple table with user definitions:

```
CREATE TABLE USERS (
  ID INT NOT NULL,
  NAME VARCHAR(50) NOT NULL,
  PASSWORD VARCHAR (50),
  LASTLOGIN DATETIME,
  FULLNAME VARCHAR(80),
  EMAIL VARCHAR(100)
);
```

12.5.2 Reading data from the database

Reading data from the database is done using a SELECT statement:

```
SELECT [DISTINCT]
  Field1, Field2, … FieldN
FROM
  TABLE
WHERE
  Condition1 [[AND|OR] Condition2 [[AND|OR] Condition3]]
ORDER BY
  Field1, Field2
```

The first part selects which fields should be returned: *Field1, Field2... FieldN* are fields from Table1, (or expressions using these fields - they can be added, subtracted, concatenated and so on). You cannot specify fields of a table that does not appear in the FROM clause.
It is possible to specify more than one table in the *WHERE* clause. Tables can be separated with commas, or with JOIN clauses. For instance the following JOIN clause

```
CUSTOMER
  INNER JOIN ORDERS ON (CUSTOMER.ID = ORDERS.CUSTOMERID)
```

will return all records in the CUSTOMERS TABLE, and for each such record will return all records in the ORDERS table for which the ID field in the CUSTOMERS table matches the CUSTOMERID field in the ORDERS table.

The WHERE clause conditions are used to limit the returned data. A record will be returned by the query if it satisfies the conditions:

```
  FieldName = SomeValue
or
  Field1 = Field2
or, a special case to test whether a field is empty:
  (Field1 is NULL)
or whether it is in a series of values:
  Field1 in (a, b, c)
```

The **ORDER BY** clause is used to order the fields. The records in the result will be ordered first on the first field, then on the second field and so on. For instance:

```
SELECT
  LOGIN
FROM
  USERS
WHERE
  (PASSWORD IS NULL)
ORDER BY
  FULLNAME
```

returns all LOGIN names from users that have no password in the USERS table and the records will be ordered by FULLNAME. If a fieldname in the ORDER BY clause is followed by DESC, then the ordering will be descending, as in:

```
SELECT
  LOGIN
FROM
  USERS
WHERE
  not (LASTLOGIN IS NULL)
ORDER BY
  LASTLOGIN DESC
```

This will return all LOGIN names in descending time of last login.

12.5.3 Creating a new record in the table.

To insert a new record in a table, an **INSERT** statement is used.
Usually the statement looks like this:

```
INSERT INTO TableName
  (Field1, … , FieldN)
VALUES
  (Value1, … , ValueN);
```

This will insert 1 new record in the table 'TableName', and will populate the record: each field specified in the INSERT clause will get the value in the same position in the 'VALUES' part of the statement.
It follows that the number of values must match the number of fields, and the type of each value must be compatible to the type of the field.
An INSERT statement need not include every field in the table. If a field is missing from the INSERT statement, then it will get the value NULL (unless there is a value specified in the DEFAULT clause for that field in the table creation statement, when it will have the default value rather than NULL).

If a field gets a NULL value, and was declared as NOT NULL, then the database engine will give an error.

12.5.3 Creating a new record in the table

The following will create a new user account in the users table:

```
INSERT INTO USERS
  (ID, LOGIN,FULLNAME)
VALUES
  (1,'michael','Michael Van Canneyt')
```

12.5.4 Deleting a record from a table

Removing a record from a table is done with the DELETE Statement.
In general it looks like this:

```
DELETE FROM TableName [WHERE condition1 [[AND|OR] condition2]]
```

If there is no WHERE clause, then all records will be deleted. The WHERE clause in general specifies a condition which uniquely determines the record that must be deleted.

For instance:

```
DELETE FROM USERS WHERE LOGIN = 'michael'
```

will delete the record for the user 'michael' from the table of users.

12.5.5 Updating records in the database.

To change the fields in a record in the database, an **UPDATE** statement is used.
The general form of the statement appears as follows:

```
UPDATE TableName SET
  Field1 = Value1,
  ...
  FieldN = ValueN
[WHERE condition1 [[AND|OR] condition2]]
```

This will update Field1 with Value1, Field2 with Value2. If the WHERE clause is not present, then the fields of all records in the table will be updated.
As with the DELETE statement, the WHERE clause in general specifies a condition which uniquely determines the record that must be updated with the new values.
For example:

```
UPDATE USERS SET
  PASSWORD = 'Secret',
  EMAIL = 'michael@freepascal.org '
WHERE
  LOGIN  = 'michael';
```

This will update the password and email address of the user 'michael'.

12.6 Reporting with Lazarus

No database application is complete without the ability to print out the data being manipulated. Traditionally, this kind of reporting is handled by specialized reporting engines. FastReport is such a reporting engine which is widely used, not only by Object Pascal developers. An old release (2.32) of FastReport was made available for free to Object Pascal developers. This version has since been developed by the Lazarus team, and forms the basis for LazReport, the reporting tool bundled with Lazarus.

Installation

The LazReport package is distributed with Lazarus, but is not installed in the IDE by default. It should be installed separately, which can be done in the '*Installed packages*' dialog. When installing LazReport, the '*Printer4Lazarus*' package is also compiled and installed. After installation, a new tab 'LazReport' appears on the component palettewith the components listed in Table 12.25.

Components	Description
TFrReport	The actual reporting component.
TFrDBDataset	This object forms the link between the TfrReport component and any *TDataset* descendant you want to use for reporting.
TFrBarCodeObject	Drop this object on a form to add support for barcode objects to the report designer. This then lets you draw barcodes in a report.
TFrRoundRectObject	Drop this object on a form to add support for rounded rectangles to the report designer. This lets you draw rounded rectangles in a report.
TFrShapeObject	Drop this object on a form to add support for all kinds of shapes (rectangles, circles, triangles etc.) to the report designer.
TfrCheckboxObject	Drop this object on a form to add support for drawing a checkbox to the report designer.
TfrCompositeReport	This object allows you to merge multiple reports into one print job.
TfrUserDataset	This object allows you to create reports based on arbitrary data. With the help of some events, you can emulate a '*TDataset*'.
TfrTextExport	Exports the generated report as text.
TfrHTMLExport	Exports the generated report as HTML.
TfrCSVExport	Exports the generated report as a CSV (Comma Separated Values) file.
TfrPrintGrid	Prints the contents of a *TDBGrid* component.

Table 12.25: Components appearing on the component palette

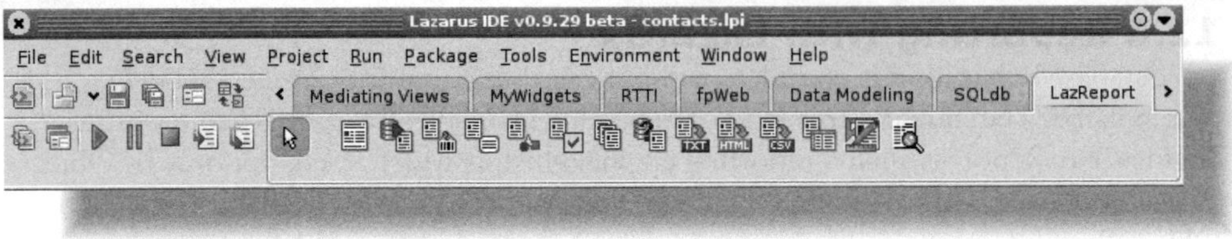

Figure 12.21: Components installed by lazreport

LazReport is a banded report generator. This means that it consists of a number of bands, each band with a number of printable elements (text, images, shapes) on it. Any elements positioned on the band are printed each time the report engine decides that the band must be printed. The elements are printed at their designed positions, but relative to the starting position of the band when it is printed.

There are several types of bands:

- Report header and report footer bands which are printed only once, the header at the start of the report, the footer at the end. This is good for an opening report title and a closing data summary.
- Page header and page footer bands. They are printed at the top and bottom of every page of the report. They can be used to display a page number, running totals, date and time of printing, or a company logo.
- Column header and footer bands. They are much like page header and footer bands, but are printed at the top and bottom of each column in the report. In a columnar listing (such as a list of customers with their contact data), a column title would contain descriptions of the columnar data ('Client name', 'Client phone', 'Client email' etc.)
- Data bands. These bands are printed once per record in the data set. The dataset can be a real *TDataset,* or can be an event-based simulation of a dataset (using the *TfrUserDataset* component).
- Group header and group footer bands. It is possible to group records based on an expression calculated for each record in the dataset.
  (This might be customer number in a list of invoices during a given period).
  As soon as this expression changes, the reporting engine starts a new group, and prints the group header band.
  When a group ends, the group footer band is printed. This allows you to provide group totals (such as a total for each customer's invoices).
  Multiple grouping levels can be defined. (Invoices can be grouped per customer per quarter).
- Child bands: Sometimes it is not possible to lay out the data correctly using just one band. In that case, child bands can be attached to the first band allowing you to choose between different bands, depending on a variable you specify.

You can drop one or more printable elements on to each report band, and there are several elements available to you:

- A text element of arbitrary size. The text can be a mixture of static text and expressions. Before the reporting engine displays a text element, it examines the template text and calculates any expressions found there. The text resulting from the combination of static and calculated text is then printed.
- Shapes. These enable you to draw lines.
- Images. The printed image can either be static, or it can be retrieved from a blob field.
- Bar codes. You can print bar codes, which are calculated from an expression.
- Checkbox. A checkbox can be used to display a check mark, depending on the evaluation of some boolean expression.

Finally, the generated report can be exported to file, either directly, or by the user when he is previewing the generated report. Currently, exports can be made to plain text, HTML, or CSV (the formatting of data is largely lost in this case, but the textual data will be exported to file).

12.6.1 Creating a report

A report can be dropped on a datamodule or a form. Creating a report consists of the following steps:

1. If the report is to display data from a *TDataset* descendant, then you have to create the dataset. Optionally a *TDatasource* may be used, but this is not required.
2. For each dataset used in the report, a *TfrDBDataset* component must be dropped on the form or datamodule. Its *Dataset* or *DataSource* property must be set to the dataset created in the first step.
3. A *TFrReport* component should be dropped on the form. Its *Dataset* property should be set to one of the *TFrDBDataset* components created in the previous step.
4. Finally, the context menu of *TFrReport* is used to start designing the report.

The Report Designer window has the elements you would expect from a GUI designer: buttons to add objects; buttons to align objects; and a Property Inspector. Some elements of the Designer are reminiscent of the font and text alignment buttons found in many text editors.
The design of a new report is usually started by adding a *Master Data* band to the report: The *[Band]* button from the toolbar to the left of the page view (this is the second button from the top) must be used for this. After clicking where it should go on the page, the kind of band must be chosen, and here *Master Data* must be selected. Once selected, the dataset to be connected to the master data band must be chosen. The band must be connected to the dataset whose data is to be displayed. Additional bands can be dropped on the page, for instance a report header band that simply displays a title, a page footer band that displays the page number and the date and finally a column header band which will display the column headers for the displayed data.

The number of columns in a report can be set in the Object Inspector since each page in the report has a *Columns* property which is the number of columns to use.

The report designer looks as in Figure 12.22.

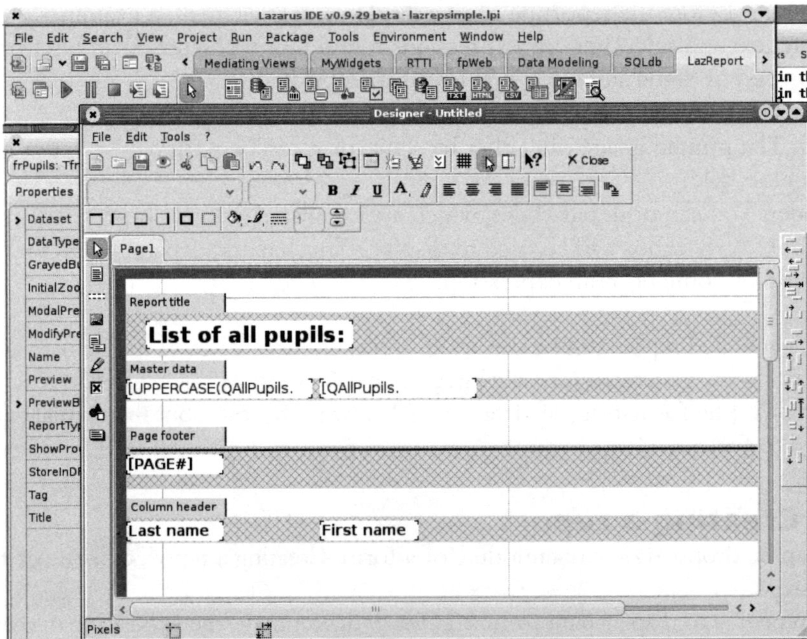

Figure 12.22 report designer window

Displaying text can be done using the *[Add text]* button, and clicking on the band where the text should be displayed. An editor appears in which you edit the text to be printed. This is a simple text editor with some special features, namely the ability to insert variables, database fields and functions, mixed with normal text. In fact, the reporting engine will treat anything between square brackets [] as a function that it should evaluate, and the result of the evaluation will be inserted in the text at the location of the brackets. Clicking the *[DB Fields]* button will present a list of fields, and one of them can be selected. The editor will insert the name of the dataset, appended with the fieldname, between double quotes.
By clicking the *[Function]* button, this can be enhanced with a function, e.g. to print the name in all uppercase. There are various special report variables which can be inserted by clicking the *[Variable]* button in the text editor. These variables include things such as the date, time, current page number etc. You might place them, for instance, in the footer band.
The *[Format]* button can be used to specify formatting of formulae or variables that have a numerical or date/time result, to give the number of decimal places in a numerical field and so on. Once the report is finished, it can be printed or previewed:

```
procedure TForm1.BPreviewClick(Sender: TObject);
begin
  if FRPupils.PrepareReport then FRPupils.ShowPreparedReport
  else
    ShowMessage('Prepare report failed !');
end;
```

The *PrepareReport* call will prepare the report in memory. If that succeeds, the report can be previewed in the preview window on screen using the *ShowPreparedReport* call. Alternatively, the report can be sent to the printer immediately with the *PrintPreparedReport* procedure:

```
procedure TForm1.BPrintClick(Sender: TObject);
  var R : TFrReport;
begin
  R:=SelectedReport;
  if R.PrepareReport then
    R.PrintPreparedReport(",1)
  else
    ShowMessage('Prepare report failed !');
end;
```

The first argument to *PrintPreparedReport* is a string specifying the set of pages that should be printed: if left empty, all pages will be printed. It can contain the usual page ranges such as '1,5-8' which would print page 1 and pages 5 through 8. The second argument is the number of copies. When previewing the report, the user can still select the printer prior to printing, or save the report to file.

12.6.2 The report designer

If a *TFrDesign* component is dropped on the form where the report is, the Report Designer is included in the application. Users can use it create new reports or modify existing reports. Provided the application contains a query builder, this can be used to create quite a powerful reporting solution for application end-users.
It is trivial to activate report design:

```
procedure TForm1.BDesignClick(Sender: TObject);
  Var R : TFrReport;
begin
  R := SelectedReport;
  R.DesignReport;
end;
```

The Report Designer is a modal window, so the *DesignReport* method will not return until the Designer is closed.
Finally, it is possible to export the report data. This feature is enabled by dropping the export components on the same form as the report. Then the *[Save]* button in the preview window will allow you to select the export format:

- **Text.** This will export the report as text, preserving as much formatting as possible. Obviously, images cannot be exported to text.
- **Html.** This will export the report as HTML, preserving as much formatting as possible.
- **CSV.** This will export the report as CSV (Comma Separated Values). All formatting will be lost, and only the report data will be exported.

To export a report via code the export component must also be dropped on the form. The following code shows how data can be exported in several formats using a radiogroup to specify the export format:

```
procedure TForm1.BExportClick(Sender: TObject);
  Const HTMLFilter = 'HTML files|*.html';TeXTFilter = 'Text files|*.txt';
      CSVFilter = 'CSV files|*.csv'; AllFilter = '|All files|*.*';
  Var C : TClass; F : String; R : TfrReport;
begin
  R := SelectedReport;
  Case RGExport.ItemIndex of
    0 : begin
          C := TfrTextExportFilter;
          F := TextFilter;
        end;
    1 : begin
          C := TfrHTMExportFilter;
          F := HTMLFilter;
        end;
    2 : begin
          C := TfrCSVExportFilter;
          F := CSVFilter;
        end;
  end;

  SDExport.Filter := F + AllFilter;

   If SDExport.Execute then
      If R.PrepareReport then
        R.ExportTo(C,SDExport.filename)
      else
        ShowMessage('Prepare report failed !');
end;
```

The case statement selects the export filter and a file filter expression for the *SDExport* save dialog. After the save dialog closes, the *ExportTo* method of *TFrReport* is called. This takes two arguments: the first is a filter class, and the second is a filename under which the export will be saved.

B

C

D

E

F

G

H

I

M

N

O

P

Q

R

S

T

U

V

W

X

Z